乙亥新春咏怀 有序

余自中学讲武,大学习文,毕业前后,始从元任诸大师,治音声之学,初入国库,遭战乱,旅食四方,几废所业。解放后,应罗师之召,始归队科研于兹四十年矣。八年前,以七八之龄休致,复蒙回聘,今春始返初服。窃维:一生未精三馀,空掷心分射鹄,志逊探骊,每临渊而羡鱼,辄为山而亏篑,读往追来,能无所愧?佇此万象更新之日,百废俱兴之年,改革奏功,兆民有庆,爰发成

图书在版编目(CIP)数据

现代语音学前沿文集/G. Fant，H. Fujisaki，J. Shen(沈家煊)主编．—北京：商务印书馆，2009
ISBN 978-7-100-06769-0

Ⅰ．现…　Ⅱ．G…　Ⅲ．语音学—国际学术会议—文集　Ⅳ．H01-53

中国版本图书馆 CIP 数据核字(2009)第 172018 号

所有权利保留。
未经许可，不得以任何方式使用。

现代语音学前沿文集
G. Fant，H. Fujisaki，J. Shen(沈家煊)　主编

商 务 印 书 馆 出 版
(北京王府井大街36号　邮政编码 100710)
商 务 印 书 馆 发 行
北 京 瑞 古 冠 中 印 刷 厂 印 刷
ISBN 978-7-100-06769-0

2009 年 12 月第 1 版　　　开本 787×1092　1/16
2009 年 12 月北京第 1 次印刷　印张 27¼　插页 40
定价：90.00 元

贺吴宗济先生百岁华诞

Festschrift for Professor Wu Zongji's 100th Birthday

现代语音学前沿文集

Frontiers in Phonetics and Speech Science

Edited by

GUNNAR FANT
Department of Speech Communication and Music Acoustics
Royal Institute of Technology
Stockholm, Sweden

HIROYA FUJISAKI
University of Tokyo
Tokyo, Japan

JIAXUAN SHEN
Institute of Linguistics, Chinese Academy of Social Sciences
Beijing, China

目录（Contents）

List of Contributors and their Affiliations
序言
Foreword
Biography
Photo Album

吴宗济
试论普通话中韵律规则与其他若干学科中韵律规则的共性   1

陈玉东，吕士楠
汉语朗读语篇的修辞结构和韵律表达   21

孔江平
语言发声研究的基本方法   33

路继伦，林茂灿
疑问句末基频"上升尾巴"与语气助词——赵元任先生"连续叠加"思想初探   49

麦耘
广西藤县岭景方言的去声嘎裂声中折调   57

石锋，冉启斌
塞音的声学格局分析   63

王韫佳
CAH、PAM 和 SLM 述评——兼论跨语言语音对比与 L2 语音习得   73

吴洁敏，吕士楠，黄华新，缪冠琼
情韵朗读的声学特征   85

熊文婷，崔丹丹，孟凡博，蔡莲红
情感语音的韵律特征分析与转换   97

张家騄
元音内在基频研究   105

祖漪清，闫润强
声调目标实现的规律及变化   117

LI Aijun
Studies on Chinese Prosody: Professor Wu Zongji's Thoughts on Prosody and their Far-reaching Implications ⋯ 127

Arthur S. ABRAMSON, Theraphan LUANGTHONGKUM
A Fuzzy Boundary between Tone Languages and Voice-Register Languages ⋯ 149

CAO Jianfen
How Do Speech Sounds Vary and Serve Efficient Communication? ⋯ 157

DANG Jianwu, LU Xugang
Investigation of the Relation between Speech Production and Perception Based on a Vowel Study ⋯ 169

Jerold A. EDMONDSON
Correspondences between Articulation and Acoustics for the Feature [Atr]: The Case of Two Tibeto-Burman Languages and Two African Languages ⋯ 179

John H. ESLING
The Control of Laryngeal Constriction and the Emergence of Speech in Infants in the First Year of Life ⋯ 191

Gunnar FANT, Anita KRUCKENBERG
Studies of Swedish Prosody in the Frame of Speech Production ⋯ 205

Hiroya FUJISAKI
The Command-Response Model for F_0 Contour Generation and its Implications in Phonetics and Phonology ⋯ 227

Louis GOLDSTEIN, Hosung NAM, Elliot SALTZMAN, Ioana CHITORAN
Coupled Oscillator Planning Model of Speech Timing and Syllable Structure ⋯ 239

Daniel HIRST, Caroline BOUZON, Cyril AURAN
Analysis by Synthesis of British English Speech Rhythm: From Data to Models ⋯ 251

Keikichi HIROSE, Qinghua SUN, Nobuaki MINEMATSU
Generation of F_0 Contours for Mandarin Speech in Combination with Rule-based and Corpus-based Methods ⋯ 263

Philip HOOLE, Lasse BOMBIEN, Barbara KÜHNERT, Christine MOOSHAMMER
Intrinsic and Prosodic Effects on Articulatory Coordination in Initial Consonant Clusters ⋯ 275

Klaus J. KOHLER
Patterns of Prosody in the Expression of the Speaker and the Appeal to the Listener   287

LEE Chin-Hui
Linking Statistical Signal Processing with Acoustic Phonetics: A New Speech Recognition and Analysis Framework Based on Automatic Speech Attribute Transcription (ASAT)   303

Ilse LEHISTE
The Latvian "Broken Tone"   317

Helen MENG
A Contrastive Phonetic Study between Cantonese and English to Predict Salient Mispronunciations by Cantonese Learners of English   321

Hansjörg MIXDORFF
Auditory-visual Perception of Mandarin Syllables   329

John J. OHALA
Understanding Variability in Speech: A Brief Survey over 2.5 Millennia   341

Louis C.W. POLS
Phonetics: Consistency and Variability   349

Yoshinori SAGISAKA, Yoko GREENBERG, Ke LI, Mingzhao ZHU, Minoru TSUZAKI, Hiroaki KATO
Prosody Modeling of Communicative Information for Synthesis and Recognition   359

TSENG Chiu-yu, SU Zhao-yu
Boundary and Lengthening — On Relative Phonetic Information   369

XU Yi
In Defense of Lab Speech in Prosody Research   381

ZHANG Jinsong, CAO Wen
Studies on Chinese Tone Information Processing and their Possible Implication for Automatic Pronunciation Training   391

List of Publications by Professor Wu   403

Messages of Congratulations to Professor Wu   409

List of Contributors and their Affiliations

蔡莲红　　清华大学计算机系
陈玉东　　中国科学院心理所，中国传媒大学
崔丹丹　　清华大学计算机系
黄华新　　浙江大学语言与认知研究中心，浙江大学人文学院
孔江平　　北京大学中文系
林茂灿　　中国社会科学院语言研究所
路继伦　　天津师范大学外国语学院
吕士楠　　中国科学院声学研究所，北京捷通华声语音技术公司
麦　耘　　中国社会科学院语言研究所
孟凡博　　清华大学计算机系
缪冠琼　　北京捷通华声语音技术公司
冉启斌　　南开大学汉语言文化学院
石　锋　　南开大学汉语言文化学院
王韫佳　　北京大学中文系
吴洁敏　　浙江大学外语学院，浙江大学语言与认知研究中心
吴宗济　　中国社会科学院语言研究所
熊文婷　　清华大学计算机系
闫润强　　摩托罗拉上海实验室
张家騄　　中国科学院声学研究所
祖漪清　　摩托罗拉上海实验室

ABRAMSON Arthur S., Haskins Laboratories and The University of Connecticut, USA
AURAN Cyril, UFR Angellier, Université Charles de Gaulle -Lille 3, France
BOMBIEN Lasse, Institute of Phonetics and Speech Processing, Munich University, Germany
BOUZON Caroline, Laboratoire Parole et Langage, Université de Provence, France
CAO Jianfen, Institute of Linguistics, Chinese Academy of Social Sciences, China
CAO Wen, Center for Studies of Chinese as a Second Language, Beijing Language and Culture University, China
CHITORAN Ioana, Department of French and Italian, Dartmouth College, USA
DANG Jianwu, School of Information Science, Japan Advanced Institute of Science and Technology, Japan
EDMONDSON Jerold A., Department of Linguistics, University of Texas at Arlington, USA
ESLING John H., Department of Linguistics, University of Victoria, Canada
FANT Gunnar, Department of Speech, Music and Hearing, Royal Institute of Technology, Sweden

FUJISAKI Hiroya, Professor Emeritus, University of Tokyo, Japan
GOLDSTEIN Louis, Haskins Laboratories and University of Southern California, USA
GREENBERG Yoko, Language and Speech Research Laboratory, Waseda University, Japan
NAM Hosung, Haskins Laboratories, USA
HIRST Daniel, Laboratoire Parole et Langage, Université de Provence, France
HIROSE Keikichi, Department of Information and Communication Engineering, University of Tokyo, Japan
HOOLE Philip, Institute of Phonetics and Speech Processing, Munich University, Germany
KATO Hiroaki, ATR Human Information Processing Research Laboratories, National Institute of Information and Communications Technology, Japan
KOHLER Klaus J., Institute of Phonetics and Digital Speech Processing, University of Kiel, Germany
KRUCKENBERG Anita, Department of Speech, Music and Hearing, Royal Institute of Technology, Sweden
KÜHNERT Barbara, Institut du Monde Anglophone, Université Sorbonne Nouvelle Paris III, and Institut du Monde Anglophone, CNRS, France
LEE Chin-Hui, School of Electrical and Computer Engineering, Georgia Institute of Technology, USA
LEHISTE Ilse, Professor Emeritus, The Ohio State University, USA
LI Aijun, Institute of Linguistics, Chinese Academy of Social Sciences, China
LI Ke, Language and Speech Research Laboratory, Waseda University, Japan
LU Xugang, ATR Spoken Language Communication Research Labs, National Institute of Information and Communications Technology, Japan
LUANGTHONGKUM Theraphan, Department of Linguistics, Chulalongkorn University, Thailand
MENG Helen, Department of Systems Engineering and Engineering Management, The Chinese University of Hong Kong, Hong Kong SAR, China
MINEMATSU Nobuaki, Department of Information and Communication Engineering, University of Tokyo, Japan
MIXDORFF Hansjörg, Department of Computer Science and Media, Berlin University of Applied Sciences, Germany
MOOSHAMMER Christine, Haskins Laboratories, USA
NAM Hosung, Haskins Laboratories, USA
OHALA John J., Department of Linguistics, University of California, Berkeley, USA
POLS Louis C. W., Institute of Phonetic Sciences, University of Amsterdam, The Netherlands
SAGISAKA Yoshinori, Language and Speech Research Laboratory, Waseda University, Japan
SALTZMAN Elliot, Haskins Laboratories and Boston University, USA
SU Zhao-yu, Institute of Linguistics, Academia Sinica, Taiwan of China

SUN Qinghua, Department of Information and Communication Engineering, University of Tokyo, Japan

TSENG Chiu-yu, Institute of Linguistics, Academia Sinica, Taiwan of China

TSUZAKI Minoru, ATR Spoken Language Communication Research Labs, National Institute of Information and Communications Technology, Japan

XU Yi, Department of Speech, Hearing and Phonetic Sciences, University College London, UK

ZHANG Jinsong, College of Information Sciences, Beijing Language and Culture University, China

ZHU Mingzhao, Language and Speech Research Laboratory, Waseda University, Japan

序　言

这次由我们所主办的语音学研讨会，中外学者会聚一堂，切磋学理，交流心得成果，同时也庆贺吴宗济先生百岁华诞。

2004 年，吴宗济先生在 95 岁高龄的时候曾经豪迈地说：你们就把我当成 59 岁好了，有什么困难任务，你们尽管压过来。又过去了五年，吴先生百岁，豪迈之情不减，我们惊喜地看到他不但完成了社科院的老年基金项目"汉语普通话韵律研究"，而且还主持编辑出版了《赵元任语言学文集》中英文版，现在又参加了《罗常培语音学文集》的编辑工作。

我 1979 年到语言研究所当研究生，除了国际音标的训练，实验语音学的启蒙知识就是看吴先生写的《实验语音学知识讲话》，后来我做汉语口误的研究，细读吴先生的文章《试论普通话语音的"区别特征"及其相互关系》，深深为吴先生将中国传统音韵学和现代语音学理论结合起来的能力所折服。再后来我自己的学生也去吴先生那儿请教语音学和音韵学，获益匪浅，对吴先生也是十二分佩服。

一个真正的语言学家首先要有听音辨调的能力，吴先生回忆自己大学毕业到史语所应考当助理，李方桂先生在钢琴上弹了几组四部和弦，考生中唯有吴先生能用五线谱把乐调谱出来交卷。回想我在语言所工作的时候参加一次出国进修选拔的考试，一道题是把录音中的一段曲调记录下来，我只能胡乱用五线谱画了个调形，跟吴先生比起来真是十分的惭愧。吴先生的过人之处是不仅"耳聪"而且"手巧"，他对实验仪器的摆弄能力也是他取得杰出成就的原因。吴先生给自己的书斋取名"补听缺斋"，给自选文集取名《补听集》，手、耳、脑并用，自然就"武艺高强"。

吴先生不仅武艺高强，还境界高远。他用王国维谈到的创业或治学必经的三个境界回顾自己的历程。要用实验方法来分析发音方法和特点，补听缺，探究语音演变规律，发现自身的差距要迎头赶上，出外取经，这是第一个境界"独上高楼，望尽天涯路"。要用机器合成或识别语言，要它"听懂"自然话语而不错、"说出"如口语般流利自然，就需要文、理双方的结合，这种结合谈何容易，孜孜不倦，锲而不舍，这个阶段辛苦而漫长，是第二个境界"衣带渐宽终不悔，为伊消得人憔悴"。把治学做人联系起来，眼光要大，认真务实，学无止境，有海纳百川、博取众长的胸襟和气魄，对人类语言的奥秘有更深的领悟。这第三个境界就是"众里寻他千百度。蓦然回首，那人却在灯火阑珊处"了。

吴先生退休 20 多年来，退而不休，与一些大学合作，完成了"汉语语调合成"的科研课题，并应用这项目的理论研究成果，开发出汉语文—语转换系统的产品，获得了相当好的经济效益，得到国家的优等奖励。他还为所内所外培养了许多语音研究的后继人才和研究骨干。他对汉语语音学如何面向信息时代的未来进行了思考和探讨，提出我的研究方向要随形势的需要而有所调整。另外，他还就汉语声调与音乐乐律的关系，以及汉语语音的科学分类等问题，回顾了从隋唐以来的许多阐述，指出了古代文献中关于汉语声调的叙述、用乐律描写调值及其变化规则等方法，至今仍有参考价值。最近他又想到汉字草书笔法与汉语语调规则的相似性，拿历史上狂草名家的运笔和连写的轨迹和普通话的连读变调和语调规则加以对照，发现书法的

"连绵"、"映带"、"错综"和语音的"协同变调"或"停延轻重"在服从语法、表达情感上有相通的规则可寻。他认为对中国传统的知识善于领会并加以援用，也许能运用东方的思维方式为未来语音学的研究开辟新的途径。

　　这次研讨会和论文集的编辑得到吴先生日本的好友和同道藤崎博也教授的鼎力支持，我们深表感谢。现在会议的论文集即将出版，我就写上面这些话算作序言。

沈家煊
中国社会科学院语言研究所所长

Foreword

Dear Professor Wu Zongji,

On the remarkable occasion commemorating your centennial birthday, it is our great honor and pleasure to address you on behalf of all the contributors to this volume.

Born as a son in a notable family, you graduated from the renowned Tsinghua University 75 years ago, with your unique training both in Science and Humanities. Since then, you have consistently been pursuing an academic career, developed an efficient laboratory for speech research within the Chinese Academy of Social Sciences with highly qualified students and associates, whose works along with your own are well known internationally. Since 1979, you have also been serving the international community as member of the Permanent Council for the Organization of International Congresses on Phonetic Sciences, where some of us had the pleasure of working with you more closely. Our admiration and friendship continues even today.

Although the main part of the contributions to this volume are based on the papers presented at the International Forum held in conjunction with the Phonetic Congress of China in Beijing, April 2008, we are very pleased to include some from your friends and admirers, both old and young, in the field of speech communication, who could not be at the meeting. Along with all these valuable contributions which are in the printed volume, we are happy to present you a DVD of photographs and other records that are worthy of commemorating the extraordinary fruitful life of a century of our great and admired friend, teacher, and father, who, to out great pleasure, continues to live an active scientific life.

Dear Professor Wu, you are the hope and pride of all those who had the pleasure of being under your scholarly influence. We wish you many more years of unprecedented, fruitful and happy life!

Gunnar Fant and Hiroya Fujisaki

Biography

Wu Zongji, alias Zhichuan, descendant of a family from Wuxing, Zhejiang Province.

1. Brief life history

1909-04-04: Born in Ji'ning, Shandong Province. In his childhood he studied at Nanyang High School in Shanghai and then Dacheng High School (old system) in Peking. After graduation, he was admitted to the Preparatory Course of Nankai University in Tianjin.

1928: Admitted into Tsinghua University, and studied first at Dept. of Civil Engineering, and later at Dept. of Chemistry, and finally at Dept. of Chinese Literature. Obtained the B.S. of Literature degree in 1934.

1934-1935: Worked at the Publication Office of Tsinghua University, and was in charge of editing, publishing and exchanging of "Journal of Tsinghua University", "Tsinghua Science Reports", and various literature and history books and other publications.

1935-1940: Admitted into the Institute of History and Languages, Chinese Central Academy of Sciences, as Assistant, first at Nanjing, and then moved with the Institute to Kunming in 1937.

1949-1950: Special reporter of Dagong Newspaper in Shanghai.

1950-1951: Chief Editor in Chinese Film and Record Corporation.

1955-1956: Head of Section of Research and Investigation on Scientific Instruments, Chinese Export Corporation, Shanghai.

1956: Joined the Institute of Linguistics, Chinese Academy of Sciences, first as Assistant Researcher, and then as Researcher up to present.

2. Working experience at the Institute of Linguistics

(1) **1956-1957**: Served as a teacher of phonetics for the Research Class of Mandarin Speech in cooperation with the Ministry of Education and the Institute of Linguistics.

(2) **1957-1958**: Sent to Czechoslovakia, German Democratic Republic, Sweden, and Denmark, to investigate and study experimental phonetics.

(3) **1978**: Became Director of the Speech Laboratory, Institute of Linguistics, Chinese Academy of Social Sciences (formerly the Institute of Linguistics, Chinese Academy of Sciences).

(4) **1978**: Became Professor and Supervisor of M.S. students in the Graduate School of CASS.

(5) **1978-1980**: Member of the Scientific Committee, Institute of Linguistics, CASS.

(6) **1979**: Researcher, Institute of Linguistics, CASS.

(7) **1979-1980**: Adjunct Professor at the Dept. of Chinese Literature of Peking University. Opened the course of Experimental Phonetics.

(8) **1979**: Elected as Member of the Permanent Council for the Organization of International Congresses of Phonetic Sciences.

(9) **1979**: Invited to be Member of the Scientific Committee of the Institute of Acoustics, Chinese Academy of Sciences, and also joined the editorial committee of the Chinese Journal of Acoustics.

(10) **1981**: Became Member of the Scientific Committee of the Chinese Society of Linguistics, and also served as the chief editor of the 5th and the 6th volumes of "Chinese Journal of Linguistics".

(11) **1981**: Elected as Vice Chairman of the Committee of Language and Music Acoustical Society, National Acoustical Society.

(12) **1986**: Retired, and then rehired during 1986-1995.

(13) **1988**: Invited to be Visiting Scholar at the Ohio State University.

(14) **1995**: Invited to be Advisor of the Language Society of Beijing.

(15) **1996**: Participated in the NNSF project "Research on Mandarin Intonation Synthesis" conducted by the University of Science and Technology of China.

3. Main Academic Career at the Institute of Linguistics

The academic career of Prof. Wu Zongji on speech can be divided into four stages as follows:

During the first stage, he mainly worked on the introduction and application of experimental phonetics and the analysis of Mandarin vowels, consonants and tones. During this stage, his main publications include "Figures of the Monosyllables of Mandarin", "Introduction to Experimental Phonetics", "Introduction to Modern Mandarin Phonetics" and dozens of other papers. In particular, from 1982 onward, he focused his work on the analysis of Mandarin tones and on the study of the variations of Mandarin tones in utterances. He published a series of papers on the rules of tone sandhi in bi-syllable, tri-syllable, quadro-syllable, and quinta-syllable sequences and their phonetic, syntactic and phonological origins.

During the second stage, he mainly worked on intonational variations. He found that the tone patterns of short words such as bi-syllabic and tri-syllabic words basically remain invariant, while phrasal intonation is mainly up-and-down variations of the baseline. Based on this, he proposed a new method for intonation analysis, namely, applying 'change key' (musical term, the so-called 'key shifting') processing without changing the tone patterns. At the same time, he changed the commonly accepted linear frequency scale into musical tone scale, thereby normalizing the data and simplifying the calculation simultaneously. This theory and method opened up a powerful way to solve various problems in the study of Mandarin intonation. The main theory can be found in his papers published during 1993-1996.

During the third stage, he mainly worked on the applied research, especially on the application of his co-articulation theory and intonation theory to speech synthesis. He designed a complete set of phonetic symbols (both segmental and prosodic) for the purpose of speech synthesis, providing conditions for improving the naturalness of synthetic speech. The main contents are found in his papers during 1996-2000.

In the fourth stage of his academic activity which started from around 2000 and is being continued up to today, on the one hand he has been summarizing his research works both in modern phonetics and traditional Chinese phonology and integrating them into speech technology, but on the other hand he has started exploring a new topic of interest in the cognitive aspects of human communication that are common to speech and handwriting. As the only one actor and witness of the progress of Modern Phonetics in China over the last 100 years, he still contributes to this field with a remarkable insight and novel ideas. The corresponding publications are partially found in *Linguistic Essays by Wu Zongji*, which was published in 2004.

Photo Album

1928, **Z. Wu** with his wife, father-in-law and mother-in-law. From right to left: **Z. Wu**, his father-in-law G. Mei (ex-president of the High Court of Shandong Province in the early period of ROC), mother-in-law, and wife J. Mei.

1934, **Z. Wu** studying at Tsinghua University.

1934, **Z. Wu** graduated from Tsinghua University.

1952, Family photo taken in Shanghai.
First row (from left to right): **Z. Wu,** second daughter Caizhu, wife J. Mei.
Second row (from left to right): first daughter Qiangzhu and son Youzhi.

July 31, 1938, **Z. Wu** in Kunming, with Prof. Chao and three other assistants.
From left to right: **Z. Wu**, Y. Chao, T. Dong, S. Ding and S. Yang.

1957, Visiting Prof. B. Hála at the Department of Phonetics of Brno University, Brno, Czechoslovakia.
From right to left: **Z. Wu**, an assistant, and B. Hála.

1957, **Z. Wu** on a bridge over Vltava river, Czechoslovakia.

1960, **Z. Wu** with the new experimental sound spectrograph in Phonetics Laboratory, Institute of Linguistics.

August 1979, at the 9th International Congress of Phonetic Sciences, held in Copenhagen, Denmark. From left to right: **Z. Wu**, J. Zhang and M. Lin.

August 31, 1982, at the Working Group on Intonation held with the 13th International Congress of Linguists, Tokyo, Japan.
First row (from right to left): **Z. Wu**, H. Fujisaki, E. Gårding and I. Lehiste.
Second row (from right to left): K. Hirose, J. 't Hart, G. Bruce, A. Abramson, M. Liberman, P. Martin, K. Kvavik and J. Ohala.

April 1983, on the occasion of Peter Ladefoged's visit to the Institute of Linguistics.
First row (from left to right): **Z. Wu**, J. Cao, L. Yang, P. Ladefoged, M. Lin and G. Sun.
Second row (from left to right): X. Wang, H. Bao, Q. Lin and Y. Xu.
Third row (from left to right): Y. Zu, J. Xing, J. Yan and S. Yang.

March 12, 1988, on the occasion of Hiroya Fujisaki's visit to the Institute of Linguistics.
From right to left: M. Lin, H. Ren, Z. Wu, H. Fujisaki, S. Wang, and S. Yang.

1988, **Z. Wu** visiting the National Gallery of Art in Washington, D. C., U.S.A.

November 10, 1990, visiting H. Fujisaki's home with Louis Pols.

November 18, 1990, at the International Conference on Spoken Language Processing held in Kobe, Japan.
From left to right: **Z. Wu**, G. Fant and H. Fujisaki (Chairman of the conference).

August 21, 1991, at the Banquet of the 12th International Congress of Phonetic Sciences, held in Aix-en-Provence, France.
With Mario Rossi
(Chairman of the Congress).

September 18, 1994, at the International Symposium on Prosody held in conjunction with the 3rd ICSLP in Yokohama, Japan.
First row (from left to right): H. Fujisaki, **Z. Wu**, I. Lehiste, J. Hirshberg and M. Rossi.
Second row (from left to right): G. Bruce, G. Fant, K. Kohler, J. Ohala and J. Terken.

March 31, 1997, at the Banquet of the First China-Japan Workshop on Spoken Language Processing held in Huangshan, China.
From left to right: Z. Wu, D. Guan, H. Fujisaki and J. Zhang.

April 2, 1997, at the First China-Japan Workshop on Spoken Language Processing held in Huangshan, China.
First row (from right to left): H. Fujisaki, K. Hirose, **Z. Wu**, R. Wang and S. Doshita.

1997, **Z. Wu** riding a horse at Yangguan in Dunhuang City, Gansu Province.

September 5, 1999, on the north hill of Yantai City (Chefu), Shandong Province. Acting "打死老虎" (beat and kill a tiger, just like Wu Song), which is also an example of quadro-syllabic tone sandhi phrases in Standard Chinese.

1999, **Z. Wu** giving a keynote speech at the 4th Phonetic Conference of China.

December 31, 2000, at home with his great-grandson Y. Wu.

October 17, 2000, **Z. Wu** giving the plenary lecture at the opening session of the 6th International Conference on Spoken Language Processing held in Beijing, China.

October 19, 2000, with friends at the banquet of ICSLP 2000 in Beijing.
From left to right: T. Huang, D. Guan, **Z. Wu**, G. Fant, H. Fujisaki and B. Yuan.

March 29, 2004, **Z. Wu** addressing at the opening ceremony of TAL 2004, held at the Institute of Linguistics.

March 29, 2004, accepting the Festschrift as a present from his close friends at the banquet for celebrating his 95th birthday.
From right to left: **Z. Wu**, G. Fant and H. Fujisaki.

March 29, 2004, **Z. Wu** cutting the birthday cake.

March 29, 2004, **Z. Wu** and H. Fujisaki at TAL 2004.

March 29, 2004, at the banquet of TAL 2004.
From left to right: K. Hirose, **Z. Wu** and T. Huang.

February 19, 2004, **Z. Wu** with all the members of Phonetics Laboratory.

2005, in Shanghai with his family members.
From left to right: **Z. Wu,** his cousin J. Sheng and second daughter Caizhu.

April 3, 2006, commenting on the studies at the Symposium on Tone and Intonation.

April 3, 2006, **Z. Wu** with three officials of the Institute of Linguistics, CASS.
From right to left: J. Shen (director), **Z. Wu**, W. Cai and K. Dong (deputy directors).

April 18, 2008, **Z. Wu** speaking at the opening ceremony of PCC2008, Beijing.

April 18, 2008, **Z. Wu** talking with L. Jiang, Director of the Academic Division of Philosophy, Literature and History of the Chinese Academy of Social Sciences.

April 18, 2008, **Z. Wu** entering the banquet hall at PCC2008 with his daughter Caizhu (right) and a friend from France, A. Grenié (left).

April 18, 2008, **Z. Wu** with friends and colleagues from home and abroad.
First row (from left to right): H. Fujisaki, **Z. Wu**, J. Ohala and J.Shen.
Second row (from left to right): G. Hu, G. Wu, L. Fang, S. Li, J. Dang, F. Zheng, X. Wang, A. Grenié, F. Shi and others.

2007, **Z. Wu** writing a message for the Chinese Journal of Phonetics.

2008, **Z. Wu** working at another desk in his study room, making full use of two computers at the same time.

April 2, 2009, **Z. Wu** was cutting the birthday cake at his 100th birthday part with Prof. Shen, Prof. Fujisaki and Prof. Cao.

April 2, 2009, **Z. Wu** with all the friends and colleagues celebrating his 100th birthday.

乙酉九六初度厚蒙同志亲友诸成七律致谢！

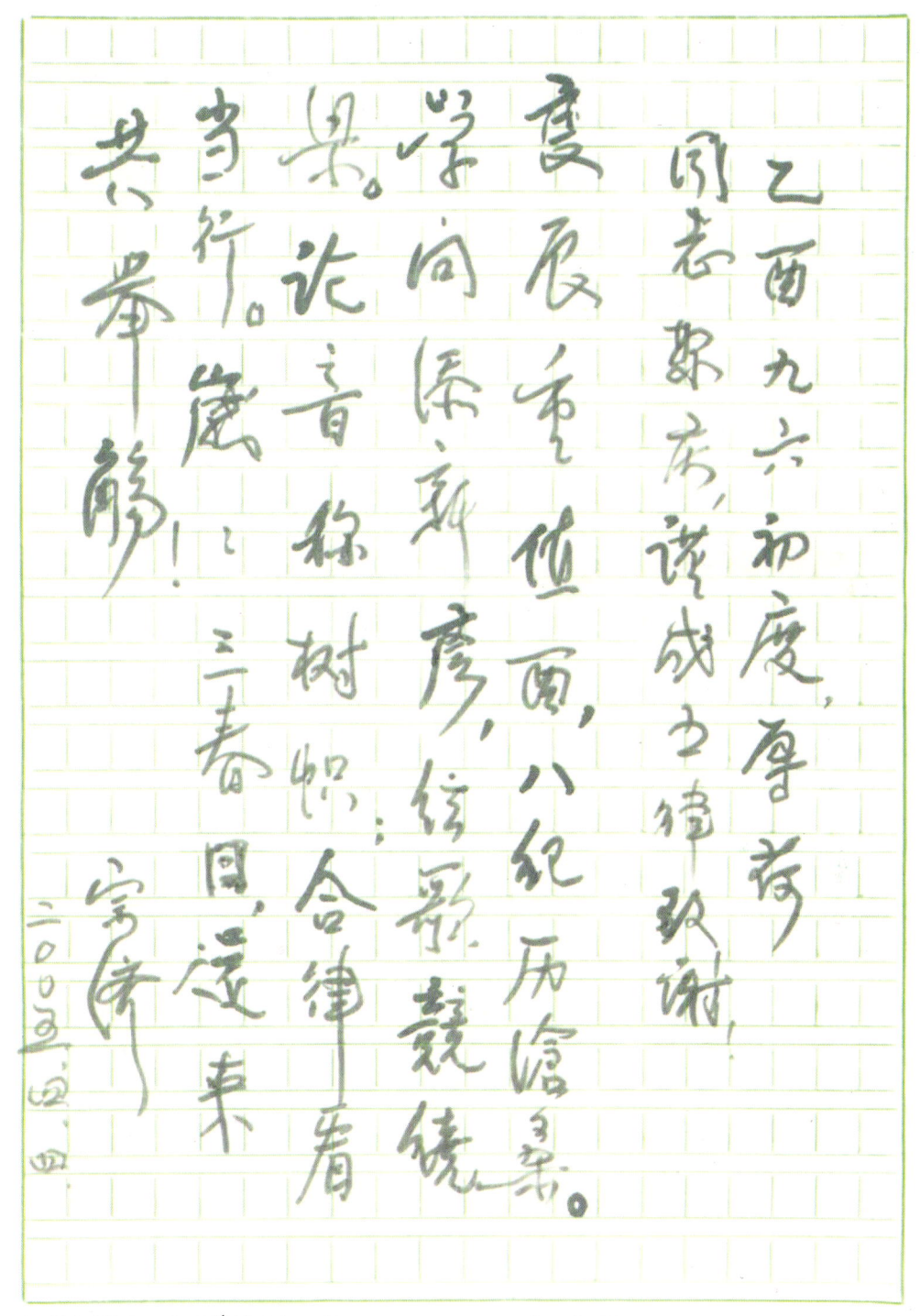

度辰不值颜，八秩历沧桑。
学问探新彦，绝歌竞饶梁。
论音称树帜，合律看当行。
俊彦三春同，远来共举觞！

宗济 2005.4.4

April 4, 2005, at the 96th birthday of **Z. Wu**, a poem was written by him.

试论普通话中韵律规则与其他若干学科中韵律规则的共性

吴宗济

摘要

语音是思维的媒体之一，口语中的抑扬顿挫、顺逆同化等韵律变化都是由思维控制的。我国的传统艺术中如诗文的格律、书画的笔法、音乐歌舞的节奏等，也都是思维的媒体，各有其韵律，它们同属汉语的思维系统，因此彼此之间的韵律规则自有许多共性值得探索。此外，现代物理学中关于相对论的理论以及生理学中关于言语神经的一些活动，也都有其韵律规则。本文选出普通话的若干连续口语中韵律变化的规则，与我国几种传统文学、艺术的韵律规则试作比较，寻绎其间的共性，并以物理、生理的有关韵律规则加以印证，或可作为今后建立汉语语音韵律规则的参考。

1. 引言

人们要传递和表达自己的思维，就得转换成一些信息或媒体，使接收者能够感知。人类常用的感知渠道是视觉与听觉。视觉感知的信息有文字、图画以及表情，听觉的有语言、歌唱以及拟声。视觉信息的艺术化有舞蹈；听觉的有音乐（当然，还有戏剧，是二者得兼的）。这些信息的质与量都由思维产生和控制。因而信息的活动和节奏与思维的是同步的。以语言来说，传统的语言学和语音学的研究，都只属于"人－人对话"的范围，新兴的"人－机对话"的语言学、语音学还没有系统地问世。语音动态的高层次规则是"韵律规则"，它包括语音的三项特征：高低、轻重和快慢。三者的搭配和变化，随思维活动而极其繁复，成为今日"人－机对话"中提高语音自然度的"瓶颈"[26]。

今日"人－机对话"中的一项主要任务，是普通话语音合成与识别质量的提高。目前，在我国的言语工程方面，通过文理的合作，针对汉语的特点，二十来年的研究，从字到词、从词到句，成果已从实验室走向市场，取得了前所未有的成就。只是过去的研究对普通话短语连读的音段和超音段的处理，虽已达到较为满意的程度，但对有关成句和成篇自然度的韵律的处理，却还有不小的差距。

究其原因，表达语句自然度的载体，除上述的特征外，还有连续语音的韵律三特征的搭配。它们的相互依存和制约的关系，因人别、因语境而异，其多变规则的分析处理还达不到应有的水平。语言学者可套用当年梁沈约论声调的说法，现在韵律的研究是："程序之法有限，韵律之变累万；以累万之繁，配程序之约，韵律变化，非思力所举。……"况且"人－机对话"中的语音韵律的授受，和"人－人对话"中的大有不同。后者是单凭口耳就能随机应变；前者就必须把表达思维的一切韵律变量的细节准确无误地编成数码，再通过相当复杂的程序来运行。

语音动态的"韵律规则"的探索成为今日"人－机对话"中提高语音自然度的关键。韵律既是思维的媒体，我们在进一步探索语音韵律规则、从事大量取样和编码之外，似乎还应该扩大一番视野，看看同属思维媒体的其他学科中有没有可供借鉴的韵律规则。最为接近汉语思维的其他学科，要属中国传统的文学和艺术了。本文对此作些尝试，选取文学中的诗、文和赋，艺术中的书画和乐、曲,简略地介绍其中的韵律理论和分析方法,来作为建立普通话语音韵律规则的借鉴。关于处理方案,还介绍一些近来物理学和生理学研究中有关韵律的新资料,来扩大思路,作为研究分析语音韵律的参考。

2. 中国文学中的韵律规则

2.1 诗

现代中国语文学课程中关于韵律的叙述,多属于诗、词、曲、赋,以及文章的节奏,其中也有一些是属于中国音韵学或普通语音学的。传统音韵学中关于语音的资料,多数是声母与韵母的考据和分类,关于声调的也只限于调位的分类而缺乏调值的描写[28]。古代的诗与歌是一体的,古诗的体由四言而发展为五言、七言,都是能吟唱的。律诗讲究平仄搭配,就完全属于韵律规则的要求[29]。语言学大师王力先生论述的汉语律诗的平仄与长短关系问题,正是与吟诵的韵律有关。他说:

"声调自然是以音高为主要特征,但是长短和升降也有关系。依中古声调的情形看来,上古的声调大约只有两大类,就是平声和入声。中古的上声最大部分是平声变来的,极小部分是入声变来的。中古的去声大部分是入声变来的,小部分是平声变来的(或由平经上变入)。依我们的设想:平声是长而不升不降的,上去入三声都是短的。这样,自然分为平仄两类了。平仄递用就是长短递用,平调与升降调或促调递用。"[17]

梁代文学评论家刘勰论诗:"人禀七情,应物斯感,感物吟志,莫非自然。"古诗中有以诗配乐的体裁,称为"乐府",刘勰说:"乐府者,'声依永,律和声'也。""故知诗为乐心,声为乐体;乐体在声,瞽师务调其器;乐心在诗,君子宜正其文。"说明诗与乐是不可分的。诗不协乐,就是不正。因此其韵律是严格的。早期的乐府诗是配乐的,至唐以后的乐府就脱离乐律而徒有其名,成为诗的一种体裁了。

2.2 文

古代文人的文章,到汉、魏以后齐、梁之际,就开始讲求声律,用乐律来描写声调的相对值。而且古代文章多主张要合乎吟诵,那就也与声调的音乐感有密切关系。梁代"永明体"的一派文人讲究四声,其中的沈约是代表。他论文章的音乐化和韵律的规则:

"夫五色相宜,八音协畅;由乎玄黄律吕,各适物宜。欲使宫羽相变,低昂舛节,若前有浮声,则后须切响。一简之内,音韵尽殊;两句之中,轻重悉异。妙达此旨,始可言文。""宫商之声有五,文字之别累万。以累万之繁,配五声之约,高下低昂,非思力所举,又非止若斯而已也。……若以文章之音韵,同弦管之声曲,则美恶妍嫱,不得顿相乖反。"[14]

这就强调了文章的声调可以完全用音乐的五音相配,而获得与弦管之音同样美妙的境界。

梁代的文学评论家刘勰也说:

"夫音律所始,本于人声者也。声合宫商,肇自血气。……古之教歌,先揆以法,使疾呼中宫,徐呼中徵。夫宫商响高,徵羽声下;抗喉矫舌之差,攒唇激齿之异,廉肉相准,皎然可分。……凡声有飞沉,响有双迭。双声隔字而每舛,迭韵杂句而必睽;沉则响发而断,飞则声飏不还,并辘轳交往,逆鳞相比。……是以声画妍蚩,寄在吟咏;滋味流于下句,气力穷于和韵。异音相从谓之和,同声相应谓之韵。"[39]

这是一段较早的相当具体的韵律评论。他主要说明语音的韵律来自人的思维。声调就靠发音机制的运动。古代的唱法是:紧唱要合宫调,慢唱要合徵调。宫、商调高,徵、羽调低。(按:古代五声音阶的"宫商角徵羽",是宫低而徵高。刘勰说,宫是"疾呼"、"响高";徵是"徐呼"、"声下",则是徵低而宫高了,如无错简,也可以按"旋相为宫"的唱法,以徵为宫,就是徵低而宫高。)双声的字不能隔开,叠韵的句不能杂乱。声调太低会隔断,太高会走调。这样,韵律就得循环而齐整。文语之美全在吟咏。韵味要传给下句,气力要用来和韵。不同的音连读叫做和,相同的调呼应叫做韵。(按:古代文献中"声"、"音"常混用。如《说文解字》:"宫商角徵羽,'声';丝竹金石匏土革木,'音'也。"则"声"与"音"是"声调"与"音质"的区别。)[25]

2.3 赋

语音韵律的变量,在语境中影响的因素,不是用简单的规则就能概括的。在古文献中,常有用非常华赡的文笔描写事物的动态,而使情文并茂的,也可用来比拟语音的韵律,如三国时曹植(子建)的《洛神赋》中,有一段想象洛神体态的描写:

"翩若惊鸿,婉若游龙……神光离合,乍阴乍阳……动无常则,若危若安。进止难期,若往若还。"

此赋的八句虽是想象洛神的姿态,但却是一段节奏完美、词义对称、极为精彩的文字。我们试把这八句借用于语音韵律的描写:节奏变化或断或连;阴调、阳调随机搭配。高调如惊鸿的起飞;连调若游龙的蜿蜒;韵律动态没有常规;语气力度或紧或松;节奏停延难于预定;同化异化有顺有逆。

这一段话把体态之美同文章之美融合无间,而用来描写语音韵律之美也是恰当的吧。

3. 中国艺术中的韵律规则

中国的艺术包罗很广。这里只选几种同属于直接表达思维的媒体:音乐、书法、绘画和戏曲。其中的韵律规则与语音的韵律规则有很多相通之处。在此择要选录一些前人的论述。

3.1 音乐

中国古代关于音乐的叙述,有"乐律"和"乐音"两大部分,文献极其丰富。乐律是声调计量的基础,王力先生对"乐律"曾有简明通俗的介绍,兹摘录如下。

"古人把宫商角徵羽称为五音,……后来再加上变宫、变徵,称为七音。……作为音级,宫商角徵羽等音只有相对音高,没有绝对音高。这就是说,它们的音高是随着调子转移的。但是相邻两音的距离却固定不变。只要第一级的音高确定了,其他各级的音高也就都确定了。古人通常以宫作为音阶的起点。……宫的音高确定了,全部五声音阶各级的音高也就都确定了。七声音阶的情况也是这样。"(按:语音的声调正是如此。在平叙句中,四声的一个基调的音高定了,其余各调的音高也都定了。参看[20])

"古书上常常把五音和六律并举。……律和音是两个不同的概念。……旧说古人用十二个长度不同的律管,吹出十二个高度不同的标准音,以确定乐音的高低,因此这十二个标准音也就叫做'十二律'。十二律各有固定的音和特定的名称,……从低到高排列起来,依次为:黄钟、大吕、太簇、夹钟、姑洗、中吕、蕤宾、林钟、夷则、南吕、无射、应钟。十二律分为阴阳两类:奇数六律为阳律,叫做六律;偶数六律为阴律,叫做六吕。"[17]

中国的传统音韵学,从来就是用宫商五声的乐律来描述声调的。到了明代,朱载堉始创的"十二平均律"的理论达到很高的水平[4]。我们的实验证明,不同人或不同语气语调的频率值各有不同,但如用十二平均律的单程来计量,其调型格局相对是守恒的。正如王力先生所言:声调的乐律是相对音高,不是绝对音高[20][25]。

3.1.1 声乐

中国从来就是用乐律来分析声调的。现代的语音实验证明，不同人或不同语气的声调高低可以不同，但同一方言中调位的乐律格局是相对稳定的。语音声调的表达有声乐和器乐。声乐主要是歌唱和戏曲。以曲调唱法非常严格的昆曲为例，明清之际，昆曲的唱法由于文人雅士的参与和切磋，流传了不少有关乐理的唱论。其中的术语换成现代词汇来说，就有：音阶、音程、音域、旋律、滑音、主题、变奏、节拍、转调、移调、尾声等等的规律，都可用来作为研究语音韵律的借鉴。

关于乐音的叙述，最早的文献有《礼记》的《乐记》，指出音乐的产生和发展：

"凡音之起，由人心生也。人心之动，物使之然也。感于物而动，故形于声；声相应，故生变；变成方，谓之音。比音而乐之，及干戚羽旄，谓之乐。……故歌之为言也，长言之也。说（悦）之，故言之；言之不足，故长言之；长言之不足，故嗟叹之；嗟叹之不足，故不知手之舞之，足之蹈之。"

这就是说，言语是由思维产生的，而音乐、歌唱、舞蹈都是言语的延伸、增强和修饰化。

3.1.2 器乐

关于演奏器乐的韵律，可以唐代大诗人白居易描写琵琶演奏之听感为例：

"轻拢慢捻抹复挑，初为霓裳后六幺。大弦嘈嘈如急雨，小弦切切如私语。嘈嘈切切错杂弹，大珠小珠落玉盘。间关莺语花底滑，幽咽流泉冰下难。水泉冷涩弦凝绝，凝绝不通声渐歇。别有幽愁暗恨生，此时无声胜有声。银瓶乍破水浆迸，铁骑突出刀枪鸣。曲终收拨当心画，四弦一声如裂帛。……"

此诗用刻画入微的状声字句，描写出琵琶声的抑扬顿挫，以及指法的入神。其中有些描写，可以拿来比拟语音的韵律，如："急雨"是快速，"私语"是轻读，"花底滑"是连绵变调，"冰下难"是降调，"凝绝"是停顿，"水浆迸、刀枪鸣"是突升的移调和突增的音量……

3.1.3 戏曲

关于戏曲的唱法，元代芝庵的《唱论》说：

"歌之格调：抑扬顿挫，顶叠垛换，萦纡牵结，敦拖呜咽，推题九转，摇欠遏透。歌之节奏：停声、待拍、偷吹、拽棒、字真、句笃、依腔、贴调。"[33]

他对昆曲韵律的格调（声调、字音）、节奏（长短、快慢）有如此详尽的描述，其中有多半可以用来作为语音韵律的规则。

声调的节奏在戏剧道白中的作用，明代李渔论昆曲"宾白"的韵律时说：

"世人但以音韵二字用之曲中，不知宾白之文，更宜调声协律。世人但知四六之句平间仄，仄间平，非可混施迭用，不知散体之文亦复如是。……如上句末一字用平，则下句末一字定宜用仄……"[11]

这就不只是描写歌唱，而是描写道白，有如今之朗诵，其韵律规则就和口语的韵律规则有更密切的关系了。

3.2 书法

书写的文字主要是思维的媒体。汉字书法的演变为：篆、隶、楷、行、草。草书的发展过程有"章草"、"今草"、"狂草"三个阶段。书法中能自由表达思维的是今草和狂草，而狂草尤其能抒发感情，达到随心所欲的自然境地，因此其韵律变化就特别丰富。这里就以狂草为例。唐代张怀瓘论草书的体势说：

"字之体势，一笔而成。偶有不连，而血脉不断。及其连者，气候通其隔行。唯王子敬明其深诣，故行首之字，往往继前行之末。"[37]

他所说草书是"一笔而成"，如果笔画不连，但"血脉"仍旧"不断"，这正是语音连读变调的两种模式。语音实验证明：两音节连读，后字的辅音如为浊辅音，调形就和前字调尾连接而一气呵成；如为清辅音，调形就断开而走势不断。他所举王子敬功力之深，写得通畅时，次行首字的起点笔势会接上前行末字之尾。这也正是语音韵律的一条重要规则：在自然口语中，下句的头会和上句的尾连读而服从"跳板规则"构成"协同变调"。[22]

宋代姜夔的《续书谱》对草书有更精辟的理论：

"草书之体，如人坐卧行立。……一切变态，非苟然者。又一字之体，率有多变，有起有应。如此起者，当如此应，各有义理。……自唐以前多是'独草'，不过两字属连。累数十字而不断，号曰'连绵'、'游丝'。……古人作草，……其相连处，特是引带。尝考其字，是点画处皆重，非点画处偶相引带，其笔皆轻。虽复变化多端，而未尝乱其法度。张颠、怀素最号野逸，而不失此法。……大抵用笔有缓有急，有有锋，有无锋，有承接上文，有牵引下字，（按："承接"、"牵引"正是"跳板规则"的头、尾调形）乍徐还疾，忽往复收。缓以效古，急以出奇；有锋以耀其精神，无锋以含其气味。横斜曲直，钩环盘纡，皆以势为主。"[9]

现代书法家欧阳中石说："草书的笔画可以'连绵'、'约简'；结字可以'变形'、'移位'；字与字可以'萦带'、'呼应'、'跌宕'、'交错'、'参差'、'间插'……。"[13]

草书的韵律如"一言以蔽之"，就是"以势为主"，综合各家之论，草书书法韵律的格局，可以简化为三种模式：

1. "连绵"：草书的上字尾笔与下字起笔连写，为不断的笔法。
2. "映带"：草书的上字尾笔与下字起笔断开，但"笔意"（走势）仍前后呼应。
3. "错综"：一幅草书中有的字形放大或缩小，行款有的离格或跨行。

正如语音的两字连读变调模式，如前节所述，"连绵"：下字为浊辅音或元音，其过渡调形不断；"映带"：下字为清辅音，其过渡调形稍稍断开，但听不出来（二者过渡的走势，都如同船与岸之间的跳板）；"错综"：例如两上声连读时，前上声的变为阳平的极化调形（"连绵"、"映带"为"语音变调"，"错综"为"音系变调"）[22]。

草书的笔法，历代论者很多，大都只说到如何心手相应、如何运笔布局，但是从未有人说清楚，在一幅草书中，为什么有些连笔而有些不连。我们现在从狂草的书法中可以回答这个问题了。这就是连笔的"书法"和"文字"（准确地说应该是"语言"）的语法是有密切关系的。试想书写既然是受思维支配，就必然会反映写者的"思路"（即刻就反映在"潜语言"上），草书是纵笔疾书，也就更和口语的语法合拍。以唐"草圣"怀素的狂草《自叙帖》真迹为例（研究前人笔法，必须根据其真迹或其影印本。再好的拓本对牵丝等笔也不免丢失）。全帖共计703字、126行；以四字的短语占绝大多数，都作连笔（除了遇到换行时，笔画不得不断开之外，但笔势仍常有呼应）；其他的短语和句子也都按语法处理，或连绵或映带。例如《自叙帖》的第一句是"怀素家长沙"："怀素"和"长沙"都是语法中"直接成分"的二字组，就各作连笔，而"家"字和上、下字断开。又多字组的短句，如"则有张礼部"，"以至于吴郡张旭"等，字数虽多，为了贯彻语气，也是一笔到底，充分反映了语法的结构，都作"连绵"的写法。（图1）

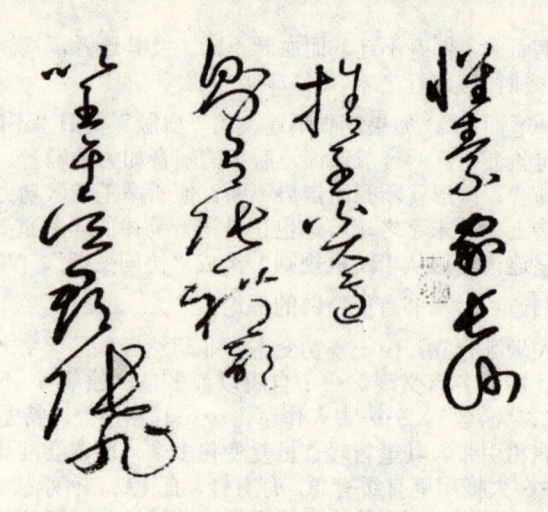

图1：怀素《自叙帖》

<u>怀素 家 长沙 舍子奚适 则有张礼部 以至于吴郡张旭</u>

近人王涣林在《自叙帖》的序中评介怀素的草书说：

"'使转'可谓草书之灵魂。……牵丝映带，气血一脉。……此帖牵丝处理，已达顶峰。连绵缭绕，生动多姿。尤其某些'借笔'牵丝……一字之末，成次字之首。浑然天成，虚实互见。狂草强调制造矛盾，又解决矛盾。故字形大小之错综，亦成为得力武器。……此卷字形大小、开合，对比极为夸张，洋溢着浓烈的浪漫主义气息。此外，《自叙帖》无行无列，行间疏密，虚实互见，大章法却能以一气团之，有全卷浑然的缜密感。"[15]

这里说到怀素的"借笔牵丝"和"大小错综"的两种笔法，可举一些例子（图2、图3）。

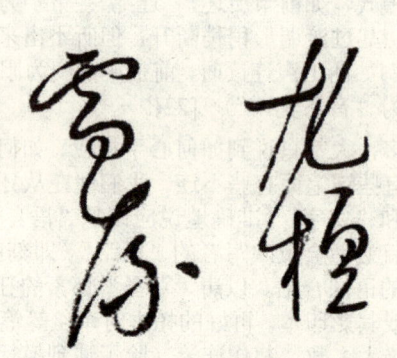

图2：怀素《自叙帖》

<u>尤极 电流</u>

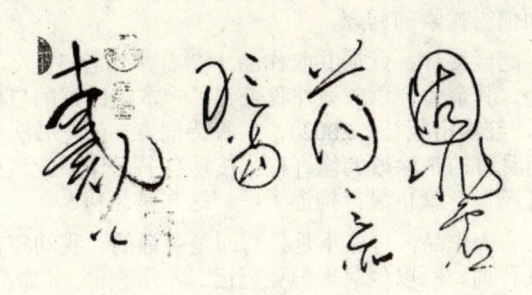

图 3：怀素《自叙帖》
固非虚薄之所敢当

图 2 是两组连绵映带的例子。"尤极"二字，上字"尤"的末笔为右上角的一个"点"，和下字"极"的首笔为左边一横的起点，距离较远，但仍拉出一条相当长的斜线（"借笔"）作为"牵丝"。再看"电流"两字，"电"的末笔为一钩在最右，"流"的首笔为一点在最左，本可拉一"牵丝"。但上字"电"的末笔一钩是向上挑的，其势不便向下，于是索性顺势将笔锋左转一圈，去和下字"流"的首笔接轨。所以草书的精神就在于"以势为主"，而这样的连绵或映带，又基本上是服从语法结构的。

图 3 是"大小错综"、"无行无列"的例子。本来每行都有五六个字，这句"固非虚薄之所敢当"八个字忽然放大，占了三行。不但大小错综，而且出行出列。

"戴公"两字更是占满了一行，不但更加出格，而且大小悬殊，淋漓极致。其他古今草书名家，如唐张旭、宋黄庭坚（山谷）、清傅山，乃至现代的毛泽东，他们的草书笔法，连绵、映带也都合乎语法和语气。但如在放诞自然上，只有毛氏可与怀素分庭抗礼[30]。

关于毛泽东的书法，评家称之为天才而与素书、黄书媲美。王涣林在怀素《自叙帖》的序言中同时评论毛书说：

"黄山谷、毛泽东学狂草有成。黄山谷得之于禅悦，毛泽东得之于天才。毛泽东以天纵奇秉超越了笔墨字形之羁绊，径与狂僧神游；笔法上虽略逊一筹，气局意象之高，似有过之。"

试看图 4 的例子，就知并非过誉。图 4 是毛氏写的古诗（采自中央档案馆编《毛泽东手书古诗词选》，档案出版社，1984）。"疏影"、"暗香"两句名句，用笔都是按短语语法作"连绵"的草法。"月明林下美人来"一句，除换行断开都是一笔到底的。"（自去）何郎无好咏，东风愁寂几回开"两句，越写越大，最后"几回开"三字的错综出列，与怀素实为异曲同工。

图 4：《毛泽东手书古诗词选》
疏影横斜/水清浅 暗/香 浮动 月/昏黄
月明林/下 美人来
何郎 无/好咏 东风/愁寂几/ 回开

这里出现一个有趣而值得探索的问题。

毛氏书写的古诗选，略经统计：此册共收作品 117 首，作者 57 人，全书 213 页，狂草就有 148 页，狂草极多连笔，其余为今草。另外我查到了一本毛氏写的自作诗词影印本（胡为雄编著《毛泽东诗词鉴赏》，红旗出版社，2002），共收诗词 75 首，书法多为行楷，很少草书，绝无狂草，更少连笔，而且有的是涂改的修订稿。按理自书己作，应该更熟悉、更自由些，但其结果恰恰相反，不作狂草，行款也显得拘谨了些。这却是为何？

据我臆测：毛泽东写古人作品，可能不是抄写而是背诵的。我幼年也是读的私塾，同有此经历，经史诗文全得熟读背诵。所以他写来但凭记忆，不用查书。（如图 4 的"疏影"两句末二字，林逋的诗原作"黄昏"，写成"昏黄"，似乎是记错了。但当年诗人为了押韵，把"黄、昏"作为形容词，与"清、浅"成对。而在今日，"黄昏"已通用作为名词，与"月"字连接就不通。毛本是诗人，就不经意地在自然思维中纵笔疾书，写成"昏黄"，来和"清浅"作对了。这正是狂草不假推敲、紧接思维的一个很好的例子。）因此他所写古诗都用草书。至于他写自己的作品，虽然内容都是熟悉的，但有时还需要改动一些，有的诗还可能是应求之笔，这就较为严谨，反而不够流畅，就用行草了。（本文发表后，作者才又见到 1984 年 7 月中央档案馆编的《毛泽东手书古诗词选》，在"出版说明"中指出："这些诗词大多是毛泽东同志凭记忆书写的。凡和原作有出入的地方，经核对，都在释文中分别作了校订和增补。……"说明毛泽东写古诗是多凭记忆而可能写错或改动的。这证明我的"臆测"是对了。）

本文对草书所引文献似乎太多了些，与其他各节不平衡。原因是：草书的连绵错综，几乎完全反映了思维中的语法规则，能和语音的韵律动态相互对应。它的离行、扩大，也同感情语调的调阶移动或/和调域展宽相合。其中多维变量的现象，更是有其共性。所以研究草书的韵律规则，可以给语音韵律研究做很好的参考[30]。

3.3 绘画

中国传统的绘画向来分为"工笔"和"写意"两大类，而"写意画"又名"水墨画"或"文人画"，最多的作品是山水画。它是表达思维、抒发情感的主要媒体之一。古往今来，关于这方面传世的作品和理论，较书法的有过之无不及。"写意"顾名思义，就是表达思维。其间的笔法和布局差不多都和草书书法的韵律在在相通，向来有"书画同源"之说，因此也能成为研究韵律规则的重要对象。

唐代大诗人兼山水画家王维（传）的《山水诀》说："夫画道之中，水墨最为上。肇自然之性，成造化之功。"他的《山水论》又说："凡画山水，意在笔先。"北宋郭熙《林泉高致集》中的《山水训》又说："人之学画，无异学书。"他论山水画法要自然、要"意在笔先"，无异于作草书之法[3]。

明代石涛论写意画的笔法更为具体：

"动之以旋，润之以转，居之以旷。出如截，入如揭。能圆能方，能直能曲，能上能下。左右均齐，凸凹突兀，断截横斜，如水之就深，如火之炎上，自然而不容毫发强也。"又说："山川万物之具体，有反有正，有偏有侧，有聚有散，……有断有连……"

石涛论写意的笔法：有旋转出入，方圆曲直，上下左右，凹凸横断，反正偏侧，聚散断连……这简直就是狂草的韵律。而特别提出笔法的变化，不可"拘于拟古"而要能"借古开今"。他说：

"'至人无法'，非无法也，无法而法，乃为至法。凡事有经必有权；有法必有化。一知其经，即变其权；一知其法，即功于化。夫画：天下变通之大法也……"

这段语录看似玄虚,实际上他提出的"经"与"权","法"与"化"的辨证关系,和春秋时孟子的一段话极其相似。孟子(轲)曾批判当时杨、墨两学派的"为我"与"兼爱"是各走极端,提出"权"的重要性:

"执中无权,犹执一也。所恶执一者,为其贼道也,举一而废百也。"(《孟子·尽心上》)

这就是说:单靠规则("执中","经")而不知变通("权"),就是墨守陈规而不问其余("执一"),这就成为真理之障碍,所以处理问题要融会贯通。石涛的这个启示,对今日一切科研工作都有指导意义。例如,口语语音的必然变调规则是"经"与"法",而韵律的或然变化则是"权"与"化"。

现代艺术家郭茂来所著绘画理论,从视觉的感知方面来衡量艺术品的美学价值,绘画的视觉规则与语言的听觉规则相通,称为"视觉语法"。其论点是:

"视觉语法是依据视觉语言所要表达的特定信息,有机合理地构成诸多视觉语词秩序的组织方法,也就是把视觉内容的各种要素,协调统一起来的结构形式。……在艺术语言中,构成不同形态、色彩语词间秩序关系的语法要素有:'平衡'、'节奏'、'韵律'、'旋律'。……视觉形态的平衡关系,可以分为以静感为主导的平衡和以动感为主导的平衡。以静感为主导的平衡是指:以'对称性'原理构成的平衡关系,也称之为'均齐关系'。依据对称关系的不同特点,可将视觉形态对称的形式分为'反射对称'、'回转对称'、'旋转对称'、'移动对称'四种主要类型。以动感为主导的平衡是指:平衡关系中的'不对称'形式。这种以不对称的形式所构成的平衡关系,也称之为'均衡'。"[6]

写意画的"平衡"与"均衡",就相当于草书的"连绵"与"错综",也相当于口语连音的"同化"与"极化",都是"韵律"的表现规则。

中国向来有"书画同源"之说,基本上都从思维与韵律的关系立论。兹举两例。如胡寿荣论水墨画与书法:

"张旭的草书,其'势'和内力达成的动态活力,给人以'流畅'、'舒旷'、'顿挫'的抽象美感。……书法的点划从生成之日起即是对抽象情怀的自由阐释。'书画同源',中国画的笔法来自书法,中国的书与画有着共同的审美特征。中国写意绘画的笔墨法则基本上是由书法的笔意、笔法发展而来的。……中国书画的笔墨是理性经验外化之迹,笔墨呈现的效果多层次地反映了智性潜能以及抽象思维美学所意含的审美情调与意境。……用笔的疾徐顿挫等,其表征乃是抽象形态。"[8]

程翔章论书法与画法的关系说:

"从早期的书法与绘画看,二者本就同出一源。往往字就是画,画就是字。"他举张芝草书一笔而成、陆探微作画连绵不断的例,"书法在章法布局上也有很多相通之处。如在疏密的处理上,都讲究'疏能走马,密不通风'。在虚实的处理上,都讲究'虚实相生,计白当黑'。在大小的处理上,都讲究'参差错落,揖让补救'等等。因为书与画具有以上特点,所以我们说,中国书画同源是有根据的。"[3]

这些资料不但把书法与画法的韵律作了充分的等同,而且认为视觉的韵律也有语法,同时,我们在语音中也找到不少与书、画相通的韵律规则,而且它们都是来自思维,因此我们也可顺理成章地说:书、画与话语都是同源[30]。

4. 语音韵律的变化规则

4.1 普通话韵律的基本单元（必然变量）

普通话的韵律，在语音学上包括声调、重音、快慢和音步的节奏；在声学上包括音高、音强、音长和停延的搭配。韵律的表现，无论是在短语、句子和篇章中，都是以单字和短语为基本单元，这就是所谓语调的底层结构。说话时根据需要，在句子中先加上一些修改而成为语调的表层结构。因此，表层语调是由若干个底层机构，通过"逻辑"（问答或祈使）或/和"语气"（感情或责难）的韵律修饰，而构成表层结构的。底层结构的变量是受生理、声学和音系规则支配的"必然变量"。表层结构的变量是受环境支配的或然变量。所以研究语句的或然变量的韵律，就必须先掌握短语的必然变量的韵律规则。短语的韵律规则包括单音节调型、双音节、三音节、四音节各短语的音节间连读变调模型，以及语音学、音系学、语法学的"三平面变调规律"、协同变调的"'跳板'规则"、逐级语法层次的"'多米诺'变调规则"，这些规则已有报告发表，并在言语工程中验证[18][19][22][32]。

4.2 普通话语调的韵律变量（或然变量）

上节指出：普通话语句的韵律，包括语句的语气、节奏等或然变量。这些或然变量是以底层的必然变量为基础的。所以对于表层的语调，如果不能澄清底层的必然变调，而直接从表层语调去分析，必将得出过多的语调模型而难于应用。我们应该掌握"法"与"权"的关系，从复式的表层语调中，先按"必然变调规则"把"基本单元"提取出来，所余下的韵律变量就浮现了。还有比较难于处理的，是接收反馈信息后的随境变量（如"应答"），也就是语音处理系统的自适应功能（这都属于韵律处理的最高层次），这些问题如不解决，自然度就永远不能提高。目前我们已经初步把或然变量之中常用的规则，如线性频率转换为乐律半音的坐标，短语韵律的"移调"和"变域"处理等规则，都是为提高语音合成的自然度和语音识别的准确度打下基础的。我们认为，这些规则对于语音合成等处理方案，是必须首先考虑的基本概念[24][26][27][32][7][2]。

4.3 篇章韵律的分析初探

现代普通话的韵律规则，属于语句的，当前已经有不少研究成果了；属于篇章的，在语法方面的研究已有不少；在语音方面的似乎还不多。这里试以普通话的四句朗诵材料为样本，用上述的韵律规则作些分析。朗诵句如下：

"他们的品质是那样的纯洁和高尚。
他们的意志是那样的坚韧和刚强。
他们的气质是那样的深厚和朴实。
他们的胸怀是那样的美丽和宽广！"

这是由一位电台女广播员发的音。经过声学分析如图 5a—5d。（原图包括：语音波形频谱、频率的赫兹调形、乐律的半音程调形、全部测量数据等五项。本文只列出半音程坐标的调形图及其数据。）

这四句中，（1）短语的语法：按赵元任先生的说法，"他们的"为"领属代名词"，是每图的第一句短语。"是那样的"为"程度副词"，也是每图都相同[36]。"品质"、"意志"、"气质"、"胸怀"四个"名词"，每图一组；"纯洁"、"高尚"、"坚韧"、"刚强"、"深厚"、"朴实"、"美丽"、"宽广"八个"形容词"，每图两组。（2）短语的语音："他们的"为"双+单"的三字调，"的"为"轻声"。"是那样的"为"单+三"的四字调，"是"作轻读，"的"为轻声[31]。此四句朗诵描写的对象是人民英雄，带有称颂的感情。其移调程度和调域的宽度含有朗诵和歌颂的双重因素,此四句是服从篇章的韵律规则的,其中逻辑重音和感情重音的成分,由代词、副词和名词、形容词同时表达。我们把名词、形容词的数据跟代词、副词的数据分别测量统计(表1、表2),是要观察一下前者跟后者各自表达感情的程度有无不同。分析的办法是:短语一概不采用末字。"调域上限"用阴平字和去声字的调形起点;"调域下限"用全上字的转折点或半上字的终点。平均后,调域上限的根据作为基调,上限下限之差作为调域的宽度。

表1:图5a—5d的名词和形容词的基调和调域的数据

采用的阴平字起点的调阶	高#D4	坚 G4	刚#G4	深 E4	胸 A4
采用的去声字起点的调阶	意 G4	气 G4			
采用的全上字转折点和半上字终点的调阶	品 C3	朴#C3			
平均基调	上限 G4	下限#C3			
调域宽度	18ST				

表2:图6a—d中的代词和图7a—d中的副词的基调上限的数据

"他们的"	图6a	图6b	图6c	图6d
基调上限	#G4	#G4	#A3	#A4
"是那样的"	图7a	图7b	图7c	图7d
基调上限	G4	#D4	B3	B4

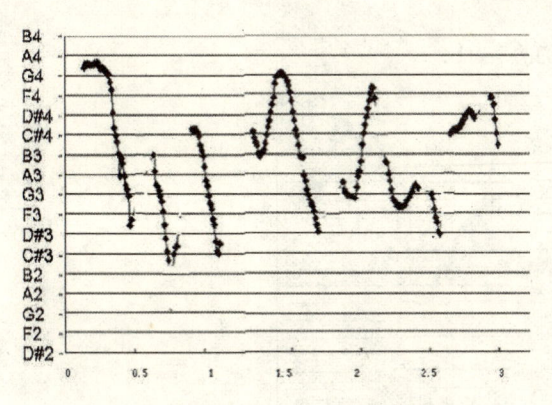

图5a:他们的品质是那样的纯洁和高尚 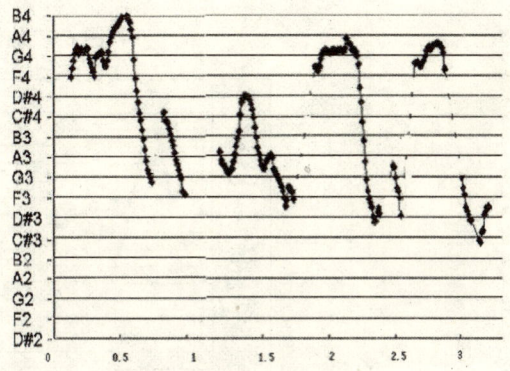   图5b:他们的意志是那样的坚韧和刚强

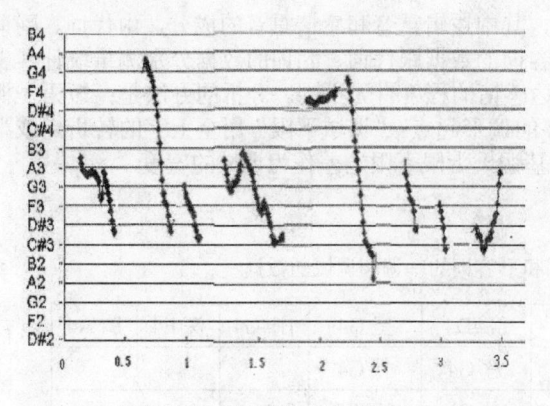

图5c：他们的气质是那样的深厚和朴实 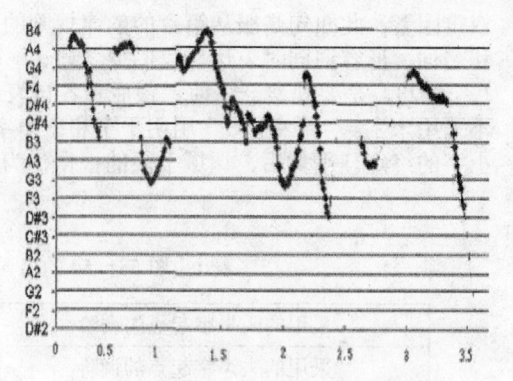　　　　　**图5d**：他们的胸怀是那样的美丽和宽广

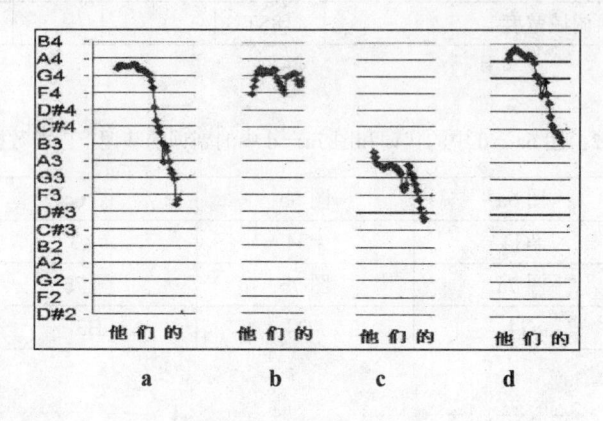

图6："他们的"对比

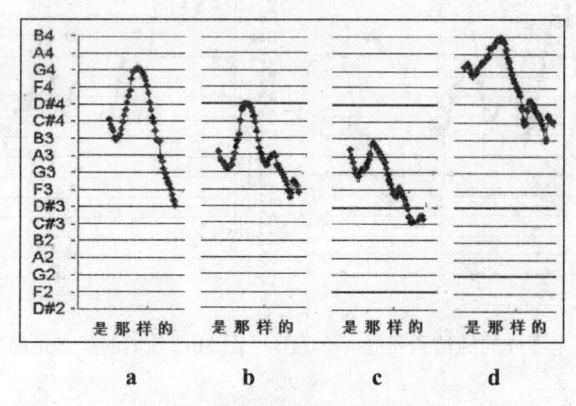

图7："是那样的"对比

　　图6、图7是四句朗诵句中重现的两组短语的比较，四句中这两类短语的字同而调形不同。这四句的背景为歌颂英雄，故除了朗诵体的韵律外，还带有一定的感情韵律。各名词和形容词的基调调阶本来都可能再有所移动，调域宽度都可能再有所改变，但是因为名词前有了"代词"，形容词前有了"副词"的前提条件，于是这个感情信息的表达就都由前者分担一部分了。试看四句中最高的声调上限是图7d的"那"字的声调（B4），它就比图5d的"胸"字（A4）的声调还高一个半音程。

这四句在语法上是自成一组篇章的，从而产生了篇章韵律的变量。试看图 6 和图 7：四句中前三句（a，b，c）的三个"他们的"和三个"是那样的"的基调，都有相当大的变化。图 5a 中这两个短语的基调都最高，调域最大。5b 中则是"他们的"基调也高，但调域变小，长度变短；"是那样的"基调降低，而调域变短。5c 中的这两个短语则是基调都最低，调域都最短。5d 中则是二者基调都最高，调域都最大。

这四句的韵律调势，总的来说应该是一个前三句递降而后一句突升的、"先抑后扬"的常见的格局。但是，我们看到，从仪器给出的这四句的实际调形却有不同程度的变体。应该降的竟然升了，应该升的又降了，简直"不合规律"。如果贸然只从调高、强度和长度的表层调形来分析，必然会得出许多五花八门无法归纳的"语调模型"来，既无从自圆其说，还给信息处理方面造成不切实用的难题。其实如果认识了本文 4.1 节所述"必然变量"的各项规则，再具备一些基本的言语生理和言语声学的知识，对这些表层上的复杂变量，就能顺藤摸瓜，搜索出这些语音变量的底层真相，可以归纳而得出简化的规则来。

试以这四句为例认真作一番解析。先看 5b 中"他们的"为什么不同于 5a 中"他们的"那样的降势，而发得那样高，这有言语声学上的原因。它后接的字是"意"，起调是高的，服从"跳板规则"而便前接短语高了。而且还有一个言语生理的原因，由于它是浊音，前后音节间的声带颤动不能停止，于是不得不产生协同发音作用（逆同化），而使前接的短语抬高。这是它首先要完成的语音的"必然变量"规律。然而，它还要完成篇章韵律的第二个"或然变量"规律，于是将长度变短（按听觉生理的规律，韵律三特征中的长度短了，音量就弱而有降低的听感），在听感上的效果就相当于低调了。这样，5b 的"他们的"在听觉上就如同低降。

再看 5c 中的"他们的"，是按篇章韵律规则降到最低了。但是后接的字"气"的调头却是高起的。如果按照跳板规则或逆同化规则，岂不是不合规律了？这又是一个言语生理问题。"气"字是清送气塞擦辅音，按发音方法的生理规则，"气"字发音的程序是先塞后擦，成阻之先声带颤动就必须停止，因此就不一定需要服从协同的逆同化规律。

如上所述，这四句的韵律变量，在听觉上是合规则的（我们必须承认，一切语音合成质量的评价，都是以听觉为标准的），前三句的短语的声调感觉呈现递降的"滑坡"之势，语气似乎已逐渐衰弱了；可是到第四句 6d 和 7d 忽然来了个"石破天惊"！二者的基调比在第一句的基调还高，调域也展宽到了极端！这一来整个四句的"情调"都被激活了，成为"先抑后扬"的"篇章韵律"的完美格局。拿怀素《自叙帖》篇末的一个字就占了一行的写法、《琵琶行》描写曲终的"水浆迸、刀枪鸣"的用词，和这四句朗诵相比，可谓"异曲同工"。这就相当于一幅草书中的"连绵"、"映带"和结尾的"错综"书法，文章中的"一简之内，音韵尽殊；两句之中，轻重悉异"的韵律规则。

4.4 传统文艺中的韵律规则与语音的韵律规则的对照

传统文学、艺术中有关韵律的规则，可与现代语音韵律规则对照的项目，初步可提出如下的各项：

现代汉语语音的韵律：
    音段的变化：同化　异化　简化　离格　省略　替换
    声调的变化：弯头　降尾　变调　轻声　同化　过渡　极化　移调
    长度的变化：延长　缩短　断开　轻声　音步　节奏
    轻重的变化：加强　减弱　轻声　递降　极化

艺术的韵律：
    书画：连绵　映带　错综　出格　简笔　藏锋
    度曲：减字　偷声　停板　迟声　循环　衬字

音乐：全音 半音 音阶 旋律 高音 低音 中音 移调 转调 滑音 装饰音
休止 延长缩短 短促 连音 强拍 弱拍 交错 重现

5. 自然科学中的韵律规则

5.1 自然科学中的韵律

　　诺贝尔物理学奖获得者李政道，在最近一次"物理的挑战"报告上，介绍"20世纪的物理成就"，其中提到中国古代的物理，引了唐杜甫的两句诗："细推物理须行乐，何用浮名了此生。"他说："什么是细？仔细观察。什么是推呢？紧密推理。所以细就是讲怎么做实验，推就是怎么做理论。对于怎么做科学实验与理论，我想很难找出比'细'跟'推'两个字用得这么准确的。"

　　他举了许多现代物理学发明的例子，并用苏州的窗格解释21世纪物理学中的对称与不对称问题。结束时说："科学跟艺术有什么关系，我觉得这很有关系。艺术，不管是诗歌、绘画，还是音乐，都是我们用新的方法唤起每个人的意识与潜意识的情感。……所以说情感越珍贵，唤起越强烈，反映越普遍，艺术越优秀。……有人类就有情感，它越普遍唤起创造性，艺术越有价值。人类情感是每个人都有的。科学呢？科学，不管天文、物理、生物、化学，对自然界的现象，进行新的准确的抽象；科学家抽象的叙述越简单，应用越广泛，科学创造也就越深刻。我们不在自然界内，可是这个抽象，把它变成原理，是我们做的。……所以，科学与艺术，它的共同基础是人类创造力。它追求的目的是真理的普遍性。"[12]

　　我们可以说：科学中的各种对称与不对称的现象，也就是它的韵律，在自然界有普遍性。研究文学、艺术，乃至语言的韵律规则，应该取法一些研究科学韵律的方法，来做到"细"和"推"。

5.2 现代科学处理物体变量的基本方法

　　现代自然科学中处理物体变量的基本方法，一是了解现象要用实验，取得结果要靠数学。二是对复杂系统的混沌问题要能即时反馈，能自适应。今日语音自然度的处理上所遇到的难题，正是：（1）如何能将实验成果转换成有效的数学规则在机器上应用；（2）如何使机器能对语音韵律的混沌变量即时反馈并作自适应的处理。这里有两位科学家的意见值得参考。

5.2.1 理论物理的实验与创想

　　杨振宁在一次报告中引用了爱因斯坦在1933年所作《理论物理的方法》演讲中的一段话："理论物理之公理基础不能自实际经验提炼出来，而是要创想出来。"他又说："创想的泉源来自数学。" 杨氏做了解释说："这句话当然值得斟酌。假如一个人不与纯粹的世界、现实的世界发生关系，光坐在那儿想，他不可能想出今天我们所了解的物理世界的结构。所以爱因斯坦是说，你应对现实的世界要有多的了解。可是，最后这个结果却不是从一个实验一个实验的数据得出来的，而是要有一个数学的东西促使你创想出来，再把这个结果与实验的结果验证一下，这才可能得到大的发展。"[35]

5.2.2 复杂系统的反馈与自适应

　　周光召在一次报告中讲如何解决现代科学中的复杂系统问题，他说：

　　"在20世纪以前，宏观系统一直是科学主流研究对象，着重研究线性相互作用的、处于平衡稳定状态附近的系统，它们具有确定的运动规律，所以我们常常能够预测它未来的行为。随着科学技术的发展，现在一个产品常常是多种技术的综合，包含的部件和结构越来越复杂。从20世纪70年代末，人们开始对混沌现象和分形理论进行研究，通过一些数值模拟，人们认识到在非线性本能相互作用下的开放系统,在特定条件下会发生混沌现象或者叫突显现象。当混沌出现在这个区域的时候,这个系统对外界的偶然因素是非常敏感的。系统长期的运动状态成为不可预测的,在一定程度上就是一种无序状态。但又不是完全无序,而是一定程度上的无序。"

"什么叫非线性,非线性就是作用和作用的效果不按相同的比例增长。……非线性相互作用会产生正反馈。非线性相互作用会引起运动中的突变。……为了保持系统的稳定,不致陷入混沌状态,因此,任何一个系统要保持稳定,就必须具有及时反馈、调控和自适应的系统。生物是这样的,一个社会组织也同样如此。"[38]

5.2.3 语音韵律变量是非线性复杂系统

汉语语音的韵律包括音高、音长和音强相互作用的三维变量,在语句中由于语气不同而变更彼此的搭配和强弱的比例,成为难定规则的非线性复杂系统,以致按过去的常规研究已感到不能应付。近来由各信息科研和工程方面所制订的韵律处理公式和模型,虽已有百花齐放的局面,但对韵律自然度的提高,数学规则的订定,还有待于更进一步的探索。目前当务之急,除了上述文艺学科的韵律规则可供启发、扩展思路外,人们口语的韵律变量在人—机对话中的多变性与模糊性以及反馈与自适应规则的缺乏,都是亟待解决的问题。语音的韵律变量,从时间、空间来说,它的多维性、多变性,也得按上述的两个基本方法来解决。语音韵律变量的时空坐标数据和数学处理,都可根据物理学"相对论"中的"对称性"、"恒定性"、"模糊性"等规则来制订,韵律变量的原理在心理学中的大脑活动规则有些解释也可参考,下面略予介绍这方面的资料。

5.3 物理学中的"相对论"

"相对论"的基础理论,对于我们韵律规则的分析是有指导意义的。现在介绍一本科普读物中的一段:

"我们观察和描述物体的运动,总是相对于另一物体或物体群而言的。物理学上将这些描绘物体运动时所参照的物体或物体群称作'参照系'。对于观察者来讲,参照系是静止的,它是其他物体在某过程中时空位置发生变化的背景。在物理学中,研究任何一个物理过程,都离不开参照系。要想定量地探讨物体的运动规律,必须建立与参照系固连的时间—空间坐标系('时空坐标系'),以及用于度量空间尺度的标准尺和用于度量时间尺度的标准钟。"[5,第三章:相对论基础]

按:在今日的韵律研究,例如要分析某人所说的一句感情话语韵律的动态,就得先测量他或她所说平叙句韵律的时—空数据,作为参照系来和其感情句的韵律数据比较,从而根据其在时空上的不同差额,来设定感情的等级,如果没有这参照系就给感情句设定等级,其科学性就成问题。

对于"时空坐标系"的作用,前书又说:

"时空坐标系的作用是相对地确定任一物理事件的空间位置和发生时刻。我们在确定一个空间点的位置时,需要且仅需要三个数,或者说,空间是三维的。采用笛卡尔直角坐标系,每一个点与三个数组成的坐标(X,Y,Z)一一对应。"

"仅有空间坐标,不能完全确定一个事件,还要有时间坐标,用以反映事件发生的时刻。将时间坐标和空间坐标联合起来的坐标系,就是'时空坐标系'。"(同上)

按:韵律三特征的"互补"和"取代"的关系,在哲学上是"相互依存"和"相互制约",在物理上正是"三维关系",用笛卡尔或矢量的分析将可得出,并能够应用于信息处理上。在我们过去的研究中,三者在韵律句中的相互关系是:

音高变,音强、音长都不一定变;

音强变,音高一定变,音长不一定变;

音长变,音高和音强都不一定变;

在听觉的重音上,音长可和音高或音强互补。

5.3.1 物理学"相对论"中的"对称"原理

关于物理学中的"对称"问题,杨振宁在一次报告中指出,"20 世纪物理学的发展有三个主要的旋律,就是量子化、对称、相位因子"[35]。现在引一段上述科普读物中关于"对称"的简明介绍:

"对称性是人们在观察和认识自然过程中产生的一种观念。……在物理学上,对称性就是变换不变性,并将所研究的对象叫做'系统'。同一个系统可以处于不同状态。如果这些不同的状态没有区别,我们就说它们是等价的,我们把系统从一个状态变到另一个状态的过程叫变换,或者称为给系统一个操作。如果一个操作使系统从一个状态变到另一个与之等价的状态,或者说状态在此操作下不变,我们就说该系统对于这一操作是对称的。由于变换或操作的不同,有各种不同的对称性。最常见的对称操作是时空操作,相应的对称性称为时空对称性。其中,空间操作有平移、转动、镜象反射、空间反演等;时间操作有时间平移和时间反演等。"[5,第六章第二节:对称性和守恒量]

按:语音的韵律变量既然是物理三特征的变量,其对称性和操作状态应该与物理学的相同。事实果然是这样。例如:句子中的短语调形尽管由于语气变换而"移调"(平移)或"变域"(时空反演),但其声调等除了加了些连绵的走势,其格局却是基本对称的。即使有些属于音系上的变体(如上声变阳平),也不外乎物理上的"镜象反射"。普通话双音节的四声连调、16 个模型有七对镜象(图 8[18],图中最后一图的"阴阴"HH 和"上上"LL 本应是一对镜象,但因两上连读,前上变了阳平 LL→RL,故少了一对)。

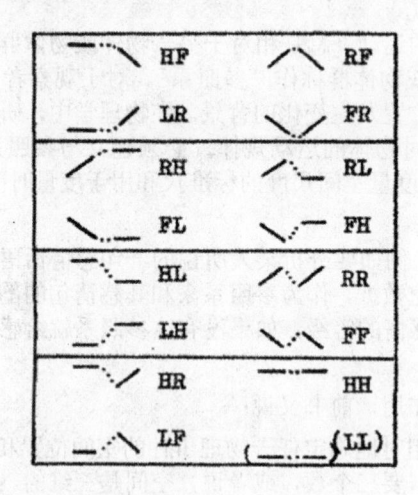

图 8:普通话双音节连读变调模型镜象图(H 高、L 低、R 升、F 降)

5.3.2 "相对论"中的"守恒性"

物理学中最重要的一条定律是守恒定律。它包括物体中的"不变元"和"对称元"两类结构的守恒量。守恒有"能量守恒"、"动量守恒"、"角动量守恒"。对称跟守恒的关系是一种非常密切的关系。[35]"在宏观物理学中,涉及的对称性都是时空对称性。原来人们司空见惯的物理规律,相对于空间坐标的'平移不变性',与动量守恒是等价对应的。……对称性所涉及的变换分为连续进行的'连续变换'和不连续进行的'分立变换'。时间平移、空间平移和空间转动等属于连续变换……与连续变换不变性相联系的守恒量是相加性守恒量（'分立变换'，暂略）。……

"人们曾经认为，守恒律在所有现象中无条件成立。然而，后来的研究进一步揭示出守恒律与系统的运动规律有关，特别与相互作用有关。我们将对所有作用都成立的守恒律称为'严格守恒律'；如果一个守恒律对某些相互作用成立，但对另一些相互作用不成立，而且在运动过程中后者的影响是次要的，则称之为'近似守恒律'。……

"对称性和守恒律是跨越物理学各个领域的普遍法则，利用对称性和守恒律我们可以回避一切复杂的过程量的演算，通过状态的不变性和状态量的守恒，探究物质结构及相互作用的奥妙。……"[5,同前]

5.4 语音韵律变量的对称与守恒

普通话语音韵律的变化，在实验中证明，句子中每个短语的连读调型是必然的变调模型，也就是说，其变调调形是（熟悉本方言的）说话人不假思索而发出的。如果遇到逻辑重音而使基调抬高了（平移），其平叙句中多音节短语的四声搭配格局仍旧是稳定不变（对称）的，也就是说，平叙句中短语的本调模型和移调后的模型是对称的，因此其首尾调值虽有些变动（如受跳板规则的首尾移动），而主调格局是"严格"守恒的。再进一步，如果遇到的句子是感情句子，其短语不但是逻辑重音，而且还是感情重音，则将不但移调，其调域还会展宽或缩小，这就是或然的变调。其调形格局由于韵律三特征的搭配比例受外加影响而改变，成为"近似"的守恒。

5.5 神经系统中语音韵律的感知

普通话韵律的变换，有的是必然的，有的却是或然的，要视环境而变的。人－人交际可以运用接收反馈信息的功能，来作随机应变的应答。人－机交际就必须有一套相当高明的智能程序来应付。语音产生的生理学和物理学方面的知识如果还不能解决，那么，似乎还得从语音感知方面的学科寻求一些办法。

一切语音的韵律，是由生理和心理的"言语链"产生的。这就需要三者综合的研究，来解决这个复杂的韵律变量问题。生理、物理的语音学已有相当规模，而心理的或神经的语音学却还在幼稚阶段。这就需要心理学或神经学的专家提起他们对语音学的兴趣，来为这项新兴的事业作"知识投资"了。语言的神经系统方面，过去多认为只是左脑和语言有关，近来已有了比较深入的研究，认为左脑主要是分析词汇定义，而右脑是综合处理语言的感知。这也许能给多变的韵律研究开一条新的路子。

美国的一位美术教师贝蒂·爱德华以她多年培训绘画人才的经验，吸收了很多美术理论家的著作，以及最近医学界对左右脑感知功能的研究成果，写了《像艺术家一样思考》一书。作为教材，20年来已用13种语言在全球行销。她引用了很多当代学者的论点，并根据许多失语症的报告和世界知名人士用左手写字（左撇子，向来被认为是右脑功能发达的）的统计，主张用左手练习绘画，训练右脑激发创造力。书中并提出书法是绘画的一种形式。她说，过去两百年间，科学家发现语言和与语言相关的能力主要位于左脑，一般认为大脑的右边没有左半边先进，这实在是偏见，后来的研究证明右脑有抽象理解的功能。[1]她在书中列表总结出左右脑模式的特征对比。兹将其中与语音韵律特征有关的项目选录如下：

表3：左脑模式和右脑模式的特征对比

	左脑模式		右脑模式
词汇性	用词汇进行命名、描述和定义	非词汇性	用非词汇性认识来处理感知
分析性	有步骤地一部分一部分解决问题	综合性	把事物整合成为一整体
象征性	使用符号来象征某些事物	真实性	涉及事物当时的原样
时间性	有时间概念,将事物排序	非时间性	没有时间概念
数字性	使用数字进行计算	空间立体性	看到各事物之间的联系和如何组成整体
逻辑性	把事物按逻辑或数学顺序排列	直觉性	根据感觉或视觉洞察事物真相
线性	进行连贯性思维,引出集合性结论	整体性	感知整体规律和结构引出分散性结论

从上表可以看出,左脑的思维比较具体；右脑的比较灵活,对多变的韵律感知和分析的能力较好。特别是语音连读时的变调多为逆同化,常常是"意在声先",因此右脑对综合、整体、非线性的韵律理解似比左脑为优。

6. 结语

本文对普通话语音与其"近亲"——文艺、"远亲"——理科三方面的韵律规则或与韵律的关系,作了些比较,旨在从它们的韵律变量方面归纳出一些共性,作为进一步探索语音韵律规则的参考。

语音韵律的变换,在话语进行中受多方面的影响(反馈),是极其敏感地随时反馈的。物质科学的最终目的是寻找事物之间的因果关系。科学定律的正确性与其可重复性和可预见性密切相关。显然,在某种物质过程中,等价的原因必定产生等价的结果……用对称性的语言来讲就是:

(1) 对称的原因必产生对称的结果；
(2) 原因中的对称性必反映在结果中；
(3) 结果中的不对称性必在原因中有反映。

以上三个结论即为对称性原理。借助这一原理,可以帮助我们在对物理机制不甚了解的情况下,定性地分析某些物理过程。[5,同上]因此,语音韵律的变换再复杂,它的每一项变量(结果)必然都有它的原因。从一切实践理论来说,都是对原因的依存和被原因所制约。无源之水、无本之木是不存在的,我们常常在实验中了解一些现象,如不追究其原因,就作出解释,或加以类推作为规则来应用,其结果就很难达到理想,甚至有错误的可能。

语音韵律多变的原因是多方面的,其形成的原因和其间"依存"和"制约"的关系,有如下表：

表4：语句中韵律变量的原因

韵律原因	依存关系	制约关系
言语生理学规则	发音方法的功能	发音部位的运动
言语声学的规则	言语声学的功能	言语感知的领域
语法学的规则	语言意义的认知	语法结构的制约
音系学的规则	语言理解的共识	历史音变的制约

本文脱稿时，适看到电视中主持人对中国"直11"直升飞机主设计师的访问，他历尽艰苦取得成功。问他为什么喜欢书法，他说这和他的研究工作是相通的。最近有不少"神州五号"载人成功的报道，"神五"中有上万个部件，其中影响安全的因素之多无法想象，考虑得稍为不彻底就会出乱子。本文所引的各学科理论似乎零散了些，但"其事虽殊，其理则一"，知者谅不河汉斯言。

（本文的朗诵例句采自中国科技大学计算机系的录音材料：魏巍《最可爱的人》；该例句的图表制作和测算由王海波同学协助，均在此一并致谢！）

参考文献

[1] 贝蒂·爱德华（2003）《像艺术家一样思考》，张索娃译。海口：海南出版社。
[2] 蔡莲红、吴宗济、蔡锐、陶建华（2001）汉语韵律特征的可计算性研究。载《新世纪的现代语音学》，第5届全国现代语音学学术会议。北京：清华大学出版社。
[3] 程翔章、曹海东编（1997）《书画同源》。武汉：武汉测绘科技大学出版社。
[4] 戴念祖（1994）《中国声学史》。石家庄：河北教育出版社。
[5] 高潮、甘华鸣主编（1998）《图解当代科技》。北京：红旗出版社。
[6] 郭茂来（2000）《视觉艺术概论》。北京：人民美术出版社。
[7] 胡其炜、蔡莲红（1998）汉语语音合成平台的设计与实践。载《第五届全国人机语音通讯学术会议论文集》，哈尔滨。
[8] 胡寿荣（2003）抽象思维和水墨特性。载中国画研究院主编《水墨研究》第三辑。北京：民族出版社。
[9] 姜夔《续书谱》。载老水番编《宋代书论》。长沙：湖南美术出版社，1999年。
[10] 李爱军（2002）汉语口语的韵律和韵律标记（英文）。载《语音研究报告》，中国社会科学院语言研究所语音研究室。
[11] 李渔《闲情偶寄·宾白第四》。北京：作家出版社，1996年。
[12] 李政道（2002）物理的挑战。载《学术报告厅——科学之美》。北京：中国青年出版社。
[13] 欧阳中石主编（1997）《书法》。北京：高等教育出版社。
[14] 沈约《宋书·谢灵运传论》。载《文选》卷五十。北京：中华书局，1977年。
[15] 王涣林（1997）《唐怀素自叙帖》。长春：吉林文史出版社。
[16] 王力（1958）《汉语诗律学》。上海：新知识出版社。
[17] 王力（2002）《中国古代文化常识图典·乐律》。北京：中国言实出版社。
[18] 吴宗济（1982）普通话语句中的声调变化。《中国语文》第6期。
[19] 吴宗济（1985）普通话三字组变调规律。《中国语言学报》第2期。
[20] 吴宗济（1994）普通话语调的短语调群在不同音阶调域下的调型分布（英文）。载《国际韵律特征研讨会议论文集》，横滨。
[21] 吴宗济（1989）补听缺斋语音杂记。《中国语文》第6期。
[22] 吴宗济（1990）汉语普通话语调的基本调型。载《王力先生纪念论文集》。北京：商务印书馆。
[23] 吴宗济主编（1991）《现代汉语语音概要》。北京：华语教学出版社。

[24] 吴宗济（1995）普通话不同语气语调的可预测性（英文）。载《第十三届国际语音科学会议论文集》，斯德哥尔摩。

[25] 吴宗济（1997）从声调与乐律的关系提出普通话语调处理的新方法。载中国语文编辑部编《庆祝中国社会科学院语言研究所45周年学术论文集》。北京：商务印书馆。

[26] 吴宗济（1997）试论"人－机对话"中的汉语语音学。《世界汉语教学》第12期。

[27] 吴宗济（1998）隋唐长安四声调值试拟。载《北京市语言学会第五届年会论文提要汇编》，北京语言文化大学。

[28] 吴宗济（2002）中国音韵学和语音学在汉语言语合成中的应用。《语言教学与研究》第1期。

[29] 吴宗济（2003）试论汉语的声调和节奏——从胡乔木的提问谈起。《语言学论丛》第二十八辑。北京：商务印书馆。

[30] 吴宗济（2003）"书话同源"——试论草书书法与语调规则的关系。《世界汉语教学》第1期。

[31] 吴宗济（2003）试从文学与艺术的韵律探索普通话的韵律规则。载《第六届全国现代语音学学术会议论文集》，天津师范大学。

[32] 吴宗济、王仁华、刘庆峰（1997）面向文－语合成的标记文本的设计（英文）。载《第一届中日口语处理研讨会议论文集》。合肥：中国科技大学出版社。

[33] 燕南芝庵《唱论》。载中国戏剧研究院编《中国古典戏曲论著集成》第1卷。北京：中国戏剧出版社，1959年。

[34] 杨振宁（2002）对称与物理学。载《学术报告厅第二辑——求学的方法》。西安：陕西师范大学出版社。

[35] 杨振宁（2003）二十世纪理论物理学发展的主旋律。载《学术报告厅第三辑——科学的品格》。西安：陕西师范大学出版社。

[36] 赵元任（1968）《中国话的文法》，丁邦新译。载《赵元任全集》第一卷。北京：商务印书馆，2002年。

[37] 张怀瓘《书断》上，草书。载潘运告编著《张怀瓘书论》。长沙：湖南美术出版社，1997年。

[38] 周光召（2003）复杂社会系统与社会发展。载《学术报告厅第三辑——科学的品格》。西安：陕西师范大学出版社。

[39] 周振甫（1988）《文心雕龙今译》声律第三十三。北京：中华书局。

汉语朗读语篇的修辞结构和韵律表达

陈玉东　吕士楠

摘要

　　本文对记叙文、新闻评论和议论文三个不同类型的汉语普通话朗读语篇，从篇章修辞结构和韵律特征两个方面进行了分析。研究结果表明，语段的韵律表达是以语篇结构和语义关系为依据的，语篇结构在专业朗读的有声语言韵律特征上得到正确的反映。主次和并列两类修辞关系反映的韵律特征明显不同，主次类关系促使语篇韵律更富有变化，并列类关系则使韵律表达趋于稳定。

　　由于在语篇修辞结构上主次和并列类分布的比例不同，上述三种类型语篇的韵律特征也显著不同。在并列类关系比例较大的记叙文朗读中，偏重采用音长和音质的变化的韵律手段，以音高突显表达逻辑重音方面有所减弱；新闻评论多主次类关系，偏重使用音高变化形式来表达语义单元结构和逻辑重音，音长和音质变化相对不突出；议论文修辞结构关系最为复杂，较多采用调节高音线、音长和音质的手段，而音节自身时长和低音线变化不大。

关键词：　语篇修辞结构　主次类　并列类　韵律特征

1. 引言

　　小句是语篇中的基本单元，语篇的衔接和连贯依靠小句之间的有机组合。在语篇的语音研究方面，陈玉东[7]对新闻播报语篇语段的构造和调节进行了初步的探讨；王蓓等[11]、郑秋豫等[2]也对语篇层面的韵律特征进行了探讨。但要想从根本上寻求语篇层面韵律特征的内在依据，还需要从篇章语法的角度来探求。

　　篇章语法研究，国内外成果颇丰，包括从 Halliday 和 Hasan[3][4]的功能主义语法，到后来的多个流派的话语分析理论等。这方面汉语的研究成果也很多，例如有关复句的研究[12]，副词的衔接功能的研究[15]，汉语语篇的衔接与连贯的研究[8]，特别是屈承熹的《汉语篇章语法》[9]系统地阐述了汉语语篇的结构功能。但目前语法方面的研究对于语音实体的表现关注还很不够，迫切需要语音学实证性研究的支持。

　　在具有影响力的语篇研究和分析的理论中，修辞结构理论（RST－Rhetorical Structure Theory）[5][14]是经典的语法理论。它以小句为基本单元，构建小句以上各层级语义关系的基本框架。修辞结构理论得到广泛的应用，在众多语种的书面语分析中，取得了很有价值的成果。本研究将采用这一理论对三种不同类型语篇的修辞关系进行分析，同时对其有声语言表达韵律的声学参数进行测量、分析，力图寻找语篇修辞结构和韵律表达之间关系的线索。

2. 研究方法

2.1 语料的选取

　　本文选取三篇朗读语料：记叙文《背影》（作者朱自清，朗诵者方明）；新闻评论《香港回归百年盛世》（中央人民广播电台播出，于芳播送，后简称《香港》）；议论文《谈骨气》（作者吴晗，朗诵者方明）。三种体裁的文稿，朗读风格各不相同。这是对不同体裁语篇的韵律表达和语法结构分析的一种尝试。

2.2 RST 分析

依据 Halliday 小句定义[3][4]和邢福义小句中枢概念[13]，并参考 RST 确定小句的原则[5][14]，本文考察的小句包括：简单句，复句中的分句，分裂的主从句中的主句和从句，表示时间、条件等的从句，嵌入成分等。在修辞结构理论中，小句是典型的基本语篇单元（EDU－Elemental Discourse Units），小句及小句以上层级的修辞结构关系总体上分为两大类，一类是单核（mononuclear）类关系，一类是多核（multinuclear）类关系，小句通过各种关系组合起来构成更大单元。结合汉语复句研究的相关成果，我们把单核类称为主次类，把多核类称为并列类。在本研究中设计的并列类关系包括：顺序（sequence）、连接（conjunction）、接合（joint）、对比（contrast）、递进（progressiveness）和选择（alternative）等六种关系；主次关系包括：背景（background）、原因（cause）、详述（elaboration）、结果（result）、转折（otherwise）、对立（antithesis）、目的（purpose）、证明（justify）、嵌入（embedded）、补充（complementarity）、解释（interpretation）、环境（circumstance）、让步（concession）、评价（evaluation）、动机（motivation）、总结（summary）、条件（condition）、推论（inference）、手段（means）、解答（solutionhood）、举例（example）等 21 种关系。我们利用 RST 分析的通用软件 RSTTool 3.0[6]，分析《背影》的一个片段，得到的修辞关系如图 1：

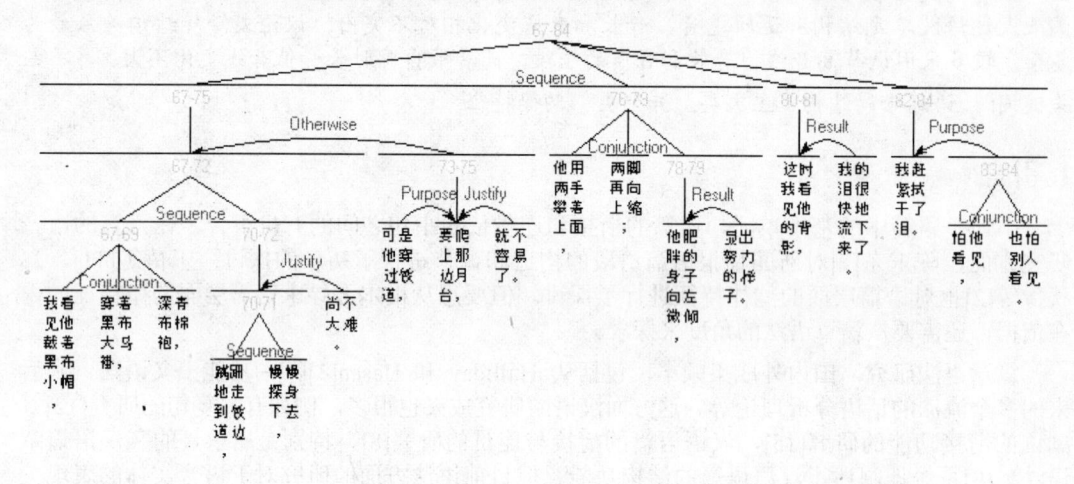

图 1：《背影》片段 RST 结构分析

2.3 语音分析

本研究采用 Praat5001 对语音进行数据采集和多层标注。根据先前的研究，语段内小句的衔接主要依靠小句首尾的音高变化和时长变化实现，语段内的主次轻重配置是依靠小句重音的重新配置完成的[7]，因此本研究主要提取小句的首尾音节和小句重音的高低音点。即重音处在小句首尾的，提取首尾的高低音点即可；重音处在句中的，除小句首尾的高低音点外，再提取句中重音的高低音点。音高特征点的数据是人工提取的，具体方法如下：依据沈炯的双线模型[10]，阴平提取高音点，阳平提取高音点和低音点，上声提取低音点，去声提取高音点和低音点。句首音节音高的高低音点都有时，以首音节的音高值作为句首音高值；当首音节缺少高音或低音点时，以后面相邻最近的音节的音高值补齐。句末音高也作了类似的处理，以最末音节为准，当它缺少高音点或低音点时，用前面相邻最近的音节的值补齐。重音位置特征点的提取规则是：提取重音词的最高点和最低点，缺少高音点或低音点时以最近音节的相应音高值为准。

本研究在需要男女声对比时，把以 Hz 为单位的基频转换为半音 st，转换公式是：st=12×lg(f/fref)/lg2。其中 f 是目标基频；fref 为参考基频，男声取 70Hz，女声取 100Hz。音高举例分析时，一般直接用基频 Hz 值。

已有研究表明小句末音节时长和小句间停顿时长是时间维最关键的韵律参数，本研究人工测量这两个时长，单位为毫秒（ms）。

3. 语篇结构分析结果

采用了 RST 修辞结构理论，我们对语篇层级内小句之间的语义关系进行了分析。分析中发现，在不同类型语篇之间是存在明显的差异的。

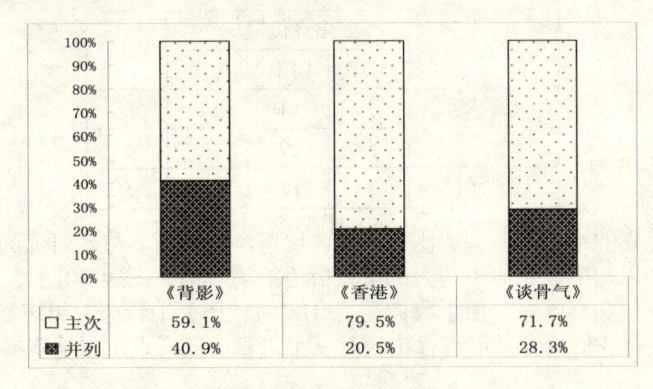

	《背影》	《香港》	《谈骨气》
主次	59.1%	79.5%	71.7%
并列	40.9%	20.5%	28.3%

图 2：三语篇的主次类和并列类关系比例

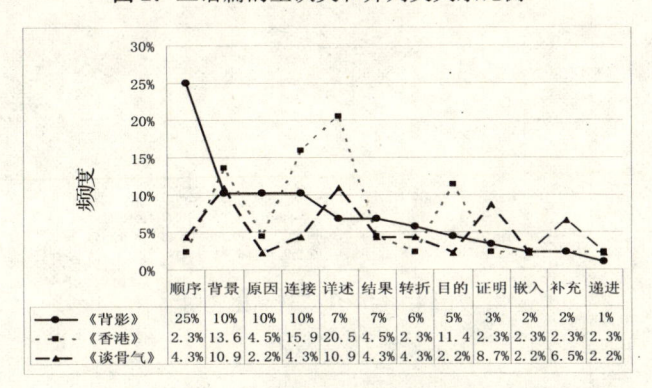

	顺序	背景	原因	连接	详述	结果	转折	目的	证明	嵌入	补充	递进
《背影》	25%	10%	10%	10%	7%	7%	6%	5%	3%	2%	2%	1%
《香港》	2.3%	13.6	4.5%	15.9	20.5%	4.5%	2.3%	11.4	2.3%	2.3%	2.3%	2.3%
《谈骨气》	4.3%	10.9	2.2%	4.3%	10.9	4.3%	4.3%	2.2%	8.7%	2.2%	6.5%	2.2%

图 3：三语篇主要修辞关系比例

图 2 显示了三个语篇中主次类和并列类修辞关系所占比例，图 3 显示了三个语篇主要修辞关系所占比例。《背影》是记叙文，叙事功能是第一位的。语篇结构以并列关系为主，包括顺序、连接、接合、对比、递进等五种关系，共占总数的 40.9%，其中顺序一种就占 25%。《香港》是新闻评论，《谈骨气》是典型的议论文，这两篇的语义关系（或逻辑关系）相对比较复杂，其中较少出现并列类关系。《香港》中包括连接、顺序、递进三种关系在内共有 20.5%，《谈骨气》中包含了六种并列类关系，但所占比例也只有 28.3%。记叙文并列关系的比例较大，使得语篇内部主次关系比例降低，语篇结构相对简单，这应该是叙事性语篇的一个突出特点。

语篇结构是语篇韵律表达的内在依据，我们期望通过韵律特征研究，找到语篇结构和韵律表达之间的关系线索。

4. 语音分析结果

4.1 音高分析

沈炯[10]提出的汉语的双线模型认为，在语调表达中，声调音域的低音线与韵律单元的完整性相关，高音线与语义重音相关。本研究进一步证实了这一结果，这一结论对于三种不同的语体都是符合的。但是，在三种语体中符合程度不完全相同。

我们首先统计了三个语篇中人工标记的焦点在小句中的分布情况，结果如表1：

表1：三语篇焦点在小句中的分布情况

语篇	焦点位置			宽焦
	句首	句中	句尾	
《背影》	3	14	14	8
《香港》	5	29	7	6
《谈骨气》	5	18	11	5

一般认为，句中焦点的小句语调构造比较典型，出现频度最高，与本研究的统计结果（表1）符合。因此，我们以句中焦点的小句为例来分析语篇的音高。图4和图5分别表示三个语篇里句中焦点音高均值和标准差。由于我们在把 Hz 值转化为半音值时男声参考频率取 70Hz、女声取 100Hz，使得我们用半音值进行比较时三个语篇的低音点下限基本持平（0值上下）。

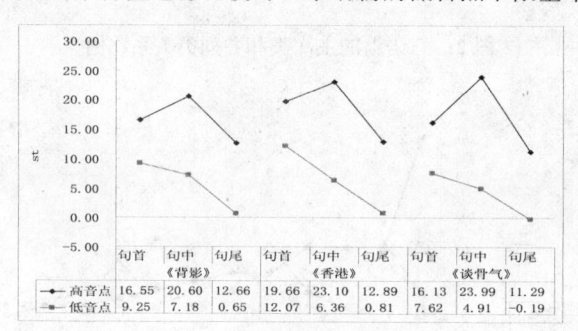

	句首	句中	句尾	句首	句中	句尾	句首	句中	句尾
	《背影》			《香港》			《谈骨气》		
高音点	16.55	20.60	12.66	19.66	23.10	12.89	16.13	23.99	11.29
低音点	9.25	7.18	0.65	12.07	6.36	0.81	7.62	4.91	-0.19

图4：句中焦点音高比较图

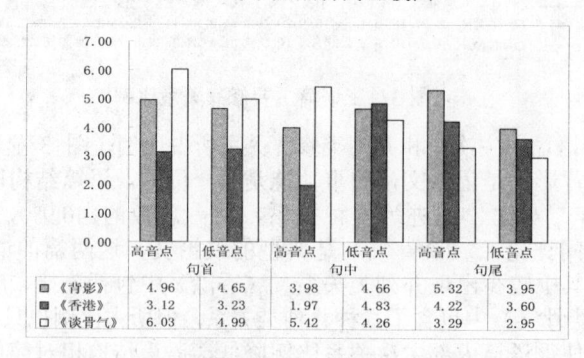

	高音点	低音点	高音点	低音点	高音点	低音点
	句首		句中		句尾	
《背影》	4.96	4.65	3.98	4.66	5.32	3.95
《香港》	3.12	3.23	1.97	4.83	4.22	3.60
《谈骨气》	6.03	4.99	5.42	4.26	3.29	2.95

图5：句中焦点音高标准差比较图

由图可见，新闻评论《香港》的特点是：低音点的下倾趋势最明显，下倾幅度最大（平均 11.89 个半音）；句中（焦点）高音点均值居中（23.1 个半音），标准差却最小（1.97）。这一现象说明在新闻评论中突出地反映了双线模型的特点，即低音线的明显下倾，体现了新闻播音的节奏鲜明稳定、重音适度的特点。图 6 中小句"特别是没有邓小平建设有中国特色社会主义理论的指引"，是低音线（下面的横线）下倾在小句前后的表现以及高音线突显语义重音都很明显的实例。

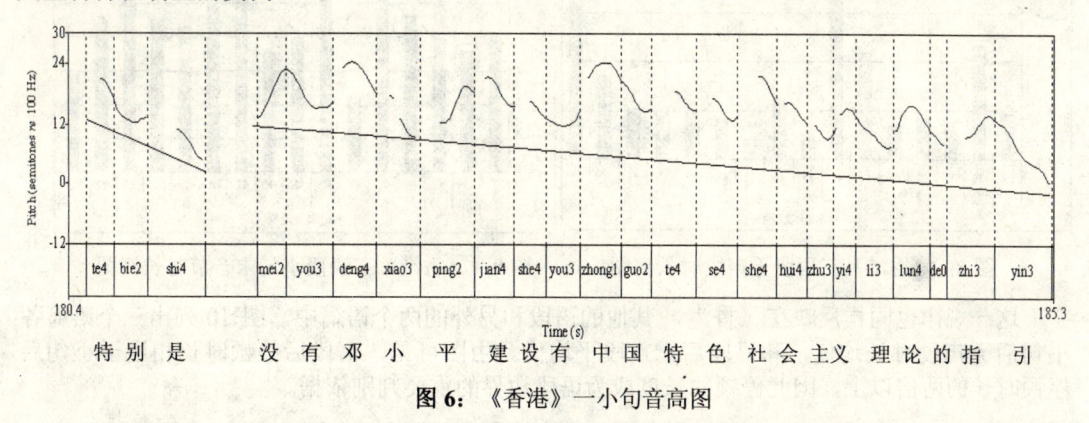

图 6：《香港》一小句音高图

从图 4 和图 5 我们也可以看到，记叙文《背影》和议论文《谈骨气》中低音点的下倾相对较弱，幅度较小（分别为 8.6 和 7.8 个半音）；在句中焦点的高音点均值方面，《背影》较低（20.60 个半音），《谈骨气》较高（23.99 个半音），但二者的标准差都较大（3.98 和 5.42），尤其是《谈骨气》的标准差最大。这表明，记叙文和议论文与新闻评论相比，低音线整体偏低，下倾趋缓；记叙文高音线偏低，整体音域偏低偏窄，表达语义重音时高音线上升，起伏较多；议论文高音线偏高，整体音域偏宽，表达语义重音时高音线上升，起伏很大。这是因为两种类型的语篇融入了更多的情感因素，随着不同强度的情绪起伏，小句焦点上高音点的高度也发生相应的变化，与新闻播音中的重音适度时的音高变化明显不同。由此可见，高音线的起伏是情感变化的反映。如图 7 所举例子，两个小句"父亲是一个胖子，走过去自然要费事些"的音高曲线图，低音线下倾在小句中显现得不明显，但高音线在表现语义重音上还是比较突显的，如图椭圆标记所示。突出"父亲"和"胖子"为"因"，强调"自然"是"果"，不仅呈现了语意上的呼应关系，也体现了父子深情。

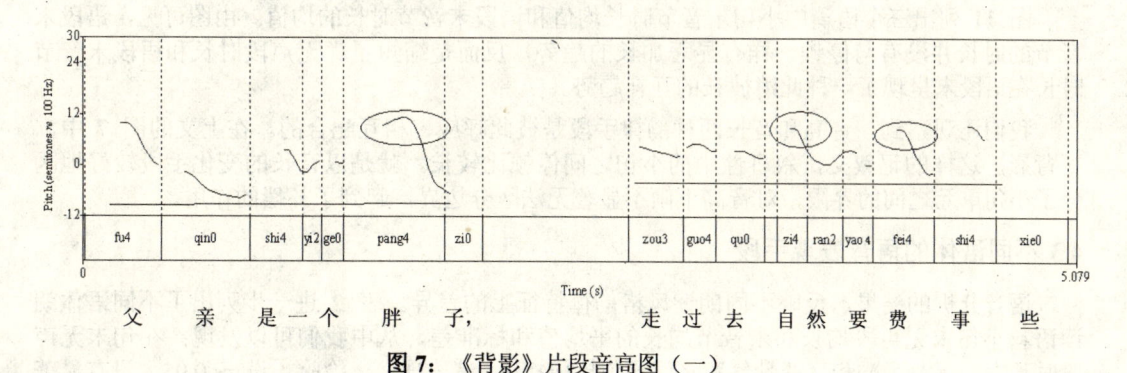

图 7：《背影》片段音高图（一）

4.2 音长分析

音长分析主要集中在小句末无声段时长，和小句末音节时长两个方面。图 8 和图 9 分别是《香港》三个语段句间无声段时长，和三个语段中小句末音节时长的直方图，段末小句直方块顶部另用方框标出。由图可见，语段末的停顿显著大于小句间的停顿；语段末音节延长小于小句末音节延长。

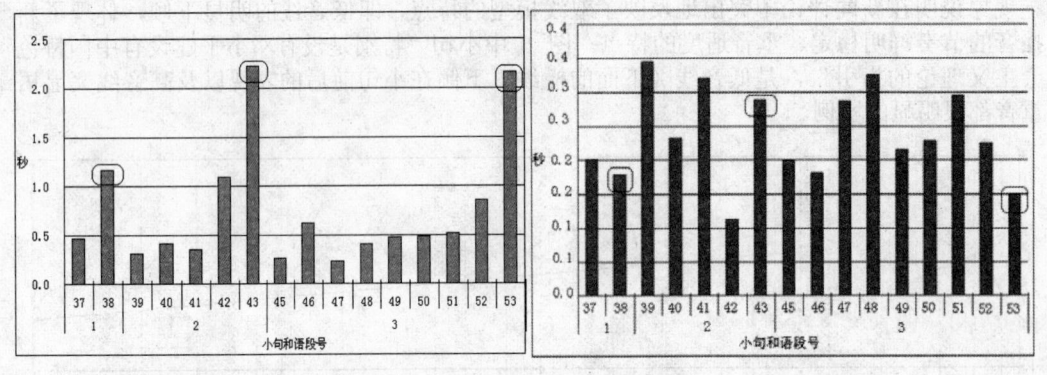

图 8：《香港》三语段无声段时长例图　　图 9：《香港》三语段小句末音节时长例图

这一规律也同样反映在《香港》其他的语段和另外的两个语篇中。图 10 列出三个语篇各小句后无声段时长均值，和语段后无声段平均值。由图可见，语段后停顿时长相当于小句后停顿时长的两倍以上，因此停顿的长度成为语段边界的重要判别依据。

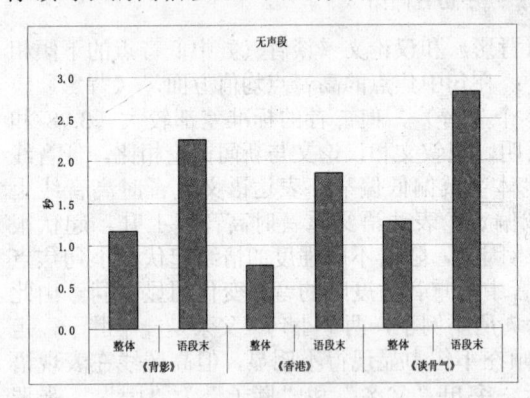

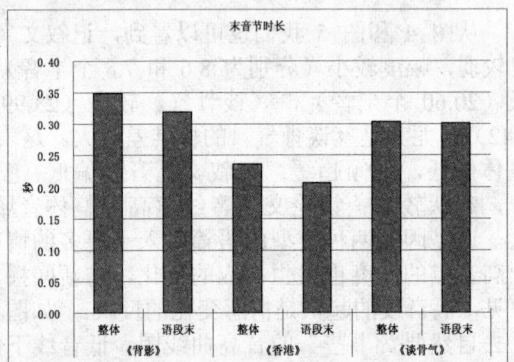

图 10：三语篇中小句后无声段均长比较　　图 11：三语篇中小句末音节均长比较

图 11 列出三个语篇中小句末音节时长均值和语段末音节时长的均值。由图可见，语段末音节的时长并没有与停顿一样有显著加长的趋势，反而是缩短了。无声段时长和语段末音节时长在语段末呈现了一种此消彼长的互补趋势。

我们还观察到，音高和音长两种韵律手段是彼此呼应、相互配合的。在上文的图 7 中，《背影》这样的记叙文，叙事性中的小句之间停顿比较长，就是以音长的变化手段较好地区分了小句单元之间的界限，对音高下倾不显著无法区分边界，起到了补偿的作用。

4.3 不同语体的语音表现手段

语音分析的结果，反映不同朗读风格韵律特征上的差异。表 2 进一步列出了不同语体朗读语料小句末无声段均长和末音节均长的平均值和标准差，从中我们可以发现：在句末无声段时长上，《背影》和《谈骨气》之间均值比较接近，都较长，t 检验，设 $p<0.05$，没有显著差别（t=-0.342，其绝对值小于单尾临界值 1.68）；而《香港》与《背影》之间有显著差别（t=1.72，大于单尾临界值 1.68），《香港》与《谈骨气》也有显著差别（t=1.78，大于单尾临界值 1.69）。这一现象可以解释为：记叙文和议论文都属于文艺性作品，朗读时利用句末停顿来表情达意的机会都较多，句末停顿的伸缩性也较大（标准差也较新闻评论大得多），

语速也因此都较慢。而新闻评论与记叙文和议论文的显著差别也主要在于新闻评论属于新闻语体，语速偏快，小句末无声段均长较短，也较为稳定（标准差最小）。

表2：不同语篇小句末无声段和小句末音节均长（ms）

篇　名	句末无声段		句末音节	
	平均	标准差	平均	标准差
《背影》	1170	952	348	102
《香港》	755	626	237	67
《谈骨气》	1275	1228	304	81

在末音节时长上，三个语篇之间都有显著差别（t检验p值均小于0.05）。但相比之下，《背影》和《谈骨气》的小句末音节均长较长、标准差较大，其中《背影》最甚。这是因为记叙文和议论文在句末利用时长手段表情达意的机会较多，小句末音节时长的变化也是重要表现之一，因此变化也较多。当音段具有较长持续时间时，也为音强和音质等方面的更复杂变化提供了必要的条件。《香港》小句末音节最短，标准差也最小，同样显示了句末时长变化较小的特点。

总体上说，新闻评论在末音节时长和小句末无声段时长上都比较短、也比较稳定（标准差都最小）。据观察，在新闻评论语篇中，没有出现小句内停顿时长达到小句后停顿时长的情况。这是因为新闻评论是一种较为规整的语体，在语调和重音的表现上，音高的作用更为重要，音长、音强和音质的作用都不是太大。上文图6，小句"特别是没有邓小平建设有中国特色社会主义理论的指引"中，音高和音长分布显得非常规整，小句重音在"邓小平"上，调核落在"平"上，音高的峰值延伸到了下一个音节"建"上，而"平"时长较前后音节也较长些。

在三类语篇中，记叙文的小句末音节平均是最长的（348ms），而且标准差也最大（102ms），显现了记叙文在韵律表达中音节长度的处理是比较从容的、灵活多变的。议论文的小句末停顿平均最长（1275ms），标准差也最大（1228ms），原因可能是议论文逻辑性较强，句末停顿可以给人更大的领悟空间。

在记叙文语篇朗读中，重音的突显、语调的表达方式往往是多变的，音高、音长、音强都可以实现，其中音质的变化会成为一种常见的手段。图12给出记叙文语篇《背影》朗读中一个小句"这时，我看见他的背影"的例子，由其语图和音高图可见，"这时"后的停顿格外的长（1168ms），相当于小句末停顿时长的平均值1170ms）。这表达一种心灵上的震颤，与后面的重音"背影"呼应，并且多用"虚声"（音质变化）表达，具有特殊的艺术效果。这是在记叙文中常见的现象。

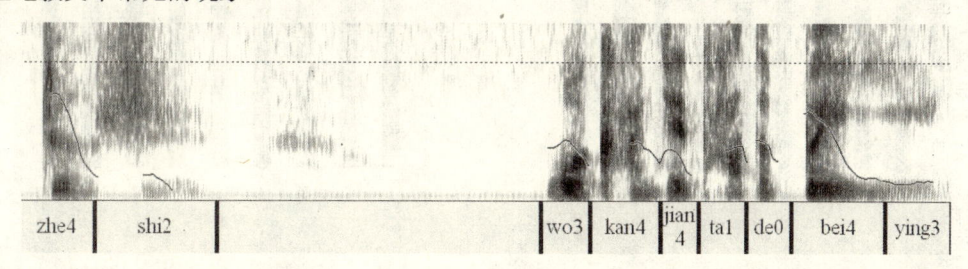

| zhe4 | shi2 | | wo3 | kan4 | jian4 | ta1 | de0 | bei4 | ying3 |

图12：《背影》小句"这时，我看见他的背影"语图及音高曲线

通过前文对语篇结构和韵律表达特征的分析，我们将三个不同类型语篇的韵律表达呈现出的不同的声学特征归纳为：

【记叙文】以记叙为核心，叙事、描写、抒情，以求得情感上产生共鸣。在语篇结构关系上（包括小句之间的关系和更大语法单元，例如话题链之间的关系），记叙文并列关系比例最大，反映出语篇结构的逻辑关系比较单一。在韵律表达上，记叙文较多地采用了音长和音质的变化形式来表达"重形象、求生动"的语篇，而以音高突显逻辑重音方面有时就显得不太突出。

【新闻评论】以评述为核心，以陈述新闻事实和观点主张为主要目的。在语篇结构关系上，新闻评论主次关系最多、并列关系最少，语篇结构的逻辑关系较记叙文复杂。在韵律表达上，新闻评论较多使用音高变化形式来表达"重逻辑、求庄重"的语篇；而在音长方面就显得中规中矩，音质方面变化也不突出。

【议论文】以论证为核心，以摆事实、讲道理为要务。在语篇逻辑关系上，议论文呈现出比新闻评论更复杂的关系，嵌套现象较多，但在语言表达方式上却与记叙文一样，有较强的文艺性特点。对于具有这种特点的语篇，韵律表达方面也有其独特的地方。议论文与记叙文相似的是，低音线的下倾趋势都有所减弱，音长和音质手段的应用显得比较多；与新闻评论相似的是，在音节时长上比较稳定一些，不像记叙文那样具有很大的灵活性。

5. 三类语篇的修辞结构和韵律表达的关系线索

在研究中我们发现，要得到不同的修辞结构关系的韵律要素相关物是困难的，可能其他因素对韵律的影响更大。包括以表义为主的新闻广播和以表情为主的艺术朗读的影响，个人对作品的理解和表现手法的影响等。但从我们的研究中还是可以看出若干端倪。

我们取图1《背影》RST分析的同一片段作对应的声学分析。其中的九个小句①－⑨：

①我看见他戴着黑布小帽，②穿着黑布大马褂，③深青布棉袍，④蹒跚地走到铁道边，⑤慢慢探身下去，⑥尚不大难。⑦可是他穿过铁道，⑧要爬上那边月台，⑨就不容易了。

它们的修辞关系分别是图1中的小句67－75所示。由图1可见，它们之间的关系大多是"连接"、"顺序"的并列类关系，典型的是小句①－④。在⑥－⑦之间是"转折"关系，⑤－⑥以及⑧－⑨之间是"证明"关系，都属于主次类关系。图13显示的分别是九个小句的平均音高和平均音强。

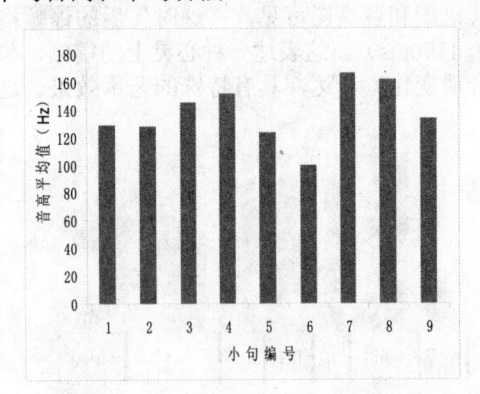

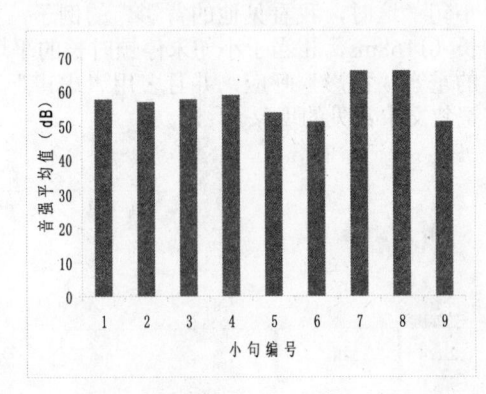

图13：《背影》片段的小句音高、音强均值

据观察发现，在并列类关系的小句之间音强和音高变化不大，①－④平均音强分别为58dB、57dB、58dB和59dB，音高为129Hz、128Hz、145Hz、152Hz，尤其是相邻小句之间的音强几乎持平、音高相差也只有1－7Hz。而在⑥－⑦之间"转折"关系处，音强和音高却

有明显变化，平均音强从 51dB 上升到 66dB；平均音高从 100Hz 上升到 166Hz。在这个例子中，⑤—⑥之间的"证明"关系表示对前面行为结果的判断，朗诵者采用轻轻点到的手法，音强和音高都很低。这是有意衬托和突显⑥—⑦之间的"转折"关系。分析还发现，这九个小句的平均音高和音强的相关性较高（相关系数为 0.87），说明音高特征和音强特征是一种相互伴随的特征。

表 3：《背影》片段音节时长和相邻小句停顿比较表

相邻小句	音节均长差（ms）	句间停顿（ms）
①—②	-18	631
②—③	105	455
③—④	-41	453
④—⑤	30	1502
⑤—⑥	-25	483
⑥—⑦	-38	2094
⑦—⑧	25	257
⑧—⑨	81	993

表 3 列出了这九个小句间的停顿和音节时长均值差。从时长上我们可以观察到小句的语速多变的特点，小句②—③、⑥—⑦、⑧—⑨之间音节均长相差较大，分别是 105ms，38ms 和 81ms，这跟小句内音节的多少相关。小句间停顿时长在不同的修辞关系上有着明显的不同，①—④四个小句之间比较均衡（都在 453—631ms 的范围内），而在④—⑨五个小句之间是不均衡的，其中④—⑤之间 1502ms、⑥—⑦之间 2094ms 和⑧—⑨之间 993ms。①—④的停顿时长均衡反映了"连接"和"顺序"关系倾向于稳定的韵律特征，与音高和音强的特征是一致的。⑥—⑦是"转折"关系，⑧—⑨是"证明"关系，需要用更多的韵律变化来显示这种主次关系，较长的停顿与较大的音高、音强变化也是一致的。

此外，值得注意的是④—⑤之间的"顺序"关系，参见这两句的音高图（图 14）：在描摹"探身下去"的情状时，采用了弱起的方式，⑤的句首起音很低，"慢慢"两音的平均音高只有 87Hz，比整个小句的平均音高 106Hz 低出 20Hz 左右，这是艺术语言表达中采用的一种特殊的变化手段，它减弱甚至抵消了小句的音高重置和下倾趋势。

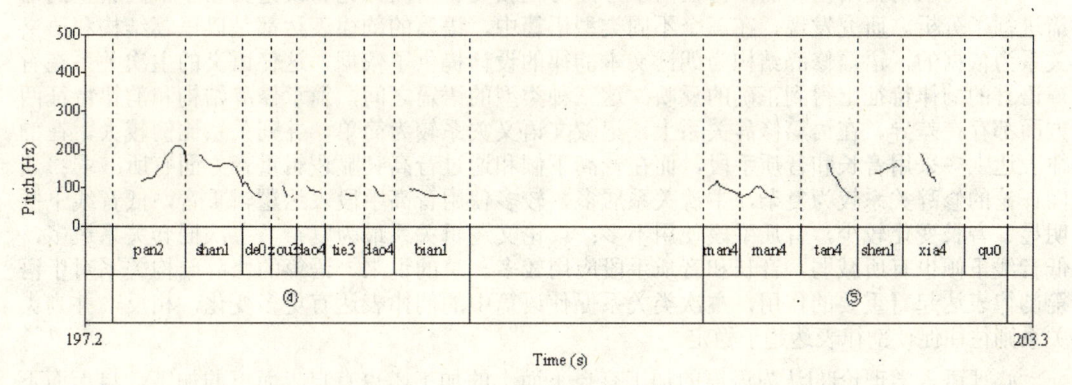

图 14：《背影》片段音高图（二）

我们再看《谈骨气》中三个小句的例子，图 15 是对这三个小句修辞结构的分析：①在上层，②和③合起来是对①的详述，属于主次关系；②是③的条件，二者也属于主次关系。在这种复杂的嵌套和主次关系下，三个小句的韵律表达也呈现出较多的变化性。图 16 可见，在逻辑重音的位置上（"多次"、"劝他"、"投降"和"大官"）音高突显非常明显。

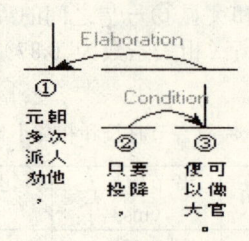

图 15： 《谈骨气》片段修辞结构分析

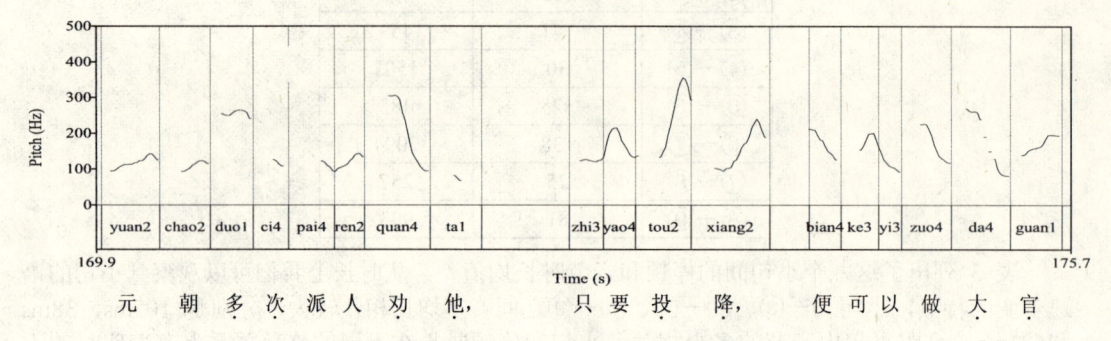

图 16： 《谈骨气》片段的音高和时长图

许多例子都显露出了语篇朗读中修辞结构和韵律表达之间的密切关系，我们的观察或许只是冰山一角，但其表征应该是一个缩影，反映的是修辞结构和韵律表达方式之间的关系线索。我们可以说，修辞结构关系的种类和组合方式不同是三类语篇的韵律表达呈现不同声学特征的重要原因之一。当然，语篇修辞结构和韵律表达之间的关系是复杂的，诸多其他因素的作用或许会影响到我们对其声学表征的准确把握。

6. 结论和讨论

本研究从语篇结构和韵律特征两个方面对记叙文、新闻评论和议论文三个不同类型的语篇进行了分析。研究发现，在三个不同类型语篇中，语篇的韵律表达都是以语篇结构和语义关系为依据的，语篇修辞结构为朗读文本韵律的设计提供了依据，这使语义的主次关系在有声语言的韵律特征上得到正确的反映。这三种类型的语篇之间，篇章修辞结构和韵律特征两方面都存在差异。在语篇修辞关系上，记叙文语义关系较为简单，并列关系比例较大，在韵律表达上多采用音长和音质手段，而在音高下倾和通过音高突显逻辑重音方面有所减弱；新闻评论的修辞关系较为复杂，主次关系居多，较多使用音高手段表达逻辑重音，低音线下倾明显、音长变化较少，音质手段使用不多；议论文逻辑关系最为复杂，主次嵌套关系最多，低音线下倾也有所减弱，音长和音质手段应用较多。总的说来，语篇的修辞结构关系对于语篇韵律表达起着重要的作用，主次类关系促使语篇中的韵律表达有更多变化，相反，并列类关系则往往促使韵律表达趋于稳定。

心理语言学理论[1]认为语篇的加工有自下而上的加工，也有自上而下的加工。自上而下的加工是按照语篇的图式规划的，图式是语义记忆里的一个结构，它对一群信息和期望的排列方式作出规定。图式对语篇细部的重组发挥重要作用，实验心理学证明语篇的图式对语篇加工具有指引功能。针对不同类型语篇的加工，在心理状态上是有明显不同的，语篇图式的构建及其语篇加工也具有不同的特点。本研究中，从小句到语段再到语篇的加工就是自下而上的加工，它表现为由小的韵律单元组合成大的韵律单元的层面。而从篇章层面的语义关系上对语篇的整体控制和把握则是自上而下的加工。抒情性和形象性较强的记叙文、时政和新闻性较强的新闻评论以及典型的议论文在语篇结构和韵律表达上所显示的不同，都是语篇在加工中整体心理图式的不同造成的。修辞关系是小句乃至小句以上的韵律单元构成语篇的纽带和桥梁，什么样的语篇类型选择什么样的结构关系是一种自上而下的加工，而以这些修辞关系为依据的韵律表达自然也呈现出了与语篇类型需要相一致的特征来。

  语篇修辞结构和韵律表达之间在语音特征上所反映出来的蛛丝马迹，表明了言语表达的心理过程是与语言学、心理学和声学密不可分的。本文仅仅是个案分析，抽取的三个语篇还不能全面涵盖各种类型，所得结论也都来源于有限的样本，尽管这些结论与我们的语感是基本一致的，但依然需要更系统、更深入的研究。下一步我们将在大规模语料库的基础上结合感知实验进行定量和定性分析，期望可以得到更可靠、更可信的结论。

参考文献

[1] Carroll D.W. 1999. *Psychology of Language*. 北京：外语教学与研究出版社，汤姆森学习出版社。

[2] Tseng, C.Y., Pin, S.H., Lee, Y.L. 2004. Speech Prosody: Issues, Approaches and Implications. In: G.Fant, H.Fujisaki, J.Cao, Y.Xu (eds.), *From Traditional Phonology to Modern Speech Processing*（语音学与言语处理前沿）. Beijing: Foreign Language Teaching and Research Press, 417-438.

[3] Halliday M.A.K. 1994. *An Introduction to Functional Grammar*. Beijing: Foreign Language Teaching and Research Press & Edward Arnold (Publishers) Limited, 2004:1-16.

[4] Halliday M.A.K., Hasan R. 2001. *Cohesion in English*. Beijing: Foreign Language Teaching and Research Press.

[5] Mann, Thompson. 1987. *Rhetorical Structure Theory: A Theory of Text Organization*. ISI: Information Sciences Institute. Los Angeles: CA, ISI/RS-87-190, 1-81. Reprinted from The Structure of Discourse, L. Polanyi, ed.

[6] O'Donnell Michael. 2004. RSTTool Version 3.45.

[7] 陈玉东（2004）《传媒有声语言语段的构造和调节》。北京大学博士学位论文（未刊）。

[8] 胡壮麟（1994）《语篇的衔接与连贯》。上海：上海外语教学出版社。

[9] 屈承熹（2006）《汉语篇章语法》。北京：北京语言大学出版社。

[10] 沈炯（1985）北京话声调的音域和语调。载林焘、王理嘉等《北京语音实验录》。北京：北京大学出版社，73-130页。

[11] 王蓓、杨玉芳、吕士楠（2005）语篇中大尺度信息单元边界的声学线索。《声学学报》第2期，177-183页。

[12] 邢福义（2002）《汉语复句研究》。北京：商务印书馆。

[13] 邢福义（2006）《小句中枢说》。长春：东北师范大学出版社。

[14] 徐赳赳（1999）复句研究与修辞结构理论。《外语教学与研究》第4期。

[15] 张谊生（2000）《现代汉语副词研究》。北京：学林出版社。

语言发声研究的基本方法

孔江平

摘要

在语音学、言语生理学、言语病理学、言语声学以及言语工程领域，语言发声的研究已经有了几十年的历史，从人们开始重视语言发声类型研究至今大约也已有二十多年，本文主要根据自己研究的经历和实践，粗略地总结了一下目前常用的一些发声类型研究的方法，它们主要有：1）谐波分析法；2）逆滤波分析法；3）频谱倾斜率分析法；4）多维嗓音分析法；5）声门阻抗分析法；6）动态声门分析法；7）发声起始状态分析法；8）嗓音音域分析法。除了个别研究方法外，这些方法大都已经很容易操作和实现，撰写此文是希望这些方法能广泛地在研究领域得到使用。

关键词：语言发声　发声生理和物理　语言发声信号分析

1. 引言

言语产生理论将语音发音（speech production）分为调音（articulation）和发声（phonation）两部分。其中，调音主要是指各部位发音器官协调运动形成声道形状，然后共鸣而产生的不同的语音，比如，通常语言里最常见的元音/a/、/i/、/u/等，都是由于不同的声道形状共鸣而产生的不同语音。发声是指声带在气流的作用下，以不同的振动方式而产生的声源，声源主要包括了声带振动的频率，即振动的快慢以及声带振动的方式，比如，正常嗓音发声，气嗓音发声，挤喉嗓音发声，气泡嗓音发声，假嗓音发声等。

在早期的语音学研究中，人们对语言的调音有较多的认识，如发音部位的定义和发音方法的定义等，根据这些语音学中的基本定义，产生了元音、辅音等基本概念，从而建立起了语音学或者说基于调音的语音学基础理论和方法，这些理论和方法在语言学的研究中起了极为重要的作用。然而，随着语言学、言语声学、言语生理学的发展，人们对语音产生的认识有了很大飞跃。另外，在语言学研究中进行的大量语言田野调查使人们发现了大量具有语言学意义的发声类型，如中国的彝语、哈尼语、景颇语、载瓦语等[32]，中国民族语言学中常用的"松元音"和"紧元音"这些语言学概念，就是对不同发声类型的语言学定义，这些都使得语言学家和语音学家逐步认识到了语言发声的重要性。

在语言发声类型的研究中，首先是信号的问题，也就是说研究发声类型要采集什么信号。通常我们研究语音最为重要的信号是声音信号，另外，在早期调音的研究中，X 光声道和腭舌信号对于语音调音研究起了非常重要的作用，当然现在有更多的信号，如核磁共振（MRI）、螺旋 CT、动态电子腭位信号等。在发声的研究中，可使用的信号主要有：1）语音信号；2）声门阻抗信号；3）气流气压信号；4）高速数字成像信号等。这些信号可以用不同的信号处理算法来处理，从中提取出有用的可以反映各种语言发声类型的参数，从而解释语言发声类型的性质和揭示语言发声的生理学、物理学和语言学本质。

发声研究的方法很多，有的主要用于嗓音生理学和病理学的研究，有的主要用于语言声学的研究，还有些方法可以用于心理语音学的研究。本文主要根据语音学的需求，介绍一些能用于嗓音发声类型研究的基本方法。它们包括：1）谐波分析法；2）逆滤波分析法；3）频谱倾斜率分析法；4）多维嗓音分析法；5）声门阻抗分析法；6）动态声门分析法；7）发声起始状态分析法；8）嗓音音域分析法。

2. 发声的生理和物理基础

本节简单介绍一下喉头的解剖，喉头主要是由软骨和肌肉组成，主要的软骨包括会厌软骨（epiglottis cartilage）、甲状软骨（thyroid cartilage）、环状软骨（cricoid cartilage）和一对杓状软骨（arytenoid cartilages）。

环甲节（cricothyroid joint）连接甲状软骨和环状软骨，环杓节（cricoarytenoid joint）连接杓状软骨和环状软骨，杓状软骨和环状软骨之间的运动改变声带的长度，杓状软骨沿着环杓节纵向运动导致声带的打开和并拢[26][28][12][15]，见图1（图片参考了 Titze [28]绘制而成）。

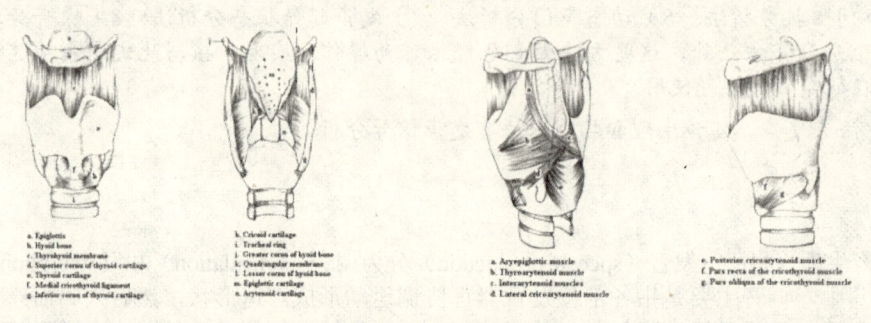

图1：喉头的整体框架（前视图和后视图）　　图2：喉内肌（后侧视图和前侧视图）

喉头大约包括十几条肌肉，它们主要是喉内肌、环甲肌（CT）、外展肌、内收肌、后环杓肌（PCA）、内杓肌（INT or IA）、侧环杓肌（LCA）、甲杓肌（TA）、发声肌（VOC）和外喉肌。喉内肌由一组肌肉组成，喉外肌则包括舌骨上肌（suprahyoid muscle）和舌骨下肌（infrahyoid muscle），见图2。

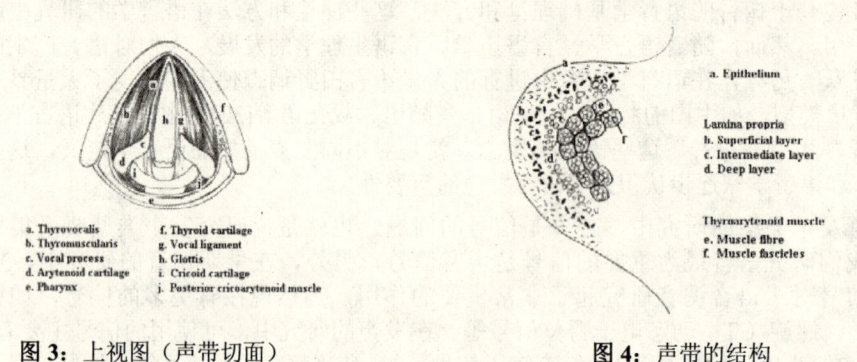

图3：上视图（声带切面）　　图4：声带的结构

环甲节和环杓节的运动由喉内肌控制，喉升高和降低的运动由喉外肌控制，如，舌骨上肌和舌骨下肌，这些肌肉支撑着整个喉头，也可能会导致音调的变化。杓状软骨的运动由外展肌（PCA）和内收肌（INT、LCA 和 TA）控制，这些肌肉导致声带的外展和内收。CT 的收缩导致声带的拉伸，VOC 在某种程度上控制声带的有效质量和紧张度。

声带由软组织构成，包括：1）上皮细胞（epithelium）；2）表面层（superficial layer）；3）中间过渡层（intermediate layer）；4）深层（deep layer）；5）肌肉（muscle）。声带结构也可以分为：1）黏膜（mucosa），它包括上皮细胞和表面层；2）韧带（ligament），它包括中间过渡层和深层；3）肌肉。声带的结构还可以简单地分成：1）声带的覆盖层，包括上皮细胞、表面层和中间过渡层；2）声带体，它包括深层和肌肉。见图3、4中的细节。

发声的生理结构和发声的物理原理是直接相关的，同时，声源的产生涉及声道的共鸣。在言语产生过程中，由于声源是通过声道发出来的，因此又叠加上了共鸣的特性，这使得研究声源变得很复杂，因为要从声波中提取声源首先就要把声道共鸣的特征去掉，在现代信号处理技术中这仍然是一个没有很好解决的问题和技术上的难点。

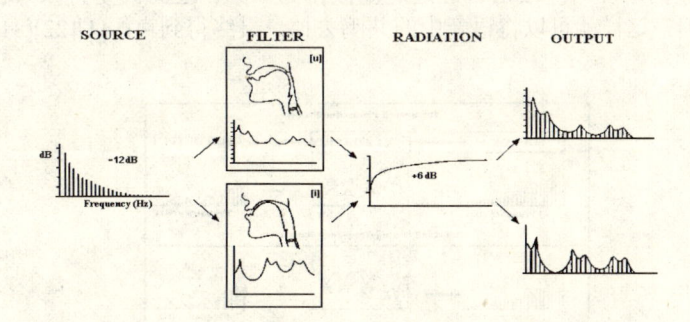

图 5：言语产生的三个部分和过程(Hardcastle et al., 1997)

图 5 是言语产生的一个基本原理的示意图，严格地讲言语产生可以分为三个部分：第一个部分是声源，用线谱图表示，它的基本特性是每个倍频程下降 12dB；第二个部分是共鸣，声源经过声道共鸣到达口部，这个过程改变了声源的共鸣特性形成了不同的元音，如图中口腔侧面图和共振峰包络图所示，一个表示/i/的形成过程，而另一个表示/a/的形成过程；第三个部分是唇辐射，用曲线图表示，其物理特性是每个倍频程提高 6dB，最后形成语音，用共振峰包络图和线谱图表示。在言语产生的过程中，唇辐射的特性极其重要，需要真正理解。

3. 谐波分析法

在语言发声研究中，谐波分析是一种最简单易行的方法，也是最早被语音学研究人员使用的方法，说它简单是因为只要有语言的录音，就可以进行声学分析，而声学分析只要作最简单的功率谱分析即可。因此在上个世纪 70 年代，美国 UCLA 的语音学家用此方法分析和研究了许多语言的发声类型，其中就包括中国的一些民族语言[17][18][21][19][20][14][29][3][32]。

谐波分析法在声学原理上主要是根据声源能量的大小，即声源谱的特性，声源谱高频能量强会导致第二以上谐波的能量大于第一谐波的能量，因此可以通过测量第一、二谐波的能量来判断嗓音发声类型的不同，一般是使用第一、二谐波之比的方法。

其优点是简便易行，但这种方法也存在很多缺点，其中最主要的缺点是在测量数据时共振峰对谐波能量会有影响，因此，有经验的语音学家在使用此方法时，往往选择元音/a/作为分析的样本，这是因为/a/的第一共振峰比较高，因而对第一、二谐波的能量影响比较小或者没有影响，这样就可以得到比较稳定和有规律的数据。如果使用了/i/、/y/、/u/作为测试样本，第一共振峰比较低，基频的能量和第一共振峰的能量会重叠，因而就得不到真实的嗓音数据。

为了解决其不足，研究人员往往会使用第二共振峰的能量和第一或第二谐波能量的比值来判断嗓音的发声类型，这种补救的方法在通常情况下对分析语言的不同发声类型也都会很有效。但是在语言发声类型的研究中，以不同发声类型作为最小对立时，声道的形状不一定完全相同，往往会有一定的差别，这就导致了要研究的嗓音发声的最小对立元音的共振峰不同，从而影响到数据的测量导致数据的误差，在这种情况下往往要考虑其他的研究方法。

4. 逆滤波分析法

图 6 是言语产生和逆滤波的原理示意图，分为上中下三张图，上图是言语产生的原理，与图 5 不同的是，共鸣部分用滤波器来说明，唇辐射和语音输出用线谱图和共振峰包络图表示。

中图为逆滤波的原理，一段语音经过逆滤波得到声源，逆滤波是将原共鸣特性反过来设计逆滤波的滤波器，这样就可以将语音中的共鸣去掉，最终得到声源[1][22][31]。

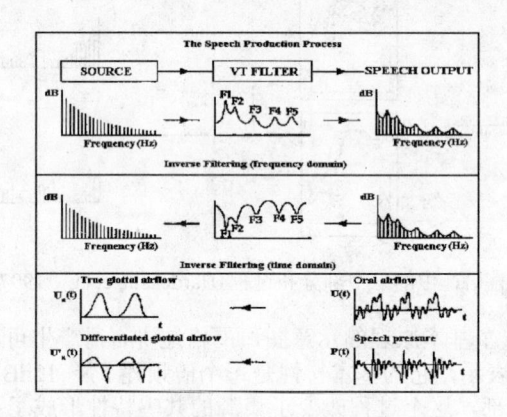

图 6：言语产生和逆滤波原理示意图

下图为声源和语音的关系，这一部分对于理解逆滤波最为重要，我们通过发声的生理研究知道，肺部气流冲破关闭的声带使声带振动产生声源，气流冲开声带形成的空隙称为声门，单位时间内通过这个空隙的气流为声门气流，一般用体积流速度表示。从下图的上半部分可以看到，如果对口腔气流进行逆滤波，得到的是声门气流，口腔气流一般是通过口腔面罩或气流计采集，逆滤波后得到声门气流。通常情况下很难直接采集到声门气流，因为很难将采集器放到声带（声门）的上方。声门气流除了从口腔气流中逆滤波得到以外，实际上还可以从声门面积推算出来。根据目前的技术，采集声门面积要用高速数字成像和图像处理的技术[32]。下图下半部分是从声压（语音）经过逆滤波得到声源，这个声源的形式是声门气流的微分，从中可以看出，口腔气流的微分形式基本就是声压。在发声的研究中，通常很少用口腔气流经逆滤波得到声源信号，一般都是对声压进行逆滤波获取声源。

下面我们来讨论一下从声压逆滤波获取声源的基本方法、过程和存在的问题。要进行逆滤波首先要提取声道共鸣的特性，在现代信号处理技术中一般使用自回归（AR）模型，具体来讲就是线性预测（LPC）。

$$s(n) = \sum_{k=1}^{p} a_k s(n-k) + Gu(n)$$

（1）

以上公式定义了言语产生的基本时间离散模型，其中 s（n）为言语信号，u（n）为激励源，G 为增益，k{αk}为滤波器系数，k 为信号的延时。

从上面的公式可以看出，逆滤波首先是对一段语音进行线性预测，计算出线性预测系数，我们知道线性预测系数代表的就是共鸣特性，那么将得到的系数直接用于逆滤波就能得到声源。

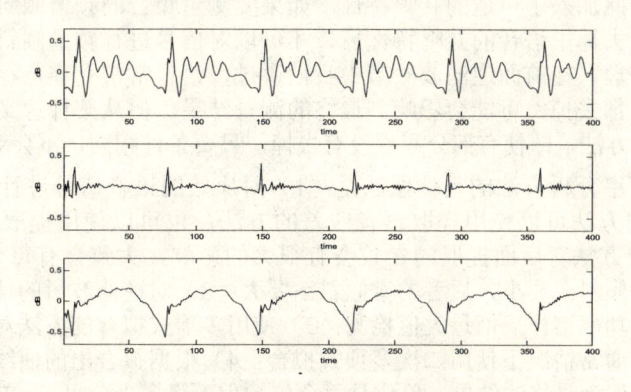

图 7：两种不同的逆滤波方法

图 7 显示了两种不同的线性预测逆滤波方法，图上为语音波形/a/，图中为直接使用线性预测系数逆滤波后的结果，在言语工程上通常使用这种方法，称为语音的残差信号，对其进行积分可以得到声门气流的波形。图下为另外一种逆滤波的方法，这种方法是首先将语音信号进行预加重（preemphasis）处理，然后提取出线性预测系数，将提取出的线性预测系数对同一段未进行预加重的语音信号进行逆滤波，得到的就是图下中的信号。这种声源信号通常用于语音学和言语产生理论的研究，这是因为利用这种微分的声源信号能够更好地解释语音声源的物理意义和语言学意义。例如，著名的 LF 模型[9]和 Klatt88 串并联共振峰参数合成器都是利用声门气流的微分形式来建立模型的。

虽然线性预测逆滤波有算法简单快捷等优点，在工程也广泛使用，但在对语音声源的研究方面，它也存在许多缺点至今不能很好地解决。这是因为线性预测是全极点（共鸣）模型，因此无法很好地提取出语音中的零点（反共鸣），而人的言语产生系统中始终都存在零点。首先，由于人的鼻腔和口腔同时参加共鸣时会出现耦合现象，因此产生了零点[5]；第二，由于咽腔底部梨状窝的存在，发音时也会导致出现零点[6]；第三，声门下气管在声门打开时同样会产生耦合，以致产生零点。这三个方面都影响逆滤波的精度和效果，因此，目前在通常的研究中，可以通过选择元音，特别是/a/元音的办法避开由于鼻音导致逆滤波不精确的问题，但总不是解决问题的根本办法。要想根本解决逆滤波的零点问题，就必须提取零点将其加入到逆滤波参数中。

逆滤波还可以用滤波器组的方法，这种方法通过改进界面的友好性，可以加入人为干涉的功能，通过人工干预极点和零点的参数，达到理想的逆滤波效果。一个简单的方法，将 Klatt88 串并联共振峰参数合成器反过来写，就是一个很好的零极点的逆滤波器。另外，我们目前正在研究开发的"基于频谱反转的逆滤波系统"也得到了很好的结果，但仍需要进一步改进才能完善。相信随着逆滤波技术的发展和改进，通过逆滤波提取语音声源将会越来越准确和简便易行。

5. 频谱倾斜率分析法

　　人类言语嗓音的特性是每个倍频程下降 12 个分贝，由于发音人、性别和语言不同，这个数字会发生变化。如果一种语言中有不同的发声类型，嗓音的频谱倾斜率就会有较大的差别，这为我们研究嗓音发声类型提供了实证测量和研究的可能，但言语声波是通过共鸣以后发出来的，因此加入了声道的共鸣特性。如果要测量嗓音的频谱倾斜率，首先就要对语音进行逆滤波，在去掉了语音的共鸣特性后，才可以对信号进行频谱倾斜率的测量，这就是语音分析前的预处理。在前面逆滤波一节中我们讲过，语音常常有零点存在，如果语音处理不能将所有的零点都去掉，可能会影响到最终的测量结果。但从某种意义上讲，如果使用一种相同的逆滤波的方法，即使有部分零点没有去掉，只要条件相同，不会对结果有很大影响。

　　频谱倾斜率分析方法的具体做法是：1）对原始的语音信号进行逆滤波，提取出声源信号，逆滤波的方法可以使用提取语音残差的方法，也可以使用提取声门气流微分形式的方法，但这两种方法对后面提取的参数会有很大的影响，大致会有每个倍频程 6 个分贝的差别，前者的谱倾斜率要小，后者的谱倾斜率要大；2）对逆滤波后的信号分帧计算功率谱，然后对每一帧的功率谱作局部最大值检测；3）使用多项式拟合的方法对检测出的局部最大值进行曲线拟合，通常情况下使用二次多项式拟合；4）根据拟合出的曲线计算出嗓音每个倍频程下降的分贝数作为最终的结果，单位是每个倍频程下降多少分贝（-dB/oct）。

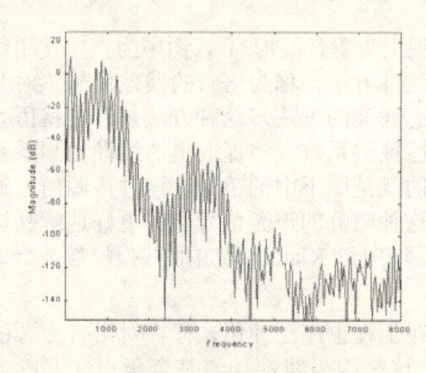

图 8：普通语音功率谱 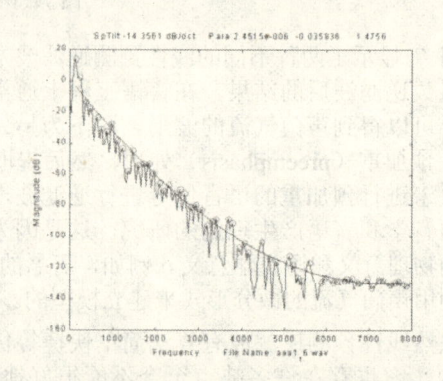　　　　　　　　　　图 9：频谱倾斜率示意图

　　图 8 是语音的普通功率谱，图 9 是频谱倾斜率示意图。可以看出，图 9 中的频谱下倾很平滑，这是因为经过了逆滤波，去掉了共振峰，小的圆圈是自动检测出的局部最大值，平滑线是根据局部最大值得到的二次多项式拟合后的曲线，图上方的参数分别是二次多项式曲线的截距、斜率、曲率和频率倾斜率（-dB/oct）。

　　频谱倾斜率分析的方法可以用在许多方面，这些研究主要包括：1）对一种语言的频谱特性进行定量分析，以便在通信等领域中作为这种语言的基本参考；2）对一种语言不同发声类型的持续元音进行嗓音特性的定量分析；3）对病变嗓音的不同类型进行性质的描写；4）对有语言学意义的发声类型进行分析和感知方面的研究；5）为语言韵律研究和韵律的建模提供基础数据；6）作为嗓音合成的基本参数。总之，嗓音频谱倾斜率（频谱下倾）在嗓音发声类型研究中是一种重要的方法。

6. 多维嗓音分析法

多维嗓音分析最早是从嗓音病理领域发展出来的一种通过声音检测嗓音质量、发声类型和诊断嗓音病变的声学方法，在国际上，特别是在欧美等发达国家，医院里常常用此方法对嗓音患者进行初步诊断并以检测的数据和图标作为嗓音的病例。

多维嗓音分析主要分信号录音、算法和参数三个方面。第一是录音，多维嗓音分析要求录音必须是二至三秒钟的持续元音，而且需要 44－48k 的采样频率。另外，根据我们的实践，声门阻抗信号也可以用于多维嗓音的分析，但需要进行一些预处理，最好是用声门阻抗信号的微分形式。第二是算法，多维嗓音分析的算法很多（见美国 KAY 公司多维嗓音分析软件的使用手册），这里我们介绍两个最重要也是最有特色的算法，绝对频率抖动和频率抖动百分比。

绝对频率抖动将一段浊音音调周期之间的变化定义为：

$$Jita = \frac{1}{N-1} \sum_{i=1}^{N-1} |T_0^{(i)} - T_0^{(i+1)}| \tag{2}$$

其中，$T_0^{(i)}$ 的 i=1，2，3，…N 是提取的音调周期参数，N 等于提取的音调周期的个数。

频率抖动百分比将一段浊音音调周期之间的相对变化定义为：

$$Jitt = \frac{\frac{1}{N-1} \sum_{i=1}^{N-1} |T_0^{(i)} - T_0^{(i+1)}|}{\frac{1}{N} \sum_{i=1}^{N} T_0^{(i)}} \tag{3}$$

其中，$T_0^{(i)}$ 的 i=1，2，3，…N 是提取的音调周期参数，N 等于提取的音调周期的个数。

常用的多维嗓音分析参数有六类 33 项。第一类是"基音基础参数"，包括：1）平均基频（Fo.Hz），2）平均音调周期（To.Ms），3）最高基频（Fhi.Hz），4）最低基频（Flo.Hz），5）F0 标准偏差（STD.Hz），6）基频半音范围（PFR）。第二类是"频率抖动参数"，包括：7）F0 抖动频率（Fftr.Hz），8）振幅抖动频率（Fatr.Hz），9）分析样本时长（Tsam.s），10）绝对频率抖动（Jita.Us），11）频率抖动百分比（Jiit.%），12）相对平均扰动（RAP.%），13）音调扰动商（PPQ.%），14）平滑音调扰动商（sPPQ.%），15）基频变化率（vFo.%）。第三类是"振幅抖动参数"，包括：16）振幅抖动（ShdB.dB），17）振幅抖动百分比（Shim.dB），18）振幅扰动商（APQ.%），19）平滑振幅扰动商（sAPQ.%），20）振幅变化率（vAm.%）。第四类是"噪音指数"，包括：21）清浊率（NHR），22）嗓音骚动（VTI），23）软发声指数（SPI），24）F0 抖动强度指数（FTRI.%），25）振幅抖动强度指数（TRI.%）。第五类是"嗓音清化参数"，包括：26）嗓音破裂级（DVB），27）次和谐级（DSH），28）清声级（DUV），29）嗓音破裂数（NVB），30）次和谐音段数（NSH），31）非浊音段数（NUV）。第六类是"基本参数"，包括：32）计算音段数（SEG），33）总测定音调周期（PER）。图 10、11 是一个正常嗓音和一个气嗓音的图形表示。

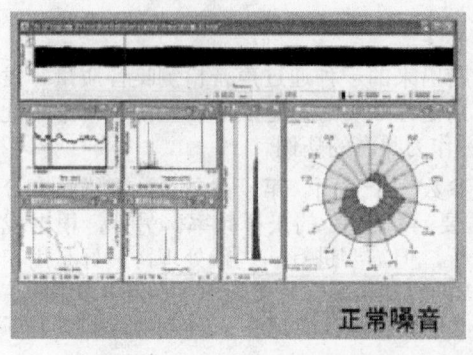

图10：一个正常嗓音的图形表示 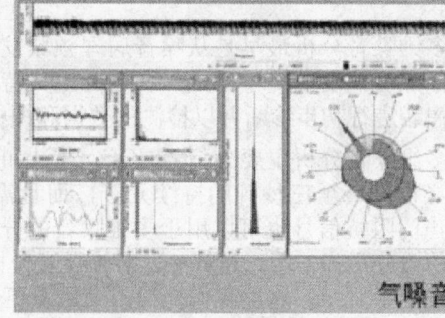　　图11：一个气嗓音的图形表示

从以上的数据可以看出，多维嗓音分析是一种从声学的角度描写个人嗓音特性、区分嗓音性别、鉴定嗓音声纹、量化不同语言嗓音和诊断嗓音病变的有效方法。虽然多维嗓音的有些算法还需要改进，但大部分的算法都是公认的已经很稳定的算法。我们在区分汉语、藏语、蒙古语和彝语四种语言的嗓音特性中得到了很好的结果[32][27][16][10][13]。

7. 声门阻抗分析法

声门阻抗信号（signal of electroglottalgraph）是通过声门仪（laryngography，通常称"喉头仪"）采集的涉及声门变化的生理电信号，这个仪器最早是由英国伦敦大学的弗森教授发明和研制的。众所周知，直到目前人们从语音信号中提取声源信号还有很多困难，因此在研究语音的声源方面还存在许多障碍，声门仪的出现确实在很大程度上推动了嗓音声源的研究，特别是在言语嗓音生理和嗓音病理的研究和诊断方面得到了很大的发展。

声门阻抗信号的出现，给研究者开辟了一个新的领域，使人们对声门的变化、声带的振动方式和嗓音声源的关系研究有了很大的发展，特别是对语言的发声类型有了更好的认识。在语音学研究方面，从声门阻抗信号中提取出来的参数可以很好地用来描写不同语言的发声类型，因而被语音学家广泛使用。从声门阻抗信号中可以提取出许多参数用于嗓音发声的描写、研究和建模。其中有三个参数最为重要，它们是：1）基频，2）开商，3）速度商。实际上，基频、开商和速度商不仅仅是从声门阻抗信号中可以提出，从语音声源信号的积分形式中也能提取出来，方特教授著名的 LF 嗓音模型中使用的开商和速度商就是指从语音信号中提取出的开商和速度商[1]。

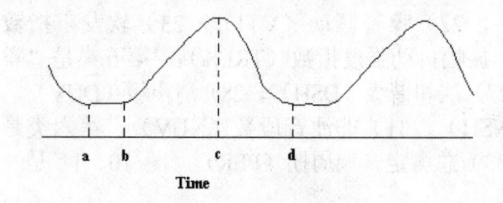

图12：声源信号的基频、开商和速度商的基本定义 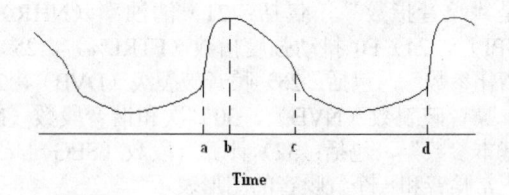　　图13：声门阻抗信号的基频、开商和速度商的基本定义

---

[1] 这几年有很多同行问我关于开商和速度商的定义，大家觉得有些文献上讲的有出入，不是很清楚，主要的问题就是因为这两个定义不仅用在声源信号上，而且用在了声门阻抗信号上，因而产生了一点混淆。

从言语信号的物理意义上讲，基频是周期的倒数，这个比较清楚。开商是指声门打开相比整个周期，同样的物理意义，我们也可以用接触商来表示，只是数据不同（见 KAY 公司的 EGG 相关分析软件）。速度商是指声门的正在打开相比声门的正在关闭相。

图 12 为从语音信号中提取出来的嗓音信号的积分形式，通常情况下其波形的峰值是右倾的，图中 ad 为周期，ab 为闭相，bd 为开相，bc 为声门正在打开相，cd 为声门正在关闭相。基频、开商和速度商可以用以下公式来定义：

    基频   = 1/周期(ad)
    开商   = 开相(bd)/周期(ad)×100%
    速度商 = 声门正在打开相(bc)/声门正在关闭相(cd)×100%

图 13 为语音声门阻抗信号的积分形式，也是原始形式，通常情况下其波形的峰值是左倾的，图中 ad 为周期，ac 为闭相，cd 为开相，bc 为声门正在打开相，ab 为声门正在关闭相。基频、开商和速度商可以用以下公式来定义：

    基频   = 1/周期(ad)
    开商   = 开相(cd)/周期(ad)×100%
    速度商 = 声门正在打开相(bc)/声门正在关闭相(ab)×100%

使用基频、开商和速度商可以用来描写和定义不同的发声类型。在语言发声类型的研究方面，这些定义可以用来描写汉语声调的嗓音发声模型、民族语言中元音的发声类型、汉语韵律研究的嗓音模型、病变嗓音的性质、声纹鉴定、声乐研究中的不同唱法和唱腔等。限于篇幅本文只是简单介绍一下，给出这些定义的嗓音区别性特征和声学发声图。

表 1：发声类型特征表

	气泡音	气嗓音	紧喉音	正常音	高音调嗓音
音调	1	2	3	4	5
速度商	4	1	5	3	2
开商	5	4	1	3	2
音调抖动	4	5	2	1	3

表 1 是发声类型特征表，列出五种发声类型及嗓音参数大小顺序的数值，参数根据基频参数的大小排序，从数据的矩阵中可以看出这五种发声类型可以完全区分开来，因此，根据这一性质，我们可以将其转换为区别性特征来描写语言的不同发声类型，因为通常情况下，这五种发声类型能涵盖大部分语言的发声类型现象。

表 2：发声类型区别特征表

	气泡音	气嗓音	紧喉音	正常音	高音调嗓音
音调	−	−	−	+	+
速度商	+	−	+	+	−
开商	+	+	−	+	−
音调抖动	+	+	+	−	+

表 2 是五种语言发声类型及其参数的区别性特征表，特征符号"+"和"-"是根据正常嗓音的参数来区分的，即，正常嗓音定义为"+-"，大于正常嗓音的参数定义为"+"，而小于正常嗓音的参数定义为"-"。从表中可以看出，紧喉音可以描写为：音调"-"，速度商"+"，开商"-"，音调抖动"+"，见表 2。当然根据嗓音的这些数据，还可以采用其他的方法来描写嗓音发声类型，建立更符合某种语言音位系统的区别性特征系统。

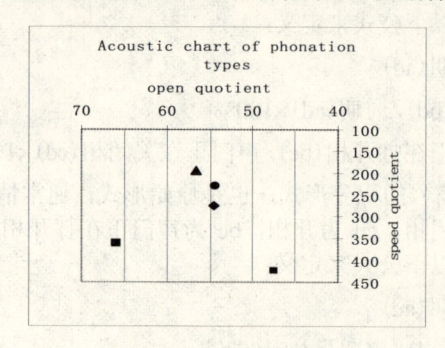

图14：声学发声图

在语音学研究中，通常用声学元音图来描写元音的位置及其特性，根据嗓音的参数，我们提出用"声学发声图"或者也可以称为"声学嗓音图"来描写语言嗓音发声类型的特性[32]，图中横轴为开商，纵轴为速度商。根据这种体系和方法，图中菱形为正常嗓音，右下角的小方形表示紧喉音，图左下角的大方形是气泡音，正常嗓音上边的圆形是高音调嗓音，三角形是气嗓音，同样我们也可加上基频画出三维的声学发声图来。另外，用"声学发声图"不仅可以从声门阻抗信号中获取参数，也可以从声学信号中获取参数，如果参数是从生理信号中获得的也可以称为"生理发声图"或者"生理嗓音图"，其内容是有区别的，但描写语言嗓音发声类型的主导思想完全一致。

8. 动态声门分析法

在语言发声研究中，动态声门分析方法的设备和技术基础是高速数字成像和数字图像处理，在设备和技术上对文科背景的语音学研究人员来说有一定的困难，但随着技术的发展，技术问题会越来越简单。众所周知，从传统的语音学到科学的语音学的一个最为重要的标志是在 X 光出现后被及时地应用到了语音学中，从而发现了舌位高低前后和语音发音的重要关系，大大推动了语音学向着科学的方向发展，但直到今天我们对声带的生理机制还知之甚少。上世纪七八十年代高速数字成像技术的进展，使我们有条件对声带的振动进行观察和研究，可以说高速数字成像技术的应用一定会大大推进语言嗓音发声的研究，其意义就在于此。

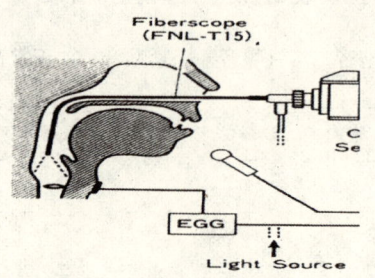

图15：高速数字成像设备（Kiritani et al., 1993）

图 15 是高速数字成像设备的示意图，内窥镜可以是软的导线也可以是硬的，前端装有镜头和冷光源，另外，还有话筒和电声门仪；通常情况下三路信号同时采集。其中图像的采样频率可以高达 4501 帧/秒（最大采样频率 9000 帧/秒），文件格式一般为 256×256 像素 8 比特灰度级。随着计算机速度的提高和内存的增加，现在已经有了彩色的高速数字成像系统。

在信号处理技术层面，主要是图像处理和语音信号处理。数字图像信号处理的目的主要是提取出视频信号中声门的面积，然后根据面积提取各种用于研究的参数。语音信号的主要目的是提取出有用的语音参数，如基频、共振峰、开商、速度商、振幅等。有了这些参数就可以进行动态声门和语音关系的研究。

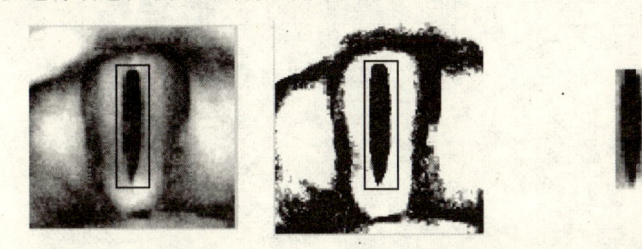

图16：图像处理的简单过程

从图 16 可以看出，为了处理的方便，一帧图像可以先加一个小窗用来确定声门的面积，然后经过调节对比度和抽取声门面积等方法最终得到动态的声门面积，当然也可以用自动的方法。这只是最简单的过程，因为实际的高速数字视频会出现光线灰暗、抖动和漂移等现象，都需要加以处理才能得到较好的动态声门。

动态声门的参数提取比较复杂，不是技术的问题而是怎样定义的问题，因为，提取声门面积有很多方法，也可以定义很多参数，这需要根据研究的目的来确定。因为高速数字成像不仅可以用于声带振动的基础研究，而且还可以用于嗓音病理的诊断和研究以及言语工程的生理合成研究。因此，只有确定了研究的目的，才能断定提取的参数。在基础研究方面有以下几种参数可以比较全面地对动态声门进行研究和建模，见图 17。

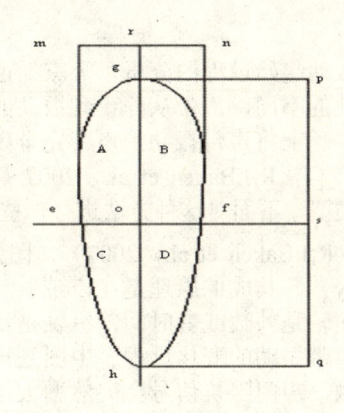

图17：参数定义示意图

第一类是基本参数，包括：1）声门面积最大值位置；2）声门开启点；3）声门关闭点；4）绝对声门长度；5）绝对声门宽度；6）声门面积长宽比。

第二类是声门面积参数，包括：7）声门总面积；8）左声门面积；9）右声门面积；10）上声门面积；11）下声门面积。

第三类是声门长宽参数，包括：12）声门长；13）声门；14）前声门长；15）后声门长；16）左声门宽；17）右声门宽。

第四类是声门面积函数参数，包括：18）声门面积函数周期；19）声门面积函数；20）声门面积函数开相；21）声门面积函数闭相；22）声门面积函数开商；23）声门面积函数速度商；24）直流分量基础参数。

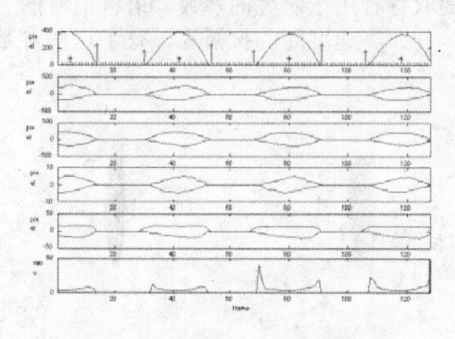

图 18：正常嗓音声门参数示意图 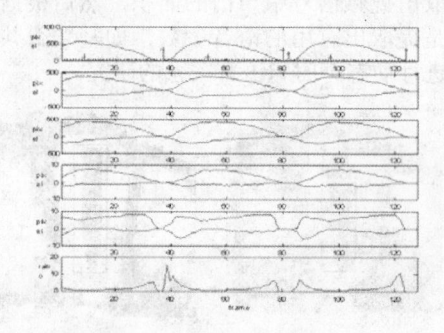　　　　**图 19**：气嗓音声门参数示意图

图 18 和 19 是正常嗓音和气嗓音声门参数示意图，图中给出了 13 个参数，从上至下分别是声门面积、左右声门面积、前后声门面积、左右声门宽度、前后声门宽度、长宽比，另外，根据声门面积可以计算出基频、开商和速度商，这样一共是 13 个参数。这 13 个参数是经过验证的，比较稳定，而且和具有物理意义的语音参数有比较密切的关系。

动态声门技术是一项比较新的技术，通过应用这一技术和研究方法，可以探索语言嗓音发声类型生理和物理之间的关系，追寻语言发声类型的本质，因而它在语言发声研究领域不仅具有理论意义，而且具有实际的应用价值，另外，这一技术在嗓音医学领域和言语工程领域具有很好的开发应用前景[15][2]。

9. 发声起始状态分析法

发声起始状态分析是指对声带振动起始过程的分析。大家知道，由于各人声带条件的不同、语言发声类型的不同和声母条件的不同，声带从静止到振动的过程会发生变化，从而导致各种不同的声带振动起始方式。生理上将声带振动到声带完全闭合（接触）称为"声带接触时间（Vocal attack time，VAT）"[4, R.J.Baken et al., 2007（正在发表中）]，通过测量 VAT 可以帮助我们确定嗓音的发声类型，下面对这种方法进行一些简单的介绍。

图 20 是 VAT 原理示意图（取自 R.J.Baken et al., 2007），图分为上中下三张，上图是声带高速数字成像单线图（kymography），其成像原理是在声带振动的高速视频图像中选一条线，然后将它们排列成一张图片，横轴是帧数或者时间，纵轴是每一帧所取的画面，通常是取声门的中间线，从上图可以看出声带振动的变化过程。中图是声门阻抗信号，从声门阻抗信号的原理我们知道，一旦声带接触，声门阻抗信号会突然增大，因为声带接触时阻抗会变得很小。下图是经过带通滤波的语音信号。

从图 20 可以看出，声带从开始振动到声带完全接触有一个较长的过程，大概有六七个振动周期，结合其他信号可以明显看出，声带一开始振动声压就出现了，但声门阻抗信号特别小，不过当声带接触时声门阻抗信号就突然变大。根据这一原理，我们就可以测量出 VAT

---

[2] 有关利用高速数字成像研究声带振动和动态声门的文章很多，有大量参考文献，但专著很少，在这本书中列出了上个世纪能找到的所有文献，可供参考。

来。从图 21 可以看出，声带的振动是突然启动的，在第一个振动周期声带就完全闭合了，体现出了另一种不同的声带启动方式。从这两张图可以看出，VAT 的定义是"声带开始振动到声带接触的时间"。根据这个定义，图 21 的 VAT 为负值（-2.25ms）。图 22 是另一张嗓音 VAT 示意图，从中可以看出 VAT 的数值为正（16.25ms）。从视频可以看出前者为硬启动嗓音（hard voice），后者为软启动嗓音（soft voice）。

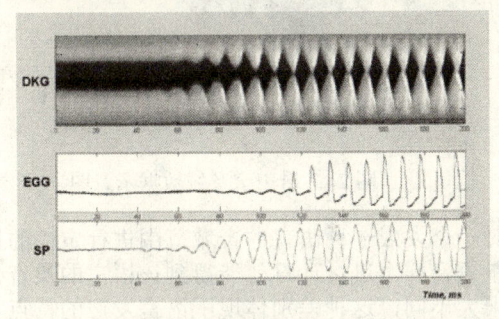

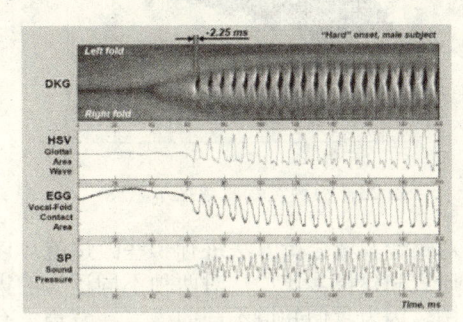

图 20：VAT 原理示意图   图 21：硬嗓音 VAT 原理示意图

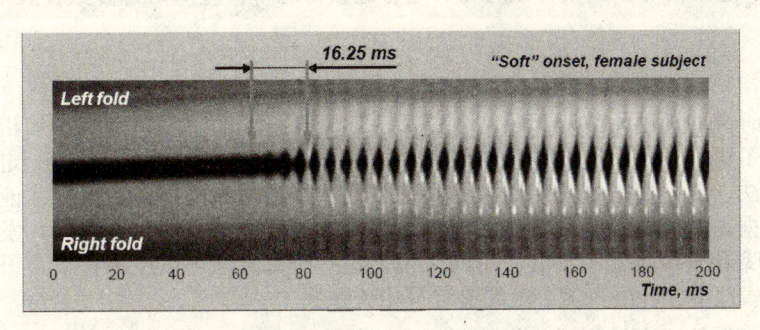

图 22：软嗓音 VAT 原理示意图

VAT 是一种最近才发展出来的语言嗓音研究的方法，它有很好的研究和应用前景，虽然目前还主要是应用在病理嗓音的诊断、分析和研究方面。很显然，这一方法经过改进可以用于语音发声类型的共时描写、发声类型和声母生理关系的分析、语言发声类型在历史音变中的作用等方面的研究。

10. 嗓音音域分析法

研究和测定嗓音有很多方法，其中有一种算法上很简单但很有用的方法，即嗓音音域分析法，这种方法主要是通过测定发音人的音域范围达到确定一个人嗓音特性的目的。具体的方法是合成一个特定音阶（通常是钢琴键盘上的某个音）音高的声音，让发音人模仿其音高，同时发音人的发音从最弱变到最强。根据语音分段计算出基频和振幅（分贝），然后将其画在二维图上，其中 x 轴为基频，y 轴为振幅，灰度变化为频度。

图 23 和 24 是两个不同男声的音域示意图（图片取自 KAY3700 语音分析系统中的音域分析软件），从第一张图可以看出，这个男声的音域很宽，有将近四个八度，几十个分贝的分布。从第二张图的数据可以看出，其音域较窄，不到三个八度，但分贝数值和第一个男声大致相同。很显然，利用这一方法可以很好地测定一个人的音域范围，了解其声带和嗓音的自然条件，在声乐考试和教学中都会很有用处。

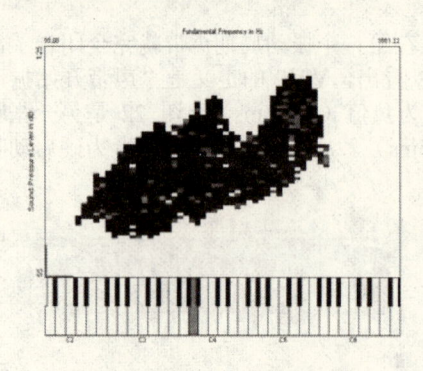

图23：男声宽音域数据示意图 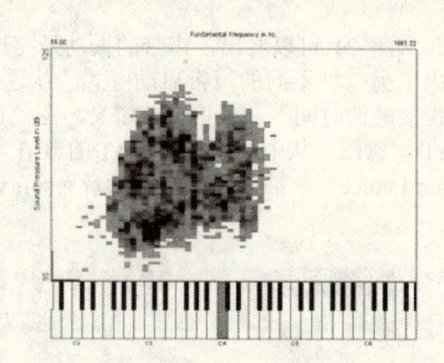　　　　　图24：男声窄音域数据示意图

对嗓音音域分析方法进行一些改进就可以对一个人或一种语言的音域范围进行定性的描写、研究和建模。比如，对两种不同语言的大量语音样本进行计算就能得到该语言的嗓音分布范围，因为我们知道不同的语言在发声上有很大不同，这种差别体现了语言发声的特点。如果加上开商和速度商等参数就可以对嗓音进行建模，这种模型对语音参数合成十分有用。

11. 结束语

语言发声研究的进展始终随着嗓音生理和声学研究技术的发展，两者相辅相成，缺一不可，从而推动了语言发声研究的进步。然而，在我们选择研究方法时，并不一定非要选择最复杂的研究方法，而是要根据研究对象和研究目的选择最适当的方法，这样才能得到最为有用和可靠的数据，从而揭示嗓音发声的内在规律，达到研究的目的。在我国，发声研究方法的进步促进了嗓音发声研究的发展。总的来说，这些研究方法可以应用在发声语音学、生理语音学、嗓音病理学、言语声学、声纹鉴定等相关领域。

在面向语言学的语音学领域，新的研究方法使我们可以开创新的研究热点。例如，VAT的应用不仅可以用来描写嗓音发声的起始状态，而且可以利用此方法研究辅音和嗓音发声生理的内在机制，从而达到解释语言历史音变生理制约的基本规律。又如，基于高速数字成像的动态声门研究可以使我们有可能建立声带振动的生理模型，从而模拟语言嗓音发声类型的产生和基本的特性。也可以用来模拟病变嗓音的振动方式和制订嗓音病变手术的方案以及模拟术后的嗓音。另外，嗓音的生理模型的不断完善，将会大大推动基于仿生学的语音生理合成的完善和建立高质量的合成系统，推动语言嗓音发声基础和应用研究的发展和进步。

致谢：本项研究由自然科学基金资助（项目批准号：10674013）。

参考文献

[1] Alku P. 1991. Glottal wave analysis with pitch synchronous iterative adaptive inverse filtering. *Proc. EUROSPEECH '91*, 1081-1084.
[2] Ananthapadmanabha T.V. 1984. Acoustic analysis of voice source dynamics. *Speech Transmission Laboratory – Quarterly Progress and Status Report*, 2-3, 1-24. Roya Institute of Technology, Stockholm.
[3] Anthony Traill, Michel Jachson. 1987. Speaker variation and phonation types in Tsonga nasals. *UCLA Working Papers in Phonetics* 67.
[4] Baken R.J., Orlikoff R.F. 1998. Estimating vocal fold adduction time from EGG and acoustic records. In: Schutte H.K., Dejonckere P., Leezenberg H., Mondelaers B., Peters H.F. (eds.), *Programme and Abstract book: 24th IALP congress*, Amsterdam, 15.

[5] Dang, J., K. Honda, et al. 1994. Morphological and acoustical analysis of the nasal and the paranasal cavities. *Journal of the Acoustical Society of America* 96 (4), 2088-2100.

[6] Dang, J., K. Honda. 1997. Acoustic characteristics of the piriform fossa in models and humans. *Journal of the Acoustical Society of America* 101 (1), 456-465.

[7] G. Fant. 1979. Glottal source and excitation analysis. *STL-QPSR*, No. 1, 85-107.

[8] G. Fant. 1982. The voice source, acoustic modeling. *STL-QPSR*, No. 4, 28-48.

[9] G. Fant, Liljencrants J., Lin Q. 1985. A four parameter model of glottal flow. *STL-QPSR*, No. 4, 1-13.

[10] Hall K. D., Yairi E. 1992. Fundamental frequency, jitter, and shimmer in preschoolers who stutter. *Journal of Speech and Hearing Research*, Vol. 35, 1002-1008.

[11] Hedelin P. 1984. A glottal LPC-vocoder. *Proceedings of IEEE International Conference on Acoustics, Speech, and Signal Processing*, San Diego. 1.6.1-1.6.4.

[12] Hirose H. 1997. Investigation the Physiology of Laryngeal Structures. In: William J. Hardcastle and John Laver (eds.), *Chapter 4. The Handbook of Phonetic Sciences*. Blackwell Publishers.

[13] Horii Y. 1985. Jitter and shimmer in sustained vocal fry phonation. *Folia Phoniatrics*, Vol. 37, 81-86.

[14] Kirk P.L., Ladefoged P., Ladefoged J. 1984. Using a spectrograph for measures of phonation types in a natural language. *UCLA Working Paper in Phonetics* 59, 102-113.

[15] Kong, J.P. 2007. *Laryngeal Dynamic and Physiological Models: High-Speed Imaging and Acoustical Techniques*. Peking University Press.

[16] Kong J.P., Caodao Barter, Chen, J.Y., Shen, M.X. 1997. Acoustic study of jitter, shammer and tremmors in Mandarin. *Theory and Application of Signal Processing*. Conference on Speech, Image and Communication Signal Processing of China (SICS'97), Zhengzhou, China.

[17] Ladefoged P. 1973. The features of larynx. *Journal of Phonetics* 1, 73-84.

[18] Ladefoged P. 1988. Discussion of Phonetics: A note on some terms for phonation types. *Vocal Fold Physiology*, Vol. 2, Vocal Physiology: Voice Production, Mechanisms and Functions. New York: Raven Press.

[19] Ladefoged P., Maddieson I., Jackson M. 1987a. Investigating phonation types in different languages. *UCLA Working Papers in Phonetics* 67.

[20] Ladefoged P., Maddieson I., Jackson M., Huffman M. 1987b. Characteristics of the voice Source. *UCLA Working Papers in Phonetics* 67 [To be appeared in the Proceedings of the European Conference on Speech Technology, Edinburgh].

[21] Laver J. 1980. *The Phonetic Description of Voice Quality*. Cambridge University Press.

[22] Lindestad P-A, Sodersten M., Maerker B., Granqvist S. 1999. Voice source characteristics in Mongolian "Throst singing" studied with hgih-speed imageing technique, acoustic spectra and inverse filtering. *Phoniatric and Logopedic Progress Report*, No. 11. Department of logopedics and phoniatrics, Karolinska institute, Huddinge university hospital, Sweden.

[23] Ljungqvist M., Fujisaki H. 1985. A comparative study of glottal waveform models. *Technical Report of the Institue of Electronics and Commmunications Engineers*. Japan, EA85-58, 23-9.

[24] Maddieson I., Ladefoged P. 1985. "Tense" and "Lax" in four minority languages of China, *UCLA Working Paper in Phonetics*, 60-99, 59-83.

[25] Rosenberg A.E. 1971. Effect of glottal pulse shape on the quality of natural vowels. *Journal of the Acoustical Society of America* 49,583-98.

[26] Sawashima M., Hirose H. 1983. Laryngeal gestures in speech production. In: Peter F. MacNeilage, Springer-Verlag (eds.), *Chapter 2. The Production of Speech*. New York, Heideberg, Berlin.

[27] Shen, M.X., Kong, J.P. 1998. MDVP (multi-dimensional voice processing) study on sustained vowels of Mandarin through EGG signal. *Proceedings of Conference on Phonetics of the Languages in China*, Hong Kong.

[28] Titze I.R. 1994. *Principle of Voice Production*. Englewoods cliffs, New Jersey, *Prentice Hall*: 07632.

[29] Therapan L. Thongkum. 1987. Phonation types in Mon-Khmer languages. *UCLA Working Papers in Phonetics* 67.

[30] William J. Hardcastle, John Laver (eds.). 1997. *Handbook of Phonetic Sciences*. Blackwell Publishers.
[31] 方特、高奋、孔江平（1994）《言语科学与言语技术》。北京：商务印书馆。
[32] 孔江平（2001）《论语言发声》。北京：中央民族大学出版社。

疑问句末基频"上升尾巴"与语气助词

——赵元任先生"连续叠加"思想初探

路继伦　林茂灿

摘要

　　早在 20 世纪 20 年代，赵元任先生就提出汉语的语调实际上是字调和语调本身的"代数和"，并指出了两种声调叠加的模式：一种是同时叠加，另一种是连续叠加。连续叠加是指在句子的最后一个字调后面加上一个尾巴。其中表示疑问的上升尾巴有如下的表现：55=56，35=36，214=216，51=513。后来，赵元任先生进一步认为把这个语调尾音当做助词处理更好，其特点是它没有自己的成段因素，而是寄生在最后一个语素上。

　　为观察和验证赵元任先生所提出的表示疑问的上升尾巴的存在，笔者做了声学实验。结果发现，主要是最后为去声字的疑问句中存在一个较为明显上扬的尾巴，所收集的数据中有上扬结尾的占了绝大多数。实验中还让听辨者分别听了原始带有上升尾巴的疑问句、去掉了尾巴的疑问句、原始不带尾巴的陈述句和加上了上升尾巴的陈述句。疑问句调的声学实验与听辨实验表明：1. 以去声结尾的疑问句一般会不同程度地出现一个上扬尾巴，但疑问功能不依赖于它。2. 去声结尾的疑问句出现的上扬尾巴，是语气助词失掉了其音段而保留下来的超音段，它作为对疑问信息的加强而依附在全句最后一个音节上。3. 边界调基频曲线的形状或斜度的改变是疑问语气的决定因素。疑问句末出现的上扬尾巴是一个类似语气助词的位置，它不大影响整个语调模式。

关键词： 连续叠加　基频　疑问句　上升尾巴　语气助词

1. 引言

　　一般说来，人们会感觉到疑问句用升调，陈述句用降调。汉语是声调语言，单字本身就具有音高升降变化的声调，当一个音高曲线呈下降趋势的去声字出现在疑问句句尾时，仍然能够看出它还是一个降的声调。那么，为什么人们还会感觉到疑问句是某种升调呢？这是因为，汉语的句调和声调是分离的，句调是不受声调支配的自主超音段，而句调的语音实现是由带有声调的字按照句调模式输出的，也就是说汉语虽然具有固定的本字调，但它也同英语一样有着不同的语调模式。汉语疑问句上升边界调的实现是通过将最后一个重读音节的音阶整体提高并加大这个音节的斜率来完成的。表现为降调的去声处在疑问句句末时，它会从音节首到音节尾逐步加大音高频率（即不如本字调下降得那么低），但这并不能改变它还是一种下降的趋势。那么，这种升调信息很可能是靠结尾处添加一个上升的小尾巴来传递的。赵元任先生早在 20 世纪 20 年代就开始了对汉语语调的研究，并注意到了这一问题。

2. 连续叠加

1929 年赵元任先生将汉语语调分为两个层次加以解释。他认为语句里的字调因地位的不同产生种种变化所形成的调子为"中性语调"；不由字调的不同所决定、几乎整个汉语都一样甚至同外语也有许多相同的地方的调子叫"口气语调"。这两种语调相互作用于同一语句中形成总语调（resultant intonation），即两种语调相加的代数和[2]。之后他明确提出"汉语的语调实际上是字调和语调本身的'代数和'"[3]。他在分析英语与汉语语调时指出汉语在毫无色彩的平叙句中，调群的结尾就变化多端，而汉语调群的调节如同英语一样可以用"升尾"和"降尾"来实现。他还提出汉语语调中能与英语语调对等的语素是语法分词（Grammatical Particle）或叫语助词（Speech-Helping Word）的用法[3]。在《汉语的字调跟语调》[4]一文中他较为深入地分析了本字调和句调的统一问题，指出了两种声调叠加的模式：一种是同时叠加，即字调受到语调的作用而产生音高水平与范围的变化；另一种是连续叠加，即在最后一个字调后加上一个尾巴。连续叠加又有上升结尾和下降结尾两种，其中表示疑问的上升的尾巴有如下的表现：

55=56，35=36，214=216，51=513。

我们可以发现当我们把具有声调的汉字组合成句子的时候必须同语调结合，这样才能完整准确地表达说话者的意思，正如赵元任先生所说"真正的语言有语言的抑扬顿挫的神气，这就是语调，有了语调，方才成为一种活的语言"[5]。赵元任先生认为同时叠加和连续叠加是构成汉语最终语调的两个成分或叫部分。后来在对连续叠加作了进一步分析之后，他在《汉语口语语法》[6]一书中进一步解释说语调尾音有特殊的形态因素性质，把这个语调尾音当做助词处理更好，其特点是它没有自己的成段因素，而是寄生在最后一个语素上。显然赵元任先生将连续叠加中的语调尾巴看成是一个超越字的声调之外的附加成分。

3. 实验与统计

本实验目的是观察和验证赵元任先生所提出的疑问句的上升尾巴的存在。实验的录音材料取自中国社会科学院语音室的语料库。句型为陈述句"这个字读作 X"和疑问句"这个字读作 X？"分别将"猜、才、彩、菜；搭、答、打、大；滔、逃、讨、套；摘、宅、窄、债"等 16 个字带入句型，共形成 32 个句子。四个发音人，每人每句读三遍。

实验结果发现，疑问句中有的确实存在一个上扬的尾巴。

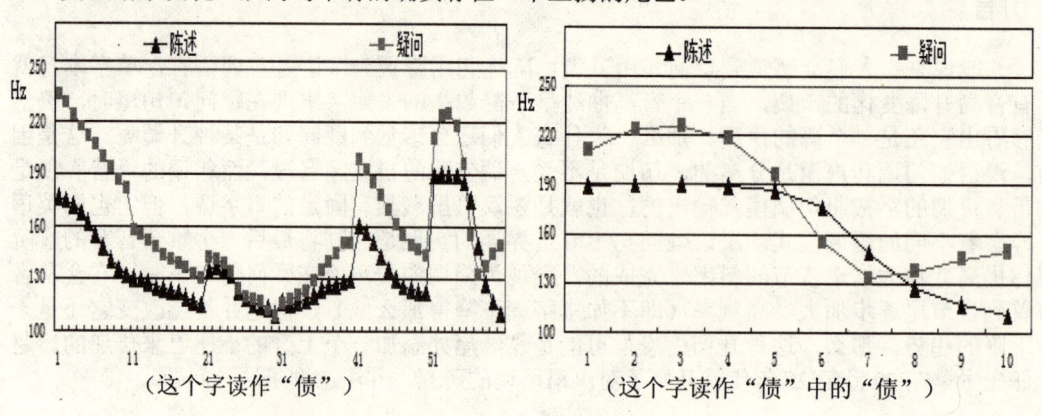

图 1：疑问句"这个字读作'债'？"中上扬的结尾

从上图中我们可以明显看到，与陈述句相比疑问句的音高曲线的确存在一个上扬的结尾。

（这个字读作"菜"）　　　　　（这个字读作"菜"中的"菜"）

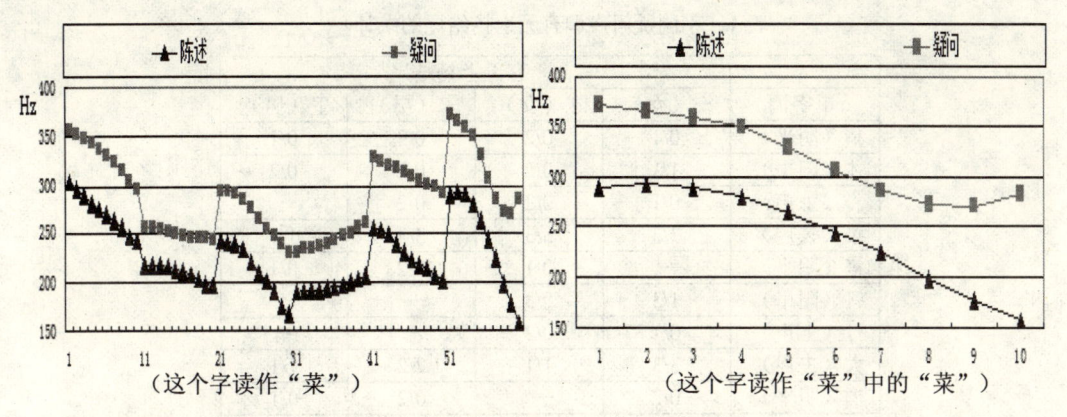

图 2：疑问句"这个字读作'菜'？"中上扬的结尾

与陈述句相比这个疑问句的音高曲线也存在一个上扬的尾巴。对录音材料分析的统计显示，疑问句中存在上扬结尾的现象不是任何声调都出现，见下图。

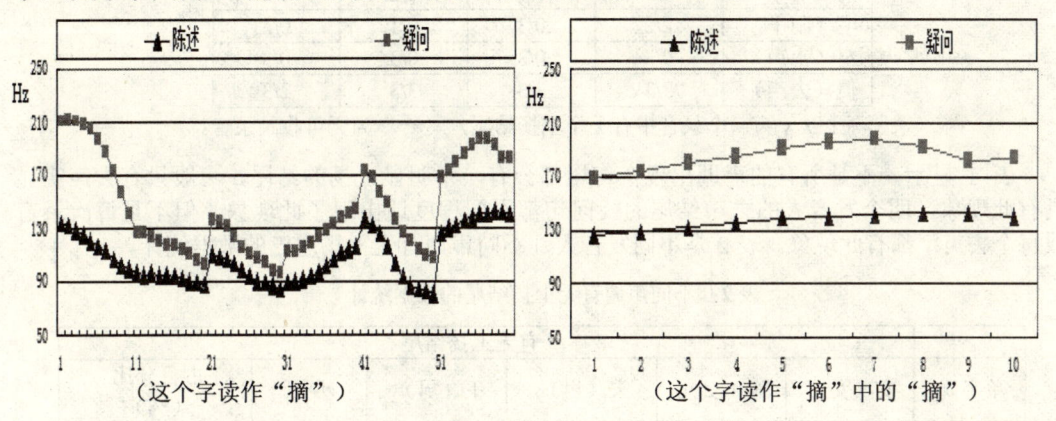

（这个字读作"摘"）　　　　　（这个字读作"摘"中的"摘"）

图 3：疑问句"这个字读作'摘'？"的结尾

图 3 的句子在句末处没有明显上扬的尾巴。一般出现上扬尾巴的句子，其句末往往是去声，而即使是去声也不一定都有上扬的尾巴，请看下图。

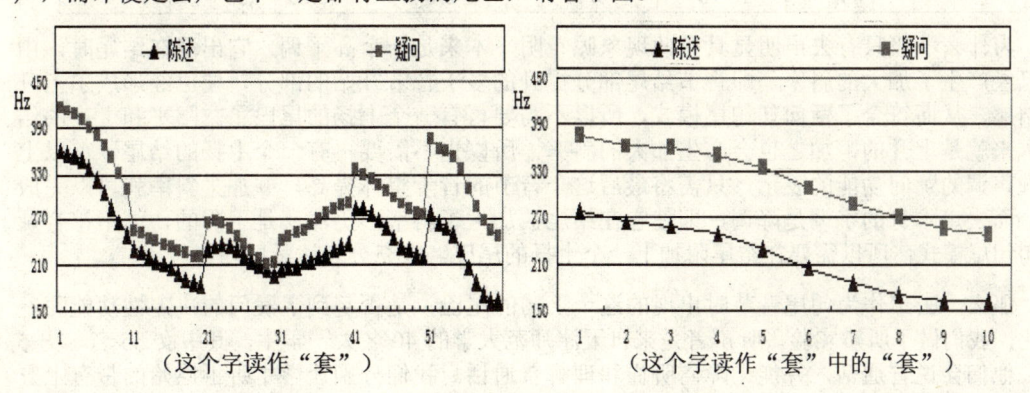

（这个字读作"套"）　　　　　（这个字读作"套"中的"套"）

图 4：疑问句"这个字读作'套'？"的结尾

根据实验数据可以发现，疑问句句尾有无上扬的尾巴总的讲是有一定规律的，其统计结果见表1和表2。

表1：不同疑问声调有无上扬结尾的统计

单字调	有无上扬结尾			
	安（女）	陈（女）	宋（男）	王（男）
猜（阴平）	0/1	0/2	0/3	0/1
才（阳平）	1/1	0/2	0/2	0/2
彩（上声）	0/1	0/2	0/2	—
菜（去声）	3/3	3/3	3/3	1/1
搭（阴平）	—	0/1	0/2	0/1
答（阳平）	1/3	0/3	—	—
打（上声）	0/1	0/2	—	—
大（去声）	3/3	1/1	2/2	1/1
滔（阴平）	0/2	—	0/2	0/1
逃（阳平）	2/2	—	0/2	0/2
讨（上声）	0/2	0/1	0/2	—
套（去声）	2/3	3/3	1/1	1/1
摘（阴平）	0/1	0/1	0/2	0/2
宅（阳平）	2/2	0/3	0/1	0/3
窄（上声）	0/3	0/3	0/3	0/3
债（去声）	3/3	3/3	3/3	2/3

注：x/y 为 y 个录音中有 x 个上扬结尾，"—"为无可收录录音。

表 1 显示，不是所有的声调出现在句尾都会有一个明显上扬的结尾，一般只有去声明显具有此现象。四个发音人的去声结尾的疑问句都不同程度地出现了此现象，但不是每次录音或每个去声字都有此现象。表 2 是不同发音人、不同声调有无上扬尾巴的数据统计。

表2：不同声调有无上扬结尾的数据统计

单字调	有无上扬结尾				小计	占百分比（%）
	安（女）	陈（女）	宋（男）	王（男）		
阴平	0/4	0/4	0/9	0/5	0/22	0
阳平	6/8	0/9	0/5	0/7	6/29	20.7
上声	0/7	0/8	0/7	0/3	0/25	0
去声	11/12	10/10	9/11	5/6	35/39	89.7

为什么一般只有去声明显具有此现象呢？阴平本来是一个高平调，它出现在结尾时，由于已经产生了加大的斜率，即音节结尾部分提升的多于音节开始的部分，便已经形成了上升的结尾，从而符合了疑问句句尾模式，所以不需要再有一个上扬的尾巴了。阳平和上声的结尾本来就是上升的，加之也会产生加大的斜率，所以也不需要再有一个上扬的结尾了。以上三种声调的疑问功能的表示，只需将最后这个音节的音阶整体提高，并加大斜率就可以完成了。而去声本身的字调是降调，即使它在结尾被加大了斜率，仍然还是下降的，而不符合疑问句句尾模式，所以需要在结尾附加上一个上扬的尾巴，来充分表达疑问功能。

那么，去声作为句尾音节时出现的这个上扬的尾巴，是否起到了疑问的决定性功能呢？为此，我们做了听辨实验。听辨者是来自天津师范大学的 40 名大一学生，其中女 35 名，男 5 名。他们会说普通话，并能无障碍听懂和理解普通话。我们分别让学生听了原始的带有上升尾巴的疑问句、去掉了上升尾巴的疑问句、原始的不带上升尾巴的陈述句和加上了上升尾巴的陈述句，句子顺序随机排列，观察他们对以上四种句子是否认为是疑问的判断。表 3、表 4 是听辨结果统计。表中 q 表示疑问，s 表示陈述，y 代表原始句，-wei 表示减掉了上扬的尾巴，+wei 表示加上了上扬的尾巴。如：cai4-q-y_s 表示"菜、去声、问句、原始句、宋氏发音人"。

表3：陈述的去声添加上扬尾巴后改认为是疑问的听辨率统计

类型	文件名	认为陈述（人）	认为疑问（人）	认为疑问率（%）	比原句增加（人）	增加率（%）
去声陈述（男）							
原句1	cai4-s-y_s	39	1	2.5		
1加尾	cai4-s+wei_s	38	2	5	1	2.5
原句2	zhai4-s-y_w	40	0	0		
2加尾	zhai4-s+wei_w	40	0	0	0	0
原句3	zhai4-s-y_s	25	15	37.5		
3加尾	zhai4-s+wei_s	10	30	75	15	37.5
原句4	da4-s-y_s	33	7	17.5		
4加尾	da4-s+wei_s	23	17	42.5	10	25
					平均增加 16.25%	
去声陈述（女）							
原句5	cai4-s-y_an	40	0	0		
5加尾	cai4-s+wei_an	39	1	2.5	1	2.5
原句6	cai4-s-y_ch	38	2	5		
6加尾	cai4-s+wei_ch	38	2	5	0	0
原句7	zhai4-s-y_an	40	0	0		
7加尾	zhai4-s+wei_an	40	0	0	0	0
原句8	zhai4-s-y_ch	40	0	0		
8加尾	zhai4-s+wei_ch	39	1	2.5	1	2.5
原句9	da4-s-y_ch	40	0	0		
9加尾	da4-s+wei_ch	40	0	0	0	0
原句10	tao4-s-y_ch	40	0	0		
10加尾	tao4-s+wei_ch	39	1	2.5	1	2.5
原句11	tao4-s-y_an	40	0	0		
11加尾	tao4-s+wei_an	39	1	2.5	1	2.5
					平均增加 1.43%	

表3显示，陈述句加上上扬尾巴后听辨率有了不同程度的变化，其中对男发音人的疑问辨别增加较高，为平均增加16.25%，而对女发音人的疑问辨别增加较少，平均只增加1.43%。不过，我们注意到这样一个细节，陈述句加上上扬尾巴后听成是疑问句的比率增加最大的句子，其原始句的陈述句听辨率就很低，如表3中的原句3"zhai4-s-y_s"，原句4"da4-s-y_s"。

我们再来看当把原来疑问句所具有的上扬尾巴去掉之后的听辨结果。

表 4：疑问的去声去掉上扬尾巴后还认为是疑问的听辨率统计

类型	文件名	认为陈述（人）	认为疑问（人）	认为疑问率（%）	比原句减少（人）	减低率（%）
		去声疑问（男）				
原句 12	cai4-q-y_s	0	40	100		
12 去尾	cai4-q-wei_s	4	36	90	4	10
原句 13	zhai4-q-y_w	30	10	25		
13 去尾	zhai4-q-wei_w	31	9	22.5	1	2.5
原句 14	zhai4-q-y_s	2	38	95		
14 去尾	zhai4-q-wei_s	10	30	75	8	20
原句 15	da4-q-y_s	3	37	92.5		
15 去尾	da4-q-wei_s	4	36	90	1	2.5
					平均降低	8.75%
		去声疑问（女）				
原句 16	cai4-q-y_an	7	33	82.5		
16 去尾	cai4-q-wei_an	30	10	25	23	57.5
原句 17	cai4-q-y_ch	0	40	100		
17 去尾	cai4-q-wei_ch	0	40	100	0	0
原句 18	zhai4-q-y_an	11	29	72.5		
18 去尾	zhai4-q-wei_an	16	24	60	5	12.5
原句 19	zhai4-q-y_ch	1	39	97.5		
19 去尾	zhai4-q-wei_ch	0	40	100	−1	−2.5
原句 20	da4-q-y_ch	0	40	100		
20 去尾	da4-q-wei_ch	1	39	97.5	1	2.5
原句 21	tao4-q-y_ch	1	39	97.5		
21 去尾	tao4-q-wei_ch	0	40	100	−1	−2.5
原句 22	tao4-q-y_an	12	28	70		
22 去尾	tao4-q-wei_an	21	19	47.5	9	22.5
					平均降低	12.86%

表 4 显示，疑问句减掉上扬尾巴后听辨率有所下降，其中对男发音人的疑问辨别平均降低 8.75%，而对女发音人的疑问辨别平均降低 12.86%。这里仍然要注意，疑问句上扬尾巴剪掉后听成是疑问句的比率降低较多的，其原始句的疑问句听辨率就是很低的，如表 4 中原句 16 "cai4-q-y_an"，原句 22 "tao4-q-y_an" 等。另外，当去声作为疑问的结尾时，去掉上扬尾巴之后，有的疑问信息确实有所下降，但有的没有变化，更有个别的反而疑问信息有所加强，如：21 去尾 "tao4-q-wei_ch"。

作者对加上尾巴或去掉尾巴是否会对听辨者对于句式的判断造成影响进行了推断统计。通过运行软件 SPSS13.0，对数据进行了配对 T 检验。当 P 值小于 0.05 时，说明有显著性差异，也就是说尾巴的加减对听辨有影响。如果 P 值大于 0.05，则没有显著性差异，说明数据中的差异是样本差异引起的，而不是加减尾巴引起的。

表 5：数据配对 T 检验（T-Test）结果

A. 去声陈述

		Paired Differences						
		Mean	Std. Deviation	Std. Error Mean	95% Confidence Interval of the Difference Lower	Upper	t	df	Sig. (2-tailed)
Pair 1	VAR00001 - VAR00002	-.06909	.12284	.03704	-.15161	.01343	-1.865	10	.092

B. 去声疑问

		Paired Differences						
		Mean	Std. Deviation	Std. Error Mean	95% Confidence Interval of the Difference Lower	Upper	t	df	Sig. (2-tailed)
Pair 1	VAR00001 - VAR00002	-.13273	.33103	.09981	-.35512	.08966	-1.330	10	.213

统计显示，去掉或加上上扬尾巴之后，疑问信息的下降或提升没有显著性变化，P 值均大于 0.05。即使陈述句添加上扬尾巴同陈述句原句对比一组检验中 P 值为 0.092 接近 0.05，也是由于个别句子所致，而这些个别句子的原始听辨率就很低。可见，疑问信息不主要依赖于疑问句句末出现的上扬尾巴，剪掉疑问句末这个上扬尾巴或是给陈述句加上它，都不大影响人们对于疑问信息的感知。这个上扬的尾巴只可以加强疑问信息，它不是疑问信息的决定因素。因此，我们把疑问句末的上升尾巴处理为一个附加的、用来加强疑问的语气助词更为合理，正如赵元任先生后来认为的那样，最好把它当做助词处理，它没有自己的成段因素，而是寄生在最后一个语素上[6]。

4. 结论

汉语的句调和声调是分离的，句调的语音实现是由带有声调的字按照句调模式输出的。正如赵元任先生主张的那样，汉语句调除了有同时叠加现象外，确实也存在连续叠加的现象。实验证明疑问句中有些确实存在一个上扬的结尾，在结尾为去声字时表现最为明显，但也不是一定出现一个上扬的尾巴。去掉疑问句末的上扬尾巴或给陈述句加上一个上扬尾巴，疑问信息的下降或提升没有显著性变化，疑问功能不是主要依赖于它。疑问信息主要来自句末边界调，同时恐怕又主要是由改变其斜率来实现的，正如林茂灿[1]所描述的那样，疑问的边界 F0 曲拱的斜率比陈述的大，或音阶比陈述的高，或者两个条件同时满足。疑问句末的这个上扬尾巴占据了一个语气助词的位置，它是一个附加的、用以加强疑问语气的助词，它不大影响整个语调模式，只是可以加强疑问信息。从音系角度我们可以认为这个上扬的尾巴是语气助词失掉了其音段而保留下来的超音段，它作为对疑问信息的加强而依附在全句最后一个音节上。

参考文献

[1] 林茂灿（2006）疑问和陈述语气与边界调。《中国语文》第 4 期。
[2] 赵元任（1929）北平语调的研究。《最后五分钟》附录。北京：中华书局。
[3] 赵元任（1932）英语语调与汉语对应语调初探。载《历史语言研究所集刊》，外编（蔡元培先生六十五岁庆祝论文集）。

[4] 赵元任（1933）汉语的字调跟语调。载《历史语言研究所集刊》第 4 本第 3 分。
[5] 赵元任（1935）国语语调。《广播周报》第 23 期；又《国语周刊》第 214 期。
[6] 赵元任（1979）《汉语口语语法》。北京：商务印书馆。

广西藤县岭景方言的去声嘎裂声中折调

麦 耘

摘要

广西藤县岭景方言是一种粤方言，其阴、阳去声都是中折调。本文分析这是嘎裂声，并认为嘎裂声性在该方言中可视为声调的区别特征。

关键词： 岭景方言　去声　嘎裂声　区别特征

1. 引言

藤县位于广西壮族自治区东部，其东边是梧州市和苍梧县，东南是岑溪市，西南是容县，西边是平南县，西北是蒙山县，东北是昭平县。县内通行一种属粤语勾漏片的方言，内部有一些差别。北部有一些讲客家方言的人口，还有一些少数民族人口。岭景镇在藤县的西南角，与平南县和容县交界，镇政府所在地与藤县县城直线距离有 30 多公里。该镇讲粤方言，镇内各村语音基本一致。

本文的材料是 2006 年 5 月中旬在藤县县城和岭景镇录制的。笔者录了三位发音人的语音，本文只用了其中一位的录音做语图。发音人黄 H.-K.，藤县岭景镇新村人，女，40 岁，高中文化，干部。自小在本村长大，现在县城工作，经常回家乡。新村在岭景镇的西北部，邻近平南县，距镇政府所在地五六公里。

岭景方言有非常整齐的八个声调：

　　　　阴平 552　　　阴上 445　　　阴去 40̰3　　　阴入 5

　　　　阳平 33　　　　阳上 335　　　阳去 30̰2　　　阳入 3

在听感上，岭景方言的去声是一种"中折调"，像在发音的当间突然折断似的，可以明显地听到在音节的偏后处有个短暂的停顿，然后再发出一个短而弱的尾音，发音时有喉头紧张感。

2. 岭景方言的阴去声

2.1 阴去声中的甲型

本文用 Praat 作图。每图除声波图和频谱图外，最下面一幅的点线是基频线（音高域取 90－250 赫，由于部分录音材料有低频噪音，影响成图质量，故音高域下限设为 90 赫。经调低参数试测，结果无实质性差异），单线是能量线（视域取 40－80 分贝）。

图 1 两例声调的前段是平或微降，后段大约三分之二处突然下降并消失，能量大幅减弱；一段时间后，基频恢复，音高比消失前略低。"粪"的前段高点为 224 赫（不计弯头，下同），"凳"是 205 赫（这在所录得的阴去字中是偏低的），恢复后都只达到 180 多赫。能量略有所恢复，中间呈现一个能量低谷。所录的字音的长度大致在 350 至 450 毫秒之间

（以下均同），这一类型音节中间基频线消失的时段，短的约 50 毫秒，长的超过 100 毫秒，多在 80 至 90 毫秒之间（"粪"是 58 毫秒，"凳"达 150 毫秒）。基频恢复后一般维持几十毫秒，个别可超过 100 毫秒（"粪"是 82 毫秒，"凳"只有 17 毫秒）。这个长度直接影响听感——音节后段重新出现的尾音，"粪"听起来清晰些，"凳"较含糊。

现在把这种型式称为"甲型"。在笔者录取的总共 28 个阴去声单字中，有 21 个属甲型，占 75%。

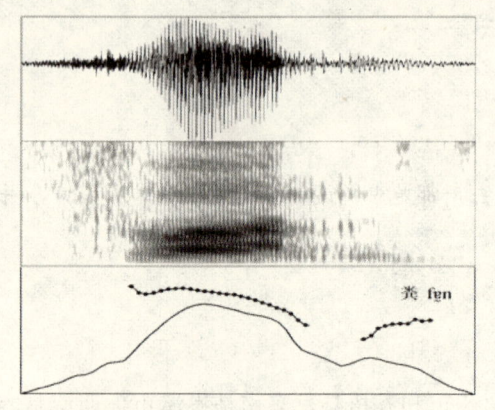

图 1-1：阴去之甲型"粪"[fen̰]　　　　图 1-2：阴去之甲型"凳"[d̰en̰]

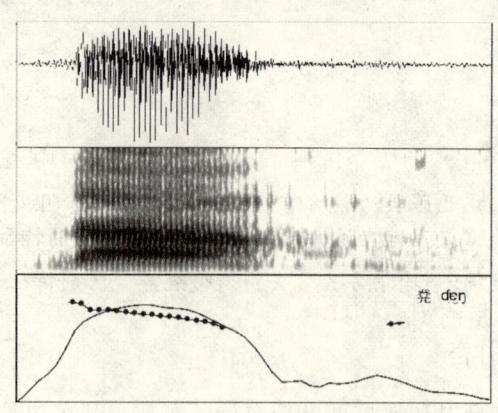

朱晓农[6]指出：嘎裂声（creaky voice）与中喉塞造成的中折调不同。其共同特点是音节中间都有声门关闭的过程，但发音生理截然相反：中喉塞往两端拉紧声带来关住声门；嘎裂声则是靠朝中间收紧声带来关住大部分声门。两者的声学特征也完全不同：喉塞音引起升调，嘎裂声导致降调，且常因声带振动不规则而使基频测不出。

上两例的基频在中断之前是下降的，显示是嘎裂声，而非中喉塞。对不同的发声态可以作声学上和生理上更严密的证明，本文仅是根据朱晓农的观点，就基频线的走向作直观的说明。又，在基频变化率较大时，各种算法都可能会测不出基频。笔者未尝试其他算法，仅依 Praat 的结果进行归纳。由于只想说明嘎裂程度的强弱，归纳出的只是音位内的变体，所以用 Praat 的算法已可以达到目的。

声带收缩得越强烈，基频线消失的时间就越长，恢复后维持的时间就越短，中间的能量缺失也越厉害。如"凳"的收缩很强烈，从语图可见，有几十毫秒时间声带基本不振动，而不仅是振动不规则。

2.2 阴去声中的乙型

"乙型"是强烈程度较低的嘎裂声。

图 2（见下页）两例的基频线基本没消失（图 2-1 有不到 10 毫秒测不出，可忽略不计），降到底以后向上反弹。两例前段高点都在 220 多赫，后段高点在 200 赫上下。最低点分别为 101 赫和 146 赫。没有能量低谷。发声时声带不很强烈地向中心挤缩一下，立刻又改为向两边拉伸，向正常状态回复，声带没达到振动不规则的地步。"冻"的挤缩程度比"醉"更弱。照理说，100 赫是能听到的，不必说 140 多赫了，但听起来这种音仍有断成两截的感觉，是音高的骤降和迅速反弹这种跳跃式的反差造成的。

乙型阴去字笔者仅录到七个，占所录阴去字的 25%。

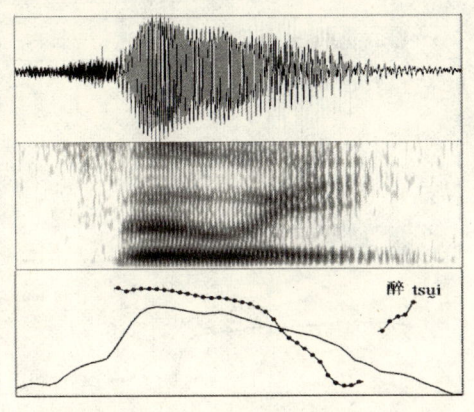

图 2-1：阴去之乙型"醉"[tsṵi]　　　　　　图 2-2：阴去之乙型"冻"[dṵŋ]

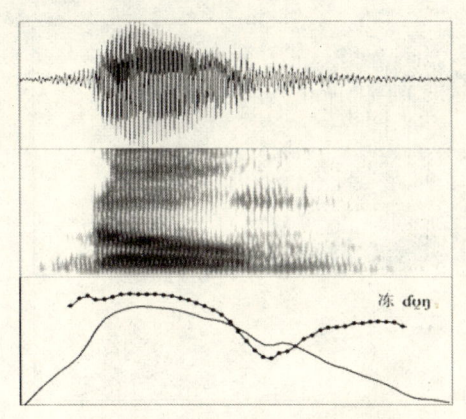

要强调指出，不论甲型还是乙型，都是同一音型的不同变体，实质是一样的，不同的仅仅是嘎裂声性有强有弱。

3. 岭景方言的阳去声

3.1 阳去声中的甲型

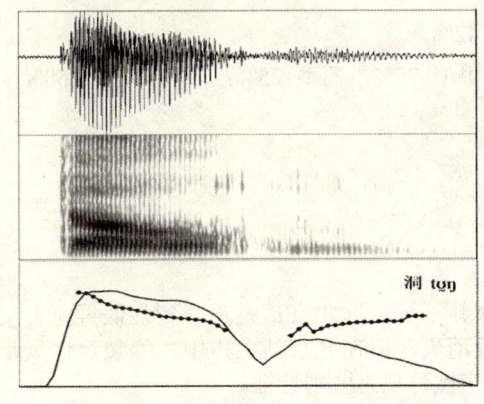

图 3-1：阳去之甲型"洞"[tṵŋ]　　　　　　图 3-2：阳去之甲型"大"[ta̰i]

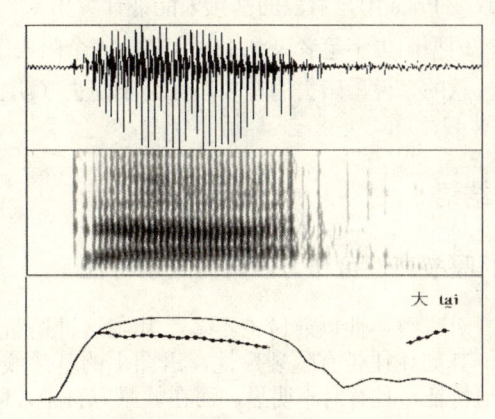

图 3 中，"洞"的前段高点为 195 赫（在阳去字中是偏高的），"大"是 175 赫，而它们的后段高点恰都是 178 赫。"洞"的基频线消失段是 58 毫秒，"大"达 133 毫秒。有明显的能量低谷。

有一点值得注意："大"的前段已经表现出声带状况不稳定，图中可见基频有颤抖（jitter）现象。依笔者的理解，这实际上是声带连续的轻微收缩，然后是一次大的收缩，正式形成嘎裂声。

在笔者所录的 26 个阳去字中有 15 个属甲型，占 58%。

3.2 阳去声中的丙型

阳去中没有嘎裂声性不强、基频线不中断的乙型，却有基频线消失之后没再恢复的情况，本文称为"丙型"。

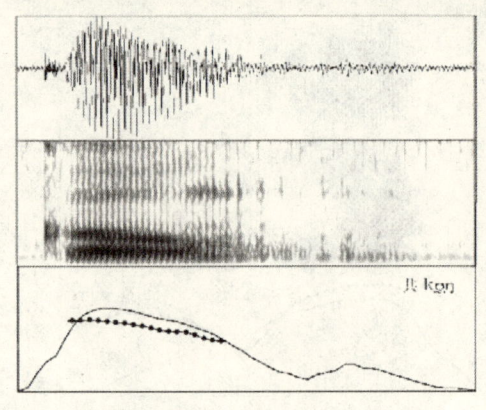

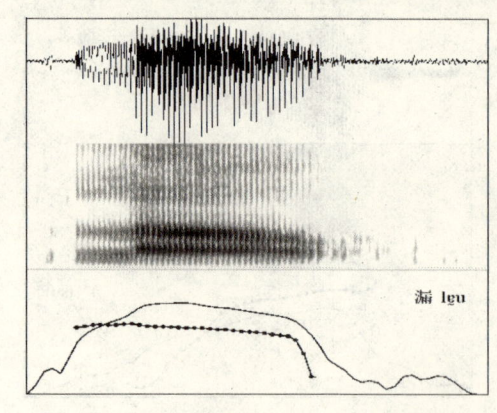

图 4-1：阳去之丙型"共" [kuŋ]　　　　　　　图 4-2：阳去之丙型"漏" [lgu]

图 4 中，"共"的高点是 181 赫，渐降到 153 赫时基频线消失。"漏"的高点也是 181 赫，渐降到约 165 赫时突然下降，最低时是 115 赫。此两例声带收缩后，始终没能恢复到非常规则的振动，是比甲型更强烈的嘎裂声。不过，尽管在这两例的语图中，音节后段没显示出基频线，但在听辨的时候，后段短而弱的尾音还是能听到。从图上看出，在基频线消失后，能量线还有过上升，达到 40 多分贝。就是说，音节并不是在嘎裂声发生后就结束的。由此可见，丙型与甲、乙型实质上仍是相同的，它们是变体关系。只是丙型的嘎裂声性更强，导致在 Praat 中，后段的基频未能被计算出来。

丙型阳去字笔者录到 11 个，占 26 个阳去字的 42%。

总的来说，阳去的嘎裂声性强于阴去（阴去：甲型 75%，乙型 25%；阳去：甲型 58%，丙型 42%）。

4. 结语

4.1 嘎裂声性可作为声调的区别特征

对嘎裂声性以前讨论不多，其实这种语音现象并不罕见。北京话上声降到最低再向上反弹，其间往往带有嘎裂声性，语图上的基频线中段消失。但在北京话上声中，嘎裂声性只是伴随特征，且有时不明显。而在岭景方言中，嘎裂声性可视为区别特征。

笔者为岭景方言声调定的区别特征矩阵如下（岭景方言的入声韵带 -p, -t, -k 韵尾，所以不必从声调上为入声划分音位，把阴、阳入分别附于阴、阳平即可）：

	阴平 552	阳平 33	阴上 445	阳上 335	阴去 403	阳去 302
高调	+	−	+	−	+	−
升调	−	−	+	+	−	−
嘎裂声	−	−	−	−	+	+

在此矩阵中，阴、阳平与阴、阳去之间靠是否带[嘎裂声]特征来区别。确切地说，以是否带出现在音节后部的嘎裂声性为区别。由于嘎裂声性出现在音节后半段，声调的主体在嘎裂声性之前，为凸降形，故与读凸降的平声形成对比。

图 5 是阴、阳平的例子。阳平有降尾，也可以标为 332 调，不过那个降尾从辨字的角度来说是羡余的。

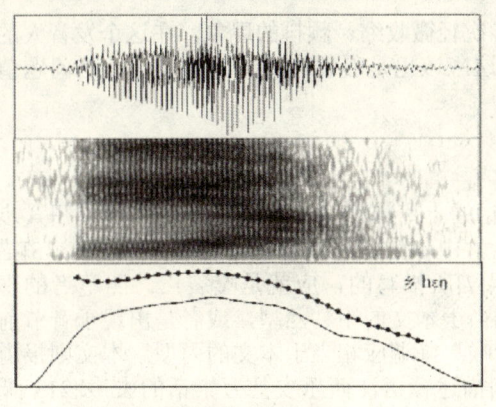

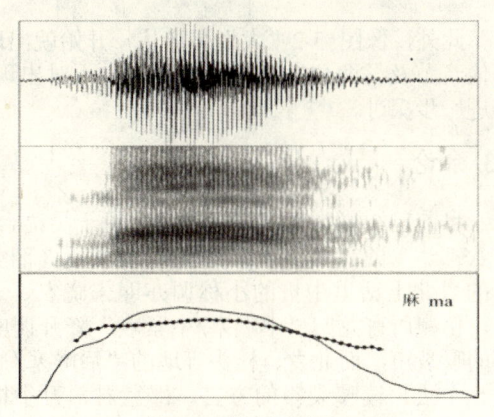

图 5-1：阴平 "乡" [hɛŋ]　　　　　　图 5-2：阳平 "麻" [ma]

阴平与阴去、阳平与阳去的主体部分相似，但它们至少有两个区别：

一、有没有喉头紧张色彩。发音人在读去声字时明显地喉头紧张，而读平声时则否。这种色彩是喉头周围的肌肉和声带本身为了声带挤缩而进行的运动造成的。

二、音节是否有断为两截的感觉。两种平声音节都是普通的、内部连续的音节，而两种去声字都在发出音节主体之后有短暂的停顿，停顿之后有一个短而弱的尾音。本文只讨论单字调。在语流中，这种尾音有可能会失去。这个问题需要另作研究。

归结起来就是：是否带嘎裂声性。把去声视为曲折调是另一种可能的处理方法。将来的研究或许可以考虑用非嘎裂的基频线替换带嘎裂声性的部分来作听辨实验，以证明嘎裂声性是否确为区别特征。又，曾有朋友提醒笔者：这种中折调会不会是塞音后加鼻音韵尾？赣语江西余干方言有这类中折调，其入声韵以塞音接鼻音为韵尾，李如龙、张双庆[1]标为 "甲" [katn]、"裂" [lietn]、"叔" [ʃukŋ]等。笔者于 2006 年七、八月间在昆明的语言调查培训班上对一名余干籍学员的发音进行过听辨，确认这是一种处于音节尾部的 "鼻除阻"（nasal release），严格地当标作[katⁿ]、[ʃukⁿ]等。这种音节在口腔中有确定的阻塞部位，后带鼻音，与没有口腔阻塞、也没有鼻音的岭景方言阴声韵的去声字差别很大，而与岭景方言阳声韵的去声字有点相似。但余干方言的音节断裂是由于口腔阻塞，似乎没有明显的喉头紧张感。希望今后能见到有关的语音实验报告。

这涉及声调的性质。除 "入声" 性质的问题一直在讨论外，学界习惯上还是把声调视为一种音高现象。但是，如果嘎裂声性确可以作为声调的区别特征之一，或将影响对 "声调" 的定义。一般情况下，声带以拉紧/放松来调节的正常振动方式影响音高，而嘎裂声性是一种特殊的声带振动方式，并以这种特殊方式影响音高。当然，无论正常的音高还是嘎裂声性，都与声带状况有关，都属于发声（voice quality）的范畴。

4.2 对发声机制的简单讨论

岭景方言的平声和去声都有音高下降的情况，但两者发声机制不同，表现也不相同：平声是声带从较紧的状态放松，声带振动自然放慢，导致音高相对平缓地下降；岭景的去声是声带向中心挤缩，迫使其振动放慢并变得不规则，这种方式会使音高的下降斜率非常大。如图 4-2 "漏" 在 17 毫秒内下降 48 赫，图 5-1 "乡" 26 毫秒下降 42 赫，图 2-1 "醉" 92 毫秒下降 101 赫，都是相当惊人的瞬时落差。这只是就测出来的基频线而言，基频线表现不出来的情况就更不必说了。

在挤缩之后有重新向两边拉伸的动作，这就造成了音高和能量的一定恢复，从而有后段 "尾音" 存在。

此外，像图 3-2"大"那样从一开始就出现多次轻微收缩、颤抖的现象，在这个发音人的其他音节及另两位发音人的发音中也不时出现。这应该也是嘎裂声性的一种表现。这问题值得进一步探讨。

4.3 余论

目前已知嘎裂声在汉语方言中见于吴语台州话的上声[6]和属于桂北土话的广西贺州八步"八都话"的入声[2][3]，以及粤北土话（韶关话）中作为形态音位的小称调[7]。伍巍[5]描写的粤北土话里中折的小称调亦即朱晓农、寸熙[7]所描写的，应就是嘎裂声。照笔者的理解，伍巍所言龙归"中喉塞/中紧喉"降升调应相当于本文的甲、乙型，或者是出现于音节前部的嘎裂声，而北乡、桂头等地的"后喉塞/后紧喉"降调应相当于本文的丙型。本文则报道了一个去声读嘎裂声的方言。邵慧君、万小梅[4]描述赣语江西乐安县万崇话的去声 213 调是：降到最低时带有喉头紧张色彩，仿佛声调中间有短暂的断裂，前半段低而促，后半段相对扬而缓。从这描述看，很像是在音节的前部带有嘎裂声性。

这都是近几年发现的。其实台州和粤北土话的中折调早已引起学界注意，只是以前多认为中喉塞作用。现在对嘎裂声性的机制和表现正逐步明了，这对指导方言调查的实践很有益处。或许未来还会在汉语方言和少数民族语言中发现更多的嘎裂声及其不同类型，包括发音学意义上和音系学意义上的不同类型。

致谢：衷心感谢朱晓农博士、胡方博士和匿名审稿专家的指教。

参考文献

[1] 李如龙、张双庆主编（1992）《客赣方言调查报告》。厦门：厦门大学出版社。
[2] 麦耘（2007）广西贺州八步鹅塘八都话入声的语音分析。《桂林师范高等专科学校学报》第 1 期，1-7 页。
[3] 麦耘（2008）广西八步鹅塘"八都话"音系。《方言》第1期，18-33页。
[4] 邵慧君、万小梅（2006）江西乐安县万崇话的小称变调。《方言》第 4 期，309-315 页。
[5] 伍巍（2003）广东曲江县龙归土话的小称。《方言》第 1 期，54-60 页。
[6] 朱晓农（2004）浙江台州方言中的嘎裂声中折调。《方言》第 3 期，226-230 页。
[7] 朱晓农、寸熙（2003）韶关话的小称调和嘎裂声。载戴昭铭主编《汉语方言语法研究和探索》，哈尔滨：黑龙江人民出版社，346-354 页。

塞音的声学格局分析

石 锋 冉启斌

摘要

本文使用嗓音起始时间（VOT）和闭塞段时长（GAP）两个参量来建立塞音的声学格局；并从塞音格局的角度对北京话、苏州话、太原话及水语中的塞音进行了分析。考察看到塞音格局分析能够有效地展示不同类别塞音之间的关系及不同性质塞音自身的特征。VOT 和 GAP 在一定程度上存在补偿关系。文章最后给出了塞音格局中的音类区域图。

关键词： 塞音 声学格局 分析

1. 引言

塞音（stop），又称爆发音，是指发音时声道完全闭塞爆发而成的音。在辅音的各种类别中，塞音占有最为重要的地位。据研究，世界语言中不存在没有塞音的语言，塞音是唯一一种所有语言都具有的辅音音类[1][2]。因此，对塞音的深入分析显得尤其重要。

语言内的各种单位都是成系统的，在语音方面，不同类别的语音单位形成一定的语音格局。各种语言和方言的语音格局对于我们认识不同语言中所表现的语音共同规律及各自的个性特征都很有意义[11]。本文打算使用声学分析的方法，提取一定特征参量，对塞音的声学格局进行探讨，并由此对相关语音现象进行分析考察，以期对塞音的分析研究有所助益。

2. 塞音的声学格局

2.1 建立塞音声学格局的方法

闭塞段时长（GAP）和嗓音起始时间（VOT）是塞音声学特征的两个重要参量。闭塞段时长是塞音发音时的持阻时间长度。嗓音起始时间是塞音从除阻到嗓音产生之间的相对时间关系。

在数学上两组数值可以在一个二维坐标中进行标示。每个塞音都具有相应的 GAP 值和 VOT 值，我们以 GAP 作为纵坐标，VOT 作为横坐标，可以根据不同塞音的 GAP 和 VOT 数据，在坐标中作出相应的样点。这些样点就是不同塞音在塞音格局图中占据的位置。

在实验中由于样本较大，以及提取数值误差等原因，不同的样点可能会出现重合、交叉等现象。和声调格局及元音格局的做法一样，我们从较大样本中计算出平均值，按平均值在格局图中标示样点。这样既能够比较清楚地提取出某语音单位内在的典型数值，也更容易体现出不同语音单位之间的相互关系。

2.2 北京话的塞音声学格局

考察北京话的塞音格局我们使用冉启斌[7]的数据。发音人为一名地道的北京女性青年。测量 VOT 的语料均为单音节，样本数在 50－70 之间。测量 GAP 的语料为双音节，样本数均为 50。在安静的居室录音，使用南开大学开发的"桌上语音工作室"（MiniSpeechLab）进行数据测量，统计分析使用 SPSS10.0 完成 [7]。这里简单列出相关平均值数据，如表 1。

表 1：北京话塞音的 VOT、GAP 数据（时长单位均为毫秒）

声学参量 塞 音	VOT 平均值	VOT 样本数	VOT 标准差	GAP 平均值	GAP 样本数	GAP 标准差
[p]	11	55	6.94	79	50	24.86
[t]	15	64	4.06	66	50	18.38
[k]	34	59	7.61	68	50	19.54
[p']	87	57	18.04	60	50	22.13
[t']	87	68	16.11	51	50	17.59
[k']	101	48	14.29	41	50	16.15

按照表 1 的数据，将各平均值样点绘入 VOT-GAP 二维坐标中。根据 VOT 和 GAP 的一般数值，坐标的纵、横轴范围均为 0－120 毫秒。这样得到北京话塞音格局图，如图 1。

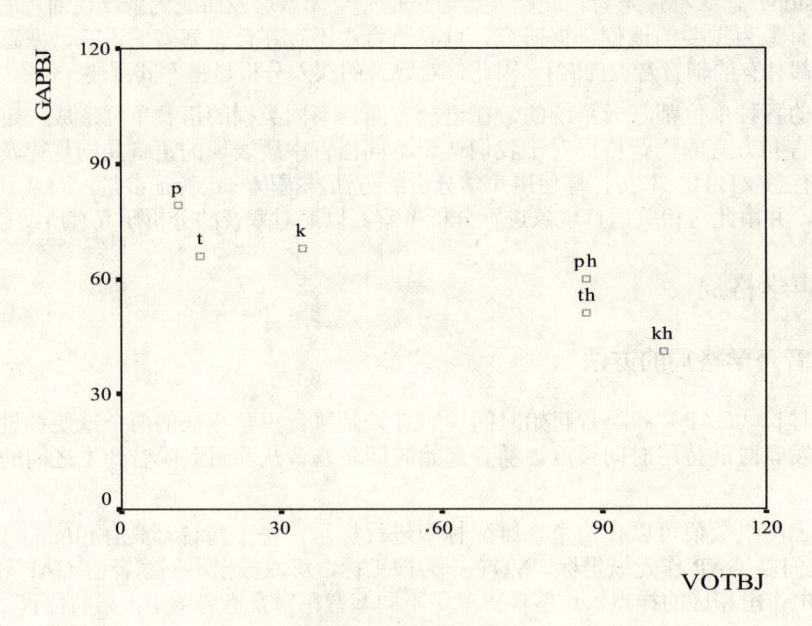

图 1：北京话的塞音格局

在图上，不带音的双唇不送气塞音[p]位置最高，且最靠近纵轴，总体位置居于左上角。其次是不带音的舌尖不送气塞音[t]及舌根不送气塞音[k]，它们的总体位置也偏高偏左。不带音的送气舌根音[kʻ][1]位置最低，且离纵轴最远，总体位置居于右下角。不带音的送气双唇音[pʻ]和舌尖音[tʻ]也偏右偏下。

从图上可以看到，北京话的六个塞音分为较为明显的两个聚合，即不带音不送气塞音（[p t k]）和不带音送气塞音（[pʻ tʻ kʻ]）。它们分别分布在格局图偏左上和偏右下的位置。

3. 几种语言（方言）塞音的声学格局

使用上述塞音格局分析方法，我们分别对太原话、苏州话和水语中的塞音进行了考察。

3.1 太原话的塞音声学格局

在音位描写上，太原话中的塞音与北京话一致，也有不带音的[p pʻ t tʻ k kʻ]共六个塞音，没有带音塞音。梁磊[5]曾经对太原话塞音的 VOT 及 GAP 数据进行过测量，得到结果如下：

表 2：太原话塞音的 VOT、GAP 数据（时长单位均为毫秒）

塞音	VOT	GAP
[p]	6.8	69.4
[t]	9.1	66.3
[k]	18.9	57.2
[pʻ]	94.3	42.4
[tʻ]	91.3	49.3
[kʻ]	99.2	46

将上述数据绘入 VOT-GAP 二维图中，得到太原话塞音格局图，如图 2。

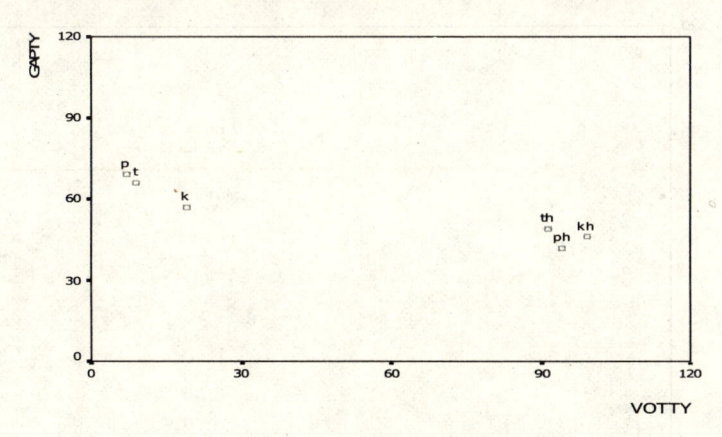

图 2：太原话的塞音格局

从上图来看，不带音的双唇不送气音[p]依然占据格局图的左上角，位置最高，最靠近纵轴。不带音的舌尖不送气音[t]和舌根音[k]略低略靠右，但都离[p]较近。不带音的送气双唇音[pʻ]位置最低，但离纵轴最远的是不带音的送气舌根音[kʻ]。六个塞音在图上分为两个聚合非常清晰。

---

[1] 因作图软件的原因，送气符号[ʻ]在图上均以[h]表示。后同，不另注。

3.2 苏州话的塞音声学格局

与北方方言不同，吴语中一般有三套塞音。苏州话中的三套塞音即一般所谓的浊塞音、清不送气塞音和清送气塞音。在音位描写上一般记为[b d g p t k p' t' k']。关于吴语中浊塞音的音值，经过很多学者的研究，一般认为在单念时是不带音的（voiceless），即没有声带的振动；在语流中可能变为带音的（voiced）音。[3][10][9]

我们曾经测量了苏州话三类塞音的 VOT 和 GAP 数据，结果如表 3。

表 3：苏州话塞音的 VOT、GAP 数据（时长单位均为毫秒）

塞音	VOT	GAP
[b]	8	63
[d]	8	48
[g]	20	55
[p]	6	109
[t]	7	105
[k]	16	89
[p']	81	87
[t']	62	85
[k']	80	69

根据上述数据作出塞音格局图，如图 3。

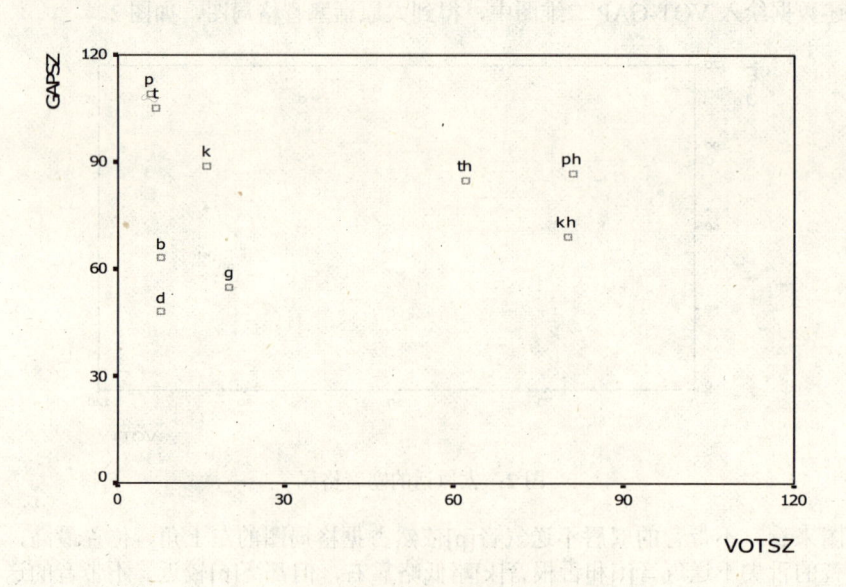

图 3：苏州话的塞音格局

在苏州话的塞音格局图中，不带音的不送气塞音[p]依然位于左上角，其他两个不送气塞音[t k]也居于左上角。三个塞音的位置都很高。不带音的送气塞音[t' p' k']位置靠右，[p' k']纵向位置几乎一致，[pʻ]离纵轴最远。浊塞音[b d g]靠近纵轴，位置略微靠下。从图上能够比较清楚地观察到九个塞音呈三个聚集区域分布。

3.3 水语（中和）的塞音声学格局

除汉语方言以外，我们还测量了水语（中和）塞音的相关数据。中和水语属于水语中的三洞土语，分布在贵州省三都水族自治县的中和区。它的塞音比较复杂，共有四套 13 个，分别是：[p t k q pʻ tʻ kʻ qʻ ʔb ʔd mb nd ŋg]。从发音部位上看，这 13 个塞音涉及双唇、舌尖、舌根、小舌四个部位；从发音方法上看，分为不送气清音、送气清音、前喉塞浊音（缩气音）和鼻冠浊音四类。对水语的塞音进行考察是很有意义的。

按我们对中和水语塞音 VOT 的测量 [12]，以及重新测得的 GAP 数值，以男发音人为例，有关数据如下表 4。

表 4：中和水语塞音的 VOT、GAP 数据（时长单位均为毫秒）

塞音	VOT	GAP
[p]	10	88
[t]	12	76
[k]	29	77
[q]	24	65
[pʻ]	70	46
[tʻ]	67	58
[kʻ]	79	60
[qʻ]	82	82
[ʔb]	-28	59
[ʔd]	-18	53
[mb]	-102	41
[nd]	-96	47
[ŋg]	-91	24

按上述数据作出塞音格局图，如图 4。

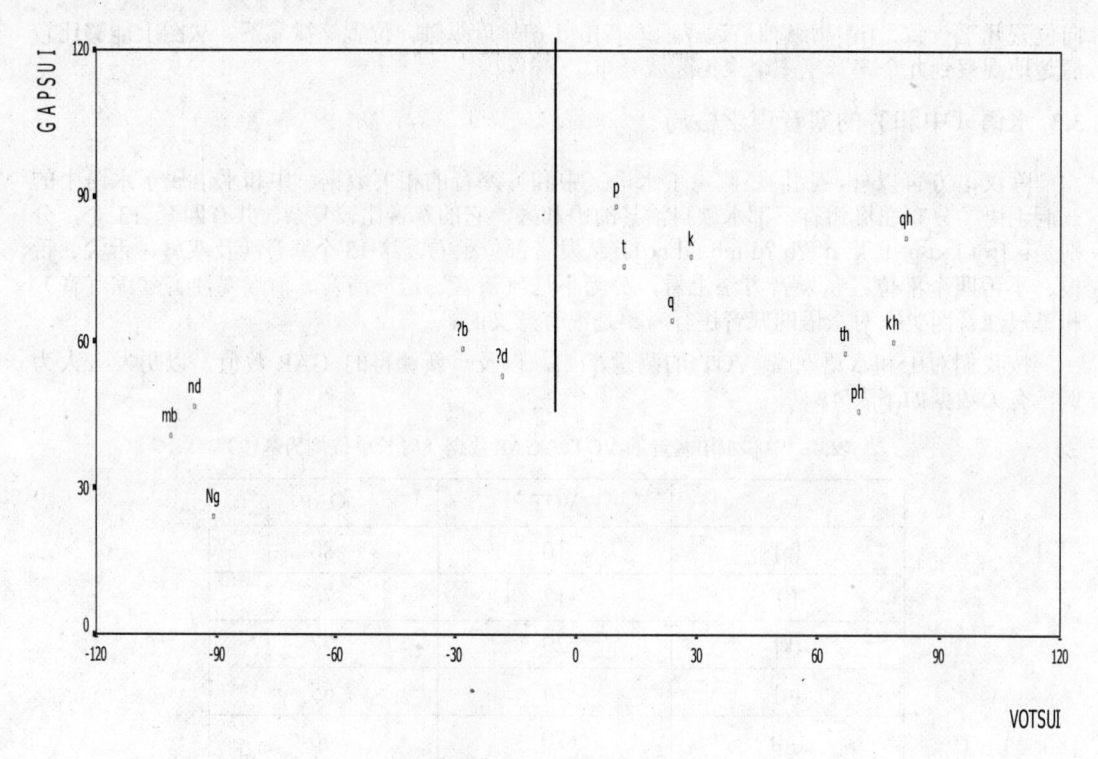

图 4：水语（中和）的塞音格局

中和水语的塞音格局图与前面的汉语方言塞音格局图不太一样，最大的区别是它分为两个大的部分。右边的部分相当于前面汉语方言的塞音格局图，我们把它称作塞音格局图的主图。左边的部分为上文的格局图所不具备，我们把它称作塞音格局图的副图。副图的存在是因为水语中具备真正带音的塞音，它们的 VOT 为负值。

从格局主图看来，不带音的不送气音[p t k q]依然处于左上角，双唇塞音[p]最靠左靠上。不带音的送气音[pʻ tʻ kʻ qʻ]居右，小舌音[qʻ]最靠上，双唇音[pʻ]最靠下。在格局副图上，带音的前喉塞音[ʔb ʔd]靠近纵轴，带音的鼻冠塞音[mb nd ŋg]离纵轴都较远。整个图上，13个塞音分为四个区域分布。

3.4 对塞音格局图的分析

前面我们给出了几种汉语方言的塞音格局图及一种塞音比较复杂的水语塞音格局图。综合起来看，我们认为有如下几个方面值得注意。

第一，塞音格局图上音类的聚集特性。在各个方言（语言）的格局图上，属于一个类别的塞音总是分布在相近的区域，形成若干个聚合。不送气的音聚集在一起，送气的音也聚集在一起。几个类别基本上相互分离。同时，相同类别的塞音在格局图上又处于相对稳定的位置。不带音不送气的塞音总是分布在格局主图的左上角，不带音送气的塞音总是分布在格局主图的右边。带音的塞音则分布在格局副图上。性质不同的塞音各自占据相应的空间范围。这一方面说明塞音的类别分布具有规律性，另一方面也说明我们所做的格局图反映了塞音本身的特性。

第二，塞音格局图上音类的位置规律。在上文各塞音格局图上，有一个很明显的规律是，不带音不送气双唇塞音[p]在主格局图中总是居于最上、最左的位置。虽然[p]在不同语言

（方言）中的具体位置有所改变，但是相对的位置关系能够维持一致。这一点可以类比于声学元音图中前高不圆唇元音[i]。[i]在元音声位图中一般总是处在最高、最左的位置，很少发生变化。格局图上的其他塞音则同元音中的[a][u]等表现相似，在前后高低上存在变动。当然，塞音[p]的稳定位置关系与元音[i]在机制上则应该存在差别。与[p]不同的是，可以观察到送气塞音[k']的位置关系也具有一定的稳定性，它常常出现在格局主图的最右位置。这一点在北京话和太原话中均是如此。苏州话中[k']以 1 毫秒的弱势与双唇塞音[p']处在最右。在水语中[k']并非处在最右，但最靠右的塞音是送气小舌音[q']。看起来送气塞音的发音部位越靠后越倾向于居右。当然，塞音的这种位置规律以不送气音表现得最为稳定清晰，送气音的规律性不如不送气音。

第三，塞音格局图对语音性质的反映。在前面的塞音格局图上，相同类别的塞音在不同方言的格局图中具体位置往往不同。例如在北京话中[p t k]的位置处在 60－90 之间，太原话中[p t k]处在 60 附近，而苏州话中[p t k]则都分布在 90 以上。这种差异我们认为是对不同语音性质的反映。对于北京话塞音的性质，赵元任[14]早在 1935 年就有过论述，他认为北京话的塞音"是弱的"，并且用清化的[b̥]来标写双唇塞音。罗杰瑞[6]也认为北京话的不送气塞音虽然是"清音"，但都是"弱音"，"对没受过语音训练的人听来好像是浊音"。在声学实验上看到，北京话[p t k]后接元音的第一共振峰（F1）过渡为升，与典型的浊塞音相同 [8]。吴语的不带音塞音赵元任[14]认为是"强的"，用[p]标写，他说"这里头[p]跟[b]一强一弱很不同的"。格局图中的纵轴是塞音发音时闭塞段时长的反映，闭塞段的时长一般反映了发音时肌肉的紧张程度。纵轴反映塞音的强弱性质是有依据的。太原话的不送气塞音在纵轴上位置较低，与北京话近似，也比较"弱"。从这里可以看出，塞音格局图的纵轴反映的是由发音时肌肉的紧张程度而产生的松紧性质。

考察前面各个塞音格局图，可以看到塞音在横向的位置关系上也颇不相同。例如太原话中的[p' t' k']分布在横轴的 90 以上，位置较为集中。北京话的[p' t' k']分布在 90 左右，位置较为分散。苏州话的[p' t' k']位置最靠左，分布在 90 以下，60 以上。这种分布上的差异也与它们的语音特点相关。赵元任[14]把北京话的送气双唇塞音记为[ph]，认为是"强送气"，"无论在什么地位，送气作用总是不失落的"。而对于太原话的送气塞音，赵元任记为[px]，认为是"强音加摩擦送气"，"是声门大开着读的"。

从上面的分析可以看出，在塞音格局图上纵轴和横轴代表不同的意义。纵轴表示的是塞音本身性质，主要是反映肌肉紧张程度的发音松紧特征。横轴表示的是塞音发音方法上的属性，与塞音的带音与否、送气程度相关。从这个角度观察，苏州话的不带音送气音看来送气不强烈。水语的不带音不送气音比较弱，送气音送气成分也不强烈。

4. 塞音声学格局的意义

塞音格局的分析是一种方法，也是一个思路。这里我们从声学分析的角度提出了塞音格局的两个维度，即嗓音起始时间（VOT）和闭塞段时长（GAP）。从理论上讲，塞音的格局分析也可以在不同的基础和方法上进行。例如在听觉混淆数据的基础上，张家騄等[13]从清－浊、送气－不送气（或长－短）等维度给出了汉语普通话的辅音格局。在动态腭位数据的基础上，李俭、郑玉玲[4]从舌腭接触的靠前性、趋央性等维度上给出了普通话的辅音格局。塞音格局分析的维度选择并不是唯一的。

在塞音声学格局的基础上，我们还可以对有关问题作进一步的探讨。例如关于 VOT 和 GAP 之间的关系、塞音的声学空间等。

4.1 VOT 和 GAP 之间的关系

从观察上看，一种方言（语言）的塞音格局中 VOT 值的分布范围较大时，GAP 值的分布范围则相对较小。例如在太原话中，横轴上的 VOT 值分布较宽，而纵轴上的 GAP 值则分布较窄。在苏州话中，GAP 值分布较宽，则 VOT 值分布相对较窄。北京话的情况居中。水语的格局主图中也存在这种关系，它的 VOT 值分布较窄，而 GAP 值分布较宽。为比较清楚地看到这种关系，可以根据上文几种方言（语言）的 VOT 及 GAP 数值计算出各自的数值范围，如下（表5）。

表 5：VOT 值、GAP 值分布范围比较

方言（语言）	VOT 范围	GAP 范围
北京话	90	38
太原话	92	27
苏州话	75	61
水语（中和）	72	42

在上表中，可以看到 VOT 的范围较大时 GAP 范围相对较小，VOT 的范围较小时 GAP 范围相对较大。从中可以得到一个大致的结论：在一种方言（语言）内，VOT 值分布范围和 GAP 值分布范围存在一定程度的补偿关系。当然，这种关系不是绝对而是相对的。

这种补偿关系说明 VOT 和 GAP 并不是两个绝对独立的量，而是具有相互联系的平衡关系。它表示的意义是，纵轴的分布范围（GAP）和横轴的分布范围（VOT）相互牵制，从而使得各语言的塞音在总体分布空间上比较接近，大致具有相对稳定的活动范围。

4.2 塞音的声学空间

从前面的塞音格局图中我们能够看到这样的事实：一定的音类常常分布在特定的区域。这种关系是很稳定的。这使得我们有可能从具体的塞音格局图中抽象出一个作为参照的塞音空间音类分布图。在这个图上，某类塞音在理论上分布在一定的区域范围。按前面的考察，我们可以给出一个参照图，如图 5。为清楚起见，这里纵轴以 20 为起点。

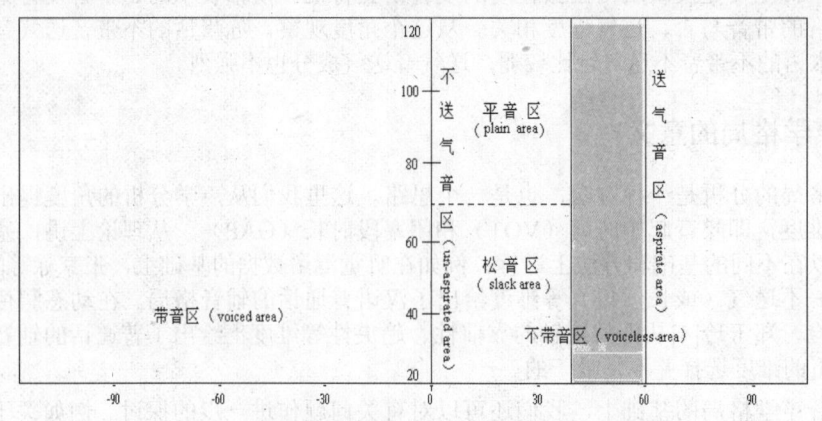

图 5：塞音空间中音类分布区域图

在图 5 中，完整的塞音空间分为主图和副图。横轴的零点将完整的塞音空间分为左右两部分，副图居左，主图居右。零点右边是不带音区（voiceless area），零点左边是带音区

（voiced area）。在不带音区，中间的阴影部分将主图分为两个部分，左部分为不送气音区（un-aspirated area），右部分为送气音区（aspirated area）。两部分之间并不是一条线，而是从上到下的一个阴影带。这表明在送气音区和不送气音区之间并不是连续的，而是存在一个断裂带。在不送气音区内部，从上到下由纵轴 70 左右的线条分为平音区（plain area）和松音区（slack area）。在苏州话的塞音格局中我们看到，苏州话的不带音不送气塞音分布在平音区，而传统所谓的浊音[b d g]分布在松音区。这一结果与有关实验和理论上的研究相符合。Henton，Ladefoged，Maddieson[1]考察了世界语言中的各种塞音，并综合实验结果认为吴语的"浊塞音"和爪哇语（Javanese）的一类塞音属于发声类型（phonation type）上的松音（slack stop）。松音发音时肌肉松弛，所以在表示闭塞段时长的纵轴上位置较低。在带音区的副图上，应该存在不送气带音塞音、送气带音塞音、鼻冠塞音等语音类别，由于本文只有水语的材料，在这里没有作进一步的细致划分。

5. 结语

本文从声学实验的角度对塞音格局的建立进行了尝试，以塞音的嗓音起始时间（VOT）和闭塞段时长（GAP）作为两个维度，考察了北京话、太原话、苏州话及中和水语的塞音声学格局。

考察看到，声学格局中的塞音具有明显的聚集特性，可以有效地区分不同类别的塞音。同时，从塞音格局的角度能够对不同塞音的具体语音特性进行分析。VOT 和 GAP 在一定程度上存在补偿关系，反映了塞音在总体分布空间上活动范围相对稳定的内在性质。从具体的塞音格局图中可以抽象出一个作为参照的塞音空间音类分布区域图。

塞音格局分析是语音格局研究的组成部分，对于塞音自身规律的揭示、语音的类型比较及语音习得等都将具有意义，相关问题我们将作进一步的探讨研究。

参考文献

[1] Henton, C., Ladefoged, P., Maddieson, I. 1992. Stops in the world's languages. Phonetica 49.
[2] Jakobson, R. 1958. Typological studies and their contribution to historical comparative linguistics.中译本《类型学研究及其对历史比较语言学的贡献》。载《雅柯布森文集》，钱军、王力译注。长沙：湖南教育出版社。
[3] 曹剑芬（1982）常阴沙话古全浊声母的发音特点——吴语清浊音辨析之一。《中国语文》第 4 期。
[4] 李俭、郑玉玲（2003）汉语普通话动态腭位的数据缩减方法。载《第六届全国现代语音学学术会议论文集》，天津师范大学。
[5] 梁磊（1999）太原话塞音的实验分析。载《现代语音学论文集》。北京：金城出版社。
[6] 罗杰瑞（Jerry Norman）（1995）《汉语概说》。张惠英译。北京：语文出版社。
[7] 冉启斌（2005）《基于普通话的汉语阻塞辅音实验研究》。南开大学博士学位论文。
[8] 任宏谟（1981）《北京话塞音特性研究》。中国社会科学院硕士学位论文。
[9] 沈钟伟、王士元（1995）吴语浊塞音的研究——统计上的分析和理论上的考虑。载《吴语研究》。香港：香港中文大学出版社。
[10] 石锋（1983）苏州话浊塞音的声学特征。《语言研究》第 1 期。
[11] 石锋（2002）北京话的元音格局。《南开语言学刊》第 1 期。
[12] 石锋、冉启斌（2007）中和水语四套塞音的声学分析。《民族语文》第 2 期。
[13] 张家騄、齐士钤、吕士楠（1981）汉语辅音知觉结构初探。《心理学报》第 1 期。
[14] 赵元任（1935）中国方言当中爆发音的种类。载《历史语言研究所集刊》第 5 本 2 分。

CAH、PAM 和 SLM 述评

——兼论跨语言语音对比与 L2 语音习得

王韫佳

摘要

  本文从理论假设和实证研究两个角度介绍了在第二语言语音习得领域比较有影响的三种框架：对比分析假设，知觉类比模型和语音学习模型。文章通过对这三种理论的介绍，分析了跨语言语音对比与第二语言语音习得之间的关系，并结合作者自己的研究结果对这三种假设中存在的一些理论和实践问题进行了初步的讨论。

关键词： 第一语言　第二语言　语音　习得　对比

1. 引言

  从语言学的角度研究对第二语言习得（SLA）产生影响的诸多要素，语言学层面的因素当然是研究者们注意的中心。如何评价母语（L1）在第二语言（L2）语音习得中的作用，L1 和 L2 语音单位之间的相似性对 L2 语音范畴的形成起到何种作用，L1 语音系统的作用和普遍语法作用之间的关系如何，这些都是在 L2 语音习得研究中得到普遍关注的话题。本文拟对在 SLA 领域和心理语音学领域比较有影响的三种理论，即对比分析假设（Contrastive Analysis Hypothesis）、知觉类比模型（Perceptual Assimilation Model）和语音学习模型（Speech Learning Model）以及与之相关的一些技术问题进行简要的介绍，并对 L2 语音习得领域存在的一些问题进行初步的讨论。

2. 对比分析假设

2.1 理论基础和基本框架

  Contrastive Analysis Hypothesis（CAH）是一个心理学假设。关于 CAH 的理论背景、要旨和它所遭遇的批评以及它后来的重新发展，Ellis[7]曾经作过比较详细的回顾和阐释，本小节的部分内容来自 Ellis 的这个综述。CAH 是为了满足 L2 教学需要而产生的一种 L2 习得理论，为了更加有效地进行教学，教师将学习者的 L1 和 L2 的语言结构进行对比，通过对比结果预测学习者的困难和偏误。从心理学的角度看，CAH 是一种基于行为主义理论的假设；从语言学的角度看，它有明显的结构主义语言学的色彩。

  行为主义心理学关注的焦点是刺激—反应关系，反应是由刺激导致的，因此，一种具体的刺激与一种具体反应之间的关联就形成了所谓的"习惯"（habit）。根据行为主义的学习理论，旧习惯将会介入新习惯的形成过程之中；对于 SLA 来说，L1 就会干扰（interfere）L2 的学习。"干扰"的概念在行为主义理论框架下的 SLA 研究中具有核心地位。干扰是心理学上所谓"前摄抑制"（proactive inhibition）的结果。当 L1 和 L2 用不同的方式表达相同的意思时，学习者就会用 L1 的实现机制去产生 L2，这样，偏误就产生了。为了建立新习惯，学习者就必须克服前摄抑制。行为主义的学习理论还认为，L1 将会迁移（transfer）到 L2 当中去。当前摄抑制存在的时候，这种迁移就是负迁移，负迁移导致偏误的产生。当 L1 和 L2 的习惯相同或近似时，就会产生正迁移，正迁移有助于 L2 的学习。行为主义的学习理论对于偏误非常关注，因此预测偏误是这一理论的重要任务，而预测偏误的手段就是对比分析。

CAH 有强式和弱式两种观点。强式假设认为，一切的 L2 错误都来自学习者的 L1 系统。弱式假设是一个诊断性的假设，它用来确认 L2 偏误中的哪一种是来自 L1 的干扰——弱式假设同时也暗示着，并非所有的偏误都来自 L1 的干扰。

由上面的介绍可知，在 CAH 的框架下，L2 的某个语言结构与相应的 L1 结构的相似性的大小，在很大程度上决定了学习者是否能够成功习得这个 L2 结构。对比分析研究在语言学上的操作过程可以分为四个步骤：（1）对 L1 和 L2 语言系统进行描写；（2）选择 L1 和 L2 系统中的某个子系统或者某些结构作为分析对象；（3）通过对比得到两种语言的相似点和不同点；（4）对可能产生偏误的地方进行预测。在语音习得的问题上，CAH 确定 L1－L2 结构相似性的方法主要是进行抽象的音系对比，用来对比的单位一般是抽象的音位或者音位的区别性特征。例如，日语的塞音和塞擦音有清浊对立而无送气对立，汉语普通话的情况正好相反，因此，日语母语者在学习普通话的送气辅音时就存在困难，他们往往用清浊对立替代送气对立，这就是所谓负迁移。又如，汉语和朝鲜语的塞音和塞擦音都有送气对立，因此，母语为朝鲜语的学习者在学习汉语的送气辅音时就不会存在困难，这就是所谓的正迁移。

2.2 质疑与批评

上个世纪 60 年代，CAH 在 SLA 研究中颇为流行，但从 70 年代开始，对 CAH 的质疑越来越多，Ellis[7]把这些批评总结为三个方面：（1）实证研究的结果中出现比率很大的反例；（2）心理学和语言学的理论基础存在问题；（3）教学实践中遭遇失败。

人们在实证研究中发现，L2 中的偏误并不都与 L1 相关，与 L1 无关的偏误可能占全部错误的一半以上[7]，导致这种情况发生的原因是，影响 L2 习得的因素是多方面的。笔者认为，CAH 最主要的问题并不在于它忽略了母语之外的影响 L2 学习的各种因素，因为即便是从 L1 对 L2 影响的角度看，CAH 的预测和解释能力依然是非常有限的。例如，Major & Kim[15]指出，仅仅使用对比分析法并不能为习得顺序或者速度提供任何解释，因为对于存在习得困难的若干 L2 结构来说，这种方法无法从理论上预测到哪些方面的困难更大。我们仍以日语母语者学习汉语普通话为例，CAH 的预测结果是学习者对于普通话送气对立的区分存在困难，但这个预测结果无法表明送气对立是否在所有语境之中的困难程度都完全相同，也无法表明送气对立的感知困难和产生困难是否一致。王韫佳、上官雪娜[26]的研究结果表明，日语母语者对普通话送气对立的区分受到了辅音所在音节的声调和辅音在词中位置的显著影响，在某些语境之下，他们对普通话送气对立的区分是相当好的。我们这项研究的结果还表明，日本学习者感知普通话送气对立和产生送气对立的困难也不一致，在感知中不送气音的错误率高于送气音，而产生中的情况恰好相反。由这个案例可以看到，过于简单和抽象的 L1－L2 音系对比对于 L2 语音偏误的预测力是相当弱的，从语言学的角度看，这一点才是 CAH 的致命弱点所在。

对 CAH 心理学和语言学的理论基础的批评源于 Chomsky 对行为主义心理学和结构主义语言学的批评，由于这一方面的批评与本文的主题距离较远，因此我们不拟介绍。需要提出的是，对 CAH 的理论层面的批评还包括这一框架对某些基本概念的混同（参见 Ellis[7]）。对比分析假设将 L1 和 L2 的差异等同于 L2 学习中的困难，同时又将困难等同于偏误。实际上，差异是语言层面的概念，而困难则是心理层面的。因此，两种语言之间的差异并不一定直接导致学习上的困难。困难和偏误之间也不一定存在直接的关系。关于差异、偏误和困难之间的关系，"后 CAH"以及近年来在理论界影响较大的 Speech Learning Model 进行了比较深入的分析，我们将在下文给予比较详细的介绍。

2.3 CAH 的自我修正和发展

尽管遭受到了广泛的批评，对比分析假设并没有完全被学界所摒弃，相反，严厉的批评以及在实证研究和教学实践中所遭遇的失败促使一些研究者对这种理论进行反省和修正，因而使它有了新的发展。其中最为重要的、与语音习得关系最为密切的进展当属对 L1－L2 相似性与 L2 习得关系的重新分析。

传统的对比分析假设认为，L1 和 L2 某个项目的差别越大，学习者的困难就越大，因此偏误就越多。但是，有研究（参见 Ellis[7]）表明，英语母语的学习者学习汉语的时候困难并不大，这是因为这两种语言的结构有很大的差别。这就是说，L1 与 L2 之间较小的相似性在某种程度上反而有利于 L2 的学习，这几乎是对传统对比分析假设中相似性的强弱与学习困难大小关系的一个颠覆。Oller & Ziahosseiny（转引自 Major & Kim[15]）更是明确提出，L2 中与 L1 相异的或者不相似的语言现象比相似的语言现象容易学习。随着实证研究的深入，这种新的观点得到日渐广泛的认可。Wode（参见 Ellis[7], Major & Kim[15]）提出，只有当两种语言的某个项目存在一种"关键相似度"（crucial similarity measure）时，学习者才会用 L1 的项目去替代 L2 的对应物，例如，德语中不存在辅音[r]，德语母语者在学习英语的时候会用母语中的[w]而不是[R]替代英语中的[r]，因为[w]与[r]存在关键相似度，而[R]与[r]差别更大。Ellis[7]认为，新的对比分析假设面临的任务是将"关键相似度"的内容具体化，以便更加精确地预测或者解释干扰会在何种情况下出现，这当然是一个非常复杂的工作，因为它需要在心理学和语言学因素之间寻求某种平衡。

如上所述，对比分析假设经历了繁荣——被批评——重新发展的螺旋式上升过程，在 SLA 研究中，它仍然是一种重要的理论框架，只不过不同的研究者对它有不同的阐释方法和使用方法而已。下面要介绍的在 L2 语音习得领域具有重要影响的两种理论模型，实际上都与对比分析假设有某种程度的关联，因为它们都是从 L1 和 L2 的关系入手来考察 L2 语音在感知和产生方面的进程的。

3. PAM 和 SLM 理论述要

如上所述，CAH 关于 L1－L2 相似性和 SLA 之间的关系的预测在实证研究和教学实践中都遭到了相当大程度的失败，这就促使人们对于二者的关系进行深入细致的实证分析和新的理论探讨。Perceptual Assimilation Model（PAM）和 Speech Learning Model（SLM）是 20 世纪 80 年代在中介语语音学（interlanguage phonetics，与之相对应的是中介语音系学，即 interlanguage phonology。这两个术语的具体含义见 Major[16]）领域产生的两个重要理论模型（Munro & Bohn[18]），这两个模型对于 L1－L2 语音相似性与 L2 语音习得的关系有完全不同于传统的 CAH 的看法。

3.1 以感知为研究对象的 PAM

非母语的语音感知包括两种情况，一是单语者对非母语语音的感知，二是 L2 学习者对目标语的语音感知。对于这两种感知来说，最直接的影响因素都是 L1 语音系统。在非母语语音感知的研究中，最著名的理论框架是 Best[2]所提出的 PAM。

PAM 的核心是：当听到非母语中两个对立的音系范畴（*phonological* categories）时，听音人会把对立体中的两个范畴与母语中发音最为相似的音系范畴进行类比，因此会产生不同类型的类比模式。常见的四种类比模式为：（1）TC 型（two categories），将非母语的两个范畴感知为母语中的两个范畴,因此能够很好地区分这对非母语的范畴。(2)SC 型(single category),将非语的两个范畴感知为母语中的一个范畴,因此对非母语的两个范畴的区分能力较差。(3)CG 型(category goodness),把非母语的两个范畴听成母语中的一个范畴,但是认为两个非母语范畴与母语中这个范畴的相似程度不同,因此能够对非母语的两个范畴进行一定程度的区分,不过区分的正确率不如 TC 型。(4)UA 型(uncategorized assimilation),无法对非母语的两个范畴中的一个或者两个与母语中的任何范畴进行类比。

Best 后来把 PAM 从单语者扩展至 L2 学习者,她认为,初始学习者感知 L2 的最小对立体也可能会有四种方式。(1)L2 对立体中仅有一个音系范畴被感知为 L1 的某个范畴。在语音层面(phonetic level),一旦最小对立体中的某个成员被感知为 L1 中某个范畴的完美范例(本文作者注:意思是 L2 的某个范畴被认为与 L1 某范畴的某个变体完全相同),那么,这个 L2 范畴在整个学习过程中的进步将是非常有限的。但是,如果学习者认为 L2 的这个范畴与 L1 范畴的所有语音变体都有所差别,那么学习者就有可能在感知中建立起这个新范畴。(2)L2 对立体中的两个范畴被感知为 L1 中的同一个范畴,但是其中的一个与 L1 对应物的相似程度较差一些,这个感知类型在 PAM 中属于 CG 型。与 L1 对应范畴相似度较差的那个 L2 范畴最终可能被学习者在音系和语音层面同时建立起来,而与 L1 对应范畴相似度较好的 L2 范畴则不会被成功习得。(3)L2 最小对立体中的两个范畴被感知为 L1 的同一个范畴,并且这两个范畴与 L1 对应物的相似度完全相同,这种感知类型相当于 PAM 中的 SG 型。大部分学习者都不能很好地区分 L2 的这两个范畴,学习者最后是否能够在感知中建立起新的对立体,一个关键性的影响因素是 L2 最小对立体的音位负担的大小。如果 L2 的某个最小对立体在言语交际中被频繁地用来区分词义,那么,学习者在感知中区分 L2 对立的压力就会加大,成功习得的机会也就因之增加。(4)非 L2 音系同化。如果初学者认为 L2 对立体中的两个范畴很难被清楚地同化为 L1 的任何音系范畴,但它们又都与 L1 的若干范畴具有一定的相似之处(在 PAM 框架下,此种情况属于 UG 型),那么,L2 最小对立体中的一个或者两个范畴在感知中都将被相对容易地建立起来。这个类型很像 SLM 中的陌生因素(new phone),但二者之间还是存在一些关键性的差别。这些差异我们将在下文加以介绍。

PAM-L2 的特点是,在界定 L1-L2 相似性时明确提出了音系学和语音学两个不同层面的相似性,从整体上来说,PAM-L2 与 PAM 没有太大的差别,但是,PAM-L2 对感知模式的描写更加细节化,同时还依据不同的感知模式,对学习者是否能够最终成功地在感知中建立 L2 的音系范畴进行了预测,也就是说,PAM 只适用于单语者或者只有极少的 L2 经验的初始学习者,而 PAM-L2 也适用于长时 L2 学习者,因为它注意到了学习过程和最终结果。

3.2 以习得过程为研究对象的 SLM

Flege 的 SLM [8][9][10][11]是针对 L2 语音学习提出的,它的目的在于探求个体学习者对 L2 音段(phonetic segment,如元音、辅音)的习得过程[12]。它的基本主张是:(1)基础学习机制,包括为语音范畴(phonetic category)建立长时记忆的能力会伴随人的一生。(2)组成 L1 和 L2 语音系统的元素共享一个音系空间(common phonological space),因此 L1 和 L2 的语音系统将会互相影响。在这个理论主张的基础上,它提出了若干理论假设,其中最著名的假设是,等值归类(equivalence classification)这种基本的认知机制对成年人的 SLA 具有重要影响,在这个机制的作用下,一个 L2 语音单位与 L1 语音单位的相似度越差,这个 L2 语音单位被成功习得的可能性就越大。

等值归类机制是人类在面对一系列范畴变体(本文作者注:例如音位变体)时能够把这些变体归为一个恒定范畴(本文作者注:例如音位)的现象。等值归类在 L1 语音系统的形成过程中无疑是重要的,因为它使得儿童可以辨认出不同说话人说出的或者在不同的语境中出现的属于同一个范畴的声音。但这种机制却会使得年龄稍长的儿童或者成年人把 L2 中的某个声音等同于 L1 中与之相似却不完全相同的对应物，因而使他们无法成功地建立这个 L2 的语音范畴。由此可见，L2 中的某个音素（phone）是否在 L1 中存在相似对应物就成为这个音素能否被成功习得的重要条件。

SLM 以 L1-L2 语音相似性为基础，把 L2 的音素分为相同音素（*identical* phone）、相似音素（*similar* phone）和陌生音素（*new* phone）三类。相同音素是指在 L1 中能够找到声学特征完全相同的对应物的 L2 音素。相似音素是指在 L1 中存在容易识别的对应物的 L2 音素，但 L2 音素与其 L1 对应物在声学上有一定的差异。陌生音素是指在 L1 中很难找到对应物，并且与 L1 中所有音素的声学差别都较大的 L2 音素。从这个分类可以看出，SLM 对 L1-L2 语音相似性的界定是在语音学的层面上进行的。从习得过程和难度上来说，相同音素是最容易习得并且在学习的初始阶段就已经形成正确发音的音素。在初始阶段，相似音素的习得显得比陌生音素好一些，但是，经过长时间的学习之后，相似音素的发音可能没有进步或者进步缓慢，最终仍然带有 L1 的口音；陌生音素的发音不仅会有长足的进展，而且有可能被成功获得。简言之，L1-L2 音素相似性较大时，L1 的音素会阻隔学习者建立 L2 的语音范畴，而 L1-L2 相似性较小时，学习者有可能成功建立新的 L2 范畴。

我们以 Bohn & Flege[6]的研究为例说明 SLM 在实证研究中的具体运用。这项研究对成年的德语母语者学习英语中的元音/i ɪ ɛ æ/的情况进行了考察。首先通过比较这些元音的声学空间，确认了德语学习者所认定的英语的"相似元音"和"陌生元音"，英语的/i ɪ ɛ/分别与德语的/i ɪ ɛ/在声学空间上有一定程度的重叠，英语的/ɛ/与德语的/ɛː/在声学空间上也有重叠，因此，英语的/i ɪ ɛ/被确认为德语母语者学习英语时的相似音素。所有的德语元音在声学元音图上都高于其英语的相似对应物，此外，德语松紧元音之间有显著的长度差异，英语的松紧元音之间只有音色差异而没有长度差异。英语的/æ/与德语的/ɛ ɛː/在语图上都没有丝毫重叠，与德语的/a/有很少的重叠，但英语的/a/与德语的/a/相似程度更高，因此，英语中的/æ/被确立为陌生音素。学习者分为长时学习者与短时学习者两组。实验结果表明，两组德语母语者所发的/i/和/ɪ/在音色或长度上都与英语母语者存在一定的差异，带有一定的德语色彩；两组学习者的/ɛ/在音色上都与英语母语者没有显著差异，但是长时学习者的/ɛ/比短时学习者和英语母语者短，短时学习者的长度与英语母语者没有显著差异。短时学习者/æ/的高度显著高于长时学习者和英语母语者，长时学习者的音色与英语母语者没有显著差异，但英语母语者的/æ/比两组学习者的都长。由于德语中没有/ɛ/和/æ/的对立，因此两位研究者也观察了学习者所发的这两个元音的声学差距，短时学习者所发的这两个元音的声学差距比长时学习者和英语母语者都小，而后两组被试之间没有显著差异，这就进一步证明长时学习者已经比较成功地建立了/æ/的语音范畴。

相似元音/i/和/ɪ/的结果与理论假设是一致的，即，学习经验对发音进步的影响是有限的，尽管学习者所发的/i/和/ɪ/在一定程度上逼近了英语母语者的发音。元音/æ/的结果也在很大程度上印证了理论假设。相似元音/ɛ/的结果表面看来与理论假设不一致，两组学习者的发音在音色上都与英语母语者没有差异，并且短时学习者在时长上更加接近英语母语者。Bohn 和 Flege 认为，短时学习者在/ɛ/上貌似成功的习得需要结合/æ/的情况进行考察。长时学习者和英语母语者的/ɛ/和/æ/在音色上是两个范畴，而短时学习者却是一个范畴。由于短时学习者混淆了/ɛ/和比它舌位低的/æ/，因此，他们很可能会降低/ɛ/的舌位，从而导致他们在/ɛ/的舌位高度和长度上接近于母语者。我们认为，/ɛ/的习得问题说明，验证"相似音素比陌生音素难习得"的假设时，需要仔细考量某个具体音素在中介语语音系统中的具体音系地位。

在这项研究中，Bohn 和 Flege 还对相似音素和陌生音素在习得中的关系进行了讨论，他们提出的一个进一步的假设是，相似音素是否能够在发音上有所进步，与它是否具有一个相邻的陌生音素有关。如果相似音素具有一个与之邻近的、具有共同音质特征的陌生音素，一旦学习者成功地建立了陌生音素的范畴,那么这个相似音素就有可能继续逼近母语者的发音。例如,英语的/ɛ/和/æ/相对于德语的/ɛ/来说都比较低、比较长,如果要在发音中区分这两个音位,学习者就必须注意格外相似音素/ɛ/的发音,这样,陌生音素/æ/的发音就促进了相似音素/ɛ/的发音。Flege 的另一个研究[8]表明,法语中的/u/对于英语母语的学习者来说是一个相似音素,法语中的/y/对于学习者来说则是陌生音素。实验结果表明,长时学习者所发的/u/仍然与法语母语者有所差别,但他们所发的/y/与法语母语者已经没有差别了。这是因为,相似音素/u/尽管存在一个邻近的陌生音素/y/,但这两个音素与英语的/u/相比并不具有相同的音质特征,法语的/y/比英语的/u/舌位靠前,而法语的/u/比英语的/u/舌位靠后,英语母语学习者即便完全用英语的发音来替代法语的/u/,他们所发的法语的/u/和/y/仍然有所区别,也就是说,他们就不必着意去纠正相似音素/u/的音色。既然学习相似音素/u/的动力不大,这个音素被成功习得的机会也就减小了。

3.3 SLM 与 PAM 的比较

从 L1－L2 相似性对 L2 习得的影响看,PAM(包括 PAM－L2)和 SLM 在很大程度上是有相似之处的。例如,PAM－L2 所归纳的第一和第二种感知类型都与 L1－L2 范畴的相似度有关,无论是被学习者认为与 L1 对应物完全相同的,还是与 L1 对应物具有高度相似性的 L2 范畴,都很难在学习者的感知中被建立起来,而与 L1 对应范畴相似性较差的 L2 范畴则有望被成功建立,这些预测与 SLM 的相关假设颇为相似。此外,PAM－L2 的第四种感知类型与 SLM 所提出的陌生音素的感知非常相似(尽管 Best 本人认为二者存在一些差异),而两种理论都认为这种感知类型中的 L2 范畴是容易被成功建立的。

当然,PAM 与 SLM 的差别也是很明显的。首先,PAM 认为,影响 L2 语音习得的 L1 因素既有语音层面的,也有音系层面的(这是 Best 一贯的主张,参见 Best et al. [1][2][3][4]),而 SLM 的理论假设和实证研究基本上是语音层面的。其次,PAM 只关注非母语的语音感知问题,它不讨论任何有关非母语语音产生的问题,而 SLM 非常关心语音感知与产生之间的关系(参见 Flege[11]),对于 L1－L2 相似性与 L2 学习的关系,SLM 的研究重点也是 L2 语音的产生而不是感知。第三,PAM 和 SLM 对影响 L2 习得因素的观察角度不完全相同,例如,PAM 关心的是 L2 的语音对立是如何被感知的,而 SLM 关心的则是每一个语音范畴的习得。第四,同时也是最值得注意的一点是,即便在一些貌似相似的细节上,PAM 与 SLM 仍然存在相异之处。例如,如 3.1 节所述,PAM－L2 中的第四种感知类型与 SLM 提出的学习者对陌生音素的感知方式颇为相似,但是,Best and Tyler[2]认为,二者在一些关键点上有所不同。在 PAM 系统中,对于 L2 语音知觉起关键作用的并不仅仅是某个具体的 L2 音段与跟它最为接近的 L1 音段之间的相似性程度,同时起到重要作用的还有 L2 音段在整个中介语系统中所处的地位。也就是说,对知觉学习造成影响的还有两方面的因素:(1)被感知为与这个 L2 音段具有相似性的所有 L1 音段有哪些;(2)这些 L1 音段与被感知为与这个 L2 音段的对立体具有相似关系的所有 L1 音段是否完全重合。如果 L2 对立体的两个成员与不同系列的 L1 音素(本文作者注:两套 L1 音素可以有所交叠,但是不能完全重叠)具有某种相似性,也就是说,在中介语的音系空间中它们是不同的,那么两个新的 L2 范畴都会在感知中被建立起来。如果两个 L2 音段被感知为与同一套 L1 音位具有相似性,也就是说这两个 L2 范畴在中介语的音系空间中是接近的,那么,学习者在感知中只会建立起混合了两个 L2 范畴的一个新范畴。在 L2 的学习过程中,这个新范畴有可能分裂成两个对立的 L2 范畴,也有可能维持原状,分裂与否的条件见 PAM 的感知模式三。

3.4 跨语言语音相似性的确定方法

PAM 和 SLM 都在理论层面对 L1−L2 语音相似性与 L2 语音习得之间的关系提出了假设，但是，如何在实证研究中确立 L1−L2 语音相似性却是一个值得继续探讨的课题，正如 Flege [10]本人所提出的那样：L2 音素与 L1 音素在多大程度上不同才能被确认为陌生音素？这里既有理论方面的问题，也有技术方面的问题。理论方面的问题包括，L1−L2 相似性应该像 Flege 早期所主张的那样离散为若干种类型，还是应该把相似性的大小看成一个连续分布？L1−L2 的相似性应该建立在声学层面上还是应该同时考虑声学、心理和音系层面的参数？技术方面的问题包括，L1−L2 的相似度如何量化以及使用何种技术手段进行量化等等。

在 Flege 及其合作者和追随者的早期研究中（1984−1993 年，参见 Flege[12]），L1−L2 的相似性是三分的，即相同音素、相似音素、陌生音素。三分的依据也多是声学比较的结果。但是，从 1994 年之后，SLM 开始注重 L1−L2 的感知相似性，并且认为感知中的相似度是一个连续统。无论是感知研究还是声学研究，SLM 都认为 L1−L2 的相似性只能通过实证研究而不能通过理论预测获得。这个原则意味着，SLM 对于单凭音系分析来预测 L1−L2 的 CAH 是完全拒绝的。通过实证研究来确立 L1−L2 语音相似性已经成为当今研究者的共识。与语音学的三个基本研究角度相对应，L1−L2 语音相似性的实证研究也可以从生理、声学和感知的角度进行。Strange[19]对跨语言语音相似性研究中的理论和技术问题进行了比较全面的综述。本小节下面的内容主要是对他的综述的扼要介绍，必要时笔者将进行简短的评论。

据 Strange 的报道，Best 和她的合作者[4][5]曾经从发音生理的角度分析跨语言语音相似性，他们用辅音的系列发音特征来描写祖鲁语和英语辅音的相似性，这些特征包括：（1）发音时调用的主动发音器官，如唇、舌尖、舌叶、舌体等；（2）声腔阻碍的程度（发音方法）和位置（发音部位）；（3）喉的姿态（gesture），即声门的开/闭、升/降；（4）软腭的姿态。以上参数和时长参数结合在一起，用来最终确定 L1−L2 辅音的相似性。但是，在这些研究中，Best 和她的合作者对发音生理的描写都是抽象的，因为他们并未给出具体的生理测量参数。另据 Strange 的考证，迄今为止还没有人从发音生理的角度来描写 L1−L2 元音相似性，这是因为元音的产生与辅音有很大的不同，元音的生理特征有较多的共性。

Strange 认为，从元音和辅音感知类型的角度看，声学特征更适合用来定义 L1−L2 元音的相似性。辅音的感知模式是范畴感知，也就是说，听音人调用声学参数来区分两个对立辅音时，在很大程度上受到了与这些参数相关的音系特征的限制。元音的感知模式是连续感知，元音声学特征的区别在一定程度上独立于音系在频谱和时长结构方面的声学关联物，因此元音之间声学特征的区分性比辅音更强。可能是由于 Strange 所说的原因，用声学特征来描写 L1−L2 元音相似性的实证研究很多，而用这种方法来描写辅音相似性的研究则鲜有见到。

Strange 提出了在 L1−L2 元音相似性研究中需要注意的几个技术性问题。首先是"发音人归一化"（speaker normalization）问题，发音人声道的个性特征可能会给元音声学空间的对比带来影响。避免这种影响的有效办法是使用比率标度和相对单位，例如用 F_1-F_0、F_2-F_1、F_3-F_2 的 Bark 值分别代替 F_1、F_2、F_3 的 Hz 值（Strange 未曾提及的这个方法的另一个好处是可以消除性别带来的共振峰频率差异，当被比较的两个或更多被试组内的男女比例不一致时，这个方法对于数据的处理就更有意义）。第二方面的，同时也是更为重要的技术问题是实验设计中一系列环节的具体处理方法，例如：a) 发音人应该是单语者还是双语者，使用多少发音人合适？b) 被比较的音段应该置于何种语境之下？c) 每种语境下的每个音段被重复多少遍才能最自然地体现出一个音位范畴在具体语境中的语音实现？Strange 认为，若想更加准确地把握影响学习者感知 L2 元音音段和对立的一个全局的 L1−L2 语音相似性的关系，就应该对多种语音环境、音位变体条件和韵律条件下的元音分布进行对比。

Strange 还提出了通过声学特征研究元音相似性的统计学问题。元音声学参数的均值比较结果只能告诉我们不同元音的声学分布是否存在显著差异，但却不能告诉我们差异的程度到底如何，因此，Strange 提出用线性判别分析（linear discriminant analysis）来比较 L1 和 L2 元音在声学空间中的分布。用 LDA 来分析 L1－L2 元音相似度的具体过程分为两步。第一步以 L1 中若干元音范畴的观察值作为训练系列，对这些参数进行加权以获得最佳的 L1 元音范畴分离，并确立参数空间中每一个 L1 元音范畴的均值重心（centroid），训练系列的分类结果决定了这些 L1 范畴在频谱或/和时长参数的基础上被区分的程度。第二步是在训练系列的权重空间和重心基础上对 L2 元音（测试系列）进行归类：每个 L2 元音范畴的每个观察值都被归类到一个或多个 L1 范畴中去，这样就可以计算出 L2 元音的分类矩阵，通过这个分类矩阵可以看到 L2 的某个元音与 L1 哪一个元音相似度更大。

如何从主观感知的角度建立 L1－L2 语音相似性也是一个值得讨论的问题。据 Strange 的综述，Best 和她的合作者建立感知中的跨语言相似性也是从辅音入手研究的（例如 Best et al. [4]），他们使用的是文字转写方法。具体做法是，听音人（英语母语者）听到 L2（祖鲁语）的语音片断后，用英文字母把它们转写下来，可以使用附加符号或者说明性文字加以辅助。通过观察 L2 中形成对立的辅音的转写形式，就可以判断出感知类型属于 Best 所提出的四种感知模式中的哪一类。Strange 认为，Best 的这种方法存在两个方面的缺陷。首先，它可以从范畴角度预测感知的相对难度，但是却不十分适合范畴拟合度型的感知模式（PAM 中的 CG 型），如果 L2 中的若干辅音对立的感知都是 CG 型，那么这种方法就无法确定哪一对辅音的感知更加困难。第二，这种方法可能也不适合对元音相似性的研究。元音的感知通常是非范畴感知，听音人即便是转写自己母语的元音也很难保持一致性，而呈现给被试听辨的元音排列顺序也会影响到转写，此外，这种方法对于非语音透明型文字（例如英语）的元音转写也不合适。

Flege 和他的合作者所使用的配对相似性比较法（Flege et al. [13]）克服了 Best 方法的缺陷。在 Flege 等人的这项研究中，西班牙语和美国英语的元音被一对一对地搭配起来，听音人对每一对元音的相似度进行九级里克特等级评估，这样就可以得到所有西班牙语元音与英语对应物相似度大小的排列顺序。这种方法俭省而且有效，不过 Strange 认为它仍然存在缺点，因为用来对比的母语和非母语的发音都被限制在一个单一的语音环境中，这就意味着，听音人不是在用母语语音范畴的内在表征（internal representation of phonetic categories），而是在用母语语音的特殊形式去与 L2 的语音范畴进行对比。如果听辨语料中的 L1 发音不能代表听音人内在的音位范畴的分布，那么听辨结果对于听音人的感知类比类型的预测性也就比较差。但是，如果研究者试图考察所有语音或者韵律条件下的相似性，那么用来听音的项目数量又会非常庞大，听音人难以高质量地完成这个艰巨的听辨任务。

与配对相似性比较法相关的是 Guion et al. [14]和近年来其他的一些研究所采用的字母转写与拟合度评价相结合的办法。在 Guion 等人的实验中，他们把英语的音节播放给日语母语者听，要他们说出其中的辅音最像日语的哪一个辅音，可以用假名表示，也可以用词。然后对每一个辅音与其相似物的拟合程度做七级里克特等级评估。最后根据被试选择相似物的一致性和拟合度分数的大小来确定相似程度。

L1－L2 相似性的等级评估在感知实验中被频繁采用，但其中也有些技术性的问题需要注意。如果使用相似度等级的均值作为统计量，那就意味着研究者认为他所使用的若干相似性等级是定距分布的，但被试在完成实验任务时很难做到这一点。因此，Strange 提出，在进行统计分析时，比较稳妥的做法是把这些等级看做定序变量，在分析中心趋势和组间差异时以非参数检验为宜。但是，如果按照 Strange 的建议使用非参数检验，又会带来检验效率比较差的问题，笔者认为，一种比较折中的做法是，采用适当的实验手段（例如增加听音人数量、在语料中适当重复每个听音项目等）使等级评估的结果尽量接近定距分布，并设法把离散的等级变量转换为连续变量，以这个连续变量作为统计量进行分析，然后对统计结果进行参数检验。

4. 老问题与新问题

4.1 对音系对比的重新评估

Best 和她的合作者最近指出[2]，常常有人认为 PAM 和 SLM 带有 CAH 的特点，这其实是一种误解，因为这两种模型并未将它们的预测完全建立在 L1 音系对立的基础之上——PAM 认为，L1 对非母语语音感知的影响既有抽象的音系层面的，也有渐变的语音细节层面的。显然，她对 CAH 的批评并非因为 CAH 进行了音系对比，而是因为它不注重对 L1 和 L2 语音范畴之间的语音（phonetic）相似性或者相异性的深入研究。

本文并不打算为 CAH 正名或者翻案，但我们关心的是，在 L2 语音习得的实证研究中，抽象的 L1－L2 音系对比是否真的毫无作用。我们的回答是否定的，理由有三。

首先，在进行 L1－L2 的范畴（无论是语音范畴还是音系范畴）对比时，只有从音系对比入手，才能初步确定进行对比的对象，例如 Flege[8]对法语和英语高元音的对比就是从音系的角度出发的。

第二，在确定 L1－L2 音素的相似性时，主观的感知评估和客观的声学分析是常用的两种手段，但是，两种分析的结果有时会出现较大的分歧。在这种情况下，对两种语言中的这两个音素关系的确定只能依据音系对比的结果。我们最近发现[25]，在日语母语者的感知中，汉语普通话的单元音 u[u]与日语中的单元音ウ[ɯ̹]的相似度很高，但是在声学空间上，这两个元音不仅没有任何重叠，而且还分离得比较远。与之相反的是，普通话的 e[ɤ]和日语的オ[o]在声学空间上的距离相对较近一些，但它们在感知中的相似度却比较小。这些分歧只能从两种语言的音系对比中才能得到合理的解释。u 与ウ虽然在声学空间上相差甚远，但在各自语音系统中的地位有相当高的相似性。u 是普通话中的唯一的后、高、圆唇元音；从客观属性上看，ウ的舌位前度和圆唇度都比较中立，但在日语中，它与イ形成了舌位前后和唇形圆展的对立，所以在音系上也可以认为它是具有[+圆]和[+后]的特征。既如此，普通话中 u 的舌位较后和唇形较圆就不会给日语母语者对它的认同感造成很大影响。e 在汉语普通话中是与 o 形成互补关系的不圆唇元音，而日语中并没有与 o 相对应的不圆唇变体，日语母语者将普通话的 o 认同为日语的オ之后，对 e 的认同感自然就比较差了。实际上，感知本身就在一定程度上反映了听音人的内在母语音系，因此感知结果不可避免地携带着音系层面的信息。

第三，在解释学习者的 L2 发音或者知觉偏误时，PAM 和 SLM 并不能解决所有的问题，而整体的音系对比仍然是不可或缺的方法。笔者关于韩国和日本学生对汉语普通话高元音感知的研究[23]就说明了 L1 和 L2 的整体音系对比在解释 L2 语音感知特点中的重要性。这个研究观察了学习时间没有显著差异的韩国和日本学生对普通话高、前圆唇元音[y]的感知情况，实验结果表明，韩国学生的感知正确率显著高于日本学生。从孤立的元音音位以及音色来看，这个现象是难以解释的，因为韩语和日语中都不存在高、前元音圆唇与展唇的对立。但如果我们整体观察韩语和日语的元音系统，实验结果或许就是可以解释的。韩语在历史上曾经存在以[±圆唇]相区别的多组平行对立，今天，这种对立在前元音中仍有残留（表现为语音系统的社会变体）。此外，在后、高元音中还存在以唇形相互区别的对立[u]：[ɯ]，也就是说，韩国人的听感中对于圆唇特征具有一定的敏感度。而日语中不存在仅以唇形相区别的对立，因此，日本人对于圆唇特征的敏感度自然不及韩国人大。

4.2 跨层的语音范畴类比

无论是 CAH 中的抽象音系对比,还是 PAM 和 SLM 所涉及的学习者对 L2 和 L1 语音范畴的类比或者等值归类,L1 和 L2 中被用来对比或者类比的对象都是属于一个层面的范畴,例如元/辅音音位或音素。但是,如果 L2 某种类型的语音范畴在 L1 中不存在,那么,学习者就可能把 L2 中的这类语音范畴与 L1 中另一个层面的范畴进行类比。例如,重音和声调最重要的声学关联物都是音高,因此,重音语言母语的人在感知声调时,就有可能把高调音节感知为重音音节,把低调音节感知为非重音音节。又如,母语中存在辅音清浊或者松紧对立的人会把非母语中的声调现象与辅音的清浊或者松紧进行类比。对于此类现象,上文所介绍的三种理论框架都没有给予考虑。

笔者在过去两个研究[21][22]中发现,美国人和日本人在加工汉语普通话双音节词的首字阳平音节时,受到后字声调的影响:如果后字是高起点的阴平或去声,阳平的高音特征就被删除(被念成半上声或者近似半上声的调子);如果后字为低调上声,阳平的高调特征就被保留(被念成阳平或阴平或与这两个声调近似的调子)。笔者认为,这种现象是学习者把声调与母语中的重音进行类比的结果。日语和英语的双音节词当中只有且必须有一个重音音节,其音高组合只能是高低或者低高的模式。由于阳平在实际发音中的高音特征不如阴平和去声显著,因此在学习者的听感中,它是一个在音高上难以归类的音节。上声的音系特征是低,因此容易被归入非重读音节。这样,当后字具有高音特征时,阳平就被处理为非高音节了;而当后字为低音时,阳平就被处理为高音音节了。

声调还可能被母语为非声调语言的学习者"借用"来类比辅音的范畴。清辅音之后元音起始处的基频高于浊辅音之后元音起始处的基频,这是人类语言的普遍规律。王韫佳和上官雪娜[26]在研究日本学习者对普通话不送气/送气对立的习得情况时发现,辅音所在音节的声调对于学习者感知不送气辅音有显著作用。阳平和上声音节中不送气辅音的感知正确率高于阴平音节中的不送气辅音,这正是学习者把声调高低与辅音清浊进行类比的结果。日语母语者把非高起点的阳平和上声条件下的辅音类比为母语中的浊辅音,把高调阴平条件下的不送气辅音类比为母语中的清辅音,而日语中的浊辅音没有送气变体,清辅音常有送气变体,因此低调条件下的不送气辅音仍然被感知为不送气,而高调条件下的不送气辅音则容易被感知为具有送气特征。这种情况是无法直接套用 PAM 或者 SLM 的框架进行处理的。

跨层的语音范畴的类比或者等值归类是否真的存在或者是否是一种普遍现象,我们现在还不能轻易下结论,因为这方面的实证研究的数量还很少。汉语是声调语言,汉语普通话的塞音和塞擦音存在送气对立而无清浊对立,因此,无论是重音语言或者有清浊以及松紧辅音对立语言的母语者学习汉语普通话,还是汉语普通话母语者学习其他语言,在跨层的语音范畴对比方面,都有相当多的空白地段等待着研究者们去填补。

4.3 关于中介语音系学

本文的主题是 L1-L2 语音相似性对 L2 语音习得的影响,影响 L2 语音习得的因素很多,仅从语言学层面的因素看,除了 L1 之外,普遍语法(UG)的作用也不容忽视。从上个世纪70 年代后期开始,人们逐渐认识到 UG 在第二语言语音习得中的重要性(参见 Major & Faudree[17])。有关 UG 与 L2 语音习得之间关系的研究,笔者也曾在另一篇文章里进行过综述[24],兹不赘言。UG 对 L2 习得的影响已经在许多实证研究中得到了证明。需要进一步讨论的是,在 L2 语音习得过程中,L1 和 UG 是如何交互作用的。邓丹[20]关于日语母语者对普通话单元音习得顺序的研究结果表明,当 L1 和 UG 对 L2 语音习得的作用方向相反时,起决定作用的是 L1 因素。除了 UG 以外,近十几年来,许多新产生的音系学理论在 L2 语音习得的研究中也得到了运用(参见 Major[16]),其中比较引人注目的是优选论(OT)的使用。把 OT 引入 L2 语音习得研究,也可以看做是以 UG 为基本理论原则的一种做法。OT 认为人类语言共用一套制约规则，但是各种制约条件的等级却是因语言而异的，OT 根据这个等级排序来说明语言的类型变化。这样，语言的普遍性和特殊性在 OT 中都得到了具体的体现。无论是用 UG 理论还是其他音系学理论对 L2 语音习得进行预测或者解释，从学科分类的角度来说都属于中介语音系学（interlanguage phonology）的研究范畴。由于篇幅和主题的限制，本文对这个方向的研究不拟进行详细介绍。

5. 结论

跨语言语音对比是 L2 语音习得研究必不可少的步骤和手段，这里既有复杂的理论问题，也有纷繁的技术问题。从理论的角度看，L1－L2 音系对比在 L1－L2 语音相似性的实证研究中不仅不应当被抛弃，而且应该得到更加深入的探讨。L1－L2 的音系对比既包括对整体音系的分析，也包括对音系范畴的具体的语音表达的分析，音系学的前沿理论应该在对比分析中得到运用。重要的理论模型，例如 PAM 和 SLM，应该在数量更多、内容更广泛的实证研究中得到检验、修正和发展。我们还应该注意到 L1 对 L2 语音习得作用的多样性，即，这种作用不一定是同一种范畴之间的作用，而且有可能是不同范畴之间的作用。从技术的角度看，如何得到定量的 L1－L2 语音范畴相似度，这个相似度是否需要以及如何进行离散化，仍然是关键之中的关键。实验手段的逐步完善，统计工具的审慎选择，都会使实验结果向着更加可靠的目标逼近。

汉语的语音系统有一些突出的特点，以汉语作为第二语言的非汉族人口数量很大，而来到中国进行浸入式汉语学习的外国人也越来越多，因此汉语作为第二语言的语音习得研究有相当好的资料来源。但是，国内的汉语作为第二语言的语音习得研究与国际水平相比还有相当大的差距，真正开始引入国际前沿研究的理论和手段只有不到十年的时间。"引入"不等于无条件地照搬前人的理论和克隆他人的方法，而是应该针对汉语自身的特点有所扬弃。今天，西方的 L2 语音习得研究已经成为语音学一个不可忽略的分支，这一领域的研究报告频频出现在重要的语音学刊物上。我们也期待着国内的 L2 语音习得研究能够不断吸收国内外语音学和音系学领域的最新成果，通过大量严谨踏实的实证研究而逐渐成为中国语音学的一个独具特色的研究方向，同时也期待着这一领域的理论研究成果能够更好地服务于汉语和外语的教学实践。

参考文献

[1] Best, C. T., Strange, W. 1992. Effects of phonological and phonetic factors on cross-language perception of approximants. *Journal of Phonetics* 20, 305-330.

[2] Best, C. T., Tyler, M. D. 2007. Nonnative and second-language speech perception: Commonalities and complementarities. In: Bohn, O. and Munro, M. J. (eds.), *Language Experience in Second Language Speech Learning*. Amsterdam /Philadelphia: John Benjamins Publishing Company, 13-35.

[3] Best, C. T., Hallé, P. A., Bohn, O.-S., Faber, A. 2003. Cross-language perception of nonnative vowels: Phonological and phonetic effects of listeners' native languages. *Proc. 15th ICPhS*, Barcelona, 2889-2892.

[4] Best, C. T., McRoberts, G. W., Goodell, E. 2001. Discrimination of non-native consonant contrasts varying in perceptual assimilation to the listener's native phonological system. *Journal of the Acoustical Society of America* 109, 775-794.

[5] Best, C. T., McRoberts, G. W., Sithole, N. M. 1988. Examination of perceptual reorganization for nonnative speech contrasts: Zulu clicks discrimination by English-speaking adults and infants. *Journal of Experimental Psychology: Human Perception and Performance* 14, 345-360.

[6] Bohn, O. S., Flege, J. E. 1992. The production of new and similar vowels by adult German learners of English. *Studies in Second Language Acquisition* 14, 131-158.

[7] Ellis, R. 1999. *Understanding Second Language Acquisition*. 上海：上海外语教育出版社。

[8] Flege, J. E. 1987. The production of "new" and "similar" phones in a foreign language: Evidence for the effect of equivalence classification. *Journal of Phonetics* 15, 47-65.

[9] Flege, J. E. 1993. Production and perception of a novel second-language phonetic contrast. *Journal of the Acoustical Society of America* 3, 1589-1608.

[10] Flege, J. E. 1997. English vowel productions by Dutch talkers: more evidence for the "similar" vs. "new" distinction. In: James, A. and Leather, J. (eds.), *Second-Language Speech, Structure and Process*. Berlin/New York: Mouton de Gruyter, 11-52.

[11] Flege, J. E. 1999. The relation between L2 production and perception. *Proc. 14th ICPhS*, San Francisco, 1273-1276.

[12] Flege, J. E. 2005. *Origins and development of the Speech Learning Model*. Unpublished presentation for the 1st ASA workshop on L2 speech learning. Vancouver: Simon Fraser Univ.

[13] Flege, J. E., Munro, M. J., Fox, R. A. 1994. Auditory and categorical effects on cross-language vowel perception. *Journal of the Acoustical Society of America* 95, 3623-3641.

[14] Guion, S. G., Flege, J. E., Akahane-Yamada, R., Pruitt, J. C. 2000. An investigation of current models of second language speech perception: the case of Japanese adults' perception of English consonants. *Journal of the Acoustical Society of America* 107(5), 2711-2724.

[15] Major, R., Kim, L. 1999. The similarity differential rate hypothesis. *Language Learning* 48(1), 151-183.

[16] Major, R. C. 1998. Interlanguage phonetics and phonology, an introduction. *Studies on Second Language Acquisition* 20, 131-137.

[17] Major, R. C., Faudree, M. C. 1996. Markedness universals and the acquisition of voicing contrasts by Korean speakers of English. *Studies in Second Language Acquisition* 18, 69-90.

[18] Munro, M. J., Bohn, O. 2007. The study of second language speech: A brief overview. In: Bohn, O. and Munro, M. J. (eds.), *Language Experience in Second Language Speech Learning*. Amsterdam /Philadelphia: John Benjamins Publishing Company, 3-11.

[19] Strange, W. 2007. Cross-language phonetic similarity of vowels: Theoretical and methodological issues. In: Bohn, O. and Munro, M. J. (eds.), *Language Experience in Second Language Speech Learning*. Amsterdam /Philadelphia: John Benjamins Publishing Company, 35-55.

[20] 邓丹（2003）《日本学习者对汉语普通话舌面单元音的习得》。北京语言大学硕士学位论文。

[21] 王韫佳（1995）也谈美国人学习汉语声调。《语言教学与研究》第3期，126-139页。

[22] 王韫佳（1997）阳平的协同发音与外国人学习阳平。《语言教学与研究》第4期，94-104页。

[23] 王韫佳（2001）韩国、日本学生感知汉语普通话高元音的初步考察。《语言教学与研究》第6期，8-17页。

[24] 王韫佳（2003）第二语言语音习得研究的基本方法和思路。《汉语学习》第2期，61-66页。

[25] 王韫佳、邓丹（2009）日本学习者对汉语普通话"相似元音"和"陌生元音"的习得。《世界汉语教学》第2期，262-279页。

[26] 王韫佳、上官雪娜（2004）日本学习者对汉语普通话不送气/送气辅音的加工。《世界汉语教学》第3期，54-66页。

情韵朗读的声学特征

吴洁敏 吕士楠 黄华新 缪冠琼

摘要

情韵朗读是具有感情韵律特征，能表情达意的朗读法。本文通过对表层朗读、节律朗读和情韵朗读的测听及声学特征分析，说明那是在语言和言语的不同层次、表情和非表情的不同水平上的三种朗读模式。它们韵律特征不同、传递信息不同、认知功能不同。通过听众对用不同模式朗读相同文本的话语感知调查，说明情韵朗读具有表情、表态功能，还可传递只能意会不能言传的信息，从而使读者、听者和作者产生共鸣，以达到高层次言语交际的目的。声学分析结果，则揭示了产生不同语音感知效应的物理基础。研究还发现：新闻广播与节律朗读声学特征相符，抒情散文和带感情色彩的杂文朗读与情韵朗读声学特征相符。根据语音实验说明，以达意为主的不带感情信息的节律朗读，表现在短语的低音线下倾和重置现象较为明显；承载感情信息的情韵朗读短语的低音线下倾不明显，而突出了高音线的作用。此研究结果，对汉语韵律研究和语音合成都具有重要的理论意义和应用价值。

关键词： 节律朗读 表意功能 情韵朗读 表情功能 韵律特征 传递言外之意

1. 引言

为了帮助外国人克服说汉语的洋腔洋调和中国南方人说普通话的土腔土调，在上个世纪80年代末，原杭州大学吴洁敏开始研究节律，找到一些规律，并首创了节律朗读法，能把文本读得抑扬顿挫富有节奏，但当时未能把中性语调和表情语调分开。在后来的教学实践中渐渐发现，节律朗读虽然能纠正洋腔洋调、土腔土调，读出言语的节奏感，却难以达到声情并茂。于是，怎样读得能表情达意的问题，就成了本世纪探讨的主要内容。课题组在对国内外汉语朗读教学进行了长达五年的调查、比较与探索，完成了国内中小学和幼儿园5000多份语言素质现状调查问卷（包括录音）统计，还辗转亚、美、非、欧等地，从国内语文教学和海外华语师资培训及示范教学中，总结出汉语的表层朗读、节律朗读、情韵朗读三种模式。认为"情韵朗读"能补节律朗读之不足，并于2007年3月，在对香港推广普通话专业委员会教师的培训试点中取得成效。本文通过多学科的合作研究，观察三种朗读法的语音波形、音高曲线和语图，力求探明情韵朗读的节律特征和它表情、表态功能的物理基础；将语音分析技术与语言教学结合起来，希望能把口耳相授的朗读技巧，具体反映到对声学参数的控制上来。本研究不但有助于汉语韵律本体研究和提高语言教学质量，也有助于提高计算机语音合成的表情功能。

2. 什么是情韵朗读

朗读和说话不同，它是一个由文字的视觉感知转换成语音的听觉感知的物理、生理、心理活动过程。记录汉语的文字是音节文字，每个汉字由声、韵、调组成。我们把机械地读出文本汉字序列的字音，称"表层朗读"，表层朗读不一定读懂文本内容。把在词句层面上以语义为基础，读出文本层次结构和思想内容的朗读称"节律朗读"，节律朗读具有表意功能，但缺乏感情信息。在节律朗读基础上，增加感情韵律特征，能表情达意的朗读叫"情韵朗读"。

情韵朗读中的"情韵"，是指由音高、音长、音强乃至音质变化等成素构成的感情韵律特征；它会冲破节律常规，激活大脑主管情绪的神经元，所以能传递感情信息。因为情韵朗读的语流中，具有能表达感情的韵律特征，正好补足了文本没有感情标记的不足。所以，情韵朗读是一种从语言到言语，从表意到表情、表态的，能把"字里行间"的思想感情一起表达出来，并能传递言外之意的朗读法。

通过实验，对表层朗读、节律朗读和情韵朗读的波形、音高曲线和语图进行分析对比，并通过测听比较听众的反馈信息，发现用三种不同模式朗读相同文本的声学参数不同、传递信息不同、听众心理反应也不同，它们代表了初、中、高三级不同认知水平。表层朗读还没有进入言语层面，但它是中、高级朗读的基础，节律朗读是情韵朗读的基础，情韵朗读是能表情达意的神似朗读。下面通过实例分析，说明这三种朗读模式的不同特征与不同功能。

3. 表层朗读、节律朗读、情韵朗读的声学特征及其功能

我们用台湾诗人彭邦桢的《月之故乡》为例，分析三种朗读模式声学特征的差异。作者通过"望月思乡"的描写，抒发了思乡至极而不可释怀的伤感。全诗如下：

（1）天上一个月亮，水里一个月亮，天上的月亮在水里，水里的月亮在天上。

低头看水里，抬头看天上，看月亮，思故乡，一个在水里，一个在天上。

下列图1、图2，是本文第一作者用表层朗读（a）、节律朗读（b）、低沉型情韵朗读（c）和高昂型情韵朗读（d）四种不同模式，朗读《月之故乡》前四个小句（第一段），所得到的四种不同语音样品的声学分析结果。图1表示不同朗读模式的语音波形。图2是相应的音高曲线。在音高图中，我们有意将短语间停顿作了调整，以便使整段话语有接近时长，忽略停顿，集中关注音高模式的差异。因为朗读模式不同，听众感受就不同。

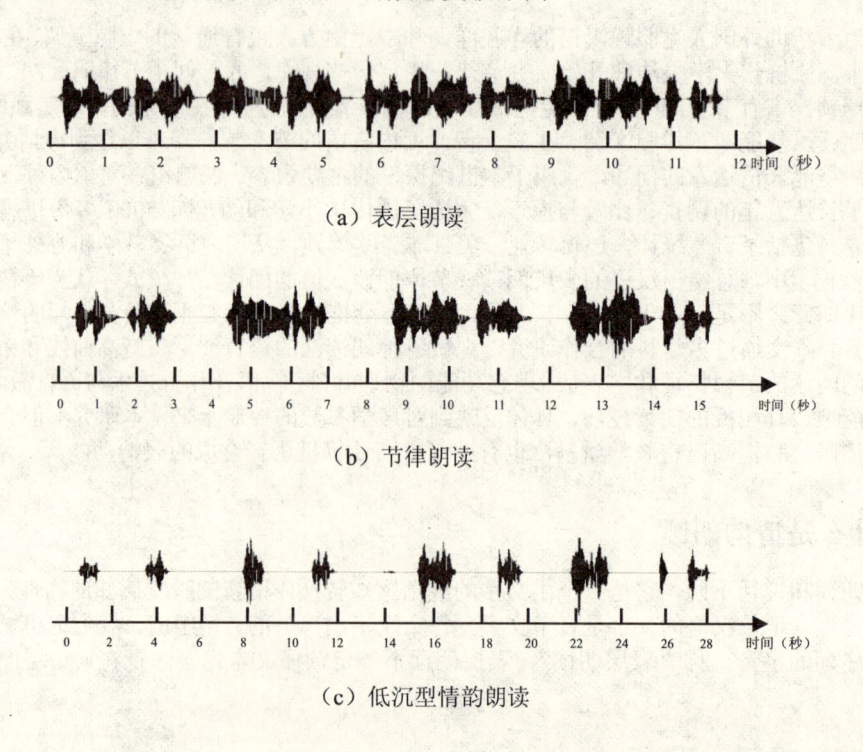

（a）表层朗读

（b）节律朗读

（c）低沉型情韵朗读

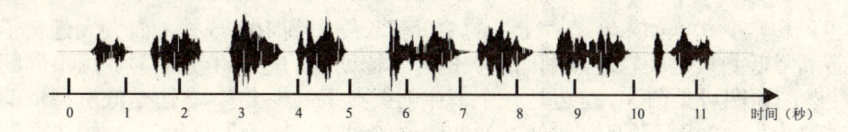

(d) 高昂型情韵朗读

图1：《月之故乡》第一段不同朗读模式的波形图

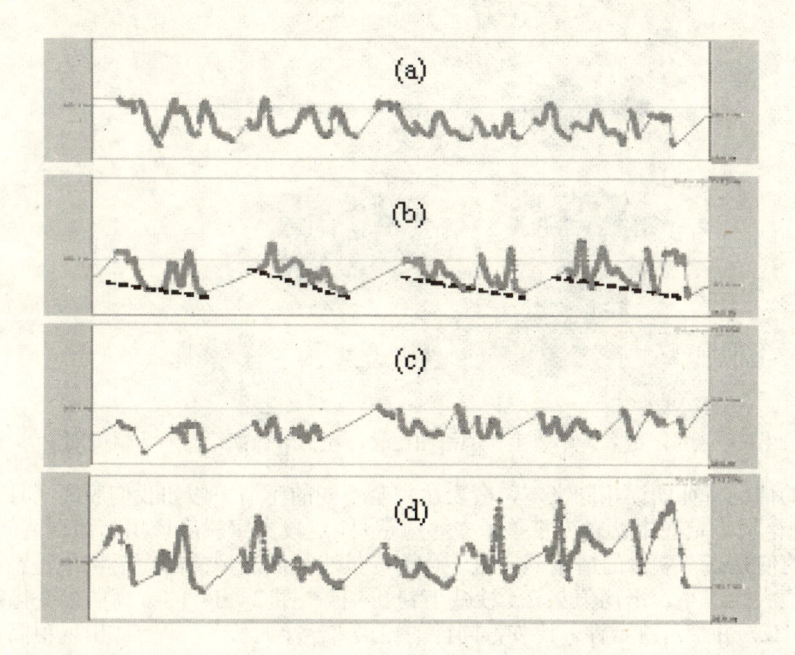

图2：《月之故乡》第一段与图1对应的音高图

表层朗读，只要求读准每个汉字的声、韵、调。但朗读无层次，缺少节奏感。由于许多小学教师要求学生读得响亮，所以表现在句中吸气多、字字响亮，虽有音步重音构成音步节奏，但表意功能不完善。由图1（a）波形图可见，音节长度和最高幅度的变化不大，短语间的间隔变化较小；音高图2（a）变化大致在120到320Hz范围内，因声调不同而上下游动。这是最底层的读书识字，不了解深层语义，没有进入言语层面，也缺乏音乐性，更谈不上表情和表态功能。但表层朗读是节律朗读和情韵朗读的基础。

节律朗读，要求读出文本的停延、节奏、基调和句调群组合规律[4]。表现在韵律短语的节奏清晰，短语间约有1.3秒的停顿，见图1（b）；还有较为明显的韵律短语低音线下倾现象[2]，见图2（b）虚线所示。如果能让学生了解字里行间节律的语意，就能把文本读得抑扬顿挫富有节奏，有可能激活大脑右半球主管音乐的神经元。实践结果证明，节律朗读能帮助克服说普通话的洋腔洋调和土腔土调。因为大脑左半球主管单词识别和语言声音、语词记忆，右半球主管复杂图形识别和音乐、形状记忆[6]，所以节律朗读调动了大脑左右半球的功能，有助于提高朗读兴趣，巩固生字、新词的准确读音及其用法。但节律朗读只有表意功能，缺乏感情信息，虽进入言语认知层面，却不能表达文本"言外之音"。所以，若采用节律朗读模式来读抒情文本，则尚属形似朗读。

情韵朗读在节律朗读基础上增加了感情韵律特征，不但能把文本读得抑扬顿挫富有音乐美，还能读得声情并茂、表情达意。由图1（c）可见，朗读者使用一种超常韵律，表达了望月思乡的哀伤情感，韵律短语的数目由四个增加到九个，短语间停顿长达2—3.5秒；音节时长和音高也出现超常变化，如末音节"上"的韵母音长缩短到100毫秒，而大大延长了肺气流的沉积段，音高降低到只是轻轻地点到而已，这与节律朗读的区别十分明显。用不同朗读模式的那两个"上"的语图可见图3：左边是一个节律朗读典型的"上"，右边是低沉型情韵朗读表达哀伤情感的"上"，白线表音高。此外，情韵朗读的第1－2短语和第3－4短语之间的"声断气连"，传递了不能言传只能意会的伤感信息。这个例子，就是通过变化音段的和超音段特征的那些语音手段，充分表达了一种极度哀伤的情感，使读者、听者和作者的思想感情起到共鸣。所以，情韵朗读属神似朗读。

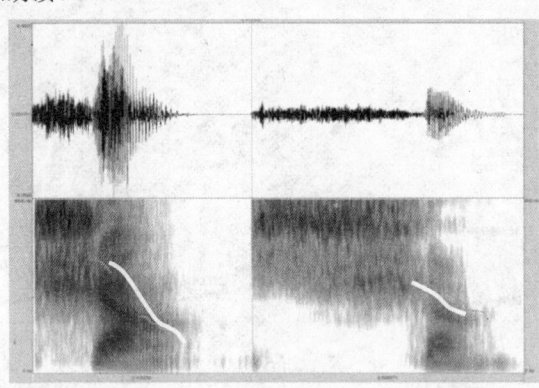

图3：《月之故乡》中"上"的语图比较，左为节律朗读，右为情韵朗读

用不同的情韵特征朗读相同文本，会表达完全不同的感情。假如我们脱离《月之故乡》的写作背景，把语境设定在中秋之夜带孩子去海边赏月，这段文字就应该用高昂型情韵特征表示，那么，传递的便是兴奋欢愉的情绪，见图1（d）。虽然和低沉型情韵短语切分差不多，但短语间的停延时值大大缩小，平均值从2.5秒减小到0.4秒。图2（d）的音高曲线变化幅度增大到152.5－612.6Hz，并带有跳跃性。比如，同样的短语"一个月亮"，第一次出现用高调，第二次用低调，这种跳跃韵律，形成了强烈的对比。再有，后面用联珠格的两个"水里"的"水"，前一个"水"的上声的调值从214扬起变为215，达到极致。那都是一般生活言语中很难见到的超常韵律表现，却又奇而不怪，新颖、活泼、可爱。我们称这种表达欢快兴奋的朗读为高昂型情韵朗读，它的节奏快，忽高忽低，像戏曲中花旦走小花步一样，使听众的欢快情绪油然而生。由此可见，同样的文本，用不同的情韵特征，可以表达不同的情绪，传递不同的感情信息。

下面综合观察音高曲线的变化。从图2可以发现，图2（b）的低音线下倾十分规则，在四个韵律短语间的音高重置明显。这些特点，与其他三个图不同，可以将它归结为节律朗读的典型音高特征。对比其他三条音高曲线，比如在图2（c）中，韵律短语多了，低音线下倾就不那么有序，音高总体上维持在320Hz以下的低水平上。图2（d）低音线的变化和图2（c）相似，但高音线明显上移，一些音节的高音点提高很多。高音点上移和增加，便是使听者感知到这段语音链表达兴奋、喜悦之情的物理基础。

通过测听，可以论证不同朗读模式形成的不同韵律特征所传递的信息不同。2007年12月，我们通过在广州的59位中小学语文教师及高校普通话测试员，对以上四种朗读模式的语音感知和听众反应进行调查。那是在讲座之前，没有任何提示的情况下进行的问卷调查。除1人没有答全，其他58位的问卷一致认为：表层朗读没什么感觉，尚未进入言语交际层；节律朗读能了解文本内容，无感情信息；情韵朗读的感情信息鲜明，能表情达意，其中低沉型情韵朗读表达了悲哀之情，高昂型情韵朗读传达的是兴奋和喜悦。而且可以反复，认同率达到100%。

总之，根据情韵朗读与节律朗读的语图比较、分析，无论音长、音高、音强特征都有明显差异。尤其是音长特征更为明显，低沉型情韵朗读的音节平均时长达到1107毫秒。以往语感测试也发现，汉语语速达 1000 毫秒/音节，是表示特殊感情的临界参数。达到这个语速，言者和听者都可能会因此动容，无论是悲哀还是愤慨。这便是人们常讲的"感动得说不出话来"的时候[5]。不言而喻，感情韵律是语意的表达手段，脱离语意是毫无意义的。通过在多年的语言教学实践中试验，对海内外上千名师生进行测听，尽管最初还没出现情韵朗读这个术语，只是实验用不同的声学特征，表达不同的思想感情，结果发现，低沉型朗读《月之故乡》表达的是思乡之苦，高昂型朗读表达的是兴奋喜悦之情，认同率达 99.9%。

4. 新闻广播和艺术朗诵

我们抽取中央人民广播电台的录音，把新闻广播《庆祝香港回归》、散文《背影》和杂文《谈骨气》三种语体的声学特征，与上述节律朗读、低沉型情韵朗读、高昂型情韵朗读三种模式对比。进一步论证"表情"和"达意"的韵律特征差异。虽然有发音技巧和个人朗读风格问题，还会涉及主观的心理感受方面的个体差异，但这里我们关注的是受声学参量控制的韵律特征对语音感知的影响，任务是揭示"表情"和"达意"所采用的声学手段的不同，观察并分析三个不同语体文本的音高曲线与不同朗读模式的声学特征的关系。我们发现，新闻广播的显著特点是韵律短语低音线下倾和重置明显。例（2）就是一个典型的例子。全句如下：

（2）在欢庆香港回归的时候，我们更加深刻地体会到，没有中国共产党的领导，没有祖国的日益强盛，没有改革开放的伟大成就，没有新中国三代人的不懈努力，特别是没有邓小平建设有中国特色社会主义理论的指引，就不可能有今天的香港回归。这是一百多年历史写下的庄重结论。

这是一个复句结构作宾语的长句，语法结构："状语+主语+状中+宾语（多重复句结构）"，充当宾语的复句结构层次及组合关系如下：

{[（①没有…②没有…③没有…④没有…⑤特别是没有…）+就不可能有…]+这是…结论}

我们注意到其中音节的音长、音强变化不太大，短语之间停顿时长也大致相同。最明显的特点是低音线下倾，图 4 表示开头的三个短语，虽然处在不同的语法层面，短语的句法结构也不同，三个短语表达的也不是一个完整的语意群。但由图 4 可见，每个短语的低音线下倾明显，如图上虚线所示，短语间还有明显的低音线重置，重置幅度达 140 Hz 左右。这和前面例（1）的图 2（b）所示的节律朗读特征相似。因此，我们说新闻广播采用的是节律朗读模式，短语的低音线下倾和重置为其主要韵律特征，而对语法、语义的依赖较少。

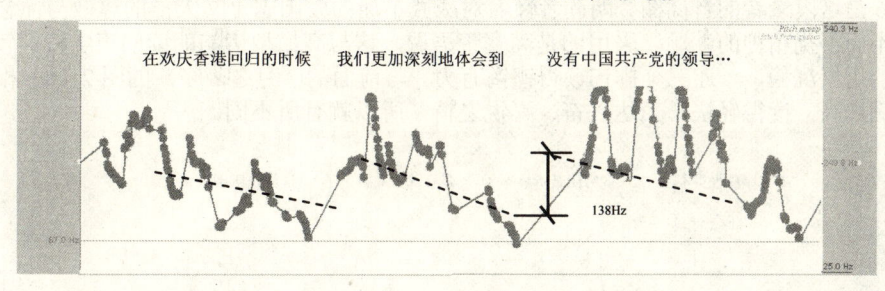

图 4：新闻广播片段的波形和音高图

作为对照，下面列举抒情散文和带感情色彩杂文的音高曲线片段。例（3）是从一位资深播音员朗读《背影》中截取的一句话：

(3) 我看见他戴着黑布小帽，穿着黑布大马褂，深青布棉袍，蹒跚地走到铁道边。

他采用的是低沉型情韵朗读的模式，其音高图见图5。这里用气沉声缓的低窄带语调朗读，描写了父亲的背影，表达了悲哀感伤之情。

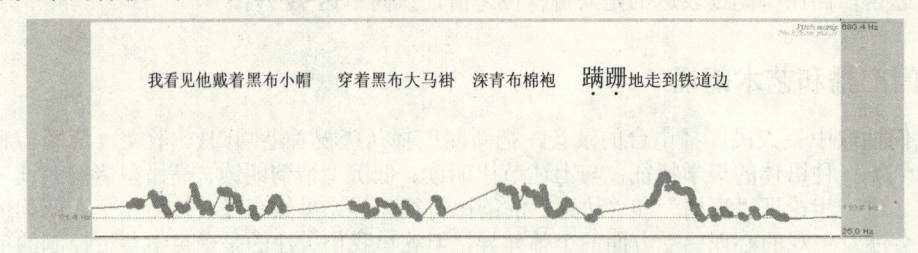

图5：《背影》片段的音高图

这个句子也是主谓结构作宾语，但重音落在"蹒跚"上，用音高、音强表示。从父亲"蹒跚"地走着，可以想象父亲的衰老和对儿子的疼爱，用高音线的提升，形成强烈的语音"突显"，表达出对父亲深深的怀念与自责。从图5的音高曲线还可以看出，在声学层面上最明显的特征是音高变化较小，除了重音词，大都沉降在低基频区，出现低窄带调域，低音线下倾不明显。其超音段声学特征与前面分析的《月之故乡》图2（c）的低沉型情韵朗读的韵律特征相符。

不仅如此，在图5的音段特征上，有些音节和正常语音有相当大的区别，比如在选用的文本后面，"他将桔子散放在地上"的"上"的语图，也是只见声母，而韵母只是淡淡地一闪而过，传递出欲言无语的悲哀之情。这与前面低沉型情韵朗读《月之故乡》图3的"上"有异曲同工之妙（限于篇幅，把"……散放在地上"的语图略去）。

这里，我们分别采用了两名素不相识的教师与播音员朗读的不同文本语音样品，只不过是朗读的都表达了悲哀之情，就出现了完全相同的声学特征，而且可以反复。应该说，那不是一种巧合，而是一种规律。可见，表达悲哀感情的散文韵律与低沉型情韵朗读特征相符。

例（4）是由同一位资深播音员朗读的杂文《谈骨气》的片段。

(4) 高官厚禄收买不了，贫穷困苦折磨不了，强暴武力威胁不了，这就是所谓大丈夫。

图6是这段录音的音高图。朗读者怀着对威武不屈的爱国志士文天祥的尊敬与怀念，表达了对他不挠精神的歌颂。采用的是高宽带语调，这与高昂型情韵朗读的声学特征较接近。但这里的用气沉稳，一连三个排句读得铿锵有力。与前面的《月之故乡》的图2（d）相比，前者是气满声高，读得轻快，表达兴奋、喜悦之情，所以就有所不同。

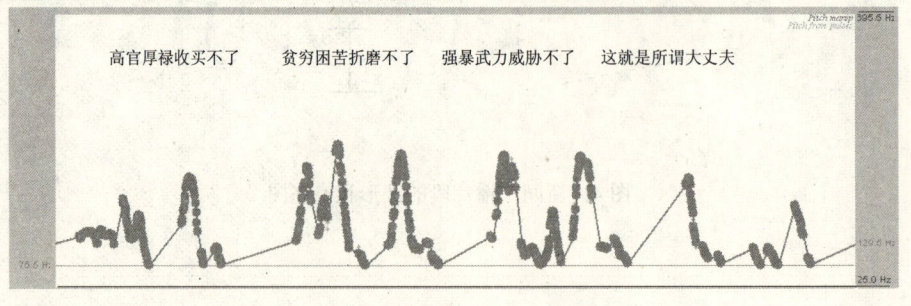

图6：《谈骨气》片段的音高图

从图 5 和图 6 两张音高曲线图分析,可看到图 5 的低音线的下倾和重置不明显,原因是采用了低窄带调域,加上短语的切分是破语法结构的。在朗读每一个气群时,"气能"总是由强变弱,出现短语低音线下倾,这是一种自然现象。但感情的强烈变化,可以冲破短语下倾的常规。如例(4)的图 6 是个指代复句,前面一连出现三个排句,可是,因为三个排句的重音不在句首,就不可能出现高音线下倾现象。又比如第三个排句短语的重音在首尾,就出现了凹曲调,最后一句有"这"和"大"两个重音,使短语出现了两个波峰。那都是为了感情表达的需要。所以,情韵朗读中短语低音线下倾和重置退居到次要地位,而高音点的升降成了情感表达的重要手段。比较图 6 和图 5,突出的区别是图 6 的音域显著展宽了。因为是同一位播音人,音域的变化和区别就可以直接从音高曲线图上看出来。

以上我们用例证的方法,来阐述我们对节律朗读、低沉型情韵朗读、高昂型情韵朗读不同的声学特点的认识,以及新闻播报和艺术朗诵需要采用不同的朗读模式。但总是不能摆脱内省式研究的缺憾,和基于数据的实证研究所得到的科学结论还有距离。下面对三个朗读语料的音长和音高特征进行总体上的统计分析对比,以期对内省式的研究结果作些补充。虽然,这三个语料对于千变万化的语言现象仍是沧海一粟,但也总能或多或少地弥补基于例句思辨所得结论的某些不足。统计语料的概貌如表 1:

表 1:用于音高和时长统计的语料

名　称	语体	文本长度(字)	发音人	朗读总时长(秒)
谈骨气	杂文	997	男(方)	415.2
背影	散文	724	男(方)	318.7
庆祝香港回归	新闻	939	女(于)	257.3

【时长统计】如果用语段的总时长被音节数除所得到的音节平均时长来比较的话,杂文、散文和新闻分别为 416、440 和 274 毫秒,显然新闻广播的语速要快得多,这也是提高新闻信息传递效率所要求的。然而,当我们注意到图 7 音节时长统计结果时,发现:

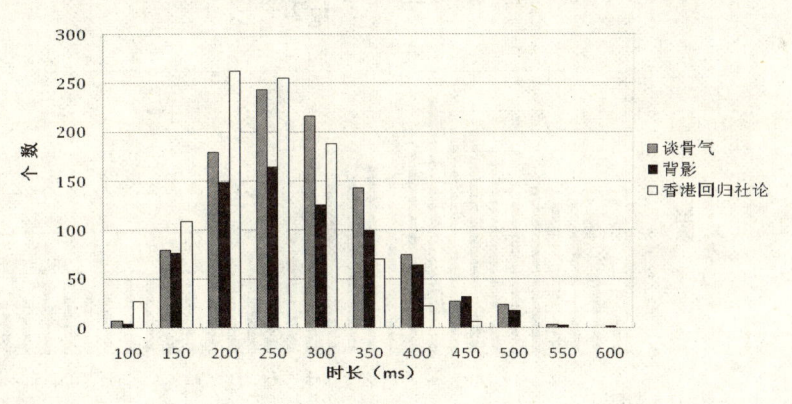

图 7:不同语体音节时长分布

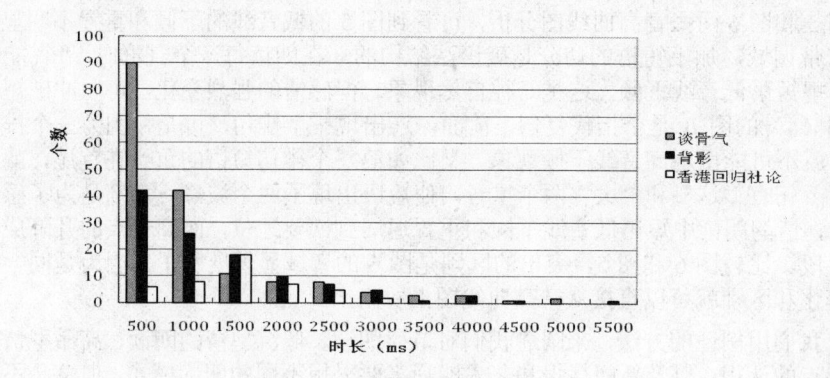

图 8：不同语体停顿时长分布

不同语体的音节时长分布差异不大，分布曲线的峰都在 250 毫秒左右。但从图 8 停顿时长统计结果可以看到，三种语体的停顿时值差异十分明显。需要说明的是，在统计停顿时，我们只关注韵律短语间有 200 毫秒以上的音空段，对于较短的韵律词之间的停顿没有计算在内。艺术朗诵中，出现 500－1000 毫秒左右的音空频繁，语流被切割得比较分散，出现停顿的概率较大，停顿时长的范围较宽，使得"语流音空"成为表达感情的重要手段之一。相对而言，新闻广播的停顿规律性强，在韵律短语之间有 500－1000 毫秒左右的音空，在语义块之间有 1500 毫秒左右的音空，停顿的次数比艺术朗诵少得多。如果扣除停顿时长，则三个文本的音节平均时长分别为 260 毫秒、278 毫秒和 212 毫秒。可见散文和杂文语速变慢，主要是由停顿引起的。

【音高统计】由于新闻播报是女声，艺术朗诵是男声，为了便于音高和音域的比较，音高的单位采用半音（st），即：

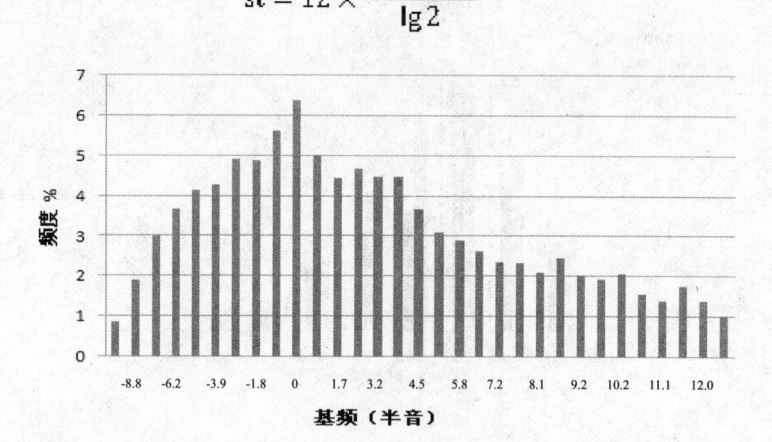

$$st = 12 \times \frac{\lg(\frac{f0}{f_{0\_ref}})}{\lg 2}$$

图 9：《庆祝香港回归》全文音高分布

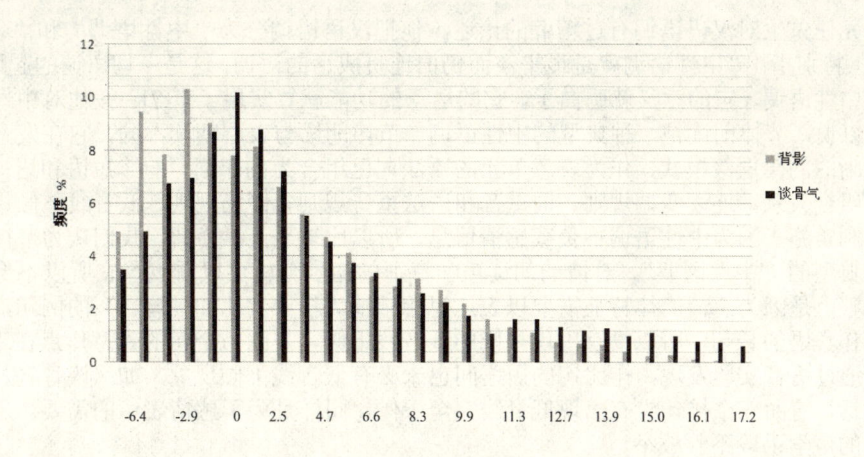

图10：《背影》和《谈骨气》两文各自的音高分布

其中 F0 表示基频的测量值，F0ref 表示基频参考值。本文的参考值分别取实验语料发音人男声和女声的基频最可机值，即女声为 200Hz，男声为 130Hz。数据获取和统计方法是提取全语篇的浊音段基频值，窗长 20 毫秒，步长 10 毫秒。测得的赫兹值被转换为半音。图 9 表示《庆祝香港回归》新闻播报提取的所有基频值的统计分布，图 10 是两篇艺术朗诵的基频分布图。以超过1%的出现概率计算，基频的覆盖范围是差不多的，约为 23 个半音，但从分布来看，新闻播音与艺术朗诵有明显的区别。新闻播音分布比较均匀，峰值频度为 6.4%；而艺术朗诵的峰值频度达到10.2%，分布明显偏向低频，其中《背影》的低频偏向更显著。这些结果与个案分析（图 4、5、6）是一致的，证明这些例子具有新闻播报和艺术朗诵的典型的音高特征。其中新闻播报的音高表现和艺术朗诵的区别也十分显著，我们将它归纳到表意的节律朗读。散文和议论文的艺术朗诵属于情韵朗读，但它们的音高特征也有区别，分别归纳为"高昂型"和"低沉型"两类，但与新闻播报比起来，音高分布都偏向低频，只是低沉型偏的较多而已。通过语句个案和有代表性的语篇统计分析，研究所发现的新闻播报的音高特征，对于传递以表意信息为主要目标的文语转换系统的研制，有实际的指导意义。虽然我们对朗读模式音高特征的研究还是初步的，但语音分析技术却为传统的内省式研究，转向客观的基于数据分析的科学研究奠定了基础，它在人文科学和自然科学之间架起了一座桥梁。

5. 讨论

　　首先说明，这里所讨论的是"朗读"，而不是即兴言语（spontaneous speech），那是有稿子的，不仅有文字，还会有少量韵律符号。书面语是经过提炼的，来自生活又高于生活的言语，比口语规范，也富有艺术性。因为许多超音段特征没有书面标记，所以，口语变成书面语，就会有许多信息被遗漏。它在转换为口语的朗读过程中，需要把那些书面符号无法记录的信息补充进去。但也正由于书面语的规范化，就会有许多约定俗成的韵律模式。加上这些限制，在韵律特征上也会比真实的生活言语规范。因此，我们有可能将朗读简单地归纳为：表层朗读、节律朗读和情韵朗读三种模式。表层朗读除了识字、背书以外，缺少言语信息，很少有交际意义。这里，我们重点关注节律朗读和情韵朗读。研究结果表明，节律朗读是以表意为主的一种言语表达方式；情韵朗读是以表情为主的言语表达方式。即兴发言一定比朗读复杂得多，从以表意为主还是以表情为主的视角考察，即兴发言是否有同样的特点，尚需进一步研究。但朗读模式主要受语体、语境、题旨及文本自身特点的影响。如果抒情散文没有写出感情，那么，即使采用情韵朗读也传递不出感情信息。

赵元任先生对汉语语调有过精辟的论述。他把汉语语调分为"中性语调"和"表情语调"两大类,特别指出"中性语调就是最平淡而仍旧连贯成话的语调,这是一切语调的起码货","国语有了中性语调,它的意义就明白了,它的达意的功能就算实现了"[7]。按他对中性语调的定义,可以说,节律朗读是一种典型的中性语调。节律朗读与表层朗读不同,它在发音规划中已形成清晰的韵律层级模式,作为表意单元的语法词已组合为韵律词、韵律短语和语调短语。根据这种组合关系,连读变调规则、词重音和语法重音规则、停延规则、低音线下倾规则等都可得以顺利实施。因为中性语调不负载感情信息,所以比较平淡。为此,我们认为节律朗读可称为一种典型的"中性语调"。对情韵朗读声学特征的初步分析可以看到,它所以不像节律朗读那样规整,是因为感情韵律特征需要以表达思想感情为核心。比如《背影》的例句,同样是复句结构作宾语的长句,所以没有出现规则的低音线下倾,是因为全句的表意焦点在"蹒跚"一词上。通过语音实验发现,排比句的短语间也未必有低音线下倾现象。如《谈骨气》开头引用孟子的话,前面三个排句没有出现低音线完全下倾,同样是为了感情表达的需要。足见实现情感表达的声学手段不胜枚举。

沈炯提出了汉语语调的双线模型[1]。本文研究发现:节律朗读的显著特点是,以韵律短语为组合单元的低音线下倾和重置,以低音线的有规则变化的节奏形式,标明了语义的块状结构。发话人按这种节奏,把语意信息板块发送出去,听话人按同样的约定俗成节奏接收,达到顺畅信息交流的目的。这一特点在新闻广播中得到充分的体现。相对而言,情韵朗读的低音线变化迟钝,高音线运动活跃,前面的许多情感事件,都可从高音点在语调系统中的变化得到解释。但不同语体的高音线活动态势不一样。因此,我们将低音线的语言学功能归纳为表意的;高音线功能是表情的。这和沈炯的模型并不矛盾。但在研究感情语调中,若能增加肺气流的表现形式,得到的结论会更加全面。如宽带语调表喜悦和愤怒,若能加上"表喜悦之情是气满声高,表憎恨之情是气足声硬",那就有了表示正负感情的区别特征。

语音实验证明,音长、音强、音空均具有表情功能。图2表兴奋的28个音节用11秒,表思乡之情用31秒,中性语调用15.5秒。从测听和语图7的不同语体时长对比中可知,语流音空是表达深沉感情的心理、生理现象。赵元任说,表情语调除掉音高跟时间,还得要注意到强度,跟"嗓子"的性质(quality of voice),有时候嗓子变得利害了还会影响到字音的声母韵母[8]。吴洁敏的"汉语基调的九宫调模矩阵"分析了音高、音长两个维度,把中间格的中语速、中语阶称为"大和"调模,把四角的高快、高慢、低快、低慢称为"四极调模",四极调模是表感情语调的[3]。但当时没有分析音强特征,现在发现,音强是不可缺少的感情韵律特征。从图3右"上"字的噪音变化,与资深播音员朗读《背影》的"上",都在短韵母后紧接着长长的语流音空。请注意,那音空并非马上出现送气段,而是紧憋着一股沉积的肺气流,它是负载着深沉的感情信息的。这是一种表达深沉感情的音强特征。

传统语音教学采用口耳传授法,费时、费力。如今有语音实验手段的帮助,把听觉感知转化为形象的视觉图像,让学生看到产生不同感知效应的言语的物理基础,认识到为什么不同说法有不同的反应,从而自觉地通过语图可视的音高、音长、音强和音色的控制,提高自己的言语表达效果,这无论对母语教学还是海外华语教学,都具有重要的应用价值。同样,在语音合成技术研究中表明,以表意为目标的系统,韵律短语的划分和低音线的控制十分关键;以表情为目标的系统,则更应关注高音线的控制。当然,研究结果也说明,我们不能用孤立的、个别的声学特征去解释或用计算机去模拟不同的情感,如惊喜、恐惧、悲哀等,因为情感表现力是诸多声学参数变化的综合结果,而且言语感情表达还有心理、生理变化的作用。

6. 总结

本研究认为,在汉语的表层朗读、节律朗读、情韵朗读三种基本模式中,后两种具有交际功能。节律朗读形成的是中性语调,主要功能是表意,其韵律特征较规范,以韵律短语为单位的低音线下倾和重置是它的重要特征。情韵朗读具有感情韵律特征,形成的是表情语调,除了表意,还有表情、表态功能;其声学表现复杂,是综合调制音长、音高、音强、音空和音质参数的结果,负载着感情信息,表现在音高点运动更为活跃。新闻广播符合节律朗读声学特征,抒情散文和带感情色彩的杂文,符合情韵朗读声学特征。朗读模式要受到题旨、语境和语体的制约。

情韵朗读的语音感知是心理的,精神的,但它的基础是物理的,物质的。相信任何语音的感知特征都可以通过实验手段,求得声学的和生理的、心理的解释。如果朗读和说话缺乏情韵特征,人们便无法获得超文本的"言外之音"。无论说话还是朗读,感情韵律特征都不可缺少。这也是在实际生活言语交际中,必须掌握的技能与艺术。此外,语言还有娱乐功能,情韵朗读是艺术语言的核心。

此项研究具有重要的理论意义和应用价值。我们对感情语调的研究才起步,还需要进一步作出三种不同水平朗读的声学层面与表征关系的深入研究,为认知心理学、应用语言学及言语工程作出贡献。

致谢:本文是国家重点社科基金项目(批准号 07AYY001)和浙江大学语言与认知研究中心项目的成果之一。本文写作中,吴宗济先生提出了宝贵意见。特此致谢!

参考文献

[1] 沈炯(1998)汉语语调构造和类型。《语言文字应用》第 1 期。
[2] 王安红、陈明、吕士楠(2003)基于言语数据库的音高下倾现象研究。《声学学报》第 28 卷第 4 期。
[3] 吴洁敏(1999)汉语基调的"九宫"调模矩阵及其参数。《中国社会科学》第 5 期。
[4] 吴洁敏(2001)汉语奇偶句调型的组合模式。《中国社会科学》第 3 期。
[5] 吴洁敏、朱宏达(2001)《汉语节律学》。北京:语文出版社。
[6] 徐科主编(2005)《神经生物学纲要·脑的高级功能》。北京:科学出版社。
[7] 赵元任(2002)国语语调。载吴宗济、赵新那编《赵元任语言学论文集》。北京:商务印书馆。
[8] 赵元任(2002)北平语调的研究。载吴宗济、赵新那编《赵元任语言学论文集》。北京:商务印书馆。

情感语音的韵律特征分析与转换

熊文婷　崔丹丹　孟凡博　蔡莲红

摘要

本文分别以整句和句内音段（句首、句中、句末）为单位对情感语音的六种典型韵律特征进行了分析，研究了当语音信号由中性变换成愤怒、高兴、惊奇和悲伤情感时，其声学特征的变化特点。根据分析结果，进一步选择时长、能量、最大基频、基频范围这四个韵律特征，进行了由中性语音到情感语音的转换实验，并对全局和局部分音段两种转换模型的转换效果进行实验比较，也对局部分音段情感转换模型的有效性进行了主观评测。实验结果表明：情感语音的韵律特征对于不同情感，语句内不同音段，其变化不尽相同。这种音段间韵律特征的局部差异对情感的表达感知有贡献，并可用于指导情感转换。

关键词：　情感语音　韵律特征　局部　情感转换

1. 引言

语音是人们在日常生活中重要的交流手段，它不仅能够表达文字所含的语义信息，还可以通过说话者的说话方式，如语气、音调变化等，表达出说话者的态度和情绪，即我们常说的"言外之意"[6]。情感语音的研究已成为语音研究的热点。

情感语音的研究表明，语音情感信息主要体现在韵律特征的变化上[1][2][6]。有的进一步指出，基本情感的声学特征差异，主要反映在基频的高低、能量的增减和语速的快慢上[6]。运用少量的韵律特征，可以较为有效地识别悲伤、高兴、愤怒、惊奇等情感[4][7]，并且通过修改韵律参数，可以在一定程度上表现出情感[5]。但遗憾的是，对于高兴、愤怒、惊奇等高激活的情感区分，一直较为困难。

已有的研究，大都是以整个情感句为单位分析语音信号的韵律特征[8][7]。但语音特征具有时变性：时长伸缩、音调升降在句中不同位置具有不同的变化规律[3]。情感的表现和感知也会随音段的位置改变。因此，有必要研究句内局部音段的韵律特征和音段间的韵律特征变化特点。这对发掘情感语音声学表达的规律，实现更高质量的情感语音转换，是非常有意义的。

为了研究韵律特征在语句内部的局部差异对情感表达的影响，本文设计了文本对齐的无意义短句，并用五种情感录制了情感句，分别从整句话和局部音段两个角度对六个情感韵律特征进行统计分析与对比，研究了不同情感下韵律特征的变化特点，总结出基于全局（整句话）韵律特征和局部（句内音段）韵律特征的两种情感转换模型。实验评测结果表明，局部分音段情感转换模型在惊奇和愤怒情感方面效果明显。

2. 分析用语料与特征

本文研究韵律特征参数的时域变化对情感表达的贡献，因此分析中应尽可能消除文本语义对情感韵律特征的影响，并尽量确保用于分析的语音，其同种情感表达方式前后一致。先以短句为单位对录入的情感语音的平均基频、最大基频、最小基频、基频变化范围、平均能量和平均时长进行统计分析；再将短句分为句首、句中、句末三个音段，并以音段为单位对以上六个声学特征进行统计，得到情感语音句内不同位置音段的局部韵律特征。

2.1 分析用语料

本文设计的语料是文本对齐的短句（5-6字），共 48 个。为了避免情感表达方式受文本内容、音调的影响，文本涵盖所有单、双音节声调组合的 24 种情况，每种组合在句首、句中、句末各出现一次。每个短句均为 5 个或 6 个音节组成。为了研究句语音韵律结构的局部特点，根据词的位置将每个短句分成句首、句中、句末三个音段，每段为 1-2 个音节。

录音者用中性、愤怒、高兴、惊奇、悲伤五种情感共录制了 240 句情感句。虽然一种情感可以有多种表达方式，但在录音时要求录音者对同一种情感保持相同的表达方式。

然后，对采集的数据进行评估，选取情感表达明显的样本，进行语句切分；再利用分析工具进行音节切分、基频提取；最后手工进行修正，剔除野点，进行平滑，并用四次曲线对基频曲线进行拟合。

2.2 韵律特征提取

本文分析研究的特征是短时能量、时长、平均基频、最大基频、最小基频、基频范围。短时能量计算的帧长 20ms，帧移 10ms，以 dB 为单位。为排除噪音干扰，只计算句中能量过某特定阈值的那些音节。时长计算的是从语句第一个音节的开始到最后一个音节结束的时间间隔，包括了音节之间的停顿部分。其他四个参数可从标注数据中得到。

为便于对比情感语音与中性语音韵律特征差异，将同文本语句的非中性情感的参数与中性情感的参数相比，得到归一化的表示。

例如愤怒的全句基频均值的计算公式如式（1），其中 $\overline{F0}_{愤怒}(x)$ 表示的是愤怒情感中第 x 句的基频均值：

$$\overline{F0}_{愤怒} = \frac{\sum_{1}^{48}\overline{F0}_{愤怒}(x)}{\sum_{1}^{48}\overline{F0}_{中性}(x)} \tag{1}$$

局部分析句内音段的韵律特征时，则是将句子分为句首、句中、句末三个部分，依次统计这三个音段的愤怒、高兴、惊奇、悲伤四种情感下的局部韵律特征（相对值）。局部统计时，每个位置（句首、句中、句末）各有 48 个音段。

3. 韵律特征分析对比

3.1 全局韵律特征分析

首先，考察统计的六种全局韵律特征在语音由中性转为愤怒、高兴、惊奇、愤怒时的变化区别（图 1）。

从图 1 看出，悲伤较中性时有所延长，而其他三种的语速均有提高。在能量方面，悲伤的能量明显小于其他三种情感。通过全局特征可以区别悲伤情感。愤怒、高兴和惊奇明显提高了基频均值。

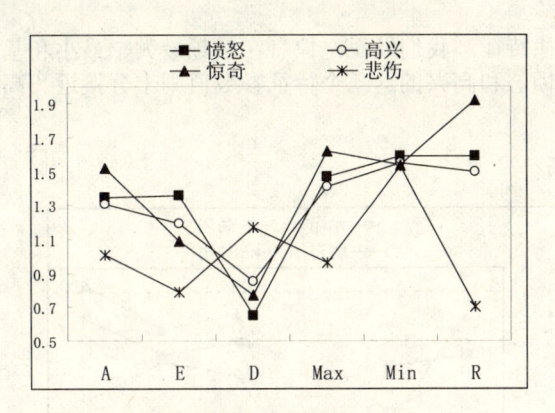

图1：不同情感的全局韵律特征变化对比
A：平均基频；E：平均短时能量；D：时长；
Max：最大基频；Min：最小基频；R：基频范围

同时该图也反映出，单从全局的角度，以语音的韵律特征来区分激活度较高的愤怒、高兴和惊奇比较困难。特别是当这三种情感的时长、最大基频、最小基频、基频范围的统计方差相对较大时，更是对这三种情感的区分造成困难（表1）。

表1：全局韵律特征变化的平均值与标准差

μ：归一化均值；σ：标准差

		愤怒	高兴	惊奇	悲伤
基频	μ	1.36	1.41	1.50	1.03
	σ	0.15	0.11	0.11	0.06
平均能量	μ	1.29	1.21	1.08	0.77
	σ	0.02	0.01	0.01	0.01
时长	μ	0.59	0.82	0.82	1.11
	σ	0.07	0.07	0.07	0.11
最大基频	μ	1.36	1.53	1.63	0.94
	σ	0.24	0.18	0.19	0.10
最小基频	μ	1.46	1.47	1.39	1.44
	σ	0.72	0.64	0.76	0.68
基频范围	μ	1.29	1.57	1.80	0.57
	σ	0.59	0.49	0.61	0.25

音节的韵律特征与其所在的韵律结构位置相关，即其特征会随音节所在的韵律词内、韵律短语、语调短语的位置变化。为了进一步研究不同情感，特别是愤怒、高兴与惊奇之间的韵律特征的差异，本文将一句话分为句首、句中、句末三个部分，分别考察语音从中性情感变至愤怒、高兴、惊奇、悲伤时的局部变化情况。

3.2 句首/句中韵律特征分析

统计句首音段的韵律特征（图2）。结果表明，愤怒的能量明显高于高兴和惊奇；高兴的时长大于愤怒和惊奇，在频率范围上则比它们要窄得多。

统计句中音段的韵律特征。我们发现：惊奇在基频最大、最小和基频均值上是可以与愤怒和高兴区分开的，而愤怒和高兴的这三个特征参数值则十分接近。高兴在句中部分的时长要比愤怒和惊奇稍长。

3.3 句末韵律特征分析

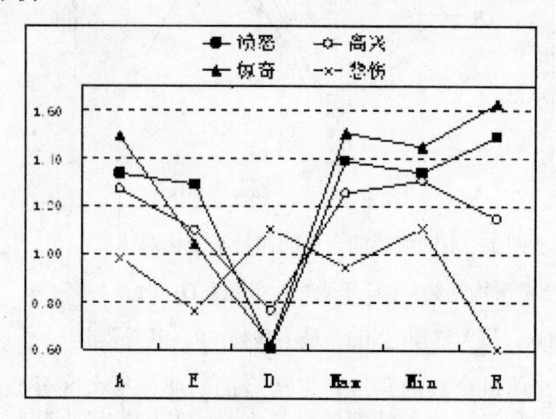

图 2：不同情感的句首韵律特征对比

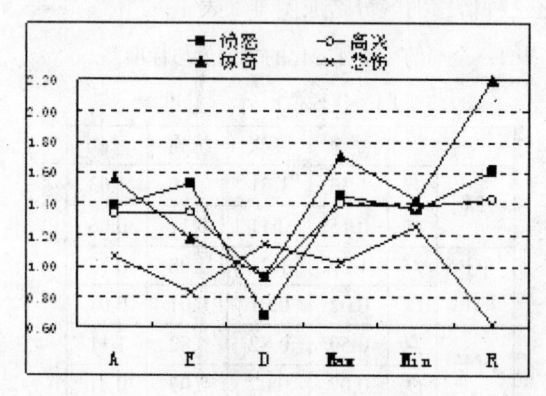

图 3：不同情感的句末韵律特征变化对比

统计句末音段的韵律特征（图 3）。结果表明，在句末部分，惊奇的基频范围的变化幅度明显增大，增幅是愤怒的两倍，是中性情感下的 2.2 倍。同时惊奇在最大基频方面进一步增大，已能较为明显地和愤怒、高兴区别开来。此外，愤怒在句末音段的时长明显短于愤怒和高兴，是愤怒区别于其他情感的又一特点。

3.4 综合分析对比

综合 3.2－3.3 的局部分析结果，激活度较高的愤怒、惊奇的区分能力已有较大改善。愤怒情感的平均短时能量在句首、句中、句末均为最大，并且其句末的时长最为短促；惊奇的句末的基频范围明显大于其他情感，句末音调提高，基频范围的显著增宽也是惊奇的特点之一。相较于愤怒和惊奇，高兴的局部特点并不十分显著，只是比愤怒、惊奇在句首、句中的语速更加缓慢，句首部分的基频范围更窄。

另一方面，横向比较这三种情感可以发现，句末音段中不同情感的韵律特征差异最为突出。这表明句末部分的说话方式是情感表达的关键之一，从而也印证了句内分音段研究的有效性。

除此之外，还可以看出局部分析对区别愤怒、高兴、惊奇有较大贡献的主要是平均短时能量、最大基频、基频范围这几个特征。

4. 转换实验及结果分析

根据以上分析，选取与情感表达感知最为密切相关的四种特征——平均短时能量、时长、最大基频、最小基频——分别从全局和局部两个角度对语音信号由自然中性语音到愤怒、高兴、惊奇、悲伤的情感语音的转换过程进行建模，得到全局和局部两种基于韵律特征的情感转换模型。例如，局部转换模型的句末段部分如下：

表2：局部转换模型——句末段

句末	愤怒	高兴	惊奇	悲伤
平均能量	1.22	1.13	1.02	0.76
时长	0.56	0.74	0.65	1.03
最大基频	1.28	1.37	1.52	0.95
基频范围	1.19	1.37	1.63	0.55

为了验证上文的分析结果，证明局部音段韵律特征对情感表达和感知的影响，进行了偏向性测试，比较了上述全局情感转换模型和基于句内分音段（句首、句中、句末）的局部模型的转换效果，然后对局部模式的情感转换结果进行了主观测试并给予评价。

4.1 实验语料

一共录制了10组集外测试用句，每组有四个不同的情感句。各组中每句话都可分成两个部分：含有情感倾向的不同文本的半句和不含情感倾向的相同文本半句。录音者先用不带情感的中性语音朗读四种情感句，然后再用相应的情感语音朗读一遍。随机选择其中两组进行本次测试。

4.2 转换方法

为了给测试者提供一个具体情感语境，令其更好地评价情感转换结果的有效性，分别截取两个半句，对其用全局模型和局部模型进行中性到四种情感的转换。再将转换结果和该句中未转换部分的录入情感语音进行拼接。为了避免录入的情感语音段给测试者造成听音干扰，对每组测试语句都给出了被转换内容的中性录入语音作为参照。

因此，四种情感各有测试句四组，每组包括一个参考句，两个转换结果句。共16组48句。参与测试的10位同学分别就每组中的两种转换结果进行比较，选出更加符合相应情感语境的转换结果。另外，也请这些同学单独对基于分音段的局部情感转换模型的转换效果进行具体评价，评测语料为16句，测试时提供情感转换句的同文本自然中性语音作为参考。

4.3 偏向性测试结果

统计每种情感中测试者认为较好的转换模型的分布情况，结果如表3所示。

表3：偏向性测试结果

	1	2	3	4	5
愤怒	0%	5%	32.5%	57.5%	5%
高兴	0%	35%	50%	15%	0%
惊奇	2.5%	25%	27.5%	35%	10%
悲伤	0%	12.5%	52.5%	35%	0%

可以看出，大多数人（77.5%）认为惊奇情感的转换使用局部模型明显优于全局模型。在高兴和愤怒上，局部略有优势。而对于悲伤情感，更多人认为全局模式的转换效果要好于局部模式。测试结果基本符合分析结果。

4.4 局部模型主观评价结果

对分音段的局部情感转换模型的转换结果进行主观评价。评价标准共分 5 级：1 没有情感信息，2 有正向的情感信息，但目标情感不清楚，3 稍有目标情感，4 能较好地表达目标情感，但可以听出与自然情感语音的差别，5 非常好地表达了目标情感，非常自然。

统计出每种情感的评价等级的分布，用百分数形式表示，如表 4 所示。

表 4：分音段局部情感转换模型的主观评测结果

	全局更优	局部更优	相当
愤怒	12.5%	17.5%	70%
高兴	22.5%	30%	47.5%
惊奇	15%	77.5%	7.5%
悲伤	35%	10%	55%

对局部情感转换模型的转换结果的主观评测表明：局部情感转换模型能较好地实现由中性语音到目标情感的转换。其中，愤怒转换效果最好，其次是惊奇和悲伤，最后是高兴。

4.5 实验结果分析

综合两项主观测试的结果，可以得到以下启示：

对于悲伤情感，采用全局韵律特征已能很好地与其他情感区分，但全局模型的基频低于局部模型。

对于高兴情感，两种转换模型的区分度不大，并且转换的结果语音在听感上虽然有较强的激活性，但与理想的愉悦性还存在一定距离。

对于惊奇，测试结果显示，韵律特征参数的局部变化，特别是句末音段的变化对该情感的表达有明显贡献。

5. 结语

本文验证了语音的韵律特征承载着主要情感信息这一结论，并进一步通过将语句分为句首、句中、句末三个音段，以音段为单位对情感语音的局部韵律特征进行了研究。研究发现：时长、平均短时能量、最大基频和基频范围这四个韵律特征的局部（尤其是句末）的变化对语音情感的表达与感知有显著贡献，并能够在一定程度上区分激活程度相近的愤怒、高兴和惊奇三种情感。

通过对基于全局情感转换模型和局部转换模型的中性到情感语音的转换实验，证明了上述结论。

不可否认，情感的语音表达具有多样性。但是，由于研究是基于排除语义、声调影响的语料进行的，所以分析得到的情感表现方式具有一定的普遍意义。这为进一步描述语音情感，及建立相应的语音情感转换模型提供了有价值的参考。

当语义本身具有情感倾向时，或者情感焦点改变时，都将会对本文研究的韵律特征产生影响，其规律也将更为复杂。而激活度较高的愤怒、高兴、惊奇情感的特征差异也还需要进一步研究。我们愿和语音学界的各位同行共同努力，不断探索。

参考文献

[1] Sobin,C., Alpert, M. 1999. Emotion Speech: The Acoustic Attributes of Fear, Anger, Sadness and Joy. *Journal of Psycholinguistic Research* 28(4), 347-365.
[2] Vergyri, D., Stolcke, A., Gadde, VRR., Ferrer, L., Shriberg, E. 2003. Prosodic Knowledge sources for automatic speech recognition. ICASSP 2003.
[3] 曹剑芬（1999）普通话节奏的声学语音学特性。载《第四届全国现代语音学学术会议论文集》。
[4] 崔丹丹（2007）《情感语音分析与变换的研究》。清华大学博士学位论文。
[5] 韩纪庆、邵艳秋（2006）基于语音信号的情感处理研究发展。《电声技术》第 5 期，58-62 页。
[6] 蒋丹宁（2005）《情感语音的声学特征分析及建模》。清华大学博士学位论文。
[7] 姜晓庆、田岚、崔国辉（2006）多语种情感语音的韵律特征分析和情感识别研究。《声学学报》第 31 卷第 3 期，217-221 页。
[8] 赵力、将春辉、邹采荣、吴镇扬（2004）语音信号中的情感特征分析和识别的研究。《电子学报》第 32 卷第 4 期，606-609 页。

元音内在基频研究

张家騄

摘要

本文在音节、单词和单句的层次上，研究了汉语元音内在基频问题并与外语作了比较。结果表明：1. 作为声调语言的汉语和其他语言一样，也具有元音内在基频并且在数值上也与外语相近。2. 元音内在基频是与声调调值有关的但与调形无关，元音基频越高，高元音与低元音的内在基频差越大。在嗓音音域的下限（上声和去声的最低点），内在基频消失。3. 男声和女声的元音内在基频，在物理标尺（Hz）上数值是相近的（平均男声为 24.8Hz，女声为 21.5Hz），但是在乐律（心理）标尺（semitone，半音）上就看出差别来了（平均男声为 2.44St，女声为 1.44St）。4. 介音会使韵母的基频提高，但并不改变元音内在基频间的关系；鼻韵尾会使中元音和低元音的基频提高而使高元音的基频降低，也不影响内在基频关系。5. 在不同的说话声级和不同的说话速度之下，元音内在基频仍然存在，只是数值上有所变化。因此，元音内在基频是元音的固有属性，是元音音质的一部分，内在基频是不受说话人主动控制的。

关键词： 元音　内在基频　内在音高　半音

1. 引言

元音内在基频（intrinsic fundamental frequency，IF0）过去也通称为内在音高（intrinsic pitch 或 IF0），是指在同样发音条件下，高（闭）元音比低（开）元音的基频要高。可是近年来有的研究表明，高元音在音高感知上要比具有同样基频的低元音为低，这种现象称为内在音高（intrinsic pitch）。因而又有把元音内在基频与元音内在音高加以区别的必要。本文不论是在分析基频的物理标度（Hz）还是把物理标度转换成心理（乐律）标度（semitone）时均称为内在基频（IF0），因为我们的工作主要是对元音基频的声学测量结果加以分析研究。

元音内在基频早就被人们注意到了（Meyer，1896-7；[1][6][3]），不过英语的内在基频研究比较多，也较深入。Shadle[7]还研究了元音内在基频与语调之间的相互作用问题。Whalen 和 Levitt[9]对涵盖 11 个语系的 31 种语言的元音内在基频的测量结果加以分析比较，从而得出元音内在基频对各种语言是普遍存在的结论。可是元音内在基频的产生机理，以及语义和韵律特征对内在基频的影响，至今仍然不十分清楚。对内在基频的全面研究，必将有助于对言语产生，特别是对基频调控的深入了解，对语调建模也会有重要作用。这不但对言语科学具有理论意义，对言语工程也会有应用价值。

汉语是具有多种调型的声调语言，调值覆盖范围很广，可高达一个倍频程，同时具有丰富的元音（普通话单元音多达 10 个）系统和多样的韵母结构。这样汉语普通话的元音内在基频问题，自然应当受到应有的注意，同时也是研究内在基频的性质及其产生机理的理想对象。石波和张家騄[8]曾对汉语普通话的元音内在基频进行了系统的测量，并且从声源和声道相互作用以及韵律特征之间的相互作用的角度加以分析讨论[10][11]。本文将在音节中协同发音、单词中不同位置和不同说话方式的语境条件下，进一步考察元音内在基频的固有属性。

2. 实验材料和实验方法

实验材料：采用音节表和词表两种语言材料，以尽可能地包含不同的协同发音和不同的语境条件。由于汉语音节在声韵母的组合上有严格的音位配列规则的约束，所以在普通话中实际存在的音节里边，不同元音和不同声调的出现频率就有很大差别。为了便于统计分析对比，最好在实验材料中，对不同元音及其声调尽量加以平衡。因而，由 10 个单元音和 22 个声母（包括零声母）组成了 404 个音节。为了考察协同发音对元音内在基频的影响，还特别选取了 28 个复韵母，只读阴平调。

除了音节表之外，还编辑了一个有 509 个双音节词（选自《现代汉语词典》）构成的词表。每个双音节词均由一个被测字和一个配字组成。被测字在前的词有 273 个；被测字在后的词有 236 个。配字的选择，主要是考虑与被测字的声调组合和韵母搭配的出现率尽量平衡。

实验方法：发音人为男女青年各五名，均说标准的普通话并熟悉汉语拼音。发音是在混响时间小于 0.5 秒的测听室中进行的。被测音节和被测单词分别置于负载句中，发音人自然朗读，但对声级加以监控。测试音节用的负载句是：我读____字。测试单词用的负载句是：我读____这个词。

3. 实验结果

3.1 音节中的元音内在基频

利用所编制的音节表，考察在不同的音节结构和不同的调类中的主要元音所表现出来的内在基频。由于汉语声调的调型比较复杂，所以在测量不同声调的元音基频时，所有声调曲线均不考虑弯头拖尾段，按下述原则确定测点提取基频：第一声（阴平）取中点，记为 T1；第二声（阳平）取最低点和最高点，分别记为 T2-1 和 T2-2；第三声（上声）取最高点和最低点，分别记为 T3-1 和 T3-2；第四声（去声）取最高点和最低点，分别记为 T4-1 和 T4-2。由于音节都是放在负载句中发音的，所以上声也就都变成了半上。汉语普通话 10 个元音在不同音节结构中，不同声调测点的基频平均值列于表 1。

由于元音/ê, o, er/出现频率很低，读音时难免不那么稳定。又由于不论男声还是女声，各元音与低元音/a/的基频差值，也就是内在基频差 $\Delta F0$，都是相近的，所以在表 1 中就把男女声的平均值也列出来，用以考察基频 F0 的高低对内在基频的影响。从表 1 可以看出，高元音与低元音的基频差，即内在基频，是与嗓音基频高低相关的，阳平调的起点 T2-1 内在基频要比阴平的 T1 和阳平的 T2-2 小得多。另一点值得注意的是，去声的调尾 T4-2 和上声的最低点 T3-2，它们都接近了正常音域的下限，高元音和低元音/a/的基频差，不但很小而且还可能出现负值，内在基频现象消失了。这一点和 Shadle[7]在经过精心设计的实验句句尾观察到的情况是一致的。这一现象女发音人表现得更加明显，既可能是基频测量技术上的问题，也可能与嗓音基频很低时常出现的气泡音（vocal fry）有关，有待进一步研究。

男声和女声在元音内在基频上表现相近的现象，在英语中也是一样的，这可以从图 1 看得出来。

表1：普通话10个元音在不同声调测点上的基频（Hz）（发音人：五男，五女）

元音[1]	发音人	T1	T2-1	T2-2	T3-1	T3-2	T4-1	T4-2
/i/	五男	175.1	118.0	167.1	112.9	89.4	196.8	96.8
	五女	290.6	204.5	265.4	219.3	168.9	312.1	180.1
	五男五女	232.9 (18.3)	161.3 (6.6)	216.3	166.1	129.2 (2.4)	254.5	138.5 (-3.3)
[ɿ]	五男	181.2	121.7	170.7	116.3	89.6	207.6	98.8
	五女	302.3	205.7	271.0	214.2	172.1	326.0	182.1
	五男五女	241.8 (27.2)	163.7 (9.0)	220.9	165.3	130.9 (4.1)	266.8	140.5 (-1.3)
[ʅ]	五男	178.5	116.1	169.1	115.4	90.3	194.7	101.3
	五女	295.2	200.4	263.9	216.2	168.0	318.9	191.7
	五男五女	236.9 (22.3)	158.3 (3.6)	216.5	165.8	129.2 (2.4)	256.8	146.5 (4.7)
/ü/	五男	180.1	119.2	175.1	115.0	90.1	196.5	101.3
	五女	299.6	208.6	277.9	218.8	170.7	318.4	176.1
	五男五女	239.9 (25.3)	163.9 (9.2)	226.5	170.6	130.4 (4.6)	257.5	138.7 (-3.1)
/u/	五男	181.4	116.6	168.3	111.5	89.7	205.9	105.2
	五女	306.9	209.1	289.1	217.9	172.1	335.2	184.2
	五男五女	244.2 (29.6)	162.9 (8.2)	228.7	164.7	130.9 (4.1)	270.6	144.7 (2.9)
/e/	五男	164.2	114.3	156.3	113.7	88.2	187.0	100.6
	五女	288.9	202.3	269.6	215.2	169.6	315.3	183.2
	五男五女	226.6 (12.0)	158.3 (3.6)	213.0	164.5	128.9 (2.1)	251.2	141.9 (0.1)
/ê/	五男	165.7	117.4	181.0	126.0	88.6	176.2	99.4
	五女	293.6	206.2	291.4	211.2	164.4	324.6	174.4
	五男五女	229.7 (15.1)	161.8 (7.1)	236.2	168.6	126.5 (-0.3)	250.4	136.9 (-4.9)
/o/	五男	167.8	117.2	160.1	115.6	89.8	184.0	99.9
	五女	278.2	199.9	269.9	213.8	170.2	309.8	183.3
	五男五女	223.0 (8.4)	158.6 (3.9)	215.0	164.7	130.0 (3.2)	246.9	141.6 (-0.2)
/er/	五男	170.2	116.0	169.6	121.6	87.8	177.6	99.8
	五女	301.8	200.2	273.6	209.4	161.2	313.8	181.8
	五男五女	236.0 (21.4)	158.1 (3.4)	221.6	165.5	124.5 (-2.3)	245.7	140.8 (-1.0)
/a/	五男	153.6	111.1	155.7	107.5	82.5	175.2	96.7
	五女	275.5	198.3	254.9	226.9	171.1	302.3	186.8
	五男五女	214.6 (0)	154.7 (0)	205.3 (0)	167.2 (0)	126.8 (0)	238.8 (0)	141.8 (0)

注：括弧中的数字是各元音的基频与低元音 a 的基频的差值 ΔF0。

---

[1] 斜线内为拼音字母，方括号内为国际音标。

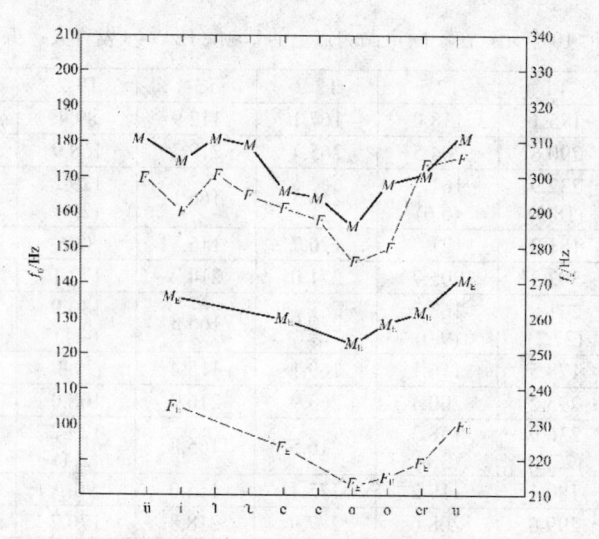

图1：汉语和英语的元音内在基频对比

（英语的数据引自 [6]，横坐标上的元音符号除两个舌尖元音外均为汉语拼音）

  图 1 上汉语的数据取自阴平调；英语的数据取自 Peterson 和 Barney [6]的实验结果，选择与汉语近似的元音画到图上。图上横坐标是按照前元音从高到低，后元音从低到高排列的。纵坐标是元音的基频（Hz）左边的标尺用于男声，右面的标尺用于女声，他们的尺度是一样的。可以看到，不论是对于汉语和英语，还是对于男声和女声来说，曲线的形状和斜率都是十分近似的，即高元音和低元音的基频差是相近的，只是 F0 的绝对值有所不同。

  我们还可以看到，同一种语言采用不同的测试方法，所产生的差别要比不同语种之间的差别还要大，见图 2。

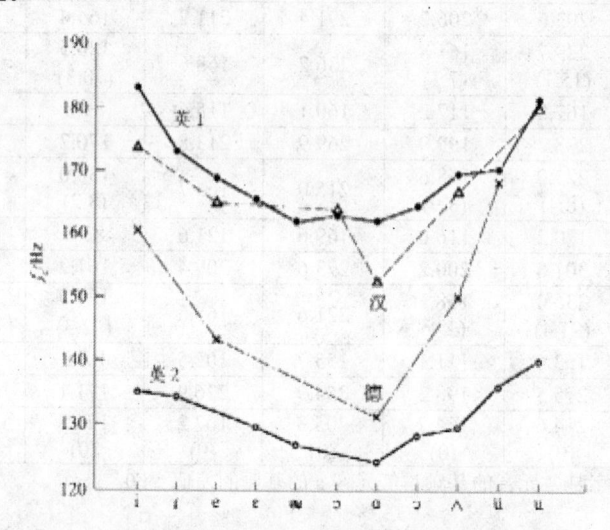

图 2：不同语种和不同测试方法测得的元音内在基频比较

  图 2 中曲线英 1 是引自 Lehiste 和 Peterson[3]对一名男发音人的测试结果。他们是将被试音节置于负载句中，处在语调突出的位置。他们的测试方法和汉语是一样的，所得结果也很相近。汉语是五名男发音人的平均。曲线英 2 是引自 Peterson 和 Barney[6]对 33 名发音人的测试结果。他们是将被测元音置于两个辅音/h/ 和/d/之间来发音的，所以总的基频都要低一

些。但是曲线的斜率，也就是内在基频是与曲线英 1 差不多一样的。德语的结果是引自 Hoole 和 Mooshammer[2]对 1 名男发音人测得的紧元音的结果。他们也是把被试音节置于负载句中，但是单句结构与英语和汉语不同。横坐标的音标是以英语为准的，汉语和德语都是与之相近的元音。可以看到，采用不同的测试方法，元音基频的绝对值有较大的不同，但是元音基频之间的相对关系，即内在基频，却是差不多一样的。

3.2 单词中的元音内在基频

为了进一步考察元音在更大的语境中内在基频的表现，利用所编制的双音词表，使被测元音分别处于词首音节或词尾音节进行测量，并将元音在音节中和处在单词的不同位置上的内在基频加以对比，所得结果列于表 2。

表 2：七个主要元音在单词的不同位置上和元音在音节中的内在基频差（ΔF0，Hz）对比（五男五女平均）

测点	语境	/i/	[ɿ]	[ʅ]	/ü/	/u/	/e/	/o/	平均
T4-1	音节	15.7	28.0	18.0	18.7	31.8	12.4	8.1	19.0
	词首	15.5	5.0	10.6	14.8	21.9	18.8	17.5	14.9
	词尾	8.2	9.5	8.5	5.7	15.5	12.9	1.5	8.8
T1	音节	18.3	27.2	22.3	25.3	29.6	12.0	8.4	20.4
	词首	20.4	24.4	29.5	23.3	20.8	20.9	21.1	22.8
	词尾	10.7	23.4	7.8	19.3	11.5	14.6	13.3	14.4
T2-2	音节	11.0	15.6	11.2	21.2	23.4	7.7	9.7	14.3
	词首	22.2	20.6	10.8	20.9	16.7	9.0	7.2	15.3
	词尾	12.9		2.2	14.6	14.1	4.2	3.3	9.6
T2-1	音节	6.6	9.0	3.6	9.0	8.2	3.6	3.9	6.3
	词首	11.9	20.9	12.3	6.6	10.4	2.5	1.5	9.4
	词尾	10.8		7.1	4.5	10.6	0.4	1.9	5.9
T3-2	音节	2.4	4.1	2.4	3.6	4.1	2.1	3.2	3.1
	词首	5.2	6.8	5.8	5.8	5.0	2.8		4.3
	词尾	2.1	4.7	3.1	1.1	2.6		1.3	1.9

从表 2 可以看出，元音在单词中的位置，对内在基频是有影响的，处于词首的元音内在基频差比处于词尾的要大。这主要是由于韵律特征和语义的影响。因为在设计负载句的时候，没有考虑对单词语义和韵律特征加以控制。负载句"我读 XX 这个词"，朗读时会读成两个韵律短语："我读 XX"和"这个词"，这样词尾音节就成了韵律短语尾音节了，由于陈述句语调下倾的影响，元音基频降低了，内在基频也就变小了。此外，虽然汉语双音词的重音模式多为中重模式，但是也有一些会读作重中（虽然词尾没有轻声音节，但可能被轻读）。发音人朗读时未对重音模式加以提示，只照发音人的习惯读法读出。总的来说，同样调值下，词尾音节的基频要比词首音节为低。

为了更细致地考察单词中主要元音的内在基频表现，现以元音/i, u, ü, a/为例，男女发音人在全部测点上的测量结果示于表 3。表中元音字符后的汉字："首"表示该元音是作为主要元音出现在词首音节；"尾"则表示该主要元音出现在词尾音节。从 T1 到 T4-2 各组符号分别代表在四种声调中的不同测点，每个测点列下的数字，是各元音的基频，基频下面括弧中的数字，是该元音与低元音/a/的基频差 ΔF0。

表3：单词中主要元音的内在基频 IF0 和高元音与低元音/a/的基频差值（△F0，Hz）
（发音人：五男，五女）

性别	元音	T1	T2-1	T2-2	T3-1	T3-2	T4-1	T4-2
男	i首	184.9 (24.3)	129.0 (11.6)	182.9 (23.7)	113.7 (2.2)	95.4 (5.1)	196.5 (19.1)	114.8 (3.6)
	i尾	169.3 (12.9)	120.6 (10.5)	162.3 (10.2)	108.1 (2.5)	88.1 (3.1)	189.5 (15.1)	103.1 (6.1)
	u首	184.5 (23.9)	129.0 (11.6)	177.1 (17.9)	117.2 (5.7)	95.9 (5.6)	202.5 (25.1)	123.6 (12.4)
	u尾	171.4 (15.0)	119.6 (9.5)	162.9 (10.8)	106.7 (1.1)	89.1 (4.1)	190.5 (16.1)	104.1 (7.1)
	ü首	184.4 (23.8)	125.9 (8.5)	179.7 (20.5)	116.5 (5.0)	97.6 (7.3)	197.9 (20.5)	114.1 (2.9)
	ü尾	176.6 (20.2)	112.9 (2.8)	169.3 (17.2)	105.9 (0.3)	87.4 (2.4)	188.0 (13.6)	104.3 (7.3)
	a首	160.6 (0)	117.4 (0)	159.2 (0)	111.5 (0)	90.3 (0)	177.4 (0)	111.1 (0)
	a尾	156.4 (0)	110.1 (0)	152.1 (0)	105.6 (0)	85.0 (0)	174.4 (0)	97.0 (0)
女	i首	302.9 (16.5)	228.7 (12.2)	295.8 (20.7)	222.5 (-5.9)	177.5 (5.3)	327.0 (11.8)	202.1 (-1.7)
	i尾	292.5 (8.6)	206.4 (11.2)	273.8 (15.6)	214.5 (-6.9)	173.7 (1.1)	311.6 (1.2)	187.3 (-6.6)
	u首	304.0 (17.6)	225.8 (9.3)	290.7 (15.6)	219.0 (-9.0)	176.6 (4.4)	333.9 (18.7)	209.3 (5.5)
	u尾	292.0 (8.1)	207.0 (11.8)	275.7 (17.5)	213.7 (-7.7)	173.6 (1.0)	325.3 (14.9)	190.3 (-3.6)
	ü首	309.2 (22.8)	221.3 (4.8)	296.5 (21.4)	224.5 (-3.9)	176.5 (4.3)	324.2 (9.0)	197.3 (-6.5)
	ü尾	302.4 (18.5)	201.5 (6.3)	270.3 (12.1)	206.8 (-14.6)	172.4 (-0.2)	308.2 (-2.2)	187.4 (-6.5)
	a首	286.4 (0)	216.5 (0)	275.1 (0)	228.4 (0)	172.2 (0)	315.2 (0)	203.8 (0)
	a尾	283.9 (0)	195.2 (0)	258.2 (0)	221.4 (0)	172.6 (0)	310.4 (0)	193.9 (0)

  从表 3 中可以看到，不论对于男发音人还是女发音人来说，词尾音节中的主要元音的基频，总是比词首音节中同样元音的基频要低。一般来说，基频低了，所表现出来的内在基频也低。基频低到音域的下限，第四声（去声）的最低点 T4-2，内在基频现象就消失了。这时女声表现出高元音和低元音的基频差出现负值，男声的基频差则很小且显得不那么规则，常出现基频低基频差反而大的现象。至于女声在上声开头 T3-1 高元音和低元音的基频差出现负值的情况，还有待于进一步考察研究。

  鉴于男声和女声在不同声调的同一个测点上，尽管基频 F0 相差很大，但是高元音与低元音的基频差 △F0 是差不多的。所以可以认为高元音与低元音的基频差——内在基频，是与调值有关的而与调型无关。也就是说，高元音与低元音之间，在语境相同的情况下，所表现出来的内在基频是一种元音内在的固有属性。为了更清楚地看出男声和女声的内在基频表现，在心理（知觉）和物理方面的异同，特将三个高元音/i, u, ü/和低元音/a/之间的内在基频分别以物理尺度和乐律尺度来表示，即分别以 Hz 为单位和以半音 Semitone（St）为单位，列于表 4。

  两个频率之间的半音数用下式计算：

$$半音数 = 39.86 \log \frac{f_2}{f_1} \tag{1}$$

其中 f_2 是较高的频率，f_1 是较低的频率。

表中 T1，T4-1，T4-2，T3-2 分别表示不同的测点，ΔF0m，ΔF0f 分别表示男声和女声的三个高元音的平均基频与低元音的基频差，$\overline{\Delta F0}$ 表示男女声 ΔF0 的平均。

表 4：普通话内在基频的物理尺度（Hz）和心理尺度（St）

性别	元音	T1 Hz	T4-1 Hz	平均 Hz	T4-2 Hz	T3-2 Hz	平均 Hz	音域 St
男	i	175.1	196.8		96.8	89.4		
	u	181.4	205.9		105.2	89.7		
	ü	180.1	196.5		101.3	90.1		
	平均	178.8	199.7	189.3	101.1	89.7	95.4	11.84
	a	153.6	175.2	164.4	96.7	82.5	89.6	
ΔF0m		25.2	24.5	24.8	4.4	7.2	5.8	2.44
女	i	290.6	312.1		180.1	168.9		
	u	306.9	335.2		184.2	172.1		
	ü	299.6	318.4		176.1	170.7		
	平均	299	321.9	310.5	180.1	170.2	175.3	9.89
	a	275.5	302.3	288.9	186.8	171.1	178.9	
ΔF0f		23.5	19.6	21.5	-6.7	-0.6	-3.65	1.24
$\overline{\Delta F0}$				23.15			1.07	1.69

从表 4 可以看出，采用物理标度，男女声的内在基频是差不多的，本文的结果是男声为 24.8Hz，女声为 21.5Hz；Whalen 和 Levitt[9]对各种语言的统计平均结果男声为 13.9Hz，女声为 15.4Hz，也是相差不多的。汉语的数据看起来比各种语言的平均数据为高，是因为汉语的数据是取在阴平和去声的基频高点，也就是接近发音人的音域上限。可是要采用心理（乐律）标度——半音（semitone，略作 St），这是一种两音相比的对数标尺的相对标度——来表示的话，那么男声和女声之间的差别就显现出来了。汉语男声的内在基频为 2.44St，女声为 1.24St；Whalen 和 Levitt 的统计结果，男声为 1.84St，女声为 1.34St。值得注意的是，对于男声和女声的平均内在基频的音高表现来说，汉语为 1.69St 而 Whalen 和 Levitt 对各种语言的平均统计结果为 1.65St，它们又是十分相近的。所以采用心理标度——半音，对研究内在音高是合适的。

在音域下限（测点 T3-2，T4-2），男女声平均的内在基频只有 1.07Hz，女声还出现了负值。对不同测点测得的数据的置信度分析表明，T3-2 和 T4-2 测点上测得数据的置信度比 T1 和 T4-1 要低，在这两个测点上高元音与低元音的基频差 ΔF0 要小于置信区间，所以可以认为没有内在基频表现。

3.3 韵母中的元音内在基频

利用汉语韵母的特殊结构，来考察韵母中主要元音在介音和韵尾协同发音影响下的内在基频。测试音节均选用零声母音节，在阴平调的条件下测得的不同韵母的基频，以主要元音来分组，按基频由低到高从左到右排列如图 3 所示。由于元音内在基频男声女声没有系统差别，图 3 表示的是五男五女的平均结果。图中点划线是所有韵母基频的平均值 $\overline{f_0}$。

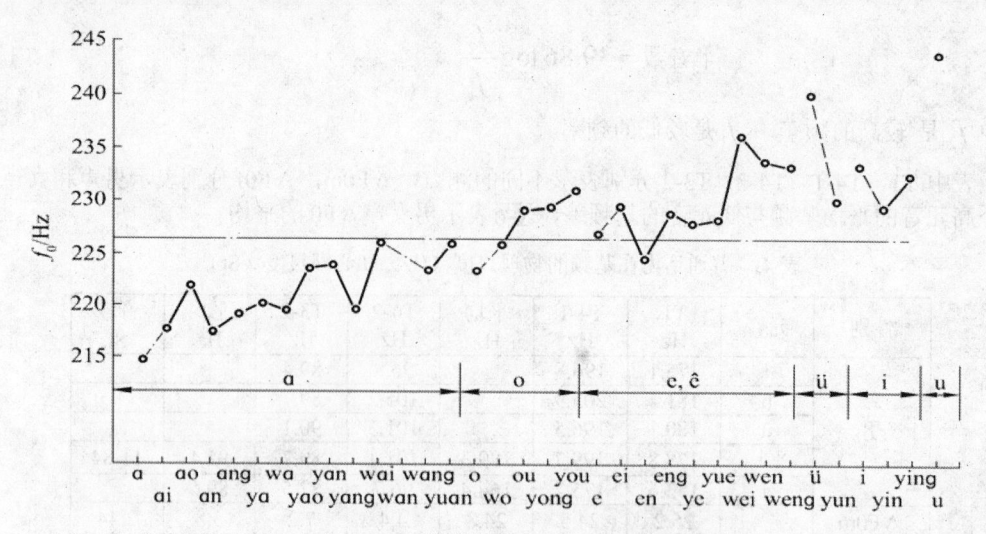

图 3：不同韵母的内在基频（五男五女阴平声平均）

从图 3 可以看出，尽管有介音和韵尾（它们都是高元音或鼻音）的影响，主要元音仍然表现出内在基频。但是，由于介音和韵尾对主要元音带来的协同发音的影响，使得高元音与低元音的基频差变小，从单元音的平均 23.9Hz 降到复合韵母的 18.6Hz。

3.4 介音对内在基频的影响

为了进一步考察协同发音对内在基频的影响，首先看介音对内在基频的影响。以元音/a/及其带有五个不同韵尾的二合韵母/ai, ao, au, an, ang/为基准，与前加不同介音的复合韵母的基频 F0 的对照关系示于图 4。同时把元音/e, o, ê/构成的复韵母/ei, wei, en, eng, wen, weng, o, wo, ê, ye, yue/也一并绘于图 4 以便比较。

可以看到，元音/a, o, e, ê/和带韵尾的二合韵母，加上介音以后基频都要升高，因为所有的介音都是高元音，由于协同发音使这些元音的舌位有所升高。与此同时，各带韵尾的二合韵母同单元音/a/相比，仍然保持内在基频关系。同样的介音对不同的主要元音的影响，在基频升高的数量上差不多是相同的。因而在图 4 上呈现出一些近似平行四边形的现象。

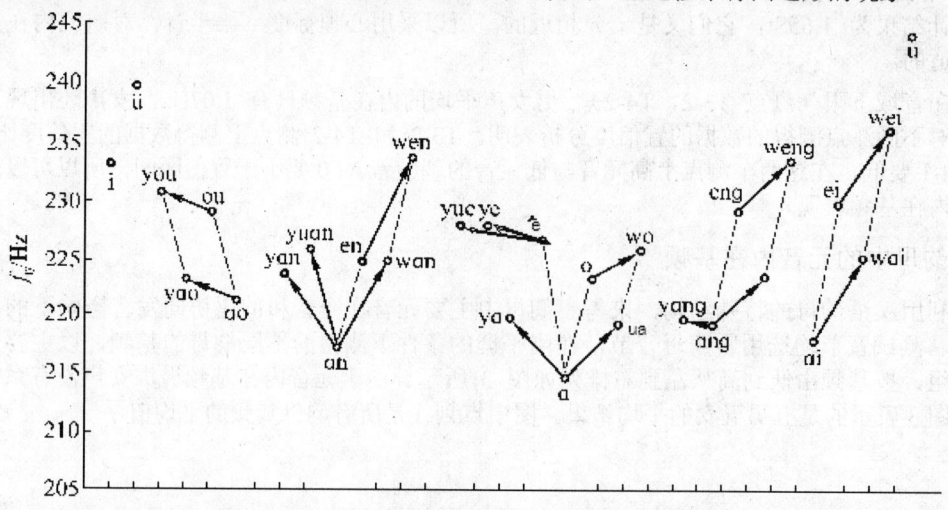

图 4：介音对内在基频的影响（五男五女阴平声平均）

3.5 韵尾对内在基频的影响

现在来考察韵尾对内在基频的影响。仍然以低元音/a/为基准，以及前有介音的两个二合韵母/ia，ua/，加上韵尾以后的基频变化，与其他几个主要元音的情况对比示于图5。

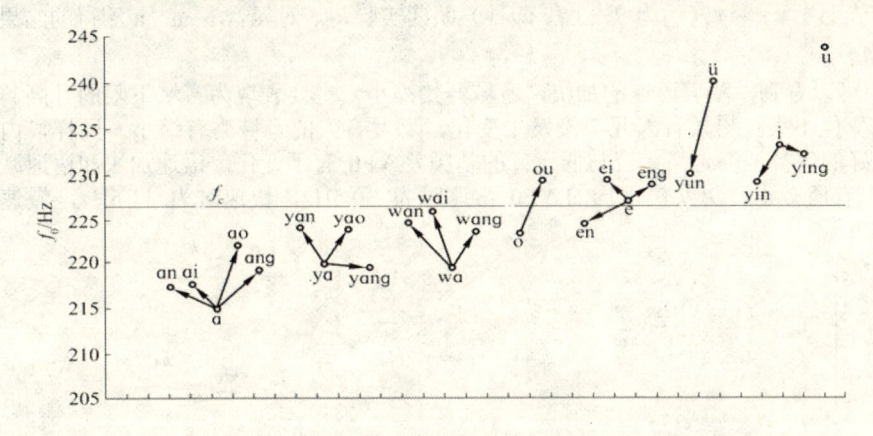

图 5：韵尾对内在基频的影响（五男五女阴平声平均）

韵尾对元音基频的影响，可以分成两类：对于低元音和中元音来说，韵尾使基频提高；对于高元音来说鼻韵尾使基频降低。因为韵尾除了高元音就是鼻音，它们的舌位都是高的。不过鼻韵尾会使高元音/i/和/ü/的基频降低，还是一个值得注意的问题。此外，韵母/yang/和/en/表现出有些不同的情况，基频有些下降，这还值得进一步调查研究。

3.6 说话声级对内在基频的影响

为了在更高的语境层次上来考察内在基频，也就是研究韵律特征对内在基频的影响。首先观察说话声级对内在基频的影响。发音人（一男一女）分别以正常声级（唇前 1m 处为 65dB）、大声（75dB）、小声（55dB）来朗读实验句。仍以测点 T1 和 T4-1 的平均值作为音域上限，T3-2 和 T4-2 的平均值作为音域下限，对元音/i, u, a/测得的结果示于图 6。由于倒频谱算法问题，女声在大声发音时基频很高，没有得到可靠的结果，图上也没有画出来。

从图 6 可以看到，随着说话声级的提高，嗓音的音域也在扩大，同时内在基频仍然在保持。在说话声级降低到 55dB 时，不但音域缩小而且内在音高逐渐消失，这名男发音人表现得比较明显。

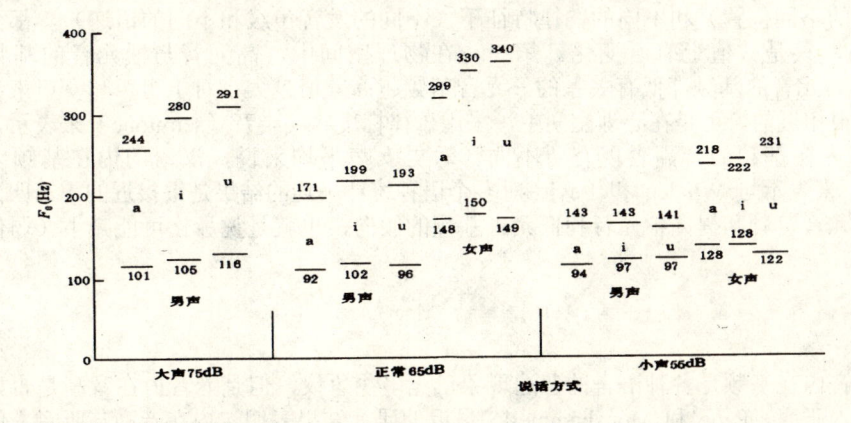

图 6：说话声级对内在基频和音域的影响（一男一女）

3.7 说话速度对内在基频的影响

接下来在保持正常说话声级（65dB）的条件下，考察说话速度对内在基频的影响。发音人（一男一女）在正常的说话声级之下，用三种不同的语速：正常（约为 4 音节/秒）、快读（约为 7 音节/秒）、慢读（约为 2－3 音节/秒）朗读实验句。对元音/i, u, a/测得的结果示于图 7。

从图 7 可以看到，随着语速的加快，音域开始缩小，主要表现为音域下限的升高。语速变慢，音域变化不大，男发音人几乎没发生变化，女发音人的音域略有缩小。同样，内在基频得到了很好的保持，但是高元音与低元音的基频差 ΔF0 有了变化。语速加快和语速减慢，都会使 ΔF0 有所减小。男女声平均的 ΔF0 常速时为 30.5Hz，快速时为 11.5Hz，慢速时为 24.5Hz。

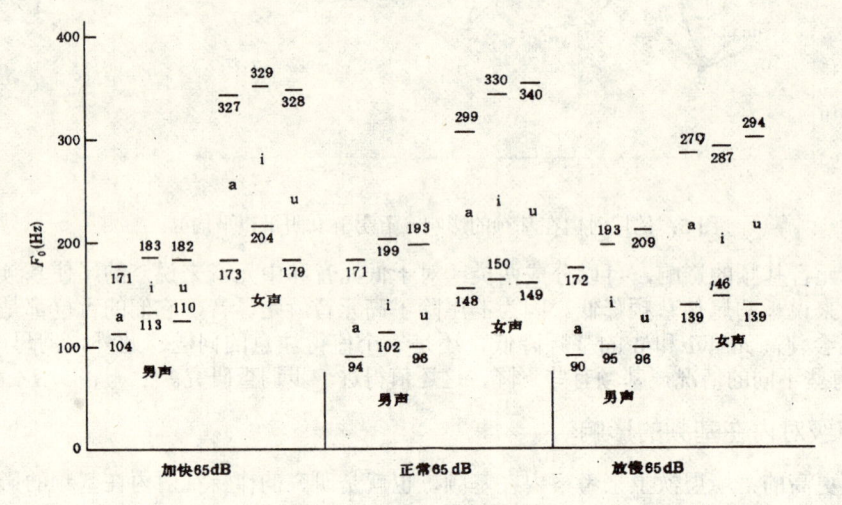

图 7：说话速度对内在基频和音域的影响（一男一女）

4. 结论

根据我们在不同的语境层次上，对元音内在基频的研究结果，可以得出如下结论。首先，元音内在基频对于具有复杂声调系统的汉语也是存在的，并且与其他语言，如英语和德语，有相同的性质和相近的数值。其次，元音内在基频在各种语境中（不同的元音辅音环境以及单词中的不同位置）和不同的韵律特征下（不同的发音声级和不同的语速），都会得到很好的保持，只是数值上有所变化。第三，在物理空间中，高元音与低元音的基频差值（Hz），是与元音的基频高低有关系的，元音基频越高差值越大；对于男声和女声来说，这一差值又是很相近的。可是在心理空间中，采用乐律标度——半音（semitone）来表示，男声和女声元音内在基频的音高表现有所不同。对男女声平均来说，汉语的内在基频以半音（semitone）来表示与 Whalen 和 Levitt 对多个语种统计平均的结果是很接近的。第四，鼻韵尾有降低高元音基频和提高中元音和低元音基频的倾向，也就是说鼻化可能减小（弱化）元音内在基频。

5. 讨论

关于元音内在基频是各种语言的普遍现象已无多少争议，但是元音内在音高是否如此似乎还值得深入研究。Pape 和 Mooshammer[5]最近的研究结果表明，内在音高与听音人的语言背景和音乐修养都有关系。他们的实验证明，母语为拉丁语系的西班牙语和葡萄牙语的听音人，对元音内在音高最不敏感；母语为德语的听音人对内在音高最敏感；而意大利语的听音人则介于两者之间。这一问题实际上也牵涉到元音内在基频的产生机理。

尽管元音内在基频现象已经发现很久了，但其产生机理却一直莫衷一是。总起来说，曾有两种有代表性的学说[4]。一种是声学耦合学说，主张高元音的第一共振峰 F1 都很低，由于声带和声道之间的耦合作用，F1 会吸引嗓音的基频 F0 向它靠近。这就像小号演奏家的唇振动频率，被小号的共振频率所吸引一样。可是越来越多的实验证明，声门阻抗比声道阻抗大很多，声源和声道是相互独立的，它们之间并不存在耦合。特别是 F1 距 F0 较远的中元音也具有内在基频，这就用耦合学说难以解释了。另一种是舌牵引学说，认为高元音的舌位较高，特别是元音/i/舌位还靠前，所以在发音时舌骨运动会牵动喉头上升，对声带产生附加的张力，以致基频升高。但是，这一学说在面对很多语言的测试结果都有元音/u/常表现出比元音/i/更高的内在基频这一现象（本文中的结果也是一样）却不能做出合理解释。因为元音/u/是后高元音，为什么会比前高元音/i/的基频要高呢？这一点至今仍不十分清楚。特别是，对于汉语来说，两个鼻韵尾，一个前鼻音/n/一个后鼻音/ng/，它们既会引起中元音和低元音的基频升高，又会引起高元音的基频下降（见图5）。这也是一个很值得进一步研究的问题，也很可能会对揭示内在基频的产生机理大有帮助。

本文是在言语信号的不同语境层次上，特别是在声调曲线的不同位置测量了元音内在基频，证明了作为声调语言的汉语，和重音时程语言（stress-timed language）与音节时程语言（syllable-timed language）一样，也具有元音内在基频，并且在数值上也是差不多一样的。可以认为，元音内在基频是元音的固有特征也是元音音质的一部分，它是不受发音人主动控制的。本文这些工作只研究了内在基频的声学表现，为阐明元音内在基频的产生机理，还需要一系列发音生理的测量数据来补充验证。

参考文献

[1] Crandall, I.B. 1925. The sounds of speech. *Bell System Technical Journal* 4, 586-626.
[2] Hoole, P., Mooshammer, C. 2002. Articulatory analysis of the German vowel system. In: Auer, P., Gilles, P. & Spiekermann, H. (eds.), *Silbenschinitt und tonakzente*. Niemeyer, Tübingen, 129-152.
[3] Lehiste, I., Peterson, G.E. 1961. Some basic considerations in the analysis of intonation. *J. Acoust Soc. Am.*33, 419-423.
[4] Ohala, J.J., Eukel, B.W. 1987. Explaining the intrinsic pitch of vowels. In: R. Channon & L. Shockey (eds.), *In honor of Ilse Lehiste*. Dordrecht: Fores, 207-215.
[5] Pape, D., Mooshammer, C. 2008. Intrinsic pitch is not a universal phenomenon: Evidence from Romance languages. *Proc. 11th Labphon (Laboratory Phonology)*. University of Wellington, New Zealand.
[6] Peterson, G.E., Barney, H.L. 1952. Control methods used in a study of the vowels. *J. Acoust. Soc.Am.*24, 175-184.
[7] Shadle, C.H. 1985. Intrinsic fundamental frequency of vowels in sentence context. *J. Acoust. Soc.Am.*78, 1562-1567.
[8] Shi, B., Zhang, J. 1987. Vowel intrinsic pitch in standard Chinese. *Proc. XIth ICPhS*, Tallinn, Estonia. 142-145.
[9] Whalen, D.H., Levitt, A.G. 1995. The universality of intrinsic F0 of vowels. *Journal of Phonetics*23, 349-366.
[10] 张家騄（1989）元音内在基频与讲话方式对共振峰的影响。《声学学报》第14卷，401-406页。
[11] 张家騄（1993）超音段特征间的相互作用。《声学学报》第18卷，263-271页。

声调目标实现的规律及变化

祖漪清　闫润强

摘要

本文通过对一个汉语普通话语音合成数据库韵律参数的统计,分析了长度不同话语的语速分布、相应的基频变化范围,以及在不同韵律位置声调目标实现的状况。结论表明:话语越长,或包括的音节数越多,语速越快,相应的基频变化范围也越大。在话语中,局部语速和基频变化范围是由韵律结构决定的。在一个韵律短语内部,前一音节声调的基频目标往往会滞后到后面音节。当语速较快,基频变化范围较大时,声调目标的实现会发生明显滞后和更明显的离散,并对后面音节的走势产生明显影响。结果表明:仅依靠文本层面的信息指导语音合成的基频生成,拼接点处的不连续性是难以克服的。

关键词:　声调目标　基频曲线　韵律结构　语音数据　自然度

1. 引言

关于基频的研究和建模包括两个层次,其一是整体语调曲线,其二是局部基频曲线。在声调语言中,基频曲线不仅携带了语调信息,还携带了声调信息,局部基频曲线反映的是声调的形状。在绝大多数非声调语言中,局部基频曲线反映了轻、重音的表现。

局部基频曲线的负载单元通常是音节。局部基频曲线的变化受制于整体语调的变化。在话语的不同韵律单位中,局部音段的韵律表现差异很大。构建局部基频曲线和音段的相互关联,也是基频模型的基本问题。

汉语普通话的声调结构属于复杂结构,即不是单纯的高或低,而是包括了上升和下降的变化过程。如果将普通话的四声在孤立音节情况下的声调作为标准声调,它们的基频曲线在连续语流中与标准情况偏离很大,这种偏离和所处整体语调、韵律结构中的位置有关,也与声调环境有关。在语流中,声调目标的实现是动态的,并遵从一定规律。

基频建模的目的是将基频变化的规律形式化。关于局部基频曲线和整体语调的相互关联的问题之一是音段和基频曲线的对准(alignment)问题。在声调语言中,即声调曲线在一个音节上是如何实现其目标的,也就是讨论在不同的语音环境下局部基频目标如何实现。汉语普通话的声调目标可简单概括为:阴平为高,阳平为上升,上声为低,去声为下降。

关于汉语普通话的基频曲线模型,多是建立在各个音节声调相连的基础上的。

Fujisaki 模型[2]是典型的叠加模型,即短语指令和重音指令造成的基频偏离以对数形式相加,构成语调。应用到汉语普通话[3][5],重音指令即声调指令,当处理阳平(上升)和去声(下降)时使用了一对指令反映方向的变化。短语指令和声调指令都采用了指数函数,声调指令函数会逼近一个目标值(ceiling level)。

Stem-ML 模型[5]的一系列控制参数掌管基本设置、间断和重音等基本语调元素的变化，模型用于汉语普通话时，这些参数也控制了相邻声调间的变化。当后一个音节较为强势（如重读）时，前一个音节的基频曲线变化会表达后一音节的声调实现[4]。

目标逼近（TA）模型[9]综合考虑了语音单元声调目标和发音器官生理结构带来的制约，使用了线性函数和指数函数组合的数学表达方式。模型的含义是音节基频曲线的形成过程是声调目标实现的过程[7][8]，并且该过程与音段的实现保持一致。当声调目标达到了，即转入下一个音节声调目标的实现，这个转换点基本就是前后两个音节的边界。因此音节基频曲线的形状既同该音节的声调目标有关，又同前一音节结尾处的基频频率值有关。在汉语普通话的应用中，TA 模型的数学表达中目标逼近的理念表现得十分明确。

无论是用什么样的模型，语音数据在其中都起了关键作用。本研究使用自然话语初步分析声调目标实现的基频表现，并试分析局部声调在话语中的实现情况。

2. 自然语音基频曲线的基本变化

实验使用的语音素材是一个汉语普通话合成语音数据库。由于语音覆盖和朗读方便的需要，合成语音数据库多考虑独立叙述句。孤立句的朗读语句被称为一个话语（在此不得不忽略孤立句对分析韵律结构存在的局限性）。为了简化问题，讨论仅限于声学层面的表现，而回避句法、语义产生的影响。

2.1 语音数据

用于实验的语音数据是一个专业女播音员朗读的约 8000 个语句。由于经过设计，在这些句子中所有带调音节都有足够的样本。采集的语音波形用 16bit 的 DAT 格式保存，采样率为 16KHz。所有的语句都有音节边界标注及韵律标注。基频信号由语音分析软件 Praat 提取。

语句的韵律结构从小到大被定义为三层：韵律词（prosodic word）、中间短语（minor phrase）和韵律短语（major phrase）。韵律词内的音节连接较为紧密，通常大于或等于语法词，其间一般没有停顿。

由于在实际数据中，中间短语和韵律短语往往很难划分，在实验中我们将它们合为一层，并统称为韵律短语。重音包括各韵律层级的重音和语句重音。重音的标注以"听到什么标什么"为原则，因此各韵律层级的重音允许存在空缺。

2.2 语句的语速和基频变化范围

语速可用语速（speech rate）和音速（articulatory rate）两个不同的物理量描述。语速的计算包含了停顿和间断[1][12][6]。音速的计算不包含停顿，因此音速纯粹反映了发音器官的变化速率。我们用音节平均时长来描写语速或音速。

图 1 为合成语音数据库中话语的语速和音速分布。结果表明，话语包括的音节数越多，语速及音速越快。但话语包含的音节数达到一定程度（七八个音节），语速不再加快，这是因为发音器官变化速度是有生理限度的，不可能无限增加。

在相同说话人的同一套语音数据库中，语速随句长的分布反映了发音人有将一个话语作为一个大的语音单元、并尽量保持相同长度的趋势。因此造成了句子越长语速越快的现象。同时由于一个话语中包含的音节个数不同，受发音器官动作变化的生理限制，发音人又无法无限制地加快语速。

不同长度的句子基频的表现又如何呢？图 1（b）给出了对应于图 1 的整个语音数据库的基频变化范围分布情况。显见，话语延续越长，基频的变化范围越大。

对语音数据库的统计表明发音人的基频变化范围会超过 200Hz（见图 1），当音节个数增加，话语中必定会插入间断，而间断的引入似乎并没有阻断基频在允许的情况下变化范围的进一步扩大。可以假设，当话语中的一个韵律短语结束、基频重置时，虽然声带停止了振动，却另有相关的发音器官没有停止工作，它帮助了重置的基频立即到位。

总之，自然语音基频和时长的变化与语速相关。话者会采用不同的策略应对不同长度的语句。

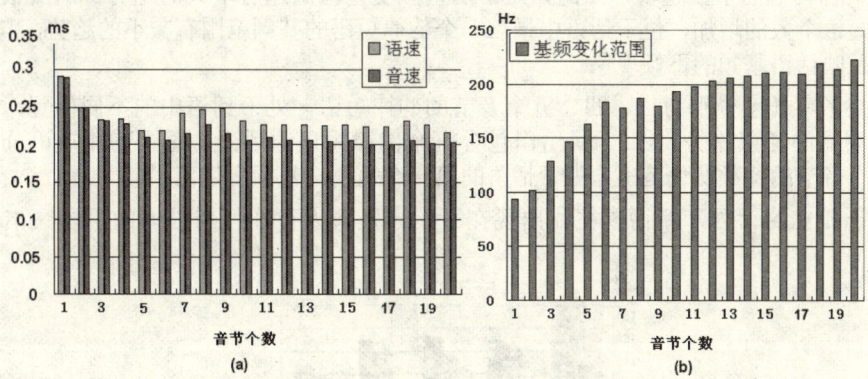

图 1：话语语速（a）及基频变化范围（b）分布

2.3 语句内不同韵律单元的语速和基频变化范围

对语音数据库的大致统计分析表明，韵律短语的长度对该韵律短语中基频的变化范围是有影响的。

如果样本足够多，可以忽略不同声调关于基频的分布带来的影响。因此我们选取样本个数较多的、长度分别为三、四、五个音节的韵律短语进行考察。

图 2 列出了出现于话语第一个韵律短语，长度分别为三、四、五个音节时的基频变化范围。图中横坐标表示整个话语包含的韵律短语个数。因此横坐标为 1 的位置表示该话语只有一个韵律短语，长度为三、四、五个音节。

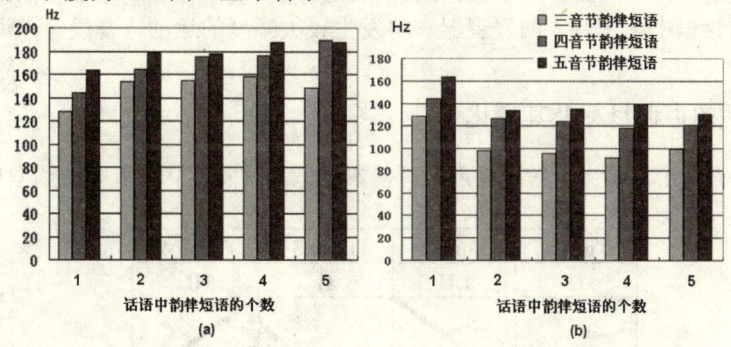

图 2：出现于话语第一个韵律短语（a）和最后一个韵律短语（b），
长度分别为三、四、五个音节时的基频变化范围

图 2（a）表明：韵律短语的长度越大，或韵律短语所含音节的个数越多，该韵律短语的基频变化范围越有增大的趋势；随着话语所包含的韵律短语个数的增加，位于话语第一个韵律短语的基频范围有扩大的趋势，似乎是为后面的下倾留出一定的空间。

为了进一步考察基频变化范围，以及对应的下倾，下面将分析话语最后一个韵律短语的状况。

图 2（b）列出了出现于话语最后一个韵律短语，长度分别为三、四、五个音节时的基频变化范围。图中横坐标表示整个话语包含的韵律短语个数。同样，横坐标为 1 的位置表示该话语只有一个韵律短语，长度为三、四、五个音节。结果表明：韵律短语的长度越大，或韵律短语所含音节的个数越多，该韵律短语的基频变化范围越有增大的趋势；随着话语所包含的韵律短语个数的增加，位于话语中最后一个韵律短语的基频范围有减小的趋势，与 3.1 节对比，可反映话语基频的下倾现象。

如果考察长度分别为三、四、五个音节的韵律短语，处于话语中的不同位置，不难发现它们有明显的递降趋势。图 3 只给出包含五个韵律短语的话语、每个韵律短语分别为三、四、五个音节的基频变化范围。处于话语的第一个短语，基频变化范围最大。

对于孤立的话语，新话题往往出现在开始，发音人往往使用强调的手段突出这一新话题。

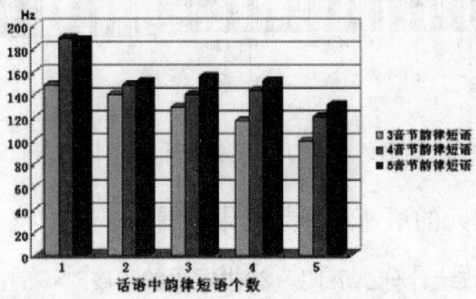

图 3：包括五个韵律短语的话语中，出现于话语不同位置的，
长度分别为三、四、五个音节时的基频变化范围

3. 话语中声调目标实现的规律及变化

随着话语长度的增加（或音节个数的增加），音速加快，并且基频变化范围加大。也就是说，在较长的话语中，发音人的发音器官将发生较大幅度的运动。音段、声调的协同发音现象更为复杂。

3.1 汉语普通话的声调目标及其变化

汉语普通话有四个声调（不考虑轻声）。基本调型，或发孤立音节时的调型见图 4。四声的声调目标分别为高、上升、低、下降。

Tone 1	Tone 2	Tone 3	Tone 4
H	LH	L	HL

图 4：汉语普通话四声的基本调型

在不同音境下，基频曲线的形状会发生变化。但同时由于存在声调目标，这种变化又存在着规律。通过聚类，也许可以刻画这种变化，聚类时考虑了如下音境：

- 当前音节声调；
- 前一音节声调；
- 当前声母；
- 当前音节在短语中位置；
- 当前音节在语调短语中位置；
- 重音情况；
- 韵律短语在句子中位置。

从语音数据库中选取 36392 个归一化的音节基频曲线进行聚类后，得到如图 5 所示的七个归一化模板。通过决策树分析的方法，用这七个基频模板预测连续话语的基频，可取得较好结果[13]。

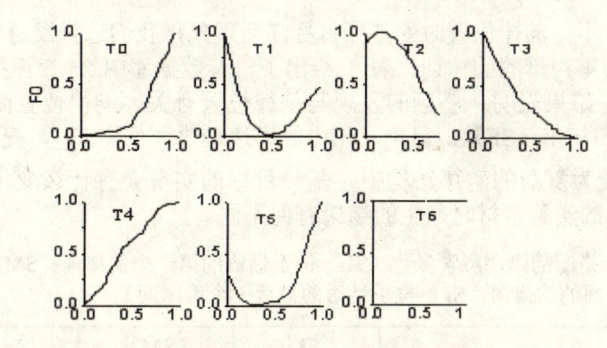

图 5：从语音数据库提取的七个变化的基频调型

3.2 自然话语中对立声调目标邻接时声调目标的实现

声调基频曲线的变化来自前、后音节声调的影响。因此音节基频曲线的形状既同该音节的声调目标有关，又同前一音节结尾处的基频频率值有关。当然不同的韵律结构环境，对当前声调目标是有影响的。在具体的实现过程中，由于生理条件的限制，某些情况下可能会产生一些滞后。当两个相连音节基频目标相互对立（如由高到低），声调目标的滞后、以及基频曲线的变化将十分明显。

汉语普通话 2—3 声搭配是典型的基频目标相互对立的例子，即一个完成上升后实现下一个低目标的事件。基于语音数据库的分析，两音节韵律词 2—3 声搭配时的平均声调曲线如图 6 所示。前一音节上升的声调目标一直延续到后一音节，上升的基频到达后一音节后，转而下降，因此出现了一个峰值，由于运动惯性的存在，峰值的位置会滞后到下一个音节。峰值的位置和音节边界的距离即声调目标滞后时间。

类似的对立搭配模式还有许多，如 2—2 声、4—4 声等，相应地，目标的变化较为离散。由于篇幅所限，在此不一一给出实验数据。

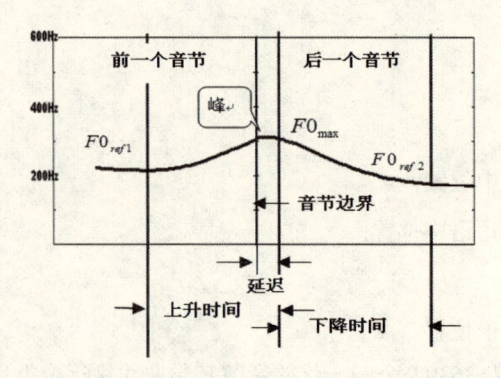

图 6：两音节韵律词 2－3 声搭配时的平均基频曲线

3.3 韵律环境与对立声调目标实现的变化

为了考察音节处于不同韵律位置时的基频目标滞后现象，我们选择汉语普通话 2－3 声搭配、第二个音节声母为零声母的韵律词。表 1 给出了语音数据库中 2－3 声搭配在不同韵律位置的基频参数统计值，结果表明：基频的表现与韵律位置有关。韵律位置简化为三个：句首（SI），句中（SM）和句末（SF）。显见，句中的语速最快（见图 7），变化也最大。

我们需要考察在较为复杂的韵律结构中，基频目标的实现会有什么变化，或者说探讨不同于许毅[8][10]所使用的实验素材时产生的结果有何不同。

表 1：两音节 2－3 声搭配韵律词声学参数（SI：位于话语的第一个韵律词；SM：位于话语中间的韵律词；SF：位于话语的最后一个韵律词）

	SI	SM	SF
平均基频峰值延迟 (ms)	3.67	12.55	8.08
基频峰值延迟标准偏差 (ms)	18.45	14.76	16.64
基频上升频率 ΔF (St)	4.05	3.75	4.86
基频下降频率 ΔF (St)	9.64	8.55	7.92
平均基频上升斜率 (Hz/ms)	0.599	0.427	0.420
基频上升斜率标准偏差 (Hz/ms)	0.260	0.236	0.178
平均基频下降斜率 (Hz/ms)	-1.130	-0.921	-0.601
基频下降斜率标准偏差 (Hz/ms)	0.308	0.329	0.250
前一音节时长 (ms)	182	134	230
后一音节时长 (ms)	189	180	220

分析表明：具有统计意义的滞后程度是有限的（参见图 7），同许毅的结果一致。语音合成数据库中提供了变化更加剧烈的韵律环境，在相同的语音环境下（如声调类型），前一个音节的基频目标为当前音节提供更多的变化，并影响到当前音节基频目标所能到达的位置。发音人在力所能及的情况下，极力保持着声调与音段的对齐。

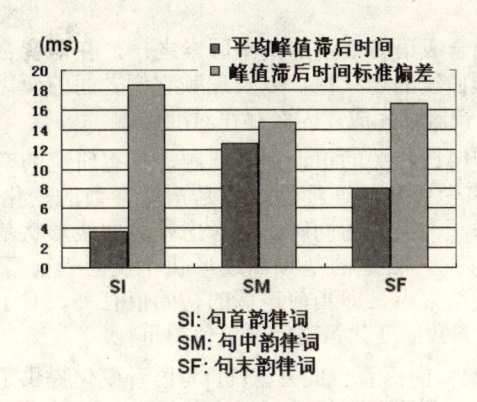

图 7：两音节 2－3 声韵律词峰值滞后统计值

在数据库中，可以发现一些极端情形，如 2－3 声搭配时，基频峰值向后延迟高达 60－76ms。然而，整个数据库中这种大幅度的滞后现象虽并不多见，但也时有发生。同时数据表明，也有不容忽略的部分数据峰值发生在边界前。总之，数据表明平均峰值是滞后的，但仍有部分例外情况，可以说，前面音节对后面音节的影响大于后面音节对前面音节的影响，或正向协同发音比逆向协同发音明显。当语速较快，基频变化较大时，情况更为复杂。正因为如此，图 2 所示的上升和下降音节声调曲线不止一种方式。图 7 给出的高方差表明语音的分类过于简单。

4. 结论及讨论

4.1 基本结论

（1）说话人有将一个话语作为一个韵律单元的倾向。一个话语包括的音节数越多，语速及音速越快。但话语包含的音节数达到一定程度，语速不再加快。随着话语所包含的音节个数增加，无论其中有无停顿，在生理限制允许的情况下，基频的变化范围越大。在孤立话语中，位于话语中第一个韵律短语的变化范围最大。

（2）自然语音平均结果表明的前一个语音单元的声调目标在音节边界完成，然后转而实现下一个声调目标。当两个相邻的语音单元在声调上存在对立时（如高和低的对立），可以更清楚地观察到由于生理条件的限制而发生的、转折点滞后到下一个音节的情况。这一点与许毅的研究结果一致。然而在不同的韵律位置，声调目标的实现情况会发生变化。当音速较快，基频变化范围较大时，声调目标滞后相对明显。

（3）在普遍支持基本结论（2）的同时，仍有不容忽略的一部分数据反映了声调目标提前实现后一个音节的声调目标。这时，前一音节的发音情况较后一音节往往处于弱势，即后音节更加到位。到位并非重读。石基琳等在软模板基频预测模型中对相邻音节可调节强势[4]（strong preferences）的设置是有数据依据的。

4.2 声调与音段的对准问题与合成语音的连贯度

关于局部声调实现的问题和语音合成密切相关。在语音研究人员研究更为复杂的语调课题的同时，语音合成并未逃脱微观问题所带来的困扰，局部声调的实现、声调与音段的对准等问题如果处理不当，会使所有在更高层次上做出的努力黯然失色。细节决定成败。

语音的连贯度是影响合成语音质量的基本因素之一，在语音合成问题中，需要解决局部音段的连续性和局部基频曲线的连续性，以及理顺它们之间的变化关系。音段目标和声调目标的实现分别由不同的发音器官完成，因而存在对准问题。

与合成语音的连贯度密切相关的声调细节问题，仍有研究的空间。在语音合成中，连贯性具有两个意义，一是声学参数的连续性，二是声学参数的变化策略。对于拼接式语音合成，在单元选择时，考虑频谱信息的同时，要考虑基频曲线形状是否合适。这时仅靠文本层面的语境信息往往是不够的，合适的基频曲线形状不仅同当前音节的声调目标实现过程有关，也同前一音节的基频结束点，即当前声调的初始值有关。对于参数语音合成，声学参数的连续性或许不成问题，参数的变化策略问题更值得重视。

基于统计模型（HMM）的语音合成方法[11]为语音变化提供了分析平台。然而对多变的语音数据，使用统计模型去刻画所有细节似乎有些徒劳，其结果可能会产生由于平均造成的过度平化的问题。

4.3 语音研究的数据平台

我们可以粗略地将语音数据分为实验室话语和自然话语。实验室语句的文本是人工设计的，有些句子在实际生活中不多见，同时对朗读方式也有严格的要求。自然语句的文本多来自报刊、文章等发表物，语句在现实生活中较为常见，对朗读往往不做过多要求。使用不同的语音数据，可能会得出不同结果。问题往往是来自对数据的控制。

（1）实验室语音和自然语音

实验室语音的文本是人工设计的，句子通常较短，同时内容有时不太常用。这时，发音人对时长的控制比较均匀，同时由于录音的控制可以做得很好，每一个音节往往容易读得比较到位。实验室话语是字正腔圆的。

在选择自然语音数据库的朗读文本时，一般是以最大音段覆盖为原则的，发音人对大多用词比较熟悉，因此朗读时比较随意，同时每个音节的朗读未必到位。自然语音表现出了更多的抑扬顿挫，即更多的时长变化和基频变化，它们在带来更自然的效果的同时，也带来了更多的发音不到位。与人类活动相关的问题一定是多变的，很难量化。这时语音研究对象的正确分类十分重要。

规整的实验室话语，语音变化较少，为语音规律的声学参数统计带来了方便[10]。语音数据量也可以得到控制，因此可简化数据处理方面的工作，同时较少的变化可以排除许多干扰。在某种意义下，迫使语音变化简单化，正是制造实验室语音的目的。我们不妨使用实验室语音研究获得基本的语音规律并应用到言语工程系统。

（2）语音的自然度

很难想象，人们会用完全相同的发音手段去实现语音的目标，可以说语音的变化是和自然度相关的。追求语音合成的自然度是语音合成技术的目标。因此用发音完全到位的语音数据预测基频曲线，难免会生成单调的结果。

如果使用自然语音，语音的分类确实棘手。例如，在实验室语音中可以得到明确的重读和非重读两种情况，而自然语音中的重读音节并非十分明确，常常难以判断。如何驾驭自然语音数据是另一个难题。

参考文献

[1] Fougeron, C., Jun, S.-A. 1998. Rate effects on French intonation: prosodic organization and phonetic realization. *Journal of Phonetics* 26, 45-69.
[2] Fujisaki, H. 1992. Modelling the Process of Fundamental Frequency Contour Generation. In: Y. Tohkura, E. Vatikiotis-Bateson, Y. Sagisasaka (eds.), *Speech Perception, Production and Linguistic Structure*. IOS Press, 313-328.
[3] Gu Wentao, Kekichi Hirose, Hiroya Fujisaki. 2004. A method for automatic tone command parameter extraction for the model of F0 contour generation for Mandarin. *Speech Prosody*.
[4] Greg P. Kochanski, Chilin Shih. 2000. Stem-ML: Language-independent prosody description. *ICSLP*, Beijing, China.
[5] Greg Kochanski, Chilin Shih. 2001. Prosody Modeling with Soft Templates. *Speech Communication* 39(3-4), 311-352.
[6] Li, A.J., Zu, Y.Q. 2008. Speech Rate effects on discourse Prosody in Standard Chinese. *Speech Prosody 2008*, accepted.
[7] Xu, Y., Wang, Q.E. 2001. Pitch targets and their realization: Evidence from Mandarin Chinese. *Speech Communication* 33 (4), 319-337.
[8] Xu, Y. 2002. Articulatory Constrains and Tonal alignment, a keynote lecture. *Proceedings of Speech Prosody 2002*, 91-100.
[9] Xu, Y., Thipakorn, B. 2007. Modeling tone and intonation in Mandarin and English as a process of target approximation. http://www.phon.icl.ac.uk/home/yi/publication.html.
[10] Xu, Y. 2008. In defense of Lab speech in prosody research. *Proceedings of the 8th Phonetics Conference of China*.
[11] HMM-based Speech Synthesis System (HTS)-Home. http://hts.sp.nitech.ac.jp.
[12] 曹剑芬（2003）语速特征及其变化。载《语音研究报告》，中国社会科学院语言研究所语音研究室。
[13] 胡文英、祖漪清（2006）语句的基频曲线预测。《声学学报》第 31 卷第 1 期。
[14] 沈炯（1992）汉语语调刍议。《语文研究》第 4 期，15-24 页。
[15] 吴宗济、林茂灿主编（1996）《实验语音学概要》。北京：高等教育出版社。

STUDIES ON CHINESE PROSODY:
PROFESSOR WU ZONGJI'S THOUGHTS ON PROSODY AND THEIR FAR-REACHING IMPLICATIONS

LI Aijun

ABSTRACT

For more than 70 years, Professor Wu Zongji's great efforts in speech studies have epitomized the glorious progress of modern Chinese phonetic inquiries since the mid-20th century. By adopting experimental approaches of modern phonetics, he has helped blaze a pioneering path to the comprehensive exploration of the phonetic features of Mandarin, has not only systematically analyzed the acoustic and physiological characteristics of phonetic segments, but also made an ineffaceable contribution to the studies of prosodic features in Chinese and their applications in speech engineering. The linguistic collections of Professor Wu Zongji [95] are the quintessence of his lifetime career as a phonetician.

To mark the celebration of his hundredth birthday, we highlight his achievements on the study of Chinese prosody, especially his ideas of contextual vs. obligatory tone sandhi rules. His recent explorations on the relationship between discourse prosody and traditional Chinese artistic forms, such as calligraphy, ink-and-wash painting, are also included.

Not only is he a down-to-earth researcher, Professor Wu also enthusiastically encourages his colleagues and students to join in his endeavors, and by doing this, he has already influenced generations of linguists. Professor Wu pays great attention to the application of phonetic research findings to speech engineering, especially the contributions in the enhancement of the naturalness of Chinese Speech Synthesis. Partly due to his leading presence, the research of Chinese prosody is becoming a flourishing area both at home and abroad, which is conducive to the progress of the marriage between phonetic studies and the technologies of speech engineering.

Keywords: Professor Wu, Chinese, prosody, intonation, tone

1. INTRODUCTION

In the early 20th century, two giants of Chinese linguistics, Liu Fu and Chao Yuen-ren launched the investigation of tones, with Kymograph as the main measuring tool for tonal frequency. Based on the systematic accounts on the definition and types of Chinese intonation as well as the relationship between intonation and word tone, Chao put forward his prestigious theory that "Chinese intonation is actually the algebraic addition from the original tones of words and sentential intonation", which is also figuratively depicted as "the small waves ridding on the large waves".

A worthy student following Chao Yuen-ren, Professor Wu had carried out a series of experimental studies on the segmental characteristics of Mandarin since the 1960's. In the 1980's, he began to examine tone sandhi in Mandarin. He inherited and further developed Chao's ideas of "rubber effect" and "small-waves-plus-big-waves effect" on the nature of intonation by realizing a tangible quantification of the relationship between the two effects and examining the variation patterns of intonation on the three levels, i.e. syntax, phonetics and phonology. Through the analysis of the tone sandhi patterns of bi-, tri-, and quadri-syllabic words, he managed to establish rules to govern tone sandhi in phrases, which are then taken as the basis for investigating sentential intonation. He proposed the hierarchical Domino Rule to express successive tone sandhi phenomenon and the Intonational Transposition Rule to explain the tonal variations of phrases. He also developed a prosody labeling system and found a series of prosodic and segmental rules applied in speech synthesis. His core conceptions on tone and intonation can be generalized as contextual vs. obligatory tone sandhi rules.

It is under his far-reaching influence that the studies on Chinese tones and intonations and other related prosodic inquiries have become thriving academic fields since the 1980's.

1.1 Intonation model

Different models have been proposed in intonation research, such as the PENTA model by Xu Yi, the Top-Bottom Line model by Shen Jiong, the STEM-ML model by Shih Chilin, etc. In addition to the intonational model, based on the AM intonation theory, Lin Maocan pointed out that there are two variables in Chinese intonation: the accents and the boundary tones. Further, Tseng Chiu-yu examined the acoustic performances of intonation from the perspective of discourse. What is more gratifying is the rising of a large number of young and promising scholars, therefore, the studies on tone, tonal linking and intonation of various dialects are gradually carried out. All these researches have enriched the Chinese intonation studies to great extent.

1.2 Stress, duration and rhythm

As for the Chinese stress, Chao [14] classified them into three categories: normal stress, contrastive stress and weak stress. Based on this classification, a series of experiments have been conducted.

First of all, many studies on neutral tone have been carried out. For example, Lin [53] explored the characteristics of neutral tone through perceptual testing from segmental synthesis samples. He argued that the variation of the duration is the major clue for distinguishing strong and weak stresses. Lin & Yan [48][50] noted the changes of neutral tone are mainly caused by the shortening of duration and the decreasing of energy. In this regard, the neutral tone can be seen as weak stress. Moreover, Cao [2][4] elaborated that the auditory impression of the neutral tone is the comprehensive effect of the variations of four phonetic elements, among which pitch is considered to be more notable but with a stable pattern. Different from the phonetic examination, Wang [83] investigated neutral tone from the phonological aspect. He investigated the neutral tone profile in Tianjin dialect. And, Lu and Wang [58] suggested that weak stress and neutral tone are two concepts defined on the stress tier and tone tier respectively.

Secondly, experimental analyses on normal stress were also launched, e.g. Lin, Yan & Sun [49], Yan & Lin [111] investigated the acoustic performances of the normal stress of bi- and tri-syllabic words in the Beijing dialect. They noted that normal stress exhibits longer duration and a comparatively full pitch pattern. Cao [2][8] further argued that the contrast between the so-called "medium" and "heavy" stresses belongs to the comparative difference within normal stress. Since then, research has gradually turned to the study of accents in the sentential level. For example, Shen's [61] study on sentential stress exhibited that the duration does not show a significant effect, whereas pitch takes the primary role and sentential stress can cause the top line of pitch to expand upward.

Experimental studies on duration and rhythm were carried out in a relatively late period. It is closely related, however, to the later-raised exploration into prosodic structure. Cao [3][4][5] explored the nature of Chinese rhythm through related evidence from linguistics and para-linguistics and reckoned that Chinese rhythm is not the pattern with an equal interval among syllables or stresses, but a kind of pattern, in which prosodic phenomena are regularly displayed, including pausing, lengthening, shortening and extending of duration, raising and lowering of pitch. Chinese rhythm has iterated loose-tense pattern: intra-foot is tense and inter-foot is loose (Wang [82]). Liu [56] proposed the concept of "Rhythm Fulcrum", which demonstrated that the Chinese pause serves as the rhythm fulcrum, whereas, in English it is realized as accent. Li [34] investigated the perceived pauses in news broadcast pertaining to the prosodic hierarchic structure, and got the pausing patterns.

1.3 Prosodic structure

From the late 1980's, studies on prosodic structure have gradually become the core of Chinese prosody research.

The first tide is on the defining of prosodic boundary and the study on its corresponding acoustic characteristics. Studies on this aspect have been growing prosperously. Li [36] analyzed the acoustic features to signal the prosodic boundaries and the sentential accents. Lin [44] discussed the relationship between stress and prosodic structure in Chinese. He put forward that stress is constrained by the prosodic structure, and furthermore, stress in the sentence is hierarchical, which can be characterized as: sentential stress, prosodic phrase stress and prosodic word stress. Cao [5] conducted research on the phonetic and linguistic cues to signal prosodic boundaries. She mainly discussed the definition of prosodic units, the relationship between pause distribution and syntactic structure as well as Part of Speech (POS), and the construction of rhythmic words.

Then, research on the aspects of prosodic labeling system of Chinese (Wu [95]; Li`[32][36]), intonation modeling (Xu [106][108][109]; Kochanski & Shih [30]; Fujisaki [16][17]; Gu et al. [22]) were fully developed during this period.

1.4 Focus, accent and functional intonation

Chao made a summary and description about functional intonation. He elaborated the relationships among sentences with different focuses and their intonational performances (Professor Wu referred the focus as the emphasis or the accent at the sentential and discourse levels, and carried out some preliminary analysis [89]). It was after the year 2000 that the large-scale inspection which integrated focus and functional intonation were conducted. This will be elaborated in the latter discussion.

1.5 Mood, emotion, attitude and discourse prosody

After 2000, studies on prosody concentrated on the following aspects: emotional prosody, prosody in spontaneous speech, the relationship between prosody and syntax, discourse prosody, prosodic issues in phonetic teaching and acquisition, and relations between prosody and other modalities that have become the hot spots.

Because of space limitation, we will concentrate on introducing the intonational viewpoints of Professor Wu and other scholars as well as the state of the research on Chinese functional intonation, such as focus and discourse prosody in recent years.

2. INTONATIONS

2.1 Viewpoints on Chinese intonation from Wu and other scholars

Wu greatly expanded Chao's idea of Chinese intonation. He proposed that the surface intonation of an utterance results from three interactive factors, i.e. the original mono-syllabic tonal pattern, the poly-syllabic phrasal tone sandhi, and the sentential intonation, with the first two serving as the basic units related to obligatory tone sandhi rules and the last one as a global contour related to Contextual tone sandhi rules which can be modified by different attitudes, emotions and discourse expressiveness.

In the following part, we will start with Chao's viewpoint on intonation.

2.1.1 Chao Yuen-ren's viewpoints on tone and intonation

Wu [96] summarized Chao's contribution to Chinese tone and intonation as follows: (1) providing the way to describe Chinese tones; (2) proposing the "Five-grades", "tone-letter" system; and (3) summarizing the tone sandhi rules of Beijing Dialect and elaborating on the relationship between tone and intonation.

Afterwards, Shen [60], Cao [6], Lin [46], Cao [11], and Liu [54] successively made statements about Chao's viewpoints on tone and intonation, which can be roughly summed up as follows: (1) Chinese intonation is made up of mono-syllabic tones, neutral intonation (tone sandhi), and mood intonation, with the first two closely related to pitch and duration and the last one mostly related to four such elements as pitch, duration, intensity and voice quality; (2) Tone and intonation bear the relationship of algebraic addition, which can be expressed by the famous theory of "the small waves riding on top of large waves"; (3) The rubber effect of intonation, which produces the up-and-down shift as well as the expansion and depression of the pitch range, is used to express various intonations through the "expansion and compression of pitch range and duration". Further, logic intonation depends on stress and intonation while emotional intonation lies in the voice quality, irregular stress (or weak stress), pitch and speed of the whole phrase; (4) Sentential intonation consists of four parts: pre-head, head, nucleus, and tail; (5) Pitch range modification is adopted to describe the form and function of Chinese intonation; (6) The proposition of the direction and methods to study Chinese intonation.

Moreover, Chao described two kinds of boundary tones: simultaneous superposition and successive superposition, which are considered to be the outstanding embodiment of the relationship between Chinese tone and intonation. When some special attitudes are expressed, the boundary tones in interrogatives are obviously in successive superposition; this phenomenon is supported by Gu's experiments on the successive pattern of the boundary tone in Cantonese [22].

Chao Yuen-ren is the first linguist who studied Chinese intonation thoroughly. He gives a penetrating description about Chinese intonation with his sensitive ears and the perspicacious thinking in the 1920's and 1930's. His achievements are still beyond praise today.

2.1.2 Wu Zongji's viewpoints on tone and intonation

Wu proposed that Chinese, as a tonal language, is quite different from the non-tonal languages. As far as "tone" is concerned, there are lexical tones and sentential tones which are normally called "intonation". For the tonal patterns of phrases (basic units), some are governed by regular rules, while others are compounds of several tones. These are always considered to be the bottleneck of phonetic research. According to the argumentation in physics, no matter how complex the changes are, there must be a cause; nothing comes out of thin air. Although variables in phonetic sounds are complicated, there must be a reason. Taking tone for granted, no matter how many variations there observes, it is always the result of interdependent and interplayed "three conditions" (or "three levels"): the first one is the condition of articulatory physiology and articulatory acoustics which does not belong to phonetics, we will not deal with the psychology here; the second condition is the word and sentence structure, which belongs to the field of grammar; and the third is the condition of diachronic and synchronic phonetic evolution, belonging to the field of phonology.

2.1.2.1 Basic units

The intonation of Mandarin is composed of some basic contours, including the "Tone" of mono-syllabic contour, "Phrasal Tone-Sandhi" of the poly-syllabic phrase and "Phrasal Contour", specifically, "Phrasal Contour" consists of phrases of immediate constituents or non-immediate constituents.

2.1.2.2 Obligatory and Contextual Tone Sandhi

Tonal variations in the Mandarin sentential level are classified into "Obligaory tone sandhi" and "Contextual tone sandhi". The tonal pattern of phrase composes the basic unit of tone sandhi which forms the "underlying tonal contour" of a sentence. These basic units together make up the sentence tone, which is realized as the "surface tone contour". "Surface tone contours" are various and complex, and it is very difficult to specify the models and rules to cover them. A given utterance may contain not only the complex obligatory tone sandhi from the perspective of phonetics, grammar and phonology, but also the optional tone sandhi related to logic mood, emotional mood, acoustic features of tone, intensity and rhythm, etc. Rules should be formulated through analyzing the underlying basic units rather than the "surface tone contour".

> *Obligatory Tone Sandhi*: caused by the interdependent and interplayed tonal combinations.
> [Manner]: co-articulation, unidirectional assimilation, bi-directional assimilation
> [Rules applied]: "Gangplank rule", "Domino rule" and "Phonological rules".

(1) "Gangplank rule" is the tone sandhi rule in phonetic co-articulation (also physiological "Gangplank rule"). Tonal onset is not only affected by the voiced or voiceless of the syllable initial but also assimilated by the previous tone. The previous tonal offset is assimilated by the following one as well.

"Gangplank rule" can be applied to all the analysis of phonetic pitch variation as the transitional part between two syllables (excluding phonological tone sandhi), no matter what their grammatical constructions are (Wu [90]).

(2) "Domino Rule" refers to the rule that generalize the successive tone sandhi phenomenon for the grammatically immediate constituents in priority. In certain conditions of phrasal tone sandhi, it can be found that a surface contour is derived from the underlying contour in several steps. These kinds of tone sandhi are carried on in successive steps: one after another, just like the Domino phenomenon. When a surface contour in an utterance can not be explained by general tone sandhi rules in the above mentioned part, the Domino rule might be taken into account. For instance, in a phrase of more than three syllables, the tone sandhi always happens for bi-syllabic immediate constituents in the first step, and then assimilates or dissimilates with other syllables. The more syllables there are, the more steps there will contain.

(3) Polarization rule refers to the extreme tonal changes caused by diachronic phonology.

1) Rules of transposition of basic registers of phrasal contours

Wu carried out substantive acoustic analysis on four functional intonations: declarative mood, imperative mood, interrogative mood and exclamative mood. He noted that the phrasal contours are quite consistent in patterns and ranges (figure 1). Their basic registers can be changed to meet the intonation modifications, resembling the change-key in music composition. Thus, phrasal tone-group in different moods is in compliance with the "Transposition of Basic Registers" rule and the "Tone Sandhi" rule for "Neutral tone" or "Weak Stress" in sentences.

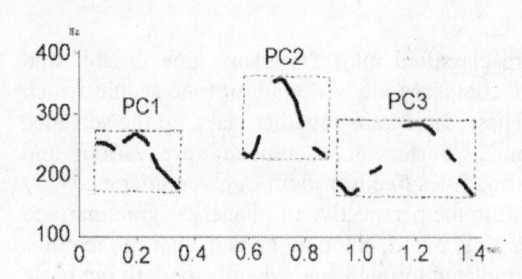

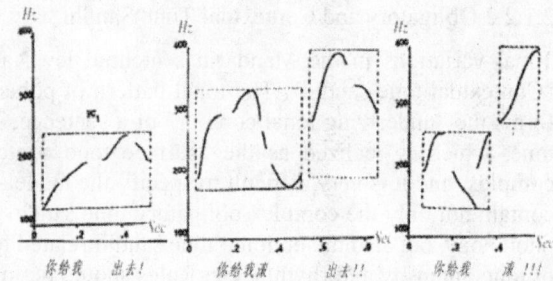

Figure 1: Wu's intonation model: Phrase PC1, PC2 and PC3 have conservational tonal range in musical calibration and are transposed by different change keys determined by attitude.

Figure 2: Tonal contour of utterances "ni3 gei3 wo3 chu1 qu4", "ni3 gei3 wo3 gun3 chu1 qu4" and "ni3 gei3 wo3 gun3".

2) Mood, Emotion and Discourse Intonation

Prosody of an utterance not only correlates with phonetics, grammar and phonology; it is more concerned with the context of semantics and pragmatics. Prosodic analysis can not be implemented in isolation; the context should be taken into account.

In declarative sentences, logical foci can exert intonational prominence, and the ranges of register transposition are in accordance with the speaker's habit and usually limited within one octave. However, for interrogative or declarative sentences, in addition of the logical prominence, attitudinal prominence takes a leading part, and the ranges of register transposition are determined by the extent of speaker's mood or emotion, which may be enlarged more than one octave.

Through analyzing imperative utterances with angry emotions, Wu demonstrated how emotional intonation can be explained through rules of "Obligatory Tone Sandhi" and "Contextual Tone Sandhi".

> *"Contextual tone sandhi"* for sentential and discourse intonation
> [Context]: interrogative, imperative, logic accent, emotional accent
> [Rules Applied]: conservation of toneme, transposition of basic registers of phrasal contours, variation of tonal range, compensation of prosodic features

In the three utterances in Figure 2, the speaker's emotion runs up step by step; the pitch and intensity follow up correspondingly. The first utterance is within the pitch range of an octave. The pitch of the second goes up 8 St (semitones), while the range width only goes up 2 St. In the third utterance, although the pitch can not go up much more, the range width changes greatly, amounting up to 19 St, thus showing that the three features of prosody are complementary to each other. Furthermore, the obligatory tone sandhi rule is applied for three low tone characters "ni3 gei3 wo3" in each utterance, while also obeying the discourse prosody. For the first phrase, the three low tone characters, as a part of a five-syllabic utterance, must follow five-syllable prosodic rule. However, according to the initial part of this three-utterance discourse, they follow the discourse prosody as well. This rule will also be applied for the second and third utterances.

These step-by-step changes, from basic unit to larger unit, lead to totally various surface tonal contours (bottom up method). Only by peeling the super crust phenomenon layer by layer, for example using the "Domino Rule" analysis strategy, can we find the truth. Firstly, the immediate constituents should be picked up, and then "Gangplank Rule" is applied. Secondly, according to the three level restrictions from the perspective of phonetics, grammar and phonology, the "Gangplank Rule" can be adopted to get the tone sandhi for poly-syllabic constituents for all three utterances respectively. Then comes the third step, following the logical and emotional needs, tonal transposition or tone sandhi rules should be applied to generate the actual surface tonal contour. What appears amusing in these three utterances is that the surface tone contour can be accounted for only when nearly all the obligatory and contextual rules of tone sandhi have been applied.

Wu illustrated the rules of intonational changes in discourse by comparing F_0 variations of two phrases in four parallel sentences of a modern poem (Figure 3-1; 3-2). Grammatically, these two phrases are different in that, the former one belongs to the "possessive pronoun", possessing the nouns that follow it; the latter belongs to "amplified adverb" by modifying the following adjective. The four utterances are depicting the people's hero, thus they are full of the feeling of praise, and the degrees of tonal transposition and range are determined by both reading and praising, submitted to the rules of discourse prosody. Pronouns and adverbs have played the role of expressing logical and emotional accents, with the prosodic variables of nouns and adjectives consequently being rather crippled.

In Fig. 3-2, the pitches of phrases "shi4 na4 yang4 de0" in the first three utterances go downwards steadily, forming a declining slope; but in the fourth one, it goes up suddenly. The pitch of "ta1 men2 de0" in sentence No. 2 is relatively high. Though it does not form a slope as the examples of No.1 and No.2 in "shi4 na4 yang4 de0", its range is quite narrow with only 3 St. At the same time, its rhythm is shorter than all the neighboring sounds, thereafter, it sounds weaker and causes a prosodic declination between the previous and following sentences. This inflectional discourse prosodic trend formed a sequence of utterances which can be found in either the rhythm of poems, lines in painting, or tunes in music. This phenomenon resembles what Shen Yue (a poem in Liang dynasty) wrote about prosodic variation in phonology: "Within one slip, prosody is different; between two sentences, melody is varied."

3) Rules of Compensation among prosodic features

According to our analysis on sentential contours of Standard Chinese, there is no doubt that tone is the main subject of prosodic features. However, in the sentential intonation, tones can not be well-done solely without the complements of the other two features, i.e. when a tone is elevated or descended in an utterance, the intensity of the syllable will accordingly be emphasized or weakened, but not vice versa. However, the function of the duration in a sentence is not weaker than that of the tone. Therefore, when the tone-range of a word is restricted under certain conditions, the lengthening of the duration may take the compensative role to fulfill the quantitative needs of the utterance. Thus, the compensatory relations among the three prosodic features are shown as follows:

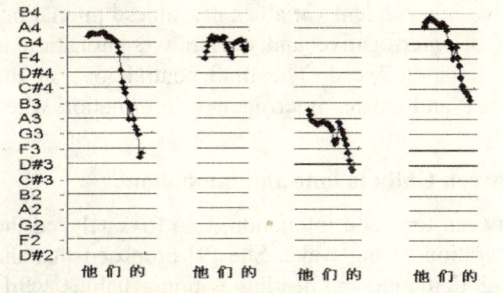

Figure 3-1: F_0 curves of the phrase "ta1 men2 de0" in a four-sentence poem.

Figure 3-2: F_0 curves of the phrase "shi4 na4 yang4 de0" in a four-sentence poem.

(1) High/Low of tone →←Long/Short of duration (one way or two ways)

(2) High/Low of tone → Strong/Weak of intensity (one way)

(3) Long/Short of duration →←Strong/Weak of intensity (one way)

2.1.2.3 Cognitive exploration on the commonness and relations between discourse prosody and other artistic expressions

"There are various natural ways or modalities to express our thoughts, e.g. 'cursive script', especially 'highly cursive script' in calligraphy, 'water ink', in particular 'spirit-drawing' in painting, and spoken languages in words, especially the emotional or attitudinal intonation."

In Wu's article "Calligraphy and Utterance Consanguinity — relations between cursive calligraphy and intonational rules" [99], he discussed the issue whether there contains commonness or relations between cursive brush-pen moving and grammatical structure. He found that cursive calligraphy grammar and Chinese tonal rules are totally consistent with grammatical relations.

2.1.3 Shen Jiong's viewpoints on intonation

Shen [60] put forward the "Top-Bottom Lines" theory to investigate the different functions of the top lines and bottom lines to express meanings and moods. He suggested that the intonation contour is produced by regulating a set of pitch ranges and the tonal contour is due to the pitch changing in the tonal range. Intonation has a modification effect for the tonal range whose variation exerts the quantitative change of the tonal contour. The variation of the top line and the bottom line of the pitch range composes the cue to the intonational pattern formation. Top line variation is triggered by semantic related prominence variation, while the variation of the bottom line is related to the rhythmic structure.

2.1.4 Xu Yi's viewpoints of tone and intonation

Starting from the Chinese tonal combination pattern, Xu Yi conducted detailed studies on segmental co-articulation and then he proposed the PENTA (Parallel Encoding and Target Approximation) model (Xu [107][109]). The key hypothesis of the PENTA model is that speech coding is realized by transmitting multiple communicative functions in parallel through encoding schemes that specify the values of the parameters to control the articulatory process of target approximation. Target approximation is a fundamental articulatory mechanism, whose controlling parameters (target, range, strength, duration) are the basic units of coding of communicative functions. Layers of information are coded concurrently through target approximation. "A target is an underlying goal specified in terms of ideal articulatory/acoustic patterns. A target can be either static or dynamic, and either simple or a composite and it has both positional and velocity specifications. The composite target consists of multiple positional and velocity specifications."

2.1.5 Lin Maocan's viewpoints on tone and intonation

Based on AM theory, Lin [47] noted that there are two independent variables in Chinese intonation: pitch accents and boundary tone. The information of interrogative and declarative intonation is carried over by the boundary syllable of the final prosodic word. The final neutral tone in the unmarked "yes-no" question changes to a stressed one and carries interrogative information when met with an interrogative mood.

2.1.6 Cao Jianfen's exploration on the relation between Chinese tone and intonation

In order to examine the super-positional relation between tone and intonation, Cao [6] analyzed the basic framework of Chinese intonation and the generation of big wave. She [9] proposed that the production of the tone lies in the pitch rising, lowering, flattening and bending within syllables, while intonation is generated from the comparison of the rising and falling of the pitch register among syllables in utterances.

2.2 Comparison of viewpoints on intonation

2.2.1 Modeling construction

Superposition view: With tone exiting above intonation, it is like big waves superposed by small ripples. The two can co-exist, and they are in the relation of an algebraic addition. Just like when the neutral tones are put on an elastomer, the value of each tone would be changed accordingly with the stretch of the elastomer. Fundamental frequency departures from the baseline following the "accent command and phrases command", then it gradually returns to the baseline, and finally the F_0 deviation caused by the two commands is added to each other in logarithm and constitute the intonation of an utterance (e.g. Chao [13][14]; Gårding [20][21]; Fujisaki & Gu [18]; Shen [61]; Wu [90][93][97]; Lin [45];Cao[6][9]) .

Linear view: Intonation of the entire sentence comes from linear connection of the local stressed pitch, the F_0 of stressed syllables and their neighboring syllables are from the result of multiple phonetic rules application, with linearity and drooping interpolation as the primary method. Further, the local ingredients are in linear distribution (pitch accent, phrase tone and boundary tone), while the overall tendency comes from local ingredients (i.e. declination comes from the multiple times of down-step effect, Lin [47]).

Parallel view: Xu [101][102] noted that the pitch of a given utterance deserves a variety of expressional functions, which are independent of each other and have their own effective means of performances. Tones, including the neutral tone, are achieved through the pitch target synchronizing with syllables while the focus and new topic of conversation is complemented through the adjustment of the local targets. Various communicative functions are coded in parallel at the same time in F_0. Overall contours come from various factors in mutual independence, and there is no unified, form-defined overall intonation pattern.

2.2.2 Basic units of construction

Chao proposed that Chinese tone and intonation consists of the mono-syllabic tone, neutral tone (tonal sandhi) and mood intonation. And Wu pointed out that the phrase tone contour is the "basic unit", which includes bi-syllable, tri-syllable, quardi-syllable, five-syllable and six-syllable combinations of different tones. Shen Jiong maintained that there are four basic elements, namely, pre-head, head, nuclear and tail. However, Xu Yi reckons that components of intonation are defined by communicative functions, and the encoding units of intonation components are the controlling parameters of the Target Approximation Model.

2.2.3 Viewpoints of overall intonation and boundary tone

There are different views on whether intonation is displayed on the entire utterance or only the final part; and opinions also differ slightly in regard to which part of intonation can be referred as boundary tone.

2.2.3.1 Overall utterance intonation

Luo and Wang [59] preferred that "mood intonation refers not only to the intonation of a particular word; it can exhibit throughout the entire utterance" with the final word showing especially significant performances.

Shen [60] Jiong proposed that intonation is formed by modifying the pitch register within a series of tone ranges; the top-bottom lines of pitch are adjusted separately.

In regard to the algebra additional relation between tone and intonation, Cao [5] proposed that this relation is not restricted to the superposition of tone and boundary tone at the end of phrase and utterance; it runs throughout the whole utterance. In contrast, intonational modulation on the tonal register is mainly reflected in the latter part of the utterance.

Wang & Ruan [86] examined the acoustic features of intonation with five kinds of interrogative and declarative sentences. They argued that intonational contours of interrogatives and declaratives are different from the beginning of the nucleus to the least extent.

2.2.3.2 Viewpoints of boundary tone

Chao [14] proposed that the ending intonation of an utterance manifests on the last several syllables. He said that declaratives are usually in normal intonation, while there is a declination trend at the end of a longer sentence, with the last several syllables showing even lower in pitch.

Xu [104] preferred that intonation is particularly shown on the last stressed syllable in an utterance. Hu [24] pointed out that the ending intonation refers to the part from the last stressed syllable to the end of an utterance.

Wu Zongji [92][95][98] adopted [BG] and [ED] to re-examine the boundary tones. He confirmed the existence of boundary tones in Chinese, "it is the syllables that locate at the initial and final positions of the intonational group". When studying the contextual tone sandhi in mood intonation, he said, "The general trend of the ending pitch in declaratives is going down slightly". When the final content words can not be unstressed, for instance, a rising tone syllable such as "hu2" dwells at the final position of a declarative sentence and it can not be read as a low-falling tone, however, it usually presented as a low-level tone, which is lower than its corresponding tone. Results of experiments demonstrated that the intonation of interrogatives (marked interrogatives) can be realized by rising the ending pitch register while keeping their tonal contour unchanged, whereas all the other basic units keep completely the same as those in the declarative. If there is any interrogative particle at the end of a question (unmarked interrogative), such as "ma0", the intonational pattern of the whole utterance resembles that of the declarative one, which shows no pitch rising at the end of the utterence.

Lin [47] insisted that boundary tone is the last stressed syllable of the prosodic word of the phrase.

2.2.4 Relationship between Tone and Intonation

Chao Yuen-ren is the first scholar who discussed the relationship between the Chinese tone and intonation. He proposed that tone and intonation can co-exist in parallel, and they are in the relation of algebraic addition. "There are at least two types of tonal additions, i.e. simultaneous addition and successive addition." For simultaneous addition, he explained it as follows: "If an upswing of a sentence coincides with a rising tone, the result will be higher than usual. If a falling intonation coincides with a rising tone, the rising tone will rise in less magnitude or be exhibited at a lower register than the first part of the sentence." He also summarized some formula for successive superposition, 55:=56, 35:=36, 214:=216, 51:=513 (for rising); 55:=551, 35:=351, 214:=2141, 55:=551(for falling), etc.

Hu [24] who observed different views and proposed that no matter what kind of intonation it is, the tone would always keep its citational form. If the tone changes to another one, it would transform to another syllable as well. "Intonation of Beijing dialect (ending intonation) is a kind of phonetic phenomenon beyond the scope of tone; the relationship of tone and intonation are not in the superpositive addition". He also reckoned that the intonation of Beijing dialect is different from that of non-tonal languages.

Wu [94] confirmed Chao's description about different ways of superposition, and summarized Chao's remarks on tone and intonation as follows: the representative means of tone is tonal contour (curve), and the function is to express meanings; while for intonation, the representative way is the pitch register (basic tone), the function is to express attitudes or emotions. Meanwhile, he advanced that the scope of tone covers word tone and phrasal tonal sandhi as well, and all these basic units "keep their citation tones", and "do not change their tonal patterns (curves)". Intonation is only the register variation of the basic tone (voice), thus generally having no significant effect on the tonal contour. As for Wu's understanding on Chao's "algebra addition", he took the algebra superposition as the average pitch registers superposition of tone and intonation.

Shen [60] noted that intonation is a kind of pitch modification consisting of a series of tonal ranges variations, while tone is a kind of contour sliding in the pitch range and intonation can regulate the tonal range. The variation of tonal range manifests in the quantitative variation of the tonal contour, and the top and bottom lines of the tone are adjusted respectively by the intonation. He also put forward that the tone, tone sandhi and intonation are not directly related to the intonation.

Lin [47] considered that the interrogative intonation is produced as the result of the moderate increase in the slope of F_0 contour of the boundary syllable and the moderate rising of the pitch register at the starting and ending points of the boundary syllable; while the generation of the declarative intonation is due to the moderate decreasing of the slope of the F_0 contour of the ending syllable and also the pitch register of the starting and ending points of the boundary syllable.

Shih [65] described two kinds of views on the relationship between tone and intonation: one is that they have no significant correlation, so the deviation in the F_0-generating model can be neglected; the other is that the two are related. And, it is essential for the F_0-generating model to clarify the circumstances under which they are correlated and the degrees of correlation between them. She considered that the accent degree related to the narrow focus or the prosodic intensity is the major factor which leads tones to exert influence upon intonations, thus the degree of the influence can be controlled by prosodic intensity.

2.2.5 The nature of tonal co-articulation

There are two different views on the nature of tonal co-articulation.

The nature of co-articulation is assimilatory and symmetric in two directions: Shen and Lin [63] argued that the tonal co-articulation is similar to the segmental co-articulation and its nature lies in assimilation. Besides, co-articulation influences the whole syllable: not only on the onsets and offsets of the tones, but also on the whole tone. Tonal co-articulation is also conducted in two directions. In contrast, it differentiates from segmental co-articulation in the way that their effects are two-way symmetrical, specifically, the anticipatory effect resembles that of the carry-over effect. Tonal co-articulation only changes the F_0 value rather than the direction of F_0 movement and it is only applied in two adjacent tones. Lin & Yan [51] presumed that, the differences of the disturbance aroused by tonal co-articulation on the onsets and offsets of each syllable are larger than the discrepancy of other parts. In regard to the direction of tonal co-articulation effects, it is unidirectional. There is a certain pattern for the disturbance of F_0 with tonal co-articulation. Tonal co-articulation effects are constrained by the word stress patterns and they are also influenced by the speaking rate of words and phrases.

Anticipatory and carry-over effects differ in both magnitude and nature: Xu [105] conducted research on the tonal patterns of bi-syllabic constituents and he found that anticipatory and carry-over effects differ in both magnitude and nature. Carry-over effects are mostly assimilatory which also exhibits greater magnitude of effect than the anticipatory ones. Further, based on the new definition of co-articulation, Xu [109] suggested that the mutual influence between tones cannot be seen as co-articulation.

2.2.6 Domain of tone sandhi

The study of tone sandhi in Mandarin mainly concentrates on the pronunciation of successive tone3 sandhis. Lu Zhiji proposed the concept of "tone sandhi domain", which demonstrated that within the identical tone sandhi domain, the application of rules may start from the underlying level, with the direction from left to right. When the structure of tone sandhi does not coincide with the rhythm of the speech, the tone sandhi rules would follow the speech rhythm.

Shen [60] considered that the disposal on rhythm can determine the elasticity among syllables. Tone sandhi happens in the successive tone3 sequences only when they are closely connected in rhythm. Shih [64] pointed out that the foot formed by direct components is the obligatory tone sandhi domain, whereas prosodic boundaries of other higher levels can block the tone3 sandhi process, and meanwhile, tone-sandhi is also influenced by other factors, such as speech rate, etc.

Kuang & Wang [31] demonstrated that the tone3 sandhi happens prior in the smallest rhythmic units and it does not spread over the boundary of intonational phrases. The authors confirmed that the motivation of successive tone3 sandhi is due to the pitch dissimilation, rather than the duration compression within the rhythmic unit. In this way, they certified that there are two aspects concerning the prosody of the Beijing dialect, i.e. "pause" and "tone-sandhi"; and each prosodic unit of different hierarchies is mainly determined by the degree of pausing.

3. FOCUS AND FUNCTIONAL INTONATION

Focus is the semantic centre of a sentence and is the core content the speaker expects to convey. Focus can be represented through syntactic, semantic and pragmatic ways, whereas the phonetic method is even more important to mark the focus. Xu Liejiong once pointed out that "like many other Indo-European languages, English also adopts phonetic means as the major way to present the focus. According to the intrinsic linguistic features of specific language, we have various strategies to make some constituents more prominent than others, such as emphasizing and lengthening it to some extent, raising or lowering the intonational contour, or combining these two ways".

Focus is usually defined based on intonation. It realizes through intonational prominence in the prosodic aspect. If a certain word or phrase is accented, the word or phrase can be taken as bearing focus (Wang & Yang [80]). There are two independent but complementary aspects for describing the focus features of a kind of sentence: 1) which part of the sentence bears focus? and 2) when the focus is identified, how the sentential accents are distributed? (Jia Yuan et al. [27])

Study on Chinese functional intonation mainly concentrates on the interrogatives. Different types of interrogatives bear different intonational patterns. Since there are biases on some basic problems in Chinese intonation, scholars have various views on the intonational features of Chinese interrogatives. An essential issue is whether there is an interrogative structure or not. Hu [24] and Jin [29] shared the same idea: the high tone (H-tone) is used at the boundary of the "yes-no" question without any interrogative structure and other kinds of interrogative sentences can observe both H-tone and L-tone. Wu assumed that the intonation of the interrogative sentence with interrogative structure resembles that of the declarative sentence.

Taking "yes-no" questions without interrogative structure as examples, scholars' views can be generalized into the following aspects: 1) the sentence final position adopts H-tone to express interrogative mood which is supported by Hu Mingyang and Jin Song; 2) the pitch of the sentence ending position in the interrogatives is rised and the whole coutour of sentence shows up-going tendency; 3) the major difference between the intonation of the interrogative sentence and the corresponding declarative one is: for the former one, the contour behind the nucleus gradually falls down and the "Top-line" rises to some extent; for the latter, the "Top-line" behind the nucleus immediately falls down and the "Bottom-line" drops. This phenomenon is supported by Shen Jiong; 4) Lin Maocan assumed that the difference can only be obtained from the boundary tone; 5) the interrogative mood starts from the focus (nucleus) and the high point of the ending position in the interrogative sentence is higher than that of the declarative one, which is supported by the research results from Liu & Xu [55] and Wang & Ruan [86].

3.1 Focus, stress and functional intonation

Wu [88] treated the influence of focus upon intonation as the grammatical tone sandhi in the sentential level. "Tonal changes may differ when speakers intend to express different emphasis; however, the surface grammatical structure remains intact. It demonstrated that although the characters, words, sentences and grammatical structures are identical, the tonal changes would be various in speech, furthermore, potential semantics can also be manifested through the tonal changes. He compared tone sandhi patterns among focused, declarative and interrogative sentences, where tonal patterns keep stable in accelerated speech, and tonal contour tends to lose its citation tonal features and become a level tone for those of un-emphasized parts. How listeners decode the intention of the utterance? It belongs to the psychological and physiological study. He summarized the relation between tone and intonation in Mandarin as follows:

Intonation={(basic units ← programmer constrain) ← attitudinal or mood effect} ← speech rate

Liu & Xu [55] investigated question intonation in Mandarin by taking the role of focus into consideration. They found that the focus obtained the same pitch range modification in questions as in statements, i.e. expanding the pitch range of the focused words, suppressing (compressing and lowering) that of the post-focus words, but leaving that of the pre-focus words largely unaffected. When the effects of focus (as well as other functions also potentially present) were controlled by subtracting statement F_0 contours from those of the corresponding "yes-no" questions, the different curves resemble exponential or even double-exponential functions. An interaction between focus and interrogative meaning is in the way of the pitch rising by the question which starts from the focused word.

Lin [47] found that the interrogative sentences show different intensities, without any contexts, namely, strong interrogative, weak interrogative, transitional tone, continuing output and statement. To change the slope or register of a boundary tone would generate interrogative mood, declarative mood and transitional tone.

Yuan et al. [114] & Yuan [115] analyzed the differences between the Chinese declarative and interrogative intonations with the Stem-ML Model and found that there are two mechanisms, i.e. the whole pitch curves of interrogative sentence are raised, and the prosodic strength values at the interrogative boundary are larger. The phrasal tones of declarative and interrogative sentences deserve parallel relation. The boundary tone is not necessary for these two intonational models. He denied the function of boundary tone in the declarative and interrogative mood.

Hu [23] investigated the prosodic realization of the interrogative words in the wh-questions, "yes-no" questions and echo-questions in Mandarin. He noted that the focused components of sentences are represented by pitch accents in the phonetic level. The results are not in favor of the duration and intensity correlated with the difference between the focused and the non-focused constituents.

Xiong & Lin [103] examined the pitch features of the ending particle word "ma0" in the "yes-no" questions. The results show that the "yes-no" questions have the identical type of boundary tones and the pitch is realized in the feature of {H} or {Raised}; the positions of the focus have no substantial impact on the boundary tone, furthermore, the changes of the tones in the sentences also have no fundamental influence on the boundary tone. Therefore, the final boundary tone in Mandarin is an intonational pitch feature independent of the focal accents and the tones; it bears stable pitch representation as well.

Boundary tone is the core factor to distinguish the declaratives and the interrogatives (Sun [66]). Final pitch is realized by combining boundary tone with the final syllabic tone, moreover, the pitch feature is realized in the intonational tier through an expanding rule, and this feature is the essential basis to estimate the sentential types in Mandarin. In contrast to the declarative sentence, pitch difference of interrogative sentence exists not only between the boundary tones, but also between the syllables preceding the boundary tone.

Shen [62] put forward that there are three basic intonational types in Mandarin. Each intonational type is corresponding to a different sentence pattern. However, she did not pay any attention to the boundary tone.

Gao [19] discussed the acoustic features of the imperative intonation in Chinese in the way of comparing the imperative and declarative intonations. She explained that the intonational type can be illustrated through the adjustment of top-line and bottom-line.

Zhou [116] dealt with the intonational patterns of Hong Kong Cantonese. The phenomenon of intonational downdraft can be presented in the natural intonations and it is especially obvious in the declarative sentences. The intonational patterns of other sentence types are mainly manifested through the F_0 of the final syllable.

Cao [10] proposed that there are nucleus unit patterns in the Chinese intonation, in which the distribution rules of nucleus accent present stable and recursive cues. Just as the tone which can be classified into High, Middle and Low, the F_0 variation values among syllables can also be divided into these three statuses. Different nucleus units adopt different variation values to make tones or syllables more prominent.

For the study of unmarked exclamatory intonation, Chen [12] found that the strong stress and broad tonal range are the most important two elements in the configuration and perception of exclamatory sentence. For imperative sentences, Lu [57] found that the durational distribution in the pitch accent bearing phrase is an essential factor in distinguishing the imperative sentence from the declarative one. The tonal combinations and the stress patterns of the prosodic phrase form the commanding intonation. The most important feature of this kind of sentence lies in the relationship between the boundary tone and the adjacent pitch accent.

Jiang [28] suggested that Chinese intonation has "intonationeme"(just as tone has toneme). Seven types of intonation are sketched out: declarative sentence, unmarked interrogative sentence, mood question, pronoun question, "yes-no" question, adverbial and alternative question.

Wang & Ruan [86] compared the acoustic features of five types of interrogatives with that of the declarative sentences and they further demonstrated the different intonational patterns among these five types of interrogatives. Their results did not support the viewpoint that the feature of interrogative intonation manifests at the boundary tone: 1) most types of interrogative sentences express the interrogative information through the overall intonation; 2) the existence of interrogative structure or interrogative mood exert some impact on the interrogative intonation; 3) there is no obvious difference in the acoustic features between the intonations with two interrogative structures and those with only one interrogative structure; 4) the difference between the interrogative and declarative sentences at least starts from the nucleus element.

Xiong & Lin [103] studied the interrogative and non-interrogative function of "ma0" as the final particle word. He pointed out that the modal word "ma0" is not the specialized interrogative particle and it does not bear interrogative mood; the reasons why interrogative and declarative sentences with final modal word "ma0" can be distinguished is due to their intonational features rather than the final modal "ma0".

Jia, Xiong and Li [26] examined the effect exerted by focal accents on sentential pitch through the acoustic and perceptual experiments. The fundamental unit applied to describes these effects is the underlying tonal target, H or L, and in this manner to observe the pitch performance. Jia , Ma and Li [27] further proposed that the effect of focus in Standard Chinese is sensitive to the metrical structure, i.e. the metrically stronger position observes greater magnitude of pitch and durational changes.

Chen [15] investigated the relationships among the stress, syllabic duration and tonal realization in Mandarin and she summarized that the realization of tones in Mandarin is the main representation of the pragmatic information.

3.2 Pitch declination and down step

Xiong [102] analyzed the pitch patterns of bi-syllabic constituents in Mandarin. When the tonal pitch feature of the bi-syllabic in Mandarin presents as "...H...L...H..." sequences, the H tone behind the L tone would have an obvious dropping phenomenon, and it is considered as "Down-step Effect". The down-step effect can be adopted to explain some regular abnormal phenomena in the pitch pattern of bi-syllabic word-combinations in Mandarin both simply and precisely. The pitch value on each tonal position is adjusted by the tonal feature (i.e. "H" and "L") and all kinds of pitch adjustment trigger effects (e.g. "Down-step Effect") on the tonal pitch feature.

Wang & Li [85] obtained the pitch-declining patterns of prosodic phrase and intonational phrase with the application of the prosodic analytical tool SFC. The slope of the declining curve gradually decreases with the increase of the amount of syllables and the curve of declination is not linear but exponential.

Wang [78][79] found that, after the prosodic phrase and intonational phrase boundary, the reset of the lowest F_0 has a systematic change, while the highest F_0 controlled by the stress are relatively free.

Wang and Chen, et al.[76][77] argued that the pitch declination appears in most intonational phrases, and the pitch reset of bottom-lines would take place at the intonational phrase boundary for the sentence consisting of several intonational phrases.

Huang, Yang and Lü [25] pointed out that the bottom lines of Chinese prosodic phrases present a regular declining phenomenon. The declining amplitude of subjective prosodic phrases is more obvious than that of the predicative prosodic phrases. The slope of bottom-line is in an inverse proportion to the phrasal length. There is an articulatory planning for prosodic phrase.

4. DISCOURSE PROSODY

The above has introduced the discourse prosodic study conducted by Wu Zongji. He proposed that the transposition of phrases and the expansion of range are restricted by the discourse types, which is also subject to the rules of contextual prosody. The function to express logic and emotional stress is basically transmitted by the pronouns and adverbs, so that the prosodic variables of nouns and adjectives are decreased comparatively.

Tseng & Lee [72] established a hierarchical discourse prosody framework named as HPG (Hierarchy of Prosodic Phrase Group) which accounts for discourse prosody organization and association. The layered HPG prosodic units from the bottom to the upward hierarchy are: the syllable, the prosodic word, the prosodic phrase, the breath group and the multiple phrase group. After a series of investigation [71][72][73][74][75], Tseng argued that the discourse prosody context provides the information of discourse planning, within-paragraph phrase association and between-paragraph topic change. Global discourse prosody context is a crucial factor for speech communication. She emphasized that the phonetic research on prosody would take a new point of view on phonetic units, research methods and research foci. The unit larger than simple clause must be taken into consideration. With respect to research methods, it is not appropriate to employ a kind of micro-method from bottom to up and only focus on those smaller units, whereas the macroscopically "top-down" research perspective would also be adopted.

Li & Zu, et al.[41] investigated the effects of speech rate on Chinese discourse prosody, which covers the perspective of prosodic structure, duration, F_0 distribution and stress placement for fast, normal and slow discourse speech. The results demonstrated that the local speech rate is closely related to the content expressed. The speaking rate effects on discourse prosody are nonlinear and need careful manipulations.

Bao [1] examined the accent distribution features in three different reading styles (lyric, critic and narrative), and in the units of sentential blocks, phrases and prosodic words. She found that the distribution of accents is different from the isolated sentence which is influenced by discourse and the reciting style.

Cao [8] found that duration varies with the discourse prosody. The syllabic lengthening can be divided into three types: pre-boundary lengthening, post-boundary lengthening and the accentual lengthening, which are cooperative and complementary with each other to express the structural information of the whole discourse.

Wu [87] systematically and vividly depicted the tone-ranges and all types of tone-patterns of the basic tone in discourse with the traditional ancient "Jiu Gong" diagram. With the register and the speech rate as two coordinates, she got a "3×3" "Jiu Gong" matrix. The acoustic features of discourse can be shown at different positions in the "Jiu Gong" matrix,

Li & Yang [42][43] explored the effect of the correspondence between accentuation and information structure on discourse comprehension and the internal mechanism of this effect. Compared to a controlled condition, inappropriate accentuation impedes discourse comprehension, but the facilitating effect of appropriate accentuation is not apparent during discourse processing; the accentuation facilitates the processing of focal words, whereas de-accentuation facilitates the processing of non-focal words. These results suggested that the effect of accentuation in discourse processing comes not only from its influence on listeners' attention allocation but also from its different ways to signal information processing.

5. PROSODY & PARALANGUAGE

Information is transmitted in various ways, besides speech sounds. It can be expressed through "oral paralanguages", such as facial expressions, actions, and gestures, etc. and also "writing paralanguages", i.e. calligraphy, fonts, and poems, etc. The exploration of the relationship among different expressional modals and the relationship between these modals and the prosodic features is not only beneficial to the cognition of our human beings but can also improving the performance of the human-machine interface system (HCI).

Li & Zhan, et al. [40] conducted a novel study on the relationship between the two modalities of speech and gesture in spontaneous conversation. They found that the speech accent is usually accompanied with stronger hand gestures while the hand and head gestures are compensatory in this case; there is no time correspondence relation between prosodic boundary and gesture boundary, whereas they have significant correlation. All their results support the "Interface Hypothesis".

Tan & Kong [69] recorded 40 broadcast texts with the EEG-EMG and RESP signals and analyzed their respiration rhythmic variations. They demonstrated that the structure of the respiration units can manifest the discourse structure; while the respiration structure can reflect the speakers' overall cognitive planning, and meanwhile, it can also express the physiological constraints. When the cognitive planning and physiological mechanisms are in conflict, a special respiration structure occurs. They [70] made a further study on breathing-reset in different types of literature-reciting and found that the breathing rhythm varies according to the types of literature.

Tao & Huang, et al. [67] conducted a perceptual analysis on friendly dialogues and put forward the concept of "Perception Vector" which consists of two dimensions: "Emotion" and "Softness". The perceptual experiment demonstrated that the degrees of friendliness and softness are positively related, while happy and angry emotions have negative relations. In addition, they found that the average F_0 values contribute in the greatest amount to emotion perception whereas the excitation strength in the LF source modal is the most related parameter to voice quality. In their another study [68],they attempt to synthesize emotional speech by using "strong", "normal" and "weak" classifications. After testing different models, such as linear modification model (LMM), Gaussian Mixture Model (GMM), and Classification and Regression Tree (CART) model, they concluded that he linear modification model gives the worst result among the three methods. The GMM method is more suitable for a small training set, while the CART method gives the best emotional speech output if trained with a large context balanced corpus.

Wang, Li & Fang [81] found that the F_0 contour can be adopted to express "happy" speech. The pitch contours of both "neutral" and "happy" speech show declination. However, the magnitude of the declination differs in the "happy" and "neutral" speech, specifically; the former one is smaller than the latter one. In addition, in contrast to the "neutral" speech, the tonal register of the prosodic word in the "happy" speech is raised. Besides that, the offsets of prosodic word are more up-going which is more obvious at the sentential final of the "happy" speech.

Li, Wang, et al.[37][39], based on an expressive dialogue corpus, made some analysis on friendly declarative and interrogative sentences. Prosodic patterns of prosodic words were statistically analyzed and compared concerning with the sentential accents. The mapping rules from neutral speech to friendly speech on acoustic parameters were achieved. They drew a conclusion that the friendliness of synthesized speech could be achieved via adjusting the perceptually distinctive acoustic parameters. Tonal pitch is the most important cue for a better expression of friendliness; only adjusting duration is effective for friendly speech synthesis. Interrogative sentences observe higher perceptual results than declarative sentences. A high boundary tone for an interrogative sentence is usually adopted by speakers to express friendly speech.

The stress pattern of expressive utterance is one of the pivotal information points for expressive speech synthesis. Li [38] claimed a kind of sentence stress-shifting phenomenon for emotional utterances. The stress shifting probability changes among different emotional states, even between speakers. No matter what the stress pattern of the neutral sentences contain, the stress tends to shift to the end of the sentences for "happy", "fear", "sadness" and "angry". The shifting probability from high to low is "angry"-"fear"-"sadness"-"happy".

Wang, Li & Fang [84] investigated the F_0 jitter of the neutral speech and emotional speech, such as "happy", "fear", "sadness", and "angry". Jitter is divided into two components, e.g. Random Jitter and Deterministic Jitter, they further modeled jitter in these two aspects by GMM.

The information of paralinguistic and non-linguistic phenomena in the spontaneous speech are of crucial importance, which express the speaking style and convey the speaker's emotion and attitude. They are referred as non-verbal information, such as breath, silence, laughing and crying, etc.

Yuan & Li [112][113] examined the relationship between the para-linguistic and non-linguistic phenomena and the expression of the emotion and attitude. They take the breath /silent pausing segments as the example to investigate the relationship between the acoustic features and the breath/silent segments (including intensity and duration) from the aspects of the emotional valence, emotional activation and other factors. Perceptual test demonstrated that the insertion of breath or some "abnormal pausing" segments in the synthesized speech give more naturalness and expressiveness.

Discourse markers mainly refer to the elements to mark discourse cohesion and to convey the exchanging information in the spontaneous speech (i.e. the discourse components without particular meaning in the spoken speech: "en4" ,"e0", "a4", "zhe4 ge0", "na4 ge0", "ran2 hou4") and the non-verbal approaches such as nodding, gestures, etc. Yin [111] systematically studied the discourse markers of "en" and "a", from four aspects: discourse function, discourse turns, emotional psychology and phonetics, which is useful for spontaneous speech recognition, synthesis and understanding.

6. ACKNOWLEDGEMENTS

Some Chinese scholars and my colleagues suggested that we should make a general review on the Chinese prosody researches in recent years, for there are so many concepts and achievements from the aspects of phonetics and speech sciences, some are identical but some are ambiguous. For example, some claimed that there is final lengthening while others not.

Therefore, apart from introducing Professor Wu's great contribution to Chinese prosodic research, I intend to enumerate various viewpoints and achievements. However, it's far beyond my ability, and due to the limited space, I only mentioned part of the research, even excluded some of Professor Wu's works on segments in Chinese.

Great thanks are dedicated to Prof. Lin Maocan, Prof. Cao Jianfen and Dr. Xu Yi for their comments and reviews, special thanks are given to my colleague, Wang Wei, and our students, Jia Yuan, Xu Hongmei, Wu Jing for their revising and editing work.

REFERENCES

[1] Bao, M.Z. 2004. *Stress distribution in discourses with different read style*. MA thesis, ZheJiang Univ.
[2] Cao, J.F. 1986. Analysis on Neutral Tone Syllable in SC. *Applied Acoustics*, Vol. 4.
[3] Cao, J.F. 1994. The effects of contrastive accent and lexical stress upon temporal distribution in a sentence. *Proc. of ICSLP1994*, Yokohama, Japan.

[4] Cao, J.F. 1995. Basic Duration Pattern of Sentence in SC. *Chinese J. of Linguistic,* Vol. 7.
[5] Cao, J.F. 2002. Rhythm of spoken Chinese: linguistic and paralinguistic evidence. *Proc. of ICSLP2000.*
[6] Cao, J.F. 2002. The interplay between Chinese tone and intonation. *Studies of the Chinese Language,* Vol.3.
[7] Cao, J.F. 2004. Tonal Aspects in Spoken Chinese: Global and Local Perspectives. *TAL2004,* Beijing.
[8] Cao, J.F. 2005. Syllabic Duration Variation vs. Prosodic Structure. *NCMMSC2005,* Beijing.
[9] Cao, J.F. 2008. Speech Variations: Generated Mechanism and Communicative Significance. *Proc. of PCC2008,* Beijing.
[10] Cao, W. 2006. Nuclear Intonation Unit. *Proc. of PCC2006,* Beijing.
[11] Cao, W. 2007. Chao Yuen-ren's Contribution to Chinese Intonation Studies. *Would Chinese Teaching,* Vol. 4.
[12] Chen, H. 2006. Unmarked Exclamatory Intonation of Chinese. *Proc. of PCC2006,* Beijing.
[13] Chao,Y.R. 1933. A preliminary study of English intonation and its Chinese equivalents. *BIHP Supplement,* No.1.
[14] Chao,Y.R. 1968. *A Grammar of Spoken Chinese* .University of California Press.
[15] Chen, Y. 2006. Durational adjustment under corrective focus in Standard Chinese. *Journal of Phonetics* 34, 176-201.
[16] Fujisaki, H., Hirose, K. 1982. Modeling the dynamic characteristics of voice fundamental frequency with applications to analysis and synthesis of intonation. In: Fujisaki, H., Gårding, E. (eds.), *Preprints of Papers, Working Group on Intonation, the 13th International Congress of Linguists,* Tokyo, 57-70.
[17] Fujisaki, H. 1988. A note on the physiological and physical basis for the phrase and accent components in the voice fundamental frequency contour. In: O. Fujimura (ed.), *Vocal Fold Physiology, Voice Production, Mechanisms and Functions.* New York: Raven Press, 347-355.
[18] Fujisaki, H., Gu, W. 2006. Phonological representation of tone systems of some tone languages based on the command-response model for F_0 contour generation. *Proc. TAL 2006,* La Rochelle, 59-62.
[19] Gao, M.S. 2001. Experimental Studied on Chinese Imperative Intonation. *Proc. of the 5th National Phonetics Conf.* , Bejing.
[20] Gårding, E. 1985. Constancy and variation in Standard Chinese tonal patterns. *Lund University Working Papers 28, linguistics-phonetics*, 19-51.
[21] Gårding, E. 1987. Speech act and tonal pattern in Standard Chinese: constancy and variation. *Phonetica* 44, 13-29.
[22] Gu,W.T., Keikichi, H., Fujisaki, H. 2006. Modeling the Effects of Emphasis and Question on Fundamental Frequency Contours of Cantonese Utterances. *IEEE Trans. on Speech and Audio Processing,* Vol. 14, No. 5.
[23] Hu, F. 2005. A Phonetic study of prosody of Wh-words in Standard Chinese. *Studies of the Chinese Language,* Vol. 3.
[24] Hu, M.Y. 1987. Aspects on intonation of Beijing dialect. *Beijing Hua Chu Tan*. The Commercial Press.
[25] Huang, X.J., Yang,Y.F., Lü, S.N. 2005. Declination pattern of prosodic phrase. *Proc. of NCMMSC 2005,* Beijing.
[26] Jia, Y., Xiong, Z.Y., Li, A.J. 2006. Phonetic and Phonological Analysis of Focal Accents of Disyllabic Words in Standard Chinese. *5th International Symposium, ISCSLP 2006.* Springer Press.
[27] Jia, Y., Ma, Q. W., Li, A. J. 2007. Durational Pattern of Five-syllable Constitutes in Standard Chinese. Technical Acoustics, Vol.26, No.4 Pt. 2, 252-256.
[28] Jiang, H.Y. 2006. Tonemes of Chinese declaritice and interrogative intonations. *Proc. of PCC2006,* Beijing.
[29] Jin, S. 1992. Mood and intonation of Beijing Dialect. *Studies of the Chinese Language,* Vol. 2.
[30] Kochanski G., Shih C.L., et al. 2003. Hierarchical Structure and Word Strength Prediction of Mandarin Prosody. *International Journal of Speech Technology*, 6(1),33-43.
[31] Kuang, G.J., Wang, H.J. 2006. Acoustic cues of successive tone 3 sandhi at different prosodic boundaries. *Proc. of PCC2006,* Beijing.

[32] Li, A.J. 1999. A national database design for speech synthesis and prosodic labeling of standard Chinese. *Proc.of O-COCOSDA'99*, Taipei, Taiwan.

[33] Li, A.J. 2002. Chinese Prosody and Prosodic Labeling of Spontaneous Speech. *Proc. of Prosody Speech 2002*, Aix-en-Provence, France.

[34] Li, A.J. 1997. Pausing in broadcast news. *Proc.CYCA'97. Harbin Engineering Unicersity Press,* 262-266.

[35] Li, A.J. 1999. Prosodic Analysis on Spoken Dialogues for Standard Chinese. *Proc. of the 4th National Phonetics Conf.,* Beijing.

[36] Li, A.J. 2002. Prosodic features of dialogue speech in SC. *Studies of the Chinese Language*, Vol.6, 525.

[37] Li, A.J. 2005. Acoustic Analysis for friendly speech. *Studies of the Chinese Language,* Vol.5.

[38] Li, A.J. 2008. Stress Pattern of Emotional Speech. *Chinese Journal of Phonetics*, Vol.1.

[39] Li, A.J., Wang, H. B. 2004. Friendly Speech Analysis and Perception in Standard Chinese. *Proc. of ICSLP2004*, Jeju, Korea.

[40] Li, A.J., Zhan, L.G., et al. 2008. A Polite Study on the Relationship between Gesture and Speech Information in Chinese Spontaneous Speech. *Tsinghua Science and Technology,* Vol. S1.

[41] Li, A.J., Zu, Y.Q., et al. 2007. A Pilot Study on Speech Rate in Chinese Discourse. *Technical Acoustics*, Vol.26, No.4 Pt.2., 242-24.

[42] Li, X.Q., Yang, Y.F. 2005. Influence of Inconsistent Accentuation on Activation of Information During Spoken Discourse Processing. *Acta Psychologica Sinica,* Vol.3.

[43] Li, X.Q., Yang, Y.F. 2005. The Influence of Correspondence Between Accentuation and Information Structure on Discourse Comprehension. *Acta Psychologica Sinica,* Vol.1.

[44] Lin, M.C. 2001. Chinese prosodic structure and stress. *Proc. of the 5th National Phonetics Conf.,* Beijing.

[45] Lin, M.C. 2002. Prosodic structure and lines of F_0 top and bottom of utterances in Chinese. *Contemporary Linguistics,* Vol.4.

[46] Lin, M.C.2006. Chao Yuen-ren's View on Intonation and Boundary . *Proc. of PCC2006,* Beijing.

[47] Lin, M.C. 2006. Interrogative and Declarative Mood vs. Boundary Tone. *Studies of the Chinese Language,* Vol. 4.

[48] Lin, M.C., Yan, J.Z. 1980. Acoustic profiles of neutral tone of Beijing dialect. FangYa, Vol.3.

[49] Lin, M.C., Yan, J.Z., Sun, G.H. 1984. Phonetic study on bisyllabic words with normal stress. *FangYan*, Vol.1.

[50] Lin, M.C., Yan, J.Z. 1990. Neutral tone and stress in SC. *Language Teaching and Research,* Vol.3.

[51] Lin, M.C., Yan, J.Z. 1992. Co-articulation pattern of Quadra-syllabic words and phrased in SC. *J. of Acoustics* , Vol.6.

[52] Lin, M.C. 2004. Production and Perception of Boundary Tone in Chinese Intonation. *Proc. of TAL2004.*

[53] Lin, T. 1984. About tone perception. *Linguistic Collations of Lin Tao.* The Commercial Press.

[54] Liu, L.L. 2007. Reviewing the Chinese Prosodic Research in the Past 80 Years. *Linguistic Research,* Vol.2, Iss. 103.

[55] Liu, F., Xu, Y. 2005. Parallel Encoding of Focus and Interrogative Meaning in Mandarin Intonation. *Phonetica,* 62, 70-87.

[56] Liu, X.Q. 2006. Acoustic feature of Chinese foot boundary. *Proc. of PCC2006,* Beijing.

[57] Lu, J.L. 2006. Profiles of Chinese commend intonation. *Proc. of PCC2006,* Beijing.

[58] Lu, J.L., Wang, J.L. 2005. On defining "qingsheng". *Contemporary Linguistics*,Vol.2.

[59] Luo, C.P. 1981. *Outline of general phonetics(PuTongYuYinXue GangYao),* The Commercial Press.

[60] Shen, J. 1992. A pilot study on Chinese intonation. *Linguistic Research*, Vol.4. Iss. 45.

[61] Shen, J. 1994. Chinese Intonation Construction and Categorical Patterns. *FangYan,* Vol. 3, 63-70.

[62] Shen, X. 1989. *The Prosody of Mandarin Chinese.* University of California Press.

[63] Shen, X.S. and Lin, M.C. 1991. Concept of tone in Mandarin revisited: A perceptual study on tonal coarticulation. *Language Sciences,* Vol. 13, Iss. 3-4, 421-432.

[64] Shih, C.L. 1997. Mandarin third tone sandhi and prosodic structure. In: Wang Jialing and Norval Smith (eds.), *Studies in Chinese phonology*. Berlin: Mouton de Gruyter, 81-123.

[65] Shih, C.L. 2004. Tonal Effects on Intonation. *International Symposium on Tonal Aspects of Languages: Emphasis on Tone Languages*, Beijing, China.

[66] Sun, N.H. 2006. *Pitch Features of Tone and Boundary Tone and Their Realization Rules*. PhD. Dissertation, Institute of Linguistics, CASS.

[67] Tao, J.H., Huang, L.X., et al. 2006. The Friendliness Perception of Dialogue Speech. *Speech Prosody 2006*, Dresden, Germany.

[68] Tao, J.H., Kang, Y.G., LI, A.J. 2006. Prosody conversion from neutral speech to emotional speech. *IEEE Transactions on Audio, Speech, and Language Processing*, Vol. 14, No. 4, 1145-1154.

[69] Tan, J.J., Kong, J.P. 2006. Pilot study on the breathy rhythm patterns for news reading. *Proc. of PCC2006*, Beijing.

[70] Tan, J.J., Kong, J.P., Li, Y.H. 2007. Breath resetting in different read discourses. *Proc. NCMMSC2007*, HuangShan.

[71] Tseng, C.Y. 2006. Fluent Speech Prosody and Discourse Organization: Evidence of Top-down Governing and Implications to Speech Technology. *Speech Prosody 2006*, Dresden, Germany.

[72] Tseng, C.Y., Lee, Y.L. 2004. Speech rate and prosodic units: Evidence of Interaction from Mandarin Chinese. *Proc. of Speech Prosody 2004*, 251-254.

[73] Tseng, C.Y., Chang, C.H. and Su, Z.Y. 2005. Investigating F_0 Reset and Range in Relation to Fluent Speech Prosody Hierarchy. *Proc. of NCMMSC2005*, Beijing.

[74] Tseng, C.Y., Chang, C.H. 2007. Pause or No Pause? — Prosodic Phrase Boundaries Revisited. *Proc. of NCMMSC2007*, Huangshan.

[75] Tseng, C.Y., Su, Z.Y. 2008. Discourse Prosody Context — Global F_0 and Tempo Modulations. *Proc. of Interspeech 2008*.

[76] Wang, A.H., Chen, M., et al. 2003. Ptich declination of intonational phrasein SC. *Proc. of the 6th National Phonetics Conf.*, Tianjin.

[77] Wang, A.H., Chen, M., Lu, S.N. 2004. Chinese pitch declination study based on speech corpus. *J. of Acoustics* 29(4), 353-358.

[78] Wang, B. 2002. *Perceptual study on prosody*. PhD. Dissertation, Institute of Psychology, CAS 2002.

[79] Wang, B., Yang, Y.F., Lü, S.N. 2005. Acoustics clues to the boundary of big information unit in discourse. *J. of Acoustics* 30(2), 176-183.

[80] Wang, D., Yang, Y.F. 2004. An Advancement in Studies on the Relationship between the Focus and the Accent in Natural Language. *Journal of XianXi Normal Univ.*

[81] Wang, H.B., Li, A.J., Fang, Q. 2005. "F_0 Contour of Prosodic Word in Happy Speech of Mandarin". In: Tao, J.H., Tan, T.N., Picard, R.W.(eds.), *Affective Computing and Intelligent Interaction, First International Conference*.

[82] Wang, H.J. 2004. On the Metrical Type of Modern Standard Chinese — A Type Based on Looseness. *Linguistic Sciences*, Vol.3.

[83] Wang, J.L. 2002. OT and tone sandhi in Tianjin Dialet vs. neutral tone. *Studies of the Chinese Language*, Vol.4.

[84] Wang, L., Li, A.J., Fang, Q. 2006. A Method for Decomposing and Modeling Jitter in Expressive Speech in Chinese. *Proc. Speech Prosody 2006*, Dresden.

[85] Wang, T.Q., Li, A.J. 2005. F_0 Pattern of Prosodic Word Analysis by Using SFC. *Technical Acoustics 2005*, Vol.24.

[86] Wang, Y.J., Ruan, L.N. 2005. Phonetic study on interrogative intonation in SC. *Proc. of NCMMSC2005*, Beijing.

[87] Wu, J.M. 1999. Chinese JiuGong Tone Matrix. *Proc. of the 4th National Phonetics*, Beijing.

[88] Wu, Z.J. 1981. Experimental phonetics and linguistics. *Linguistic Research*, No.1

[89] Wu, Z.J. 1982. Rules of Intonation in Standard Chinese, Reprints of Papers for the Working Group on Intonation. *Proceedings of the 13th International Congress of Linguists*, Tokyo, Japan.

[90] Wu, Z.J. 1988. Tone-sandhi Patterns of quadro-syllabic combinations in Standard Chinese. *Report of Phonetic Research. Institute of Linguistics, Chinese Academy of Social Sciences.*

[91] Wu, Z.J. 1990. Basic contour patterns of intonation of Standard Chinese. *Essays in Honor of Professor Wang Li.* The Commercial Press.

[92] Wu, Z.J. 1993. A new method of intonation analysis for Standard Chinese Frequency transposition processing of phrasal contours in a sentence. *Report of Phonetic Research. Institute of Linguistics, Chinese Academy of Social Sciences.* also 1996, In: G. Fant et al. (eds.), *Analysis, Perception and Processing.* Elsevier Science B. V.

[93] Wu, Z.J. 1994. Further experiments on spatial distribution of phrasal contours under different range registers in Chinese intonation. *Proc. of ICSLP*, Yokohama, Japan.

[94] Wu, Z.J. 1995. Predictability of different attitudinal intonation in Standard Chinese. *Proc. of the 13th ICPhS*, Vol. 2, Stockholm, Sweden.

[95] Wu, Z.J. 1996. The design of Prosodic Labeling Text for the phonetic synthesis of Standard Chinese, *Proc. of the 3rd National Symposium on Phonetics.* Beijing Broadcasting Institute, Beijing.

[96] Wu, Z.J. 1996. Chao Yuen-ren's contributions to the study of the tones of Chinese. *Journal of Tsinghua University Philosophy and Social Sciences,* No.13.

[97] Wu, Z.J. 1997. A new method of Standard Chinese intonation processing based on the relation between tone and melody. *Collected Essays Dedicated to the 45th Anniversary of the Institute of Linguistics, CASS.* The Commercial Press.

[98] Wu, Z.J. 2000. From traditional Chinese phonology to modern speech processing — realization of tone and intonation in Standard Chinese. *Proc. of ICSLP 2000*, Beijing.

[99] Wu, Z.J. 2003. The same source between Chinese calligraphy and speech — the relationship between cursive script and Chinese intonation rules. *Chinese Teaching in the World*, No.1.

[100] Wu, Z.J. 2004. *Linguistic Anthology by WU Zongji.* The Commercial Press.

[101] Xiong, Z.Y., Lin, M.C. 2003. Prosodic features of "a"(啊) and their conversational communicative functions. *Proc. of the 6th National Phonetics Conf.*, Tianjin.

[102] Xiong, Z.Y. 2005. Downstep Effect on Disyllabic words of Citation Form in Standard Chinese. *Proc. of NCMMSC2005*, Beijing.

[103] Xiong, Z.Y., Lin, M.C. 2003. "Ma0" as an interrogative or an un-interrogative modal word. *Proc. of NCMMSC2003*, Xiamen.

[104] Xu, S.R. 1999. *Pu Tong Hua Yu Yin Chang Shi.* Language Literature Press.

[105] Xu, Y. 1997. Contextual tonal variations in Mandarin. *Journal of Phonetics* 25, 61-83.

[106] Xu, Y. 2004. Transmitting tone and intonation simultaneously — the parallel encoding and target approximation (PENTA) model, in *International Symposium on Tonal Aspects of Languages — with Emphasis on Tone Languages.*

[107] Xu, Y. 2005. Speech Melody as Articulatorily Implemented Communicative Functions. *Speech Communication* 46, 220-251.

[108] Xu, Y. 2006. Speech prosody as articulated communicative functions. *Proc. of Speech Prosody 2006*, Dresden, Germany, SPS5-4-218.

[109] Xu, Y. 2007. Speech as articulatory encoding of communicative functions. *ICPhS XVI*, Saarbrücken.

[110] Yan, J.Z., Lin, M.C. 1988. Phonetic analysis on trisyllabic words in SC. *FangYan*, Vol.3.

[111] Yin, Z.G., Li, A.J., Wang, X. 2007. Phonetic study on "ng, a" type of discourse markers in dialogue of standard Chinese. *Technical Acoustics,* Vol.26, N0.4 Pt.2., 248-251.

[112] Yuan, C., Li, A.J. 2007. The Pause in Expressive Speech. *Proc. of NCMMSC2007*, Huangshan.

[113] Yuan, C., Li, A.J. 2007. The Breath Segment in Expressive Speech. *Computational Linguistics and Chinese Language Processing,* Vol. 12, No. 1, 17-32.

[114] Yuan, J.H., Shih, C.L., Kochanski, G. 2002. Comparison of Declarative and Interrogative Intonation in Chinese. *Proc. of Speech Prosody 2002*.
[115] Yuan, J.H. 2004. Perception of Mandarin Intonation. *Proc. of ISCSLP 2004,* Hong Kong.
[116] Zhou, X. 2001. The Intonation Patterns in Hong Kong Cantonese. *Proc. of the 5th National Phonetics Conf.*

A FUZZY BOUNDARY BETWEEN TONE LANGUAGES AND VOICE-REGISTER LANGUAGES

Arthur S. ABRAMSON, Theraphan LUANGTHONGKUM

ABSTRACT

A pure case in which tone uses only pitch for phonological distinctions, while voice register uses only phonation type for the same purpose, is fairly rare. More often than not we see pitch combined with phonation types and other properties in phonemic tones and phonation types combined with pitch and other properties in registers. Many a language traditionally classified as one or the other seems to be more of a hybrid of the two. Furthermore, phonation type is probably a stage in tonogenesis. The worth of a sharp typological distinction is surely in doubt.

Keywords: register, tone, F_0, phonation, typology

1. INTRODUCTION

Now that some decades of instrumental and experimental work on tone languages and voice-register languages have passed, the conventional boundary between the two types turns out to be not very sharp. Tones and voice registers are phonologically relevant prosodic units typically taken to have the syllable as their domain. The frequent considerable overlap of their phonetic properties gives rise to the blurring of the boundary between the two linguistic categories.

The imprecision surely arises from the classical view of tones as expressed by Kenneth Pike [19, p. 3]: "A tone language may be defined as a language having lexically significant, contrastive, but relative pitch on each syllable." This, it would seem, continues to be the normative expectation of linguists, although such an outlook obscures e.g. the important role of creakiness and breathiness in Vietnamese, which is always taken to be a tone language [18]. It was the work of experimental phoneticians in making measurements of the major acoustic correlate of pitch, the fundamental frequency (F_0) of the voice that led to the discovery of the importance of other phonetic properties. Ilse Lehiste [14, p. 79] comments, "It is not impossible that in two words presumably differing in tone, the fundamental frequency differences may happen to be minimal, while concomitant features of intensity, quantity, or segmental quality may carry the chief distinctive burden." This concession on her part certainly speaks to the question addressed herein.

In some languages, syllables are phonemically distinguished by complexes of phonetic properties called voice registers [11]. The term was introduced by Eugénie Henderson [13] as a construct to cover such features as phonation type, pitch, vowel quality, and length, with one of them, commonly phonation type (heard as voice quality), found to be dominant. In some instances, however, in languages conventionally described as having voice registers the dominant property now appears to be pitch [1][25][2] with fundamental frequency (F_0) serving as a powerful and sufficient acoustic cue in perception. The question arises then as to whether we must treat such a language as having voice registers or as having changed to a tone language. Given the existence of phonetic properties concomitant with pitch even in languages generally accepted as tonal, it may be hard to say just when such a change has occurred.

Some of the thinking presented here has been expressed in the past but seems to have been limited mainly to circles of Sino-Tibetan and Mon-Khmer scholarship. It may be helpful to disseminate it further afield.

2. TONE LANGUAGES

Pitch-accent languages, such as Japanese and Swedish, are not considered here. Even if some scholars might argue that they fit into the category of tone languages, the distributional limiting of the accents to certain kinds of syllables renders them quite different from our frame of reference.

There are indeed languages in which F_0 heights and contours [10] underlie pitch percepts that alone are essential to the distinction of phonemic tones. For example, Mandarin Chinese and Standard Thai are generally taken to be such "pure" tone languages. That is not to say that in certain contexts there are no concomitant properties unique to one tone or another, nor that in those contexts these properties are inaudible. Rather, we mean that in such a language the dominant and pervasive carrier of tone is pitch. Such languages do present challenging problems, including rate of pitch change [30] and the constraints of coarticulation and perception [31].

There are also "phonation-prominent" tone systems [15] or "mixed pitch/phonation-type tones" [5][8], yet in an important edited book on tone [9] only one paper [4] out of nine mentions them. The category covers tonal systems in which both pitch and other properties, mainly phonation types, share in phonologically distinguishing the tones. Burmese [16][29], Vietnamese [18], and Green Mong [4][5] are examples of such languages.

Let us look briefly at Green Mong of the Hmong-Mien family. The study by Jean E. Andruski and Martha Ratliffe [5] is concerned with seven tones, focusing on the two with phonation types, which also have pitch contours. (There is an eighth "minor" tone of limited distribution.) Five of the tones on modal (clear) voice can be described as having high, high falling, mid, rising, and low falling pitch contours, as suggested by their F_0 contours. The two tones characterized by phonation type are breathy and creaky respectively. As for pitch, the low falling creaky tone and the mid falling breathy tone are rather similar to the low falling modal tone. Discriminant analysis of the authors' extensive acoustic measurements of the three tones with similar F_0 contours but differing in phonation type, showed that of all the potential acoustic cues the best discriminator for the modal, creaky, and breathy tones of Green Mong is the relative amplitudes of the first and second harmonics, a good reflex of the changes in duty cycle of the larynx. Perceptual validation of the results, presumably with synthetic speech, remains to be done. A step in that direction has been taken [6] with listening tests using tokens of natural speech to assess the relative intelligibility of the three tones.

A study has just been completed [17] of a somewhat similar situation in Tamang, a Bodic language of the Sino-Tibetan family spoken in Nepal. An elaborate and meticulous examination of the four tones of the language, combining acoustic analysis with electroglottography of the larynx, reveals here too a phonologically complex set of "tonal" contrasts. Apparently both phonation type (modal vs. breathy voice) and F_0 have the same level of importance in differentiating the four tones. That is, according to the investigators, there is no hierarchical ordering of distinctive features. With no distinctive voicing of consonants in the language, at least a minor role in differentiating tones is the occasional voicing of initial obstruents in syllables with breathy voice.

3. VOICE-REGISTER LANGUAGES

Upon first encountering languages that later became known for their voice registers, linguists, who were mostly trained in the West, must have been struck by seemingly unusual properties of voice quality in elicited lexical items. Only later after much experience, perhaps, did they also become aware of concomitant differences of pitch and other features. Even so, in such cases the empirical question remains as to whether, in the presence of an apparently salient difference in phonation type, other properties that are linked to it are themselves sufficiently salient to play a role in perception. Thus, breathy voice as a phonation type is likely to occur with a lower F_0 contour than modal voice; nevertheless, only an experimental approach can determine the relative power of these two potential cues in the perception of the register distinction. Our extensive fieldwork with Mon, for example, leads us to believe that pitch plays at most a rather minor role in differentiating its modal and breathy registers; this observation has yet to be validated experimentally. Be that as it may, we are confronted today with many languages of this type. In the Mon-Khmer family, for example, three types are commonly recognized: languages with neither registers nor tones, languages with voice registers, and languages with tones. As for the group with registers, present-day observation finds among them a state of transition toward tonal systems; for some of them it is likely that the tonal stage has been reached. A brief account of our recent studies of two Mon-Khmer languages may be illustrative here.

3.1 Suai

In a fairly recent study [1] we have been innovative in that we examined the acoustics of both production and perception of voice registers in the Kuai dialect of Suai, a Mon-Khmer language. The language is said to have two registers, modal (clear) and breathy.

The work was done with a sampling of speakers in a Suai village of northeastern Thailand. A control test with natural-speech utterances of good exemplars of the registers revealed mixed levels of perceptual acuity, ranging from mere chance to rather good identification. This left eight out of 16 listeners whose data in the later synthesis experiments could be evaluated.

The utterances of six speakers were analyzed for ratios of harmonic intensities (spectral slope), F_0 and overall amplitude contours, vowel duration, and formant frequencies. The significant factors were a greater spectral slope and a lower F_0 contour for the breathy register.

For the perception tests, five parameters of the speech synthesis program SynthWorks® were used to make combinations of variants in contours of overall amplitude and F_0, level of turbulence, duration of the open quotient of the simulated voice source, and spectral tilt. The responses showed F_0 to be the primary factor. The open quotient, physiologically relevant to spectral tilt, was also significant.

The language, at least in this village, appears to be in a state of flux. We wonder whether the register distinction is on the brink of extinction or is on its way toward a stable tonal system.

3.2 Khmu'

In a more recent paper [2], we have studied the Mon-Khmer language Khmu' in its Rawk dialect spoken in a village of Nan, a province of northern Thailand. It is also described as a language with a modal register (R1) and a breathy one (R2). We did an acoustical analysis of all the seemingly relevant properties in the recorded utterances of 25 speakers (9 men and 16 women). For the possible relevance of phonation type we measured the ratio of the relative intensities of the second harmonic (H_2), the principal harmonic of the first formant (H_{F1}), and the principal harmonic of the second formant (H_{F2}) to that of the first harmonic (H_1). These ratios are taken to be an acoustic reflex of the open quotient of the vocal folds during phonation. The essence of the results of an ANOVA of the data broken down by sex is given in Table 1.

As can be seen in the first row of the table, the men show no significant difference between the registers. That is, the acoustic evidence for a distinction between modal (clear) and breathy voice is not statistically significant. For the women, however, there is a significant difference but only for the first ratio. This is a sign that the language is undergoing change. The women, who spend most of their time in the village, are linguistically somewhat more conservative. The men, who generally work outside the village in contact with Thai and Lao speakers, no longer systematically produce two phonation types, although they may well respond to them auditorily when used by their womenfolk. It would be interesting to study the speech of young children.

Table 1: The probability p that ratios. H_2/H_1, H_{F1}/H_1, H_{F2}/H_1 are independent of voice register abridged from Table 6 of [9].

Ratio:	H_2/H_1	H_{F1}/H_1	H_{F2}/H_1
Male p	0.4566	0.0645	0.4002
df	(1,7)	(1,7)	(1,7)
F	0.621	4.806	0.802
Fem. p	0.0005	0.0106	0.4232
df	(1,15),	(1,15),	(1,15),
F	19.442	8.508	0.678

The measurements of F_0 yielded significantly different contours for all the speakers. The results, converted into pitch in semitones, are shown in the graph of Figure 1. The difference is mainly one of height.

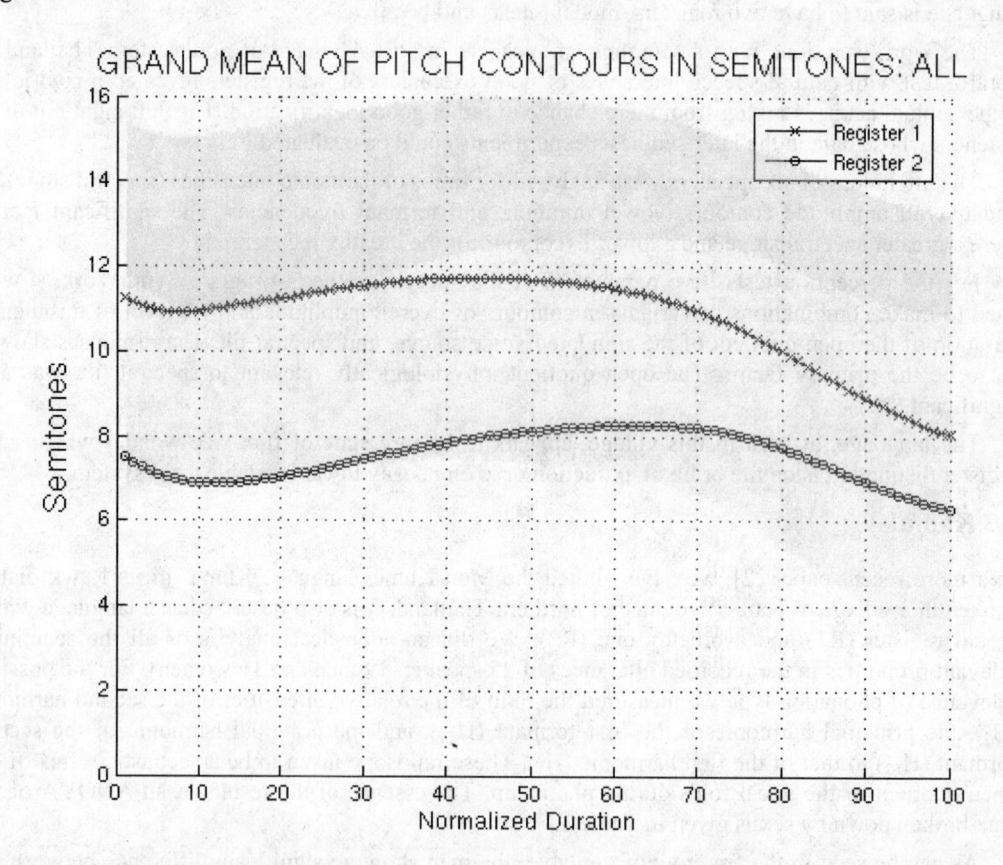

Figure 1: Normalized pitch contours averaged over the Register 1 and Register 2 utterances of 25 Khmu' speakers. The dark and lighter shaded regions indicate the standard deviations of the Register 1 and Register 2 contours respectively. (Adapted from [2])

Because of the exigencies of scheduling the running of perceptual experiments in Thailand, it was necessary to prepare the listening tests and run them before we had fully analyzed the acoustic data. Having no knowledge at that time of the significance of the harmonic ratios, at least for the women, we limited our speech synthesis to seven F_0 variants from low to high that we imposed upon a syllable that might be heard, as determined by voice register, as one member or the other of the minimal pair meaning "tooth" (R1) or "flower" (R2).

The mean responses of 29 listeners are shown in Figure 2. The stimuli rise in pitch incrementally from left to right. The categories are quite good even though neither register exceeds 90 percent identification. Perhaps the stimuli could be made a bit more natural.

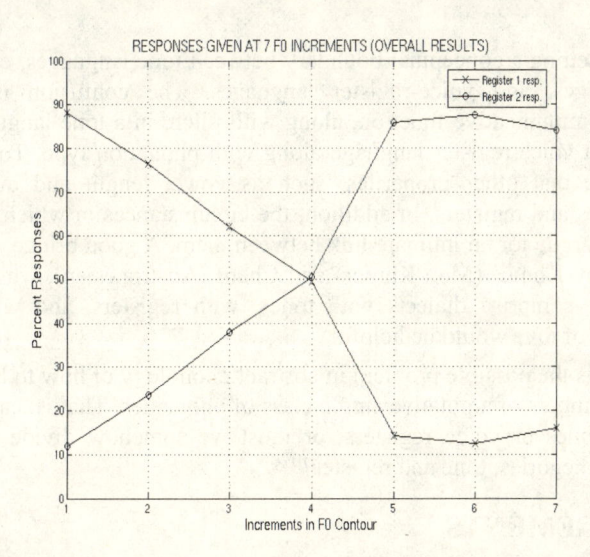

Figure 2: The percentages of Register 1 vs. Register 2 responses of 29 listeners to incremental changes in the F_0 contours of synthesized versions of the Khmu' syllable [ra˜N]. (Adapted from [2])

The contrast between the two voice registers of Khmu' Rawk is stable, although this stability floats on the surface of an underlying instability in the properties that differentiate the registers in speech production. We predict the disappearance of phonation type and the consequent dominance of pitch in both production and perception of speech. If this happens, the only reason for not calling this variety of Khmu' a tone language might be out of sentiment. Indeed, we are convinced that even among scholars there is a reluctance to depart, for a given language of interest, from a traditional classificatory nomenclature. This is perhaps illustrated by the conventional treatments of the Chong and Burmese languages. Both of them have four-way phonologically relevant prosodic distinctions. Concomitant phonetic properties make it hard to conclude whether they are tonal or register languages. Since Chong [26] is a Mon-Khmer language, the bias is to decide that it has four registers. Burmese [29], on the other hand, is a member of the Tibeto-Burmese branch of the Sino-Tibetan family, so it must be tonal.

4. DIACHRONIC OUTLOOK

Putting aside the possibility of the emergence in a language of new phonological units solely through intensive contact with another language, we see from the reconstructions of historical linguists that both tones and voice registers were apparently born in similar environments. That is, to make a long story short, the changing nature of final consonants and the loss of some, together with the loss of the consonantal voicing contrast in initial position gave rise to tones [12][15][27][28] and registers [7][8]. Other treatments with a focus on Mon-Khmer languages are to be found e.g. [20][21][22][23][24]. A critical review of the phonetic data and arguments [3] furnishes many additional references.

The classical explanation of the origin of tones was formulated by André-G. Haudricourt [12] and helpfully clarified by James Matisoff [15], who also gave us the term *tonogenesis*. Credit goes to Graham Thurgood [27][28] for revising the model and building a bridge between tone and voice register. That is, he argues convincingly that the appearance of phonation types is a stage of tonogenesis.

5. CONCLUSION

Confusion can arise in setting a conceptual boundary between tone languages, especially phonation-prominent tone languages, and voice-register languages. The confusion is heightened when phonation type has a communicative function, along with pitch, in a tone language and pitch has a communicative role in a voice-register language along with phonation type. To this must be added the at least minor role that other properties, such as vowel length and quality, may play in differentiating both tones and registers. In addition, the circumstances in which both prosodic types apparently arose would argue for an intimate link between them. A good bridge, in Thurgood's sense, may well be provided by Khmu' (Mon-Khmer) and Cham (Austronesian), which are typologically alike as languages that comprise dialects with tones, with registers, and with neither. Perhaps broadening the meaning of *tone* would be helpful.

Not to be neglected is the possible problem in abstract phonology of how to handle such complex distinctions between members of a putative single class of phonemes. That is, can we still speak of a single class of either tones or voice registers, or must we somehow divide the units in such a language between two categories, tone and register?

6. ACKNOWLEDGEMENTS

This work was supported by NIH Grant DC-02717 to Haskins Laboratories and a grant from the Thailand Research Fund to the second author.

REFERENCES

[1] Abramson, A.S., Luangthongkum, T., Nye, P.W. 2004. Voice register in Suai (Kuai): An analysis of perceptual and acoustic data. *Phonetica* 61, 141-171.

[2] Abramson, A.S., Nye, P.W., Luangthongkum, T. 2007. Voice register in Khmu': Experiments in production and perception. *Phonetica* 64, 80-104.

[3] Abramson, A.S. 2004. The plausibility of phonetic explanations of tonogenesis. In: Gunnar Fant, Hiroya Fujisaki, Jianfen Cao and Yi Xu (eds.), *From Traditional Phonology to Modern Speech Processing: Festschrift for Professor Wu Zongji's 95th Birthday*. Beijing: Foreign Language Teaching and Research Press, 17-29.

[4] Anderson, S.R. 1978. Tone features. In: Fromkin, V.A. (ed.), *Tone: A Linguistic Survey*. New York: Academic Press, 133-175.

[5] Andruski, J.E., Ratliffe, M. 2000. Phonation types in production of phonological tone: The case of Green Mong. *J. Intl. Phonetic Assoc.* 30, 37-61.

[6] Andruski, J.E. 2006. Tone clarity in mixed pitch/phonation-type tones. *J. Phonetics* 34, 388-404.

[7] Diffloth, G. 1982. Registres, dévoisement, timbres vocaliques: Leur histoire en Katouique. *Mon-Khmer Studies* 11, 1-33.

[8] Ferlus, M. 1980. Formation des registres et mutations consonantiques dans les langues Mon-Khmer. *Mon-Khmer Studies* 8, 1-76.

[9] Fromkin, V.A. (ed.). 1978. *Tone: A Linguistic Survey*. New York: Academic Press.

[10] Gandour, J.T. 1978. The perception of tone. In: Fromkin, V.A. (ed.), *Tone: A Linguistic Survey*. New York: Academic Press, 41-76.

[11] Gordon, M., Ladefoged, P. 2001. Phonation types: A cross-linguistic overview. *J. Phonet* 29, 383-406.
[12] Haudricourt, A.- G. 1954. De l'origine des tons en vietnamien. *Journal asiatique* 242, 69-82.
[13] Henderson, E. 1952.The main features of Cambodian pronunciation. *Bull. School Orient. Stud.* 17, 140-174.
[14] Lehiste, I. 1970. *Suprasegmentals.* Cambridge, Mass.: MIT Press.
[15] Matisoff, J.A. 1973. Tonogenesis in Southeast Asia. In: Hyman, L.M. (ed.), *Consonant Types & Tone.* Southern Calif. Occas. Papers in Linguistics, No. 1. Los Angeles: Linguistics Program, U. of Southern California, 71-95.
[16] Matisoff, J.A. 1999. Tibeto-Burman tonology in an areal context. In: Kaji, S. (ed.), *Cross-Linguistic Studies of Tonal Phenomena, Tonogenesis, Typology, and Related Topics.* Tokyo: ILCAA, Tokyo U. of Foreign Studies, 1-32.
[17] Mazaudon, M., Michaud, A. (in press). Tonal contrasts and initial consonants: A case study of Tamang, a "missing link" in tonogenesis. *Phonetica.*
[18] Pham, A.H. 2003. *Vietnamese Tone: A New Analysis.* New York: Routledge.
[19] Pike, K.L. 1948. *Tone Languages.* Ann Arbor: University of Michigan Press.
[20] Premsrirat, S. 2001. Tonogenesis in Khmu dialects of SEA. *Mon-Khmer Studies* 31, 47-56.
[21] Premsrirat, S. 2003. Khmu dialects: a case of register complex and tonogenesis. In: Kaji, S. (ed.), *Proceedings of the Symposium Cross-Linguistic Studies of Tonal Phenomena: Historical Development, Phonetics of Tone, and Descriptive Studies, December 17-19, 2002.* Tokyo: ILCAA, Tokyo University of Foreign Studies, 13-36.
[22] Svantesson, J-O. 1989. Tonogenetic mechanisms in northern Mon-Khmer. *Phonetica* 46, 60-79.
[23] Svantesson, J-O., House, D. 2006. Tone production, tone perception and Kammu tonogenesis. *Phonology* 23, 309-333.
[24] Thongkum, T.L. 1987. The interaction between pitch and phonation type in Mon: Phonetic implications for a theory of tonogenesis. *Mon-Khmer Studies* 16-17, 11-24.
[25] Thongkum, T.L. 1988. Phonation types in Mon-Khmer languages. In: Fujimura, O. (ed.), *Vocal Physiology: Voice Production, Mechanisms and Functions.* New York: Raven, 319-393.
[26] Thongkum, T.L. 1991. An instrumental study of Chong registers. In: J.H.C.S., Davidson (ed.), *Austroasiatic Languages: Essays in Honour of H.L. Shorto.* London: School of Oriental and African Studies, University of London, 141-160.
[27] Thurgood, G. 2002. Vietnamese and tonogenesis: Revising the model and the analysis. *Diachronica* 19, 333-363.
[28] Thurgood, G. 2007. Tonogenesis revisited: Reviving the model and the analysis. In: Harris, J.G., Burusphat, S., Harris, J.E. (eds.), *Studies in Tai and Southeast Asian linguistics.* Bangkok: Ekphim Thai, 241-262.
[29] Watkins, J. 1997. Can phonation types be reliably measured from sound spectra? Some data from Wa and Burmese. *SOAS Working Papers in Linguistics and Phonetics,* 7, 321-339.
[30] Xu, Y., Sun, X. 2002. Maximum speed of pitch change and how it may relate to speech. *Journal of the Acoustical Society of America* 111, 1399-1413.
[31] Xu, Y. 2004. Understanding tone from the perspective of production and perception. *Language and Linguistics* 5, 757-797.

HOW DO SPEECH SOUNDS VARY AND SERVE EFFICIENT COMMUNICATION?

CAO Jianfen

ABSTRACT

This paper discusses how speech sounds vary and serve efficient communication by analyzing the phonetic realization of pitch movements in context, and by reviewing the results of some former studies on segmental and suprasegmental features of spoken Mandarin Chinese. The main data were obtained from the utterances of the speakers in a multi-speaker discourse corpus. Obtained results clearly show that locally observed pitch variations, just like segmental and other suprasegmental variations, are not only related to the interaction with their neighbors, but also sensitive to their position distribution and status discrimination, both within the same domain and between different domains in the prosodic hierarchy. The results also indicate that phonetic realizations of speech sounds in a discourse are mainly rooted in the natural mechanism of speech production and its communicative function. Therefore, speech sound variations can be classified roughly into two types in terms of their generating mechanism: one is the local effect, driven by the factors operating within a small scope of the utterance; the other is the global effect, driven by the factors operating in whole scope of the utterance. Specifically, the former type of variation is mainly caused by the physiological constraints of articulation, and is governed by the co-production mechanism between neighboring segments or syllables; the latter type depends on the global organization of the utterance, and is governed by the pre-planning mechanism in speech production. These two aspects, however, do not interfere with each other, but simultaneously implement and organically unify through the same segment or syllable. They are both based on the essential requirement of achieving an efficient communication. Consequently, speech variations of the utterance are the foundation stone in keeping the life-force of natural speech.

Keywords: speech variation, phonetic realization, generating mechanism, efficient communication

1. INTRODUCTION

The phonetic realizations of speech sounds, i.e. the specific articulatory modality and the corresponding acoustic shape of the sounds, are varied in real speech. Many studies have pointed out that sound variations are closely tied to the mechanism of speech production. Thus, reinforcing the investigation in this aspect will not only improve our knowledge on the rules of speech variations, but also help us to understand the deep operational mechanism of natural speech, and to enrich the theoretical treasury of phonetics in general. On the other hand, one of the serious problems faced in speech technology, especially in automatic speech recognition, is to overcome the variability of segmental and suprasegmental features in natural speech. Consequently, it has become an urgent task in phonetics to investigate speech variations and extract the related rules. As pointed out by John Local [15], "One of the 'grand challenges' we face as phoneticians is how to make sense of the phonetic detail and phonetic variation we observe in everyday talk". Thus, he proposed that "we should take seriously the possibility that the phonetic aspects of language *should in the first instance* be analyzed and understood as shaped by interactional considerations — specifically by the organization of utterance into sequences of turns."

The variations of speech sounds include segmental and suprasegmental aspects.

Segmental variations are multifold, such as assimilation, dissimilation, voicing, devoicing, centralization, laryngealization and so on. In addition, another relevant aspect of the variation, i.e. articulatory strengthening and weakening (or reduction), has attracted more attention recently. As we know, sometimes, the term used in different literatures may not be identical, and the connotation of the same term used in phonetics and phonology may be different. In fact, such diversity might reflect the different levels of speech variation due to complicated reasons. For example, coarticulation and assimilation are usually mentioned in the same breath, but it is actually in the relationship of cause and effect, in which coarticulation is the cause, while assimilation is an effect [9]. Similarly, strengthening and reduction is the basic means of modifying articulatory accuracy in natural speech; while the voicing, devoicing, centralization and laryngealization, etc. are the specific effects caused by articulatory strengthening or reduction.

The majority of segmental variations are the variations of sound quality due to articulatory strengthening or reduction. In the case of a vowel, reduction usually results in centralization and strengthening usually exhibits as the typification of lingual features. For instance, a vowel is often strengthened when in an initial position, where it may be presented with an additional fricative or a glottalized stop, the fricative occurring mostly in high vowels and the glottalized stop in low vowels. On the other hand, in the case of a consonant, the reduction is often exhibited as neutralization of the position of lingua-palatal contact and as weakening in the degree of lingua-palatal contact [4], thus resulting in voicing of voiceless consonant, disappearance of the nasal coda and substituted by nasalization of the front vowel, and so on.

Phonetic variations in suprasegmental aspects include the variations in pitch, duration and intensity. They are caused by coarticulation between adjacent segments, as well as by large-scale prosodic factors including tone, intonation, rhythm, stress, and accent in the discourse. Moreover, as for the role in perception distinction, the variations caused by prosodic factors are much greater than those caused by coarticulatory factors [25].

Compared with segmental variations, suprasegmental variations are less well studied. Therefore, it is urgent to reinforce the research, whether it is for the theoretical development in phonetics or for practical applications in speech technology.

We then discuss how speech sounds vary and serve efficient communication, by analyzing the phonetic realization of pitch movements in context, and by reviewing the results of some former studies on segmental and suprasegmental features of spoken Mandarin Chinese. The investigation focuses on the examination of pitch variations of syllables in disyllabic words, including the variations driven by local factors operating within a small scope of the utterance and those governed by global factors operating in whole scope of the utterance. Based on the results, a general discussion is given on their generation mechanism and communicative functions.

2. GENERATION OF PITCH VARIATIONS IN MANDARIN CHINESE

2.1 Generation of tonal junctures between adjacent syllables

In earlier studies, pitch variations were investigated mainly in relation to tonal junctures between adjacent syllables. Professor Wu Zongji is one of the pioneers in this field in China. During the early 80's of last century, he investigated tonal variations through systematic analysis of the coarticulatory phenomena occurring both intra- and inter-syllablic positions in Mandarin Chinese, and further indicated the generating mechanism of pitch variation at syllable boundaries [20][21]. For instance, according to Y. R. Chao [6], the tone of mid syllable in a trisyllabic word usually change from the 2nd tone (i.e. rising tone) to the 1st tone (i.e. high level tone) in the case of preceding syllable with the 1st or the 2nd tone. In fact, however, this mid-tone does not always change to a high level tone in that case, but change to a high falling tone, which is similar to a 4th tone. Professor Wu analyzed this phenomenon and found that the direction of change of the mid-tone is conditioned not only by the category of the preceding tone, but also by the category of following tone. Consequently, when it is followed by a 2nd tone or 3rd tone in a grammatically 1+2 type trisyllabic word, this mid-tone will be changed to a high falling tone, otherwise, it will be changed to a high level tone.

The significance of Wu's finding not only fully discovered the origin of the junctures between adjacent tones, but also helped further explore the rules of pitch variation in a discourse. Wu's finding enlightens people to examine more closely on the process and to find the principle of pitch variations occurring at a syllable boundary. For instance, Xu's TA theory [24] has provided a most elaborate model so far.

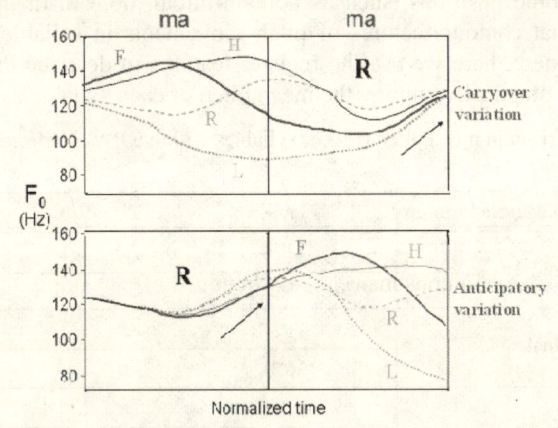

Figure 1: Nature of contextual variability (from [24])

Following Xu's theory [23], pitch target of each tone must be approximated within a syllable and reached at the end of the syllable, and there exist carryover and anticipatory variations in tonal context. Figure 1 gives an illustration of these variations.

From Fig. 1, a generating process of pitch variations at syllables boundary can be observed clearly. On the one hand, the carryover effect caused by the ending pitch target of the preceding tone can change not only the pitch at the onset of the next tone, but also the transition state from this value to its own beginning target. On the other hand, the specific pitch realization for the ending target of the preceding tone also varies delicately due to the dissimilation effect coming from the beginning target of the next tone. Specifically, when the feature of the beginning target of the next tone is low, as in the case of L (3rd) or R (2nd) tone, the ending pitch of the preceding tone will be elevated. On the contrary, it will be depressed when the beginning feature of the next tone is high, as in the case of H (1st) or F (4th) tone.

At the same time, some interesting phenomena can be observed from Fig.1. Firstly, in a certain tone, regardless of its position within the word, approximately the first one third of the tone is basically in a transition state. Obviously, it reflects a process of withdrawing from the carryover influence and of approaching to its own beginning target gradually. Secondly, only the remaining portions can match with its corresponding tone contour that represents the approximation process from its own beginning target to the ending target. At the same time, this part also bears the beginning pitch information of the next tone through the anticipatory effect, which can be seen from the different ending pitch in the case of the same rising tone followed by different tones, though the difference appears quite small and imperceptible, but it does exist in the fact. Consequently, adjacent tones are actually co-produced, and the realization of their pitch targets involves both assimilation and dissimilation.

2.2 Generation of pitch variation in a discourse

Discussion of this part is based on the pitch variation of syllables in reference to a larger scale of speech context. The speech materials for this study are the pitch realization of syllables within the disyllabic words in context. This is because a disyllabic word in Mandarin Chinese is not only a basic domain for the operation of phonological rules, such as tone sandhi and lexical stress distribution, but also the minimal context for observing the sound variation of a syllable. Therefore, studying disyllabic words in an utterance is appropriate for observing pitch variation of a syllable both in the minimal context and in a larger context. The test materials were extracted from the utterances of four speakers in a discourse corpus (ASCCD, ling.cass.cn/yuyin/product), where disyllabic words are located in different prosodic positions, such as domain-initial, domain-final, stressed, or accented positions. Considering that contour features of pitch movements in syllables are already used for lexical distinction in Chinese, here we use the register features to describe the pitch variations of a syllable in discourse, and practically employ the mean pitch of each syllable as a measure.

Table 1: Comparison in mean pitch (Hz) of syllables within a PW at different positions

PW position / syllable location	1st syllable	2nd syllable
IP initial	Av. 187.9	Av. 183.3
	Sd. 23.2	Sd. 25.6
IP final	Av. 115.4	Av. 113.6
	Sd. 16.1	Sd. 13.5
PP initial	Av. 180.0	Av. 174.4
	Sd. 31.3	Sd. 26.8
PP final	Av. 152.1	Av. 144.1
	Sd. 24.9	Sd. 15.8
Non-terminal	Av. 176.9	Av. 157.9
	Sd. 22.4	Sd. 18.8
General mean	Av. 162.5	Av. 154.6
	Sd. 33.1	Sd. 30.2

The data summarized in Table 1 represent the mean value of pitch of a syllable, calculated from the measurements of the highest point and the lowest point of each syllable within these words. The IP, PP and PW used in the table are abbreviations of intonation phrase, prosodic phrase and prosodic word respectively. Hence the figures listed in the first 4 lines show the pitch realizations of syllables in the PWs at the domain-initial and domain-final of both IP and PP, while those in the last two lines serve as references.

2.2.1 Position-determined pitch variation

Table 1 lists the specific realizations of mean pitch of each syllable within certain PW in a discourse, where extreme variations in mean pitch can be observed. Comparing the figures in the table, we find that the variations are not random, but show a systematic tendency depending on the position of the PW within the utterance and the location of the syllable in the PW.

First, the mean pitch of a syllable in the PW at domain-initial positions, regardless of whether it locates at the IP-initial or the PP-initial position, is systematically higher than that at domain-final positions, regardless of whether it locates at IP-final or PP-final position. Second, comparing with the mean value in non-terminal PWs or the general mean value of the whole utterance, the mean pitch of a syllable is obviously elevated in domain-initial PWs and descends in domain-final PWs respectively. Moreover, this tendency exists for both syllables within the PW. Third, the mean pitch of both syllables in the initial PW of an IP is higher than that of a PP, while those in the final PW of an IP is lower than those of a PP. And finally, the mean pitch of the 1st syllable is usually higher than that of the 2nd syllable in a PW, except for the case when the 2nd syllable is accented.

What is interesting is that all the pitch variations described above are matched with the corresponding prosodic structure of speech, though all the variations take place in local PWs. Specifically, (1) the mean pitch of a syllable in the domain-initial PW is systematically higher than that in the domain-final PW, which matches not only with the feature of pitch declination in the IP and PP, but also with the feature of pitch resetting at prosodic boundaries; (2) the systematic pitch difference between pre- and post-phrase boundaries matches with the feature of pitch resetting, which is one of the boundary markers in the prosodic structure; (3) the prominence of pitch of both syllables in the initial PW matches with the feature of prosodic strengthening taking place at the domain-initial PW [4]; and (4) the mean pitch of a syllable in the final PW of an IP is lower than those of syllables of PWs in all PP-final positions within this IP. This matches either with the level distinction of prosodic hierarchy and the feature of boundary tone types, i.e. it matches with the distinction between the L% feature at the end of an IP and NON-Low feature at the end of a pp within the IP.

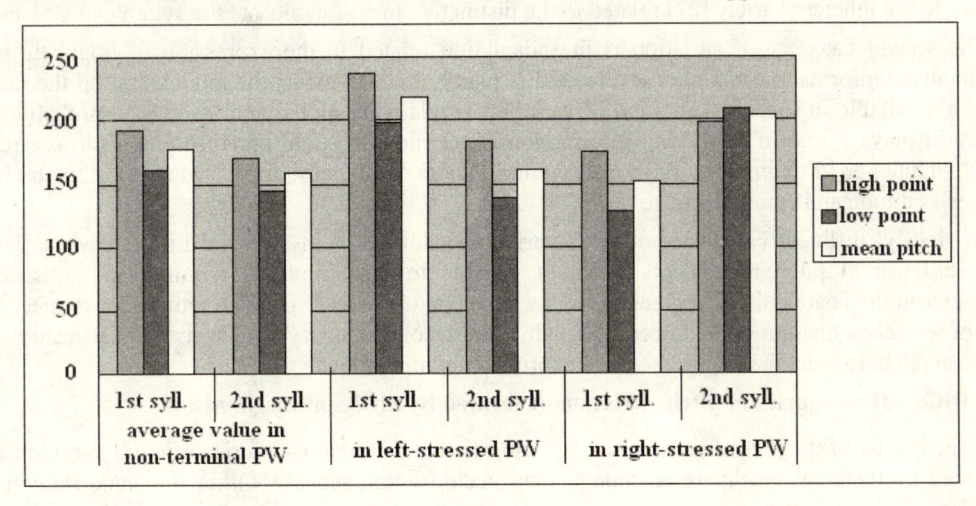

Figure 2: Comparison of pitch realization among the syllables in different types of stressed PWs

At the same time, we also find another interesting phenomenon. The mean pitch of the syllables in a non-terminal PW is close to the level of general mean, and it does not seem to conform to the rule of reduction generally taking place in this position. We suspect that it might be influenced by accentual factors in speech. To check whether it is true or not, a study was conducted and the result showed that about 20% of non-terminal PWs were stressed in the test materials. A further study was then conducted on the stressed PWs. The results are illustrated in Fig. 2, where the terms "left-stressed" and "right-stressed" indicate a difference on the degree of stress of the syllables in the PW: perceptually, the 1st syllable sounds more salient in the former type, while the 2nd syllable more prominent in latter type.

We can see from Fig. 2 that the pitch is prominent obviously in more stressed syllables. Specifically, the pitch value of the 1st syllable in a left-stressed PW and the 2nd syllable in a right-stressed PW is more prominent than that of other syllables, while that of the 2nd syllable in a left-stressed PW and the 1st syllable in a right-stressed PW is close to the mean pitch of the 2nd syllable averaged over all non-terminal PWs. Obviously, this situation corresponds to the degree of perceptual accentuation of certain syllables, and indicates that pitch realization of certain syllables in context is controlled, not only by the stress status of the PW to which they belong, but also by the degree of stress of itself within that PW.

In summary, all the variations observed in this section clearly reflect an outline of prosodic structure of the speech. Therefore, we can predict that speech variations in discourse are definitely motivated by the expression requirements for the prosodic organization of the discourse, though they appear in local words and syllables. Obviously, such manner of variation can not be an accidental coincidence, but a necessary result due to the pre-planning mechanism in speech production and the constraint of speech communication.

2.2.2 Role-determined pitch variation

On the basis of observations in the previous sections, pitch variations in Mandarin speech can be roughly classified into two main categories depending on their roles in speech and the manner of manifestation.

The first category of variation is the adaptation taking place between adjacent tones due to coarticulation, it is manifested mainly as a smooth transition between the ending pitch of previous tone and the beginning pitch of next tone, as well as the under-shoot of the tonal target of itself. This type of variation, relatively local, produces a stable pattern of pitch contour within a syllable, and belongs to the inherent variety [22] related to the distinctive tonal function of the syllable in Chinese.

The second category of variation is the adaptation related to the expression of linguistic and paralinguistic information in higher layers, and is mainly manifested as the modulation on the mean pitch of a syllable in speech. This kind of variation is relatively global and belongs to probabilistic variety. It plays a role in conveying information concerning prosodic organization, such as stress, accent, intonation, rhythm, and further discourse factors like focus, topic switching, tern taking, speaker's attitude and emotion and so on.

Obviously, different categories of pitch variation manifest themselves in different ways. They make full use of pitch movements within a syllable to meet multiple requirements in speech communication. That is, the first category utilizes the contour feature of pitch movement to meet the need of lexical distinction in the lower level; while the second category utilizes its register feature, i.e. the mean pitch, to meet the requirements of expression at higher levels.

2.2.3 Different categories of pitch variation generated by different mechanisms

From the results of the preceding sections, we can see that different categories of pitch variation are generated by different mechanisms, though they occur simultaneously within the same individual syllables.

Specifically, the first category of variation takes place between adjacent tones due to coarticulatory overlapping, and comes mainly from the "look ahead" mechanism in the lower level of speech production, while the second one is controlled by the factors concerning larger scale constraints of the discourse, and comes from the pre-planning mechanism operating in the higher levels of speech production. These two categories, however, are well-unified on the natural mechanism of speech production and driven by its function in speech communication.

In summary, pitch realization of a syllable in Mandarin speech is sensitive, not only to its adjacent tones, but also to its status and roles within a discourse. All the variations observed in individual syllables are constrained by the deep-rooted requirements of speech communication.

3. DISCUSSION: HOW DO SPEECH SOUNDS VARY AND SERVE EFFICIENT COMMUNICATION?

The factors that cause speech variations are multiple, being either internal or external. However, the ultimate factor is internal, which comes from the natural mechanism of speech production and perception, as well as the purpose of serving an efficient communication.

3.1 General mechanism of speech variation

3.1.1 Co-production of adjacent segments and biological limitation of articulators in target achieving

The natural mechanism of speech production involves following two factors in generating the varieties of speech sounds.

At first, just like the gesture overlapping during the process of athletes' handing and taking over the baton in the relay race, gesture overlapping between adjacent segments in articulation is inevitable and has been observed in real speech including Mandarin Chinese [1]. Such overlapping phenomenon is determined by coarticulatory factor, especially by the "look ahead" mechanism. It needs to introduce the interaction between one sound and its immediate neighbors, and results in the occurrence of transitions and the deviation from phonological target of the segment, so-called target-undershoot.

Next, the inherent limitation in articulation must lead to adjustment of articulatory precision in real utterance. Take vowel production as an example, as pointed out by Van Son, R.J.J.H. [18], each vowel has a unique target-position for each of the articulators. When there is ample time for the different articulators to reach their respective target positions, it will produce the ideal or canonical realization of that vowel. However, if there is not enough time and the context forces the articulators to cover relatively large distances, it will result in target-undershoot of that vowel. Such biological limitation of articulators in achieving a target also exists in tonal realization. According to Xu's model [24], contextual tonal variations are articulatorily inevitable, since all elements in speech are coded through articulation, which is limited both in time and velocity in reaching its target. Therefore, it is impossible to completely achieve every target in speech, and their real articulatory precision must be modified depending on actual requirements and constraints in a certain context.

3.1.2 Adaptation determined by specific role of the element in the utterance

It is true that the information for lexical distinction is fundamental in realizing communication, but that is not enough for an efficient communication. At least, more information related to the basic structure of speech has to be provided in order to achieve this purpose. Therefore, certain adaptations to the role of the element in the utterance need to take place correspondingly.

For instance, speaker's utterance cannot last without any break due to the requirement of perception, because perception studies have shown that listeners are sensitive to different size of chunks rather than individual syllables or words. Moreover, in the perception process, the size of speech chunk processed each time is restricted because of the limited span of immediate-memory [17] and the nature of timing control of language [12][11][2]. Hence, besides the information for lexical distinction, the information indicating both boundary and connection between different speech chunks must be provided in speaker's utterance as well. Therefore, as the markers of this role, a corresponding adaptation needs to take place naturally.

In addition, human speech is organized in a hierarchy. Hence, all the information referring to the hierarchical structure of the discourse must be provided at the same time, and the related adaptation of speech sounds must occur correspondingly.

All these indicate that natural speech is just like a complex network in which every constituent, such as a syllable or a word, stands at a certain node and is engaged in the complex relationship of the network, thus their phonetic realization must be adjusted to conform with their status or roles in speech [2][3]. Therefore, the occurring of multiple variations of speech is inevitable.

3.2 Speech variation as the adaptation to the requirements of efficient communication

What is the essential requirement of efficient communication? Van Son, R. et al. [19] provided a concise answer that speech communication is efficient if the speech signal contains enough information to be identified, and not more, because speaking is for listening [7].

Then, what does "enough information" mean?

First of all, based on the study on speech production and perception so far, we know that the information that is required for an efficient communication includes at least two basic aspects. One is needed for lexical distinction in the lower level of linguistics, the other is needed for structural expressing in higher levels of linguistics and paralinguistics, such as prosodic organization, semantic focus, modal or intonation, expression or attitude and so on. It is being realized that the latter aspect is as essential as the former in communication. Moreover, some relevant perception tests show that the latter aspect is even more important for hearing and understanding [25]. In order to meet the multiple needs with limited resources in speech communication, the individual elements need to carry both lower level and higher level information at the same time.

However, "enough information" does not mean "everything" that can be contained in an element. In terms of the organizing principle of natural speech [19], for the perception to identify a word, not all information has to be present in the word itself, and a part of it can be extracted from the context. That is to say, "enough information" does not contain the part that "can be extracted from the context". So the speakers have to estimate the ease with which the listener can understand their utterance, and adapt some aspects of their speech to strike a balance between their own efforts and those of the listener. This adaptation not only can increase the efficiency of communication, but also can lighten speaker's articulatory effort and listener's perceptual cost at the same time. Therefore, "enough information" also means that the speaker need not provide more information than they consider necessary to be understood.

3.3 Speech variation and the relationship of contradiction-unification between speech production and perception

The next question likely to be raised is: in what sense the information is necessary, and how to achieve this goal in communication? It might be helpful to realize the relationship of "contradiction-unification" between "speech production and perception".

Linguistically, there are multiple relationships of contradiction-unification in speech communication, among which the most essential one is the relation between production and perception.

3.3.1 Contradiction-unification relationship between the requirements from speakers and listeners

From the viewpoint of speech function, the basic requirement of the two parties in communication is that, on the one hand, the speaker always follows the rule of labor saving, i.e. tries to accurately convey speech information as much as possible by using articulatory resources as less as possible; on the other hand, the listener wants to listen and understand with effort as less as possible, i.e. try to receive effective information as much as possible but spend the resource of hearing and perception as less as possible.

The requirements from the two parties seem to be incompatible. However, it is unified on the same base, i. e. both sides require speech to transmit information as much as possible but spend effort as less as possible. In short, they both require speech to transmit maximum amount of information with the minimum cost. In this sense, the requirements by the speaker and the listener are unified. Thus the real contradiction is between "maximum information" and "minimum cost".

3.3.2 Contradiction-unification relation between the "maximum information" and "minimum cost"

As mentioned above, it is accordant both for the speaker and listener to require speech transmitting maximum information with minimum cost. Then, what is "maximum information" and "minimum cost"?

At first, "maximum information" does not mean every information that can be contained in a speech sound, because it is not only impossible to sufficiently achieve every target of speech sound due to the articulatory limitation in production, but also unnecessary to do so due to the psychological limitation in perception. It is well-known that natural speech is organized as a hierarchical structure, in which the syllable or words are grouped into certain size of chunks according to the needs of semantic expression [12][3]; and in perception, listeners are also sensitive to such kind of chunks, instead of individual syllables or words, this phenomenon is based on human cognitive mechanism [13]. This fact indicates that there also exist physiological and psychological restrictions in speech hearing and perception. Therefore, the information required for perception should be more related to the chunking strategy.

Accordingly, the so-called "maximum information" should be the "necessary information" that is just enough, but no more, to achieve the communication, instead of everything contained in it.

Secondly, it is also clear that the so-called "minimum cost" just means the effort expended in speech is necessary for executing an efficient communication only without redundancy. So in this sense, the "maximum information" and "minimum cost" is actually unified at the same goal, i. e. to pursue the greatest efficiency in communication.

Thus, the key point here is that how to achieve this goal properly.

3.3.3 Speech variations as proper strategy in adapting to the relationships of contradiction-unification in speech communication

All the relationships described above indicate that, for the purpose of achieving efficient communication, speakers must manipulate and adapt their speech, in order to achieve a balance between articulatory precision and perceptual distinctiveness.

To achieve this goal, the most economical and possible strategy should be: (1) to strengthen the articulation for the unpredictable part, and weaken those for more predictable part, in order to increase perceptual distinction without excess effort; and (2) to make adequate use of different aspects of the features, in order to meet different requirement by the same carrier of information simultaneously. As an inescapable result, the variations of speech sounds emerge as the times require.

Moreover, this strategy is feasible and supported by objective foundations. First, it is theoretically in accord with the rule of information distribution in natural speech, for it is commonly realized that distribution of speech information is nonlinear in both temporal and spectral dimensions, instead of averaged linearly [2][3]. Next, it is in accord with the principle of perception. As mentioned above, not all detailed features of themselves have to be heard clearly, but part of them could be extracted from the context to identify a component or a word. For example, some information related to the non-terminal components can be detected according to the context. Therefore, it is not necessary to articulate such a part very precisely, but it is possible to allow hypo-articulation, which will naturally lead to reduction. On the contrary, however, the information about terminal position or stress/accent location, and the information related to topic switching or turn-taking, as well as focus shift in discourse, are not easy to be detected. Thus, they usually need to be shown by distinctive indications through precise and even hyper-articulation, in order to ensure their prominence in perception. Consequently, it is quite natural to find the alternation between hyper- and hypo-articulation in real speech communication.

In addition, this strategy has been validated by real evidences in different languages [14], and the most powerful illustration is the articulatory strengthening at prosodic domain edges, commonly observed in many languages [16][10][8]. Generally, as we know that the information on prosodic boundary or accentual status in an utterance is relatively unpredictable, and thus needs more accurate articulation of the corresponding element to ensure enough distinctiveness for the perception; while the information on an non-terminal element is relatively predictable from the context, thus allowing reduced articulation. For example, in Mandarin Chinese, articulation of the syllables at the edges of prosodic domains shows a systematic strengthening as compared with that of non-terminal elements [4], and that is manifested by both segmental and suprasegmental parameters. Furthermore, segmental strengthening at a pre-boundary position is referred mainly to the vowels, while those at a post-boundary position are referred to the consonants. In the case of stress or accent, the lengthening of both vowels and consonants is employed in the same syllable at the same time [3]. This situation is similar to the manner of pitch variations described in section 2, and provides another instance to account for the way, by which speech sounds vary to fulfill different requirements in communication.

Accordingly, speech variation is the proper solution in adapting to the relationships of contradiction-unification existing in speech communication.

4. CONCLUSION

The results from this study indicate how pitch variation of individual syllables in Chinese ensures their lexical distinction on the one hand, and carries the information related to the interaction between adjacent tones and the organization of global discourse on the other hand at the same time. That is, the basic lexical information is distinguished by relatively stable pattern of pitch contour within a syllable, while the interaction relationship between adjacent tones is carried by coarticulatory assimilation or dissimilation occurring between syllables, and the structural information of discourse is carried through the accommodation in the mean pitch of the syllable. These results indicate that speech variation of a syllable can be used to recognize not only its lexical meaning, but also its status within an utterance. The key point is that different forms of variation carry different linguistic and paralinguistic information.

Pitch variations, just like those found in segmental and other suprasegmental aspects in Mandarin Chinese, strongly show that the exact phonetic realization of individual speech sounds must be modified in context. The ultimate motivation of these modifications is to enhance perceptual distinction with less effort in order to achieve optimal efficiency in communication. They are obliged by the demands of efficient communication, which requiring speech sounds to transmit maximum amount of information at minimum cost. To achieve this goal, the most economical and possible way is to adjust the articulatory strength of individual elements according to their specific status or roles in the utterance. The main strategy is to strengthen the articulation of unpredictable elements, such as those at domain-terminal positions or in accentual status; and to weaken more predictable ones, such as those at non-terminal or unstressed positions. Hence specific effects such as assimilation, dissimilation, voicing, laryngealization, etc., occur naturally.

Accordingly, speech sounds have to be modified at any moment and any place in order to adapt the relationship of contradiction-unification between the demands and possibilities in speech communication. In this sense, speech variation is the indispensable means in achieving efficient communication.

It is hard to imagine how speech can convey so profuse and polychrome linguistic and paralinguistic information with so contracted sound system without phonetic variations. Therefore, speech variation is the foundation stone in keeping the energy and liveliness of spoken language.

Phonetic variations of speech sounds are very complicated and sometimes even bothersome. Fortunately, however, they are not irregular but follow certain rules systematically. Anyhow, if proper information is given, the direction of variation can be predicted. Consequently, phoneticians should try to discover the variation rules, and make good use of them for both human-to-human and human-to-machine speech communication.

REFERENCES

[1] Cao, J. 1999. Comprehending of speech integration and variation from coarticulation. In: Shi, F., Pan, W.(eds.), *Recent Advances in Chinese Linguistics*. City University of Hong Kong Press.

[2] Cao, J. 1999. The rhythm of Mandarin Chinese. *The Proc. of International Workshop on the Stress, Tone and Rhythm of Spoken Chinese*. Prague, Czech; Full paper published in *Journal of Chinese Linguistics*, Monograph Series No. 17, 2001, University of California, Berkeley, USA.

[3] Cao, J.2004. Restudy of segmental lengthening in Mandarin Chinese. *Proceedings of Speech Prosody'2004*, Nara, Japan.

[4] Cao, J., Zheng, Y. 2006. Articulatory Strengthening and Prosodic Hierarchy. *Proc. of Speech Prosody'2006*, Dresden, Germany.

[5] Cao, J. 2006. Articulatory strengthening and reduction: Linguistic motivation and phonetic mechanism. *Journal of Phonetics of China*, Vol.1 (The start publication).

[6] Chao, Y. R. 1948. *A Grammar of Spoken Chinese*. California: University of California Press.

[7] Cutler, A. 1987. Speaking for listening. In: Allport, A., McKay, D., Prinz, W. and Scheerer, E. (eds.), *Language perception and production*. London: Academic Press, 23-40.

[8] Fougeron, C., Keating, P. A. 1997. Articulatory strengthening at edges of prosodic domains. *J. Acoust. Soc. Am*. 101(6), 3728-40.

[9] Keating, P. A. 1988. Coarticulation and timing. *UCLA Working Papers* 69, 1-2.

[10] Keating, P. A., Cho, T., Forgeron, C., Hsu, C. 1998. Domain-initial articulatory strengthening in four languages. *Draft of LabPhon6 paper*, August 1998.

[11] Kohno, M., Tsushima, T. 1989. Rhythmic phenomenon in a child's babbling and one word sentence. *Bulletin, The Phonetic Society of Japan*, No.191.

[12] Kohno, M., Tanioka, T. 1990. The nature of timing control in language. *Proceedings of ICSLP'90*, Kobe, Japan.

[13] Laver, J. 1994. *Principles of phonetics*. Cambridge: Cambridge University Press.

[14] Lindblom, B. 1990. Explaining phonetic variation: A sketch of the H&H theory. In: Marchal, A. (ed.), *Speech Production and Speech Modeling*. Dordrecht: Kluwer Academic Publishers.

[15] Local, J. 2007. Phonetic detail and the organization of talk-in-interaction. *Keynote talk given at 16th ICPhS*, Saarbrucken.

[16] Meynadier, Y. 2004. Gradient linguopalatal variations due to a 4-level prosodic hierarchy in French. *9th Conference on Laboratory Phonology*, Urbana-Champain, IL, USA.

[17] Miller, G. A. 1956. The Magical Number Seven, Plus or Minus Two: Some Limits on Our Capacity for Processing Information. *The Psychological Review* 63, 81-97.

[18] Van Son, R.J.J.H. 1993. *Spectro-temporal features of vowel segments*. In series: Studies of language and language use, IFOTT3. PhD. Dissertation, University of Amsterdam.

[19] Van Son, R.J.J.H., Koopmans-van Beinum, F., Pols, J.L.C.W. 1998. Efficiency as an organizing principle of natural speech. *Proc. of ICSLP'98*, Sydney.

[20] Wu, Z. 1980. Tonal variation in Standard Chinese. *Studies of the Chinese Language*, No. 6. Also appears in *The Collection in Linguistic Articles of Wu Zongji*. The Commercial Press, Beijing, 2004.

[21] Wu, Z. 1983. Tone sandhi rules of trisyllables in Standard Chinese. *The Transaction of Chinese Linguistics*, No.2, 1984. Also appears in *The Collection in Linguistic Articles of Wu Zongji*, The Commercial Press, Beijing, 2004.

[22] Wu, Z. 1997. Discussion on the Phonetics in Human-Machine Communication. *Teaching of Chinese in the World*, No.4.

[23] Xu, Y. 1997. Contextual tonal variations in Mandarin. *Journal of Phonetics* 25, 61-83.

[24] Xu, Y. 2007. Target approximation as core mechanism of speech production and perception. Invited lecture given at Institute of Linguistics of CASS, Beijing, China.

[25] Zhou, X. 2001. *A perception test to the syllables in Chinese using multidimensional method*. MA thesis, Institute of Psychology of Chinese Academy.

INVESTIGATION OF THE RELATION BETWEEN SPEECH PRODUCTION AND PERCEPTION BASED ON A VOWEL STUDY

DANG Jianwu, LU Xugang

ABSTRACT

In this paper, we investigated the relationship between speech production and perception based on vowel structures in articulatory and auditory spaces. By using a nonlinear dimensional reduction method, we extracted the low dimensional vowel structures based on vocal tract shapes and acoustic features of the vowels segmented from continuous speech in an electromagnetic articulography data corpus. The extracted three dimensional vowel structures have clear physical meanings for the coordinated dimensions. In articulatory space, the first dimension represents the tongue height, and the second one is related to the lip opening ratio, and the third dimension is curved in the space which seems to relate to vowel articulation place along the vocal track. In auditory perception space, we obtained a consistent structure with that in articulatory space. The consistent structures reflect some intrinsic relation between the articulatory and auditory spaces via the topological compatibility. The topological compatibility in the articulatory and auditory spaces suggests that an efficient mapping among the structures may be used in human speech chain in the brain, which supports the motor theory for speech perception.

Keywords: speech production and perception, vowel space, motor theory, dimension reduction

1. INTRODUCTION

How speech communicates between speech production and perception in the human brain is one of the long-standing questions. Many studies have been conducted to answer this question, but there is still no clear answer.

When a sound source is modulated by a proper vocal tract shape, speech sounds would be generated. Since vowels are the central parts of speech, the sound quality and vocal tract shape for vowels have been well investigated. In phonetic aspect, vowels are described as a distribution in a coordinate-structured space with a few dimensions related with distinctive features based on vowel articulation [1][2]. The cardinal vowel chart is a traditional way to describe the relationship between vowel sounds and the tongue positions in a typical position [3], because the tongue plays the most important role in configuring the vocal tract shape. In vowel perception space, the different vowel qualities are realized in acoustic analyses of vowels by relative values of the formants, acoustic resonances of the vocal tract. The first formant (F1) corresponds to vowel openness (vowel height), while the second formant (F2) corresponds to vowel frontness. The acoustic space constructed from F1 and F2 has a similar topology to that of articulatory space with tongue height and frontness [4]. Based on this relation, the speech communication in the brain is speculated to be a topological mapping [5].

The above observation is usually carried out on isolated vowels or the vowels in a given carrier sentence. If we adopt the same parameters on the vowels extracted from the continuous speech, the distinctive structure no longer appears in either articulatory space or acoustic space. Figure 1 shows the tongue height distribution of five Japanese vowels which were extracted from read sentences obtained using electromagnetic articulography system (see details of the data in Sec. 3.1). One can see that there are heavy overlaps among the vowels.

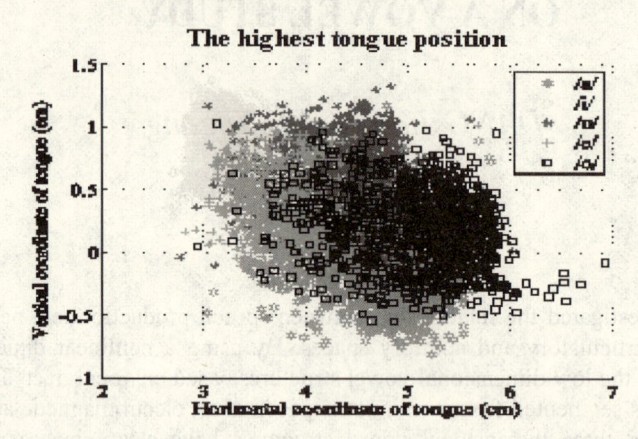

Figure 1: Distribution of five vowels using the tongue height and backness parameters

However, many studies have shown that there is a close relationship between speech production and perception [6][7][8]. "McGurk effect" is a good example to demonstrate how important the articulation for speech perception is [9]. In the experiment, they made a video by composing a sound of /BA/ to a video of the talking head that was producing sound /GA/. The subjects were asked to alternate between looking at the talking head while listening, and listening with their eyes closed. Most adult subjects think they are hearing /DA/ when they are looking at the talking head. However, they are hearing the sound as /BA/ when closing their eyes. What the experiment tells us is that subjects perceive a sound not only according to the acoustic stimuli but also using additional visual information simultaneously, which is the lip articulation. In other words, this may suggest the objects of speech perception are articulatory gestures, while some others argue that the objects are auditory in nature. Liberman [10][11] proposed a theory, the motor theory of speech perception, to explain the close relation of the speech production and perception. The essential point of this theory is that the speech sounds are perceived in terms of articulatory gestures that humans are innately able to produce.

As shown in figure 1, the traditional description could not offer a distinctive structure in the articulatory space for continuous speech. It is difficult to imagine that such tongue position based representation can be used as a reference in speech perception, especially for continuous speech. As seen in McGurk effect and learned from the motor theory of the speech perception, articulatory information is an important cue for speech perception. Therefore, a clear category organization of vowels in articulatory space should also exist in continuous speech. Since speech production and perception are co-developed in human brain during language acquisition and have a close relationship, we also speculate that there exists a similar structure in the auditory space. In this study, we are going to find such structures based on articulatory observation and acoustic measurement.

2. TRADITIONAL VOWEL SPACE EXPLORATION AND PROBLEMS

This study is going to uncover the vowel inherent structure that is not only involved in isolated vowels but also in the vowels in continuous speech. For this purpose, we must rethink the potential problems with the current researches in exploring such a kind of structure for vowels.

Descriptions of vowel articulation are a long-standing concern in phonetics. For years, there were descriptive frameworks based on linguistically and phonologically important properties of vowels such as descriptions in terms of the height and backness of the tongue (e.g. [3][12]), or in terms of the cardinal vowels of Jones [13]. Here, we question what are the problems with such studies by reviewing couple of recent researches on the structure of vowels [14][15][16].

Jackson [14] thought that the descriptions of vowels in terms of the height and backness of the tongue are felt to be perceptually motivated, even though the terminology is articulatory [14]. He used a factor-analytic model, namely PARAFAC, to analyze the tongue position using the midsagittal plan of x-ray images, where the cross-sectional width of whole vocal tract was employed except the lips. He extracted a number of factors from the vocal tract shapes of vowels, and demonstrated the relation between the factors and the tongue shapes. However, there was no clear interpretation for vowel articulation in the plane of the first factor and the second factor. Hoole (1999) focused on determining how many dimensions underly the tongue shapes that can be observed for vowel articulation, and tried to answer what their nature is [15]. He applied a hybrid PARAFAC and principal-component model on an EMA corpus of German vowels in consonant-vowel-consonant (CVC) contexts to extract the tongue configuration in vowel production. In his results, the first factor was almost corresponding to the tongue height. For the second factor, the vowel weights were heavily consonant-dependent, where almost vowels were collapsed in the median portion of the second factor. Zheng et al. (2003) analyzed three-dimensional (3D) tongue shapes during vowel production using the three-mode PARAFAC model on three-dimensional MRI images [16]. They derived the shape factors from the 3D analysis. In the vowel loading space, they showed a similar structure to that obtained by Hoole [15].

In extracting the vocal structures, the above studies employed the same analysis method PARAFAC, while used different measurements to obtain the data: X-ray picture [14], EMA data [15] and MR Images [16]. They obtained the same tendency of the tongue shape changes in varying the vowel weights of the factors. In a low-dimension (2D or 3D) description, however, the location of the vowels in the vowel loading space consisting of the factors did not show clearly intrinsic relation concerned with vowel articulation. In other words, the results in these studies did not give so much information as the description using the height and backness of the tongue [3][12].

There are two considerable problems with most of the researches in description of vowel patterns in articulatory space. The first problem is that the analysis approaches used so far is linear statistical methods, where the representative method is PCA or factor analysis (PARAFAC). The methods focus on finding a linear combination based on a few basis shapes (vectors), and explain the whole data set by data distribution variances. The second problem is that such studies so far mainly focused on the data variance, while our humans focus more on the similarity when cognizing patterns. Therefore, nonlinear properties of the articulations and similarities of the vowels are taken into account in our study.

As seen in Hoole's study, the vowel locations in the vowel loading space are sensitive to context. That may be why the studies on the vowel structure have not dealt with the vowels out of continuous speech. In this study, we will deal with these challenging issues, and attempt to extract some inherent structures from the vowels in continuous speech.

3. METHODOLOGY AND APPROACH

The vowel structure of a language is considered to be formed during language acquisition with co-development of human functions of speech production and perception. Accordingly, it can be speculated that the vowel structure may have the same or similar topology in both articulatory space and auditory space. In extracting the vowel structure, therefore, we focus on not only the articulatory aspect but also the auditory perception aspect, which is clearly different from studies above.

In human cognition, the similarity of the objects is the basic criterion. It is possible for human to use the similarity in categorizing the vowels. In terms of the similarity concept, the data patterns belonging to the same category should distribute in a neighboring region in its intrinsic hidden space. For this reason, we use the similarity for categorizing vocal tract shapes and acoustic data of the vowels, respectively. The neighboring relationship of the categories can be maintained in the low dimensional space after dimension reduction using this measure. In contrast, the factor analysis or PCA is to find the dimensions to keep most of the data distribution variance but does not guarantee the inherent structure. For a data set lying in a nonlinear space, therefore, they are not valid any more since it can not explore the nonlinear relationship of degrees of freedom of the speech production system or the intrinsic degree of freedom of the data set [17].

Based on the above considerations, we proposed a similarity measure for representation of the underlying data set, and find a low dimensional space that is able to keep their similarity relationship. For a general description, the data sample of a vowel is represented as one discrete vector. Thus, all collected data vectors X_i form a data set X, $\mathbf{X} = \{X_i \in \mathbb{R}^n, i = 1, 2, ...N\}$ where N is the data number. The similarity of the data vectors is defined as a non-linear distance between each other as described in (1).

$$w_{ij} = exp\left(-\frac{\|X_i - X_j\|^2}{\sigma}\right) \quad (1)$$

where X_i and X_j are i-th and j-th data vectors respectively. σ determines the diffusion effect of the heat kernel [18]. w_{ij} is the similarity distance between the data vector X_i and X_j. By connecting each vector to its neighbors in the data space, a similarity graph is constructed based on the similarity measurement. Each data vector is regarded as a vertex on the graph, and two neighboring vertices are connected by an edge. The similarity of the vectors is defined as a heat kernel on the graph [18]. Figure 2 illustrates a graph with five vertices, where the edges show their relation and the values on the edges are the distance obtained from (1).

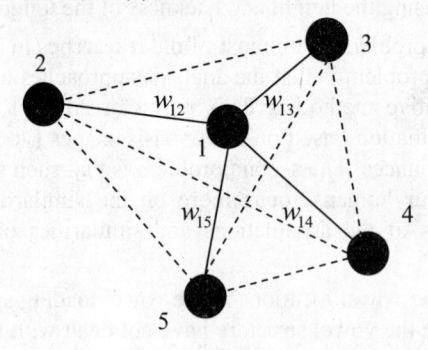

Figure 2: Construction of similarity graph of vocal tract shapes

Thus, we can obtain a similarity distance matrix (or weighting matrix) for the graph with a matrix as:

$$W = [W_1, W_2, W_3, ..., W_i, ..., W_N]$$
$$W_i = \left[w_{i,i(1)}, w_{i,i(2)}, w_{i,i(3)}, w_{i,i(4)}, ..., w_{i,i(k)} \right]^T \quad (2)$$

where $i(k)$ is the k-th nearest neighbor of the vertex i. W is a sparse matrix defined by the similarity relationship (neighboring relationship) of the data set. In constructing the discrete graph, for any vertex i, we choose k nearest vertices from its neighbors, where k is set to be six in this study. Based on the vertices and edges we construct a Laplacian graph to simulate the Laplace-Beltrami operator of the manifold [18][19]. A neighborhood keeping map can be obtained based on the discrete graph by minimizing the objective function (3):

$$L\hat{f}(\mathbf{X}) = \frac{1}{2} \sum_{i,j} \left(\hat{f}(X_i) - \hat{f}(X_j) \right)^2 w_{ij} \quad (3)$$

where L is the Laplacian matrix calculated as:

$$L = D - W$$
$$\text{with } d_{ij} = \begin{cases} \sum_{n=1}^{k} w_{i,i(n)} & j = i \\ 0 & \text{otherwise} \end{cases} \quad (4)$$

where d_{ij} is the element of matrix D. $\hat{f}$ is a mapping function of the vector vertices, and $\hat{f}(X_i)$ is the value of the mapping on the i-th vertex of the graph. The mapping function $\hat{f}$ can be obtained by solving the generalized eigenvalue problem as:

$$L\hat{f} = \hat{\lambda} D \hat{f} \quad (5)$$

To obtain a low dimensional embedding, the generalized eigenvalues and eigenfunctions for Laplacian matrix are:

$$L\hat{f}_i = \hat{\lambda}_i D \hat{f}_i, \quad i = 0, 1, 2, ..., N \quad (6)$$

The eigenvalues satisfies $0 = \hat{\lambda}_0 \leq \hat{\lambda}_1 \leq ... \leq \hat{\lambda}_j \leq ...$, then the corresponding low dimensional embedding can be described in (7), where d is the number of embedding dimension.

$$X_i \to \left[\hat{f}_1(X_i), \hat{f}_2(X_i), ..., \hat{f}_j(X_i), ... \hat{f}_d(X_i) \right]^T \quad (7)$$

Based on this mapping, the topological relationship of the data set is kept mostly when using some principal dimensions. The embedded manifold reflects the most principal degree of freedom of the data set which keeps the topological relationship.

4. EXPLORATION OF VOWEL STRUCTURES

In this section, we use the analysis method in section 3 to extract low dimensional structures from the observed articulatory data and acoustic data.

4.1 Vowel inherent structure in articulatory space

The articulatory data used in this study were recorded using Electromagnetic Midsagittal Articulographic (EMMA) system for read speech, and the acoustic signals were recorded simultaneously. The data were collected by NTT communication science laboratories [20].

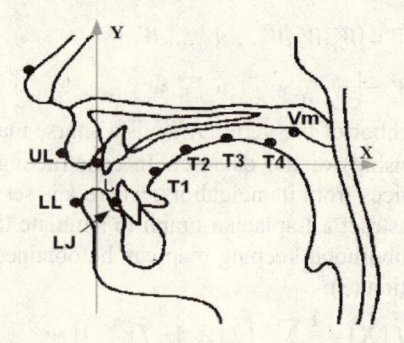

Figure 3: Placement of the receiver coils in the electromagnetic articulographic experiment, and the coordinate system used in this study.

Observation points of the measurement are shown in Figure 3: the Upper Lip (UL), Low Lip (LL), Low Jaw (LJ), four points on the tongue surface (T1 to T4 from the tongue tip to tongue rear), and the Velum (Vm). Each point is recorded by a coordinate with x and y, where x dimension is back-front horizontal direction and y dimension is up-down vertical direction. The sampling frequency was 16kHz for acoustic signal, and 250Hz for articulatory signal.

In order to investigate the topological manifold structure of the vowel space, we used five Japanese vowels /a/, /i/, /u/, /e/ and /o/, which are segmented out of the continuous speech. The vowels were automatically extracted from the stable parts of the vowel segments of EMMA data from 360 sentences of a male Japanese subject [21]. In this study, we use a vector, which consists of the x-y coordinates of the lips, jaw and tongue, to represent one vocalic configuration. One vocal tract occupies one point in the vowel production manifold. Since the velum plays a minor role in vowel production, it is not taken into consideration in this study. Thus, the articulatory data set becomes $\{X_i \mid X_i \in R^n, n=14, i=1,2,3,...,N\}$, where

$$X_i = [x_{LL}^i, y_{LL}^i, x_{UL}^i, y_{UL}^i, x_{LJ}^i, y_{LJ}^i, x_{T1}^i, y_{T1}^i, x_{T2}^i, y_{T2}^i, x_{T3}^i, y_{T3}^i, x_{T4}^i, y_{T4}^i]^T \tag{8}$$

As the result, the articulatory data set has 5725 vowels coming from 360 sentences, which almost included all of the phonetic environments of Japanese. The vowel inherent structure is explored by carrying out the nonlinear dimensional reduction on the collected data set.

The proposed method in Section 3 is adapted to the collected data set for extracting the vowel inherent structure. To do so, we first construct a discrete graph [18][22] using the collected vowel articulatory data set.

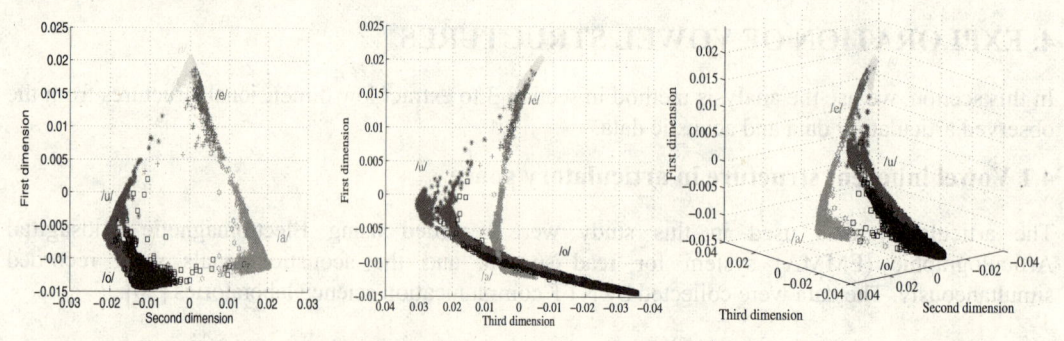

Figure 4: Intrinsic vowel structure in articulatory space. Left panel: projection in first-second dimension; Middle panel: projection in first-third dimension; Right panel: projection in three dimensions.

On the graph, for a given vertex, we choose six nearest neighboring vertices as the neighboring region patch, and assign weighting coefficients to each edge, and derive the weighting matrix W from the connections. The mapping function $\hat{f}$ is obtained by decomposing the weighting matrix using (5) and (6). Finally, a low dimensional structure of the vowels is derived from the high dimensional data, while their topological relationship is maintained. The structure is shown in Figure 4 in different views. In Figure 4, each point represents one vocal tract shape vector of the vowels. From this figure, one can see that the vowels are well clustered and separated to five vowel categories. The left panel of Figure 4 shows the relation of the vowels in the first and second dimensions. With reference to speech articulation, one can see that the first dimension concerns the tongue height. Vowel /i/ has the highest tongue position, vowels /a/ and /o/ have the lowest tongue positions, and vowels /e/ and /u/ are in middle position. This fact is consistent with that of the traditional description. The second dimension concerns the opening ratio of the lip to the oral cavity. Vowel /a/ and /e/ have a larger opening ratio while /o/ and /u/ have small ratios. This fact has been ignored by most vowel studies [14][15][16].

The middle panel of Figure 4 shows the relation of the first dimension vs. the third one. The third dimension of the inherent structure shows a curved distribution. It is a new finding of this study. This dimension is well related with the articulation positions of vowels along the vocal tract with /a/ and /o/ in the posterior region and /i/ in the anterior region (as shown in the three dimension space in right panel).

4.2 Vowel inherent structure in auditory space

A clear inherent structure has been obtained for vowels in articulatory space. The following question is what the intrinsic vowel image is in auditory perception space. In terms of the evidence that the speech production and perception interact with each other during language acquisition, we can speculate that the vowel structure possibly has the same or similar topology in articulatory space and in auditory space. This subsection will focus on how to find the vowel structure in auditory space with the same method as used for articulatory space.

Some parameter spaces were proposed to describe the auditory space for vowels. Miller [23] proposed to use his auditory-perception theory to explain vowels which concerns the speaker normalization problem. In his space, the first three formants and fundamental frequency were used. Based on auditory image analysis, Wang et al. [24] suggested that the response of the image of speech sound in auditory system can be regarded as the affine wavelet transform, which encodes the spectral profile.

In this study, we follow Wang's idea, and use the Mel Frequency Cepstral Coefficient (MFCC) in the primary step to represent acoustic parameters. Speech sound was recorded simultaneously with the articulatory measurements (see subsection 4.1 for detail). Speech signals of vowels were extracted in the stable period of each vowel, which is corresponding to the articulatory data. The number of dimensions for MFCC was chosen to be 14, as many as used for articulatory data vector. Using the same processing approach as that used for articulatory data, the vowel inherent structure is explored in auditory space. The vowel structure in auditory space is shown in Figure 5 in the similar views as those in Figure 4. One can see that the consistent structures are obtained in auditory perceptual space and in articulatory space.

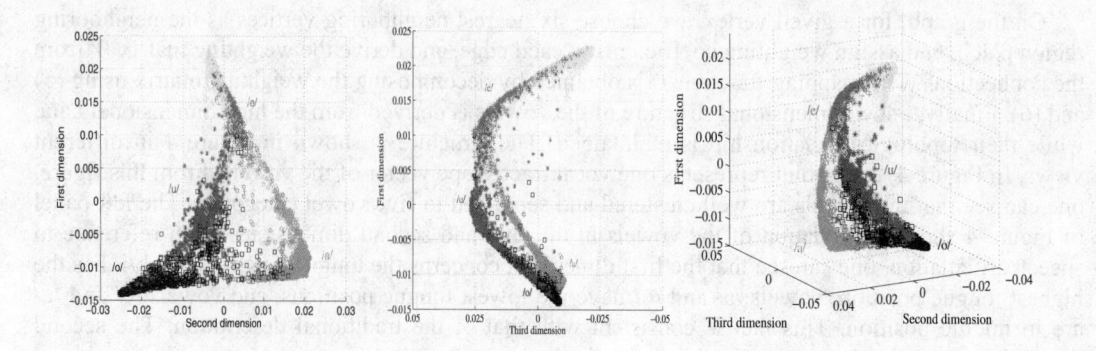

Figure 5: Intrinsic vowel structure in auditory space. Left panel: projection in first-second dimension; Middle panel: projection in first-third dimension; Right panel: an oblique projection in three-dimensional space.

5. DISCUSSION

In this study, we explore the vowel structures in terms of similarity concept that is usually used in human cognition. As the results, the clear vowel structure was explored in articulatory space from vowel data set segmented from continuous speech. This structure implies that the first three most important factors for vowel production are the tongue height, lip opening ratio, and the constriction place in the vocal tract. The finding gives more information than traditional studies. In the studies mentioned earlier [14][15][16], the vowel structures were explored using different speech materials that were obtained by different observation approaches, but using the same analysis method. There were larger differences seen in the topologies derived from the three studies. Our preliminary experiment showed that the three different structures were possibly derived from our explored vowel structure. For this reason, we may say that the similarity based vowel structure is a universal inherent structure for vowels.

It is believed that speech chain is formed in developing human functions of speech production and perception during language acquisition [25]. Accordingly, we can reasonably speculate that the image of the speech chain in the brain is somehow concerned with vowel structures in articulatory and auditory spaces. Based on this hypothesis, it is expected that a compatible vowel structure also exists in both articulatory and auditory spaces. To verify it, we adopted the same analysis method to acoustic data. Fortunately, a consistent vowel structure was obtained in auditory space. This is a big step toward proving our hypothesis.

The following question is whether the inherent structure is built in the motor space or not. Honda [5] suggested that there is a topological mapping between motor space and sensory space during speech based on his results that the equilibrium position of EMG in producing vowels is consistent with vowel location in F1-F2 plane. Dang et al. [21] used a physiological model to realize the speech process from the articulatory target to the sound generation. The simulation supported Honda's hypothesis [5]. Honda et al. [26] measured the compensations in speech production side for the auditory perturbation under a normal condition, and the condition applying an anesthetic on the tongue surface of the subjects. Their results showed that the compensation is faster with somatosensory than that without the somatosensory. Based on the evidences, it is reasonable to speculate that the inherent structure of vowels also exists in the motor space as a somatotopic map. According to the above analysis, the relation among the motor space, sensory space and articulatory space can be illustrated as a schema in Figure 6, where the inherent structure of vowels is shared in the motor space, articulatory space and sensory space. The auditory-motor linkage shown by the arrows closes the internal loop of the speech chain, which permits a direct mapping between intended articulatory and auditory patterns. Vowels have analogous motor and sensory representations in the anterior and posterior cortical areas, which connect to each other via a sensorimotor linkage [5]. The backward arrow from the articulatory to auditory spaces is equivalent to the efferent copy from motor to sensory areas. In the case of the speech process, the efferent copy is thought to generate articulatorily-induced auditory images, which are evaluated in comparison with somatosensory information as well as with perceived speech sounds. The forward arrow represents the general idea of sensory-guided motor execution, which may be applicable to a situation of auditorily-guided speech production. The looped flow of information between compatible sensory and motor representations further suggests that the two cortical areas for production and perception may work in unison to share the same information. The topological compatibility suggests that an efficient mapping among the structures may be used in human speech communication. This was what has been argued, in part, by the motor theory of speech perception [11].

6. CONCLUSION

In this study, we extracted the inherent structures of vowels out of continuous speech, which show the topological compatibility in articulatory and auditory spaces. These structures reflect the organization of the articulation and perception relationship of vowels which support the motor theory of speech perception. In addition, the inherent structure of vowels may be impressed in the motor space as a somatotopic map. Efficiency of human speech communication may result from such compatible topologies in the motor and sensory spaces. Verification of this hypothesis is remained for future study.

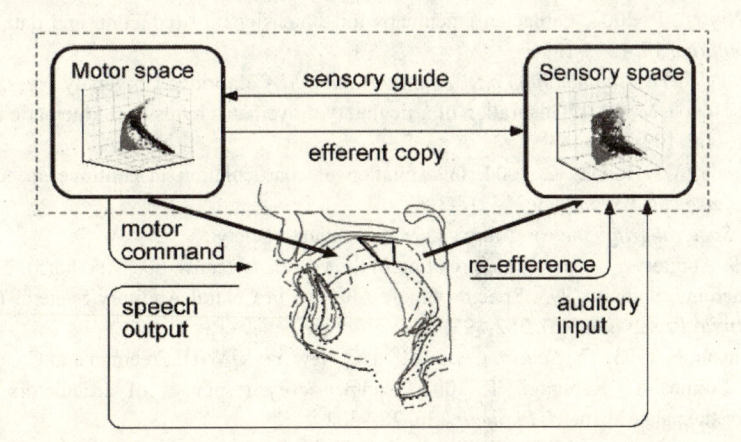

Figure 6: A hypothesis of modular organization of vowel production and perception in the brain. (Modified after [27])

7. ACKNOWLEDGEMENTS

This study is supported in part by SCOPE (071705001) of Ministry of Internal Affairs and Communications (MIC) and in part by Grant-in-Aid for Scientific Research of Japan (No.20300064). We would like to thank NTT communication science laboratories for permitting us to use the articulatory data.

REFERENCES

[1] Cardford, J. 1977. *Fundamental problems in phonetics*. Bloomington and London: Indiana University Press.
[2] Ladefoged, P. 1975. *A Course in Phonetics*. New York: Harcourt Brace College.

[3] I. P. Association (ed.). 1949. *Principles of the International Phonetic Association*. London: International Phonetic Association.
[4] Stevens, K. 2000. *Acoustic phonetics*. The MIT Press.
[5] Honda, K. 1996. Organization of tongue articulation for vowels. *J. Phonetics* 24, 39-52.
[6] Lombard, E. 1911. Le signe de l'elevation de la voix. *Annales Maladies Oreilles Larynx Nez Pharynx* 37, 101-119.
[7] Lee, B.S. 1950. Effects of delayed speech feedback. *J. Acoust. Soc. Am.* 22, 824-826.
[8] Kawahara, H. 1994. Interactions between speech production and perception under auditory feedback perturbations on fundamental frequencies. *J. Acoust. Soc. Jpn.* 15, 201-202.
[9] McGurk, H., MacDonald, J. 1976. Hearing lips and seeing voices. *Nature* 264, 746-748.
[10] Liberman, A., Cooper, F., Shankweiler, D., Studdert-Kennedy, M. 1967. *Perception of the speech code*. 74(6), 431-461.
[11] Liberman, A., Mattingly, G. 1985. The motor theory of speech perception revised. *Cognition* 21, 1-36.
[12] Chomsky, N., Halle, M. 1968. *The Sound Pattern of English*. New York: Harper.
[13] Jones, D. 1957. *An Outline of English Phonetics*. London: Hefther.
[14] Jackson, M. 1988. Analysis of tongue positions: Language-specific and cross linguistic models. *J. Acoust. Soc. Am.* 84(1), 124-143.
[15] Hoole, P. 1999. On the lingual organization of the German vowel system. *J. Acoust. Soc. Am.* 106(2), 1020-1032.
[16] Zheng, Y., Hasegawa-Johnson, Mark, Pizza, Shamala. 2003. Analysis of the three dimensional tongue shape using a three-index factor analysis model. *J. Acoust. Soc. Am.* 113(1), 478-486.
[17] Venna, J., Kaski, Samuel. 2006. Local multidimensional scaling. *Neural Networks* 19, 889-899.
[18] Belkin, M., Niyogi, P. 2003. Laplacian eigenmaps for dimensionality reduction and data representation. *Neural Computation* 15, 1373-1396.
[19] Rosenberg, S. 1997. *The Laplacian on a Riemannian manifold*. Cambridge University Press.
[20] Okadome, T., Honda, M. 2001. Generation of articulatory movements by using a kinematic triphone model. *J. Acoust. Soc. Am.* 109, 453-463.
[21] Dang, J., Honda, M., Honda, K. 2004. Investigation of coarticulation in continue speech in Japanese. *Acoustical Science and Technology* 25, 318-329.
[22] Fan, C. 1997. *Spectral graph theory*. American Mathematical Society.
[23] Miller, J. 1989. Auditory-perceptual interpretation of the vowel. *J. Acoust. Soc. Am.* 85(5), 2114-2134.
[24] Wang, K., Shamma, Shihab. 1995. Spectral Shape Analysis in Central Auditory System. *IEEE Trans. on Speech and Audio Processing* 3(5), 382-395.
[25] Denes, P., Pinson, E. 1993. *The Speech Chain*. (2nd ed.) New York: W.H. Freeman and Co.
[26] Honda, M., Fujino, A., Kaburagi, T. 2002. Compensatory responses of articulators to unexpected perturbation of the palate shape. *J. Phonetics* 30, 281-302.
[27] Dang, J., Akagi, K., Honda, K. 2006. Communication between Speech Production and Perception within the Brain-Observation and Simulation. *J. Computer Science and Technology* 21, 95-105.

CORRESPONDENCES BETWEEN ARTICULATION AND ACOUSTICS FOR THE FEATURE [ATR]: THE CASE OF TWO TIBETO-BURMAN LANGUAGES AND TWO AFRICAN LANGUAGES

Jerold A. EDMONDSON

ABSTRACT

The phonetic feature *Advanced Tongue Root* has proven to be a great aid to phonology but has remained mired in phonetic controversy. Two acoustic correlates have been proposed for the differences of vowel quality found in many West African [±ATR] languages, cf. [3]: (a) differences of *glottal wave shape* and (b) differences of *spectral timbre*. Thus, if (a), then ATR belongs to the domain of the *acoustic wave source*, but if (b), then ATR belongs to the domain of the *acoustic resonance filter*. An integrative approach has been suggested with a feature *flatness* that combines spectral tilt and vowel differences, cf. [6].

This paper will compare laryngoscopic video images captured during articulation and acoustic data from Yi and Bai, with corresponding data from two paradigmatic ATR languages, Akan and Kabiye. The Asian, like the African, data show two vowel sets with one ATR-like member possessing a consistent pattern of F_1 differences. That is, all languages demonstrated such *spectral timbre*. But, frame-by-frame comparison of the videos showed a pattern of selective differences. Bai, the language with robust phonatory voice quality differences had the widest range of source and filter features: (1) *ventricular incursion*, (2) *aryepiglottic compacting onto the epiglottal surface* as well as, (3) increased *first formant frequency and bandwidth*. Yi and the African languages showed only the last two of the three features, (2) and (3). We, thus, propose that the source feature *ventricular incursion* is not the articulatory basis for [ATR], but instead a source feature. The movement of the aryepiglottic folds toward the epiglottal surface is responsible for the increase of F_1 frequency and bandwidth. We also propose that ATR articulation involves flattening of the *aditus laryngis*.

Keywords: ATR, source, filter, formant, bandwidth

1. INTRODUCTION

In [1] we presented still images from video recordings of two Tibeto-Burman languages, Yi (四川省德昌县 Dechang County, Sichuan Province) and Bai (云南省剑川县 Jianchuan County, Yunnan Province), cf. [17][18] for a more complete description of Yi and Bai. We have also investigated the ATR articulations of Kabiye, a Garunsi language of Togo, and Akan, a Kwa language, of Ghana [2]. Akan was the first for which the ATR phenomenon was proposed, cf. Stewart [13].

Articulatory images of all four languages were obtained by using transnasal laryngoscopy, in which a small fiberoptic tube is inserted into a nostril and then led into the pharyngeal cavity, as shown in Fig. 1. Speakers are then asked to produce speech examples demonstrating minimally contrasting sets of data from their languages. The fiberscope is interfaced to the Kay Elemetrics Rhino-Laryngeal Stroboscope System. Audio and video signals are recorded in an anechoic environment with a Panasonic Digital Camcorder at 30 frames/second.

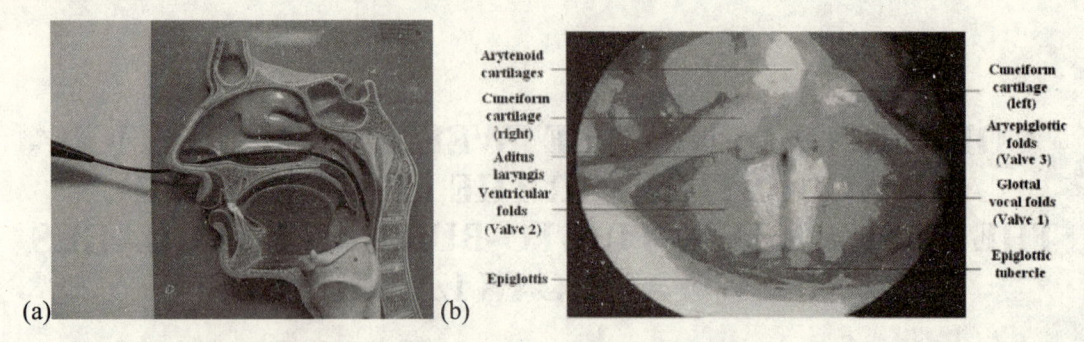

Figure 1: The fiberoptic bundle in position for video/audio capture taken in (1a), diagram from [19] and the view, in (1b), of the laryngeal plane and its structures visible with the device, retouched and modified from [2].

Additional audio recordings of the same persons involved in the laryngoscopic experiment were made at a later time in quiet surroundings with direct digital capture (Zoom H4 Handy Recorder interfaced to a Dell Inspiron 1521 computer running Cool Edit 2000). These recordings involved 10 repetitions of the test data, which were subsequently analyzed for formant frequency, bandwidth, and center of gravity values using PRAAT.[1]

Kabiye, Akan, and Yi have been reported to have two distinct pairs of vowel contrasts. Kabiye and Akan distinguish the pair members with the feature [+ATR], cf. [13][7]. Yi also distinguishes two sets, which are described in Chinese language materials with the feature 紧~松, translated here as [±Tns] [17]. The vowel pairs in these languages are organized as in Table 1:

Table 1: Vowel pairs for Kabiye, Akan, and Yi

	[+ATR]	[−ATR]
Kabiye	[i e u o]	[ɪ ɛ ʊ ɔ]
Akan	[i e u o a]	[ɪ ɛ ʊ ɔ ɑ]
	[−Tns]	[+Tns]
Yi	[i vᴮ i̪ᶻ u ɯ]	[e v̠ᴮ i̪̠ᶻ o ɑ]

As Table 1 shows, Kabiye has a nine-vowel contrast with [ɑ] assigned to the [−ATR] set, whereas Akan has a five-pair or ten-vowel system. Yi has vowel pairs that do not correspond exactly to those in Kabiye and Akan, whereby [vᴮ i̪ᶻ] represent fricativized vowels, one bilabial [vᴮ] and one with the tongue on the back of the upper teeth [i̪ᶻ], see [1] for more detailed description. The [+Tns] counterparts of these have retracted tongue position. Note as well that the vowel height differences between the pairs [i e], [u o], and [ɯ ɑ] are much greater than for the African languages.

Bai vowels have not been described in terms of sets of vowel pairs. But its syllable shapes can exhibit four types of phonatory quality (Modal, Harsh, Breathy, Harsh with aryepiglottic trilling), five or six pitch patterns (tones), and nasalization that allow it to distinguish 15 contrastive patterns. Moreover, these non-segmental features interact with resonance settings to change vowel quality [1]. An indication of the similarity of articulations among the languages can be seen in Figs. 2 and 3. Arrows represent the vectors of compacting by the aryepiglottic folds.

---

[1] The laryngoscopic investigations of Yi, Bai, Kabiye and Akan were performed under IRB approval from the University of Victoria, Victoria BC, Canada and The University of Texas at Arlington, USA by John H. Esling, Jimmy G. Harris, and myself assisted by Michael Mawdsley, MD and Michael Ross, MD, attending physicians, and the STR-Speech Tech Ltd team, Victoria BC. Native speaker participants were Li Shaoni (Bai), Lama Ziwo (Yi), Cecile Padayodi (Kabiye), and Ivan Omari (Akan). Nancy Rowe provided outstanding help with statistics.

Consider first the images of the Akan and Kabiye vowel pairs set, exemplified here by the Akan [u ʊ] and Kabiye [i ɪ] pairs. Of special interest is the compacting of the aryepiglottic folds onto the epiglottal surface.

The images (3a) & (3b) show the contrast of Bai modal with harsh vocal register and the images (3c) & (3d) contrast the Yi tense/lax pair; both languages are similar to the [±ATR] pairs in Fig. 2.

Figs. 2 and 3 show the arytenoid cartilages and the aryepiglottic folds attached to them adducting onto the epiglottal surface with concomitant flattening of the laryngeal *aditus*. This stucture is the triangular opening formed by the epiglottis, the aryepiglottic folds, and the apexes of the arytenoid cartilages, cf. Fig. (1b) and description in [16]. It is the vestibule or entrance for the flow of air between the glottal and supraglottal structures and has not figured prominently in past phonetic literature.

In (2d) as well as in (3d), (6b), (6d), (7b) and (7d), there is clear pharyngeal narrowing in evidence of still greater tension in the area around the aryepiglottic fold.

Though the two groups of languages share the buckling maneuver of the aryepiglottic folds toward the epiglottis, as these still images demonstrate, close study of the video images reveals crucial differences. The African languages and Yi do not evidence covering or damping of the adducted glottal vocal folds by the ventricular folds, viz. [2] and Fig. (4c) below.

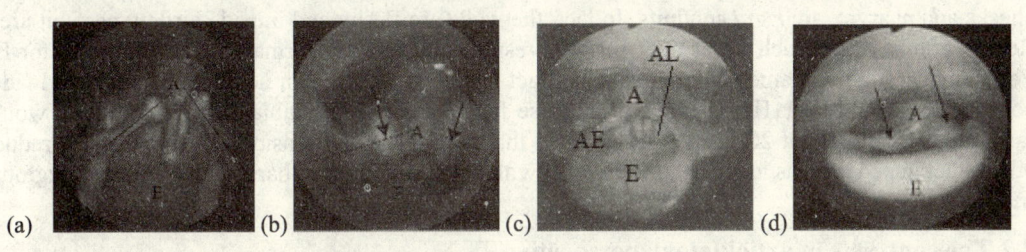

(a) (b) (c) (d)

Figure 2: Images from the videos of Akan (2a) *tu* [tú] [+ATR] "to pull out by the roots" and (2b) *to* [tʊ́] [–ATR] "to throw" at the point of maximum closure and, Kabiye (2c) *li* [lì] [+ATR] "swallow (IMP)" vs. (2d) *sɪ* [sɪ̀] [–ATR] "die (IMP)". Images (2c) and (2d) show also that the pharyngeal wall has narrowed so that the margins of the epiglottis contact the pharynx. A=arytenoid cartilages; AE=aryepiglottic folds; E=epiglottis; AL=*aditus laryngis*.

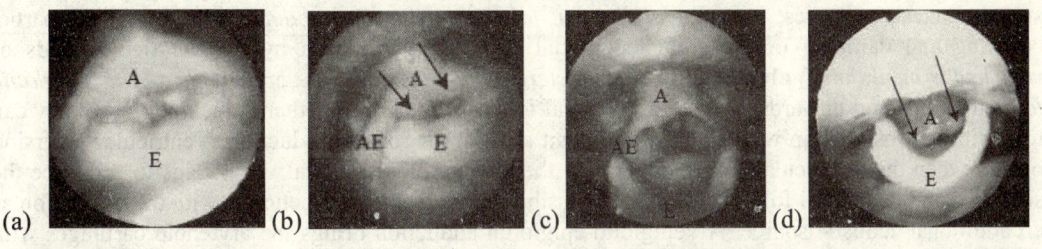

(a) (b) (c) (d)

Figure 3: Contrastive images from the videos of Bai (3a) [tɕi³³] "pull" and (3b) [tɕɛ³³] "leech", and, similarly for Yi (3c) [u³³] "head" and (3d) [ɔ³³] "hen's call to chicks". Note the distance between the epiglottis (E) and the arytenoid cartilages (A); the symbol (AE) labels the aryepiglottic fold.

2. METHODS

2.1 The phonological contrast in acoustic perspective

In Akan and Kabiye, the sets [i o e u a] and [ɪ ɔ ɛ ʊ ɑ] are phonologically unlike vowel contrasts in Western languages. In fact, [13] is credited with discovering that Akan (and analogously Kabiye) divides its vocabulary into two harmonic sets so that, in any word, members of only one of the two sets may appear. Therefore, any well-formed Kabiye word will have vowels from the set [i e u o] or from [ɪ ɔ ɛ ʊ ɑ]; mixing within a word is not allowed. Stewart [13] goes on to claim that the contrast is based not on tongue height but on "...the *position of the root of the tongue.*" In subsequent works, [8][9][10][15], there are further arguments from x-ray tracings and MRI imaging that "...the difference [in the vowel sets] is not simply in the tongue root gesture, but in the *enlargement of the whole pharyngeal cavity*, partly by the movement of the tongue root, but also by the lowering of the larynx." The works [8][9] also document a characteristic formant frequency shift in Akan such that [–ATR] vowels possess larger F_1 values than the [+ATR] vowels. Thus, larger F_1 values is the same as saying that vowels with [–ATR] values are located lower in vowel space than [+ATR] vowels. Finally, results from the perceptual perspective [2] suggest that "...voice quality along a tense-lax dimension covaries with advancement of the tongue root in vowels: a laxer voice quality co-occurs with a more advanced tongue root. As laxing the voice increases energy in the first harmonic relative to higher ones and advancing the tongue root lowers F_1, the acoustic consequences of these two articulations may *integrate perceptually into a higher-level perceptual property, here called spectral 'flatness'.*" [3] points out that the contrast may reside in a difference of *spectral timbre*, noting in particular that the flattening of the pharyngeal cavity will cause the *formant bandwidth to broaden*. This claim is substantiated in Stevens [12], where flattening of the pharynx is a resistive element in the transfer function, called *Impedance of Vocal Tract Walls*. The usual assumption is that the tongue, cheeks and pharynx are *rigid* conduits. In fact, the walls are fleshy and impede airflow per unit area. Resistive losses from such vocal tract surfaces result in increase in formant bandwidth, esp. for F_1. For a circular tube of diameter 1cm and vocal tract length of 17.7cm (for adult males), the bandwidth contribution would be 11Hz. Bandwidth increase for a fricativized bilabial vowels, as in Yi, would raise the values to about 20Hz. It is to be noted that great muscular tension of the walls will reduce vocal tract impedance, as happens in Bai vowel with pressed voice and harsh voice with aryepiglottal trilling [1].

2.2 The contrasts in articulatory perspective

In Figs. 2 & 3 above we have shown images of the [+ATR] or [–Tns] versions of vowels in comparison to those of the [–ATR] or [+Tns]. However, there are, in addition, relevant features in the full motion video images of these utterances that deserve further comment. We have argued in [2] that valve-like closures existing in many sound articulations involve not only laryngeal but also supralaryngeal structures, i.e. (a) *glottal vocal fold adduction and abduction*, **Valve 1**; (b) partial covering and damping of the adducted glottal vocal fold vibration by the ventricular folds or *ventricular incursion*, **Valve 2**; and (c) *sphincteric compression of the arytenoids and aryepiglottic folds* forwards and upwards, **Valve 3**. The vocal folds are brought together at the midline so they can touch in their oscillation with resulting efficient airflow for sound production. Ventricular incursion occurs when the ventricular folds adduct atop the already closed glottal vocal folds to reinforce the seal, to damp the glottal fold vibration, and possibly to interact sympathetically with the oscillation as an additional acoustic source. Aryepiglotto-epiglottal adduction brings the arytenoid cartilages with their associated aryepiglottic folds, to a position atop the glottal plane, thus, shortening the vowel tract and flattening the *aditus laryngis* beneath. Synergistically, the pharyx narrows to constrict the airflow even more to the centerline.

Many types of articulation require these three valves to work in synergy; for others only one or two of the three are engaged. The activation of the epiglottal constrictor shows all three in action, cf. Fig. 4. Another important combination of the valves is illustrated in creaky vocal register, Fig. 5. Aryepiglotto-epiglottal constriction is active, but there is no ventricular incursion, as the uncovered glottal vocal folds are visible in Fig. 5a. The sequence in Fig. 4 should be contrasted with pressed voice or harsh vocal register with high pitch, cf. Fig. 5b. For this vocal register, the ventricular folds engage but the aryepiglottic folds cannot close completely because of strong posterior-anterior muscle tension from high pitch.

(a) Frame 31   (b) Frame 37   (c) Frame 40   (d) Frame 44

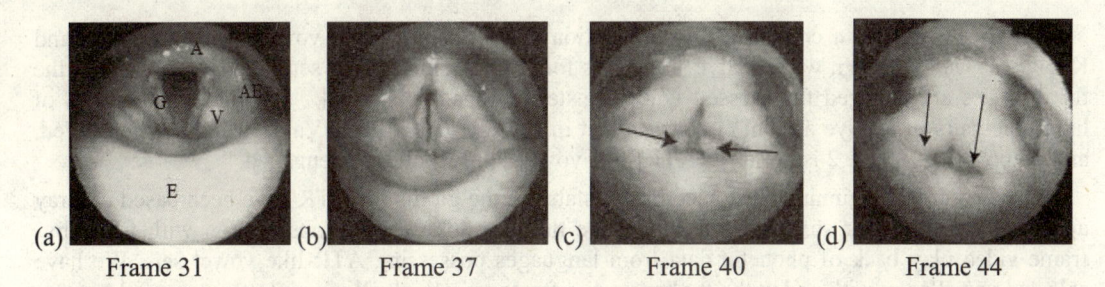

Figure 4: The three valve-sequence for Bai [pʰi⁵⁵] "fart" begins with (4a) breath position, (4b) glottal vocal fold adduction (G), (4c) ventricular incursion, and (4d) engagement of the aryepiglottic folds. The sequence is indicated by frame number from the video timeline. The ventricular folds (V) engage strongly in (4c) by closing toward the midline and covering the glottal vocal folds. But in (4d) the aryepiglottic structures move posterior-to-anterior (and thus at right angles to (4b) and (4c)) in the third sphincteric constriction).

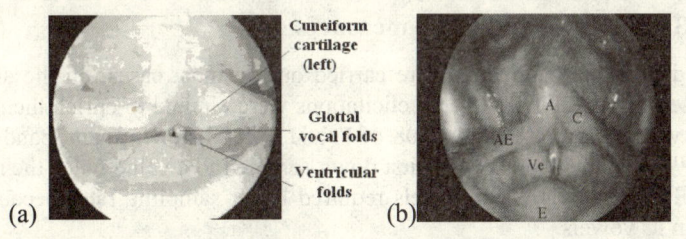

Figure 5: Comparison of creaky vocal register in (5a) vs. harsh vocal register with high pitch in (5b), also called *pressed voice*.

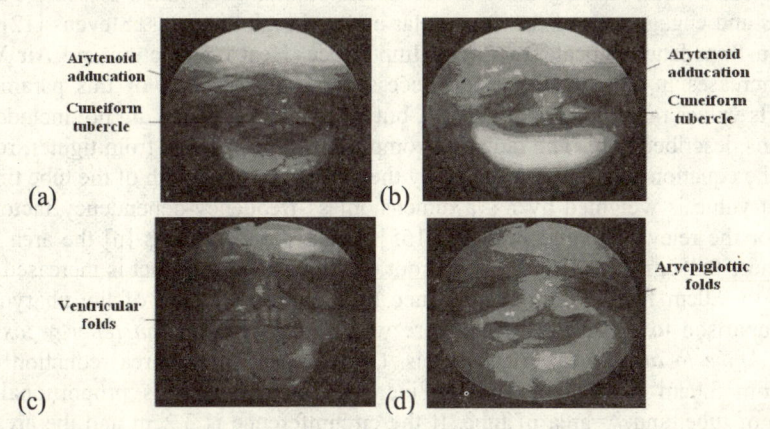

Figure 6: Comparative images for the Kabiye vowel sets showing the engagement of Valve 3, flattening of the aditus laryngis, (6a) [lè] "dry (IMP)" vs. (6b) [tɕɛ] "cut (IMP)" and (6c) [lì] "swallow (IMP)" vs. (6d) [sɪ] "die" (IMP).

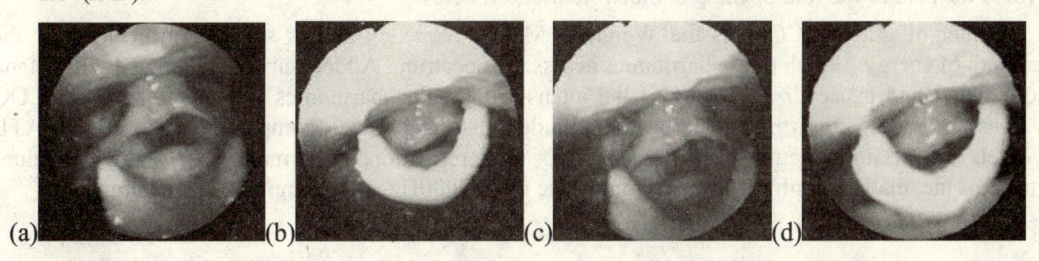

Figure 7: Comparative examples for Yi showing (7a) [i³³] "self" (indirect discourse) vs. (7b) [e³³] "a duck" and (7c) [v̩³³] "intestine" vs. (7d) [v̩³³] "kidney".

Valves 1 & 3 play a crucial role in production [–ATR] and [+Tns] vowel quality in Akan and Kabiye, as well as in Yi, while Valve 1 engages for [+ATR] and [–Tns] settings. By contrast all the three valves are engaged the pressed voice register in Figs. 3a,b and 4. Examining other sets of harmonic-pairs in Kabiye and in Yi confirm that in [–ATR]-like vowels Valve 1 and 3 are engaged, and, importantly, Valve 2 is not for [+ATR]-like vowels, only Valve 1 is engaged.

As stated at the beginning, past accounts of states of the glottis for ATR have been based on xray and MRI imaging. Our study has the advantage that it employs direct observation with frame-by-frame video play back of phonetic data from languages possessing ATR-like vowel sets. We have selected vowel pairs with and without phonatory differences, which allows us to tease apart these two aspects of the correspondences between articulation and acoustics. Our methods thus compares: (a) frame-wise video recordings from Yi, Akan, and Kabiye, which are examples of ATR-like languages without phonatory contrasts, but having F_1 and bandwidth effect and (b) videos from Bai with phonatory features, as well as the F_1 frequency bandwidth differences.

2.3 Formants, Bandwidths, and COG measures

Formant and bandwidth measurements were carried out, in most cases, on the audio tracks of the laryngoscopic video files. Additional audio elicitations were elicited to enrich the data inventory and then investigated with PRAAT (Version5008 of Feb. 11, 2008) for formant, bandwidth, and center-of-gravity values. The sound objects were first down-sampled to a value twice the maximum formant frequency (10000Hz). Yi fricativized vowels required lower sampling rates because of the acoustic frication present in its vowels.

The languages studied here make use of articulations that affect acoustic energy losses (acoustic impedance) or bandwidth. Among those mentioned here that cause such losses are flattening the *aditus laryngis* and engagement of the ventricular and aryepiglottic folds. Stevens [12] mentions, as well, Radiation Impedance, Vocal Tract Wall Impedance, Heat Conduction and Air Viscosity. All these cause increases in Bandwidth, which necessitates consideration of this parameter. Stevens [12:259] reports values ranging from 30-120Hz, but these measurements did not include vowels with the constrictions described here. The radiation component of impedance from tighter, rounded lips is expressed by the equation f^2 times A_m divided by the product of the length of the tube times the speed of sound. That value is weighted by K_S, a dimensionless frequency-dependency factor taken to be equal to 1.5 for the relevant frequencies [12: 155]. For a vowel such as [u] the area of the mouth narrows to a mere 0.28cm^2. The length of the front cavity of the vocal tract is increased by 0.9cm for lip protrusion to 9.0cm for an adult male. Since there is compression of the pharynx in [–ATR] vowels in comparison to [+ATR] vowels, there will be *heat conduction (energy loss) as well as viscosity impedance to airflow* for such vowels. Our estimate of the area reduction of the *aditus laryngis* is from 3.0cm^2 to 1.0cm^2 and the increase in bandwidth is proportional to S/A, S= circumference of tube, and A=area of tube. If the circumference is 3.2cm and the area is 1cm^2, cf. Figs. (2b,d) and (3b,d), the viscosity and heat conduction impedance could have a trebling influence on the bandwidth. Our measured values can be more than that, because of Bai aryepiglottic trilling, where the area of the fold opening is much smaller, cf. below.

Center of gravity (COG) is the Weighted Mean Frequency and is strongly influenced by the amount of energy in each of the harmonics across the spectrum. Added tension in Valve 3 will extend to Valve 1 and cause slower decay of the intensity of higher harmonics and therefore larger COG values. In order to confirm less decay of amplitude in [–ATR] vowels compared with those in [+ATR] vowels, a wideband spectral slices were taken for three repetitions of harmonic pair, and mean values in dB of the relative amplitude for each harmonic up to 5000Hz were computed and examined.

3. RESULTS

3.1 Results of frame-by-frame study of the video images

The most important observation about Akan and Kabiye is that the [+ATR] vowel types show only the expected adduction of the Vocal Glottal Folds (Valve 1), whereas in the [–ATR] vowel images the cuneiform cartilages, which have connective tissue to the aryepiglottic folds, approach the epiglottal surface near the epiglottal tubercle. This motion causes the entrance to the larynx, the *aditus laryngis*, to flatten in the posterior-to-anterior dimension and the pharyngeal wall has narrowed to touch the sides of the epiglottis.

Table 2 lists the major phonetic features of concern here. So, Akan and Kabiye, for instance, have only two tones, high and low. These tones do not appear to interact with the ATR feature. The *aditus laryngis* was flattened whenever the aryepiglottic folds compacted sphincterically onto the epiglottis. One key difference among the languages was the role of the ventricular folds. None of those languages with ATR-like phonetic features showed ventricular incursion. Only Bai possesses true phonatory quality, e.g. pressed voice (harsh voice at high/mid pitch) and aryepiglottic trilling at low pitch (it also possesses Breathy voice, but that is not relevant in this experiment). Furthermore, the *aditus laryngis* is not flattened in pressed voice in Bai, in this special case because the high pitch necessitates strong posterior-anterior tension of the crico-thyroid muscles to produce these upper frequencies. Occlusion of the aryepiglottic valve is proscribed by the inherent operation of the glottal folds at high pitch.

Table 2: Summary of the articulatory features of vowels in Kabiye, Akan, Yi and Bai from video

Language	Flattened *aditus laryngis*	Tone/Phonatory Quality	Ventricular folds engaged	Aryepiglottic folds engaged
Kabiye	Yes	High, Low	No	Yes
Akan	Yes	High, Low	No	Yes
Yi	Yes	33	No	Yes
Bai	No	55 pressed voice	Yes	No
Bai	Yes	33 pressed voice	Yes	Yes
Bai	Yes	21 aryepi trilling	Yes	Trilling

3.2 Results of the acoustic analysis

In order to present results in a space-saving but also perspicuous manner, I present in Figs. 8-10 the differential for each vowel-pair in regard to F_1, F_2, B_1, and COG values, i.e. for Kabiye the $\Delta F_1(i\sim\text{\textsc{i}}) = F_1(i) - F_1(\text{\textsc{i}})$, $\Delta \text{COG}(i\sim\varepsilon) = \text{COG}(i) - \text{COG}(\text{\textsc{i}})$, etc.

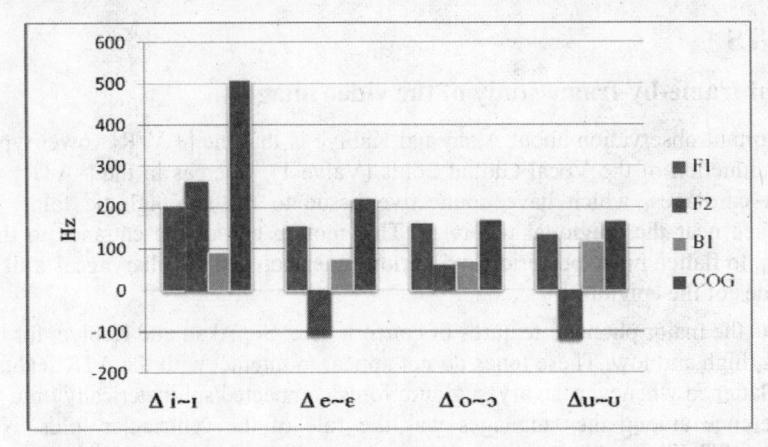

Figure 8: Results of the Kabiye F_1 F_2, B_1, and COG (Differential Vowel Pairs)

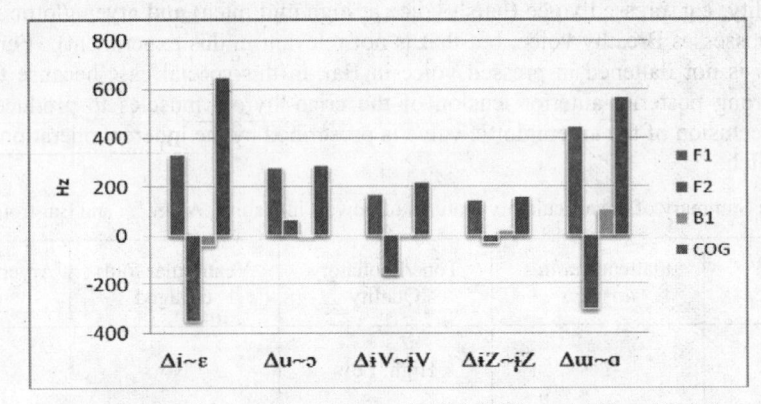

Figure 9: Results for Yi F_1 F_2, B_1, and COG (Differential Vowel Pairs)

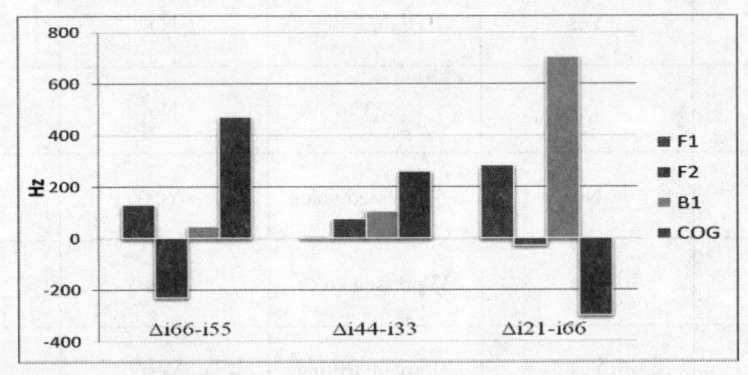

Figure 10: Results for Bai i-vowels F_1 F_2, B_1, and COG (Differential Vowel Pairs)

3.3 Statistical modeling

In order to test the level of significance of the results, a Repeated Measure within a Mixed Model Analysis was performed. Ten repetition of the vowel pairs, such as [i ɪ], [u ʊ], [e ɛ], etc. were compared with dependent variables: formant frequencies (F_1, F_2), bandwidth of F_1 (B_1), and Center of gravity (COG). There was insufficient data to perform this statistic on Akan, so it is not included here. For most, but not all dependent variables there was a significant vowel by ATR interaction at the 0.0001 level of significance. Thus, the difference in means between the [±ATR] values was tested for each vowel set separately with the following results.

3.3.1 Kabiye

For dependent variables there was a significant vowel by [ATR] interaction ($p<0.0001$) for F_1 and COG, but not for F_2 and B_1.

Main Effect results

Vowel set (10 reps)	F_1	F_2	B_1	COG
[i ɪ]	<.0001	0.6384 n.s.	<.0001	<.0001
[u ʊ]	<.0001	0.1034 n.s.	<.0001	<.0001
[e ɛ]	<.0001	<.0003	<.0001	<.0001
[o ɔ]	<.0001	0.4244 n.s.	<.0001	<.0001

Figure 11: Main Effect of statistical analysis of Kabiye data; the COG spectrual analysis showed less amplitude decay for [–ATR] vowels than for [+ATR] vowels.

3.3.2 Yi

For each dependent variable there was a significant vowel by [ATR] interaction ($p<0.05$).

Main Effect results

Vowel set (10 reps)	F_1	F_2	B_1	COG
[i e]	<.0001	<.0001	<.0001	<.0001
[u o]	<.0001	<.0001	0.9924 n.s.	<.0001
[i^z $\underline{i}^z$]	<.0001	<.0001	0.5903 n.s.	<.0001
[v^B $\underline{v}^B$]	<.0001	<.0254	0.0062	<.0001
[ɯ ɑ]	<.0001	<.0001	<.0001	<.0001

Figure 12: Main Effect of statistical analysis of Yi data; the COG spectrual analysis showed less amplitude decay for [–Tns] vowels than for [+Tns] vowels.

3.3.3 Bai

For dependent variables there was a significant vowel by [ATR] interaction ($p <0.0001$) for F_1, for F_2 ($p <0.0001$), for COG ($p <0.0485$) and B_1 ($p <0.0001$).

Main Effect results

Vowel set (10 reps)	F_1	B_1	COG
[i] for tone 55 vs. 21	<.0001	<.0001	0.0096
[i] for tone 55 vs. 5̣5	0.0018	.7497 n.s.	0.0037
[i] for tone 5̣5 vs. 21	<.0001	<.0001	0.0096
[i] for tone 3̣3 vs. 21	<.0001	<.0001	0.8885 n.s.
[i] for tone 33 vs. 3̣3	.0010	.5394 n.s.	0.5736 n.s.
[a] for tone 55 vs. 21	.0130	.7404	0.0147
[a] for tone 55 vs. 5̣5	<.0001	.0002	0.6759 n.s.
[a] for tone 5̣5 vs. 21	.0598 n.s.	.0005	0.7374 n.s.
[a] for tone 3̣3 vs. 21	.0598 n.s.	.8487 n.s.	0.9707 n.s.
[a] for tone 33 vs. 3̣3	.0003	.7673	0.7055 n.s.

Figure 13: Main Effect of statistical analysis of Bai data; the COG spectrum plots for Bai did not show clear difference in amplitude decay between the prosodic categories, but there was difference for most of the F_1 values.

4. DISCUSSION

This investigation of the correspondences between articulations and acoustics indicates three tentative generalizations: (a) ventricular incursion can act independently of aryepiglottic action to produce phonatory difference as is seen in Bai pressed voice registers, (b) the shortening of the back cavity by covering the glottal area by the aryepiglotto-epiglottal sphincter and the pharyngeal narrowing causes the F_1 to increase and the decay of amplitude in higher harmonics to decrease, and (c) the flattening of lowest part of the back cavity (the *aditus laryngis*) increases the B_1, which produces a change in the spectral timbre. But, countering the effects of heat conduction in a tube of smaller diameter, there is the tensing gesture clearly visible in Fig. 5b that makes the cavity walls much less fleshy and subject to less Wall Impedance and Airflow Viscosity. Therefore the differential values are far less significant in Bai than in the other languages with no pressed vowels. Note as well that phonatory difference and extremely tense settings for glottal, ventricular, and aryepiglottic folds seem to swamp the bandwidth and COG differences.

In regard to aryepiglottic compacting onto the epiglottis, that is the most obvious difference between the Kabiye, Akan and Yi vowel sets, cf. Figs. 2, 3, 4, 5, 6 & 7 as well as the vowel quality plots in Figs. 8, 9 & 10, which show vowels with [–ATR] features are lowered in regard to their position in the vowel quadrangle.

Finally, ΔB_1 (bandwidth differences for F_1) is an indicator of increased impedance to airflow (from viscosity, from lip radiation, or from the exposed surface of the pharyngeal cavity). Kabiye, Akan and Yi vowel sets all show significant ΔB_1 (except Yi fricativized vowels).

In sum, this study can tentatively support the view that the articulatory correlate of F_1-spectral timbre (bandwidth broadening) as well as F_1-increase is the engagement of the aryepiglottic sphincter. It does not seem to support the proposal for a combined source-resonance feature "flatness" [2], but instead suggests that phonatory quality and vowel lowering effects are distinct and that:

I. phonatory-quality is a consequence of ventricular-fold adduction.

II. F_1-frequency and F_1-bandwidth increases are consequences of the engagement of the aryepiglottic sphincter and pharyngeal narrowing. Clearly if the aryepiglottic folds trill at low pitch, then that would also constitute phonatory quality.

III. in ATR languages and Yi the anatomical structure is flattened in the *aditus laryngis*.

REFERENCES

[1] Edmondson, J., J. Esling, J. Harris, Li, S., Lama, Z. 艾杰瑞，艾思麟，李绍尼，吉米哈里森，拉玛兹偓. 1999. 论彝语,白语的音质和勺会厌肌带的关系——喉镜案例研究. The aryepiglottic folds and voice quality in the Yi and Bai language of Yunnan Province: laryngoscopic case studies. 民族语文 *Minzu Yuwen* 6,47-53 and (in English) *Mon Khmer Studies* 31, 1-21.

[2] Edmondson, J., J. Esling. 2006. The valves of the throat and their functioning in tone, vocal register and stress: laryngoscopic case studies. *Phonology* 23,157-191.

[3] Fulop, S., E. Kari, P. Ladefoged. 1998. An acoustic study of Tongue Root Contrast in Degema vowels. *Phonetica* 55, 80-98.

[4] Halle, M., K. Stevens. 1969. On the feature ATR. *MIT Research Laboratory Progress Report* 94,209-15.

[5] Kakusho, O., H. Hirato, K. Kato, T. Kobayashi. 1971. Some experiments of vowel perception by harmonic synthesizer. *Acusta* 5,132-42.

[6] Kingston, J., A. Macmillan, L. Dickey, R. Thorburn, C. Bartels. 1997. Integrality in the perception of tongue root position and voice quality in vowels. *JASA* 101, 1696-1709.

[7] Lébikaza, K. 1999. *Grammaire kabiyè: une analyse systématique*. Köppe: Köln.

[8] Lindau, M. 1978. Vowel features. *Lg*, 54, 541-63.

[9] Lindau, M. 1979. The feature expanded. *J. of Phonetics* 7,163-176.

[10] Painter, C. 1973. Cineradiographic data on the feature "Covered" in Twi vowel harmony. *Phonetica* 28, 97-120.
[11] Son, R. van, L. Pols. 1996. An acoustic profile of consonant reduction. Interspeech 3, http:// www.asel.udel.edu/icslp/cdrom/vol3/200/a200.pdf.
[12] Stevens, K. 2000. *Acoustic phonetics*. Cambridge: MIT Press.
[13] Stewart, J. 1967. Tongue root position in Akan vowel harmony. *Phonetica* 16, 185-204.
[14] Stifka, J. 2003. Tense/lax vowel classification using dynamic spectral cues. *15th ICPhS* Barcelona, Universidad de Barcelona, 921-24.
[15] Tiede, M. 1996. An MRI-based study of pharyngeal volume contrasts in Akan and English. *Journal of Phonetics* 24, 399-421.
[16] Zemlin, W. 1998. *Speech and Hearing Science Anatomy and Physiology*. (4th ed.). Allen & Bacon: Boston.
[17] 陈士林、李秀清、边仕明（1984）《彝语简志》Yiyu Jianzhi (A brief introduction to the Yi language)。北京：民族出版社。
[18] 徐琳、赵衍荪（1984）《白语简志》Baiyu Jianzhi。北京：民族出版社。
[19] http://homepage.mac.com/changcy/endo.htm.

THE CONTROL OF LARYNGEAL CONSTRICTION AND THE EMERGENCE OF SPEECH IN INFANTS IN THE FIRST YEAR OF LIFE

John H. ESLING

ABSTRACT

Our research into the earliest vocalizations by infants in English (Victoria), French (Paris), Arabic (Morocco), and Bai (China) shows that (1) speech begins in the pharynx, (2) the production of phonation begins with laryngeally constricted settings, (3) infants explore their phonetic production capacity by employing (a) 'phonetic alternations' and (b) 'pharyngeal priming'. Data from the Infant Speech Acquisition (InSpA) Project typify instances of 'phonetic play' that demonstrate how infants systematically acquire basic control over the speech mechanism and the arrays of place and manner of articulation during their first year of life.

Keywords: laryngeal, constriction, infants, pharynx, acquisition

1. INTRODUCTION

To determine how infants acquire the phonetic modality of speech production, a research project has been established to observe infant vocalizations during the first year of life in four separate language contexts where the phonological inventories of the adult languages contrast. The initial hypothesis is that speech-production processes begin in the laryngeal vocal tract rather than the oral vocal tract. A secondary hypothesis is that manner of articulation is 'learned' at one place of articulation first and then transferred to subsequent places of articulation. A tertiary hypothesis is that infants exposed to ambient languages that exploit the laryngeal vocal tract in their phonological inventories will use selected laryngeal elements of speech earlier in their babbling behaviour than do infants whose ambient languages do not contain laryngeal phonological components.

2. THE LARYNGEAL ARTICULATOR MODEL

In a program of experimental phonetic research spanning two decades, it has been shown that the laryngeal articulator plays a key role in differentiating linguistic phonetic meaning in a surprisingly large number of languages of the world [11][17][18]. In the Laryngeal Articulator Model [12][13] [7], it has been demonstrated that the glottis is not the only source of periodic energy in the larynx, that the aryepiglottic folds also generate vibrations attested in speech sounds, and that the laryngeal constrictor, as the shaper of pharyngeal articulations and of pharynx volume, contributes primary cavity resonance in 'tonal register' and 'vowel harmony' sound systems.

2.1 The two-part vocal tract

In view of the laryngeal articulator, pharyngeals are considered to be laryngeal articulations, i.e. a function of the aryepiglottic sphincter mechanism, rather than being primarily a function of tongue position. The tools of investigation that we use in our phonetic research have allowed us to formulate a theory whereby the production of pharyngeal sounds is isolated within the 'laryngeal articulator'. We have examined laryngeal articulation in over 20 languages from diverse language families across the world to demonstrate the laryngeal states [14], phonatory postures [6], and manners of articulation [5][9] that the laryngeal articulator can produce. We have shown that various complex adjustments within a relatively simple mechanism — the laryngeal constrictor — are responsible for the production of multiple manners of pharyngeal consonants, secondary sound source vibrations, and changes in pharyngeal cavity resonance, and we have shown how some languages use these articulatory parameters to generate phonological distinctions such as [tense/lax] or [+ATR/–ATR] [10].

The vocal tract is reconceptualized into two primary articulatory domains in the Laryngeal Articulator Model [13]. The laryngeal section of the vocal tract is conceived of as a series of valves, each of which is responsible for a range of articulatory configurations and is made up of its own unique anatomical structures [7]. Fig. 1 illustrates this conceptual expansion of the articulatory capacity of the laryngeal vocal tract and the primacy of the aryepiglottic folds in the production of sounds that have been termed pharyngeals and epiglottals. For infant speech, regardless of the differences in vocal tract shape from adults, it will be important to identify accurately sounds that originate in the laryngeal sector.

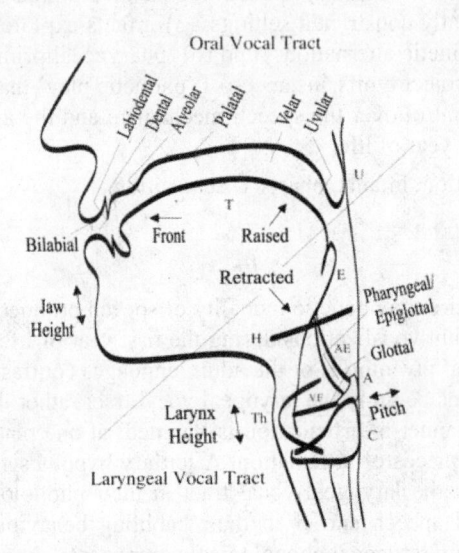

Figure 1: The 'two-vocal-tract' reconceptualization of the standard articulatory model of the vocal tract (minus the nasal tract) with jaw height determining close/open vowel setting at the front, and tongue raising/retracting determining vowel quality at the back. T, tongue; U, uvula; E, epiglottis; H, hyoid bone; AE, aryepiglottic folds; A, arytenoid cartilages; VF, vocal folds; Th, thyroid cartilage; C, cricoid cartilage. This figure is reproduced from Esling's original 2005 work in the Canadian Journal of Linguistics [13].

2.2 Laryngoscopic evidence of laryngeal behaviour

Using this model, we have determined, for example, what the mechanism of pharyngeal trilling involves and where it occurs in the speech sounds of a language with pharyngeals in its phonology. We have also identified the mechanism of pharyngeal shaping that generates contrasting laryngeal features such as [+ATR/–ATR] vowels. The supplementary source mechanism and the resonance features resulting from narrowing of the pharyngeal space are illustrated particularly well in studies of Bai, Iraqi Arabic, Somali, Yi, Akan, and Kabiye [10]. Laryngeal/pharyngeal production in each language has been studied articulatorily by means of transnasal laryngoscopy. Bai was chosen because of its vocal register contrast that involves a complex of glottal and supraglottic phonatory modification [17]; Iraqi Arabic because of its extreme and phonetically challenging pharyngeal reflexes [23]; Somali because it has pharyngeals as well as a vocalic harmony system that interacts with shaping in the pharynx; Yi because of its register series that do not induce phonatory contrasts [17]; Akan because much is known about its phonetics, and because it is historically the model language for 'ATR' harmony [28]. Kabiye, a Gurunsi language of Togo, Ghana and Benin, compares closely with Akan with extremely regular vowel series and virtually exceptionless adherence to the rules of 'ATR' vowel harmony.

The experimental phonetic equipment in our laryngoscopic research facility consists of a Kay Elemetrics Rhino-laryngeal-stroboscope (RLS 9100) with a constant halogen cold light source to photograph the actions of the larynx. An Olympus ENF-P3 fibreoptic nasendoscope is attached to the camera (Panasonic GP-US522) and light source with a 28mm lens for optimal wide-angle framing of larynx mechanisms during extreme pharyngeal articulations and of laryngeal postures during the varying pitch conditions in which tonal paradigms occur. Recordings are made directly on a Sony DCRTRV17 Mini-DV Digital Camcorder. Video images are postprocessed with Adobe Premiere 6.5 software.

Canonical phonetic profiles obtained in baseline research [11][12][13][14][19] serve as the basis for comparing the production of phonemic contrasts by native-speaker subjects in the array of languages we have studied. Languages in the video database of the larynx and pharynx include: Nuuchahnulth (Wakashan), Nlaka'pamuxcín (Salish), Tigrinya (Semitic), Palestinian Arabic (Semitic), Iraqi Arabic (Semitic), Somali (Cushitic), Amis (Austronesian), Yi (Tibeto-Burman), Bai (Sino-Tibetan/ Tibeto-Burman), Tibetan (Tibeto-Burman), Sui (Kam-Sui), Thai (Daic), Pame (Oto-Manguean), Cantonese (Sinitic), English (whisper studies), Chinese (whisper studies), Korean (Altaic), Dinka (Nilotic), Chong (Mon-Khmer), Akan (Kwa), and Kabiye (Gur).

2.3 Laryngeal qualities and place and manners

In the same way that canonical phonetic profiles obtained in baseline research constitute the basis for comparing sounds produced by native-speaker subjects of various languages, the data that we have obtained from the various native-speaker subjects constitute the basis for comparing sounds produced by infants in the Infant Speech Acquisition (InSpA) Project. Whereas invasive laryngoscopic experimentation can be carried out with adult subjects, invasive procedures are not possible with infant subjects; and they are not needed. The principal phonetic classification that takes place in the adult language studies remains largely auditory, with instrumental data providing support for the auditory distinctions that we identify in the various phonologies. The phonetic classification that takes place in the infant language studies is wholly auditory. Classifications are developed and assigned on the basis of intensive training in the system of the Laryngeal Articulator Model, with which all members of the research team are intimately familiar. Categories follow those developed while working with the data from the array of languages listed above and which are taught in undergraduate classes and in postgraduate seminars at the University of Victoria.

The categories of analysis from languages observed laryngoscopically include qualities and place and manner designations. Some examples of categories from our previous research are epiglottal stop (widely distributed in Semitic, Cushitic, Wakashan, Salish and Austronesian languages), glottal stop (with an even wider distribution), and voiceless pharyngeal trill (in Iraqi Arabic and Somali as well as in Tibeto-Burman register). In Somali, in a voiceless pharyngeal, an effect of harsh trilling of the aryepiglottic folds co-occurs, and it also appears that the combination of tight, harsh phonation at the glottis propagates through the supraglottic tube, inducing vibrations of the narrowed structures above it, including the tip of the epiglottis. A pharyngeal tap has also been identified in our data from Iraqi Arabic (a speech sound category not yet attested in the chart of the IPA). Most of these sound types, in fact, had been underattested among the world's languages prior to the results of our laryngoscopic research; so it is now possible to say that many if not most of the categories of sounds generated by the laryngeal constrictor occur far more commonly than had been previously thought. It is also possible to specify more clearly how each category is related articulatorily to the others. Examples of the posture of an epiglottal stop and of a point during voiceless aryepiglottic trilling are shown in Fig. 2. In both, the aryepiglottic folds are raised up and forwards towards the retracting tongue and epiglottis. During the trill, the aryepiglottic folds are vibrating vigorously while the glottis is open beneath in the state of breath.

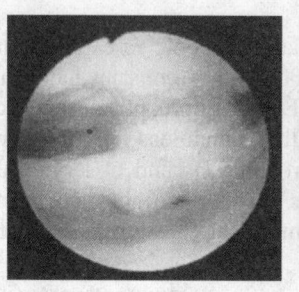

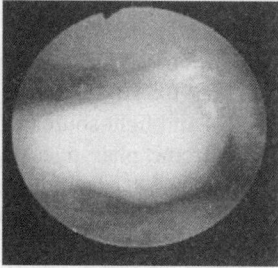

Figure 2: Maximum stricture of medial epiglottal stop [ʔ˗] in Iraqi Arabic /faʕʕal/ 'made active' (left) and voiceless epiglottal trill [ʜː] in /sahhar/ 'made magic' (right).

The qualities (due to pharyngeal resonance) that we have identified as a function of the laryngeal articulator are an example of how source generation and articulatory dynamics in the laryngeal space interact with other phonological specifiers that are not considered to be 'pharyngeal' per se. The 15-way tonal register syllable distinction in Bai (Tibeto-Burman) based on pitch, phonation type, laryngeal-constrictor tension and nasal quality is a good example of this relationship [8][17]. The Bai registers have been called 'lax' and 'tense', which are good phonological terms to differentiate the qualities. Phonetically speaking, we have argued that 'lax' reflects [–constr] syllabic register, while 'tense' reflects [+constr] syllabic register. The feature [+constr] represents the engagement of the laryngeal constrictor mechanism and results in qualities that are articulatorily the same as pharyngealization. Yi (Tibeto-Burman) is an example of a language whose vocalic system is characterized primarily by a [–constr/+constr] syllabic register contrast, which is also called lax/tense. But this is not a really isolated phenomenon. West African languages that have been labelled with [+ATR/–ATR] harmony series demonstrate the same contrast in laryngeal behaviour as those Tibeto-Burman languages with [–constr/+constr] (lax/tense) distinctions. Dinka as well as Somali also share the use of this phonetic property but in a paradigm where quality plays a more subtle role. The West African 'ATR' paradigm is virtually identical to the Tibeto-Burman lax/tense paradigm. Examples are Akan/Twi (Kwa) and Kabiye (Gur), which can each be thought of as having one set of vowels that is [–constr] (+ATR) [i, e, u, o, a], and a parallel set of vowels that is [+constr] (–ATR) [ɪ, ɛ, ʊ, ɔ, ɑ]. That the distinction is pharyngeal, i.e. a function of the laryngeal constrictor mechanism, was hypothesized in 1996 [11] and eventually confirmed through laryngoscopic observation [7][10]. The constricted series of these paradigms will be used here to make the connection between the possibilities available for contrastive purposes in adult phonologies and the way that infants begin their articulatory phonetic experience. The laryngoscopic examples that follow are of adults, but the constricted postures are very similar to the innate shape of the infant vocal tract [20].

In the [+constr] (–ATR) vowels in Akan, shown on the right in Fig. 3, the flatter forward-bending aryepiglottic angle, the more retracted tongue and raised larynx, and the narrowed posture of the laryngeal constrictor reflect the constricted state of the laryngeal vocal tract. Anatomically speaking, the constricted posture on the right resembles somewhat the shape of the naturally straight and short infant vocal tract. This comparison will be relevant when discussing what kinds of sounds infants produce in their first months of life. The existence of this body of auditorily catalogued laryngoscopic data will also assist us in understanding what inventories of laryngeally generated sounds infants produce at what stages of vocal development. The same situation exists in Kabiye (Gur), which has a similar [+ATR/–ATR] vowel harmony series. Each one of the vowels in the [+constr] (–ATR) set [ɪ̱, ɛ̱, ʊ̱, ɔ̱, a̱] demonstrates a tightened configuration of the laryngeal articulator, as seen in the image on the right in Fig. 4.

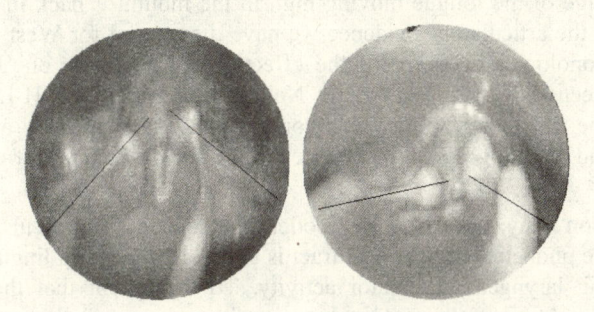

Figure 3: Mid-initial-vowel laryngeal posture of Akan /midif/ 'I am eating' (left) and /mɪ̱fdɪ̱t̪/ 'I am called' (right). The lines trace the aryepiglottic fold angle: low and open on the left; raised and closing on the right.

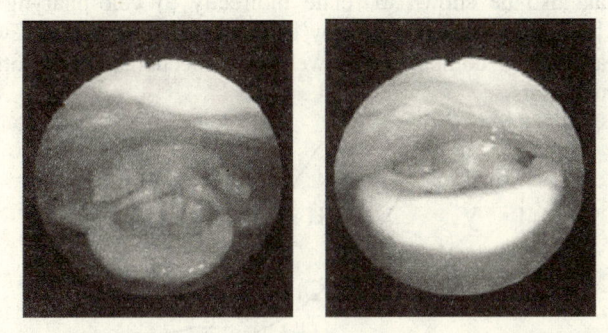

Figure 4: Mid-vowel laryngeal/pharyngeal posture of Kabiye /tú/ 'elephant' (left) and /tʊ̱́/ 'bee' (right)

2.4 The IPA vowel system, revised

In addition to consonantal place and manner, therefore, vowels are also affected by the action of the laryngeal constrictor. This is clear in the evidence from Akan and Kabiye, where vowel quality (noted by differing symbol shapes) changes as pharyngeal quality (noted by the subscript retracting symbol) changes. The flatter forward-bending aryepiglottic angle, retracted tongue and raised larynx during constriction and the consequent narrowed configuration of the pharyngeal resonator produce a vowel that is 'lower' and 'backer' on the vowel chart (i.e. retracted), whatever the individual vowel quality is due to oral lingual position.

These considerations imply that the 2005 International Phonetic Alphabet vowel chart may need revision in terms of its traditional 'Front-Back' and 'Close-Open' dimensions. The issue revolves around identifying articulators. If the tongue is taken to be the main articulator defining vowel quality and the vowel space, then the effect introduced by the laryngeally constricted set of vowels in the West African phonologies reviewed here occupies an ill-defined place in the system. If 'Back' does not account adequately for the movement of the laryngeal constrictor mechanism, then another parameter is needed in the deepest part of the vocal tract. And if opening of the jaw only applies to the 'Front' section of the vocal tract, then 'Open' is not a particularly apt qualifier for what happens to vowels in the lower right region of the vowel chart.

In many familiar systems of vowel location, vowels are described as lingually high or low and front or back. This conceptualization implies a model of lingual movement within the dimensions of a square space — four-cornered in two-dimensional terms — with the tongue moving up or down and from front to back. The tongue is usually represented in this model as the articulator responsible for changes in vowel quality along the high-low and front-back dimensions. This can be called the H-L-F-B model. This image of the tongue moving high in the mouth or back in the mouth, however, does not conform with the articulatory evidence we have discovered for West African languages or for Tibeto-Burman phonologies or even for the effects of pharyngeals on 'low back' vowels in Semitic languages, as seen above for Iraqi Arabic. Neither is the traditional H-L-F-B model as useful an image as it could be for understanding how sound quality is shaped by articulator movement, vocal tract postures, and resulting cavity resonances in a multi-faceted set of chambers such as the vocal tract.

The principal reason why the H-L-F-B model inadequately represents (and perhaps even mistakenly portrays) the phonetics of the vocal tract is that it assumes oral lingual articulator activity while virtually ignoring laryngeal articulator activity. To the extent that the H-L-F-B model is intended to account for auditory quality, it has also misinformed acoustic theory. The assumption that H-L-F-B movement of the tongue drives vowel quality is not entirely adequate in the light of what we have discovered about how the laryngeal articulator controls the pharyngeal resonator. In fact, the laryngeal articulator can also be shown to relate indirectly to velo-pharyngeal and mandibular settings in addition to lingual movement. The key in the development of a revised paradigm is to integrate a laryngeal articulator component between the mechanism of glottal airflow and the oral/front vocal tract articulators.

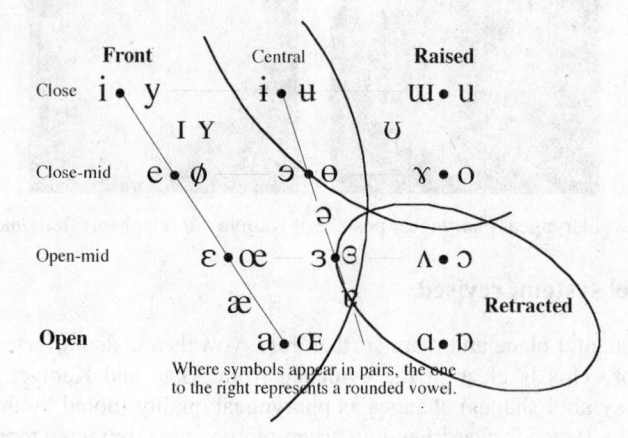

Figure 5: A revised IPA vowel chart to reflect three-way tongue movement: fronting, raising, and retraction, where retraction is a function of the laryngeal constrictor mechanism [13] [7].

The development of the Laryngeal Articulator Model [13] therefore prompts a revision of the conceptualization of the vowel chart, as suggested in Fig. 5. At the front, the tongue may be 'Fronted', but the articulator responsible for 'Open' quality is the jaw; at the back, it is the laryngeal constrictor. Tongue 'Raising' is also oral (and dorsal); but vowels affected by the action of the laryngeal constrictor will move in the direction of lingual 'Retraction', which is part of the laryngeal/pharyngeal constrictor mechanism that connects to the oral tract (cf. Fig. 1). The principal action of laryngeal constriction (aryepiglottic fold sphinctering) precedes lingual retraction and larynx raising in the hierarchy of the complex maneuvre [7][15].

These experimental articulatory phonetic findings lay the groundwork for the auditory description of infant speech production. In the past, descriptions of sound qualities emanating from the laryngeal vocal tract have lacked the phonetic precision afforded by the Laryngeal Articulator

Model. As a consequence, the labelling of infant speech sounds has been impressionistic rather than auditory phonetic [3][4][22][25][26][27]. Our goal is to integrate the present findings, based on the Laryngeal Articulator Model, with the findings of these previous studies. The research findings summarized in this paper provide a phonetic account of the components of the laryngeal mechanism, including effects on vowel quality that can be used to characterize infant vocalizations. It has been proposed that [+constr] is the feature that captures the articulatory generalization of the laryngeal constrictor [7][10], including pharyngeal consonants, tonal register and quality harmony, by creating an independent designation for the action of the lower part of the vocal tract. With this knowledge, it is possible to ask new questions about the ontogenetic development of the speech modality and to introduce new conjectures about phylogeny.

3. SPEECH SOUNDS IN THE FIRST YEAR OF LIFE

3.1 The InSpA Project — approach and method

The four language contexts in the InSpA (Infant Speech Acquisition) Project, where phonological inventories of the ambient languages are designed to contrast, are English in Canada and French in France, which do not have laryngeal features, and Arabic in Morocco and Bai in Yunnan, China, which do have laryngeal features. The initial hypothesis tested with our data is that speech-production processes begin in the laryngeal vocal tract rather than the oral vocal tract. Findings thus far in the initial part of the study are based on data from 19 infants' vocalizations (4 English, 9 Arabic, 6 Bai), classified by trained phoneticians using auditory analysis supplemented by wide-band spectrograms of 3197 utterances (English: 932; Arabic: 1011; Bai: 1254). While not all infants were recorded each month, the data presented here include a recorded session of at least one infant per month from 1 to 12 months. A digital camera with an integrated microphone was used to film the infants interacting with caregivers in their home environments. Phonatory settings (constricted vs. unconstricted) occurring in babbling sequences towards the end of the first year were also extracted from the data, but all CV(C) utterances, whether monosyllabic, reduplicative, or variegated, were considered babbling and became part of the second step of the Project.

3.2 Speech begins in the pharynx

From an anatomical point of view, laryngeal constriction as an available phonetic mechanism can be considered to be predisposed in the infant [20]. In our analysis of the phonetic production data [2][16][1][21], even babies who are surrounded by English produce the laryngeal/pharyngeal sounds that have been identified in the languages described in section 2 that have pharyngeal series, vowel harmony or register phonatory contrasts. All infants from all four ambient language environments in the study demonstrate the phonetic principle that speech production develops from a laryngeal/pharyngeal basis. In terms of phonation type, infants begin by using phonatory configurations where laryngeal constriction dominates, e.g. harsh voice, whispery voice, and creaky voice. Gradually, while continuing to employ constriction, infants develop phonation types that do not have constriction, e.g. modal voice, breathy voice, and falsetto. These tendencies are illustrated in Fig. 6, where laryngeally constricted production dominates initially in the three languages compared. The significant association between age group and constriction (χ^2(3)=93.34, p<.001) indicates that the incidence of laryngeal constriction in the utterances of the infants varies primarily as a function of age, irrespective of linguistic background.

3.3 Exploring phonatory capacity: phonetic alternations

Infants appear to use their speech production ability to explore laryngeal settings actively and systematically, beginning with phonation, based on physiological predispositions but clearly under the infants' control. In vocalizing, infants are observed to 'play' by manipulating degrees of constriction and increasing the length of utterances but also by alternating phonetic parameters in sequence and then alternating them in increasingly rapid succession over the months. For example, at 5 months, an infant may vary from a phonatory setting with less constriction to a setting with more constriction in a rudimentary pattern of alternation. At 7 months, an infant may alternate phonatory settings with and without constriction; or vocalizations at high pitch without constriction (falsetto) may alternate with high pitched vocalizations with constriction (tight harsh voice). At 8 months, an infant may explore degrees of glottal opening, alternating breathy phonation with modal phonation. At 10 months, constricted events may vary with unconstricted sequences, e.g. harshness with laryngeal closure followed by breathy voice, as unconstricted babbling sequences proliferate. It is the timing-control aspect of these alternations, as well as the nature of the phonetic values being alternated, that suggests to us that these patterns constitute a controlled 'intentional' activity.

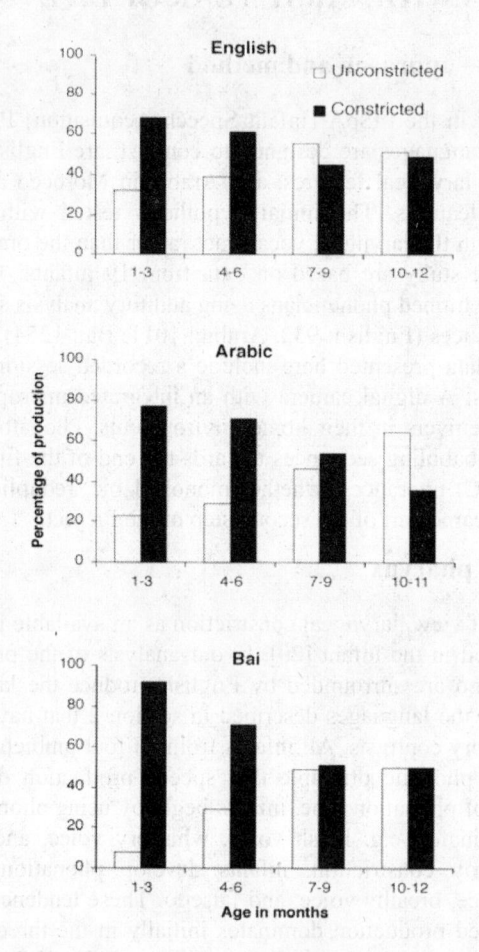

Figure 6: Proportion of constricted vs. unconstricted voice quality settings produced by English, Arabic, and Bai infants over the first year of life [1].

3.4 Expanding place of articulation: pharyngeal priming

In addition to alternating their new phonetic 'discoveries', we have evidence that infants explore new places of articulation by 'priming' the new sounds with a pharyngeal 'starter'. In the first 6 or 7 months, infants produce mainly stop strictures and fricatives that arise from laryngeal constriction (pharyngeals and glottals). In the second half of the first year, infants begin to 'specialize' in the use of consonants that predominate in their ambient languages. The 'first sound' that infants can be said to produce, from a stricture point of view and other than crying with a constricted (retracted) vowel, is epiglottal stop [ʡ], as in Fig. 2, since this stricture is a function of the laryngeal constrictor and the maneuvre is the primary airway-protection reflex. Glottal stops [ʔ], requiring more careful control with slightly more openness, only begin to appear in month 2 or 3. Fricative, approximant and trill manners are all observed to occur early in the laryngeal constrictor region (at the pharyngeal/epiglottal place, see Fig. 1).

Furthermore, we have found that oral places of articulation do not develop spontaneously as purely oral articulations. Instead, velars, uvulars, labials, alveolars and palatals appear first in combination with a pharyngeal sound. The deeper event primes the higher oral event. For example, a constriction in the pharynx (harshness, friction, aryepiglottic trilling or just pharyngeal resonance) may precede and prime the oral stricture of a labial [m]; the pharyngeal event acting as a secondary articulation to the labial. Fricatives at various places are observed to be primed with pharyngeal-stricture onset. In months 7-12, infants play by producing sequences to explore all manners at each particular place of articulation (manners which were learned initially in the pharynx). We have ample evidence of infants 'playing with the phonetic instrument', for instance producing uvular trills in long sequences once the uvular place of articulation is discovered, even where uvulars are not found in the ambient language (English).

3.5 Constriction in babbling vs. non-babbling

Once babbling begins, babbled utterances tend to be less constricted (more oral) than co-occurring non-babbled vocalizations. In our results thus far, English babbling is the least likely to feature laryngeal constriction, even at an age when the English infants' utterances overall contain a high proportion of constriction. Given that English does not use laryngeal constriction contrastively, this finding was expected. We also found that Arabic babbling consistently included a higher proportion of laryngeally constricted voice quality settings than English babbling. This finding is intriguing, since laryngeal constriction in Arabic contrasts mainly at the segmental level. It is possible that the Arabic infants have noticed the parameter 'laryngeal constriction' in their ambient language but have not yet differentiated between segmental and suprasegmental features. Alternatively, it is possible that voice quality settings are more constricted in language contexts where laryngeal constriction is employed at the segmental level. The rate of laryngeal constriction in the babbling of the Bai infants exhibited the most complex pattern: in months 4-6 and 10-12, the incidence of constriction was similar to that found for the Arabic infants; while for months 7-9, the babbling was primarily unconstricted and more closely resembled the English babbling. It is likely that phonetic acquisition of laryngeal contrasts is more complex in Bai than in English or Arabic, given that Bai employs a range of pitch-dependent phonatory settings in its tonal register system, contrasting harsh voice, modal voice, breathy voice, and five pitch patterns [8][17]. Where and when these phonetic contrasts first begin to appear contrastively in meaningful syllables in Bai will require observations of production from the second year of life.

4. DISCUSSION

Our first hypothesis - that speech-production processes begin in the laryngeal vocal tract rather than the oral vocal tract -has strong support. The secondary hypothesis, that manner of articulation is 'learned' at one place of articulation first and then transferred to subsequent places of articulation appears to be true of the laryngeal articulator. Alternations occur initially with phonation types, exercising states of the larynx, before patterns of oral combining can be performed. Furthermore, it is in the laryngeal region that these alternating patterns learn to be manipulated more and more quickly as control over the articulators grows. Then, sounds that are learned at new, oral places of articulation occur first with clear secondary 'accompaniment' from the original laryngeal/ pharyngeal articulator in the performance of 'pharyngeal priming'. The tertiary hypothesis, that infants exposed to ambient languages that exploit the laryngeal vocal tract in their phonological inventories will use selected laryngeal elements of speech earlier in their babbling behavior than do infants whose ambient languages do not contain laryngeal phonological components, appears not to be supported. By the end of the first year, none of the Arabic or Bai infants had begun to babble using pharyngeal segments or clearly identifiable laryngeal registers in their CV(C) forms. We have not yet been able to identify, towards the end of the first year or beginning of the second year, that the Arabic or Bai infants had begun to use pharyngeal segments or clearly identifiable laryngeal registers in meaningful contexts. Thus, our working hypothesis has had to be modified to consider that infants whose ambient languages contain laryngeal phonological components will have to 'reacquire' these forms once the acquisitional 'clock' is right. Although the phonetic capacity to perform the pharyngeal/laryngeal forms has been mastered by all infants during the first several months, the actual use of that capacity must be activated by other conditions that do not coincide with the beginning of babbling. Hence, it is hypothesized that the emergence of pharyngeals/laryngeals in meaningful contexts will only occur during events in the second year of life. These findings indicate that there is a disjuncture in continuity as far as overt articulatory speech production by infants is concerned, requiring some additions to and reformulation of the early stages of the continuity hypothesis [29]. Our data collection is continuing into the second year, and analyses with native-language fieldworkers of the production data in the one-word stage in both Arabic and Bai contexts are being designed to address these theoretical issues.

5. CONCLUSION

There are four main points that need to be emphasized in describing the process of the first steps in the acquisition of the speech modality. The first is that we 'learn speech from the inside out', and we do virtually all of it in the first several months of life. The 'inside' is the 'laryngeal vocal tract' component of the articulatory model, and the 'outside' is the 'oral vocal tract' component of the articulatory model. Laryngeal (including initially pharyngeal and then subsequently glottal) sounds are acquired first; then oral sounds begin to be learned, still employing a laryngeal 'base,' but not necessarily in a predictable order of places of articulation. The 'base' has three aspects: first, the laryngeal base serves as the point at which manner of articulation is acquired; secondly, the laryngeal base serves as the 'pivot point' against which other sounds are practiced in sequences of componential learning; and thirdly, the laryngeal base serves as a motor platform against which new sounds at the oral places of articulation are generated articulatorily.

Secondly, we have shown that manner of articulation can be adequately acquired in the pharynx. This has become clear as a result of our research into various languages with laryngeal phonological distinctions, and as a result of our research on infant speech, where stop, fricative, trill and approximant articulations emerge first as pharyngeals before appearing at later, oral places of articulation. A third finding is that productions of new vocalizations are 'tested' in patterns of alternating sequences that become increasingly supple in their temporal fluidity over the months of practice by the infants. For example, vocalizations with laryngeal constriction are 'tested' in alternation with new vocalizations that do not have laryngeal constriction in patterns of increasingly rapid switching of the articulatory parameters. Finally, we have established that babbling is 'primed' by the innately (i.e. initially reflexively) acquired laryngeal components of the speaking modality, so that the primarily oral sounds that occur typically in babbling emerge not as isolatedly oral articulations at the given place of articulation but rather are 'jump started' by a background, 'secondary' vocalization originating at the laryngeal place of articulation.

With regard to the babbling stage of infant speech, in the second part of the first year, babbling generally prefers new, oral, unconstricted sounds over those sounds that occurred in the first part of the first year and which are characterized primarily by laryngeal constriction. This phenomenon may relate to the split between brain stem neural control and cortical neural control, where brain stem control can be posited to account for the reflexive emergence of the innate use of the laryngeal articulator (responsible for the production of 'pharyngeal' and 'epiglottal' sounds in the taxonomy of the IPA). Later, cortical control is hypothesized to coincide with the shift from phonetic prebabbling practice (as described above) to the primarily oral control exhibited in the babbling stage, beginning around 6 to 8 months. From babbling into the word-development and word-combining stages in the second year of life, it may well be that we 'rediscover' the more basic, innate sounds we learned initially (if they are needed in the target language). Thus, our new working hypothesis is that the original, innately acquired constricted sounds will re-emerge 'from the outside in' in languages where they have to emerge eventually in the developmental phonology. The fundamental phonetic principle to be articulated here, as the result of our research, is that 'motor-phonetic awareness' is acquired very early — just as early as or even earlier than perceptual awareness is known to be acquired [24]. Furthermore, speech production abilities accompany perceptual abilities in a complex array of motor performance that begins as early as the first few weeks of life.

These results provide evidence for universal and language-specific patterns in the use of laryngeal constriction in the first year of life. In the first months of life, all infants produce primarily constricted voice quality settings. Over the course of the year, as infants systematically explore their evolving phonetic capacities, unconstricted settings make up an increasing proportion of their vocal repertoires. Within this general pattern, the distribution of laryngeal constriction in the infants' utterances may vary according to laryngeal features exploited in the infants' ambient language. Of the range of prelinguistic vocalizations produced by infants, babbling is the most likely to reflect emergent phonological properties and to exhibit cross-linguistic differences.

To summarize, we have identified the pharynx as the origin of earliest speech vocalization and the site of the earliest acquisition of manners of articulation. We have found evidence of phonetic alternation and pharyngeal priming as active strategies in the speech acquisition process. We have identified a preference for oral articulations over laryngeal units in babbling progresses. Our initial hypothesis that pharyngeal sounds will proliferate linearly when the ambient language contains those sounds is only weakly supported by the evidence of laryngeals in late vocalizations in Arabic and in Bai but not in the babbling of either of these languages. Our new working hypothesis is that pharyngeals are used first, oral sounds are preferred in babbling, and pharyngeals follow a hierarchy of 'reacquisition' in the second 12 months of life.

6. ACKNOWLEDGEMENTS

Funding support from the Social Sciences and Humanities Research Council of Canada grants 410-2003-1624, 410-2007-2375 is gratefully acknowledged. Appreciation is extended to Chris Coey, Greg Newton, Allison Benner, Izabelle Grenon, Qian Wang, Breanna Loster, Martin Holmes, Scott Moisik, Thomas Magnuson, Becky Stott, Soo Youn Ham, Dr Michael Mawdsley, Dr Michael Ross, Jimmy G. Harris, to Craig Dickson, Roy Snell and Steve Eady of STR–SpeechTech, and to Jerold A. Edmondson and Cécile M. Padayodi (University of Texas at Arlington), Chakir Zeroual (Université de Taza/ Paris III), Zeki Majeed Hassan (University of Göteborg), Pierre Hallé (CNRS, Paris III) and Dr Lise Crevier-Buchman (CNRS, Paris III/HEGP).

REFERENCES

[1] Benner, A., Grenon, I., Esling, J.H. 2007. Infants' phonetic acquisition of voice quality parameters in the first year of life. *Proc. 16th International Congress of Phonetic Sciences*, Vol. 3, 2073-2076.

[2] Bettany, L. 2004. *Range Exploration of Pitch and Phonation in the First Six Months of Life*. M.A. thesis, University of Victoria.

[3] Boysson-Bardies, B. de, Sagart, L., Durand, C. 1984. Discernible differences in the babbling of infants according to target language. *J. of Child Lang.* 11, 1-15.

[4] Boysson-Bardies, B. de, Vihman, M.M. 1991. Adaptation to language: evidence from babbling and first words in four languages. *Language* 67, 297-319.

[5] Carlson, B.F., Esling, J.H., Harris, J.G. 2004. A laryngoscopic phonetic study of Nlaka'pamux (Thompson) Salish glottal stop, glottalized resonants, and pharyngeals. In: Gerdts, D.B., Matthewson, L. (eds.), *Studies in Salish Linguistics in Honor of M. Dale Kinkade, Occasional Papers in Linguistics*, No. 17. Missoula: University of Montana Press, 58-71.

[6] Catford, J.C., Esling, J.H. 2006. Articulatory phonetics. In: Brown, K. (ed.), *Encyclopedia of Language and Linguistics* (2nd ed.), Vol. 9. Oxford: Elsevier, 425-442.

[7] Edmondson, J.A., Esling, J.H. 2006. The valves of the throat and their functioning in tone, vocal register, and stress. *Phonology* 23, 157-191.

[8] Edmondson, J.A., Esling, J.H., Lama, Z., Harris, J.G., Li Shaoni. 2001. The aryepiglottic folds and voice quality in the Yi and Bai languages: laryngoscopic case studies. *Mon-Khmer Studies* 31, 83-100. [*Minzu Yuwen, 2000* (6), 47-53 (in Chinese)].

[9] Edmondson, J.A., Esling, J.H., Harris, J.G., Huang, T-ch. 2005. A laryngoscopic study of glottal and epiglottal /pharyngeal stop and continuant articulations in Amis — an Austronesian language of Taiwan. *Language and Linguistics* 6, 381-396.

[10] Edmondson, J.A., Padayodi, C.M., Hassan, Z.M., Esling, J.H. 2007. The laryngeal articulator: source and resonator. In: *Proc. 16th International Congress of Phonetic Sciences*, Vol. 3, 2065-2068.

[11] Esling, J.H. 1996. Pharyngeal consonants and the aryepiglottic sphincter. *Journal of the International Phonetic Association* 26, 65-88.

[12] Esling, J.H. 1999. The IPA categories 'pharyngeal' and 'epiglottal': laryngoscopic observations of pharyngeal articulations and larynx height. *Language & Speech* 42, 349-372.

[13] Esling, J.H. 2005. There are no back vowels: the laryngeal articulator model. *Canadian Journal of Linguistics* 50, 13-44.

[14] Esling, J.H. 2006. States of the glottis. In: Brown, K. (ed.), *Encyclopedia of Language and Linguistics* (2nd ed.), Vol. 12. Oxford: Elsevier, 129-132.

[15] Esling, J.H. To appear. Phonetic notation. In: Hardcastle, W.J., Laver, J. (eds.), *Handbook of Phonetic Sciences*. Oxford: Blackwell.

[16] Esling, J.H., Benner, A., Bettany, L., Zeroual, C. 2004. Le contrôle articulatoire phonétique dans le prébabillage. In: *Actes des XXVes Journées d'Étude sur la Parole*. Fès: AFCP, 205-208.

[17] Esling, J.H., Edmondson, J.A. 2002. The laryngeal sphincter as an articulator: tenseness, tongue root and phonation in Yi and Bai. In: Braun, A., Masthoff, H.R. (eds.), *Phonetics and its Applications: Festschrift for Jens-Peter Köster on the Occasion of his 60th Birthday*. Stuttgart: Franz Steiner Verlag, 38-51.

[18] Esling, J.H., Fraser, K.E., Harris, J.G. 2005. Glottal stop, glottalized resonants, and pharyngeals: a reinterpretation with evidence from a laryngoscopic study of Nuuchahnulth (Nootka). *J. of Phonetics* 33, 383-410.

[19] Esling, J.H., Harris, J.G. 2005. States of the glottis: an articulatory phonetic model based on laryngoscopic observations. In: Hardcastle, W.J., Beck, J.M. (eds.), *A Figure of Speech: A Festschrift for John Laver*. Mahwah, NJ: Lawrence Erlbaum, 347-383.

[20] Fitch, W.T., Giedd, J. 1999. Morphology and development of the human vocal tract: a study using magnetic resonance imaging. *J. Acoust. Soc. Am.* 106, 1511-1522.

[21] Grenon, I., Benner, A., Esling, J.H. 2007. Language-specific phonetic production patterns in the first year of life. In: *Proc. 16th International Congress of Phonetic Sciences* Saarbrücken, Vol. 3, 1561-1564.

[22] Hallé, P.A., Boysson-Bardies, B. de, Vihman, M.M. 1991. Beginnings of prosodic organization: intonation and duration patterns of disyllables produced by Japanese and French infants. *Language & Speech* 34, 299-318.

[23] Heselwood, B. 2007. The 'tight approximant' variant of the Arabic ayn. *Journal of the International Phonetic Association* 37, 1-32.

[24] Kuhl, P.K., Stevens, E., Hayashi, A., Deguchi, T., Kiritani, S., Iverson, P. 2006. Infants show a facilitation effect for native language phonetic perception between 6 and 12 months. *Developmental Science* 9 (2), F13-F21.

[25] McCune, L., Vihman, M., Roug-Hellichius, L., Delery, D., Gogate, L. 1996. Grunt communication in human infants (Homo sapiens). *J. of Comp. Psych.* 110, 27-37.

[26] Oller, D.K. 2000. *The Emergence of the Speech Capacity*. Mahwah, NJ: Lawrence Erlbaum.

[27] Stark, R.E., Rose, S.N., McLagen, M. 1975. Features of infant sounds: the first eight weeks of life. *J. of Child Lang.* 2, 205-221.

[28] Tiede, M.K. 1996. An MRI-based study of pharyngeal volume contrasts in Akan and English. *J. of Phonetics* 24, 399-421.

[29] Vihman, M.M., Macken, M.A., Miller, R., Simmons, H., Miller, J. 1985. From babbling to speech: a re-assessment of the continuity issue. *Language* 61 (2), 397-445.

STUDIES OF SWEDISH PROSODY IN THE FRAME OF SPEECH PRODUCTION

Gunnar FANT, Anita KRUCKENBERG

ABSTRACT

As an outcome of more than 20 years of research we have developed a system of speech analysis and synthesis, labelled FK, intended as a tool for prosodic research and text-to-speech synthesis. It has resulted in a system for converting an orthographic input to an output in terms of fundamental frequency and duration data, at present tested in the frame of MBROLA diphone synthesis for Swedish, but it has also been applied to English and French. The processing allows a detailed analysis and prediction of structures from a syntactical base with rules for realization of prosodic boundaries and associated pauses. We have a support from our earlier studies of speech production including voice fundamental frequency, intensity and duration, as well as respiratory and voice source parameters in a linguistic frame. Of special interest is the co-variation of F_0 and other parameters and occasional temporal asynchrony observed within a prosodic group. These data also add insights in speech productions of value for articulatory oriented speech analysis and synthesis. A novelty lies in the intonation modelling based on a semitone scale that allows representative averaging of male and female data. It is consistently used in all data processing. It is a superposition model of local accentual modulations added to continuous prosodic base curves with normalized time scales. A backbone in the system is the introduction of the continuously scaled prominence parameter, RS, which controls both F_0 and duration data. We may thus refer to a more detailed prominence scaling than merely to a phonological labelling of words as focal versus non-focal. It allows us to quantify pre-focal and post-focal reductions within a sentence. We have collected a representative set of data on pausing for each of our subjects that displays common trends as well as large individual variations. The extensive framework of our prosody model makes it suited for applications in studies of speaking style and dialects.

Keywords: prosody, intonation, production, synthesis, Swedish

1. INTRODUCTION

The main purpose of our presentation is to summarize our recent and earlier studies contributing to a coherent view of prosodic realisation.

An early major study [13] was concerned with duration patterns and prominence related to duration. It provided an initial report on our perceptual grading of word and syllable prominence RS, then interpreted as "received stress". It also reported on studies of pausing and other juncture cues and their relative perceptual importance.

A comprehensive study of the growth of RS with a large number of acoustical parameters was published in Fant et al. [17]. It also illustrated the distribution of pre-focal and post-focal reductions in F_0 intensity and duration at varying positioning of focus within a short sentence.

The main outline of our prosodic modelling towards text-to-speech synthesis first appeared in Fant & Kruckenberg [9] and a more complete version in Fant et al [20].

Studies of the voice source were initiated at an early stage [7]. Detail studies of individual patterns and voice topology have appeared in Fant [11][13].

Insights in speech production modelling were greatly enhanced by studies of true subglottal pressure [13]. We now have a documentary material covering 20 sentences illustrated in a multi-parameter speech analysis frame [18] as exemplified in Fig.1.

More recent findings of asynchronous timing at prosodic boundary regions and of analytical relations between intensity, F_0 and subglottal pressure [24] provide a support for the understanding of observed parameter co-variation.

2. SPEECH ANALYSIS TOOLS

A most important tool which has been used from the early stage of our prosody work is the speech processing and display system Wspec, see [30] and recent applications in Fant [22][23]. Besides oscillogram and spectrogram it generates F_0 on a log scale, with a standard of one semitone per 2 mm.

Two intensity traces are provided, the regular SPL and one with a high frequency pre-emphasis, SPLH [13] defined by a gain

$$G(f)=10\log_{10}\{(1+f^2/200^2)/(1+f^2/5000^2)\} \quad \text{dB} \tag{1}$$

In relation to SPL, SPLH emphasizes the second and higher formants. Accordingly, SPLH-SPL serves as a measure of spectral tilt within the constraints of a given formant pattern and it increases with stress [16][17]. High frequency spectral tilt was suggested as a stress correlate by Sluijter & van Heusen [34].

When available, synchronous records of true sub- and supra-glottal pressures, Psub and Psup, have been included. They were obtained from a sond inserted externally into the larynx. A male laryngologist served as a subject [13][24].

A large material of subglottal data from prose reading has been collected [18].

Our standard display, see Fig. 1, also includes our estimates of syllable prominence RS. It was introduced by Fant & Kruckenberg [9] and tested on a single speaker with a listening crew of 15 people. Our present data derive from a more recent perceptual grading of all words and accented syllables in the prose reading. It was undertaken by the two authors.

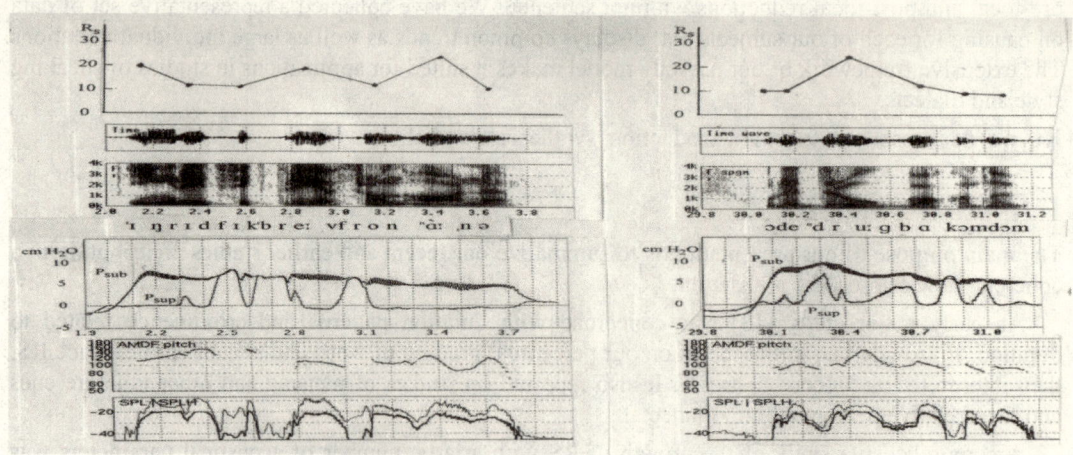

Figure 1: Examples of Wspec display. Left, a simple declarative sentence: "Ingrid fick brev från Arne" (Ingrid received a letter from Arne). Right, the first part of a sentence: "Å de drog bakom dom" (*and there was a draught behind the* ...). Emphatic high emphasis on the verb "drog".

3. INTONATION MODELLING

The main corpus of our data is from five subjects, three males and two females, reading a passage of one-minute length from a novel. In addition, we had separate recordings from studies of respiratory activity in speech and data from news reading over the radio.

All F_0 data was recorded on a log frequency scale, a feature inherent in the Wspec processing, Fig. 1. We have established a semitone scale St with 100Hz as an absolute reference.

St is derived from frequency in Hz by the equation

$$St=12[\ln(Hz/100)/\ln 2] \qquad (2)$$

The conversion from semitones to frequency is accordingly

$$Hz=2^{St/12}100 \qquad (3)$$

employed in the final phase of synthesis processing.

The significance of the log F_0 scaling was established by comparison of average data from unstressed syllables for each of our subjects. These turned out to be the same as with reference to their long time average values.

The following individual values of St were found:

Male speakers: SH=+1, GF=+1, JL=0

Female speakers: AÖ=+7, IK=+9,5

The F_0 normalization now proceeds by subtracting each subject's average scale factor from his or her recorded data which accordingly is reduced to St=1, which is close to the male average data.

We have also introduced a temporal normalization. The time scale is substituted by a sequence scale of equally spaced slots for location of F_0 points superimposed on major prosodic base curves.

The notational system for Swedish word accent of Bruce (1997) has been adopted, but with some modifications. Accent 1 and accent 2 primary syllables attain two F_0 points each. These have been labelled L* and Ha for accent 1 and H* and L for accent 2. The accent 2 secondary syllable is denoted Hg. The Bruce system contains a high tone H preceding L*. It is missing when the L*H occurs initially in a sentence. Unstressed syllables are denoted Lu and a group-terminal low F_0 juncture is marked Lt. These attain one point each.

A disyllabic accent 1 word thus contains the sequence HL*Ha and a dissyllabic accent 2 word H*LHg. These accent domains also occur in polysyllabic words. In compound accent 2 the secondary syllable Hg is shifted to the right one or more unstressed syllables. An example is the word "huvudpostkontorets", to appear in Fig. 3 and 7, transcribed as H*L Lu Lu Lu Hg Lu.

We have adopted a target-oriented frame for F_0 sampling. It provides a stable base for intonation modelling and normalization. Thus, Lu and H syllables are sampled in the middle of the vowel. The accent 2 high starting point H* is located at the vowel onset or 20-40ms later. The following low point L is of major importance. It cannot be directly observed in unvoiced segments. It has the significance of a locus for the drop from H*. It is usually found 7-10 semitones below H*, at a distance of about 120-180ms, which can be observed in voiced contexts. The location of Hg varies somewhat with relative prominence. At medium stress levels it is found at the end of the voiced part of the secondary stressed syllable and can overshoot to a following unstressed syllable. At higher stress levels Hg is displaced to an earlier position approaching the centre of the vowel.

The main tonal contrast between accent 1 and 2 at a medium or high prominence level is the rising versus falling tone in the vowel onset of the primary stressed syllable as reflected by the traditional notation "ánden" for accent 1 and "ànden" for accent 2.

The accent 2 secondary stressed syllable Hg carries the degree of prominence and may be highly reduced or even absent in pre- and post-focal positions, while the H*L drop remains a phonological marker. At high prominence levels we find a similarity in the shape and magnitude of Ha and Hg peaks and they are followed by a low tone terminal juncture.

We have derived a set of four different base curves for the superposition of F_0 data. These have smooth outlines with some degree of initial rise followed by decay to a lower value. One of these, labelled Ob1a, pertains to a sentence initial non-final group. When additional non-final groups follow, these are labelled Ob2a. A single prosodic group spanning a complete sentence is labelled Ob1b. Ob2b pertains to a sentence final position of a group when preceded by other groups. Ob1b and Ob2b end with a low value, -4 semitones on the St scale.

As a consequence, short and long prosodic groups of a selected category attain the same overall F_0 rise and fall independent of their length. This is partly explained by the concept of a breath group but has a wider significance for prosodic grouping within an utterance.

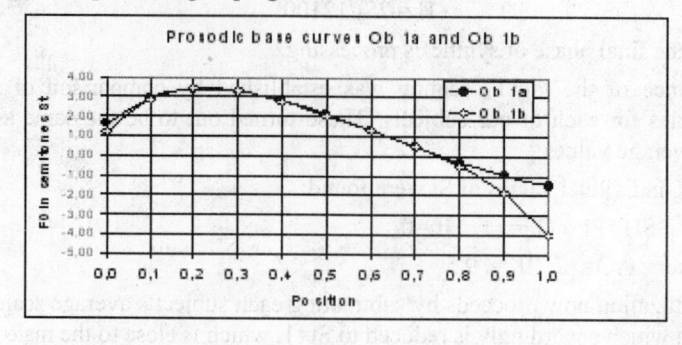

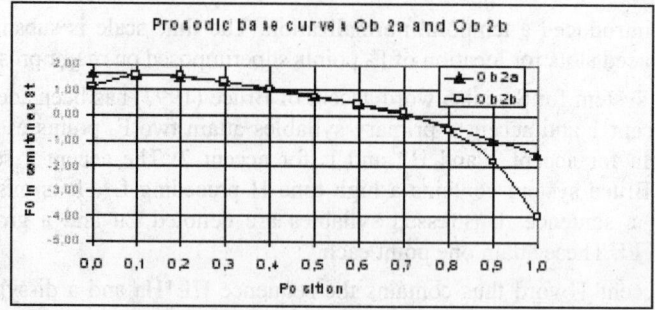

Figure 2: Our prosodic base curves for sentence initial position above and non-initial position below

Examples of the outcome of frequency and temporal normalization are shown in Fig. 3.

A major trend in Fig. 3 is the appearance of a stable overall declination curve in the five subjects' average data, including that of the female subject, AÖ. Observe that the close match is achieved by individual scale factors in F_0 and not by curve fitting. We note a tendency of AÖ to start higher and to end lower than the average, and also to favor smooth internal contours.

The major spread in the five-speaker data of Fig. 3 occurred in the word "uppångat" (*steam-opened*) reflecting varying emphasis. A stable point across all speakers is the accent 2 H*.

A close-up view of the intonation patterns of this word spoken by two of the subjects is shown in the upper part of Fig. 4. There is a 7 semitones higher accent 2 Hg for GF than for SH reflecting difference in prominence while their preceding H* indicating the onset peak of accent 2 are almost the same.

The data points in the lower part of Fig. 4 exemplify two speakers differing in prominence of the accent 1 word "barn" (*child*). Observe that subject JL has a falling branch from L* to Ha reflecting low prominence. This is a consequence of our labelling of accent points with respect to sample positions irrespective of relative height.

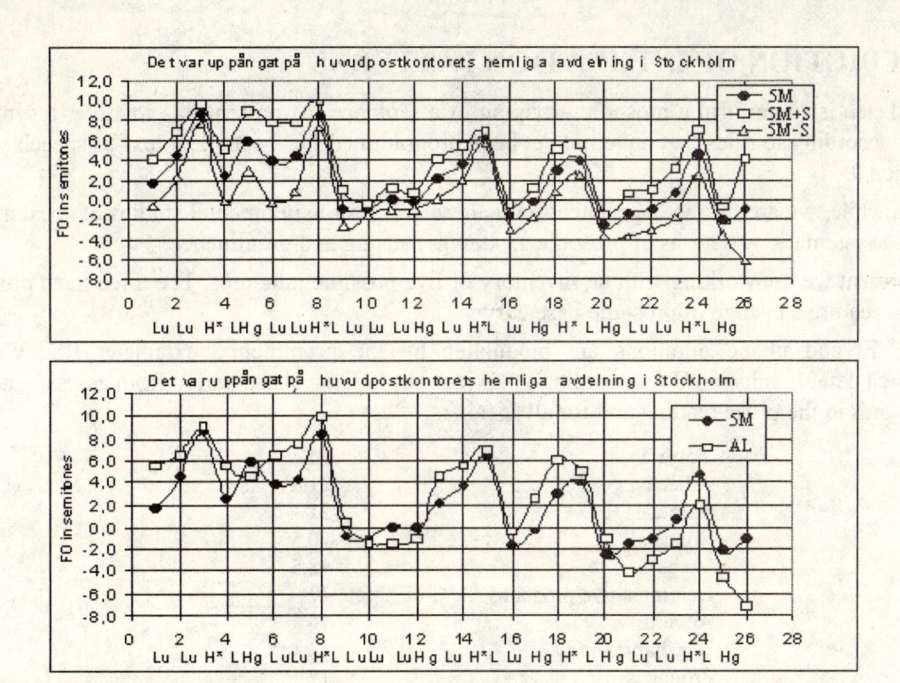

Figure 3: Time and frequency normalized F_0 contours. Above, the average of the five speakers plus and minus one standard deviation. Below, the average, 5M, solid points, and the female speaker AÖ, open squares. Sentence translation: *"It was steam-opened at the Central Post Office secret department in Stockholm."*

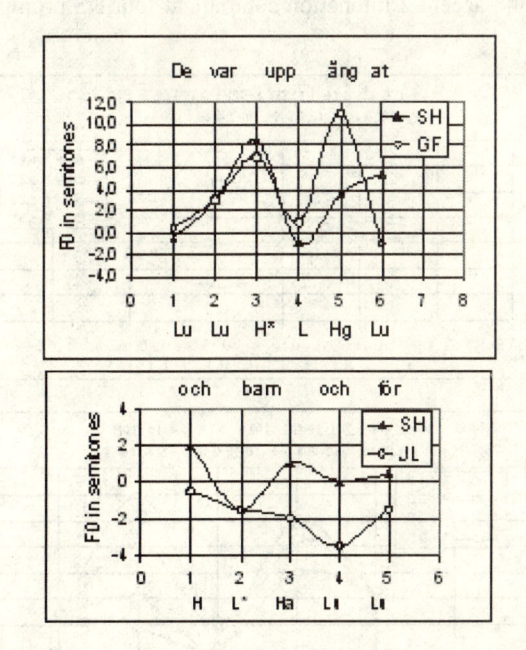

Figure 4: Detailed view of accent 1 and accent 2 speaker specific patterns contrasting in prominence level. Accent 2 above: "De var uppångat" (*It was steam-opened*), speakers SH and GF. Accent 1 below: "och barn och för..."(*and children and for...*), speakers SH ad JL.

4. PREDICTION OF INTONATION PATTERNS

The first step is to perform a prosodic grouping of a sentence. At present this involves a syntactical analysis according to rules that have not yet been programmed for a complete text-to-speech version, see section 9.

Meanwhile, we are free to experiment with alternatives for experimental studies of speaking style involving systematic variations of prosodic grouping, pausing and prominence.

At present we are working with an inventory of five possible junctures. The three most prominent junctures require a change of prosodic base curve.

Both F_0 and phone durations are modulated by the prominence parameter RS. We have established default values of RS according to lexical word class. These derive from assessment of RS for all words in the prose reading and for all speakers.

Table 1	RS
Adjectives	21,5
Numerals	21
Nouns	20,5
Verbs	18,5
Determinative pronouns	17
Adverbs	16
Auxiliary verbs	12
Pronouns	12
Average unstressed	11
Stressed unaccented	12-17
Focal stressed	>23

Normalized accent 1 and accent 2 intonation contours at four RS prominence levels are shown in Fig. 5.

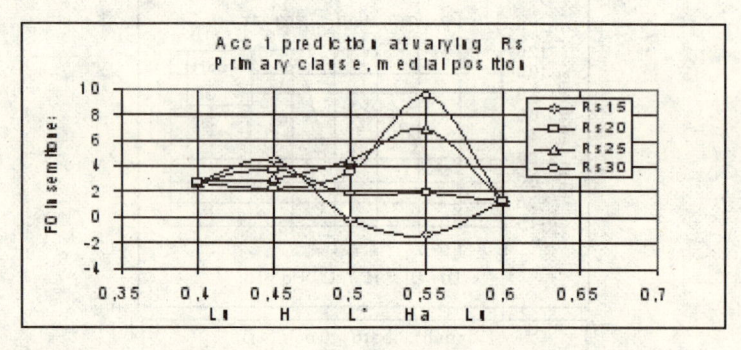

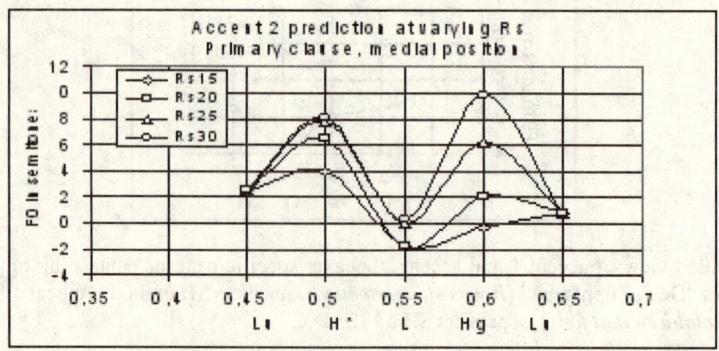

Figure 5: Normalized accent 1 and accent 2 parameters within a primary clause medial position

The accent 1 H parameter displayed a considerable variability and as a result a compressed range. As already mentioned, the L*H contour becomes falling at low RS values, a consequence of our notion system. The increase of accent 1 Ha with RS is similar to that of accent 2 Hg. Both convey prominence.

Observe that H* of accent 2 saturates at RS above 22, whilst the Hg parameter continues to increase with RS. We may conceive of H* as a phonological marker of accent 2, whilst Hg conveys the degree of sentence stress.

These general trends are illustrated in the speech analysis displays of Fig. 6.

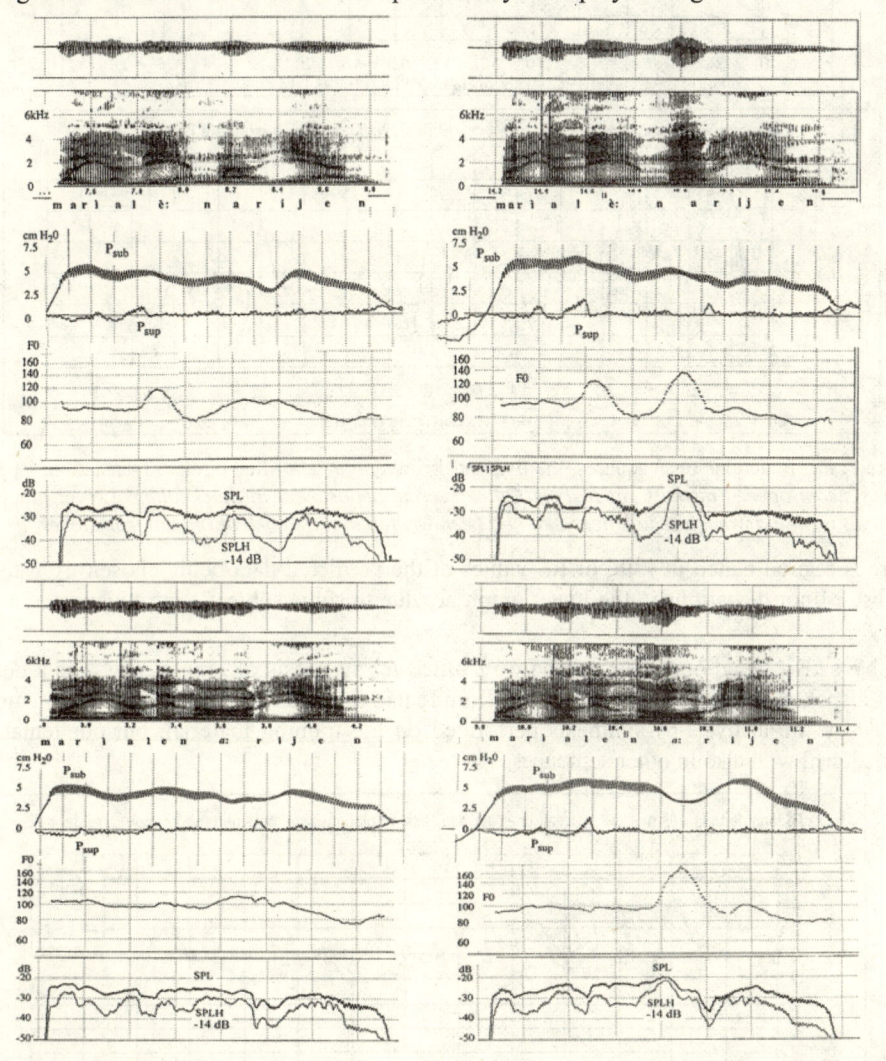

Figure 6: Upper parts: neutral and high prominence of the accent 1 word **Lena:r** in "Maria Lenar igen" [maria le'na:r ijen] (*Maria Lenar again*). Lower parts: neutral and high prominence of the accent 2 verb **lenar** in "Maria lenar igen" [maria lè:nar ijen] (*Maria is soothing again*).

4.1 Examples of F$_0$ prediction

A complete prediction of any F$_0$ value requires data on accent category, its position within a prosodic group and the established word class RS, Table 1. In Fig. 7 a prediction of the intonation within a sentence is compared with the mean data of our five subjects derived from individual RS assessments of each sample.

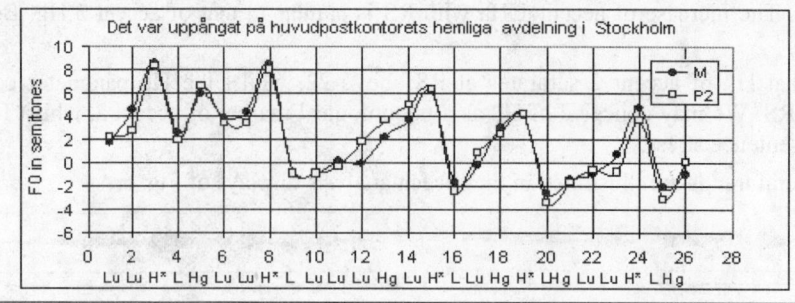

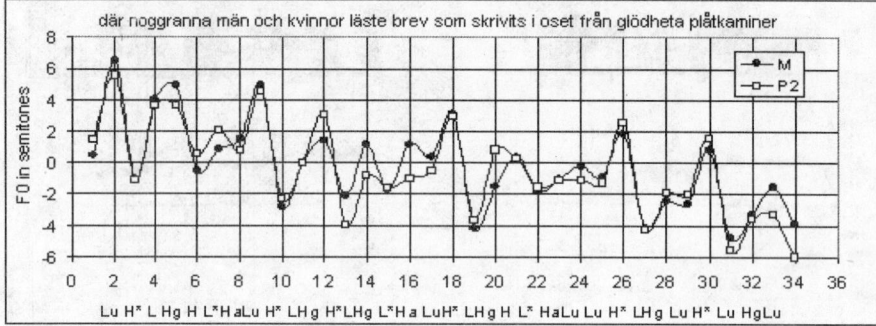

Figure 7: F_0 predictions open squares, the five-speaker average data filled circles. Translation: Upper graph: *"It was steam-opened at the Central Post Office secrete department in Stockholm."* Lower graph: *"where ambitious men and women read letters that had been written in the smoke of red hot iron stoves."*

There is a good match in spite of RS values of the predicted data being chosen from the lexical default list. Minor deviations in the lower graph are due to some subject's introduction of a prosodic boundary.

We have also found our system to be well suited for synthesis of French. Fig. 8 is a normalized graph of a spoken sentence and a prediction from tentative rules. The close match is to some extent influenced by the analysis-by-synthesis performed on the training material, but our tentative rules have functioned well also in other sentences.

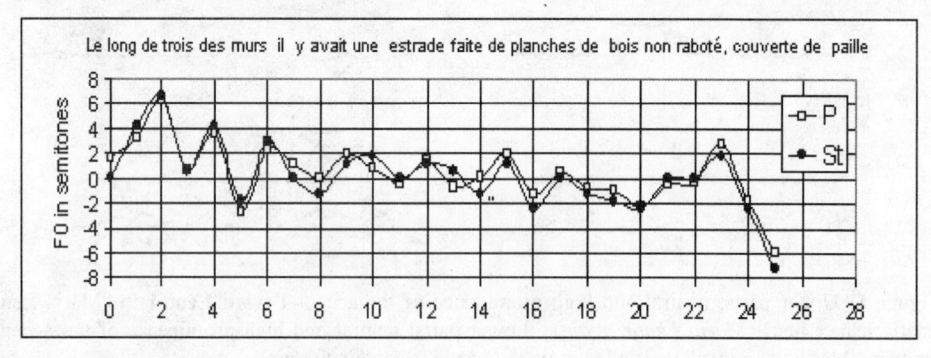

Figure 8: Measured F_0, St, and predicted F_0, P. The text is: "Le long de trois des murs il y avait une estrade faite de planches de bois non raboté, couverte de paille."

Here we have introduced a modified version of our Swedish accent 1, which accounts for the typical iambic pattern of word intonation within a prosodic group in French [10]. The final rise, typical of major prosodic groups inside a sentence, can generally be introduced without a specific intonation module by a high RS value in the last content word. Sentence final groups have the same or a larger declination towards a low F_0 than in Swedish and the pre-pause lengthening is more apparent. Duration rules were discussed in Kruckenberg and Fant [24].

4.2 Auditory smoothing of intonation related to production

The final stage of synthesis involves the conversion of the normalized time scale of intonation to a real time representation, resulting in an output of F_0 sample points at prescribed time locations. Intermediate values can be derived by an appropriate interpolation function. However, straight-line connections between sample points are generally sufficient in synthesis, which suggests an auditory smoothing in F_0 perception [22][23].

There is considerable evidence of a time constant of the order of 150ms in the generation of F_0 contours. It derives from data on the initiation of intonation in a sentence and from examples of single prominent F_0 peaks with rise times and decay times of the order of 150ms. Their shape fits well with a symmetrical Gauss function, see the F_0 peaks in the right hand parts of Fig. 6. Such single peaks have been referred to as "hat patterns" [5].

Apart from occasional more rapid F_0 fluctuations to be observed, it seems reasonable to assume a time constant of the order of 150ms in production as well as in perception of F_0.

5. MODELLING DURATION

A substantial amount of work has been devoted to rules for predicting duration. It has involved both phoneme size units and syllables. Our main resource has been a database of 8-minute text reading from an expert speaker, ÅJ. A detailed derivation of contextual rules within a phonetic frame was undertaken [15].

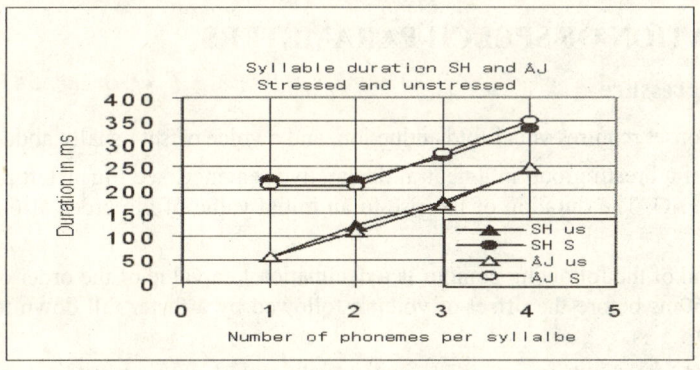

Figure 9: Stressed and unstressed syllable duration as a function of the number of phonemes per syllable. Two subjects: ÅJ and SH, the major male reference in our five-subject prose reading group. Note the similarity of data.

The stressed-unstressed dichotomy of syllable duration is illustrated in Fig. 9. Syllable duration increases with the number of phonemes per syllable. In the stress group, single phoneme syllables have the same duration as two-phoneme syllables. This is because they carry a long vowel. Of primary interest is that the stressed-unstressed contrast is about 100ms for both speakers. In terms of the prominence parameter RS, this is a step from approximately 11 to 20 units.

Phoneme durations are derived with respect to phonetic category and position within a prosodic group and a syllable. We have specific rules for determining syllable boundaries. They are based on phoneme sequences rather than on morphological criteria. In addition we apply an RS dependency by interpolation and extrapolation between phoneme class specific data for stressed and unstressed reference durations.

The procedure involves the following steps for consonants:

1. Selection of five groups of phonetic category: unvoiced stops, voiced stops, voiceless fricatives, nasals, or a group (/v/, /j/, /l/, /r/, /h/).

2. Position within the syllable: before a vowel or after a short vowel or after a long vowel.

3. Now read the reference durations, Do for RS=11 and Db for RS=20, listed for the particular phoneme category and position.

4. For other RS values perform a linear interpolation-extrapolation with respect to Do and Db.

Vowels follow the same but a less selective procedure. At present our main categories are /a/ versus all other vowels, and if they are phonemically long or short.

A well established rule in Swedish phonetics illustrated by Fant & Kruckenberg [9], is that a stressed syllable may contain either a long vowel followed by a short consonant or a short vowel followed by a long consonant. These relations are preserved by our rules and tabulated data. Thus for the contrasting words "mat" and "matt" we derive duration patterns of 64+158+97 versus 64+99+145. For the words "man" and "mann" we obtained 64+158+74 versus 64+99+99, i.e. a less expansion for the consonant [n] after the short vowel. In order to preserve consistency of this basic rule we do not allow a syllable boundary to occur before the stressed consonant. Thus: "be-mann-a." Even an unstressed vowel can have a syllabic function [26], We can not accept the gemination "be-man-na".

Phoneme, more generally phone durations, were less sensitive to the particular location of the syllable within an utterance. An exception was final lengthening, which occurred in all syllables terminating a prosodic group, even those of the lowest category.

These data pertain to text reading. In utterances composed of a few words only, the time scale is considerably expanded, of the order of 10-25%.

6. CO-VARIATION OF SPEECH PARAMETERS

6.1 Subglottal pressure

The initial voice onset requires vocal fold adduction, and a voice offset usually abduction.

At the onset of a breath group in a neutral declarative sentence, see Fig. 1 left part, voicing starts at a Psub of 3-5 H_2O. The duration of the rise to an initial value of the order of 6-8cm H_2O is 120-180ms.

The main trend of the following contour is a declination to a value of the order of 4-5cm H_2O at a location about 150ms before the offset of voicing followed by a faster fall down to a final value of about 1.5cm H_2O.

An example of high focal stress was illustrated in the right hand part of Fig. 1: "å de *drog* bakom dom…" (there *was a draught behind the*...) The F_0 peak occurs in a region of falling Psub, a general tendency that will be discussed in more detail later.

As required, Psub equals Psup at vocal tract closure, which usually are regions of pressure build-up. At less complete degrees of articulatory constrictions the driving pressure becomes Ptr=Psub-Psup.

The aero-dynamical consequences of articulatory interaction in specific phonetic frames have been studied in detail by Fant [22][23] and by Fant & Kruckenberg [24]. Here follows the main outline.

6.2 The F_0 midfrequency, F_0ref

Of special interest is the extent to which the intensity contour follows the F_0 contour and how the co-variation is mediated by subglottal pressure. We have found evidence for the relevance of a mid-frequency F_0ref in a speaker's available F_0 range, below which the SPL intensity follows the F_0 contour. In the upper frequency range, $F_0 > F_0$ref, SPL measures tend to saturate with increasing F_0.

These relations are governed by the subglottal pressure, which rises with F_0 up to F_0ref and then tends to level off. This is less so in the speech of singers who usually maintain a rising Psub and SPL above their F_0ref [35].

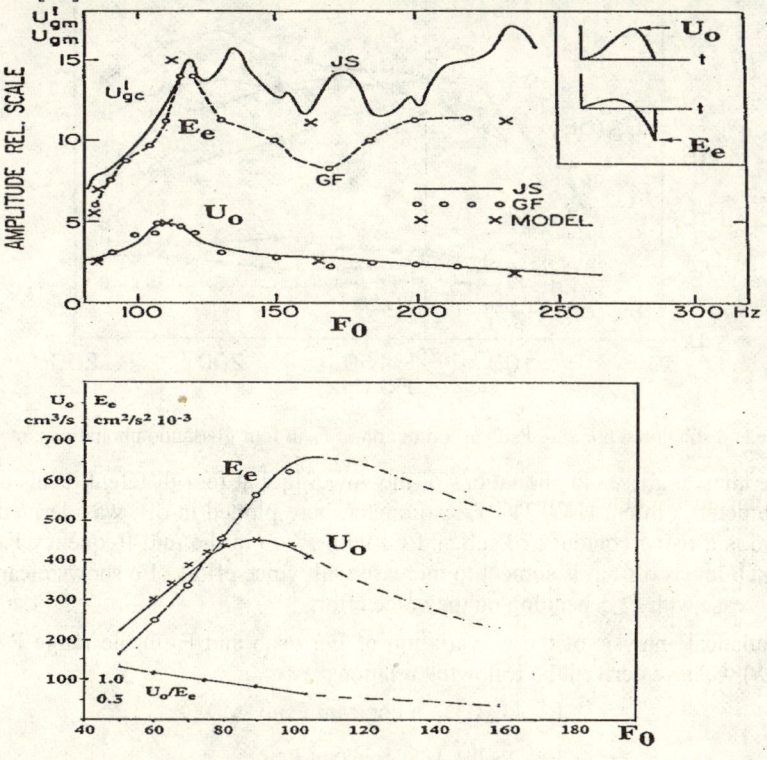

Figure 10: Voice source parameters Ee and Uo as a function of F_0. Above, subjects JS and GF in glissando phonation. Below, subject ÅJ, data sampled from prose reading.

The upper part of Fig. 10 pertains to glissando phonation, i.e. sustained phonation with gliding pitch of a vowel [ae:]. The glottal flow parameter Uo and the corresponding voice source amplitude Ee are plotted as a function of F_0 for two subjects, JS and GF.

The Ee parameter is a direct determinant of SPL as governed by the basic proportionality between Ee and formant amplitudes [13][22][23].

The two subjects have quite similar patterns of Uo rising as a function of F_0, but they differ in Ee. Both show the same breaking points of 110Hz for Uo and 120Hz for Ee, but subject JS maintains higher Ee levels above the breaking point.

The lower graph of Fig. 10 shows Uo and Ee data as a function of F_0 obtained from inverse filtering of passages from a prose text read by our reference subject ÅJ in earlier studies. His Uo data levels off at F_0=90Hz and his Ee at an F_0ref =105Hz.

6.3 Co-variation of F_0, Psub and SPL

Our major source for deriving analytical rules connecting F_0, Psub and SPL is the data in Fig. 11.

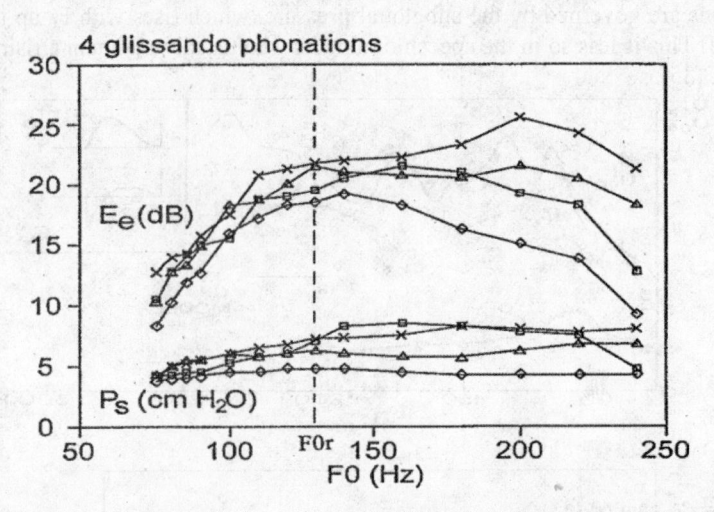

Figure 11: Ee and subglottal pressure Psub as a function of F_0 in four glissando phonations, male subject SH

Fig. 11 pertains to glissando phonations of the vowel [ae] at four different levels of voice effort. The Psub parameter is in cm H_2O. The Ee parameter, here plotted in dB, was derived from inverse filtering. There is a rising contour of Psub and Ee with F_0 up to the mid-frequency F_0ref. At higher frequencies Psub levels off but is subject to increase with voice effort. Ee shows clear tendencies to increase or decrease with F_0 depending on the voice effort.

From a statistical analysis of the co-variation of Ee, Psub and F_0 in the range $F_0 < F_0$ref (Fant, 2004, 257-258) we have derived the following relations:

$$Ee \sim F_0 1.35 \text{ at constant Psub} \tag{4}$$

$$Ee \sim Psub 1.1 \text{ at constant } F_0 \tag{5}$$

$$Psub \sim F_0 0.7 \text{ at constant Ee} \tag{6}$$

Here Ee is not in dB but a scalar value and F_0 is in Hertz.

Accordingly, with co-varying Psub:

$$Ee \sim F_0 1.35 \times Psub 1.1 \sim F_0 2.1 \tag{7}$$

which implies that Ee is increased by 12.5dB/oct in F_0 when the co-varying Psub is taken into account. This is roughly one dB per semitone increase of F_0. On the other hand, in terms of Psub and a normal co-varying F_0 we find:

$$Ee \sim Psub3 \tag{8}$$

A general model of Ee in dB, as a function of Psub and F_0, valid for the entire F_0 range has been derived:

$$Ee = K + 20\log 10 \{Ptr 1.1 xn 1.35[(1-xn2)2+xn2/Q2]-0.5\} \tag{9}$$

where $xn = F_0/F_0$ref and Q is of the order of 1.25. For more general conditions the transglottal pressure Ptr=Psub–Psup has been introduced. A higher Q will enhance the turning point. An interesting property of Eq. 9 is that it allows solving Ptr given F_0 and SPL:

$$Ptr = \{10(SPL-K/20) xn-1,85[(1-xn2)2+xn2/Q2]0.5\}-1.6 \tag{10}$$

Extending this formula to the sound pressure level SPL we arrive at:

$$SPL = K + 20\log 10\{Ptr 1.6 xn 1.85[(1-xn2)2+xn2/Q2]-0.5\} \tag{11}$$

In Eq, 10 and 11 we have included an additional exponent of 0,5 in x_n from the F_0 dependency of SPL at increasing pulse rates. The theoretical motivation is that a doubling of the number of voice periods in a given time would account for a 3dB increase. However other factors may come into play.

Also, results from our prediction experiments suggest a better fit to experimental data with the use of a higher Ptr exponent, i.e. $Ptr^{1,6}$. Equations 10 and 11 have been successfully tested in the two-word Swedish sentence "Ja adjö" [jɑ: a'jØ:]. There is a close match except at the word boundary. Observe that the SPL measure saturates in a region prior to the F_0 peak, which occurs in a falling branch of Psub. There was a fairly close match between predicted and measured SPL and also in Ptr=Psub. The F_0ref of the subject was 130Hz.

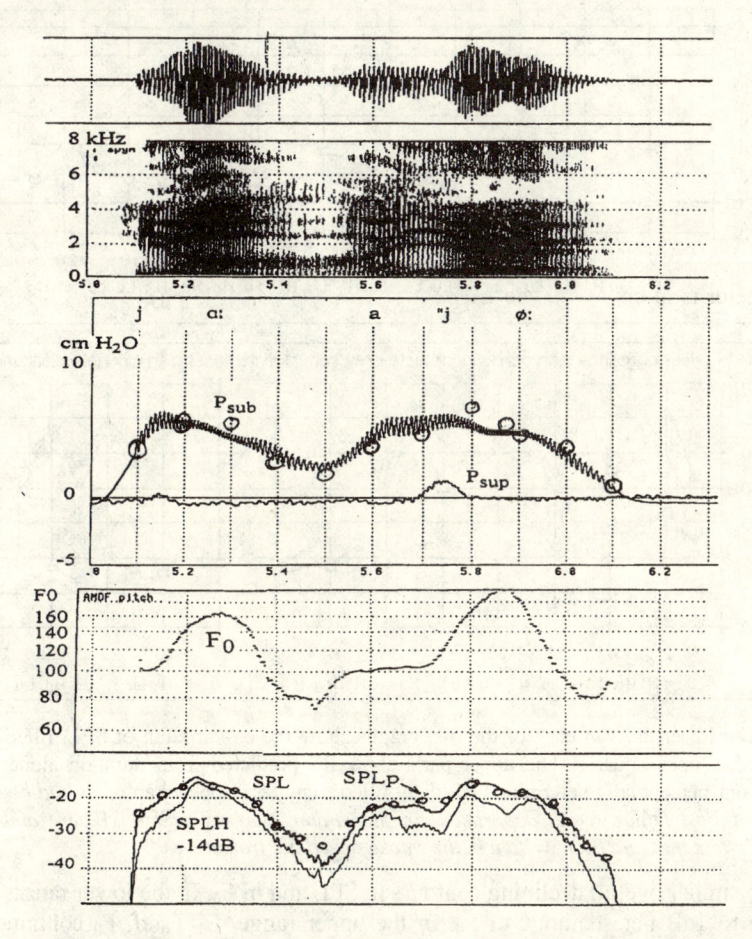

Figure 12: Illustrating the predictability of SPL from Psub and F_0, and of Psub from F_0 and SPL in a two-word phrase "Ja adjö". Predicted values are marked by solid points for SPL and by open circles for Psub.

These data add to our insight in the realization of accent 1 Ha at high prominence levels. The subglottal pressure is raised at the syllable boundary with an increase of the SPL and the SPLH intensity measures, and shows a falling contour in the region of the F_0 peak. The following steep F_0 drop accounts for a prosodic terminal low tone boundary.

Essentials of this pattern also appeared in the right hand part of Fig. 1 and in the upper right hand part of Fig. 6. It is also found in the realization of accent 2 Hg, but to a less extent.

6.4 Prose reading

F_0 and duration follow rules set by position and prominence RS. But what about the intensity parameter SPL? In our MBROLA synthesis [6] intensity is not under control, but it is of some interest to follow the co-variation of SPL with F_0 and duration.

Since durations are highly dependent on RS, we may also test the reverse relation, the predictability of RS from duration alone.

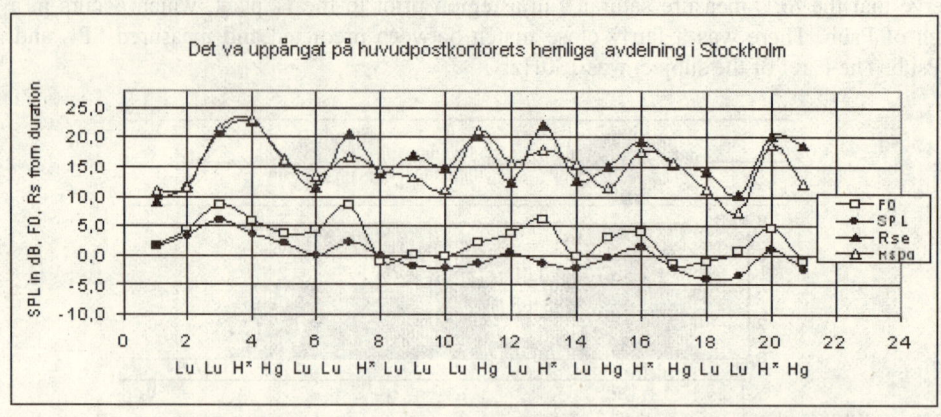

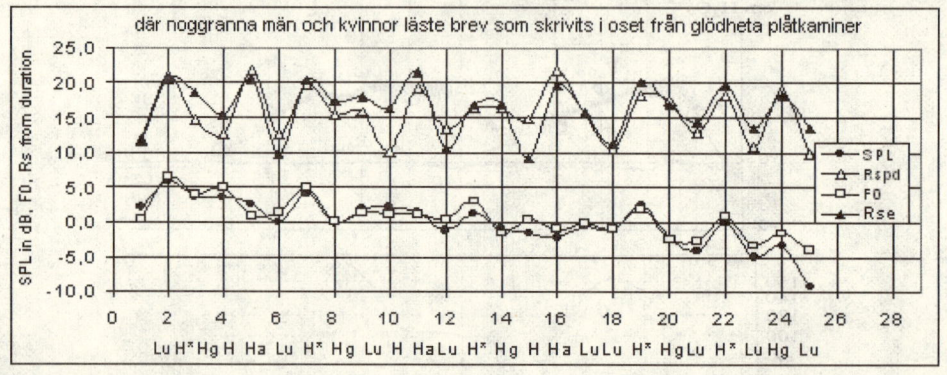

Figure 13: The lower parts in each of the two graphs show the co-variation of SPL, filled squares, and F_0 peak amplitudes, open squares. The upper parts show RS predicted from duration alone, open triangles, compared to our perceptually determined RS data, filled triangles. Upper graph: *"It had been steam-opened at the Central Post Office secret department in Stockholm."* Lower graph: *"Where ambitious men and women read letters that had been written in the smoke of red hot iron stoves."*

We observe similar overall declining contours in SPL and in F_0. In the lower range, $F_0<F_0\text{ref}$, SPL increases close to 1dB per semitone of F_0. In the upper range, $F_0>F_0\text{ref}$, F_0 continues to rise with prominence RS at a higher rate than SPL, indicating the occurrence of syllables with a potential focal accentuation. The lower graph, a relative clause, shows less signs of prominence. Here, F_0 is maintained below F_0 and the predictability of RS from duration alone is better than in the major clause above.

7. PRE-OCCLUSION ASPIRATION

The example illustrated in Fig. 14 pertains to pre-occlusion aspiration in a stressed vowel followed by an unvoiced stop.

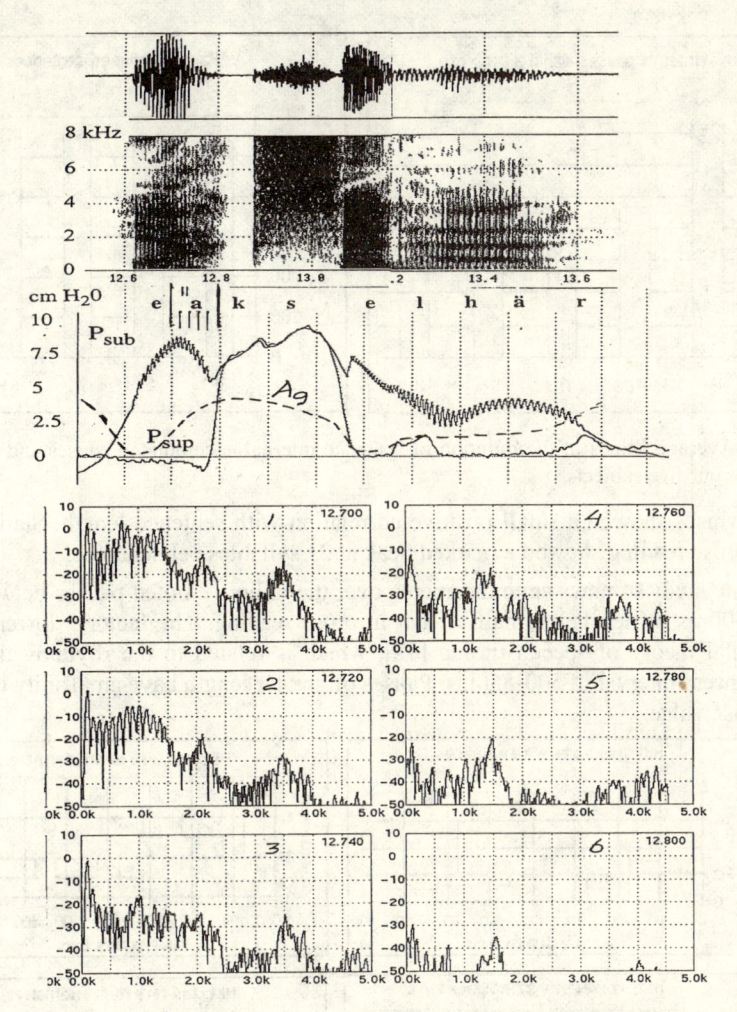

Figure 14: Pre-occlusion aspiration in a stressed vowel preceding an unvoiced stop. Text: "E Axel här?" (*Is Axel here?*) The synchrony with respect to Psub and Psup and an anticipated glottal area Ag is indicated.

The glottal opening starts well ahead of the consonantal closure [22][23]. In this process the early onset of abduction causes a drastic shift in the vowel spectrum towards a breathy quality, similar to a normal termination of a breath group [13]. Formants are gradually damped out and a noise component takes over as indicated by the sequence of spectral sections, anticipating the frication noise at the closure.

Fig. 14 also illustrates the interplay of aerodynamic and articulatory gestures within the sentence.

8. PAUSE DURATION DATA

The variability of pause durations has been documented by Fant et al.[21]. It involved our 5 subjects, 3 males and 2 females, reading a 2-minute long passage from the novel. As shown in Fig.15 we found large individual variations in the accumulated sum of pauses within sentences contrasting with a small spread of pauses between sentences, which were close to 1100ms. A somewhat lower value, 950ms, was noted for speaker JL. This subject made exceptionally few pauses within sentences.

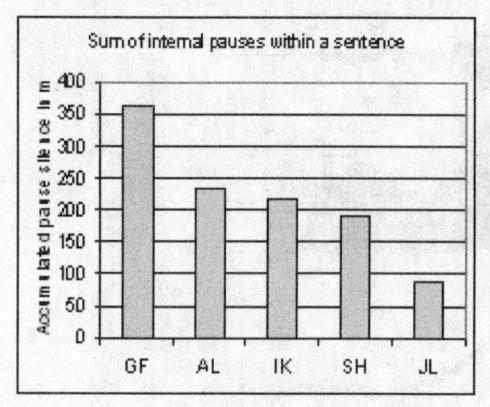

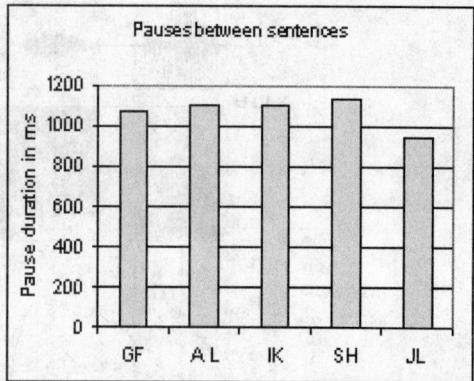

Figure 15: Average values of the duration of sentence internal accumulated pauses and of pauses between sentences for our five subjects.

Sentence pauses showed a small positive correlation with sentence length. Statistics of sentence length in the prose reading showed a marked peak at 21 syllables per sentence.

In a separate study of news announcements over the radio we noted pauses between sentences of the order of 500ms, which is one half of that in prose reading. The factor 2 lower value conforms with our quantal theory of speech timing [12], which is related to the rhythmical influence of an average inter-stress interval of 500-550ms. Pauses of greater length have an affinity to occur at 2, 3 or 4 times this base value.

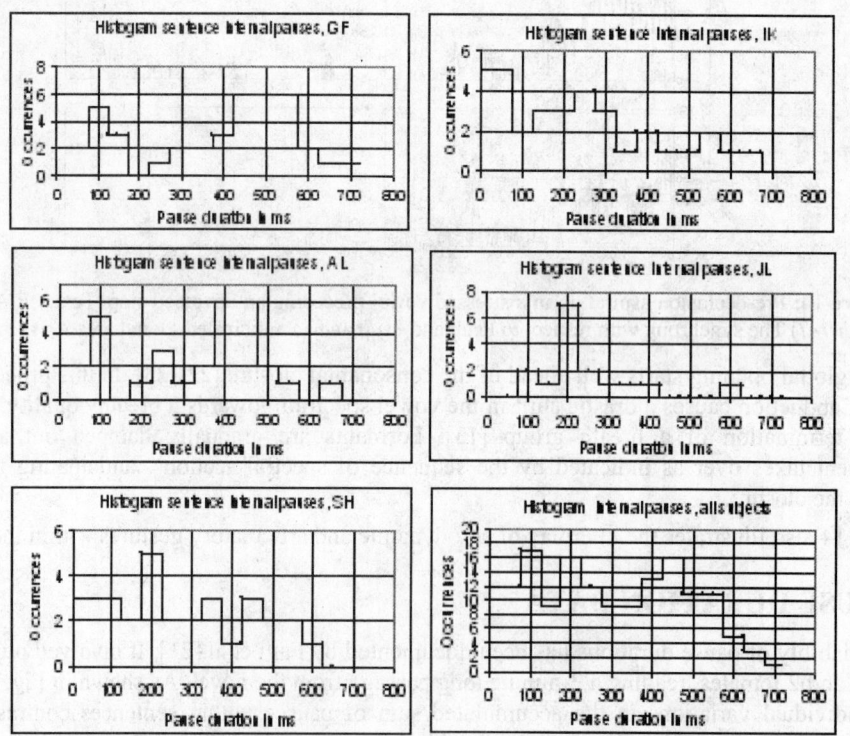

Figure 16: Histograms of sentence internal pauses for all five subjects and their average data

Histograms of sentence internal pauses for our five subjects from Fant et al. [21] are shown in Fig. 16. The main trend is a clustering around 450ms and one or two peaks around 100 and 200ms.

We have found a great variability in which subjects select prosodic boundaries within a sentence and how they were realized in terms of true and filled pauses and other criteria. An early study [8] also cited in Fant & Kruckenberg [9] provided a grading of individual variations in the realization of syntactically potential boundaries within one of the sentences of our prose text. The study engaged 15 subjects reading a text and 10 listeners for grading the subjective strength of the junctures in a scale from 1 to 5. At the boundary before a preposition phrase a pause greater than 350ms and a noticeable F_0 reset was needed for maximum prominence score. The lowest score involved pre-boundary lengthening only. Occurrence of creaky voice was found at intermediate values of subjective strength. The average grading for the preposition phrase juncture was 2. 2.

9. PROSODIC PARSING

We have developed a simplified parsing system. It involves a preliminary marking of boundaries at two levels of potential prominence in a sentence and an ordering of their positions according to distances to previous and following marks. In a second round, each juncture is allotted magnitudes in terms of pause duration and final lengthening. Minor prosodic boundaries may be realized by final lengthening alone. A most important consideration is whether a tentative prosodic group qualifies for a new base curve, see Fig. 5.

When testing these rules against our five-speaker corpus, it became evident that the individual variability was so great that the data mainly backed up essentials of our tentative parsing system. In synthesis, detailed variations generally produced quite acceptable results that could suit a specific speaker. Larger variations were associated with changes in speaking style.

10. FOCAL ACCENTUATION. ENHANCEMENT AND REDUCTION

In an earlier publication [17], we reported on how our five subjects realized focus within a short sentence. It involved F_0, duration and intensity in SPL. This study and more recent experiments confirmed that increasing the prominence of a word is associated with post-focal as well as pre-focal reductions.

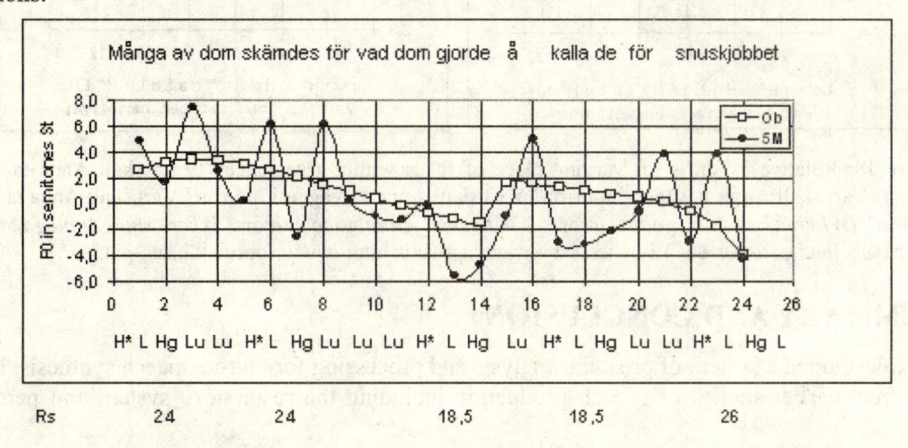

Figure 17: Examples of post-focal (Hg of **gjorde**) and pre-focal reduction (Hg of **kalla**) in a sentence of two major prosodic groups. Average data from our five subjects, 5M. Combination of two base curves. Ob. Text: "**Många** av dom **skämdes** för vad dom gjorde, å kalla de för **snuskjobbet**." (*Many were ashamed of what they did, and called it the dirtjob.*)

Fig. 17 illustrates a sentence of two major clauses. It shows the mean normalized intonation curves of our five subjects 5M superimposed on the prosodic base curves Ob1a and Ob2 b. The first two words were produced with high prominence, RS=24, followed by a post-focal reduced verb. The sentence final, emphatically high prominence word, RS=26, was preceded by a pre-focal reduced verb. In both cases the reduction affected the accent 2 Hg parameter, which at the prosodic boundary attained a bottom value.

In Fig. 18 a systematic variation of the prominence of four key words in a synthesized sentence has been carried out. The data pertain to the difference between the F_0 pattern of a specific utterance and that of a neutral pronunciation of the same utterance, thus sharpening the effect of the selection. The local increase in the Hg and Ha peaks was of the order of 6 semitones. Post-focal reductions are apparent. The processing of the final word in this sequence involved a terminal F_0 question rise, but it could have been executed by prominence marking only. This type of analysis-by-synthesis approach will be an important experimental tool in future projects.

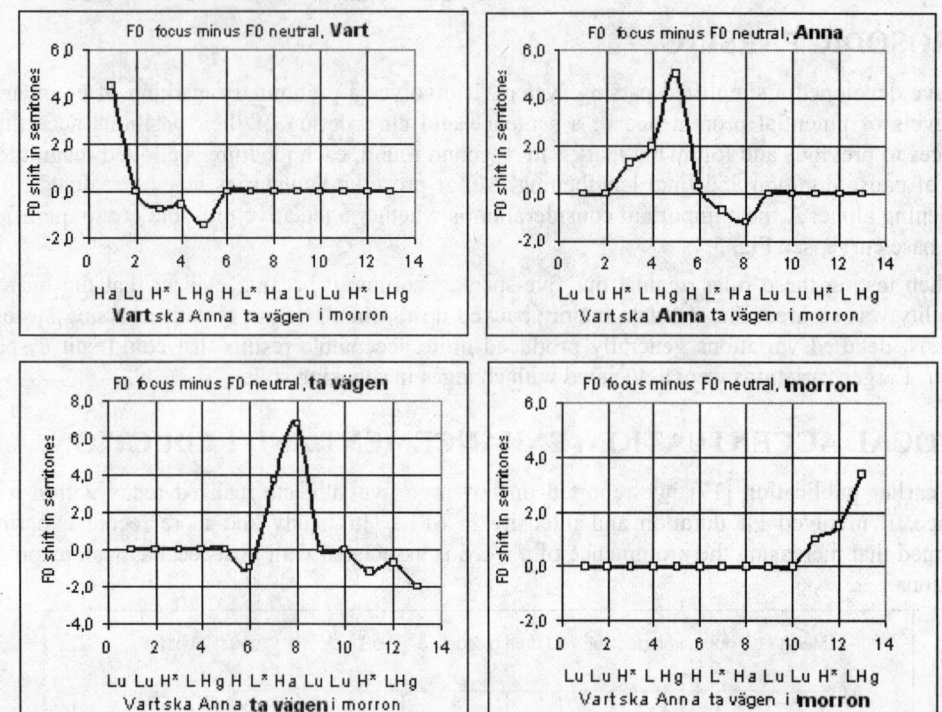

Figure 18: Relative F_0 shifts for varying place of focus within a sentence: "**Vart** skall Anna ta vägen i morron? Vart skall **Anna** ta vägen i morron? Vart skall Anna **ta vägen** i morron? Vart skall Anna ta vägen **i morron**?"(*Where shall Anna go tomorrow? Where shall **Anna** go tomorrow? Where shall Anna **go** tomorrow? Where shall Anna go **tomorrow**?*) Synthesized versions appear in http://www.speech.kth.se/~gunnar/.

11. SUMMARY AND CONCLUSION

We have developed a system of prosodic analysis and processing for text-to-speech synthesis. It has a support from earlier studies of speech production including the respiratory system and perceptual aspects.

A major part of the study pertains to two males and three females reading passages from a novel. Additional data derive from news reading over the radio.

The following novel features are incorporated:

(1) F_0 data are specified on a semitone scale, Eq. 2, and are normalized with respect to each subject's average F_0 level, thus allowing the derivation of representative group average data for mixed male and female speakers and a comparison of individual speakers, as in Fig. 3. Our processing rules have enabled a close prediction of average intonation contours for our five subjects, Fant et al. 2002. A preliminary version was published in Fant & Kruckenberg [19].

(2) We employ a superposition system of local accent data added to continuous base curves of major prosodic groups. It involves a temporal normalization, whereby the time scale is substituted by a position scale. Syllables carrying primary accent receive two positions and all other syllables, those of secondary accentuation and unstressed syllables, receive one slot each on the sequence scale.

A consequence of the temporal normalization is that longer and shorter prosodic groups will display the same overall F_0 fall. This has a support in tendencies observed in production data.

(3) A unique aspect of our system is the continuously scaled prominence parameter RS, which executes a control of accent peaks. In synthesis, RS controls both F_0 patterns and duration. Their co-variation accounts for some degree of predictability of RS from duration data alone.

The first complete Swedish text-to-speech synthesis was that of Carlson & Granström (1977). Intonation modelling involved F_0 rules for transitions between turning points. This is a widely adopted representation, e.g. Gårding [29]. Our system is target-oriented but with more explicit rules than in ToBI.

The notation system for Swedish word accents introduced by Bruce [1][2] has been adopted with some modifications. Major aspects of Swedish intonation in a superposition frame appeared in Bruce et al. [3]. Our system, Fant et al. [20], has a wider scope, subject to normalization and the introduction of the RS prominence parameter.

The main phonological marker of accent 1 versus accent 2 is a rise versus fall of tone at the vowel onset in the primary stressed syllable as indicated in the traditional notation of the accent 1 word "ánden" versus "ànden" for accent 2. The tone hights in accent 2 Hg and in the accent 1 Ha have a similar function of marking prominence.

Related systems are those of Fujisaki et al. [27], Fujisaki et al. [28] and Mixdorff [31]. They were inspired by the early work of Öhman [32][33] who introduced a linear filter impulse response modelling of accent peaks and superimposed phrase contour in a superposition frame.

We claim that our target-oriented modelling with specific time constants of F_0 rise and decay is simpler to program than that of Fujisaki and his followers, and should have a similar physiological and auditory relevance.

A fundamental object of our system is that it aims at group average data for synthesis, and also individual departures from the average data whilst all other studies in the literature have been directed to rules for analysis of specific utterances. Fujisaki derives both a phrase component and an accent component as linear filter responses in close relation to physiological constraints. As in our studies he operates with a log frequency scale. We have introduced a quantified definition of the semitone scale St with a reference at 100Hz, see Eq 2 and 3.

We operate with a combination of syntactically determined Ob base curves upon which the accent data is superimposed with a phonologically based temporal normalisation. The base curve is usually disregarded in other studies. Investigations are generally restricted to short utterances.

Studies of isolated prominent F_0 peaks support the notion of hat patterns introduced by Collier [5]. We find rising and falling branches of the order of 150ms that could be modelled with a Gaussian shape. The time constant of 150ms also fits well with auditory integration of F_0, supported by observations that interpolation between discrete F_0 points in our MBROLA [6] synthesis output does not improve naturalness.

Access to respiratory data has served as a foundation for studies of the co-variation of the subglottal pressure Psub with F_0 and intensity in SPL. Analytical expressions have been derived that enable estimates of SPL from F_0 and Psub, and of Psub from F_0 and SPL. These relations promote an understanding of the normal co-variation of F_0 and SPL. We have evidence from several studies including fiberscope glottography, glissando phonation and connected speech of the existence of a speaker specific mid-frequency F_0ref, below which SPL varies in proportion to F_0. At frequencies above F_0ref, SPL saturates, while F_0 continues to increase with prominence.

A more complex co-variation of speech parameters that we have studied is the modification and cancellation of the voice source by glottal abduction. Our example in Fig. 8 pertains to pre-occlusion aspiration in the termination of a stressed vowel followed by an unvoiced stop. Studies of this type could promote high quality, articulatory oriented synthesis.

We have introduced a system of prosodic grouping in five categories within a sentence. The three most prominent are associated with a change in base curves for superposition of F_0 data and choice of pause duration.

Of special interest is the timing of subglottal pressure, intensity and F_0 within a prosodic group, see Fig. 12. Psub is raised at the boundary of a stressed syllable raising SPL, while a prominent F_0 peak is delayed to a location of decaying Psub. At a marked prosodic boundary a final fall of Psub and F_0 set a terminal juncture.

Pause data for each of our five subjects have been collected. They differ much in terms of accumulated duration within sentences but show quite similar values close to 1000ms between complete sentences. Of interest is data from a radio news recording that showed sentence pauses of the order of 500ms, which we interpret in the frame of our quantal theory of speech timing.

Speech analysis data have provided an insight in the nature of post-focal and pre-focal reduction of F_0 data adding to more detailed findings from our earlier studies Fant et al.[16][17][18]. They have guided attempts to introduce rules for systematic shifts of focus within synthesized sentences,

A high quality of MBROLA based text-to-speech synthesis for Swedish and also for French has been demonstrated. At present, we are limited to a time consuming manual processing which could be speeded up by adequate computer programming.

Our system could be used as a tool for experimental analysis-by-synthesis reading style. The extensive prosodic frame could find applications also in studies of dialog systems.

12. ACKNOWLEDGEMENTS

We are highly indebted to Johan Liljencrants for speech recording, data processing and display.

Stellan Hertegård contributed with innovative studies of the respiratory system, which has resulted in documentary material of great value.

Kjell Gustafson introduced us to MBROLA synthesis with language specific phonetic inventories and selected voices. He has also been of help in experiments and data processing.

REFERENCES

[1] Bruce, G. 1977. *Swedish Word Accents in Sentence Perspective*. Lund: Gleerup.

[2] Bruce, G. 1995. Modelling Swedish intonation for read and spontaneous speech. *Proc. of the XIII ICPhS*, Stockholm, 28-35.

[3] Bruce, G., Filipsson, M., Frid, J., Granström, B., Gustafson, K., Horne, M., House, D. 2000. Modelling of Swedish Text and Discourse Intonation in a Speech Synthesis Framework. In: A. Botinis (ed.), *Intonation Analysis Modelling and Technology*. Kluwer Academic Publishers, 291-230.

[4] Carlson, R., Granström, B. 1973. Word accent, emphatic stress, and syntax in a synthesis-by-rule scheme for Swedish. KTH STL-QPSR 2-3/1973, 31-35.

[5] Collier, R. 1991. Multi-language intonation synthesis. *Journal of Phonetics* 19, 61-73.

[6] Dutoit, T. 2003. MBROLA. Faculte Polytechnique de Mons.

[7] Fant, G. 1982. Preliminaries to analysis of the human voice source. *KTH STL-QPSR* 4/1982, 1-27.

[8] Fant, G., Nord, L., Kruckenberg, A. 1986. Individual Variations in Text Reading. A Data-Bank Pilot Study. *KTH STL-QPSR* 4/1986, 1-17.

[9] Fant, G., Kruckenberg, A. 1989. Preliminaries to the study of Swedish prose reading and reading style. *KTH STL-QPSR* 2/1989, 1-83.

[10] Fant, G., Kruckenberg, A., Nord, L. 1991. Durational correlates of stress in Swedish, French and English. *Journal of Phonetics* 19, 351-365.

[11] Fant, G. 1995. The LF model revisited, transformations and frequency domain analysis. *STL-QPSR* 2-3/1995, 119-156.

[12] Fant, G., Kruckenberg, A. 1996. On the quantal nature of speech timing. *Proc. ICSLP 1996*, 2044-2047.

[13] Fant, G. 1997. The voice source in connected speech. *Speech Communication* 22, 125-139.

[14] Fant, G., Hertegård, S., Kruckenberg, A., Liljencrants, J. 1997. Covariation of subglottal pressure, F_0 and glottal parameters. *Eurospeech* 97, 453-456.

[15] Fant, G. 1998. DS-tabeller. *Internal report KTH Department of Speech Music and Hearing* 1998.

[16] Fant, G., Kruckenberg, A., Liljencrants, J. 2000a. The source-filter frame of prominence. *Phonetica* 57, 113-127.

[17] Fant, G., Kruckenberg, A., Liljencrants, J. 2000b. Acoustic-phonetic analysis of prosody in Swedish. In: A. Botinis (ed.), *Intonation, Analysis, Modelling and Technology*. Kluwer Academic Publishers, 55-86.

[18] Fant, G., Kruckenberg, A., Liljencrants, J., Hertegård, S. 2000c. Acoustic phonetic studies of prominence in Swedish. *KTH TMH-QPSR* 2/3 2000, 1-52.

[19] Fant, G., Kruckenberg, A. 2001. F_0 analysis and prediction in Swedish prose reading. In: N. Grønnum and J. Rischel (eds.), *To honour Eli Fischer-Jørgensen. Travaux du Circle Linguistique de Copenhague*, Copenhagen, Reitzel, 124-147.

[20] Fant, G., Kruckenberg, A., Gustafson, K., Liljencrants, J. 2002. A new approach to intonation analysis and synthesis of Swedish. *Speech Prosody*, Aix-en-Provence.

[21] Fant, G., Kruckenberg, A., Barbosa-Ferreira, J. 2003. Individual variations in pausing. A study of read speech. *Proceedings of Fonetik 2003*, Umeå University, Phonum, 193-196.

[22] Fant, G., Kruckenberg, A. 2004a. Prosody by Rule in Swedish with Language Universal Implications. *Speech Prosody 2004*, Nara, 405-408.

[23] Fant, G., Kruckenberg, A. 2004b. Analysis and synthesis of Swedish prosody with outlooks on production and perception. In: G. Fant, H. Fujisaki, J. Chao, Y. Xu (eds.), *Festschrift Wu Zongji, From traditional phonology to modern speech processing*. Beijing Foreign Language Teaching and Research Press, 73-95.

[24] Fant, G., Kruckenberg, A. 2005. Covariation of subglottal pressure F_0 and intensity. *9th European Conference on Speech Technology and Processing, Interspeech Lisboa*, Paper ID #2411.

[25] Fant, G. 2006. Speech Acoustics and Phonetics. *Selected Writings*. Kluwer Academic Publishers: Springer.

[26] Fant, G., Kruckenberg, A. 2006. Stavelseregler mars 06. *Internal report KTH Department of Speech Music and Hearing*.

[27] Fujisaki, H., Ljungqvist, M., Murata, H. 1993. Analysis and modelling of word accent and sentence intonation in Swedish. Proc. 1993 Intern. *Conf. Acoustics Speech and Signal Processing*, Vol. 2, 211-214.

[28] Fujisaki, H., Tomana, R., Narusawa, S., Ohno, S., Wang, J. 2000. Physiological mechanisms for fundamental frequency control in standard Chinese. *ICSLP 2000*, SS (01)-3, 1-4.

[29] Gårding, E. 1989. Intonation in Swedish. Lund University Linguistics Department Working Papers 35, 63-88. Also in: D. Hirst and A. Di Cristo (eds.), *Intonation Systems*. Cambridge University Press 1998, 112-130.

[30] Liljencrants, J. 2006. Wspec. http://www.fonema.se/wspect/wspect.html.

[31] Mixdorff, H. J. 2002. An Integrated Approach to Modelling German Prosody. *Studientexte zur Sprachkommunikation*, Band 25, w.e.b. Universitetsverlag, Dresden.

[32] Öhman, S. 1967. Word and sentence intonation: a quantitative model. *KTH STL-QPSR* 2-3/1967, 20-54.

[33] Öhman, S. 1968. A model of word and sentence intonation. *KTH. STL-QPSR* 2-3/1968, 6-11.

[34] Sluijter, A., van Heuven, V. 1996. Spectral balance as an acoustic correlate of linguistic stress. *J. Acoust. Soc. Am.* 100/4, 2471-2484.

[35] Sundberg, J., Andersson, M. and Hultqvist, C. 1999. Effects of subglottal pressure variations on professional baritone singers' voice sources. *J. Acoust. Soc. Am.* 105/3, 1965-1971.

More references on the subject and examples of speech synthesis are to be found in
http://www.speech.kth.se/~gunnar/.

THE COMMAND-RESPONSE MODEL FOR F_0 CONTOUR GENERATION AND ITS IMPLICATIONS IN PHONETICS AND PHONOLOGY

Hiroya FUJISAKI

ABSTRACT

The command-response model for F_0 contour generation, presented by the author for the F_0 contours of utterances of common Japanese in 1969, have since been proved to apply to a number of languages. The ability of the model to produce extremely good approximations to observe F_0 contours of natural speech comes from the fact that it is based on precise formulations of the physiological and physical properties of the human mechanisms of F_0 control. The present paper first describes its background, gives its formulations for both non-tone languages and tone languages, and presents some implications of the model to phonetics and phonology.

Keywords: the command-response model, F_0 contour generation, implications to phonetics and phonology

1. INTRODUCTION

For historical reasons, let me start by quoting Fujisaki and Nagashima [3].

"Temporal variations of the fundamental frequency of human voice are characterized by comparatively slow and systematic changes that are controlled by linguistic and physiological factors and by small rapid fluctuations whose origin is considered to be purely physiological. Though both of these contribute to naturalness, the former is of primary interest from the point of view of speech synthesis by rule.

The main linguistic factors that control the pitch contour of an utterance are word accent, breath group, stress and intonation. Some of these are inherent in a particular language, but others are subject to dialectal changes. The pitch contour is also affected by acoustic or articulatory influences of phonemes as well as by non-linguistic factors such as emotion, individual difference and other stochastic phenomena.

Prosodic rules can be derived by formulating quantitative effects of these linguistic factors on the observed pitch contour, and a number of studies have already been made toward the establishment of prosodic rules for the synthesis of several languages including English, Swedish and Japanese.

Although these studies are quite instructive, they fall far short of the validity and the generality of the rules. This can be ascribed to the fact that most of the rules have been derived without any reference to the actual control mechanisms of the glottal frequency, of which much is still left unknown.

In this respect, the work of Öhman [35][36] is conspicuous since it postulates a functional model of pitch control and tries to obtain quantitative representations of its mechanisms by the method of 'analysis-by-synthesis'[1]. This approach is of particular significance since it gives prosodic rules for speech synthesis and at the same time gives an insight into the human mechanisms of pitch control. From my point of view, however, the model leaves much to be desired."

Namely, in Öhman's first paper [35], the model was formulated in the domain of liner frequency. To me it seemed to be unacceptable since different speakers of the same language/dialect, including male and female adults as well as young children, can produce approximately the same intonation except for the absolute pitch level (key), so that a model for pitch contours should be formulated in the domain of logarithmic frequency, which is equivalent to formulating the model on the musical scale.

In his second paper [36], the formulation was in the domain of logarithmic frequency, but the sentence intonation inputs were assumed to be an initial positive step followed by negative steps to produce the basic phrase contour, and the word intonation inputs were assumed to be always negative pedestals. For me this was counter-intuitive, for in utterances of declarative sentences of Japanese, the F_0 contour consists of one or more slow phrasing curves which always rise first and then decay toward a level, and for the word accent is always marked by a rise in pitch followed by a fall, which can most naturally be considered as a consequence of a driving input shaped as a positive pedestal. Furthermore, there was no provision in his model to account for the fact that the initial frequency of an F_0 contour is always higher than the frequency at the end of the contour, which can be explained by the presence of hysteresis in the control mechanism of F_0.

2. THE COMMAND-RESPONSE MODEL

These considerations led me to propose a model of the mechanisms of F_0 contour generation for common Japanese shown in Fig. 1. The model assumes that a positive pedestal-shaped voicing command produces the sentence intonation, while another positive pedestal-shaped input produces the word accent. Note that the formulation of the control mechanisms is in the domain of logarithmic frequency, but their combined outputs are converted at the final stage to produce an output in the linear frequency domain. Using the method of analysis-by-synthesis, we have shown that the model can generate very close approximations to observed F_0 contours of short utterances of common Japanese [3].

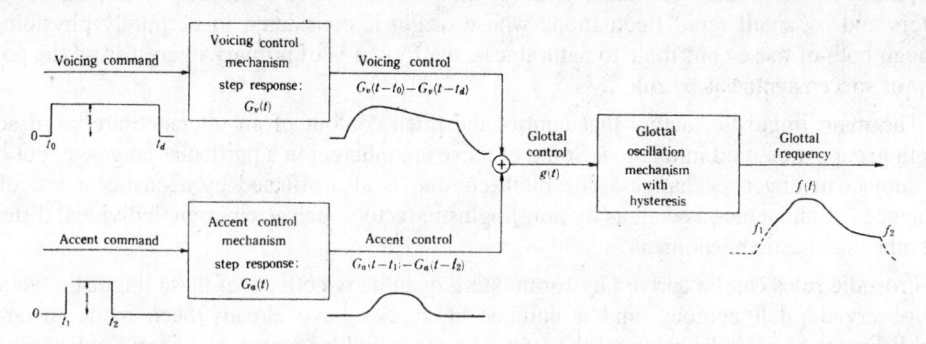

Figure 1: A model for the mechanisms of F_0 contour generation of short utterances of common Japanese [3]

Analysis of longer, more complex utterances indicated, however, the need for assuming more input commands for sentence intonation in the course of an utterance. Instead of a single voicing command, therefore, we introduced positive impulse-shaped phrase commands of varying magnitudes for producing sentence intonation, and one negative impulse-shaped phrase command to account for the rapid final fall of log $F_0(t)$ often observed at the end of an utterance. For the sake of theoretical simplicity and clarity, we also redefine the F_0 contour to be log $F_0(t)$ rather than $F_0(t)$. In this case, the logarithmic F_0 contour, i.e. $\log F_0(t)$, can be expressed as the sum of three kinds of components; phrase components, accent components, and the logarithm of the base frequency, as shown in Fig. 2 [4].

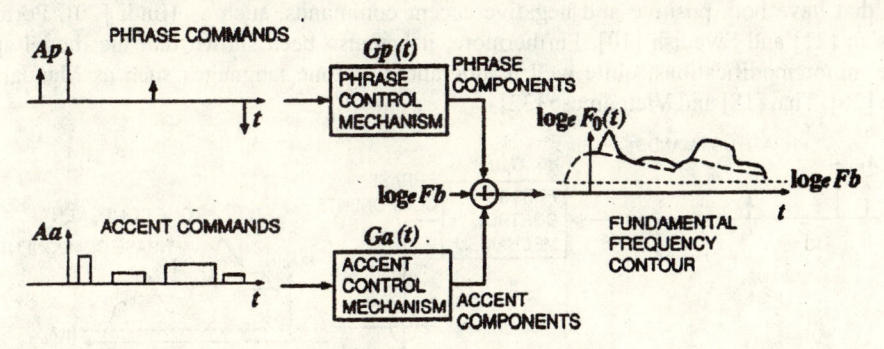

Figure 2: The command-response model for languages with only positive accent commands

In this model, the F_0 contour can be expressed by

$$\log F_0(t) = \log F_b + \sum_{i=1}^{I} A_{pi} G_p(t - T_{0i}) + \sum_{j=1}^{J} A_{aj} \{G_a(t - T_{1j}) - G_a(t - T_{2j})\}, \quad (1)$$

where

$$G_p(t) = \begin{cases} \alpha^2 t \exp(-\alpha t), & t \geq 0, \\ 0, & t < 0, \end{cases} \quad (2)$$

and

$$G_a(t) = \begin{cases} \min[1 - (1 + \beta t)\exp(-\beta t), \gamma], & t \geq 0, \\ 0, & t < 0, \end{cases} \quad (3)$$

where $G_p(t)$ represents the impulse response function of the phrase control mechanism and $G_a(t)$ represents the step response function of the accent control mechanism. The symbols in these equations indicate

F_b : baseline value of fundamental frequency,
I : number of phrase commands,
J : number of accent commands,
A_{pi} : magnitude of the i th phrase command,
A_{aj} : amplitude of the j th accent command,
T_{0i} : timing of the i th phrase command,
T_{1j} : onset of the j th accent command,
T_{2j} : end of the j th accent command,
α : natural angular frequency of the phrase control mechanisn,
β : natural angular frequency of the accent control mechanisn,
γ : relative ceiling level of accent components.

Parameters α and β are assumed to be constant within an utterance, while the parameter γ is set equal to 0.9.

A complete explanation for the underlying physiological and physical mechanisms and processes has been given by the author elsewhere [19]. The model was first shown to apply to F_0 contours of longer utterances of common Japanese and was also used for speech synthesis from texts, for it is capable of producing natural intonation even if the F_0 contour itself is not exactly equal to that of a natural utterance. The model has since been shown to apply to F_0 contours of utterances of a number of other non-tone languages, including English [12], Estonian [5], German [29], Greek [14], Korean [13], Polish and Spanish [11], in which accent commands are almost always positive. Although the accent commands shown in Fig. 2 are all positive, however, the model itself is applicable to languages that have both positive and negative accent commands, such as Hindi [20], Portuguese [17], Russian [21] and Swedish [10]. Furthermore, it has also been shown that the model applies, with some minor modifications, quite well to utterances of tone languages such as Mandarin [7], Cantonese [26], Thai [18] and Vietnamese [32].

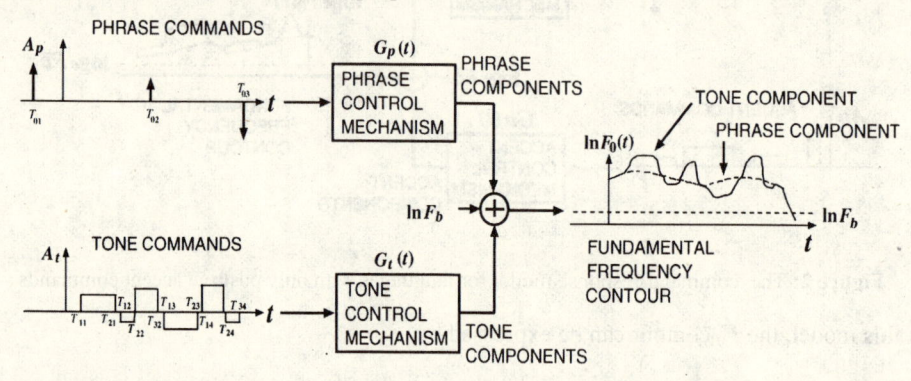

Figure 3: The command-response model for tone languages, where each syllable may have up to two tone commands, whose polarity can be positive and negative.

Figure 3 shows the model for tone languages in which the accent commands in Fig. 2 are replaced by tone commands of both positive and negative polarities. In most tone languages thus far studied, it is sufficient to assume up to two tone commands for a syllable. For example, in the four tones of Mandarin, Tone 1 has a positive tone command, Tone 2 has a negative tone command followed by a positive one, Tone 3 has a negative tone command, and tone 4 has a positive tone command followed by a negative one. In certain languages, however, we may have to assume more than two tone commands [22].

Exactly speaking, parameters α and β are different for positive tone connands and negative tone commands, but our experiments on both analysis and synthesis of F_0 contours of tone languages indicate that common values are acceptable for practical applications.

It may be worthwhile to mention here that the tone components and the phrase components in the command-response model are mathematical and quantitative representations of what Prof. Y. R. Chao called small ripples and large waves respectively [2], while the baseline value ($\log F_b$) corresponds to the keynote of the phrasal contour which varies with attitudinal or emotional changes in the speaker, as shown by Prof. Z. Wu [40].

3. IMPLICATIONS TO PHONETICS AND PHONOLOGY

3.1 Typological classification of languages based on the polarity of local commands

The command-response model has already been shown to apply to the F_0 contours of utterances of more than 20 languages, in a number of studies by the present author and his coworkers, as well as by others [30][31][33][34][39]. The results of these studies indicate that these languages fall broadly into the following two groups:

(1) languages in which only positive local commands are commonly used.

(2) languages in which both positive and negative local commands are commonly used.

The second group can further be divided into two sub-groups:

(2a) those in which the use of negative commands is lexically determined and thus is not optional (this sub-group includes both non-tone languages and tone languages).

(2b) those in which the use of negative commands is more or less optional, but is rather common.

Table 1 shows the classification of the languages thus far studied.

Table 1: Grouping of languages on the basis of tone/accent command polarity

Group	Polarity of accent/ tone commands	Languages
1	Positive only	English*, Estonian, German, Greek, Japanese, Korean, Polish, Spanish
2	Positive, zero and negative	Hindi, Portuguese, Russian, Swedish, Cantonese[†], Mandarin[†], Thai[†], Vietnamese[†]

* Certain speakers of English (both American and British) occasionally use negative accent commands, especially in order to express paralinguistic information.

† Tone languages.

It is to be noted, however, that the classification is never exact in reality. Even in languages of Group (1), paralinguistic factors such as expression of incredibility, etc., may induce the speaker to invert the polarity of the accent command from positive to negative. Also, different dialects of a language may differ significantly in such use of negative commands.

3.2 Phonological structure of the tone system of a tone language

Let us first look at the local (i.e. tone) commands of the four tones of Mandarin. As shown in Fig. 4, the tone commands for the four tones are: a single positive tone command for the most part of the final (viz. the vowel plus the coda) in Tone 1, a negative tone command for the earlier part but then switched to a positive tone command for the later part of the final in Tone 2, a single negative tone command for the most part of the final in Tone 3, and a positive local command for the earlier part but switched to a negative tone command for the later part of the final in Tone 4.

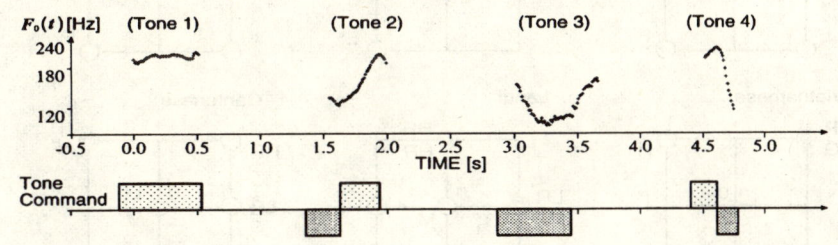

Figure 4: The F_0 contours and the underlying tone command patterns for the isolated words "yi" of four lexical tones of Mandarin [22].

If we assume, however, the existence of two tone commands for each tone, by regarding the single positive command of Tone 1 as a pair of positive tone commands of the same amplitude occurring respectively at the earlier part and the later part of the final, and by regarding the single negative tone command of Tone 3 as a pair of negative tone commands of the same amplitude occurring respectively at the earlier part and the later part of the final, we get the qualitative constellation of the four tones of Mandarin Chinese shown in Fig. 5, where the polarity of the local command for the earlier part of the final is indicated on the horizontal axis, while that for the later part of the final is indicated on the vertical axis.

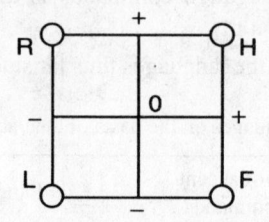

Figure 5: Phonological structure of the tone system of Mandarin. H: High (Tone 1), R: Rising (Tone 2), L: Low (Tone 3), and F: Falling (Tone 4).

In the case of Mandarin, the polarities of the tone commands are always positive or negative, but in other tone languages the tone commands can be partially or entirely null in certain tones. For example, The five tones of Thai can be represented by the constellation shown in Fig. 6 with positive, null, and negative tone commands on both axes.

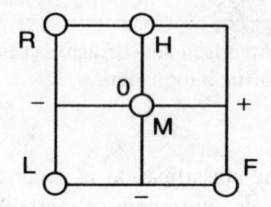

Figure 6: Phonological structure of the tone system of Thai. H: High, R: Rising, L: Low, F: Falling, and M: Mid.

Figure 7 shows the constellations of tones of six tone languages including Mandarin and Thai already shown in Figs. 5 and 6. A single circle indicates a tone, while a double circle indicates overlapping of two tones, such as an entering tone and its non-entering counterpart [30].

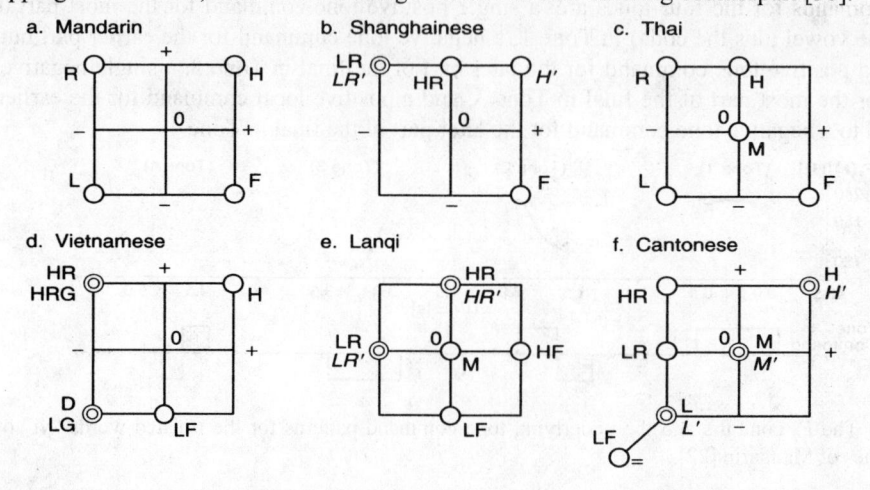

Figure 7: Phonological structure of the tone systems of six tone languages on the basis of timing and polarity of tone commands. For the tone system of Lanqi, see [24].

The figure shows the phonological structures of the tone system of these tone languages in a clear and compact manner, as compared with the traditional ways of representing the tone systems, either in terms of binary features or in terms of 5-tone levels. It is to be noted, however, that this system of representation is not meant to be final and complete. For instance, the tone system of Suzhou dialect requires more dimensions for representation [27].

3.3 Units of prosody

3.3.1 Units of prosody within an utterance

To the best of knowledge of the present author, there are no clear definitions on the units of prosody of speech beyond the word. For instance, Pierrehumbert and Beckman [37] posit "word", "accentual phrase" and "intermediate phrase" between "syllable" and "utterance" for spoken Japanese. According to the example given by them, "word" in their book is not a word as a lexical item, but is something similar to "Bunsetsu", i.e. a content word followed by zero or one or more function word(s). Also, "accentual phrase" and "intermediate phrase" are used without clear definitions.

On the basis of analysis of F_0 contours of speech of Japanese text reading, the author defined "prosodic word", "prosodic phrase", "prosodic clause" and "utterance" as the units of prosody of spoken Japanese [6].

In the first place, a prosodic word is defined as a lexical word or a sequence of lexical words spoken with a definite word accent type allowed within a particular dialect of Japanese. In many cases it is identical to a "Bunsetsu" but is different in certain cases.

For instance, the sequence of words "yama no ue no ie ni" (in a house on the top of a mountain) is pronounced as if they were a single compound word with the accent kernel at the end of the penultimate mora, and thus constitutes a prosodic word by the current definition, but is a sequence of three Bunsetsu (<yama-no> + <ue-no> + <ie-ni>) according to Hashimoto's definition. In this example, a prosodic word is larger than a Bunsetsu.

On the other hand, there are cases where a prosodic word is smaller than a Bunsetsu. For instance, in the Kinki dialect of Japanese, the compound word "idoosee-kookiatsu" (a moving high-pressure zone) is pronounced as two prosodic words, but is a Bunsetsu by definition. Hence the Bunsetsu cannot be regarded as a unit of prosody of Japanese. Also, a lexical word should not be regarded as a unit of prosody. The unit next to the "syllable" is the "prosodic word". This is one of the evidences that syntax and prosody are different.

The above definition of "prosodic word" is based on the existence of an accent component for a lexical (hence syntactic) word or sequence of lexical words. From the results of analysis of F_0 contours, however, a phrase component clearly marks a prosodic unit larger than a prosodic word, for a single phrase component can cover more than one prosodic word. Hence a prosodic phrase is defined as the portion of a phrase component that covers one or more prosodic words. It is terminated by the onset of another phrase component that is superposed onto the current phrase component, or by the onset of an utterance-medial pause that resets previous phrase components. Thus a prosodic phrase may be identical in size to a prosodic word, but is generally larger, and an utterance consists at least of one prosodic phrase.

The next unit in the prosodic hierarchy is the prosodic clause. It is defined as a part of an utterance containing one or more prosodic phrases delimited by pauses, which may be utterance-initial, utterance-medial, or utterance-final.

An utterance is defined as the next higher prosodic unit, delimited by pauses that are generally much longer than utterance-medial pauses, and is usually the counterpart to a sentence at the syntactic level.

There are, however, exceptions. For instance, in an emergency it is possible that the two sentences: "Fire! Get out of here!" may be uttered without a pause in between. In this case, the two sentences are produced as one prosodic unit — an utterance. On the other hand, a sentence may be interrupted by a very long pause intentionally or unintentionally, and then the rest may be uttered later. In such a case, the two parts of the sentence constitute two utterances. For the moment, however, we shall disregard these exceptional cases.

In the following Table 2, the first column shows various components of the observed F_0 contour of an utterance of common Japanese, the second column shows the prosodic units defined on the basis of these components, while the third column shows the syntactic units that roughly correspond to these prosodic units. As already mentioned, however, the correspondences are only approximate, and there are numerous cases where they do not apply.

Table 2: Manifestations of various prosodic units in terms of components of the observed F_0 contour, prosodic units of speech of common Japanese defined on the basis of these components, and the syntactic units that roughly correspond to these prosodic units.

MANIFESTATIONS	PROSODIC UNITS	SYNTACTIC UNITS
AN ACCENT COMPONENT	PROSODIC WORD	'BUNSETSU' (a content word followed by $n(\geq 0)$ function words)
	sandhi	
A PHRASE COMPONENT	PROSODIC PHRASE	ICRLB (Immediate Constituents with Recursively Left-branching Structure)
PHRASE COMPONENT(S) DELIMITED BY UTTERANCE-MEDIAL PAUSE(S)	PROSODIC CLAUSE	CLAUSE
PHRASE COMPONENT(S) DELIMITED BY UTTERANCE-FINAL PAUSES	**UTTERANCE**	SENTENCE

If we consider the "accentual phrase" in [37] to be roughly equivalent to our "prosodic word", then the current system can be said to have one more tier as compared to their system.

It is also to be noted that the definitions of prosodic words and phrases may be language-dependent, for languages differ in the way they use both local (i.e. tone or accent) components and global (i.e. phrase) components. For instance, in Japanese the accent component serves to combine several words together to form a prosodic word, but the tone components in tone languages such as Mandarin and Cantonese are more rigidly tied to each syllable, so that a prosodic word requires a different definition. Also, we have observed that the use of phrase components is more frequent in Mandarin and Cantonese than in non-tone languages, and may serve to mark a prosodic word rather than a prosodic phrase [7][26].

3.3.2 Units of prosody beyond an utterance

The above definitions are based on the analysis of consequences of speech production that can be observed as accent components, phrase components and pauses. In this section I will present definitions of units of prosody for a multi-utterance discourse, based purely on the analysis of speech production [16][25].

The speech material for this study is a 15-minute reading of a Japanese text by a professional announcer, at an average speech rate of 8.5 morae per second. The discourse (mainly monologues) consists of 88 utterances whose length varied quite widely from 14 morae to 116 morae.

Preliminary analyses of the durations of pauses as well as of the F_0 contours of all the utterances indicated that pause duration preceding an utterance (Dpi) and magnitude of the initial phrase command of an utterance (Api) are two good indicators of discourse segment boundaries. According to the analysis of distributions of Dpi and Api, the entire discourse can be regarded as consisting of 19 **major discourse segments**, while each major segment consists of one or more **minor discourse segments**. All the utterances then belong to either one of the following three groups:

(a) initial utterances of major discourse segments,

(b) initial utterances of minor discourse segments (except for those that belong to (a)),

(c) utterances that belong to neither (a) nor (b).

Table 3 summarizes the results of analysis of variance in both Dpi and Api between the three groups of utterances, where ** indicate differences being significant at 95% level, while *** indicate differences being significant at 99% level. These results indicate that larger prosodic units beyond an utterance are being signaled highly reliably, at least as far as the current speech material is concerned, but do not mean that every discourse segment is always unmistakenly marked.

Table 3: Results of analysis of variance

Dpi	(b)	(c)	Api	(b)	(c)
(a)	***	***	(a)	**	***
(b)		***	(b)		**

*** significant at 99%   ** significant at 95%

Although the analysis of variance has been done on the averaged data, it may be possible that the actual cues are more local, viz. that listeners can detect discourse segment boundaries on the basis of local cues, and also on the basis of lexical, syntactic and semantic cues.

These results lead to a hierarchy of prosodic units of a discourse shown in the first column of Table 4, where the second column shows syntactic units that roughly (but never exactly) correspond to the prosodic units.

Table 4: The units of prosody of a discourse and the units of syntax of a text of Japanese

PROSODIC UNITS	SYNTACTIC UNITS
UTTERANCE	SENTENCE
MINOR DISCOURSE SEGMENT	PARAGRAPH
MAJOR DISCOURSE SEGMENT	
DISCOURSE	TEXT

Note that the units of prosody of a discourse are finer than those of syntax, since major and minor discourse segments are generally not differentiated in syntax.

3.4 Influences of para- and non-linguistic information on parameters of the F_0 contour

The model-based analysis can provide a clear and quantitative interpretation on the effects of various factors on the prosody, in particular on F_0 contour characteristics. Because of space and time limitations, only brief mention will be made based mainly on past studies by the present author and his coworkers.

3.4.1 Manifestation of paralinguistic information — emphasis

Although focus is a phenomenon at the symbolic level so that the information on its location is linguistic, its realization, emphasis/prominence, involves gradations; hence the information is paralinguistic by the author's definition [19]. In one of our early works [6], we have shown that realization of a focus in Japanese involves both accent components and phrase components in a rather complex manner. Namely, the presence/absence of a focus (both narrow and wide) and the degree of emphasis/de-emphasis exert influences on

(a) the formation of prosodic words as well as the relative amplitudes of accent commands, which in turn depend on the word accent type of the lexical words in focus as well as their immediate neighbors.

(b) the formation of prosodic phrases as well as the relative magnitudes of phrase commands, which in turn depend on the scope of focus as well as the local syntactic structure of the sentence.

Realization of emphasis, at least in spoken Japanese, thus involves interactions of three levels of information: lexical (word accent), syntactic and pragmatic (focus). We have even demonstrated that there are cases in which a speaker fails to meet the requirements from all three levels, and thus has to sacrifice one in favor of others. Since some of the factors are highly language-specific, these results cannot be generalized to other languages. The actual process of realization of focus as emphasis has thus to be studied and formulated for each individual language.

3.4.2 Manifestation of non-linguistic information — emotion

The information on speaker's emotion is primarily independent from the linguistic information of the message that is to be spoken, but comes from the speaker's mental state, so that it is non-linguistic by the author's definition. Its realization involves gradations. Studies based on the analysis of F_0 contours using the command-response model (e.g. Higuchi et al. [28]) have shown that the value of the baseline of the F_0 contour (i.e. $\log F_b$) increases when the speaker is emotionally excited, like in anger, and the amount of increase is roughly proportional to the degree of excitation. This is consistent with the findings by Prof. Wu, who quite properly called it a "change-key"[40]. In most cases, it also decreases the magnitudes of phrase commands, thus reducing the dynamic range of the F_0 contour, i.e. $\log F_0 (t)$.

4. CONCLUDING REMARKS

In this paper I have shown the background and development of the command-response model and its formulations both for non-tone languages and tone languages. The unique ability of the model to produce extremely close approximations to actually observed F_0 contours comes from the fact that it is not an *ad hoc* copy of some observed data, but is based on precise mathematical formulations of the physiological and physical properties of the human mechanisms for controlling the fundamental frequency of vibration of the vocal folds [19].

I have then shown a few examples of its applications, mainly in phonetics and phonology of tone, accent, and intonation.

Although I did not discuss modeling of other prosodic features of speech such as duration, intensity and voice quality, I am fully aware of the importance of studying their temporal variations.

Since they are also caused by some neuromotor commands, I believe that we can represent the process of their realization also by their respective command-response models.

REFERENCES

[1] Bell, G., Fujisaki, H., Heinz, J., House, A., Stevens, K. 1961. Reduction of speech spectra by analysis-by-synthesis techniques. *J. Acoust. Soc. Am.* 33, 1725-1736.

[2] Chao, Y. 1968. *A Grammar of Spoken Chinese*. Univ. of Calif. Press, 121-134.

[3] Fujisaki, H., Nagashina, S. 1969. A model for synthesis of pitch contours of connected speech. *Annual Report of the Engineering Research Institute, University of Tokyo* 28, 53-60.

[4] Fujisaki, H., Hirose, K. 1982. Modeling the dynamic characteristics of voice fundamental frequency with applications to analysis and synthesis of intonation. In: H. Fujisaki, E. Gårding (eds.), Preprints of *Working Group on Intonation, the 13th International Congress of Linguists*, Tokyo, 57-70.

[5] Fujisaki, H., Lehiste. I. 1982. Some temporal and tonal characteristics of declarative sentences in Estonian. In: H. Fujisaki, E. Gårding (eds.), *Preprints of Working Group on Intonation, the 13th International Congress of Linguists*, Tokyo, 121-130.

[6] Fujisaki, H., Hirose, K., Takahashi, N., Yoko'o, M. 1984. Realization of accent components in connected speech. *Transactions of the Committee on Speech Research, Acoust. Soc. Jpn.* S84-36, 2.

[7] Fujisaki, H., Hallé, P., Lei, H. 1987. Application of F_0 contour command-response model to Chinese tones. *Proc. 1987 Autumn Meeting, Acoust. Soc. Jpn.* 1, 197-198.

[8] Fujisaki, H., Kawai, H. 1988. Realization of linguistic information in the voice fundamental frequency contour of the spoken Japanese. *Proc. ICASSP '88*, 663-666.

[9] Fujisaki, H. 1992. The role of quantitative modeling in the study of intonation. *Proc. International Symposium on Japanese Prosody*, Nara, 163-174.

[10] Fujisaki, H., Ljungqvist, M., Murata, H. 1993. Analysis and modeling of word accent and sentence intonation in Swedish. *Proc. ICASSP 93*, Minneapolis 1, 211-214.

[11] Fujisaki, H., Ohno, S., Nakamura, K., Guirao, M., Gurlekian, J. 1994. Analysis of accent and intonation in Spanish based on a quantitative model. *Proc. 1994 Int'l Conf. on Spoken Language Processing*, Yokohama 1, 355-358.

[12] Fujisaki, H., Ohno, S. 1995. Analysis and modeling of fundamental frequency contours of English utterances. *Proc. 4th European Conference on Speech Communication and Technology*, Madrid 4, 2231-2234.

[13] Fujisaki, H. 1996. Analysis and modeling of fundamental frequency contours of Korean utterances — A preliminary study. In *Phonetics and Linguistics — in Honour of Prof. H. B. Lee*, Seoul, 640-657.

[14] Fujisaki, H., Ohno, S., Yagi, T. 1997. Analysis and modeling of fundamental frequency contours of Greek utterances. *Proc. 5th European Conference on Speech Communication and Technology*, Rhodos 1, 465-468.

[15] Fujisaki, H. 1997. Prosody, models, and spontaneous speech. In: Y. Sagisaka, N. Campbell, N. Higuchi (eds.), *Computing Prosody*. New York: Springer, 27-42.

[16] Fujisaki, H., Tamura, Y., Ohno, S. 2000. Units and structures of prosody of Japanese text reading based on phrase commands of fundamental frequency contours. *Proc. 2000 Spring Meeting, Acoust. Soc. Jpn.* 1, 295-296.

[17] Fujisaki, H., Narusawa, S., Ohno, S., Freitas, D. 2003. Analysis and modeling of F_0 contours of Portuguese utterances based on a quantitative model. *Proc. 8th European Conference on Speech Communication and Technology*, Geneva 3, 2317-2320.

[18] Fujisaki, H., Ohno, S., Luksaneeyanawin, S. 2003. Analysis and synthesis of F_0 contours of Thai utterances based on the command-response model. *Proc. Int'l Congr. of Phonetic Sciences* 2, 1129-1132.

[19] Fujisaki, H. 2004. Information, prosody, and modeling — with emphasis on the tonal features of speech. In: G. Fant, H. Fujisaki, J. Cao, Y. Xu (eds.), *From Traditional Phonology to Modern Speech Processing*. Beijing: Foreign Language Teaching and Research Press, 111-128.

[20] Fujisaki, H., Ohno, S. 2005. Analysis and modeling of fundamental frequency contours of Hindi utterances. *Proc. International Conference on Speech Science and Technology (INTERSPEECH) 2005*, Lisbon, 1413-1416.

[21] Fujisaki, H., Ohno, S. 2005. Analysis of fundamental frequency contours of Russian utterances using the command-response model. *Proc. 2005 Autumn Meeting, Acoust. Soc. Jpn.* 337-338.

[22] Fujisaki, H., Wang, C., Ohno, S., Gu, W. 2005. Analysis and synthesis of fundamental frequency contours of Standard Chinese using the command-response model. *Speech Communication* 47, 59-70.

[23] Fujisaki, H., Wang, C., Ohno, S, Gu, W. 2005. Analysis and synthesis of fundamental frequency contours of Standard Chinese using the command-response model. *Speech Communication* 47, 59-70.

[24] Fujisaki, H., Gu, W. 2006. Phonological representation of tone systems of some tone languages based on the command-response model for F_0 contour generation. *Proc. TAL 2006*, La Rochelle, 59-62.

[25] Fujisaki, H., Ohno, S. 2007. On the units and structures of a spoken discourse of Japanese. *Proc. 2007 Autumn Meeting, Acoust. Soc. Jpn.* 371-372.

[26] Gu, W., Hirose, K., Fujisaki, H. 2004. Analysis of F_0 contours of Cantonese utterances based on the command- response model. *Proc. INTERSPEECH 2004*. Cheju, 481-784.

[27] Gu, W., Hirose, K., Fujisaki, H. 2006. Modeling the tones in Suzhou and Wujiang dialects on the basis of the command-response model. *Proc. TAL 2006*, La Rochelle, 59-62.

[28] Higuchi, N., Hirai, T., Sagisaka, Y. 1997. Effect of speaking style on parameters of fundamenal frequency contour. In: J. van Santen, R. Sproat, J. Olive, J. Hirshberg (eds.), *Progress in Speech Synthesis*, New York: Springer, 417-428.

[29] Mixdorff, H., Fujisaki, H. 1994. Analysis of voice fundamental frequency contours of German utterances using a quantitative model. *Proc. 1994 Int'l Conf. on Spoken Language Processing*, Yokohama 4, 2231-2234.

[30] Mixdorff, H., Amir, N. 2002. The prosody of Modern Hebrew. *Proc. Speech Prosody 2002*, Aix-en-Provence, 511-515.

[31] Mixdorff, H., Vainio, M., Werner, S., Järvikivi, J. 2002. The manifestation of linguistic information in prosodic features of Finnish. *Proc. Speech Prosody 2002*, Aix-en-Provence, 516-519.

[32] Mixdorff, H., Nguyen, H., Fujisaki, H., Luong, C. 2003. Quantitative analysis and synthesis of syllabic tones in Vietnamese. *8th European Conference on Speech Communication and Technology*, Geneva 1, 177-180.

[33] Möbius, B., Pätzold, M., Hess, W. 1993. Analysis and synthesis of German F_0 contours by means of Fujisaki's model. *Speech Communication* 13, 53-61.

[34] Navas, E., Hernáez, I., Armenta, A., Etxebaria, B., Salaberria, J. 2002. Modelling Basque intonation using Fujisaki's model and CARTs. *Proc. Seminar on State of the Art in Speech Synthesis*, London, 3/1-3/6.

[35] Öhman, S., Lindqvist, J. 1965. Analysis-by-synthesis of prosodic pitch contours. *Speech Transmission Laboratory Quarterly Status and Progress Report (STL-QPSR)*, KTH 4/1965, 1-6.

[36] Öhman, S. 1967. Word and sentence intonation: A quantitative model. *Speech Transmission Laboratory Quarterly Status and Progress Report (STL-QPSR), KTH* 2-3/1967, 20-54.

[37] Pierrehumbert, J., Beckman, M. 1988. *Japanese Tone Structure*. Cambridge, Mass.: The MIT Press, 21.

[38] Richard, K. 2005. *An acoustic-phonetic descriptive analalysis of Lanqi citation tones*. Unpublished Honours Thesis, Australian National University.

[39] Rossi, P., Palmieri, F., Cutugno, F. 2002. A method for automatic extraction of Fujisaki-model parameters. *Proc. Speech Prosody 2002*, Aix-en-Provence, 615-618.

[40] Wu, Z. 1996. A new method of intonation analysis for Standard Chinese: frequency transposition processing of phrasal contours. In: G. Fant, K. Hirose, S. Kiritani (eds.), Analysis, *Perception and Processing of Spoken Language*. Amsterdam: Elsevier Science B. V., 255-268.

COUPLED OSCILLATOR PLANNING MODEL OF SPEECH TIMING AND SYLLABLE STRUCTURE

*Louis GOLDSTEIN, Hosung NAM, Elliot SALTZMAN,
Ioana CHITORAN*

ABSTRACT

A fundamental problem in understanding speech production is how the temporal coherence of the speech units associated with a given lexical unit is maintained despite changes due to speaking rate, prosodic embedding, and transient perturbations. To address this, a dynamical model of temporal planning of speech has been developed [21][13][26][27]. In this model, each speech unit (constriction gesture) is associated with a planning oscillator, or clock, and the oscillators within the ensemble associated with a particular lexical item are coupled to one another in a pattern represented as a coupling graph.

Given this model, it is possible to account for syllable structure in terms of intrinsic modes of coupling and the topology of the coupling graph. Onset consonant gestures are hypothesized to be coupled in-phase to the tautosyllabic vowel (regardless of how many there are in an onset), while coda consonant gestures are coupled in an anti-phase pattern. This topology can account simultaneously for regularities in relative timing and variability, and examples of this will be discussed.

Despite successes obtained with the model, it is clear that there are examples in which the same syllable structure can exhibit different patterns of timing, depending, e.g. on the place of articulation of the consonants in the cluster [10], manner [7][17] or language. In this paper, we will also illustrate how these different patterns of timing can be modeled using coupling graphs with differing topologies and/or with different quantitative specification of coupling strength associated with the graph's edges.

Keywords: articulatory phonology, coupling graph, syllable structure

1. INTRODUCTION

Like other combinatorial systems, phonology can be analyzed into a set of primitive atoms and some glue that holds them together in combinations. From the perspective of articulatory phonology [3], the atoms are the distinct vocal tract actions (gestures) used by talkers and listeners to distinguish words from one another in a communication system. Words are composed of an ensemble of gestures, organized in time in a particular fashion. The temporal organization is itself informational. An example of this can be seen in Figure 1, which shows gestural scores for the words "mad" and "ban." The scores show the temporal intervals during which gestures of the various vocal tract constriction devices are active and control their corresponding articulator sets to produce the constriction task goals. The time at which the velic lowering (wide) gesture occurs is the only difference between the scores. Thus, the speech production system must include some kind of glue that insures the temporal stability of the informational pattern, for example in the case of Fig. 1, insuring that the velum lowering gesture does not stray too far during the production of "mad," so that "ban" is perceived instead.

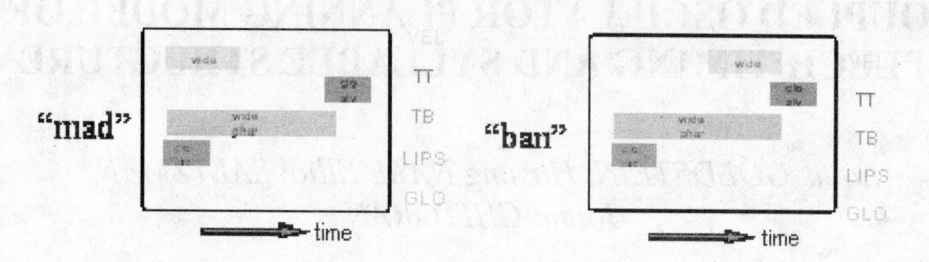

Figure 1: Gestural Scores for "mad" and "ban"

The hypothesis that underlies our recent modeling efforts [23][26][27] is that the required glue is to be found in dynamical coupling in a system of planning oscillators, or clocks. Coupled oscillators, when entrained, can exhibit the property of phase-locking. They oscillate with a stable relative phase and if perturbed, they return to their stable relative phase. If the gestures are associated with such clocks, and if their activations are triggered at particular phases of their clocks, stable relative phasing would be ensured.

Given the decision to employ coupled oscillators in speech production planning, there are at least two alternative system architectures that could be constructed. In one, each of the gesture oscillators is coupled to an external master clock. This will allow the temporal stability of the gestural pattern to be maintained, and will allow some flexibility: as the master clock changes its frequency, this will induce temporal changes in the patterns of gestural triggering. This type of system is similar in several ways to the C/D model of Fujimura [12], in which each gesture is timed to some phase of a syllable pulse. The alternative, which we have pursued in our model, is to couple the gesture's clocks to one another in a pair-wise network, described as a coupling graph. (In more recent work [27] hierarchical coupling of gesture clocks to foot and phrase level oscillators is also implemented, but not every gesture is coupled to a higher-level oscillator.)

There are at least two reasons for preferring the pair-wise coupling network to the master clock:

- The stability of relative phase of neighboring gestures can vary as a function of several factors. For example, [7] the relative phase of consonant gestures in a syllable onset is less variable than that of the same gestures in a syllable coda. If all gestures were coupled to an external clock, such differential stability would not be expected.
- Coupled oscillators can entrain in intrinsically accessible modes, and applying those modes to pair-wise inter-gestural coupling provides the basis for an embodied theory of syllable structure. As discussed in section 2, this theory can account for macroscopic universals of syllable structure, and at the same time, microscopic properties of gestural relative timing and its variability.

2. COUPLING MODES AND SYLLABLE STRUCTURE

In the model of speech production we have been developing [27], the planning of gesture relative timing (the gestural score) takes place through an oscillatory process. Each gesture of the utterance is associated with a planning oscillator, or clock, and gestures are coupled pairwise to one another in an utterance specific manner. As planning for an utterance is initiated, all of the gesture clocks begin oscillating at random phases with respect to one another. Over time (oscillator cycles) coupling forces cause local changes in phase of individual planning oscillators, and the system eventually settles into a stable pattern of oscillator relative phases. Once the system stabilizes, activation of a gesture (left edge of its gestural score box) is triggered at phase 0 of its component oscillator.

The pattern of inter-oscillator coupling associated with a particular lexical unit is represented in a coupling graph. The nodes of the graph represent the oscillators associated with individual gestures, and the edges of the graph connect pairs of coupled oscillators. The edges (or links) specify the target relative phase of the associated pair of oscillators. In the task-dynamic model of relative phase planning, the target relative phase acts as the minimum of a potential function [24], that induces forces on the component oscillators so that relative phase of the pair is attracted to its target value.

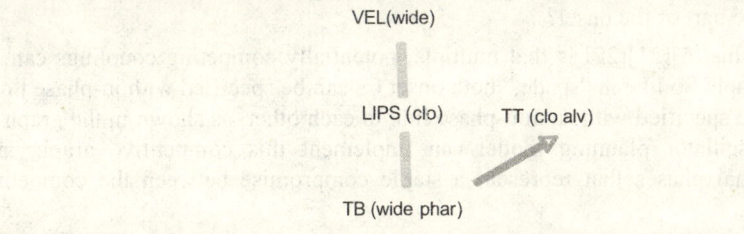

VEL(wide)

LIPS (clo)   TT (clo alv)

TB (wide phar)

Figure 2: Coupling graph for "mad"

The coupling graph for the word "mad" is shown in Figure 2. The four gestures (also seen in the gestural score in Figure 1) composing the word are the nodes. Edges come in two types: lines and arrows. The lines represent edges whose target specification is in-phase (zero degrees relative phase), the arrows represent edges whose target specification is anti-phase. For anti-phase targets, an additional bit of information is required to specify the order in which gestures are triggered (which oscillator's phase 0 triggers its oscillator first). The arrow points from the earlier gesture to the later one.

2.1 Coupling Modes and syllable structure

Research on coordination of multiple rhythms has shown that there are two intrinsically accessible, stable modes in which subjects can, for example, coordinate the movements of multiple limbs—in-phase and anti-phase [15][29]. Intrinsic accessibility means that the subjects can perform the task in one of these modes without training or learning. Of these two modes, in-phase is more accessible and stable. We have hypothesized that these same stable modes are also relevant to the coordination of multiple planning oscillators. Further, we hypothesize that for a system such as speech, which can be successfully acquired spontaneously (without explicit training) by most members of the population, intrinsically accessible modes are exploited as much as possible.

If a consonant (C) gesture and a vowel (V) gesture are to be coordinated in an intrinsic mode, there are just two possibilities: in-phase and anti-phase. We have hypothesized [13] that selecting in-phase mode produces the coordination underlying CV structures (C is a syllable onset), while selecting anti-phase produces VC structures (C is a syllable coda). Evidence for the in-phase coordination of onset C and V can be found in [19], which shows that onset C and V gestures are triggered in rough temporal synchrony. The example of "mad" in Figure 2 shows the onset gestures (lip closure and velum opening) coupled in-phase with the V gesture (wide pharyngeal constriction of the tongue body), and the coda gesture (tongue tip closure) coupled anti-phase with the V.

The coupling hypothesis constitutes a grounded (or embodied) theory of syllable structure. It explains the fact that there are syllables in language that have onsets or codas from the necessity of coordinating the timing of multiple gestures in one of two accessible modes. It can also explain macroscopic universal patterns associated with syllable structure, for example, why syllables with onsets (CV) are universal while those with codas are not [13]. This follows the fact that the in-phase mode is more accessible and more stable. Similarly, it can account for the fact that onsets and Vs combine relatively freely, while combinations of V and coda Cs can be more restricted [13] and for the fact that onsets emerge earlier in phonological development [21].

2.2 Complex Onsets

A challenge to the modal theory of syllable structure can be found in syllables with consonant cluster onsets (e.g. "spade"). The oral constriction gestures associated with the /s/ and /p/ must be at least partially sequential with one another (otherwise we could not recover them both perceptually). Therefore, they cannot both be in-phase with the V gesture. If in-phase coordination defines syllable onsets, how can they both be part of the onset?

A possible solution to this [5][21][27] is that multiple, potentially competing couplings can be specified in the coupling graph. So like in "spade," both onset Cs can be specified with in-phase links to the V, while they are also specified with an anti-phase link to each other, as shown in the graph in Figure 3. The coupled oscillator planning model can implement this competitive graph, and oscillators will settle at final phases that represent a stable compromise between the competing coupling forces.

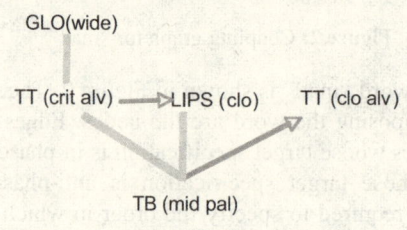

Figure 3: Coupling graph for "spade"

Evidence of this kind of competitive structure can be found in the relative timing of gestures in a complex onset [5]. In the word "spade," /s/ is shifted earlier (leftward) with respect to the vowel, compared to its timing in words in which /s/ is the only onset C. Similarly, the timing of /p/ in "spade" is shifted later (rightward), compared to its timing in words in which /p/ is the only onset C. These leftward and rightward shifts have also been dubbed the C-center effect [2][6], and they have been shown to emerge from competition in the planning model. Additional evidence for the coupling model has been found in the variability associated with C clusters. Model simulations [26][27] have shown that loops in the coupling graph (e.g. the multiply-linked onset structure in "spade" in Fig. 3), help stabilize the final oscillator relative phases, and make them less sensitive to noise. This graph property can then explain the relative temporal stability of onset clusters [7], compared to coda clusters and heterosyllabic clusters, whose relative timing does not show the C-center effects exhibited by onsets [16].

While the coupling model of syllable structure has shown promising results, there is as yet only a very small amount of data demonstrating both leftward and rightward shifts in onset clusters. Moreover, the symmetry (or lack of it) between the leftward and rightward shifts has not been systematically evaluated. In the next section, we will report on an experiment designed to investigate the robustness and symmetry of these shifts. Some evidence for systematically asymmetrical shifts will be presented, and mechanisms accounting for the asymmetries within the coupling model will be considered. In the final section, data on onset stop clusters in Georgian will be presented. These have been shown [10] to exhibit different lags as a function of the order of place in the cluster. We will consider how this kind of asymmetry can be modeled in the coupling model.

3. ENGLISH REVISITED

3.1 Method

X-ray microbeam data [20] were collected from 6 subjects producing the utterances shown in Table 1. The utterances were designed to allow comparison of the C-V timing in words beginning with single Cs (/p/, /s/, /l/) with words beginning with CC clusters (/sp/, /pl/). Two of the six subjects were asked to produce the utterances in two different accent pattern conditions (A: accent on pa, B: accent on _eets). The other 4 subjects produced only accent pattern B. Gold markers were positioned in the mid-sagittal plane at the following locations: upper lip, lower lip, lower teeth, tongue tip (actually about 1 behind the tongue tip), and tongue dorsum (as far posterior as a subject was comfortable with) and 2 on the body of the tongue, approximately equally spaced between the tongue tip and dorsum markers. Each subject produced between 5 and 10 repetitions of each utterance.

Table 1: English Utterances

I read *pa* **seats** again.
I read *pa* **peets** again.
I read *pa* **leets** again.
I read *pa* **speets** again.
I read *pa* **pleats** again.

The kinematic data were used in conjunction with a trace of the subject's palate outline to estimate constriction time functions for the relevant consonants and the vowel /i/: LA (Lip Aperture) — the distance between the upper and lower lips, TTCD (Tongue Tip Constriction Degree) — the distance from the tongue tip marker to the palate, and TBCD (Tongue Body Constriction Degree) — the distance from the more posterior tongue body marker and the palate. Constriction gestures were located in the appropriate time functions (LA for /p/, TTCD for /s/ and /l/, TBCD for /i/). For each gesture, three points in time were detected using a velocity threshold — onset of constriction formation, achievement of constriction target, and release.

Mean relative timing of consonant gestures to the vowel /i/ for each subject were calculated using the lag between achievement of constriction of the C and /i/. For the subjects who produced two accent patterns, means were calculated separately for the two patterns. By comparing a given subject's mean lags for single Cs with CC clusters, we calculated the subject's leftward and rightward shifts associated with the clusters /sp/ and /pl/. For /sp/, leftward shift was calculated as the difference between /s/-/i/ timing in "seats" and /s/-/i/ timing in "speets." Rightward shift was calculated as the difference between /p/-/i/ timing in "peets" and /p/-/i/ timing in "speets." Similarly for /pl/, leftward shift was calculated as the difference between /p/-/i/ timing in "peets" and /p/-/i/ timing in "pleats." Rightward shift was calculated as the difference between /l/-/i/ timing in "leets" and /l-/i/ timing in "pleats."

3.2 Results

Figure 4 shows the leftward (light-colored bar) and rightward (dark bar) shifts for /sp/ and Figure 5 shows /pl/. The top pair of bars show the mean shifts over all subjects, and the eight pairs below show the results for the individual subjects (separated by accent for two subjects — s1A, s1B, s2A, s2B).

In general, clusters exhibit both leftward and rightward shifts, supporting the multiply-linked onset (MLO) hypothesis. For /sp/, all subjects/accents show both leftward and rightward shifts, except for subject s1, accent pattern B, which fails to show a rightward shift. The mean leftward shift is 47ms, somewhat greater than the mean rightward shift is 25ms. However, this left-right asymmetry is not consistent across speakers/accents. Five cases show a greater leftward than rightward shift, but three show the reverse. For /pl/, leftward and rightward shifts are found for all subjects except s2 (both accent conditions). The left-right asymmetry of the means is greater than for /sp/ (mean leftward=68ms, mean rightward=13ms), and it is consistent across subjects. All 8 subjects/accents show a greater leftward shift than rightward shift.

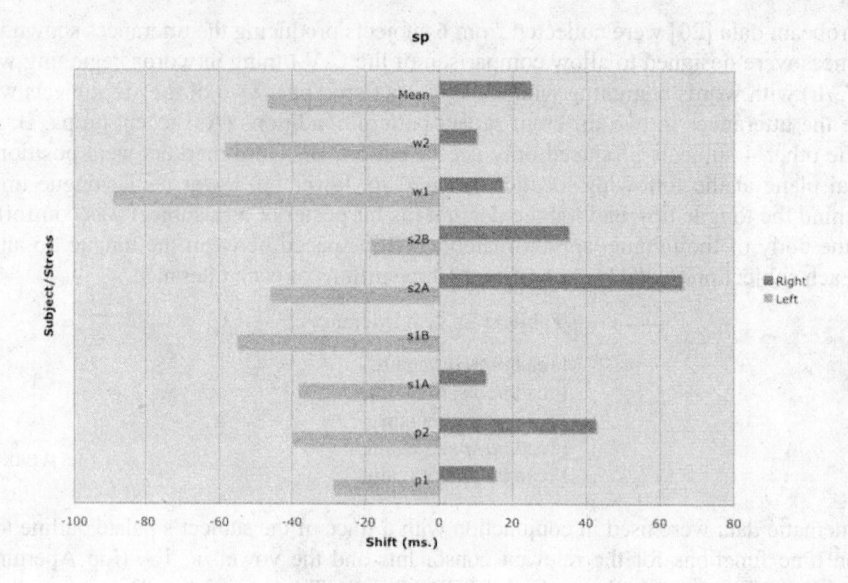

Figure 4: Leftward and rightward shifts in /sp/

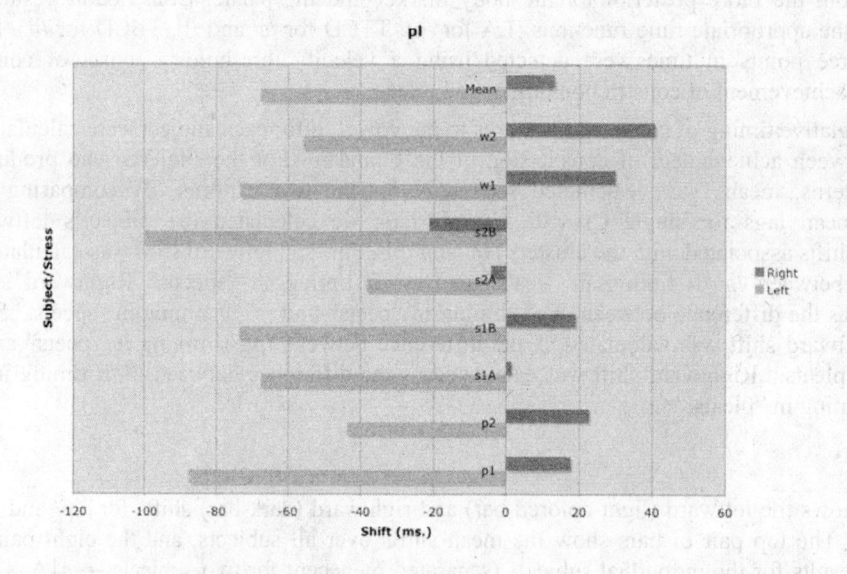

Figure 5: Leftward and rightward shifts in /pl/

How the difference in asymmetry between /sp/ and /pl/ clusters is accounted for? Since the leftward bias in the case of /pl/ appears to be quite systematic, it would be desirable to capture it in the topology of the coupling graph, i.e. a different pattern of links (edges) between nodes for /sp/ and /pl/. One possible source of such a difference is that the /l/ is, in fact, composed of two gestures: a tongue tip constriction and a body constriction at the uvula [4][28]. It is possible that both of these gestures are coupled with the vowel. This is shown in Fig. 6, along with graph for /sp/. The extra link in the /pl/ graph should result in a tighter coupling of the /l/ with respect to the vowel. This tighter coupling should also cause a reduction in rightward shift, as is confirmed in the quantitative modeling in the next section.

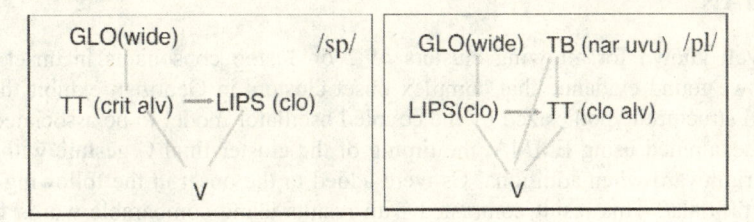

Figure 6: Hypothesized coupling graphs for /sp/ and /pl/

3.3 Quantitative modeling

While these results are in a general sense consistent with the coupling graph model that includes a competitive, multiply-linked graph of onset clusters, the details of these results are not consistent with simplest parameterization of the model that assumes that all coupling strengths are equal. That parameterization should predict an equal left and right shift. How can we model the weak left-right asymmetry exhibited by the /sp/ cluster, the much stronger leftward bias of /pl/, and an individual difference in both asymmetries?

Beginning with the weak leftward bias of /sp/, we reasoned that it would be possible to induce a leftward bias by reducing the coupling strength of C1 with V to a value less than 1, while keeping the C2-V and C1-C2 coupling strengths equal to 1. This should resolve the conflicting C-V and C-C coupling in favor of keeping C2 relatively synchronous with V at the expense of C1-V coupling. To determine if the obtained results could be predicted by adjusting the coupling strengths, we varied the coupling strengths of all links in the graph from 0.1 to 1.0 in increments of 0.1. The resulting coupling graphs were input to TADA, the coupled oscillator simulation model [22], and the resulting gestural activations were calculated. Setting all coupling strengths to 1 resulted, as expected in symmetry, with leftward and rightward shifts equal to 30ms. The data for the mean values of /sp/ were most closely modeled when C2-V and C1-C2 strengths remained equal to 1, and C1-V strength was reduced to 0.7 (yielding shifts left=40ms, right=30ms) or 0.6 (left=50ms, right=20ms). (Since the temporal resolution of the model is in terms of 10ms frames, it is not possible to model the results exactly.) Individual subject results can be approximated by reducing either C1-V or C2-V strengths.

For the /pl/ clusters, we manipulated coupling strength in the models with and without the TB link to the V. Coarser increments (0.135) were employed because there were more links to manipulate. Results for simulations without the additional link showed that reducing the coupling strength for C1-V to a value similar to that used to model /sp/ (0.74) while keeping all other strengths equal to 1 gave the same results as for /sp/ (shifts: left=40ms, right=30ms). However, when adding the additional in-phase link between the TD gesture for /l/ and the V, the shifts change to values that are close to those observed for /pl/ in our experiment: (left=60ms, right=10ms).

In summary, the English data support a view that patterns of coupling that seem to be regular aspects of the phonological knowledge of a language (in that they generalize across individual talker) can be well represented qualitatively (discretely) in terms of the set of edges that define the coupling graph. Individual differences in coordination patterns can then be modeled by quantitative variation in the coupling strength values of the graph's edges. In this sense (though not in the formal sense of the mathematics of the models), coupling strength functions like articulator weights in the constriction formation task-dynamics [25], which can show individual variation in, for example, how much lip vs. jaw raising an individual talker employs to produce a lip closure. These articulatory weights, like the coupling strengths, are assumed not to carry phonological information, which can be viewed as shared structure across community members.

4. GEORGIAN

Georgian is well known for allowing clusters of 2 or 3 stop consonants in onset position [30]. Recently [14] we found evidence that complex onset clusters in Georgian exhibit the competitive, multiple-linked structure hypothesized by the coupled oscillator model to be associated with syllable onsets. When examined using EMMA, the timing of the cluster-final C gesture with respect to the vowel shifted rightward when additional Cs were added to the onset in the following words: /riala/, /k'riala/, and /t^{s}k'riala/. This result contrasted with results using comparable words from Tashlhiyt Berber, a language in which words can also begin with complex sequences of Cs, but which are not syllabified as a complex onset, but rather as additional syllables with consonantal nuclei [11]. No evidence for the rightward shift was found in Berber. Therefore, it was argued that rightward shift could be used as a diagnostic for syllabification of consonant sequences as part of the onset.

Stop clusters in Georgian have been shown to exhibit different phonological [8][30] and phonetic behaviors when they are sequenced such that more anterior constrictions precede more posterior constrictions ("front-to-back"), as opposed to the reverse ("back-to-front"). Most relevantly, kinematic analysis has revealed that the front-to-back sequences are produced with a shorter lag between the gesture onsets [9] than back-to-front sequences. While the earlier studies on this effect [10] hypothesized that the basis for this asymmetry could be found in the affordance of perceptual recoverability, more recent work both on Georgian [9] and other languages that also appear to show this effect (e.g. French [18]) casts some doubt on this account. But whatever the underlying cause of the evolution of this pattern, the planning of sequences in Georgian must produce different relative timing of controls for two gestures, depending on their sequential order. How can this be accomplished in a model in which coordination is controlled by means of only two intrinsically stable modes?

Since the lag difference between two place orders appears to generalize across speakers and to be phonologically relevant in Georgian, it would be desirable to derive them from topological differences in the coupling graph. One possibility involves participation in the coupling graph of the release gestures associated with stop closures. Active release gestures have been shown to be necessary to account for the kinematic and perceptual properties of stops (and other consonants) [1], and to participate in some cases in planning by constituting nodes in the coupling graph [21]. However, for simplicity of exposition, the release gestures have been left out of the coupling graph figures in this paper so far (though they have been included in the actual simulations that these figures are based upon). Figure 7(a) shows a possible coupling graph for an initial /bg/ (front-to-back) cluster in Georgian, based on the MLO principles considered so far, but with the release gestures displayed. The LIPS and TB closures are both coupled in-phase with the V, and anti-phase with each other. The release gestures are coupled only to their corresponding closures, so their presence does don't affect the relative timing of the other gestures in the graph.

This topology would predict a rightward shift of C2, as has been found for Georgian. If the same graph (with the opposite ordering of the two stops) were used for a /gb/ cluster, no lag difference between /bg/ and /gb/ would be predicted by such graphs. Figure 7(b) shows an alternative hypothesis for /gb/. The only difference from Figure 7(a) is that it is now the release of C1, not its closure that is coupled in-phase with the V. This change should, however, produce an increase in C1-C2 lag (since it is a later point in C1 that is now in-phase with the V). In fact, since C1 (clo) is now anti-phase with both C1 (rel) and C2 (clo), and both of these are in-phase with the V, the coupling specifications are all consistent-there is no competition. The final phasing of the oscillators that is expected to result from this graph should have C1 (rel) in-phase with both C2 (clo) and V, and C1 (clo) anti-phase with all of these.

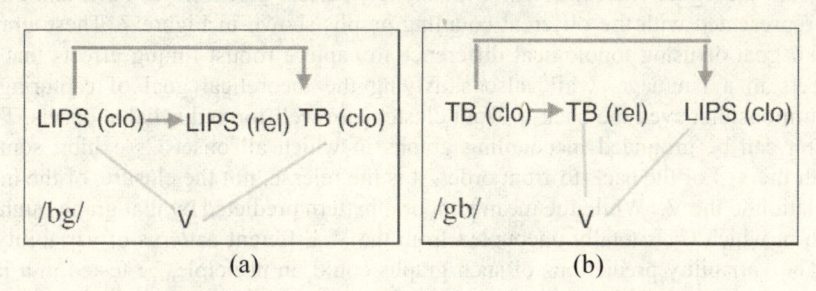

```
┌─────────────────────────────────┐   ┌─────────────────────────────────┐
│   LIPS (clo)→LIPS (rel)  TB (clo)│   │  TB (clo)→TB (rel)   LIPS (clo) │
│                                  │   │                                 │
│     /bg/         V               │   │    /gb/        V                │
└─────────────────────────────────┘   └─────────────────────────────────┘
              (a)                                     (b)
```

Figure 7: Hypothesized Georgian Coupling Graphs

Simulating these graph in 7(b) in TADA confirmed this phasing pattern. In the resulting gestural score, the lag between C1 (clo) and C2 (clo) was 90ms. C1 (rel), C2 (clo) and V were all synchronous. This 90ms lag can be compared to the C1 (clo) - C2 (clo) lag that results from the graph in Figure 7(a), which was 60ms. This difference approximates closely the difference in lag reported in back-to-front (99ms) vs. front-to-back (67ms) in [14], averaged across the two speakers. Thus, if front-to-back stop sequences are controlled by graphs such as that in Figure 7(a), and back-to-front sequences by graphs such as in Figure 7(b), then the contrasting values in these sequences can be well accounted for, while retaining the theoretically desirable property that both onset Cs are coupled to V.

One prediction of the coupling graph in Figure 7(b) is that there is no rightward shift. In the output from this graph, C2 is synchronous with V, just as it would be if it were the only C in the onset. Here we test this prediction by examining evidence for rightward shift in Georgian stop sequences with front-to-back vs. back-to-front order.

Method. The words in Table 2 were recorded by two speakers of Georgian, the same two who participated in [14]. Articulatory kinematics were measured using EMMA, with markers placed similarly to those described for the English study in the preceding section, except that only one marker was placed on the tongue body, instead of the two employed in English. Words were recorded in a frame (**Sit'q'va __ gamoit^{h}k^{h}mis ord3er**), and between 6 and 12 repetitions of each word type were acquired. A Lip Aperture (LA) time function was computed as the distance from the upper lip marker to the lower lip marker, and Tongue Tip (TTCD) and Tongue Body Constriction Degree (TBCD) time functions were computed as distances from the relevant marker to the palate outline. Gesture onsets, achievement of constriction target, and release were measured using the following time functions: /b/ (LA), t^s' (TTCD), k' (TDy), Vowels (TBCD). The time from the constriction achievement of the C gestures to the syllable's V gesture was calculated.

Table 2: Georgian words for rightward shift

Back-to-front	Front-to-back
bil-i "bill"	k'ar-eb-I "door" (pl.)
k'bil-i "tooth"	t^s'k'ar-eb-i (nons.)

Results. For the front-to-back cluster, a 19ms rightward shift was obtained (time from /k'/ to vowel was 133ms in /k'/ and 114 in /t^s'k'/). The direction of shift was consistent across the two subjects. This indicates that a graph like that in Figure 7(a) is appropriate (with an initial TT gesture substituting for the initial LIPS gesture). However, for the back-to-front example, the mean shift was only 7ms (146ms in /k'/ and 139ms in /k'b/) and was not consistent in direction across subjects. This result would be predicted by a coupling graph like that in Figure 7(b) (with the addition of a glottal closure gesture).

Results from Georgian are consistent with the hypothesis that front-to-back and back-to-front clusters are represented with the different coupling graphs shown in Figure 7. These graphs satisfy the theoretical goal of using topological difference to capture robust timing effects that generalize across subjects in a language, while also satisfying the theoretical goal of capturing Georgian speakers' intuitions that even the back-to-front clusters are well-formed syllable onsets. The syllable onset intuition can be grounded in coupling graphs in which all onset Cs exhibit some in-phase coupling with the V. For the back-to-front order, it is the release, not the closure, of the initial C that bears that relation to the V. While the mean temporal pattern predicted by that graph might not differ from a graph in which C_1 is totally uncoupled from the V, different patterns of variability would be predicted. The variability predictions of such graphs could, in principle, be tested in a language in which some CCV sequences are analyzed as complex onsets and others are analyzed as an "extra-syllabic" C followed by a CV syllable.

Finally, the coupling graph differences between 7(a) and 7(b) can also be used to model other examples where different types of onset clusters have been shown to exhibit systematically different patterns of lag. The lag differences between the German initial /gl/ and /gn/ clusters as reported in [17] can be modeled in this way. Such a model also predicts that /gl/ should exhibit the rightward shift, but /gn/ should not. It is not yet known whether that prediction is born out.

5. ACKNOWLEDGEMENTS

Thanks to Aaron Jacobs for help with the analysis. The work was supported by NIH grants DC008780 and DC03172 and NSF grant 0703048.

REFERENCES

[1] Browman, Catherine P. 1994. Lip aperture and consonant releases. In: P. Keating (ed.), *Papers in laboratory phonology III: Phonological structure and phonetic Form*. Cambridge: Cambridge University Press, 331-353.

[2] Browman, C., Goldstein, L. 1988. Some notes on syllable structure in Articulatory Phonology. *Phonetica* 45, 140-155.

[3] Browman, C. P., Goldstein, L. 1992. Articulatory phonology: An overview. *Phonetica* 49, 155-180.

[4] Browman, C.P., Goldstein, L. 1995. Gestural syllable position effects in American English. In: F. Bell-Berti and L. Raphael (eds.), *Studies in Speech Production: A Festschrift for Katherine Safford Harris*. Woodbury NY: American Institute of Physics, 19-34.

[5] Browman, C., Goldstein, L. 2000. Competing constraints on intergestural coordination and self-organization of phonological structures. *Bulletin de la Communication Parlé* 5, 25-34.

[6] Byrd, D. 1995. C-centers revisited. *Phonetica* 52, 285-306.

[7] Byrd, D. 1996. Influences on articulatory timing in consonant sequences. *Journal of Phonetics* 24, 209-244.

[8] Chitoran, I. 1998. Georgian harmonic cluster: phonetic cues to phonological representation. *Phonology* 15, 121-144.

[9] Chitoran, I., Goldstein, L. 2006. Testing the phonological status of perceptual recoverability: Articulatory evidence from Georgian. Laboratory Phonology 10, Paris.

[10] Chitoran, I., Goldstein, L., Byrd, D. 2002. Gestural overlap and recoverability: Articulatory evidence from Georgian. In: C. Gussenhoven, N. Warner (eds.), *Laboratory Phonology VII*. Berlin: Walter de Gruyter, 419-448.

[11] Dell, F., Elmedlaoui, M. 1985. Syllabic Consonants and Syllabification in Imdlawn Tashlhiyt Berber. *Journal of African Languages and Linguistics* 7, 105-130.

[12] Fujimura, O. 2000. The C/D Model and Prosodic Control of Articulatory Behavior. *Phonetica* 57, 128-138.

[13] Goldstein, L., Byrd, D., Saltzman, E. 2006. The role of vocal tract gestural action units in understanding the evolution of phonology. In: M. Arbib, (ed.), *Action to Language via the Mirror Neuron System.* New York: Cambridge University Press, 215-249.

[14] Goldstein, L., Chitoran, I., Selkirk, E. 2007. Syllable structure as coupled oscillator modes: Evidence from Georgian vs. Tashlhiyt Berber. *Proc. XVIth Int. Cong. Phonetic Sciences*, Saarbrücken, 241-244.

[15] Haken, H., Kelso, J. A. S., Bunz, H. 1985. A theoretical model of phase transitions in human hand movements. *Biological Cybernetics* 51, 347-356.

[16] Honorof, D., Browman, C. 1995. The center or edge: How are consonant clusters organized with respect to the vowel? In: K. Elenius and P. Branderud (eds.), *Proceedings of the XIIIth International Congress of Phonetic Sciences,* Vol. 3. Stockholm: KTH and Stockholm University, 552-555.

[17] Hoole, P., Bombien, L., Kühnert, B., Mooshammer, C. 2008. Intrinsic and Prosodic Effects on Articulatory Coordination in Initial Consonant Clusters. *Frontiers in Phonetics and Speech Science*(to be published), Beijing.

[18] Kühnert, B., Hoole, P., Mooshammer, C. 2006. Gestural overlap and C-center in selected French consonant clusters. *Proc. 7th Int. Seminar on Speech Production*, Ubatuba, 327-334.

[19] Löfqvist, A., Gracco, V. 1999. Interarticulator programming in VCV sequences: lip and tongue movements. *Journal of the Acoustic Society of America* 105, 1854-1876.

[20] Nadler, R. D., Abbs, J. H., Fujimura, O. 1987. Speech movement research using the new X-ray microbeam system. *Speech Motor Control Laboratories Preprints*, 181-184.

[21] Nam, H. (in press). A competitive, coupled oscillator model of moraic structure: Split-gesture dynamics focusing on positional asymmetry. In: Cole J., Hualde J. (eds.), *Papers in Laboratory Phonology IX*.

[22] Nam, H., Goldstein, L., Proctor, M. 2007. TADA (TAsk Dynamics Application) Available for downloading http://www.haskins.yale.edu/tada_download/.

[23] Nam, H., Saltzman, E. 2003. A competitive, coupled oscillator of syllable structure. *Proc. XVth International Congress of Phonetic Sciences* , Bracelona, 3-9.

[24] Saltzman, E., Byrd, D. 2000. Task-dynamics of gestural timing: Phase windows and multifrequency rhythms. *Human Movement Science* 19, 499-526.

[25] Saltzman, E. L., Munhall, K. G. 1989. A dynamical approach to gestural patterning in speech production. *Ecological Psychology* 1, 333-382.

[26] Saltzman, E., Nam, H., Goldstein, L. Intergestural timing in speech production: The role of graph structure. *Human Movement Science*.

[27] Saltzman, E., Nam, H., Krivokapic, J., Goldstein, L. (in press). A task-dynamic toolkit for modeling the effects of prosodic structure on articulation. In: Barbosa, P. A., Madureira, S., Reis, C. (eds.), *Proceedings of the Speech Prosody 2008 Conference*, Campinas, Brazil.

[28] Sproat, R., Fujimura, O. 1993. Allophonic variation in American English /l/ and its implications for phonetic interpretation. *Journal of Phonetics* 21, 391-311.

[29] Turvey, M. T. 1990. Coordination. *American Psychologist* 45, 938-953.

[30] Vogt, H. 1971. *Grammaire de la langue géorgienne.* Oslo: Universitetsforlaget.

ANALYSIS BY SYNTHESIS OF BRITISH ENGLISH SPEECH RHYTHM: FROM DATA TO MODELS

Daniel HIRST, Caroline BOUZON, Cyril AURAN

ABSTRACT

This paper presents results from the analysis of the rhythmic characteristics of a corpus of five and a half hours of authentic speech of British English. It is shown (as suggested by Wiktor Jassem over 50 years ago) that the most appropriate unit to describe the relative lengthening of phones is the Narrow Rhythm Unit, beginning with the stressed syllable and finishing at the next word boundary. No lengthening effect was found at the level of the syllable or the anacrusis (the syllables preceding the first stressed syllable). Furthermore no specific effect of stress or word boundaries was found in the data although a considerable effect of final lengthening was observed at the level of the intonation unit. These results were incorporated into a model of analysis by synthesis and it is shown that such a model provides a very promising approach to the analysis of speech rhythm.

Keywords: English, rhythm, analysis, synthesis, model

1. INTRODUCTION

It is unfortunate that today there is still an enormous gap between the community of linguists and phoneticians on the one hand and that of engineers and computer scientists on the other. Each community needs the other and, in an ideal world, linguists would provide theoretical frameworks and data which are useful to engineers, while engineers would provide tools which are useful to linguists. The exchange between the two communities, however, is in practice very slow. It often takes decades for ideas which are current in one community to be adopted by the other. The ideas of non-linear phonology, which have dominated phonological analysis since the 1970's, for example, are only recently being integrated into speech synthesis and speech recognition systems. At the same time, many linguists and phoneticians working on corpus analysis use extremely primitive tools and software: there is still today, for example no widely available tool for robust automatic alignment of a waveform with a transcription. Although such tools do exist they are generally not available in a form which the average linguist or phonetician can easily use. The result is that linguists working on spoken corpora can spend hundreds of hours providing manual alignment of their data and, worst of all, this manual alignment is very often not even fed back as a resource for evaluating automatic alignment algorithms.

In this presentation we present a language independent framework for the analysis by synthesis of speech prosody. After a general presentation in the following section we present some recent data from the analysis of the rhythm of a five and a half hour corpus of authentic speech of British English. In the final section we try to show how the results from this analysis can be incorporated into a model of rhythm.

2. ANALYSIS BY SYNTHESIS OF SPEECH PROSODY

In recent work [20][19], it has been argued that the separation of form and function in the representation of speech prosody is a highly desirable condition for the analysis of the prosodic systems of natural languages. In the area of speech synthesis, by contrast, the representation of prosody often combines both form and function. In the project described here (see also [15]), the aim is to develop and implement a symbolic representation system for prosodic form without direct reference to prosodic function.

The symbolic representation system described can be derived automatically from acoustic data via a specification of the domains and units relevant for the analysis. The analysis is reversible so that the result of the symbolic coding of the data can be compared empirically with the original data in order to evaluate the appropriateness of the analysis. The specification of domains and units for each prosodic parameter thus becomes an explicit step in the modeling of the prosodic system in order to allow the user to implement and test different models of representation.

The prosodic parameters currently implemented in the model are segmental duration and fundamental frequency but the same general framework could, and it is hoped will, be extended to include other parameters such as spectral tilt and voice quality. One specific characteristic of the framework is that different domains and units can be specified for different parameters so that the units used to define the rhythm of an utterance, for example, are not necessarily the same as those used to define its pitch.

The system implements the symbolic representation of speech prosody as a set of hierarchical structures defining specific units for the interpretation of discrete symbols coding the absolute and relative pitch and duration of different units of speech.

The representation of melody has been described elsewhere [18][19][20] while that of rhythm is presented in more detail below. The two levels of representation have a certain number of characteristics in common. For both levels, a distinction is made between, on the one hand, local, short-term variability (i.e. lexical or non-lexical distinctive tone and quantity), for which specific units are assumed, and on the other hand longer term variability involving higher order domains. Thus, speech melody is described by means of melody domains, within which the speaker's overall pitch reference level, referred to as his *key*, and the extent of variability, referred to as his *range*, are assumed to be constant [8]. In the same way, for rhythm, it is assumed that within a specific rhythm domain, a constant *tempo* is defined which then serves as a default reference with respect to which shorter term variability is described.

3. ANALYSING SPEECH RHYTHM

It is generally accepted that, next to phonemic identity, prosodic structure is one of the major characteristics influencing segmental duration, where prosodic structure is taken as the organisation of phonemes into such higher-level units as syllables, stress feet and intonation units. As Klatt [23] noted, nearly twenty years ago, however:

> "One of the unsolved problems in the development of rule systems for speech timing is the size of the unit (segment, onset/rhyme, syllable, word) best employed to capture various timing phenomena." (p. 760)

There has been considerable speculation by phonologists as to the nature of prosodic representations, conceived of as an autonomous hierarchical structure [10][26]. There has, however, been comparatively little experimental evidence to justify these theoretical constructs, so that their relationship to phonetic and acoustic data remains somewhat obscure and very much a subject for empirical investigation.

Among the units most frequently cited in phonetic studies as playing a role in the determination of segmental duration are:

(1) the **syllable** [6] — with, generally, a binary distinction between stressed and unstressed syllables.

(2) the **stress-foot** [1][12] — consisting of a stressed syllable and any following unstressed syllables up until (but not including) the next stressed syllable or until the boundary of an intonation unit.

(3) the **word**.

(4) the **intonation unit** — (also known as phonological phrase, tone unit etc.) delimited by a full intonation boundary.

To these, our own recent research, presented in more detail below, has suggested that, following Wiktor Jassem's pioneering work [22], we should add:

(5) the **narrow rhythm unit** — consisting of a stressed syllable and any following unstressed syllables up until the end of the word. (in recent work this unit has also been referred to as the "within word foot" [28][29].

(6) the **anacrusis** — consisting of any unstressed syllables not included in a narrow rhythm unit.

Note that once the boundaries of the word and of the stressed syllable are given, the limits of the foot, narrow rhythm unit and anacrusis are automatically defined.

These potential phonological units are illustrated in Fig. 1:

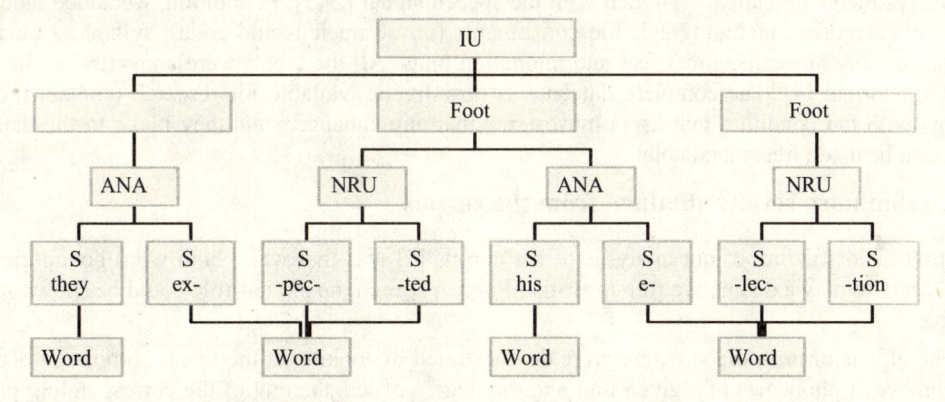

Figure 1: The Intonation Unit (IU) "They expected his election" parsed into syllables (S), narrow rhythm units (NRU), anacruses (ANA), stress feet and words.

The status of the initial anacrusis is represented here as an empty node at the level of the foot, reflecting the fact that this has been analysed in different ways by different authors. For some, the initial anacrusis is assumed to be an immediate constituent of the superordinate intonation unit, for others it constitutes a defective foot, which Halliday [12] described as having a "silent ictus".

4. AN ANALYSIS OF A CORPUS OF AUTHENTIC SPEECH

The majority of studies of segmental duration are based on corpora of carefully constructed sentences pronounced in laboratory conditions. For a recent study using this type of material, including an extensive bibliography see [29]. The motivation behind this restriction has been to systematically manipulate the prosodic structure of utterances in order to test different hypotheses. In recent work we have started analysing a large database of spoken English, the Aix-Marsec database, described in the following section, on the assumption that with a large enough database the different prosodic effects we wish to test should be sufficiently represented without needing to construct artificial utterances.

4.1 The Aix-Marsec database

The Aix-Marsec database contains about five and a half hours of speech representing a number of different speaking styles, all of which can be characterised as what we have termed "authentic speech", that is speech produced with the intent of communicating its meaning to listeners, unlike laboratory speech where the communicative function of the speech act is generally lacking.

The database derives originally from the SEC (Spoken English Corpus), a collection of BBC recordings from the 1980s, grouping eleven different radio speech styles ranging from news and interviews to poetry reading. The data consists of recordings of British English from 53 different speakers (17 male and 36 female) and includes about 55000 orthographically transcribed words as well as a manually transcribed prosodic annotation (G. Knowles and B. Williams) using a series of fourteen tonetic stress marks.

The SEC was subsequently adapted to facilitate computer use and was renamed the MARSEC (MAchine Readable Spoken English Corpus); changes consisted in manually aligning the word and (minor-major) intonation unit boundaries with the sound and changing some of the tonetic stress marks (TSM) into ASCII symbols in order to have a computer compatible annotation system [24] [25][27].

Our contribution to the database was to provide broad phonetic transcription for the corpus, which was then automatically aligned with the speech signal [2][3]. In addition, we added labels for prosodic categories, including syllable constituents (onset, nucleus and coda), syllables, anacruses and narrow rhythm units, stress feet and intonation units. All the labels were converted to the Praat TextGrid format [4]. The complete database is now freely available for research (contact the first author) with the condition that users must agree that any enhancements they make to the database shall also be made freely available.

4.2 Preliminary results obtained from the corpus

The first major finding of our analyses of the corpus [5] was that while both word boundaries and stress seem to play a distinctive role in British English speech, no similar role could be shown for the syllable.

The effects of prosodic structure were demonstrated by looking at the linear correlation between the number of phonemes in a given unit and the degree of lengthening of the corresponding phones as compared to the mean duration of the phoneme throughout the corpus. Strong negative correlations were found between the lengthening of segments and the number of phonemes in the stress-foot, in the narrow rhythm unit and in the word but not in the syllable or the anacrusis.

This confirms the findings of Hill [13] who analysed the effect of prosodic structure on segmental duration in a passage of read speech and found a certain degree of compression on the level of the stress foot and the narrow rhythm unit but not on the level of the syllable, and concluded:

"there is no evidence in our data of any syllable timed feature of spoken British English".(p.5)

The negative correlations were taken as evidence that the units in question play a role in planning the pronunciation of the utterance. A tendency to shorten segments on the level of suprasegmental units can be interpreted as a tendency to make these units more nearly equal in duration than they would be if there was no compression at all.

A second finding was that the degree of compression at the level of the narrow rhythm unit was greater than that at the level of the foot or of the word. This is understandable, since words can always be parsed into an anacrusis and/or a narrow rhythm unit and feet can always be parsed into a narrow rhythm unit followed by an optional anacrusis, as can be seen from the illustration in Fig. 1.

It follows logically, then, that if there is a significant effect within the narrow rhythm unit but not in the anacrusis, the effect found at the level of the word as well as that at the level of the foot can be interpreted as the indirect effect of that of the narrow rhythm unit, diluted by the presence of any anacrusis.

A third major finding of these studies was that once the number of phonemes in the narrow rhythm unit was determined, no further orthogonal effect of stress was found. Phones in stressed syllables, in other words, are not intrinsically more lengthened (in our corpus) than phones in unstressed syllables in the same narrow rhythm unit, once the specific contribution of the identity of the phoneme is neutralised by a z-transformation of the raw segmental duration:

$$z_{i/p} = \frac{d_{i/p} - \mu_p}{\sigma_p} \qquad (1)$$

where $z_{i/p}$ is the z-score of a given instance i of a phoneme p, $d_{i/p}$ is the corresponding raw duration, μ_p and σ_p are the mean and standard deviation for the duration of that phoneme.

In fact, if we plot the z-score of the duration of phones as a function of the number of phonemes in the narrow rhythm unit for stressed and unstressed phonemes, we see in Fig. 2 (reproduced from [5]) that stressed phones are more lengthened than unstressed phones only when they occur in very short narrow rhythm units, containing no more than three phonemes. For longer units, the stressed phones are, in fact, most of the time actually relatively *less* lengthened than the unstressed phones.

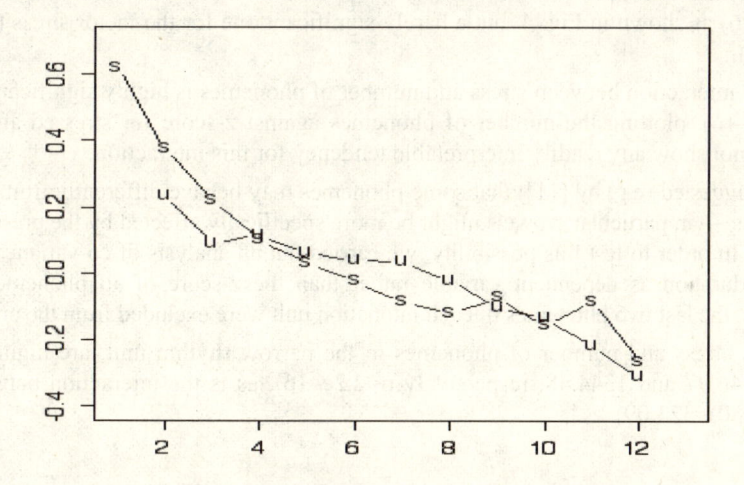

Figure 2: Duration of segments in z-score (y-axis) as a function of the number of phonemes in the narrow rhythm unit (x-axis) for stressed (s) and unstressed (u) phones.

A plausible explanation for this non-linear effect for stressed and unstressed phone duration [16] is that these results are in fact conflating the effect of stress with an effect of final lengthening affecting the last few phonemes of an intonation unit. When the units are very short and occur at the end of an intonation unit, the stressed phones themselves undergo this lengthening effect; when the units are longer, only unstressed phones are affected.

Indeed, if we plot the relation between the distance of a phoneme from the end of the intonation unit against the corresponding z-transformed duration (Fig. 3) we can see clearly that the effect is very strong for the last two or three phonemes of the intonation unit but that it quickly tails off and then after about 30 phonemes becomes erratic as the distance from the end of the unit gets greater and the corresponding number of data points gets smaller.

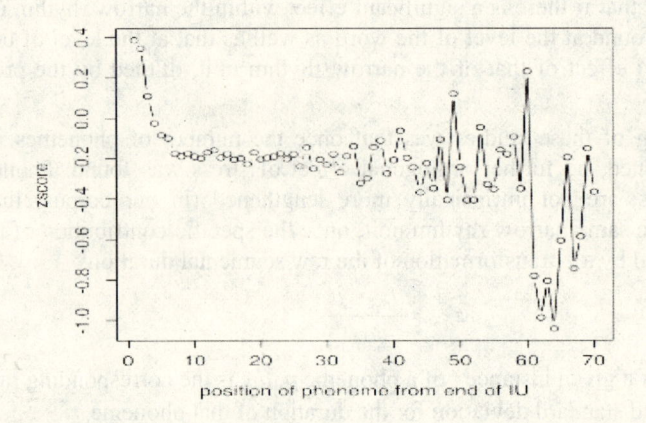

Figure 3: Z-score of duration of segments as a function of their position (in number of phonemes) as measured from the end of the intonation unit.

When the last two phonemes of the intonation unit are excluded from the analysis, an analysis of co-variance on the z-score of segmental duration as a factor of stress and of the number of phonemes in the narrow rhythm unit shows a very strong effect of the number of phonemes (F(1,140503)= 529.703; p<2e–16) as shown in Fig. 4, but a barely significant one for the factor stress (F(1,14053)= 5.6124; p=0.018).

Although the interaction between stress and number of phonemes is highly significant (F(1,14053) =76.7915; p<2e–16), plotting the number of phonemes against z-score for stressed and unstressed phonemes, does not show any readily interpretable tendency for this interaction.

It has been suggested (e.g. by [11]) that some phonemes may behave differently from others under the effect of stress — in particular, vowels might be more specifically affected by the presence of stress than consonants. In order to test this possibility, we carried out an analysis of co-variance using the z-score of vowel duration as dependent variable rather than the z-score of all phonemes. As in the previous analysis, the last two phonemes of each intonation unit were excluded from the analysis.

Both factors, stress and number of phonemes in the narrow rhythm unit, are highly significant (F(1, 43080)=1746.97 and 1344.48, respectively p<2.2e–16), as is the interaction between the two factors (F(1, 43080)=323.09).

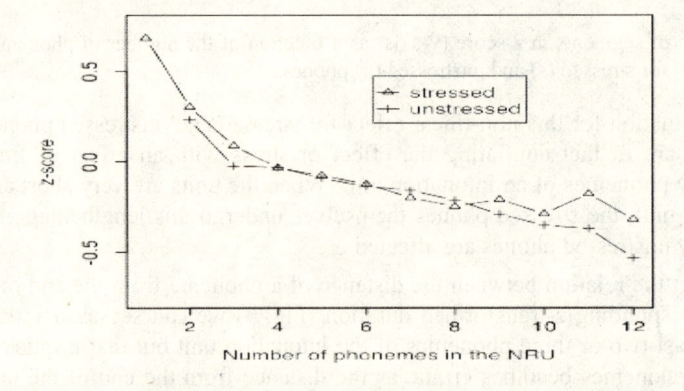

Figure 4: Z-score of segmental duration as a factor of number of phonemes in the narrow rhythm unit (NRU) for stressed and unstressed phones excluding the last two phonemes of each intonation unit.

Plotting the number of phonemes against z-score for stressed and unstressed phonemes (Fig. 5) seems, however, rather to show that if anything, unstressed vowels are more lengthened than stressed vowels within narrow rhythm units of the same size.

One other possibility, which our work had not so far taken into account, is that just as we showed that our results conflated final lengthening in the intonation unit and stress, so perhaps there is a further effect of final lengthening in the word. Since the stressed syllable of a polysyllabic word is most frequently on the first syllable, any word final lengthening would most often be affecting final unstressed syllables and might be compensating for a specific lengthening effect of stress. To test this, we coded all phonemes for their position with values: *non-final*, *word-final* (last or penultimate phoneme of word) or *iu-final* (last or penultimate phoneme of intonation unit).

An analysis of co-variance with these factors showed both position and number of phonemes in the NRU to be highly significant ($F(2,140502)=2270.4742$; $p<2e-16$ and $F(1,140502)=2057.8252$; $p<2e-16$, respectively) while once again the factor stress itself was barely significant ($F(1,140502)=5.7906$; $p=0.016$).

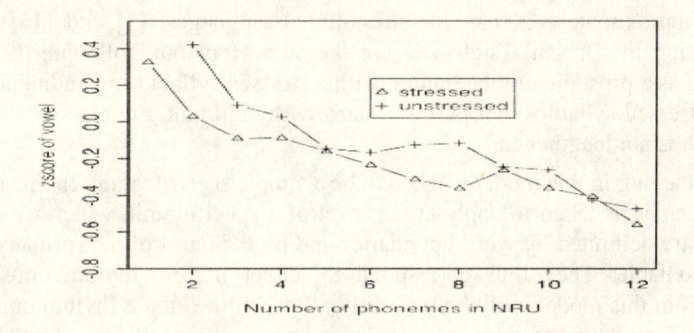

Figure 5: Z-score of duration of vowels as a function of the number of phonemes in the narrow rhythm unit (NRU) for stressed and unstressed phones excluding the last two phonemes of each intonation unit.

As can be seen from Fig. 6, however, this effect of position appears to be exclusively one of intonation unit final lengthening — word final and non-final phonemes do not show any readily interpretable pattern of difference.

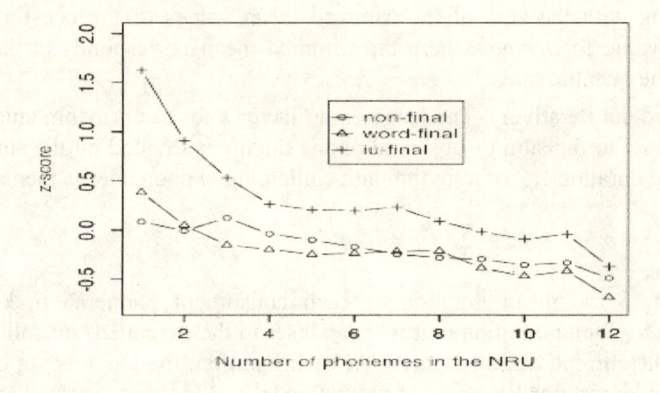

Figure 6: Z-score of the duration of phones as a function of the number of phonemes in the narrow rhythm unit (NRU) for iu-final (last two phonemes of each intonation unit), word-final (last two phonemes of each word) and non-final phonemes.

5. MODELLING SPEECH RHYTHM

The rhythm of speech can be modeled as the interaction of a number of components. In languages with lexical quantity (like Finnish) there is a lexical specification of length. In other languages, segmental duration is influenced by the accentual structure of the utterance and by more subtle longer-term variations of global duration called *tempo*.

We propose here, as an illustration of our methodology, a model of rhythm for British English that we have implemented with the ProZed environment.

In [17], as a first approximation, a simple scalar feature of length was proposed, with 5 degrees: *extra-short, short, normal, long* and *extra-long*. This feature was assumed to apply directly at the level of the segment.

There is, however, evidence that lengthening can be better handled at a higher level. Eriksson [9] showed that, for a number of European languages, when the stress foot is taken as the domain of lengthening, its duration can be satisfactorily modeled as a linear function of the number of constituent syllable, with a language specific offset of approximately 100ms for syllable-timed languages and of approximately 200ms for stress-timed languages. [1] and [16] argue that the domain of lengthening in (British) English is not the stress-foot but, following [22], the *narrow rhythm unit*, defined as a prosodic unit beginning with a stressed syllable and ending at the next word boundary. Any unstressed syllables, not part of a narrow rhythm unit, are classified as belonging to the *anacrusis*, which is not lengthened.

As in [17], lengthening in this model is taken to be a simple scalar feature. In this implementation, however, the lengthening is taken to apply at the level of a specific unit, which we call the *rhythm unit*. Rhythm units are delimited by word boundaries and by the onset of the (primary or secondary) lexically stressed syllable. They thus correspond to, either narrow rhythm units or anacruses. Monosyllabic words in this model, will consequently all constitute single rhythm units; polysyllabic words will consist of one or more rhythm units depending on the position and number of stresses. Thus a word like "communication" will be taken to consist of three rhythm units "co-", "-mmuni" and "-cation". Another difference with [17] is that whereas in that presentation, the scalar values corresponded to five discrete categories: *extra-short*, *short*, *normal*, *long* and *extra-long*, in this model there are only two discrete categories: *unlengthened* and *lengthened* where *lengthened* is associated with a scalar factor k. This model allows us to code the observed duration patterns of an utterance as a combination of two factors: a global factor of *tempo* and a local scalar degree of lengthening k applying to each rhythm unit. The lengthening factor for a given rhythm unit is calculated by comparing with the sum of the trimmed mean values of the constituent phonemes corrected by a global value for *tempo*, where the trimmed mean corresponds to the mean of the central 80% values of the quantile range.

The coding is carried out iteratively. The lengthening factor k for each rhythm unit is initially set to 0 and the tempo t is set to the sum of observed phone durations divided by the sum of predicted durations. The predicted duration $\hat{d}_{ru}$ of a rhythm unit containing m phonemes is then adjusted to:

$$\hat{d}_{ru} = \left(\sum_{i=1}^{m} (\overline{d}_{i/p}) + k * q \right) * t \qquad (2)$$

where $\overline{d}_{i/p}$ corresponds to the mean duration of each constituent phoneme p, k is the scalar lengthening factor, q is a quantal duration unit which we set to the (trimmed) overall mean duration of all phones and t is the current value of tempo. At each iteration, the lengthening coefficient k of the rhythm unit with the largest positive error of prediction $[d_{ru} - \hat{d}_{ru}]$ is incremented and the value of the tempo coefficient t is recalculated. This is reiterated until there are no positive errors greater than a given proportion (e.g. 0.75) of the quantal factor q multiplied by the current tempo t.

As an illustration of this modelling technique, a recording from the Eurom1 corpus [7] was analysed. In Fig. 7, the rhythm units are transcribed orthographically. When a word contains more than one rhythm unit as in "arrange" or "engineer", these are separated by hyphens. The figure in square brackets after each rhythm unit corresponds to its estimated lengthening factor k, the parameters t *(tempo)* and q *(quant);l* are specified at the beginning of the passage.

In this example it is assumed that the whole passage is the domain for the parameters t and q. It is, however, perfectly possible to split a passage into several separate domains and to optimise the coding for each sub-passage with specific values of t and q for each domain.

Figure 8 shows the comparison of observed and fitted durations for the passage coded in Fig. 7. As can be seen, the fit is very close (r=0.9946) and could be adjusted to an arbitrary degree of granularity by modifying the threshold conditions on the iterative process.

tempo=0.761 quant=50
I have a problem [1] with my water [3] softener [7]. The [1] water [3]-level [1] is [1] too[4] high [5] and the [2] over [1]-flow [2] keeps [2] dripping [4]. Could you [1] a-rrange [3] to send [2] an engi-neer [2] on Tuesday morning [2] please [6]. It' s the [2] only day [1] I [1] can manage [1] this [1] week [3]. I'd be grateful if you could con-firm [2] the a-rrangement in [1] writing [6].

Figure 7: A sample passage from the Eurom1 corpus coded for duration using the automatic coding scheme described in the text. Hyphens and spaces separate rhythm units, numbers in square brackets correspond to the scalar lengthening factor k as applied to the preceding rhythm unit.

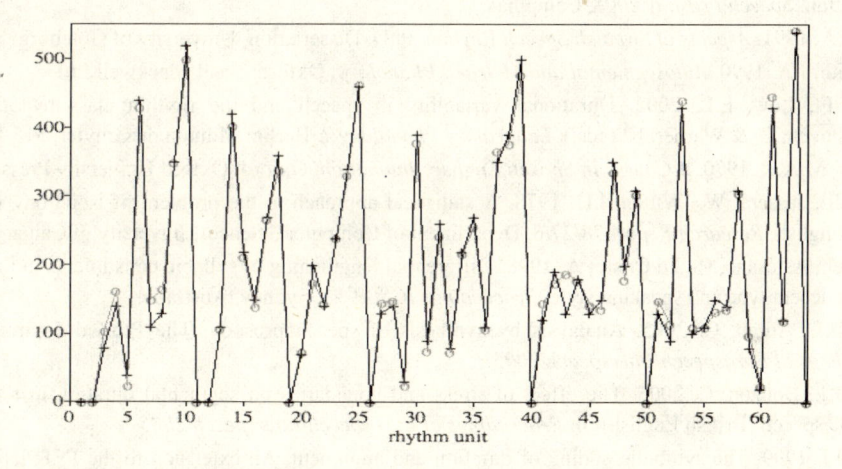

Figure 8: Observed (+) and fitted (o) durations of rhythm units for the Eurom1 passage in table (1) above

6. CONCLUSION

The model presented in the preceding section is obviously incomplete in a number of important ways. In particular, it makes the incorrect simplifying assumption that lengthening applies uniformly within a given rhythm unit. A number of studies, including some of our own work, have shown that in fact differential lengthening occurs either at the beginning or at the end of rhythm units, correlating respectively with boundaries and prominence (cf [14]). It remains to be seen however, how such differential lengthening could most appropriately be incorporated into a more complete model of rhythm.

We hope, however, to have shown here, at least in the area of speech rhythm, that an analysis by synthesis approach to prosodic modeling is a very promising direction of research and that the analysis of data from large speech corpora can provide useful insights into ways to incorporate such knowledge into more efficient and realistic prosodic models.

REFERENCES

[1] Abercrombie, D. 1964. Syllable quantity and enclitics in English. In: Abercrombie, D., Fry, P., MacCarthy, N. & Trim, J. (eds.), *In Honour of Daniel Jones.* London: Longman, 216-222.

[2] Auran, C., Bouzon, C., Hirst, D.J. 2004. The Aix-MARSEC project: an evolutive database of spoken English. In: Bel, B. & Marlien, I. (eds.), *Proceedings of the Second International Conference on Speech Prosody*, Nara, Japan, 561-564.

[3] Auran, C., Bouzon, C., Hirst, D.J., Lévy, C., Nocéra, P. 2004. Algorithme de prédiction d'élisions de phonèmes et influence sur l'alignement automatique dans le cadre du projet Aix-MARSEC. In: *Actes des XXVèmes Journées d'Etudes sur la Parole*, Fès Maroc, 57-60.

[4] Boersma, P., Weenink, D. 2005. Praat. Doing phonetics by computer. [computer program]. Version 4.3.04 Retrieved March 31, 2005 from http://www.praat.org/.

[5] Bouzon, C. 2004. *Rythme et structuration prosodique en anglais britannique contemporain.* Doctoral dissertation, Université de Provence.

[6] Campbell, N. 1992. *Multi-level Timing in Speech.* PhD. Dissertation, University of Sussex.

[7] Chan, D., Fourcin, A., Gibbon, D., et al. 1995. EUROM — A Spoken Language Resource for the EU. In *Proceedings of Eurospeech'95*, Madrid, Spain, (1), 867-870.

[8] De Looze, C., Hirst, D.J. 2008. Detecting changes in key and range for the automatic modeling and coding of intonation. *Speech Prosody 2008*, Campinas.

[9] Eriksson, A. 1991. *Aspects of Swedish Speech Rhythm.* PhD. Dissertation, University of Göteborg: Sweden.

[10] Goldsmith, J.A. 1990. *Autosegmental and Metrical Phonology.* Oxford: Basil Blackwell Ltd.

[11] Grabe, E., Low, E.L. 2002. Durational variability in speech and the rhythm class hypothesis. In: Gussenhoven, C. & Warner, N. (eds.), *Laboratory Phonology* 7. Berlin: Mouton de Gruyter, 515-546.

[12] Halliday, M.A.K. 1970. *A Course in Spoken English: Intonation.* Oxford: Oxford University Press.

[13] Hill, D.R., Jassem, W., Witten, I.H. 1978. A statistical approach to the problem of isochrony in spoken British English. *Research Report* 78/27/6, Department of Computer Science, University of Calgary.

[14] Hirst, D.J., Astésano, C., Di Cristo, A. 1998. Differential lengthening of syllabic constituents in French: the effect of accent type and speaking style. *Proceedings ICSLP'98*, Sydney, Australia.

[15] Hirst, D.J., Auran, C. 2005. Analaysis by synthesis of speech prosody. The ProZed environment. In *Proceedings of Eurospeech/Interspeech 2005*.

[16] Hirst, D.J., Bouzon, C. 2005. The effect of stress and boundaries on segmental duration in a corpus of authentic speech (British English). In *Proceedings of Eurospeech/Interspeech 2005*.

[17] Hirst, D.J. 1999. The symbolic coding of duration and alignment. An extension to the INTSINT system. *Proceedings Eurospeech'99*, Budapest.

[18] Hirst, D.J. 2001. Automatic analysis of prosody for multi-lingual speech corpora. In: E. Keller, G. Bailly, A. Monaghan, J. Terken & M. Huckvale (eds.), *Improvements in Speech Synthesis.* London, John Wiley, 320-327.

[19] Hirst, D.J. 2005. Form and function in the representation of speech prosody. In: K.Hirose, D.J. Hirst & Y. Sagisaka (eds.), *Quantitative prosody modeling for natural speech description and generation* (*special issue* of Speech Communication).

[20] Hirst, D.J., Di Cristo, A., Espesser, R. 2000. Levels of representation and levels of analysis for intonation. In: M. Horne (ed.), *Prosody : Theory and Experiment.* Dordrecht: Kluwer Academic Publishers, 51-87.

[21] Hirst, D.J., Astésano, C., Di Cristo, A. 1998. Differential lengthening of syllabic constituents in French: the effect of accent type and speaking style. *Proceedings ICSLP '98*, Sydney, Australia.

[22] Jassem, W. 1952. *Intonation in Conversational English.* Polish Academy of Science, Warsaw.

[23] Klatt, D.H. 1987. Review of text-to-speech conversion for English. *Journal of the Acoustical Society of America* 82, 737-793.

[24] Knowles, G., Wichmann, A., Alderson, P. 1996. *Working with Speech: perspectives on research into the Lancaster/IBM Spoken English Corpus.* London: Longman.

[25] Knowles, G., Williams, B., Taylor, L. 1996. *A Corpus of Formal British English Speech*. London: Longman.
[26] Nespor, M., Vogel, I. 1986. *Prosodic Phonology*. Dordrecht: Foris.
[27] Roach, P., Knowles, G., Varadi, T., Arnfield, S. 1993. MARSEC: A machine readable Spoken English corpus. *Journal of the International Phonetic Association* 23(2), 47-53.
[28] Turk, A., White, L. 1999. Structural influences on accentual lengthening in English. *Journal of Phonetics* 27, 171-206.
[29] White, L. 2002. *English speech timing. A domain and locus approach*. PhD.Dissertation, University of Edinburgh.

GENERATION OF F_0 CONTOURS FOR MANDARIN SPEECH IN COMBINATION WITH RULE-BASED AND CORPUS-BASED METHODS

Keikichi HIROSE, Qinghua SUN, Nobuaki MINEMATSU

ABSTRACT

A method has been developed for synthesizing sentence fundamental frequency (F_0) contours of Mandarin speech. It is based on representing an F_0 contour in logarithmic frequency scale as a superposition of tone components on phrase components as in the case of generation process model (F_0 model). The tone components are realized by concatenating their fragments at tone nuclei predicted by a corpus-based method, while the phrase components are generated by rules under the F_0 model framework. To keep the time-alignment between the phrase and tone components, the phrase components are first generated and their information is added to the inputs for the prediction of tone nucleus F_0 patterns. Result of listening tests on synthetic speech with the synthesized F_0 contours verified the validity of the developed method. Furthermore, it was shown through an experiment of word emphasis that a flexible F_0 control was possible by the proposed method.

Keywords: speech synthesis, F_0 contour, tone nucleus, superposition, emphasis

1. INTRODUCTION

Introduction of selection-based waveform concatenation in speech synthesis has largely improved quality of synthetic speech. However, there still remain problems seen from the prosodic aspect. Although the control of prosodic features is an important issue in speech synthesis for any language, it becomes crucial for Chinese. As is well known, Mandarin is a typical tonal language where each syllable with the same phoneme sequence has up to four tone types, each indicating different meaning. Fundamental frequency (F_0) contours of utterances should include these local tonal features in addition to the sentential intonation corresponding to syntactic/utterance structures. This situation makes F_0 movements of Mandarin speech to be more complicated than non-tonal languages. Therefore, control of F_0 contours (together with other prosodic features) becomes an important issue in Mandarin speech synthesis.

Several rule-based methods have been developed for controlling F_0 contours in Mandarin speech synthesis [7]. Although the rule-based methods are ideal in realizing various speech styles, it is not an easy task to extract rules from observed F_0 contours. The benefit of corpus-based methods over rule-based methods increases when handling complicated features. Naturally, most F_0 controls adopted in Mandarin speech synthesis are corpus-based using decision trees, neural networks, linear regression analysis and so on [1][12]. Among all, the hidden Markov model (HMM) is now commonly used for synthesizing speech of many languages, including Mandarin, for it can handle segmental and prosodic features simultaneously and concatenates speech segments in a statistical basis [2]. Flexible control of speech styles is possible by adapting HMM to a new style with a small-sized speech corpus of that style. However, it still requires a certain size to keep the speech quality.

Moreover, the method handles F_0 in a frame-by-frame manner, which is not appropriate for prosodic features: prosodic features cover wider spans of utterances, such as words, phrases and so on.

A better control of prosodic features for the F_0 movement in longer units in synthetic speech is possible using the generation process model of F_0 contour model (F_0 model), which represents a logarithmic F_0 contour as a superposition of tone components on phrase components placed on a baseline level [5]. This model was used successfully in the corpus-based method of generating F_0 contours of Japanese [3]. The method required speech corpus with F_0 model commands for the training process, which was arranged efficiently from speech waveforms using the method of automatic extraction of F_0 model commands. However, in the case of Mandarin speech, automatic extraction comes difficult because of its complicated F_0 movements [14].

While a syllable F_0 contour shows a stable pattern when it is uttered in isolation, it changes a lot when uttered in a sentence. This situation requires a number of templates for syllable F_0 contours, when a sentence F_0 contour is generated as a concatenation of syllable F_0 contours. Close observation of syllable F_0 contours indicates that a syllable F_0 contour consists of beginning and ending parts, which are transients from and to adjacent syllables, and mid part, which possesses rather stable F_0 pattern regardless of the tonal context [9]. The mid part with a stable F_0 pattern is often called as "tone nucleus".

These considerations led us to propose a method of F_0 contour generation for Mandarin speech synthesis, where the tone components were generated by concatenating F_0 patterns of tone nuclei, predicted by a corpus-based method, and were superposed onto the phrase components, which were generated by a rule-based scheme on the basis of F_0 model [10]. By first generating F_0 patterns for tone nuclei of constituting syllables and then concatenating them, a smooth sentence F_0 contour can be generated only from a limited speech corpus.

The most significant benefit of the proposed method over others without decomposition is the flexibility in F_0 contour generation: by manually controlling phrase components, we can easily generate F_0 contours with different utterance structures. In Mandarin, it is claimed that a word with emphasis is usually accompanied by a new phrase component with a large magnitude. Following this claim, an experiment was conducted whether the control of emphasis position in a sentence is possible or not, by manually changing phrase component and generating F_0 contours using the proposed method.

The rest of the paper is organized as follows. After an introduction of the two-step scheme, which was developed to keep time-synchrony between phrase and tone components, in Section 2, differences found in Japanese and Chinese phrase components are shown in Section 3. Section 3 also gives rules for phrase component generation. In Section 4, tone nucleus is first explained and then the method of tone component generation is given. Generated F_0 contours are evaluated through a listening test of synthetic speech in the same section. For comparison, F_0 contours are also generated in a similar way, but without decomposing them into phrase and tone components. Section 5 describes the full speech synthesis system constructed using the developed methods. It also includes comparison of synthetic speech quality with that by HMM-based speech synthesizer. An experiment on word emphasis is conducted in Section 6. Section 7 concludes the paper.

2. TWO-STEP SCHEME

Although speech synthesized with generated F_0 contours sounds natural, there is occasional degradation when phrase components and tone components are handled independently. In the case of Japanese, the independent handling of components do cause no clear degradation [3]. This is because, in Japanese, inter-syllabic movements of F_0 contours, viz. relative F_0 values of syllables, are important for realization of lexical accent, which is not corrupted so much due to changes in phrase components. However, in Mandarin, intra-syllable movements represent tone types, and they are often largely affected by the phrase components; for instance, rising F_0 contour characterizing T2 may appear as a falling contour when the phrase component position shifts. To cope with mismatches between two components, we developed a two-step scheme, where the phrase components were generated first, and then the tone components were generated taking the features of generated phrase components into account (Figure 1).

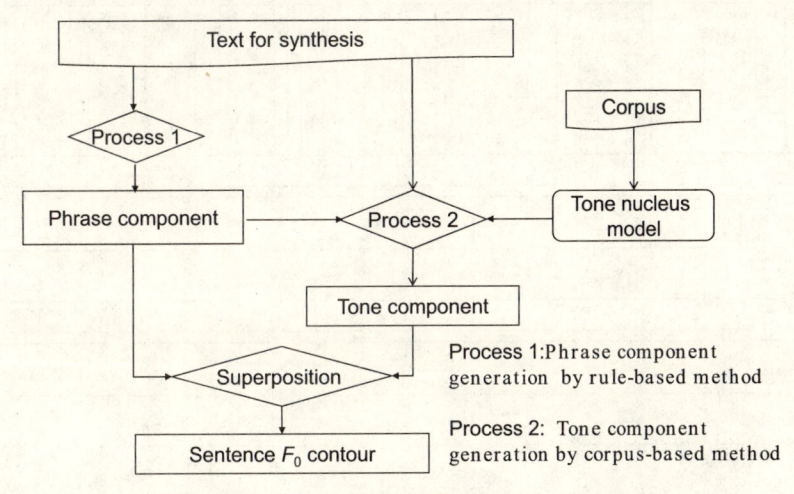

Figure 1: Two-step scheme of F_0 contour generation

Process 1: Phrase component generation by rule-based method
Process 2: Tone component generation by corpus-based method

3. GENERATION OF PHRASE COMPONENTS

F_0 contours are considered to consist of both language specific and universal characteristics. Features for tone components may be mostly language specific, while those for phrase components may be mostly language universal, for they are tightly related to higher-level linguistic information, such as syntactic structure, discourse structure and so on. Therefore, rules developed for other languages are somewhat applicable for the control of phrase components in Mandarin. We tried to apply the rules developed for the control of phrase components of Japanese to Mandarin, and found out some differences in phrase components between two languages: in the case of Mandarin, phrase components occur more frequently than Japanese [4].

3.1 Phrase components of Mandarin speech

It is generally observed that phrase components are related to syntactic structures, and therefore, their commands tend to occur at deeper syntactic boundaries. However, phrase components are also affected by the human habits of utterance: there is a certain limit in the distance between two succeeding commands. We showed that a proper control of phrase components was possible for Japanese by a set of simple rules, which were based on placing larger phrase commands at deeper syntactic boundaries, and adding supplementary phrase commands at shallower syntactic boundaries to keep the distance between two succeeding phrase commands blow a threshold [11]. These rules, however, cannot be applied to Mandarin speech as they are.

Figures 2 and 3 respectively show F_0 contours of Japanese and Mandarin utterances with the best approximations by the F_0 model. It is clear from the figures that phrase commands occur more frequently in Mandarin than in Japanese. It was observed that, in normal speech rate, the distance between two adjacent phrase components were around 15 mora (2.1 sec) for Japanese, while it is mostly less than 7 syllables (1.4 sec) for Mandarin. Frequent phrase commands in Mandarin are considered to be due to the fact that tone components can have negative values causing sharp declination in F_0 contours below phrase components. Phrase component should always be kept above a certain level so that, in principle, F_0 does not go below the baseline even with negative tone components. Based on these observations, rules on phrase command generation for Mandarin speech synthesis are developed in the next section by placing priority on keeping certain values of phrase components at prosodic word boundaries.

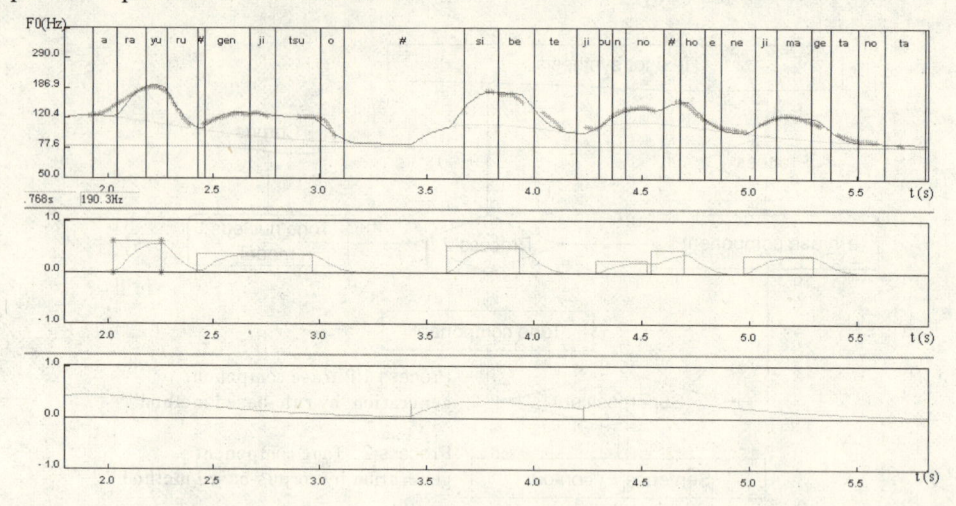

Figure 2: Example of F_0 contour of Japanese utterance "arayuru geNjitsuo subete jibuNnohooe nejimagetanoda ((He) twisted all the reality to his side)". From top to bottom: observed F_0 contour with its F_0 model approximation, accent components/commands, and phrase components/commands.

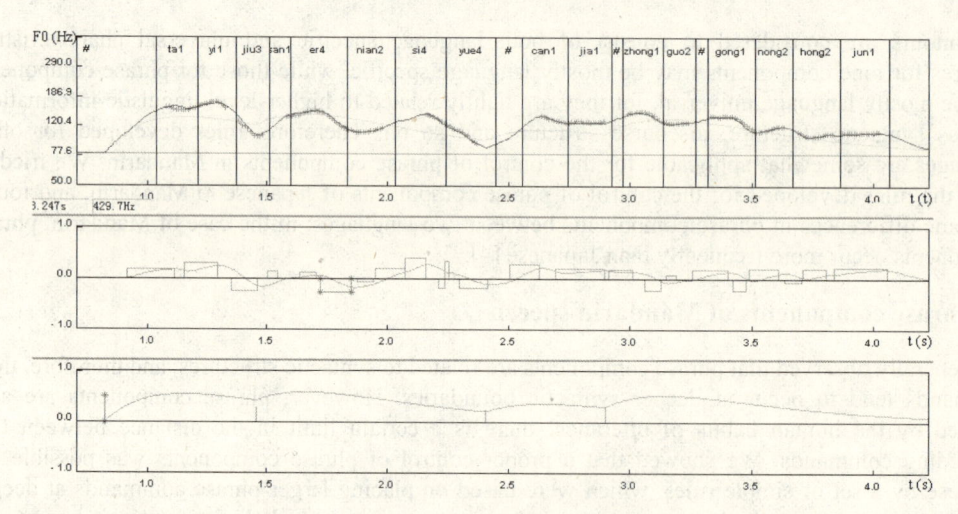

Figure 3: Example of F_0 contour of Chinese utterance "ta1 yi1 jiu3 san1 er4 nian2 si4 yue4 chan1 jia1 zhong1 guo2 gong1 nong2 hong2 jun1 (He joined the Chinese Workers' and Peasants' Red Army in April 1932)".

3.2 Rules for phrase component generation

From a Mandarin speech corpus for speech synthesis consisting of 300 utterances by a native female speaker, arranged at University of Science and Technology of China, 100 utterances were selected for the analysis of phrase components. After extracting F_0 contours from the utterances, their phrase components were manually decomposed. Based on the statistics of 1264 samples found, the following rules were constructed, which assign phrase commands at "prosodic word" boundaries. Here, prosodic word is defined as a chunk of syllables usually uttered in a tight connection; a prosodic word can be a word, a compound word, or a word chunk uttered together frequently. Since prosodic words are subject to change by the speaking styles, such as speech rates, it cannot be decided uniquely only from the texts. Although assignment of prosodic word boundaries is an importance issue, boundaries labeled in the corpus were used in the current paper.

Rule 1: Place a phrase command with magnitude 0.6 at the silence locating at the beginning of the sentence (SilB) or after a pause longer than 300ms. Also, place a phrase command with magnitude 0.47 after a pause shorter than 300ms but longer than 200ms. (The pause lengths are predicted beforehand by a separate process. See section 5.)

Rule 2: Check all the prosodic word boundaries without pauses longer than 200ms in a left-to-right manner from the utterance initial. If phrasal F_0 (F_0 value of phrase component plus baseline value) at the current boundary falls into a range (set to 150Hz~190Hz for the speaker), place a phrase command with magnitude as shown in Table 1, depending on the number of preceding phrase commands between preceding SilB/pause and current phrase command (counting the current one). If the phrasal F_0 is larger than 190Hz, skip to the next prosodic word boundary without placing any phrase command.

Rule 3: During the process of rule 2, when phrasal F_0 at the current prosodic word boundary falls below the range, go back to the preceding boundary and place a phrase command there with magnitude shown in Table 2 depending on the feature of preceding phrase commands. If a phrase command has already been placed at the preceding boundary, or if "number of phrase commands" or "phrasal F_0" does not fall into the cases listed in Table 2, skip to rule 4.

Rule 4: Split the prosodic word before the current word boundary into two smaller prosodic words. Then apply rules 2 and 3 on the newly inserted prosodic word boundary.

An additional rule is applied to the timings of phrase commands. The phrase command is placed ahead of the corresponding prosodic boundary as follows: 150ms for the phrase commands with magnitude 0.6, 50ms for the commands smaller than 0.3, and 80ms for others.

Table 1: Magnitude of phrase command placed at the current prosodic word boundary when phrasal F_0 falls into the range.

Number of phrase commands	2	3	4	5	≥6
Magnitude of phrase command	0.36	0.35	0.35	0.29	0.29

Table 2: Magnitude of phrase command placed at the preceding prosodic word boundary when phrasal F_0 falls below the range at the current prosodic word boundary.

Phrasal F_0 at immediately preceding prosodic word boundary	190Hz~230Hz				230Hz~280Hz
Number of phrase commands	2	3	4	5	2
Magnitude of phrase command	0.32	0.28	0.28	0.26	0.29

4. GENERATION OF TONE COMPONENTS

4.1 Tone nucleus model

In Mandarin, there are four lexical tones attachable to a syllable. They are referred to as T1, T2, T3 and T4, and are characterized by high-level, mid-rising, low-dipping, and high-falling F_0 contours respectively. Besides the lexical tones, there is also a so-called neutral tone (T0), which does not possess its inherent shape in the F_0 contour. Its F_0 contour varies largely with the preceding and following tones.

For a syllable, not only its early portion but also voicing period at the ending portion is regarded as physiological transition period to/from the neighboring syllables. Based on this observation, a tone nucleus model, which divides a syllable F_0 contour into three segments according to their roles in the tone generation process, was proposed and applied to tone recognition successfully [9]. The three segments are called onset course, tone nucleus, and offset course respectively. Only the tone nucleus is a portion where F_0 contour keeps the intrinsic pattern of the tone; the others are only the portions for physiological transitions.

Figure 4 illustrates syllable F_0 contours for the four lexical tones with possible articulatory transitions. It shows how the three segments are defined on the F_0 contours. Among the three segments, only tone nucleus is obligatory, whereas the other two are optional; their appearance depends on voicing characteristics of initial consonant, syllable duration, context, etc.

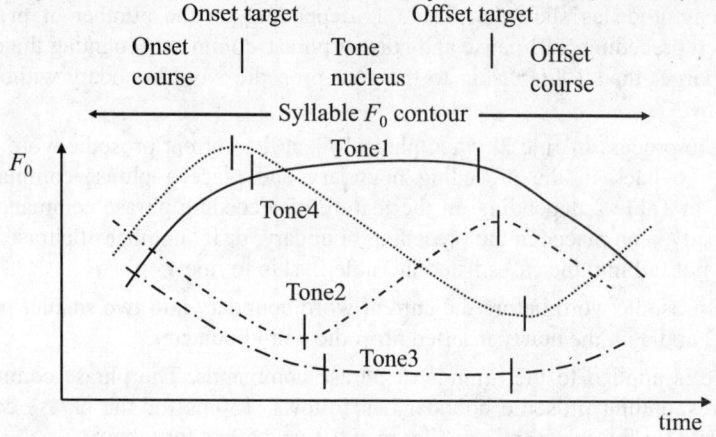

Figure 4: Tone nuclei for the four lexical tones

4.2 Method of tone component generation

Our method of tone component generation first predicts tone components only for tone nuclei of constituting syllables in a corpus-based way, and then concatenated them to generate an entire component for the utterance [8]. It consists of the following processes:

(1) For each syllable in the sentence to be synthesized, the onset time of tone nucleus is predicted.

(2) For each syllable in the sentence to be synthesized, the offset time of tone nucleus is predicted.

(3) For each tone nucleus, several parameters representing the tone component are predicted. The parameters are different depending on the tone types as explained later.

(4) Based on the predicted parameters, an F_0 pattern is generated for each tone nucleus.

(5) The patterns are concatenated with each other to produce the entire tone components.

In the first to third steps above, each parameter is predicted using a binary decision tree. Inputs to a tree are the information, which can be extracted from input text, such as phonemic constitutions of syllables, number of syllables in words, depths of syntactic boundaries and so on (Table 3). Information predicted in the former process is added to the inputs of succeeding prediction process: onset time is added to input parameters for offset time prediction, for instance. Taking the limitation of training data into account, consonants are grouped into 5 categories according to their manner of articulation. The final vocalic parts are categorized into two cases: with and without nasal coda. In the current paper, labels attached to the corpus were used as these inputs. The inputs also include the information of generated phrase components, such as number of syllables in current phrase, magnitude of phrase command, and so on (two-step scheme). Information on phoneme durations and pauses is also used, which is predicted in a separate process in a total system of text-to-speech conversion (see Section 5). As for the fifth step, the concatenation is done by interpolating adjacent F_0 patterns by a straight line, though smoother interpolation is possible such as by third order polynomials. This is because no difference is observable in speech quality depending on the interpolations, when generated F_0 contours are used for speech synthesis. For a syllable locating at a sentence initial (or after a long pause), concatenation with a tone component of preceding tone nucleus is not appropriate. Tone component at the beginning of the syllable is assumed zero and is linearly increased to the tone onset point of tone nucleus.

Table 3: Inputs to the predictors

Inputs to the predictor	Category
Initial consonant of current syllable	5
Final vocalic part of current syllable	2
Final vocalic part of preceding syllable	2
Initial consonant of following syllable	5
Tone of current syllable	5
Tone of preceding syllable	5
Tone of following syllable	5
Duration of initial consonant	Continuous
Duration of final vocalic part	Continuous
Duration of voiced part	Continuous
Boundary depth between preceding and current syllables	6
Boundary depth between current and following syllables	6
Position of syllable in current breath group	Natural num.
Number of syllables in current word	Natural num.
Position of current word in sentence	Natural num.
Duration of short pause preceding to current syllable	Continuous or 0
Duration of short pause following to current syllable	Continuous or 0
Position of syllable in current phrase	Natural num.
Number of syllables in current phrase	Natural num.
Number of phases in current breath group	Natural num.
Position of phrase in current breath group	Natural num.
Position of breath group in sentence	Natural num.
Current phrase command magnitude	Continuous
Timing of current phrase	Continuous

Parameters for tone components of tone nuclei are defined as follows:

(1) T1 and T3 are known as the "level tones", characterized by flat F_0 contours. Based on this observation, their tone nuclei are defined as portions with flat F_0 contours. Their tone components are represented by straight lines having slope coefficients with opposite sign to those of the slopes of the linear regression lines of the phrase components of the tone nuclei, so that the resulting F_0 contours become flat. Average F_0 value of each tone contour is used as the parameter.

(2) For each of T0, T2 and T4, F_0 contours of tone nuclei are first normalized in time and frequency ranges, and then are clustered into 11 groups. The average contour for each group serves as a template to represent the shape of tone component of tone nucleus. The parameters include the absolute pitch range, average F_0 value, and template identity. When predicting, templates for T2 are allowed to appear for T4 syllables and vice versa.

The same 100 news utterances used to construct rules for phrase component generation in section 2 were again used to train the method. Each utterance consists of about 50 syllables. Totally, the 100 utterances include 4839 syllables. First, all the F_0 contours were manually decomposed into tone and phrase components. And, tone nucleus was searched for each syllable. For T2 and T4, the tone nucleus can be detected rather easily by searching peaks and valleys in F_0 contours. On the other hand, it is rather difficult to automatically find the flat F_0 portion for T1 and T3. Therefore, their tone nuclei were manually extracted. These syllables were used to train binary decision trees for predicting tone component parameters.

Figure 5 shows examples of the observed (target) and generated F_0 contours for the sentence shown in Figure 3. In most cases, the F_0 contours quite similar to the original F_0 contours are generated in the method.

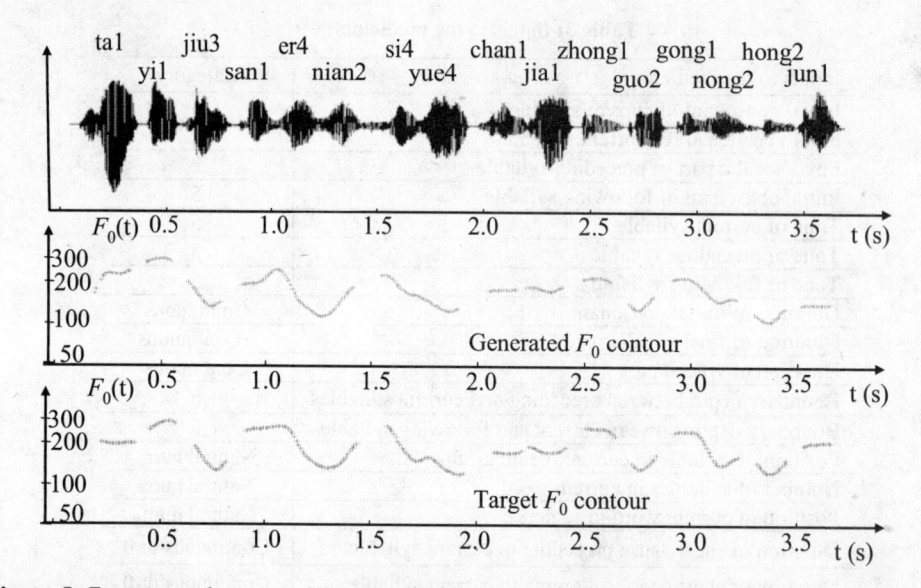

Figure 5: From top to bottom: original waveform, F_0 contour generated by the method, and one extracted from original speech.

4.3 Generation without decomposition

It is possible to generate F_0 contours without decomposing them into phrase and tone components. By doing so, a time consuming process of extracting tone components from observed F_0 contours, which is necessary to prepare speech corpus to train binary decision trees for tone component prediction, can be avoided, though flexibility in F_0 control decreases. By comparison, F_0 contours are also generated by concatenating tone-nucleus F_0 contours, which are predicted in a similar way. Since it is not necessary to compute the shape of phrase components, tone-nucleus F_0 contours for T1 and T3 syllables are represented as level lines. Different from the concatenation of tone components, at the beginning of a sentence (or after a long pause), no point is given for interpolation. To cope with this situation, an F_0 initial point is further predicted as the point of concatenation. For ease of explanation, this method predicting F_0 contours directly is denoted as direct method, while the proposed method based on representing F_0 contours as superpositions of tone components onto phrase components is denoted as superpositional method.

Fundamental frequency contours of 30 sentences not included in the training of binary decision trees are generated in both of the two methods. Speech synthesis is conducted by substituting the original F_0 contours to the generated F_0 contours by TD-PSOLA [6]. Five native speakers of Mandarin were asked to evaluate the synthetic speech with a focus on prosody, using a five-point scoring: 5 (excellent), 4 (good), 3 (marginal), 2 (poor), and 1 (very poor). Totally, 60 utterances were synthesized and presented randomly to the listeners. Although the difference is not significant, 4 listeners gave better scores for the superpositional method (Figure 6). This result shows the feasibility of the superpositional method, though it is necessary to carefully prepare the speech corpus for training the method.

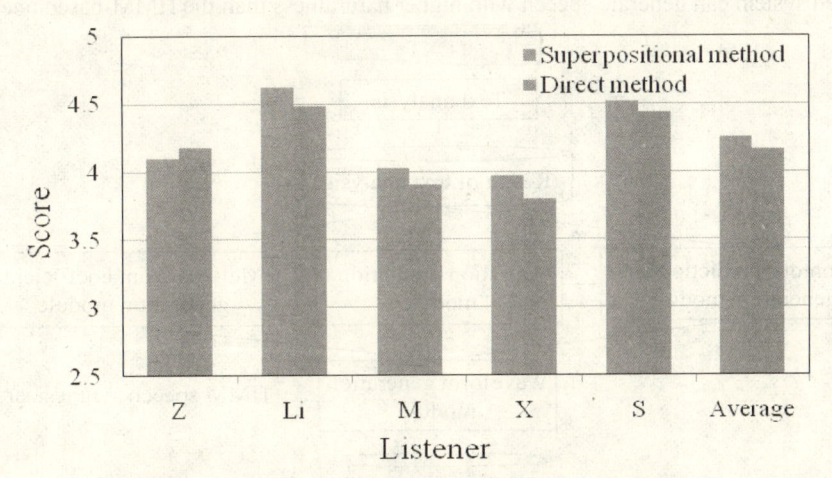

Figure 6: Result of the listening test on the quality of F_0 contours

5. EXPERIMENTS ON SPEECH SYNTHESIS

To investigate the validity of the proposed method of F_0 contour generation when applied in a TTS system, a full speech synthesis system was constructed using the HMM-based speech synthesis (instead of TD-PSOLA) [15]. The phone HMMs were Mel-cepstrum based. As shown in Figure 7, it consists of the following processes:

(1) Analyze the input text to extract information necessary for speech synthesis. The information is the same as the one used in the F_0 contour generation.

(2) Predict phone durations and short pauses using a decision tree.

(3) Generate F_0 contours in the method.

(4) Generate 24-order mel-cepstrum coefficients and make the voice/unvoiced decision for each frame by the HMM-based speech synthesis.

(5) Generate speech waveform using MLSA filter.

170 utterances from the same female speaker were added to the 100 utterances used in the previous sections, resulting in 270 utterances, which included 15392 phones and short pauses, were used to train the decision tree for duration prediction and the (context dependent) phone HMMs. Firstly, an experiment of duration prediction was carried out. By comparison, durations were also predicted by the HMM-based method, where durations were calculated from probability of state transitions. Although phone HMMs are usually trained after concatenating them without apparently using phoneme boundary information of the training corpus (concatenated training), they are also trained using the manually extracted phoneme boundaries as constraints. This is because the phoneme boundary information is used to train the decision trees. 855 phones and short pauses for 30 utterances, which were not used for the training, were predicted by the decision tree-based method and the two versions of HMM-based method respectively. The root mean square (RMS) errors between observed durations and predicted ones are shown in Table 4. The result shows advantages of the decision tree-based method over the HMM-based methods.

Speech synthesis was conducted for the 30 utterances used for the duration prediction by the two speech synthesis systems: one using the proposed methods of F_0 contour generation, and the other (full HMM-based speech synthesis system) achieved using the speech synthesis toolkit (HTS) [15]. Again the five native speakers of Mandarin were asked to evaluate the naturalness of synthetic speech using the five-point scoring. The result of evaluation shown in Figure 8 clearly indicates that the developed system can generate speech with higher naturalness than the HMM-based one.

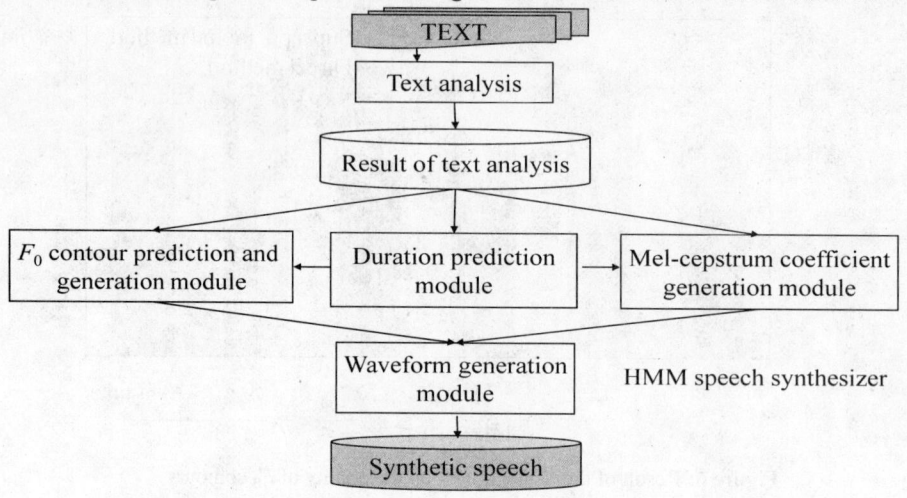

Figure 7: Total configuration of the Mandarin speech synthesis from text

Table 4: Result of duration prediction

Method	Decision tree	HMM (With boundary information)	HMM (Concatenated training)
RMS Error	0.017	0.021	0.028

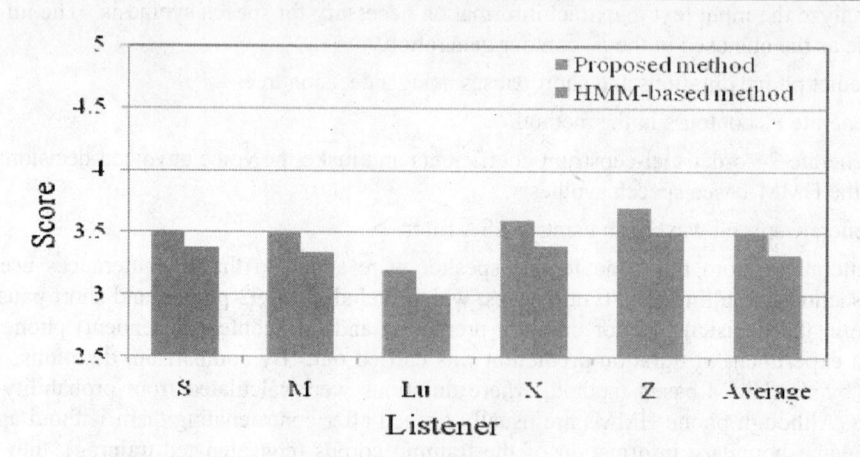

Figure 8: Result of the listening test on synthetic speech quality

6. WORD EMPHASIS

Although word emphasis is not handled explicitly in most of current speech synthesis systems, its control becomes important in many situations, such as when the systems are used for generating system's response in spoken dialogue systems: words conveying key information to the user's question need to be emphasized. Word emphasis associated with narrow focus in speech can be achieved by contrasting the F_0's of the word(s) to be focused from those of neighboring words. This contrast can be realized by placing the word(s) at the phrase component initial, by increasing the accent/tone command amplitudes of the word(s), and by decreasing the accent/tone command amplitudes of the neighboring words. Ways of using these three controls may be different from language to language. Our observation of Mandarin speech indicated the first one being dominant [11]. Since amplitudes of tone commands generally take larger values when they are placed at the phrase command initial, the second and the third controls are somewhat realized automatically.

Ten sentences, different from the 100 sentences used to train the method, were prepared. For each sentence, focuses were placed on one of 3 pre-selected words. A phrase command was inserted immediately before the word to be emphasized. After generating other phrase commands by rule, tone commands were predicted by the two-step scheme. Three different F_0 contours were generated for a sentence. TD-PSOLA type speech synthesis was then conducted by substituting the original F_0 contours to the generated ones. Totally, 30 test utterances were synthesized. For the phone durations, we used the original ones extracted from the target speech.

Table 5: Results of listening test

Testee	W	Z	S	X	Average
Focus position	86.7%	83.3%	80.0%	76.7%	81.6%
Score	4.30	4.77	4.42	4.31	4.45

These 30 synthetic utterances were randomly presented to four native speakers of Mandarin, who were asked to mark the word where he/she perceived an emphasis. The marked parts coincided with the original emphasis assignment in 81.6% on average. This result indicates that an appropriate emphasis control is achieved. Quality of the synthetic speech was also checked in the same way (in 5-point scoring) as explained in sections 4 and 5. The result in Table 5 again confirms that a good quality is obtainable by the two-step scheme. If we compare F_0 contours shown in Figure 9, it is clear that tone components are generated differently for different phrase components.

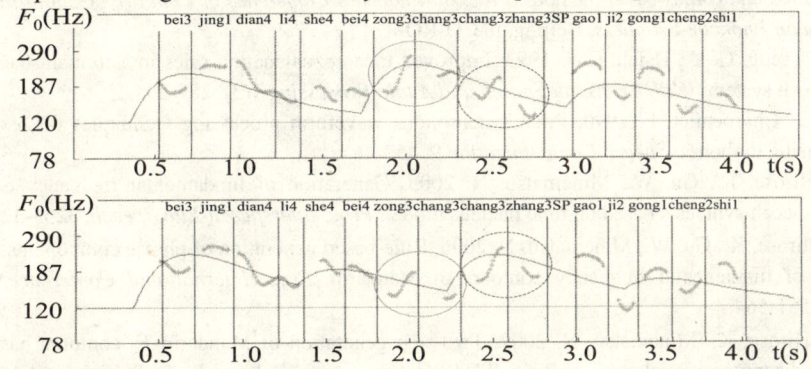

Figure 9: Generated F_0 contours for "bei3 jing1 dian4 li4 she4 bei4 zong3 chang3 chang3 zhang3, gao1 ji2 gong1 cheng2 shi1 ((He is) the director of Beijing Power Equipment Group and senior engineer)". The first and the second panels show when "zhong2 chang2" and "chang2 zhang3" are emphasized respectively. Stars indicate generated F_0 contours, while solid curves indicate phrase components.

Surely, more precise control of F_0 contours can be realized for word emphasis by training the binary decision trees using corpus with word emphasis. However, we should note that emphasis control in this section is realized without such a corpus. This comes from the ability of "flexible" F_0 contour control of the proposed method.

7. CONCLUSION

A method was proposed for synthesizing sentence F_0 contours of Mandarin speech. It first generates phrase components in a rule-based way, and then predicts tone components through a corpus-based method. By adding the information of phrase components to the inputs for the predictors of tone components, both components are time-aligned. A full speech synthesis system was realized using HMM-based speech synthesis. Listening experiments on synthetic speech indicated that a better speech quality was realized by the proposed method as compared to generating F_0 contours by the HMM-based speech synthesis. It was also shown that, by using the 2-step scheme, an empirical control of word emphasis is possible still to keep a good quality in synthetic speech. Future research includes realization of various styles in synthetic speech by the proposed method.

The authors' sincere thanks are due to Prof. Renhua Wang at the University of Science and Technology of China for providing us the Mandarin speech corpus.

REFERENCES

[1] Chen, S., Hwang, S., Y. Wang. 1998. An RNN-base prosodic information synthesizer for Mandarin text-to-speech. *IEEE Trans. on Speech and Audio Processing* 6(3), 226-239.
[2] Fujisaki, H., Hirose, K. 1984. Analysis of voice fundamental frequency contours for declarative sentences of Japanese. *J. Acoust. Soc. Japan (E)* 5(4), 233-242.
[3] Gu, W., Hirose, K., Fujisaki, H. 2006. A general approach for automatic extraction of tone commands in the command-response model for tone languages. *Proc. Speech Prosody*, 561-564.
[4] Hirose, K., Fujisaki, H. 1993. A system for the synthesis of high-quality speech from texts on general weather conditions. *IEICE Trans. Fundamentals of Electronics, Communications and Computer Sciences*, E76-A(11), 1971-1980.
[5] Hirose, K., Sato, K., Asano, Y., Minematsu, N. 2005. Synthesis of F_0 contours using generation process model parameters predicted from unlabeled corpora: Application to emotional speech synthesis. *Speech Communication* 46 (3-4), 385-404.
[6] Hirose, K., Sun, Q., Minematsu, N. 2008. Generation of F_0 contours for Mandarin speech in combination with rule-based and corpus-based methods. *Proc. 8th Phonetics Conference of China (PCC2008)/International Symposium on Phonetic Frontiers*, Beijing, in CD-ROM.
[7] Lee, L.-S., Tseng, C.-Y., Hsieh, C.-J. 1993. Improved tone concatenation rules in a formant-based Chinese text-to-speech system. *IEEE Trans. on Speech and Audio Processing* 1(3), 287-294.
[8] Moulines E., Charpentier, F. 1990. Pitch synchronous waveform processing techniques for text-to-speech synthesis using diphones. *Speech Communication* 9, 453-467.
[9] Sun, Q., Hirose, K., Gu, W., Minematsu, N. 2005. Generation of fundamental frequency contours for Mandarin speech synthesis based on tone nucleus model. *Proc. Interspeech-Eurospeech*, 3265-3268.
[10] Sun, Q., Hirose, K., Gu, W., Minematsu, N. 2006. Rule-based generation of phrase components in two-step synthesis of fundamental frequency contours of Mandarin. *Proc. International Conference on Speech Prosody*, 561-564.
[11] Sun, Q., Hirose, K., Minematsu, N. 2007. Two-step generation of Mandarin F_0 contours based on tone nucleus and superpositional models. *Proc. ISCA Workshop on Speech Synthesis (SSW-6)*, 154-159.
[12] Tao, J., Cai, L. 2002. Clustering and feature learning based F_0 prediction for Chinese speech synthesis. *Proc. ICSLP*, 2097-200.
[13] Tokuda, K., Masuko, T., Miyazaki, N., Kobayashi, T. 1997. Hidden Markov models based on multi-space probability distribution for pitch pattern modeling. *Proc. IEEE ICASSP*, 229-232.
[14] Zhang, J., Hirose, K. 2004. Tone nucleus modeling for Chinese lexical tone recognition. *Speech Communication* 42(3-4), 447-466.
[15] HMM-based Speech Synthesis System (HTS): http://hts.sp.nitech.ac.jp/.

INTRINSIC AND PROSODIC EFFECTS ON ARTICULATORY COORDINATION IN INITIAL CONSONANT CLUSTERS

Philip HOOLE, Lasse BOMBIEN, Barbara KÜHNERT, Christine MOOSHAMMER

ABSTRACT

EMA was used to study the coordination of the articulatory gestures for C1 and C2 in onset clusters, firstly as a function of the segmental make-up of the clusters, and secondly as a function of stress and prosodic boundary conditions. The segmental results, which compared German and French, indicated a much lower degree of overlap of C1 and C2 for C2=/n/ compared to C2=/l/ (with C1=/p, b, k, g/). Overlap was also less for voiceless compared to voiced C1 for German. Prosodic boundary strength affected the duration of the C1 articulatory constriction more strongly than that of C2, while, conversely, differences in lexical stress affected C2 more strongly than C1. The coordination relations between C1 and C2 were, however, not systematically affected by prosodic conditions. Nor did the different clusters studied (/kl, kn, sk/) appear to differ in their internal cohesiveness. The results are discussed with respect to how articulatory coordination is constrained to allow acoustic recovery of segmental information by the listener; the possibility of cross-language differences in these constraints is raised.

Keywords: consonant clusters, articulatory coordination, prosodic strengthening

1. INTRODUCTION

This study examines how articulatory coordination in heterorganic initial consonant clusters is modulated firstly by the segmental make-up of the cluster itself, and secondly by the prosodic conditions in which the cluster is spoken. The relevant background as well as the results to these two areas will be presented in two fairly self-contained sections (section 2: segmental make-up; section 3: prosodic conditions), and will be followed by general discussion in section 4.

2. SEGMENTAL STRUCTURE OF CLUSTERS

2.1 Background

The main impetus for this first area comes from the contention advanced in Chitoran et al. [4] that generalizations about preferred syllable structures (such as the sonority hierarchy) reflect at a more fundamental level the outcome of successful compromises between parallel transmission of segmental information, i.e. a high degree of overlap among gestures (assumed to be efficient for the speaker) and clear modulation of the acoustic signal (assumed to be efficient for the hearer). One illustration of this is the place-order effect in stop-stop clusters reported for Georgian by these authors: C1(back)+C2(front) clusters show less overlap than the reverse order, presumably to ensure recoverability of C1 by the listener (see also Gafos et al. [7] for Moroccan Arabic).

Nonetheless, relative to the very large number of complex syllabic onsets found across languages there has still been little detailed exploration of these principles. We focus here on a potentially revealing comparison among onset clusters found, for example, in German and French, but not in English, namely plosive+/l/ vs. plosive+/n/. The latter appear to be less stable diachronically than the former (cf. Vennemann [14]), and occur less frequently in extant languages. Why might they then be less suitable for the formation of complex syllable onsets? One possibility is that C1 and C2 need to overlap less (than in the case of plosive+/l/) to ensure that acoustic properties of the C1 burst are not compromised by velar lowering.

As a further manipulation of the phonetic properties of the syllable onset, the study also systematically varies the voicing category of the C1 plosive. This can be assumed to have a substantial effect on the nature of the acoustic information available to the hearer particularly in the C1 to C2 transition. But whether this may in turn lead to different preferred coordination patterns for C1 with C2 is, to our knowledge, essentially unknown. German and French were considered to be particularly appropriate for study here, since they are known to differ substantially in the timing of voice onset following voiceless plosives.

2.2 Material and Recordings

The main structure aimed for in the material for both German and French was to use real monosyllabic words (CCVC) with all combinations of C1=/p, b, k, g/, C2=/l, n/, V=/i, a/.

Not all of these combinations are lexically attested; for example, /bn/ combinations are missing in both languages and /pn/ is lexically somewhat marginal in German.

Since preliminary analysis indicated no consistent effects of vowel category on overlap between C1 and C2, and since gaps in the lexicon occasionally required the use of vowels other than /i/ and /a/, for the purposes of the present paper we will present the results averaged over vowels. In short, results can be presented for all four combinations of C1 with /l/, and three with /n/ (/bn/ missing).

Each target word was embedded in a carrier phrase with additional material not of concern here and recorded 10 times in randomized order.

Movements of the articulators were measured by means of a 3D EMA system (AG500, Carstens Medizinelektronik; cf. Hoole et al. [10]). Of the three sensors located on the tongue the frontmost one was used to analyze the tongue-tip gesture for /l, n/, the rearmost one for the tongue-dorsum gesture for /k, g/. The sensors located on lower and upper lip were combined to a lip aperture measure for analysis of the labial gesture for /p, b/. The key dependent variable is the measure of overlap between C1 and C2. This is illustrated in Fig. 1. Different measures of overlap have been used in previous investigations (Chitoran et al. [4], Gafos et al. [7]). The one used here is based on the constriction phases of C1 and C2. Specifically, the time point of the onset of the constriction phase of C2 (phase 4 in the figure) is subtracted from the time point of the offset of the constriction phase of C1 (phase 2 in the figure). This time difference is normalized by the time interval from the onset of C1 constriction to offset of C2 constriction and expressed as a percentage. The important point to bear in mind for the interpretation of the results is that, with this definition, increasingly positive values correspond to increasing overlap of C1 and C2 (negative values in effect mean that the constriction phases do not overlap)[1].

---

[1] The pattern of results presented below remains essentially the same if an absolute rather than normalized measure of overlap is used, and also if C2 timing is indexed by the onset of movement towards constriction (i.e. onset of phase 3 in Fig. 1) rather than the onset of constriction itself.

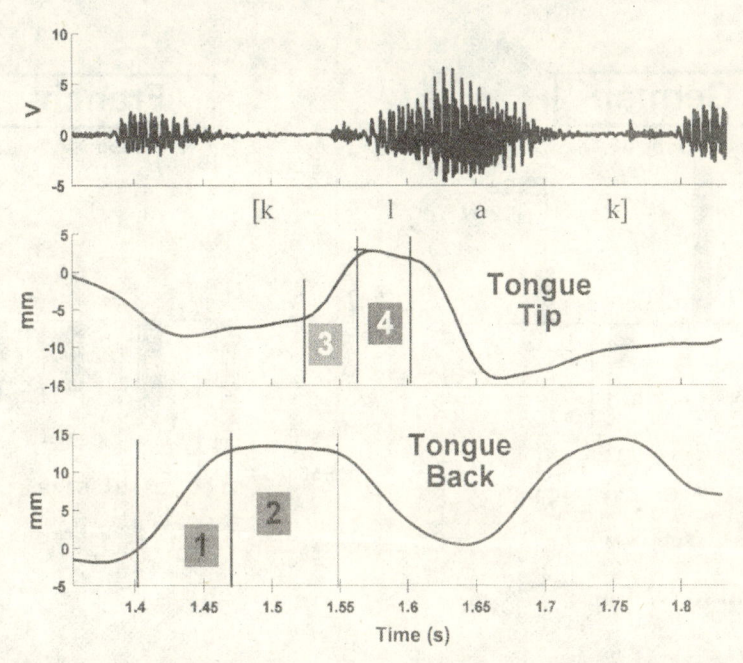

Figure 1: Illustration of determination of C1-C2 overlap for a /kl/ sequence. The constriction phases for the two consonants (labeled "2" and "4") are determined using a 20% velocity criterion in the tongueback and tongue-tip signals respectively. For illustrative purposes only the vertical movement component is shown.

2.3 Results

Regarding the manner of articulation of C2 (lateral vs. nasal), for German there is a clear effect in the form of the anticipated lower degree of overlap for the plosive-nasal sequences (see Fig. 2, left column). This appears to be a very robust effect because the same effect is observed (for the cluster pair /kl/, /kn/) in the different corpus used for the prosodic investigation reported in section 3 below. Moreover, with the prosody corpus used in section 3 the effect has been observed not only for the speakers analyzed there with EMA but also for an additional 7 speakers recorded by electropalatography (Bombien et al. [1]).

For French the pattern is less consistent, the speakers showing strong, weak and non-existent trends in the expected direction for AM, NN and CG, respectively (see Fig. 2, right column). For CG the overlap between plosive and /n/ often seemed large enough to lead to nasal release of the plosive.

Regarding voicing of C1 there is a very consistent effect for German showing less overlap between C1 and C2 when C1 is voiceless. For French no consistent effect of voicing is seen. On the basis of only three speakers per language it is, of course, too early to be confident about possible cross-linguistic differences. Nonetheless, it is intriguing that voicing-related differences are observed in that language, namely German, where acoustic properties of C2 are more strongly affected by the voicing status of C1. Perhaps this fits in with the first finding too: The constraint to maintain low overlap between plosive and /n/ may be stronger in languages where glottal opening is wide at the release of C1.

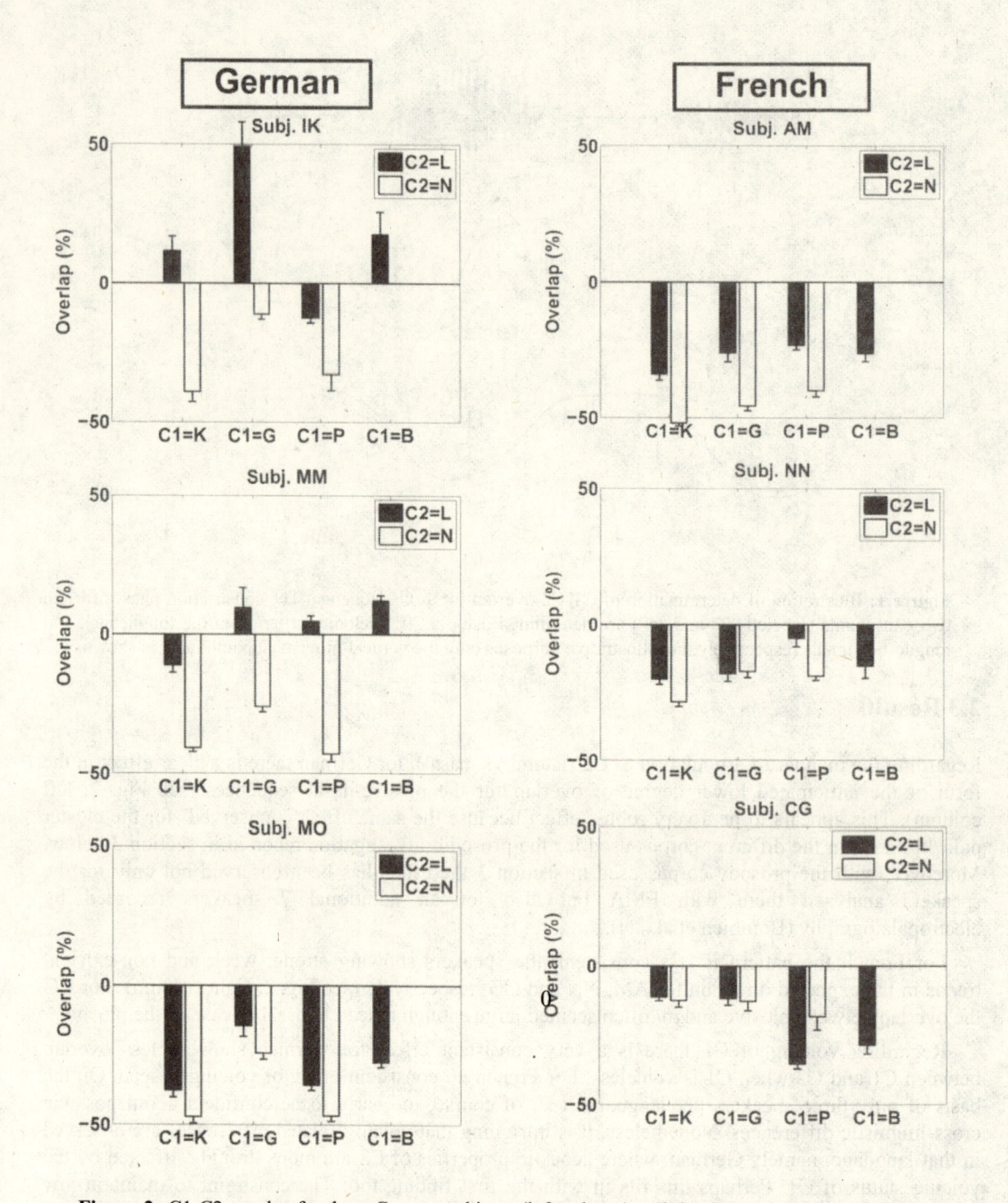

Figure 2: C1-C2 overlap for three German subjects (left column) and three French subjects (right column). See text for definition of overlap measure (expressed here as percentage). More positive values indicate more overlap. From left to right, bars in each panel are /kl, kn, gl, gn, pl, pn, bl/ (/bn/ not in corpus). Error bars give standard error of mean.

3. PROSODIC INFLUENCES ON CLUSTERS

3.1 Background and material

The second main area of the study extends to clusters the well-established experimental paradigm (e.g. Fougeron & Keating [6]; Keating et al. [11]) of investigating articulatory strengthening at prosodic boundaries, as part of an overall concern to better understand what information on prosodic structure the speaker makes available to the listener. A plausible hypothesis — consistent, for example, with the pi-gesture approach of Byrd & Saltzman [2] — is that prosodic boundary effects on articulation decrease with increasing distance from the boundary. However, with a few exceptions (e.g. Byrd & Choi [3]), most work within this paradigm has used rather simple syllable structures. Thus it is currently difficult to estimate whether boundary effects are indeed best modeled as a simple function of distance from the boundary, or whether structural properties of the syllable (e.g. consonantal onset versus vocalic nucleus) have an independent influence.

The material investigated included the clusters /kl, kn, sk/; they formed the onset of the target words, i.e. the words immediately following the prosodic boundaries. These were varied in four steps of assumed decreasing boundary strength from utterance initial to no boundary, as shown in the following examples for the /kl/ cluster at the onset of the target-word "Claudia":

Utterance initial   Thomas studiert in Fulda. Claudia geht noch zur Schule.
(*Thomas goes to college in Fulda. Claudia is still in school.*)

Phrase initial   Olga sagt immer, Claudia sei zu jung.
(*Olga always says that Claudia is too young.*)

List element   Thomas, Peter, Claudia und Elke fahren in den Süden.
(*Thomas, Peter, Claudia and Elke are travelling south.*)

Word boundary   Gestern war Claudia noch gesund.
(*Yesterday, Claudia was still well.*)

(Notes: (1) "Word boundary" is used to refer to the condition where no prosodic boundary is expected; the punctuation of the English translation is misleading. (2) "Utterance initial" might be better referred to as "Sentence intial". Here it simply indicates the condition where the strongest prosodic boundary is to be expected.)

With respect to the location of prosodic effects in the articulatory patterns, the basic expectation was that C1 would exhibit more boundary-induced variation than C2.

In addition to the boundary condition the experiment also contained orthogonal variation of a second prosodic variable, namely word stress: The target clusters formed the onsets of words with lexical stress on either the first or second syllable (e.g. "Claudia, vs. Klau'sur"). For this prosodic manipulation the literature gives even less to go on than for the boundary condition. A tentative hypothesis was based on the assumption that stress effects are centered on the nucleus of the stressed syllable and decline towards the syllable margins. Accordingly, stress effects were expected to be more visible in C2 than in C1.

Analyses focused on whether C1 or C2 showed durational or spatial enhancement at higher boundary levels and in the stress condition. In addition it was hypothesized that overlap between C1 and C2 would be reduced at higher boundary levels and in the stress condition.

In addition to the interest in prosodic effects in their own right, the manipulation of prosodic conditions in the present experiment can also be regarded as a probe to elucidate the internal cohesion of clusters (cf. Byrd & Choi [3]), thus linking up with the topic of segmental organization dealt with in Section 2 above. We saw there that /kn/ had less overlap of the component oral gestures than /kl/. Could it also be the case that the components are also less cohesive in /kn/, such that the coordination relations (as captured by the overlap measure) are more strongly affected by "external" conditions? (See Rialland [13] for distributional arguments in favor of analyzing /k/ in /kn/ as extrasyllabic in French.)

3.2 Recordings and analysis procedures

EMA recordings have been analyzed for the three German speakers who participated in section 2 above. For this part of the recording session, in addition to the EMA data, respiratory activity of the speakers was monitored by means of Respitrace in order to give additional information on prosodic divisions into breath groups.

As a preliminary stage in the analysis the actual prosodic realization at the target word of the four boundary categories given above was assigned to one of three prosodic categories, which will be referred to as follows (cf. Cho and McQueen [5]):

Big Boundary (**BG**): Pause and boundary tone

Small Boundary (**SM**): No pause but boundary tone

Prosodic Word (**WD**): No pause, no boundary tone

In the present dataset only very few big boundaries (BG) have been found, so for the following results only the SM and WD categories will be considered. The breakdown of the syntactically defined boundary categories with respect to the the SM and WD prosodic categories came out as follows:

	SM	WD
Utterance initial	51	8
Phrase initial	28	62
List element	14	76
Word boundary	2	89

This makes clear that the range of syntactic conditions was successful in generating different prosodic realizations. It also makes clear that particularly for intermediate syntactic conditions such as Phrase Initial it is important to determine the actual prosodic realization on a case-by-case basis; it cannot be assumed a priori. More refined approaches to prosodic categorization are currently also being explored.

The virtual absence of big prosodic boundaries (as defined above) in the present material is the reason why the results of a previous experiment in which 7 speakers were recorded with basically the same corpus by means of EPG will not be examined here: In the EPG experiment a large number of BG realizations were found (essentially for the utterance-initial condition), which would unduly complicate the comparison with the present EMA results. The results of the EPG experiment will be considered in detail in a separate publication (Bombien et al. [1]).

3.3 Results

We will first present the results for the durations of the target phases of C1 and C2, i.e. the durations of the phases labeled "2" and "4" in the example utterance given in Fig. 1 above.

The results for C1 are shown in the left column of Fig. 3. There is a very consistent trend in the hypothesized direction of longer durations at the more prominent prosodic boundary (i.e. the "SM" boundary compared to the "WD" boundary): Of 18 SM-WD pairs matched for stress level (and cluster and speaker), 17 are in the predicted direction. In ANOVAs carried out separately for each combination of speaker and cluster type the main effect of boundary is significant at p<0.01 in 6 out of 9 possible cases. On the other hand, the effect of stress on C1 appears to be very inconsistent. Of the eighteen stress-unstress pairs matched for boundary type (i.e. immediately adjacent bars in the figure), 10 are in the direction of longer duration for the stress condition, and in the ANOVAs only one of nine cases showed a main effect of stress in this direction that was significant at p<0.01 (/sk/ for speaker MO).

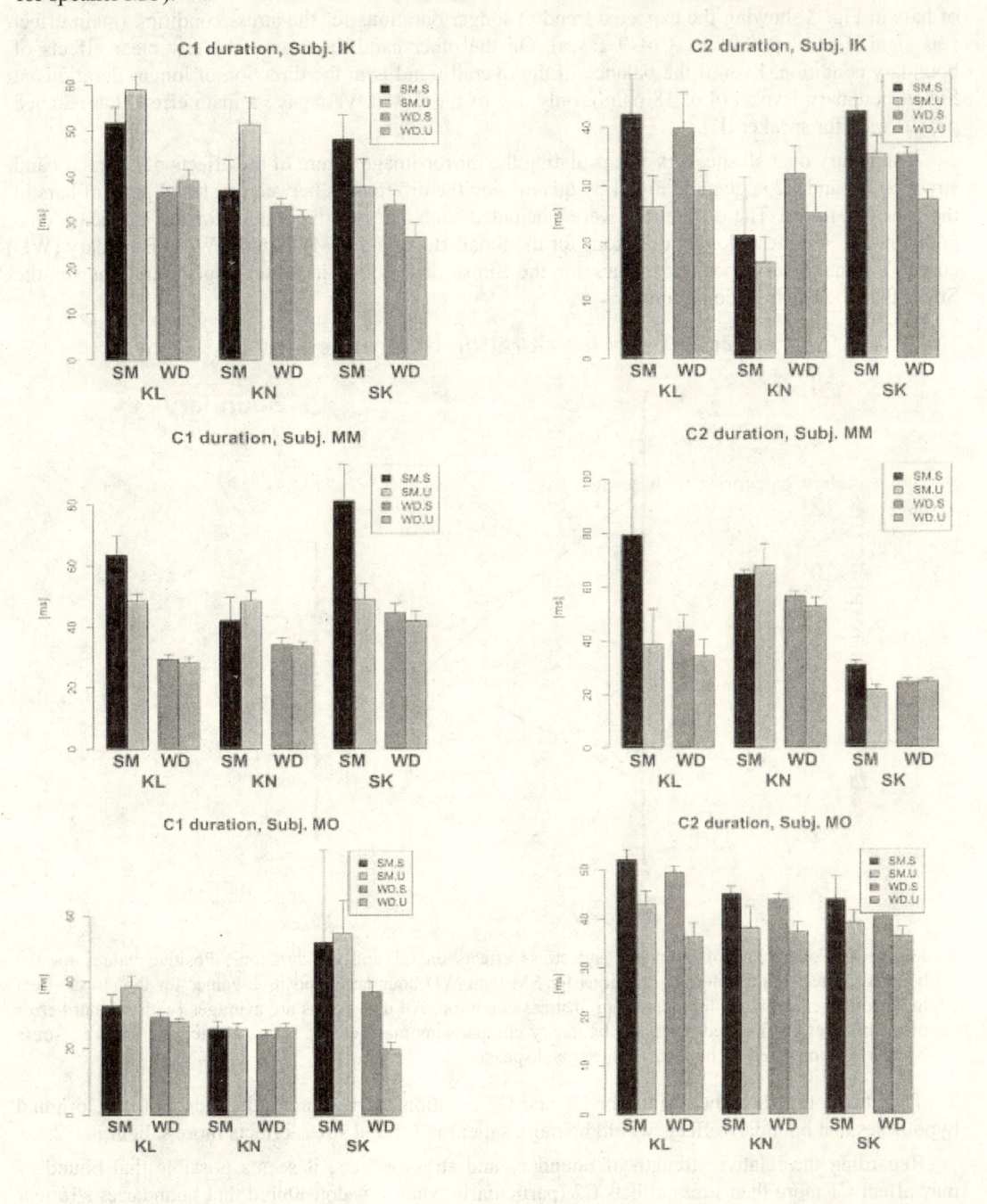

Figure 3: C1 (left column) and C2 (right column) constriction durations for three German subjects for the onset clusters /kl, kn, sk/. Each pair of bars gives the results for one prosodic boundary condition; left (darker) bar the stressed (S), right (lighter) bar the unstressed (U) condition. For each cluster, small boundary (SM) and prosodic word (WD) prosodic boundary conditions are given in adjacent pairs of bars. Error bars give standard error of mean.

The results for C2 are effectively a mirror-image of those for C1 (see right column of Fig. 3 for detailed results of each subject): The effect of stress is highly consistent, with 16 of 18 matched pairs of bars in Fig. 3 showing the expected trend of longer durations for the stress condition (main effect was significant at $p<0.01$ in 3 of 9 cases). On the other hand there are very few clear effects of boundary condition: Even if the balance of the overall trend is in the direction of longer durations at higher boundary levels (14 of 18 pairs), only one of the 9 ANOVAs gave a main effect that reached $p<0.01$ (/sk/ for speaker IK).

A summary over all speakers encapsulating the mirror-image nature of the effects of boundary and stress on C1 and C2 is given in Fig. 4 by quantifying the differences between matched pairs of bars in the previous figure. The differences were calculated such that positive values for the Boundary data points in Fig. 4 indicate longer durations for the Small Boundary (SM) than the Word Boundary (WD) condition; analogously positive values for the Stress data points indicate longer durations for the Stress than the Unstress conditions.

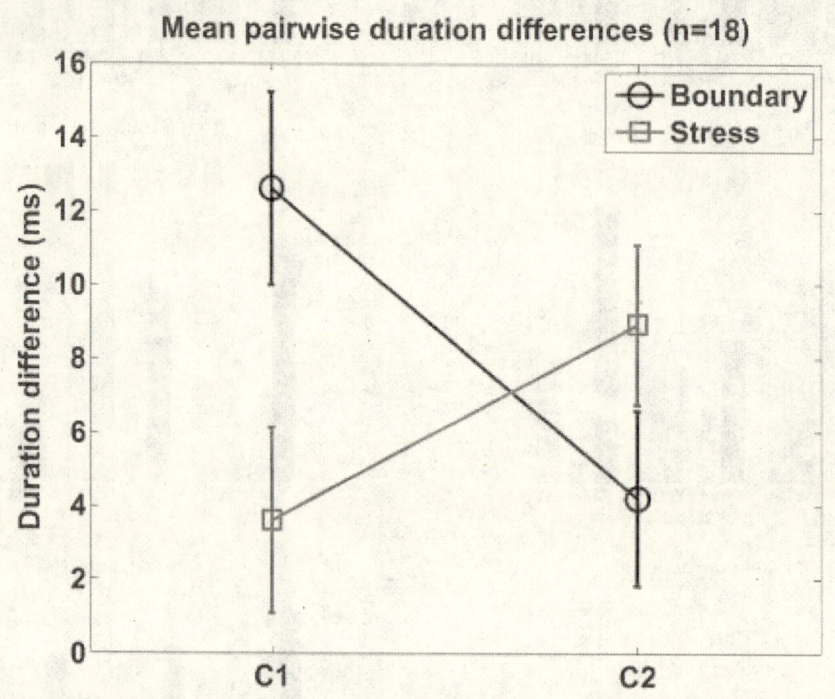

Figure 4: Comparison of boundary and stress effects on C1 and C2 durations. Positive values for the boundary effect indicate longer durations for SM than WD boundaries; positive values for the stress effect indicate longer durations for stress than unstress condition. All data points are averages (with standard error of mean) over 18 matched pairs, i.e. boundary comparisons matched for stress, cluster and speaker; stress comparisons matched for boundary, cluster and speaker.

Thus taken together, the results for C1 and C2 durations correspond quite closely to the original hypotheses that boundary effects would be more salient in C1 and stress effects more salient in C2.

Regarding the relative strength of boundary and stress effects, it seems possible that boundary may affect C1 more than stress affects C2 (particularly when it is considered that boundaries stronger than our so-called "small boundaries" could potentially occur, but did so only very rarely in these recordings); regarding the maximum temporal extent of the effects, it also seems conceivable that boundary effects may extend into C2 more often than stress effects extend to C1, but judgment on this must be reserved: Several more speakers and clusters have been recorded, but not yet analyzed.

The other main parameter relating to the temporal organization of the clusters is the overlap between C1 and C2 (defined exactly as in section 2.2 above). This is shown in Fig. 5.

The main point to note is that there is a strong contrast with the durational results for C1 and C2 just shown above: No trends with respect to either boundary or stress condition can be observed. In fact, counting matched pairs for the boundary comparison and the stress comparison gives 9/18 in both cases. There is effectively only one clear case where the hypothesized greater degree of overlap in the unstressed condition is found (/kl/ for speaker IK), and even this is counterbalanced by one clear case in the opposite direction (/sk/ for speaker MO).

In short, while prosodic conditions clearly — and not surprisingly — affect the durational properties of gestures they appear to have relatively little influence on the coordination relations between gestures in onset clusters. This result is consistent with that of Byrd & Choi [3], at least in the sense that in their data it appeared much less easy to demonstrate with respect to overlap a consistent effect of boundary condition on onset clusters compared to clusters in other syllabic positions.

This absence of prosodic effects on overlap contrasts markedly with the effect of the segmental make-up of the clusters: Fig. 5 reinforces the results of the first part of the investigation with the radically different coordination patterns between the two superficially very similar clusters /kl/ and /kn/.

This leads to the final issue to consider with respect to overlap, namely whether the varying prosodic conditions can reveal differences in the internal cohesion of different clusters. Byrd & Choi [3] considered this issue for /sp, sk/ vs. /kl/, hypothesizing that the fricative-onset clusters could represent particularly cohesive gestural "molecules". However, no clear differences were found. Similarly, here, there is little evidence from Fig. 5 that the three clusters /kl, kn, sk/ differ in the degree to which the prosodic manipulation affects the degree of overlap (we had speculated, in particular, that /kn/ might show less cohesion than /kl/).

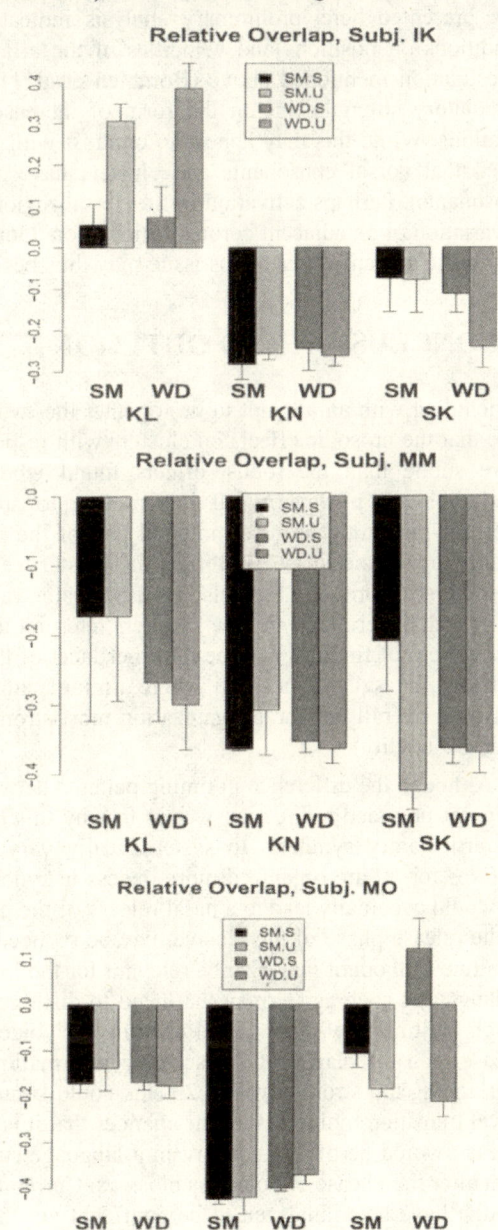

Figure 5: C1-C2 relative overlap. A value of +1.0 would indicate 100% overlap. Other details as for Fig. 3.

The final aspect of the results to consider is whether prosodic influences manifest themselves not only temporally but also spatially. While this has not yet been exhaustively explored for the EMA data presented here, preliminary analysis indicates negligible effects of the boundary and stress conditions on positions and velocities of the articulators. This fits in with the results of our EPG investigation mentioned above (Bombien et al. [1], which also found little consistent evidence for articulatory strengthening in the form of increased tongue-palate contact at prosodically stronger locations. While this may appear to contrast with some earlier findings in the literature it should be noted that dorsal consonants and clusters have scarcely been investigated (unlike single coronal consonants). Perhaps activation in the dorsal region tends to simultaneously reduce the susceptibility to variation of an adjacent coronal articulation. Our corpus actually includes a wider range of clusters than those presented here. This issue may thus become clearer when this material has been analyzed, too.

4. CONCLUSION AND OUTLOOK

Concluding with an attempt to tie together the two different areas of this study, it was interesting to note that the prosodic effects on clusters with respect to patterns of overlap, for example, were much more subtle than the robust effects found when contrasting the different segmental structures plosive+/l/ vs. plosive+/n/. It is tempting to speculate that the robust effects emerge because intergestural timing forms an integral part of the phonological representation of words, whereas the weaker prosodic effects may reflect the greater lee-way at the disposal of speakers for implementing prosodic structure, and may also reflect greater variability (particularly, perhaps, in the context of a lab-speech experiment) in how speakers interpret the communicative demands of specific utterances. This pattern of findings may be a further facet of the often observed stability of onset clusters: this is probably the syllable-position where timing patterns specified in the phonological representation dominate overall temporal organization most strongly (see Goldstein et al. [9] for further discussion of onset stability).

Although the difference in timing patterns between plosive+/l/ and plosive+/n/ appears robust, we have not provided a direct answer as to why this pattern occurs. The obvious next step would be to use articulatory synthesis to systematically vary gestural organization: Assuming oral and velar gestures for /n/ are organized more or less in synchrony then earlier timing of /n/ relative to plosive C1 would eventually lead to a nasal release of the plosive. Even before this stage the acoustic salience of the release phase of the plosive may be reduced, leading to a situation that speakers try to avoid. This line of thought may also be relevant for the lower degree of overlap for voiceless vs. voiced C1. In languages such as German that need to distinguish a very large number of syllable onsets and in which the timing of peak glottal opening for voiceless plosives is close to the time point of the oral release then the clarity of the acoustic information on the release of C1 may be improved by not overlapping too strongly with C2. This could simultaneously also enhance the salience of the C2 to vowel transition by increasing the chances that it is voiced rather than voiceless. The latter constraint, at least, would be of less concern in a language such as French where voice onset is timed to occur soon after the release of voiceless plosives. Currently, although more subjects have been recorded, not enough have been analyzed to be confident yet that cross-language differences in laryngeal timing may be accompanied by different preferred patterns in overlap of supraglottal gestures. But the results are suggestive enough to make this avenue appear well worth exploring further. Note that the whole thrust of the argument in this paragraph is based on the fact that the crucial acoustic information for initial plosives is concentrated at their release. Thus this account predicts that the constraints on articulatory organization may be different for syllable initial fricatives, for the simple reason that fricatives make sali nt acoustic information available to the listener throughout their constriction phase. And indeed, data for French /fl/ vs. /fn/ initial clusters reported in Kühnert et al. [12] show that, unlike for C1 plosive, the timing of C2 /l/ vs. /n/ relative to C1 does not differ when C1 is a fricative (this is all the more remarkable because /fn/ onsets are very rare in French, and thus might have been expected to be biased towards low overlap compared to /fl/).

From the modelling point of view, recent developments in coupled-oscillator models of articulatory coordination (Goldstein et al. [9]) in which separate oscillators are implemented for closure and release phases appear to give sufficient flexibility in coupling topologies to capture the differences in overlap that we have empirically observed for the clusters with plosive C1 in the present paper.

A final area to follow up with the present data is whether the clusters show a stable pattern of timing with the following vowel, such as the C-center effect, despite the differences in within-cluster timing (see Goldstein et al. [8] for a revealing example of how cross-linguistic differences in syllable structure are reflected in different patterns of timing of consonant clusters with the following vowel; also Goldstein et al. [9] for recent modelling of cluster-vowel coordination, comparing /sp/ and /pl/ clusters in English). For two of the French speakers presented here Kühnert et al. [12] found quite stable C-center locations; this is currently being followed up for the German speakers.[2]

REFERENCES

[1] Bombien, L., Mooshammer, C., Hoole, P., Kühnert, B. Submitted. Prosodic and segmental effects on EPG contact patterns of word-initial German clusters.
[2] Byrd, D., Saltzman, E. 2003. The elastic phrase: Modeling the dynamics of boundary-adjacent lengthening. *Journal of Phonetics* 31(2), 149-180.
[3] Byrd, D., Choi, S. In press. At the juncture of prosody, phonology, and phonetics — The interaction of phrasal and syllable structure in shaping the timing of consonant gestures. In: Fougeron, C., Kühnert, B., d'Imperio, M., Vallé, N. (eds.), Laboratory Phonology 10, *"Variation, Detail and Representation"*. Berlin/New York: Mouton, de Gruyter.
[4] Chitoran, I., Goldstein, L., Byrd, D. 2002. Gestural overlap and recoverability: Articulatory evidence from Georgian. In: Gussenhoven, C., Warner, N. (eds.), *Laboratory Phonology 7*. Berlin: Mouton, 419-448.
[5] Cho, T., McQueen, J. 2005. Prosodic influences on consonant production in Dutch: Effects of prosodic boundaries, phrasal accent and lexical stress. *J. Phonetics* 33, 121-157.
[6] Fougeron, C., Keating, P. 1997. Articulatory strengthening at edges of prosodic domains. *J. Acoust. Soc. Am.*, 101, 3728-3740.
[7] Gafos, A., Hoole, P., Roon, K., Zeroual, C. In press. Variation in timing and phonological grammar in Moroccan Arabic clusters. In: Fougeron, C., Kühnert, B., d'Imperio, M., Vallé, N. (eds.), *Laboratory Phonology 10, "Variation, Detail and Representation"*. Berlin/New York: Mouton, de Gruyter.
[8] Goldstein, L., Chitoran, I., Selkirk, E. 2007. Syllable structure as coupled oscillator modes: Evidence from Georgian vs. Tashlhiyt Berber. *Proc. 16th ICPhS*, Saarbrücken, 241-244.
[9] Goldstein, L., Nam, H., Saltzman, E., Chitoran, I. This volume. Coupled Oscillator Planning Model of Speech Timing and Syllable Structure.
[10] Hoole, P., Zierdt, A., Geng, C. 2003. Beyond 2D in articulatory data acquisition and analysis. *Proc. 15th ICPhS*, Barcelona, 265-268.
[11] Keating, P., Cho, T., Fougeron, C., Hsu, C. 2003. Domain-initial articulatory strengthening in four languages. In: Local, J., Ogden, R., Temple, R. (eds.), Papers in *Laboratory Phonology 6: Phonetic Interpretation*. Cambridge: University Press, 143-161.
[12] Kühnert, B., Hoole, P., Mooshammer, C. 2006. Gestural overlap and C-center in selected French consonant clusters. *Proc. 7th Int. Seminar on Speech Production*, Ubatuba, 327-334.

---

[2] Work supported by German Research Council (DFG) grants HO 3271/3 and MO 1687/1 to Phil Hoole and Tine Mooshammer for the project "Articulatory cross-language study of initial consonant clusters in varying prosodic conditions" within DFG Schwerpunkt program 1234 "Phonological and phonetic competence: between grammar, signal processing, and neural activity".

[13] Rialland, A. 1994. The phonology and phonetics of extrasyllabicity in French. In: Keating, P. (ed.), *Phonological Structure and Phonetic Form — Papers in Laboratory Phonology III*. Cambridge: Cambridge University Press, 136-159.
[14] Vennemann, T. 2000. Triple-cluster reduction in Germanic: Etymology without sound laws? *Historische Sprachforschung (Historical Linguistics)*, 113, 239-258.

PATTERNS OF PROSODY
IN THE EXPRESSION OF THE SPEAKER
AND THE APPEAL TO THE LISTENER

Klaus J. KOHLER

ABSTRACT

On the basis of Karl Bühler's *Organon Model* and the *Kiel Intonation Model (KIM),* this paper develops components of a paradigm of *Speech Communication,* which integrates the functions of Expression of the Speaker and Appeal to the Listener with the function of Representation of the Factual World into a comprehensive framework of language. In particular, prosodic manifestations are discussed of argumentation structure, of categories of emphasis, and of attitudes towards the listener in questions.

Keywords: information/argumentation structure, emphasis, questions, prosody

1. INTRODUCTION

Modern linguistics delimits its territory by many frontiers, creating such dichotomies as phonetics and phonology, linguistics and paralinguistics. The frontier between the former two fields has become permeable in Laboratory Phonology and has been broken down in Experimental Phonology. However, the currently prevalent paradigm locates paralinguistics at the linguistic frontier and centres on the function of the linguistic sign that has been called the representation of objects and factual relationships. In this wake, phonetic science is preoccupied, at the lexical level, with the differentiation of words by segments, stress and tone, and at the utterance level, with the coding of phrasal chunking, sentence mode, focus and information structure by prosody. In tone languages, such as Chinese, the superposition of phrasal prosodies onto lexical tones has been studied very extensively, again largely limited to the linguistic function of representation. In such a framework, the expressive function of the linguistic sign related to the sender, and its appeal function to the receiver are, therefore, excluded from the core domain of linguistics and relegated to its frontiers.

Since de Saussure, two main questions have dominated this linguistic perspective:

(1) What is the relationship between formal categories and their variations, more particularly between phonological units, such as the phoneme, and their phonetic substance?

(2) What is the relationship between formal categories and meaning?

In the pursuit of these questions, the formal categories are determined negatively by abstraction from observable phenomena according to the principle of otherness. For example, the phonemes /b/ and /p/ or the pitch accents H* and HL* must be different, and the phonetic measures, VOT or F_0 alignment, must be such that they form two disjunctive sets with clear boundaries between them. This categoriality was also generalised to perception, resulting in the Haskins principle of discrete category identification coinciding with a maximum of discriminability across the category boundaries and a minimum inside them. The paradigm persists to this day in spite of the well-founded objections right from the moment it was put forward [28], and has even seen a renaissance in the field of prosody [36][3][7][35][38]. It reflects the assumption that speech communication is based on these formal linguistic categories and their *discrete differences* in manifestation, rather than on *substantive identification*.

Phenomena that linguists find difficult to reduce to such a frame of discrete otherness are relegated to *paralinguistics* and thus differentiated clearly from the formal level of linguistics. As long as the dichotomies of linguistics vs. paralinguistics and of phonology vs. phonetics are heuristic devices for making the phenomenology of speech accessible to scientific investigation, they are useful in advancing our knowledge. Eminent phoneticians like Peter Ladefoged have dedicated a great part of their academic career to the study of sounds in the world's languages, as used to differentiate words [25][26]. Since to a large extent they work on unwritten languages that have not been studied before, they have no option but to approach the language by a very simple formal framework of sound units distinguishing words. Phrase-level and paralinguistic sound phenomena enter this research procedure as distorting noise.

However, if the central focus on formal linguistic categories is reified, it makes researchers ask questions as to whether a particular phenomenon IS linguistic or paralinguistic, IS phonological or phonetic. Such questions give no insight into the functioning of speech communication, which should be the ultimate goal in speech science, because they result in futile ontological disputes and at the same time exclude a large part of speech interaction from scientific phonetic and linguistic investigation. Speech modelling on such a basis will always remain a torso, unable to handle everyday spontaneous speech communication fully and satisfactorily. The point has come when, in languages whose linguistic structures have been well-described, such as Arabic, Chinese, Danish, Dutch, English, French, German, Hindi, Italian, Japanese, Russian, Spanish, Swedish, we should pull down the formal scaffoldings that helped to build them, and develop new concepts that can bridge the dichotomies of phonology and phonetics, of segments and prosodies, and of linguistics and paralinguistics, and provide a more adequate theoretical basis for the insightful analysis of speech communication.

2. A PARADIGM OF SPEECH COMMUNICATION

2.1 Theoretical bases

2.1.1 The Organon Model

This paper illustrates a paradigm of speech communication which moves the expression of the speaker and the appeal to the listener into the centre of phonetic investigation, complementing the narrow linguistic functions. Its theoretical point of departure is Karl Bühler's "Organon Model" [4], which is schematically portrayed in Fig. 1. It relates the linguistic sign to the SENDER, the RECEIVER, and the FACTUAL WORLD of objects and factual relationships. This threefold link establishes the functions of Expression, Appeal and Representation by *symptoms*, *signals* and *symbols* respectively. This three-faceted concept of the linguistic sign integrates paralinguistics and linguistics into a comprehensive field of speech communication. The speaker's Expressions are attitudes towards the listener and the factual world in communicative settings, or emphatic evaluations, or emotions; the Appeal to the listener is carried by commands, requests and questions. Within this frame of Expression and Appeal, this paper discusses the prosodic manifestations of

- argumentation structure: concluding, opening, contrasting or expressively opposing argumentation, showing different kinds of speakers' reactions in the unfolding of communicative interchange
- categories of negative and positive expressive intensification, as in "It stinks!" vs. "It's marvellous!"

- attitudes towards the listener in questions, prejudging answers or leaving them open to the listener, or expressing surprise.

The data will be mainly from German and English, but suggestions are advanced as to how this communicative paradigm can be introduced into the study of other languages, and how the phonetic exponents may be related to deep-seated features in human behaviour.

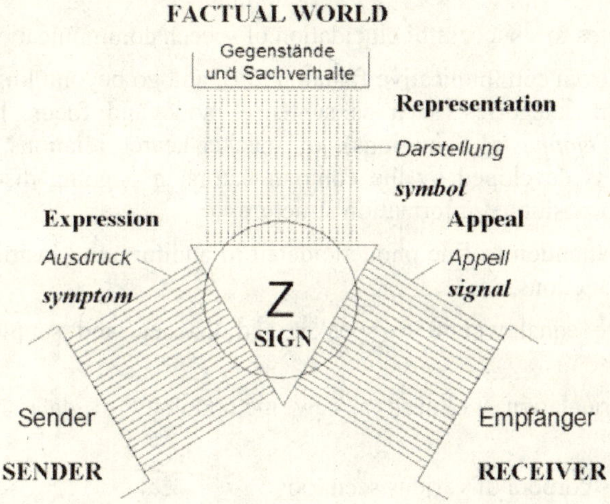

Figure 1: Schematic diagram of the Organon Model

2.1.2 The Kiel Intonation Model (KIM)

To investigate the prosodic exponents of the Expression and Appeal functions, the categories of *The Kiel Intonation Model (KIM)* are applied to the data [12][13][14][15][16][21]. KIM is a superpositional model of intonation, which parameterizes global patterns that are either (rising-)falling *"peak contours"*, (falling-)rising *"valley contours"*, (rising-)falling-rising *"combined contours"* or *"flat contours"*, for the differentiation of meaning. This pitch — meaning relationship implies that the listener is the ultimate judge for categories in a prosodic phonology; patterns are established auditorily, and acoustic features are then related to the auditory categorization.

The movement patterns are further differentiated by different synchronizations with vocal tract dynamics: *peaks* may have their F_0 maximum before the accented-vowel onset (*early*), after the accented-vowel onset (*medial*) or *"late"* in the accented syllable (or in a subsequent unaccented syllable), see [21].

These prosodic categories were established by perception experiments with series of F_0 peak shifts generated across the natural German utterance *"Sie hat ja gelogen."* ("She's been lying", *-lo-* being the only accented syllable in the sentence) [12][13][21]. The transition from *"early"* to *"medial"* is such that identification in the series switches abruptly as the peak maximum enters the accented vowel, and concomitantly, pair discrimination shows maximal sensitivity across this point. So there is not only category identification in the stimulus series, but also categorical perception in the Haskins sense. However, transition from *"medial"* to *"late"* shows gradient perception, albeit change of category. These results are extremely robust and have been found over and over again with different groups of German listeners from different parts of the country. A similar valley shift in relation to the accented vowel onset also produces a switch in identification, but only between *"early"* and *"late"*, and there is no categorical perception [31].

Niebuhr [29][30] has refined the phonetic detail of peak category manifestation by adding shape and height of F_0 peaks as well as duration and energy of the accented vowel to the parameter of synchronization, and by analysing the interplay between these physical properties in the coding of the associated functional categories. All parameters converge in focussing a waning high-low vs. a waxing low-high pitch and prominence trajectory into the accented vowel for the *"early"* and *"medial"* categories respectively. For the *"late"* category, the waxing pitch and prominence trajectory is shifted to the end of the accented syllable and beyond into an unaccented one if there is one.

2.2 Methodological prerequisites

There are six prerequisites to a successful elucidation of speech communication:

- We need to start from communicative function [39], and go beyond linguistic functions as they surface in formal categories, such as sentence mode and focus, including categories of expressiveness (*"emphasis"*, emotions), of speaker-hearer relations, and of argumentation structure, which is developed by the communicators in ongoing discourse, parallel to, and different from, propositional information structure.

- We need to pay attention to fine phonetic detail in auditory and instrumental investigation as carriers of such functions.

- We need to give equal weight to speaker and listener, and supplement production with perception studies.

- For this new orientation we need a new methodology of data acquisition by dialogue contextualization

    — in spontaneous corpora of various scenarios

    — as well as in systematically stylized experimental discourse frames.

- Any modelling of speech needs to be based on data sets appropriate for the scientific goal. If the model is to account for paralinguistic structures, the database must be collected in such a way that it can be considered an adequate representation of paralinguistic phenomena. It will, therefore, no longer do to generate databases from isolated sentences out of context which are constructed according to formal linguistic criteria and are often of doubtful semantics, and which are read in a rote fashion or reproduced after acoustic prompts by speakers selected at random without proper screening as to their aptitude for the task. This is standard practice in studies of peak alignment [35][2], which either ignore communicative function or handle it rather poorly. In another type of data acquisition, sentences are enacted with different emotions by actors. This begs the question because it presupposes that actors realize the phonetic manifestations of different emotions in such a reading task in the same way as speakers in natural communicative settings.

- Inferential statistics needs to be applied to data sets in accordance with the design of the research question and interpreted with regard to plausibility of productive *and* perceptual differentiation in speech communication. Tests, such as ANOVAs, should not be used mechanistically nor to establish the discreteness of data sets for formal linguistic categorization.

2.3 Expression of the speaker

2.3.1 Argumentation structure

In German, the categories of *"early"*, *"medial"*, and *"late F_0 peak"* contour synchronizations signal the expression of different kinds of argumentation structure — *"conclusion"*, *"opening"*, *"unexpectedness"*. Contextualization of the *"early"* peak in the example given in 2.1.2 may be "Once a liar, always a liar. ___": the speaker signals the end of an argumentation, summarizes, and expresses finality as (s)he knows or sees it. For the *"medial"* peak it may be "Now I understand. ___": the speaker signals the beginning of an argumentation and expresses openness as to a new observation or experience. For the *"late"* peak it may be "Oh.___": the speaker again signals the beginning of an argumentation, but expresses contrast to expectation, and personal evaluation of this contrast as surprise.

On the basis of further data observation, the categories of argumentation structure have been expanded by introducing an additional peak function *"late-medial"* between *"medial"* and *"late"*. It differs from *"medial"* by having a more pronounced F_0 upward glide and by adding contrast to information selection in an opening argument; and it differs from *"late"*, which has a low plateau before the rising part of the contour and superimposes an affective component on contrast [21, 30]. Figures 2-5 illustrate the 4 peak positions in the German utterance *"Er war mal schlank."* ("He used to be slim."), for instance in a context of situation where two people are looking at old photos and come across one of an old friend.

(1) In a concluding argument, the speaker describes his/her own apperception as something obvious.

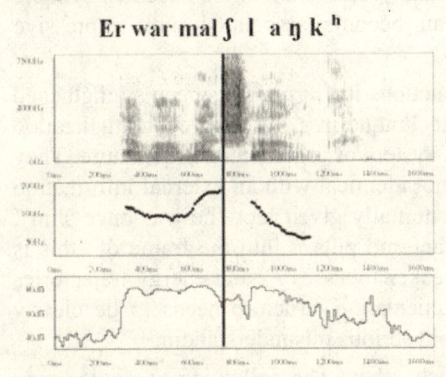

Figure 2: Spectrum, F_0, energy in German *"Er war mal schlank."* ("He used to be slim.") — *"early peak"*; male speaker kk (the author).

(2) In an opening argument, the speaker indicates that s/he has observed, and become aware of, something.

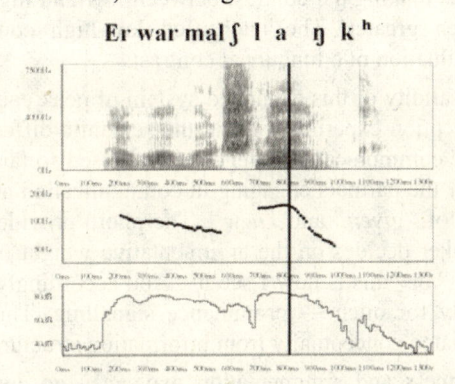

Figure 3: Spectrum, F_0, energy in German *"Er war mal schlank."* ("He used to be slim.") — *"medial peak"*; sp. kk.

(3) In an opening argument with an overlay of contrast, the speaker indicates that the observation contradicts the expectation.

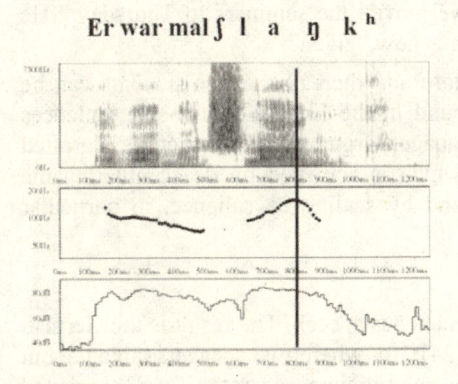

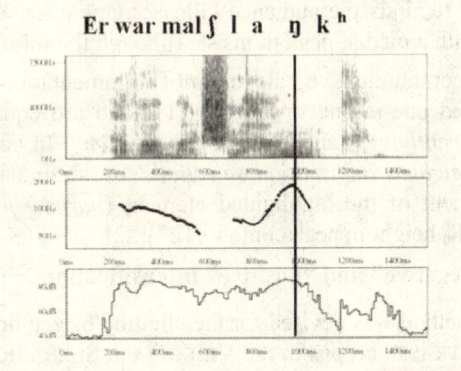

Figure 4: Spectrum, F_0, energy in German *"Er war mal schlank."* ("He used to be slim.") — *"late-medial peak"*; sp. kk.

(4) In an opening argument with overlays of contrast and expressive evaluation, the speaker shows feeling over an unexpected observation.

Figure 5: Spectrum, F_0, energy in German *"Er war mal schlank."* ("He used to be slim.") — *"late peak"*; sp. kk.

The F_0 and energy time courses show parallelism.

- For the *"early"* peak, they both descend into the vowel. This waning profile accentuates the low-falling pitch, which becomes an associate of finality in argumentation.
- For the *"medial"* peak, both contours rise into the vowel. This waxing profile accentuates the high-rising pitch in the first half of the sonorous syllable, which becomes an associate of openness in argumentation. *"early"* and *"medial peaks"* are thus opposites in pitch and prominence courses from the pre-accent to the accent syllable, and this may be the reason why the perceptual change in an F_0-shift series is so clear-cut and robust.
- In the *"late-medial"* peak, high pitch is strengthened in a more extensive low-high movement contrast in the vowel, and by energy staying high longer. This is where a gradient pitch-prominence feature enters and becomes associated with degrees of functional contrast.
- This continues right into the *"late"* peak, where the waxing F_0 and energy profile is not only shifted to late in the vowel but is preceded, concomitantly, by a low level in both parameters thus making the contrast between low and high pitch and prominence in the accented syllable even greater. The intensified low-high contrast can become associated with expressive evaluation of a functional contrast.

The validity of this expanded system of peak contour functions in German has been strengthened in a perception experiment using the semantic differential technique in a frame of contextualization [20]. The communicative categories discussed so far form a system of argumentation structure. They are set by the partners engaging in communication and are not identical with an external information structure of *"given"* and *"new"*. The photo provides the externally given fact "he was once slim". The speaker decides on the argumentative weight of this fact and puts it into the frame of "this is what it is" or "this is how I see it". And accordingly the speaker focusses F_0 and energy trajectories differently for pitch — prominence signalling. Thus, argumentation structure needs to be clearly differentiated conceptually from information structure to avoid serious misunderstanding.

Givenness and argumentation may even go against each other. The following examples may illustrate this.

(1) After a long discussion at the beginning of term about finding a suitable alternative time and day for a series of seminars to accommodate all who want to attend, the tutor says "We are going to move the seminars to Thursday." He says it with an early peak on the last word to indicate to the audience that this is final and the discussion is now closed, although this is "new" information.

(2) The session then continues to discuss other course matters, and at the end, before departing, the tutor reminds the audience "Please remember. We have moved the seminars to Thursday." He says it with a medial peak to insist, although the information is now "given".

The communicative categories of argumentation structure and their phonetic exponents can be transferred one-to-one to English [11] and are equally found in the English equivalent sentences *"She's been lying."* and *"He used to be slim."* In both languages, argumentation structure is grafted onto *"weighted information selection"* by accentuation, which is achieved by deaccentuating the environment of the highlighted element (*narrow focus*) and by scaling its salience, in particular through F_0 height in peak contours [27][22].

2.3.2 "Negative" and "positive" intensification

A new method was devised for the eliciting of genuine spontaneous speech. The result is the German LINDENSTRASSE corpus in the VIDEO TASK SCENARIO [34][24][10], where two speakers talked about differences between two sets of video clips, which were presented to them separately, each excerpted and spliced together from the German TV series. The speakers were quite familiar with the series and knew each other very well, so they achieved a high degree of spontaneity and naturalness.

This data acquisition design produced a great deal of expressive speech. In the labeling of these data, a problem arose with a sentence accent that was not coded by the pitch patterns of KIM and did not fit into the functional categories associated with them. The communicative function is expressive intensification (*negative intensification*), and is manifested prosodically by the strengthening of non-sonority, the lengthening of initial consonants, especially voiceless ones, at the expense of the accented vowel, and by non-modal phonation, even voicelessness, in the accented vowel. This accent was termed *"force accent"* [17].

There were 41 "force accents" in the corpus, which were contrasted with 35 pitch accents in segmentally comparable words and analysed in the signal parameters of duration and energy, as well as by auditory assessment of pitch pattern and voice quality, all pointing to a strengthening of non-sonority features for an emphatic negative intensification [19]. It can be concluded from these analyses that "force accents" constitute a separate prosodic category with at least three phonetic features in speech production — onset duration, energy and voice quality.

Reference to the literature [1][5] and informal data observation prompted the hypothesis that a function of *"positive intensification"* needed to be distinguished both from *"negative intensification"* and from *"weighted information selection"*. The functional difference seems to be coded by raised pitch level and sonority in the accented syllable rhyme. To test this hypothesis in German, a new database was required. It had to be obtained in a systematic data acquisition of the three functional categories with control of segmental and prosodic structures in corresponding utterances, and it needed to be as natural as possible. Utterances were designed and arranged in written texts to provide a linguistic and situational context frame that provokes the elicitation of the respective function on a selected key word, helped by pictures of facial expressions. The texts were read by pairs of speakers (one male, one female) in face-to-face communication. The speakers were known to be extrovert, and they knew each other very well.

The data analysis [23] showed a clear difference between the strengthening of non-sonority in *"negative"* and of sonority in *"positive intensification"* in relation to *"weighted information selection"*. Figure 6 compares the realizations of the utterance *"das stinkt!"* ("it stinks!") in the contexts *"Sag mal, hast du in der Klärgrube gebadet? boa! __ zum Kotzen!"* ("tell me, did you bathe in the sewers? boa! __ it makes you vomit!") and *"Ich liebe diesen alten Limburger. Wie__ Herrlich!"* ("I love this old Limburg cheese. __Wonderful!")

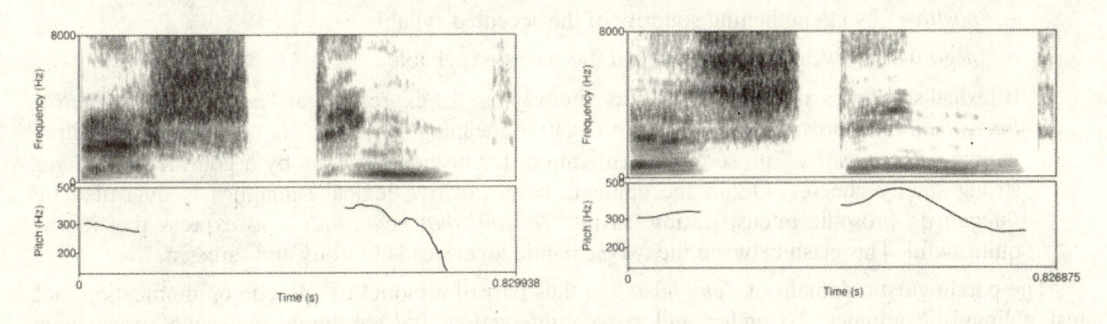

Figure 6: Spectrum and F_0 in German *"das stinkt!"* with *"negative"* (left) and *"positive intensification"* (right) from systematic data collection of *"emphasis"*; female speaker kl.

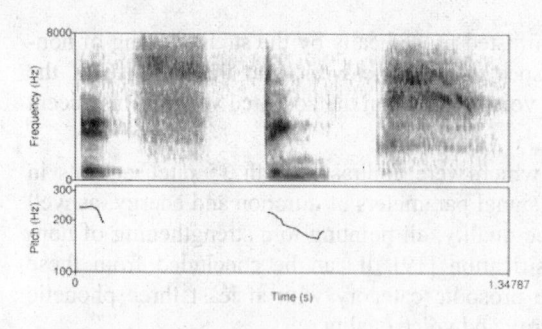

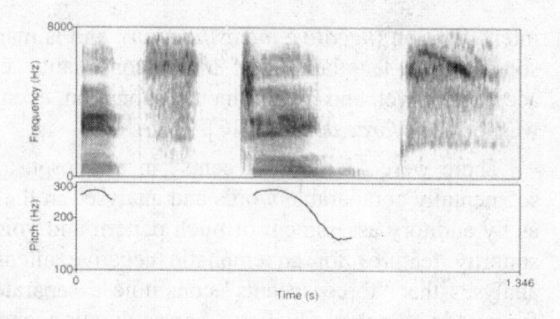

Figure 7: Spectrum and F_0 in English *"it stinks!"* with *"negative"* (left) and *"positive intensification"* (right) from data collection of *"emphasis"*; female speaker rb.

These differentiations between *"negative"* and *"positive intensification"* can be transferred to English [22] and are found with the same exponents in the corresponding English utterances in Figure 7.

2.3.3 "Emphasis" categories in the Expression function of the Organon Model and their integration into KIM

Through the corpus and the systematic data analysis the following *"emphasis"* components are added to KIM:

- *"weighted information selection"*, signalled by F_0 range
- *"contrast to one's expectation"* — degree of affective evaluation of a discrepancy between observed fact and expectation, signalled by *"medial"* to *"late F_0 peak"* synchronization with the accented syllable
- *"expressive intensification"*, signalled by special prominence for amplifying the verbal meaning
  — *"positive"* by strengthening sonority of the accented syllable
  — *"negative"* by weakening sonority of the accented syllable
- If lexical semantics and prosody go opposite ways in the expression of *"positive"* or *"negative intensification"*, prosody wins. So, the negative meaning of *"stink"* is turned into a positive feeling with *"positive"* prosodic intensification, for instance, spoken by a gourmet who loves strong smelly cheeses. Or, in the opposite case, positive lexical semantics is overruled by *"negative"* prosodic intensification, as in *"You did that beautifully"*, to express that it was quite awful. This clash between the two semantic levels leads to irony and sarcasm.

The paralinguistic domain of *"emphasis"* is thus part of a model of speech communication, not just a linguistic adjunct. To understand speech interaction, the paralinguistic use of prosody is essential.

2.3.4 "Argumentation structure" and "emphasis" in other languages

It has already been pointed out in 2.3.1 and 2.3.2 that the same peak synchronizations occur as manifestations of the same argumentation structures in English as in German, and that the semantics and phonetics of positive and negative intensification are also comparable. On the hypothesis that *"argumentation structure"* and *"emphasis"* functions are basic in human communication, they will find their expression in languages generally, and thus also in tone languages, such as Mandarin Chinese. The question then is how. There are some indications that *"finality"* vs. *"opening argument"* are signalled in Mandarin Chinese by superimposing aspects of a waning or a waxing pitch — prominence pattern, namely pitch height, onto the word tones. Figure 8 compares the word *"hao"* ("OK", with the low tone) and the word *"xing"* ("OK", with the rising tone), each spoken as *"closing"* or *"opening argument"*, respectively. (I am very grateful to Yi Xu, London, for providing the recordings.)

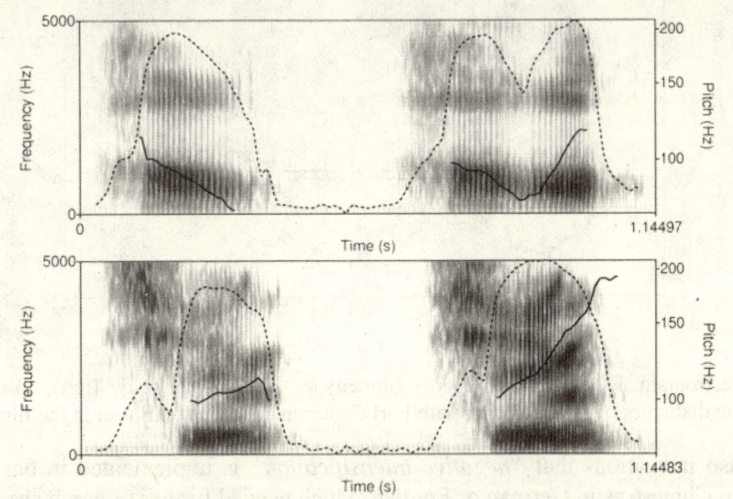

Figure 8: Spectrograms, F_0 (plain) and energy (dotted) traces of Mandarin Chinese *"hao"* (above) and *"xing"* (below) with *"closing argument"* (left) and *"opening argument"* (right); male speaker yx.

For *"closing argument"*, the low tone ends low and concomitantly acoustic energy decreases towards the end, whereas for *"opening argument"*, they both rise towards the end. Similarly, the high tone ends lower or higher and concomitantly the time course of acoustic energy is on a lower or higher level for *"closing"* vs. *"opening argument"*. So, the waning or waxing pitch — prominence patterns seem to be at work again, adapted to the conditions set by the tone language.

These Mandarin Chinese data mirror the use of prosody for similarly contextualized *yes* in English. The following excerpts from the film *The Queen* with Helen Mirren in the role of Queen Elizabeth II are to illustrate the actors' awareness of these communicative potentials of prosody. The scene at the beginning of the film introduces Queen Elizabeth in full regal robe in a portrait painting session, watching a television report on the final stage of Tony Blair's 1997 general election campaign on election day, and talking to the portrait artist, played by the Jamaican Earl Cameron:

P. *"But it is [late peak] your government."*

Q. *"Yes. [early peak] Suppose that's some consolation."*

In a telephone conversation between the Queen and Tony Blair, played by Michael Sheen, the following dialogue takes place:

B. *"Let's keep in touch."*

Q. *"Yes, [medial peak] let's."*

Figure 9 compares the two prosodies of *"Yes"*; with *"early peak"* it expresses resigned acceptance of a political fact, with *"medial peak"* it suggests an initiative for further contacts. Again F_0 is lower initially in the former, and the energy trace follows the more gradual descent of F_0 but is more sharply peaked for *"medial"*, which is not phrase-final and therefore much shorter.

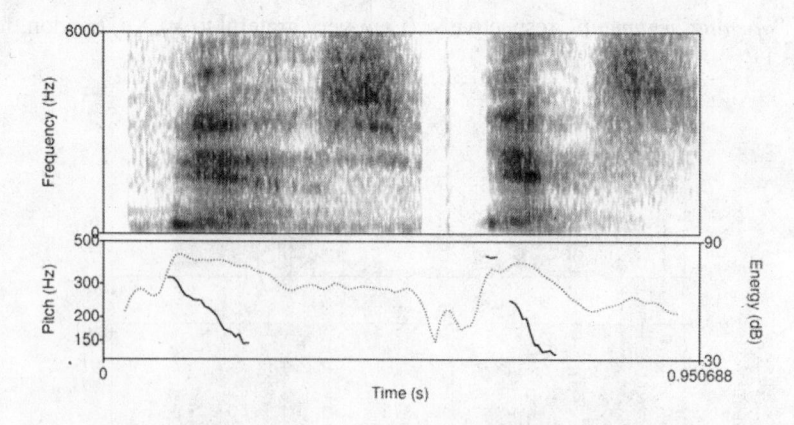

Figure 9: Spectrogram, F_0 (plain), and energy (dotted) in *"Yes."[early peak]* (left), *"Yes."[medial peak]* (right) from the dialogues of Helen Mirren with Earl Cameron and Michael Sheen in the film The Queen.

There are also indications that *"negative intensification"* is implemented in basically the same way in Mandarin Chinese as in German or English. Much needed further research should tell.

It has been extensively discussed in the literature that French, which lacks lexical stress, has an *"accent d'insistance"* that reinforces the statement being made by strengthening the beginning of a word, especially lengthening its initial consonant and raising the acoustic energy and F_0 of this syllable. If the word begins with a vowel it may be strengthened by a glottal stop, or the *"accent d'insistance"* occurs on the next syllable and affects its initial consonant. [8] The discussion seems to conflate two functions of this type of accent, *"reinforcement"* and *"intensification"*, which most probably differ in fine phonetic detail, particularly as regards the relative weighting of C and V in the accented syllable and the type of voice quality.

Grammont takes the word *"épouvantable"* to introduce the notion of *accent d'insistance*, which he describes as follows: "...il peut se faire qu'au lieu de dire cette phrase avec calme on la prononce avec une certaine émotion, que l'on éprouve le besoin de mettre en relief l'appréciation que l'on formule."[8, p.140] This example, like many others he quotes, illustrates the function of *"negative intensification"*, i.e. expressive emphasis, not insisting *"reinforcement"*. But he also lists cases like *"Cette conception n'est pas romaine, mais doit être **punique**"*, which clearly represent a different function, namely insistance and reinforcement. It is an empirical question as to whether the two uses of *"accent d'insistance"* are carried by different phonetic exponents; I presume they are, in parallel with the German data. Future research will tell.

2.4 Appeal to the listener

2.4.1 Functional and formal definitions of questions

Questions are typical means of appealing to the listener. They fulfill at least three different functions:
- asking for specific factual information
- asking for a decision along a positive-negative polarity scale
- asking for repetition or further specification with an expression of surprise.

For languages like German, English, French and many others, questions have been defined formally with reference to syntax and lexical items. Thus, in German or English, question-word questions and word-order questions are differentiated. According to common textbook opinion, the former are associated with falling, the latter with rising intonation. Among the lexically marked questions, a subclass is defined prosodically by having rising pitch from the question word to the end of the sentence: these are the repeat questions insisting on the factual information focussed on by the question word.

2.4.2 Questions in the Kiel Corpus of Spontaneous Speech

Based on the Appointment-Making Scenario data of the *Kiel Corpus of Spontaneous Speech* for German [9], which are available in orthographic transliteration and phonetic as well as prosodic transcription, search operations were carried out for the four combinations of lexical/syntactic question type and falling/rising pitch. Table 1 gives the results.

Table 1: Distribution of frequencies of falling (f), high rising (hr), low rising (lr) and other (o) pitch patterns in word order and question-word questions.

	f	hr	lr	o	total
word-order	21%	39%	30%	10%	100% (121)
question-word	57%	10%	24%	9%	100% (172)

Falling and rising patterns occur in both interrogative structures. Word-order questions predominantly show rising patterns, question-word questions predominantly falling ones. There is a negligible proportion of high-rising contours in question-word questions, whereas they dominate in word-order questions. Subsequently, instances of each of the four pairings, syntactic/lexical and f/r, were semantically interpreted in their contextual settings; selected examples were resynthesized, changing the pitch pattern from falling to rising or vice versa in each case, and interpreted in the same naturally produced context with regard to contextual compatibility and paralinguistic change of meaning.

One female speaker produced a set of all four combinations of linguistic form and prosody in the Appointment-Making Scenario corpus. Here are two of her examples to illustrate the functions of the prosodic patterns. For further details cf. [18]. With an original high-rising pitch pattern in the word-order question *"Würde Ihnen das passen?"* ("Would this suit you?") the speaker leaves the decision as to the polarity to the listener. In the resynthesis with a *"medial peak"* pattern, the speaker expects the answer "yes". In the resynthesis with a *"late-medial peak"*, the speaker expects the answer "yes" and sets it against a negative answer, thus indicating that a different answer would not be appropriate, giving the utterance a tone of irritation and impatience. With an original *"early peak"* pattern in the question-word question *"Was würden Sie denn davon halten?"* ("What would you think of that?") the speaker terminates her turn by asking the dialogue partner to make a final suggestion. This is the *"closing argument"*. In the resynthesis with a high-rising pitch pattern, the speaker requests a comment from the dialogue partner on the date that has been proposed, and the Appeal to the listener takes over.

2.4.3 A function-form framework of questions

The data from the German spontaneous corpus and the systematic F_0 manipualtion and contextual interpretation show quite clearly (a) that both rising and falling pitch patterns occur with both formal sentence structures, (b) that there is a statistical link between word-order questions and rising pitch as well as between question-word questions and falling pitch, (c) that the opposite pitch pattern introduces different functional aspects in each case.

These results fit into a function-form framework which may be illustrated by the following contextualized question types in German.

(1) Speaker B:

   "Wo?" ("Where?")

   in the dialogue context of

   Speaker A:

"Das Treffen findet in Hademarschen statt."

"The meeting will take place in Hademarschen." (a small town in the north, not widely known in Germany)

(1.1) With a *"medial peak"*, B asks for more information about the location of the venue in the town. This introduces the function of *"opening argument"* of a *"medial peak"* contour into the question context.

(1.2) With a *"late-medial peak"*, B sets the need for more information about the venue against the insufficiency of the information so far given by A. This introduces the superimposed functions of *"contrast"* and *"opening argument"* of a *"late-medial peak"* into the question context. The utterance has a tone of irritation and impatience.

(1.3) With a high-rising *"late valley"*, where the rise starts in the accented vowel, B still asks for more information about the venue, but appeals to the listener to give it. The utterance sounds less categorical and more friendly than with a peak pattern.

(1.4) With a high-rising *"early valley"*, where the rise starts before the accented vowel, Speaker B appeals to the listener to repeat the name of the place because s/he has not heard it properly or finds it strange.

Figure 10 provides these four pitch patterns.

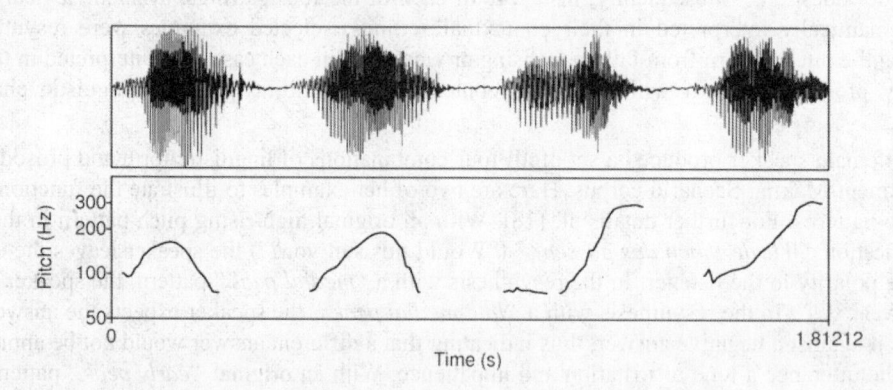

Figure 10: Speech waves and F_0 traces of 4 pitch categories in the question-word question *"Wo?"* ("Where?") From left to right: *"medial peak"*, *"late-medial peak"*, high-rising *"late valley"*, high-rising *"early valley"*; male speaker kk (the author).

(2)   Speaker A2: *"Ist er in Rome?"* ("Is he in Rome?")

in the dialogue context of

Speaker A1: *"Wo ist er denn eigentlich?"* ("Where does he happen to be?")

Speaker B: *"Er ist nach Italien gefahren."* ("He has gone to Italy.")

(2.1) With a *"medial peak"*, A wants more information about the person's whereabouts and suggests a place, expecting the answer to be "yes". This introduces the function of *"opening argument"* of a *"medial peak"* contour into the question context.

(2.2) With a *"late-medial peak"*, A wants more information, as in (2.1), but sees his/her suggestion as being different from what one might have expected. This introduces the superimposed functions of *"contrast"* and *"opening argument"* of a *"late-medial peak"* into the question context.

(2.3) With a high-rising *"early valley"*, where the rise starts before the accented vowel, A does not prejudge the answer but appeals to the listener for a polarity decision.

(2.4) With a high-rising *"late valley"*, where the rise starts in the accented vowel, A still appeals to the listener for a polarity decision, but this time with an expression of surprise at the person perhaps being in Rome.

Figure 11 provides these four pitch patterns. Such function-form relationships need to be investigated in other languages; they may be expected to be comparable in, e.g. English and Dutch.

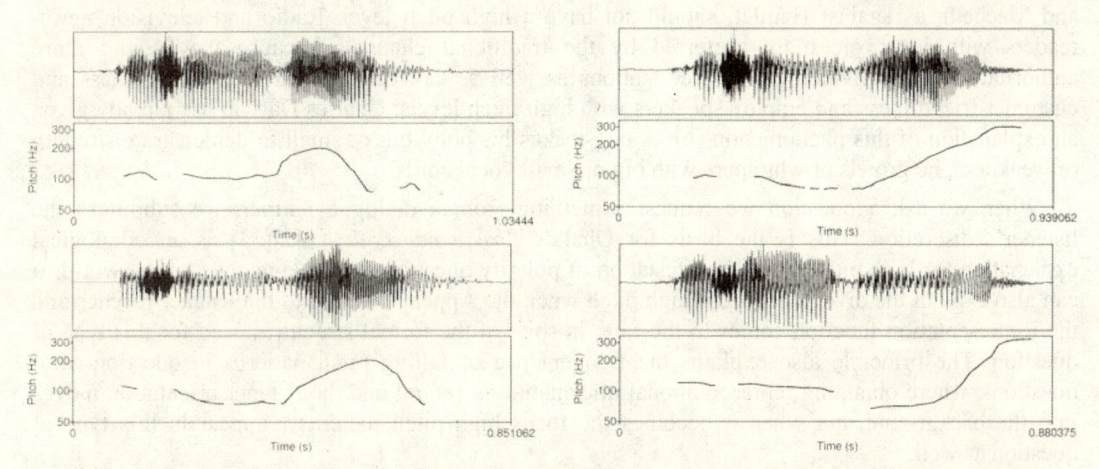

Figure 11: Speech waves and F_0 traces of 4 pitch categories in the word-order question *"Ist er in Rom?"* ("Is he in Rome?") From top to bottom: left — *"medial peak"*, *"late-medial peak"*; right — high-rising *"early valley"*, high-rising *"late valley"*, in each case on *"Rom"*; male speaker kk (the author).

2.4.4 Questions in a paradigm of speech communication

To lead the discussion of types of questions and their formal manifestations, from syntax to prosody, into a framework of Speech Communication it is essential to approach the phenomena from the functional point of view and to ask what bundles of formal features code various relationships between the SENDER, the RECEIVER, and the FACTUAL WORLD in the transmission of questions. In the case of requesting specific factual information by question-word questions, the Representation function figures prominently in the speaker's intention. So, a matter-of-fact request message will have a prototypical falling intonation. Contrariwise, a polarity question is more prominently oriented towards the RECEIVER, if the speaker leaves the decision between the polarities entirely to the listener; so, the prototypical realization will be raising intonation for an Appeal to the listener.

However, if the Representation function in a factual information question is supplemented by a consideration for the addressee, requesting rather than matter-of-fact asking for information, this friendliness coloring will result in a rising intonation from the last sentence accent to the end. Or, if the speaker asks for repetition or further specification of the focused factual aspect, the Appeal to the listener comes to the fore, and the intonation rises from the question word to the end of the sentence. On the other hand, if the speaker prejudges the decision between polarities and is therefore not primarily listener-oriented, the question loses some of its Appeal character and may be realized with falling intonation.

In such a speech communication perspective, the prosodic despondency of questions is not determined by the formal linguistic structures but by the way the speaker constructs his/her relationship with the listener and with the external world in ongoing communication.

3. THE ETHOLOGICAL BASIS OF EXPRESSION AND APPEAL

In all languages, polarity questions are associated with high pitch, either high register, or rising or expanding and strengthening the maximum of peak patterns. Why should this be so? High pitch is commonly perceived as a signal of uncertainty and submissiveness, whereas low pitch reflects self-confidence and dominance. Actors are chosen for roles according to their voice register. Richard III and Macbeth, as against Hamlet, should not have a high pitch level. Radio and television news-readers with low voices are preferred by the traditional channels because they sound more authoritative and convincing. But free stations as well as call centres cultivate youthfulness and customer friendliness and employ speakers with high pitch levels. Charles Darwin has already given an explanation of this phenomenon [6]. A dog makes his body big or small to demonstrate strength or weakness; he growls or whimpers with big or small vocal cords.

When we ask a question we request something from a dialogue partner, we submit to the listener's discretion. This is the basis for Ohala's *"frequency code"* [32][33] as an ethological explanation for high pitch in the manifestation of polarity questions in the languages of the world. It can also explain the divergence from high pitch when the Appeal function to the listener recedes and the Representation function comes to the fore, in spite of the formal structures used for this type of question. The principle also explains the frequent use of falling pitch patterns in question-word questions, where obtaining representational information is central and the listener orientation moves into the background, but when it becomes the focus high pitch patterns reappear in this type of question as well.

Even peak contour synchronizations can be related to the *"frequency code"*. Their decisive differentiating features are syntagmatically contrastive waxing or waning pitch — prominence patterns synchronized around an accented syllable. All the acoustic properties converge in establishing such low-high or high-low trajectories for the listener.

Thus, argumentation structures as part of the Expression function, and questions as part of the Appeal function can be seen as being rooted in the ethological basis of human behavior, and captured by the *"frequency code"*.

As for the emphasis categories of the Expression function, *"negative emphasis"* may be assumed to be a universal function expressing anything from dislike to disgust, and as such may be considered an adaptation of the biological function of vomiting [37] to human speech communication. Like its vegetative root, this communicative stylization would be characterized by vocal tract, more particularly pharyngeal, narrowing and raising of the larynx. The phonetic properties of heightening non-sonority by lengthening initial voiceless consonants, by fricativizing nuclear vowels, and by using non-modal phonation would result naturally from such a production basis. *"Positive emphasis"* has the opposite articulation basis, i.e. vocal tract widening, with the observed phonetic properties following from it, and, of course, the differences go together with different facial expressions.

4. OUTLOOK

What we need now is a comprehensive investigation into the function-form-substance relationships of the Expression and Appeal functions across a variety of structurally different languages in the world. This is a large-scale project, encompassing different accent, tone and rhythm types. It presupposes a different attitude towards paralinguistics and its relationship to linguistics. When they are treated as integral parts in a paradigm of Speech Communication, our understanding of how human interaction by language works and why it operates the way it does, will be greatly advanced.

REFERENCES

[1] Armstrong, L. E., Ward, I. C. 1926. *A Handbook of English Intonation*. Cambridge: Heffer.

[2] Atterer, M., Ladd, D. R. 2004. On the phonetics and phonology of "segmental anchoring" of F_0: evidence from German. *Journal of Phonetics* 32, 177-197.

[3] Baumann, S., Grice, M., Steindamm, S. 2006. Prosodic marking of focus domains — categorical or gradient? *Proc. of Speech Prosody*, Dresden, 301-304.

[4] Bühler, K. 1934. *Sprachtheorie*. Jena: Gustav Fischer.

[5] Coustenoble, H. N., Armstrong, L. E. 1934. *Studies in French Intonation*. Cambridge: Heffer.

[6] Darwin, C. 1872. *The Expression of the Emotions in Man and Animals*. London: John Murray.

[7] Falé, I., Hub Faria, I. 2006. Categorical perception of intonational contrasts in European Portuguese. *Proc. of Speech Prosody*, Dresden, 69-72.

[8] Grammont, M. 1934. *La prononciation française*. Paris: Librairie Delagrave.

[9] IPDS. 1995-1997. *The Kiel Corpus of Spontaneous Speech*, Vols. 1-3. CD-ROM#2-4. Kiel: IPDS.

[10] IPDS. 2006. *The Kiel Corpus of Spontaneous Speech*, Vol. 4, *Video Task Scenario: Lindenstrasse*. DVD#1. Kiel: IPDS.

[11] Kleber, F. 2006. Form and function of falling pitch contours in English. *Proc. of Speech Prosody*, Dresden, 61-64.

[12] Kohler, K. J. 1991. Terminal intonation patterns in single-accent utterances of German. Phonetics, phonology and semantics. *Arbeitsberichte des Instituts für Phonetik der Universität Kiel (AIPUK)* 25, 115-185.

[13] Kohler, K. J. 1991. A model of German intonation. *Arbeitsberichte des Instituts für Phonetik der Universität Kiel (AIPUK)* 25, 295-360.

[14] Kohler, K. J. 1995. The Kiel Intonation Model (KIM), its implementation in TTS synthesis and its application to the study of spontaneous speech. http://www.ipds.uni-kiel.de/kjk/forschung/kim.en.html visited Aug-08.

[15] Kohler, K. J. 1997. Modelling prosody in spontaneous speech. In: Sagisaka, Y., Campbell, N., Higuchi, H. (eds.), *Computing Prosody. Computational Models for Processing Spontaneous Speech*. New York: Springer, 187-210.

[16] Kohler, K. J. 1997. Parametric control of prosodic variables by symbolic input in TTS synthesis. In: H. van Santen, J. P., Sproat, R. W., Olive, J. P., Hirschberg, J. (eds.), *Progress in Speech Synthesis*. New York: Springer, 459-475.

[17] Kohler, K. J. 2003. Neglected categories in the modelling of prosody: pitch timing and non-pitch accents. *Proc. 15th ICPhS*, Barcelona, 2925-2928.

[18] Kohler, K. J. 2004. Pragmatic and attitudinal meanings of pitch patterns in German syntactically marked questions. In: Fant, G., Fujisaki, H., Cao, J., Xu, Y. (eds.), *From Traditional Phonology to Modern Speech Processing, Festschrift for Professor Wu Zongji's 95th Birthday*. Beijing: Foreign Language Teaching and Research Press, 205-214.

[19] Kohler, K. J. 2005. Form and function of non-pitch accents. *Arbeitsberichte des Instituts für Phonetik der Universität Kiel (AIPUK)* 35a, 97-123.

[20] Kohler, K. J. 2005. Timing and communicative functions of pitch contours. *Phonetica* 62, 88-105.

[21] Kohler, K. J. 2006. Paradigms in experimental prosodic analysis: from measurement to function. In: Sudhoff, S. et al. (eds.), *Methods of Empirical Prosody Research*. Berlin, New York: de Gruyter, 123-152.

[22] Kohler, K. J. 2006. What is emphasis and how is it coded? *Proc. of Speech Prosody*, Dresden, 748-751. (ppt presentation http://www.ipds.uni-kiel.de/kjk/forschung/lautmuster.en.html) visited Aug-08.

[23] Kohler, K. J., Niebuhr, O. 2007. The phonetics of emphasis, *Proc. 16th ICPhS*, Saarbrücken, 2145-2148.

[24] Kohler, K. J., Peters, B., Scheffers, M. 2006. The Kiel Corpus of Spontaneous Speech, Vol. IV. German: Video Task Scenario (Kiel-DVD #1). pdf document. http://www.ipds.uni-kiel.de/kjk/forschung/lautmuster.en.html visited Aug-08.

[25] Ladefoged, P. 2001. *Vowels and Consonants: An Introduction to the Sounds of Languages*. Oxford: Blackwells.

[26] Ladefoged, P., Maddieson, I. 1996. *The Sounds of the World's Languages*. Oxford: Blackwells.

[27] Liberman, M., Pierrehumbert, J. 1984. Intonational invariance under changes in pitch range and length. In: Aronoff, M., Oehrle, R. (eds.), *Language Sound Structure*. Cambridge, MA: The MIT Press, 157-233.

[28] Massaro, D. W. 1998. Categorical Perception: important phenomenon or lasting myth? *Proc. 5th Inter. Conf. of Spoken Language Processing*, Sydney, Australia, 2275-2278.

[29] Niebuhr, O. 2007. *Perzeption und kognitive Verarbeitung der Sprechmelodie. Theoretische Grundlagen und empirische Untersuchungen*. Berlin, New York: de Gruyter.

[30] Niebuhr, O. 2007. The signalling of German rising-falling intonation categories — the interplay of synchronization, shape, and height. *Phonetica* 64, 174-193.

[31] Niebuhr, O., Kohler, K. J. 2004. Perception and cognitive processing of tonal alignment in German. *Proc. Inter. Symposium on Tonal Aspects of Languges. Emphasis on Tone Languages*. The Institute of Linguistics, Chinese Academy of Social Sciences, Beijing, 155-158.

[32] Ohala, J. 1983. Cross-language use of pitch: an ethological view. *Phonetica* 40, 1-18.

[33] Ohala, J. 1984. An ethological perspective on common cross-language utilization of F_0 of voice. *Phonetica* 41, 1-16.

[34] Peters, B. 2001."Video Task" oder "Daily Soap Scenario" — Ein neues Verfahren zur kontrollierten Elizitation von Spontansprache", manuscript. http://www.ipds.uni-kiel. de/pub_exx/bp2001_1/Linda21.html visited Aug-08.

[35] Radtcke, T., Harrington, J. 2006. Is there a distinction between H+!H* and H+L* in Standard German? Evidence from an acoustic and auditory analysis. *Proc. of Speech Prosody*, Dresden, 783-786.

[36] Schneider, K., Lintfert, B. 2003. Categorical perception of boundary tones. *Proc. 15th ICPhS* Barcelona, 631-634.

[37] Trojan, F., Tembrock, G., Schendl, H. 1975. *Biophonetik*. Mannheim, Wien, Zürich: Bibliographisches Institut.

[38] Vanrell, M. M. 2006. A scaling contrast in Majorcan Catalan interrogatives. *Proc. of Speech Prosody*, Dresden, 807-810.

[39] Xu, Y. 2005. Speech melody as articulatorily implemented communicative functions. *Speech Communication* 46, 220-251.

LINKING STATISTICAL SIGNAL PROCESSING WITH ACOUSTIC PHONETICS: A NEW SPEECH RECOGNITION AND ANALYSIS FRAMEWORK BASED ON AUTOMATIC SPEECH ATTRIBUTE TRANSCRIPTION (ASAT)

LEE Chin-Hui

ABSTRACT

Recent speech synthesis system designs benefit a lot from past technical advances in automatic speech recognition (ASR). On the other hand, state-of-the-art speech recognition algorithms rely little on information in the speech knowledge hierarchy, ranging from acoustics and phonetics to syntax and semantics, in order to integrate the required set of knowledge sources into a top-down, finite-state network representation of the recognition task constraints. Therefore, it is hard to utilize knowledge available in a vast collection of literature in acoustic phonetics to enhance performance of speech recognition system. It is believed that some of these ASR limitations can be overcome by speech analysis algorithms that can take full advantage of the acoustic phonetic properties in speech signals. This calls for a bottom-up knowledge integration framework that links statistical signal processing with acoustic phonetics, spots cues in speech with a bank of speech attribute detectors, incorporates acoustic and auditory evidences in speech, weighs and combines these evidences with a set of event mergers to form cognitive hypotheses, and validates these hypotheses until a consistent decision can be reached. The recently proposed ASAT (automatic speech attribute transcription) paradigm is an attempt to implement the above framework of asynchronous speech event detection and bottom-up speech knowledge integration. We report on recent progresses that show promising results in the ASAT approach to ASR, especially in the area of cross-language attribution and phone recognition in universal attribute and phone detection. It is believed that the ASAT paradigm provides a set of new speech analysis and visualization tools that will be beneficial to speech research and education, and facilitate close international cooperation in multilingual ASR.

Keywords: attribute detection, speech analysis, speech recognition, acoustic phonetics, knowledge discovery and integration

1. INTRODUCTION

It is well-known that Prof. Wu Zongji has a formal training in both phonetics and physics. This allows him to appreciate the interactions between two vastly different sets of skills, and used them to his advantage in his studies. Researchers in speech synthesis have recently enjoyed techniques started in speech recognition, especially statistical modeling tools, such as HTK [62] with *hidden Markov model* (HMM) [46] for unit selection and smoothing, and developed tools, such as HTS [57], for their own benefit. To move from one well-trained voice to another new voice, speaker adaptation techniques, such as maximum a posteriori (MAP) [15] and maximum likelihood linear regression

(MLLR) [33] are fully taken advantage of. To deal with adaptation with a very limited number of training sentences advanced speaker adaptation algorithms, such as structural MAP in Shinoda [50], MAPLR in Siohan [53], and SMAPLR in Siohan [54], were adopted and implemented in HTS, e.g. Yamagishi [61]. It is now becoming a general practice to use HMM-based adaptation for voice conversion to the extent that speech recognition researchers will be amazed because they did not do the same.

At the dawn of the 21st Century the automatic speech recognition community is at a crossroad which calls for an increasing collaboration between speech scientists and technologists [31]. On one hand, we have learned a great deal about how to build practical speech recognition systems for almost any spoken languages without the need of a detailed understanding of the language. Data-driven, machine learning techniques, such as HMM [46] and *artificial neural network* (ANN) [5, 18], are becoming so prevailing that software packages and development kits have been developed and made available to the public, e.g. Young [61], to develop user applications with ease. With the vast collections of speech and language corpora sponsored by many business and government-funded projects in many countries, it is now quite straightforward to demonstrate *automatic speech recognition* (ASR) capabilities of new tasks for almost any spoken language. Advances in hardware, algorithms and data structure have also made implementation of large vocabulary, continuous speech recognition (LVCSR) systems affordable. On the other hand, these systems are often so restrictive that their users have to follow a very strict set of protocols to effectively utilize spoken language applications. The technology is so fragile that careful designs have to be rigorously practiced to hide technology deficiencies. Furthermore, the ASR accuracies often degrades dramatically in adverse conditions to an extent that it becomes unusable even for cooperative users.

To date, the prevailing approach to ASR is to treat speech as a stochastic pattern and adopt a statistical pattern matching paradigm. Textbooks and reference books, e.g. Rabiner [47], Jelinek [22], DeMori [9], Furui [14] and Lee [26], are good sources for ASR fundamentals. Assume a source-channel speech generation model [2] in which the message source produces a sequence of words, *W*. Because of uncertainty and inaccuracy in converting from *W* to an observed speech signal, *S*, we model the process as a noisy channel. ASR is then formulated as a *maximum a posteriori* (MAP) decoding problem as shown in Figure 1.

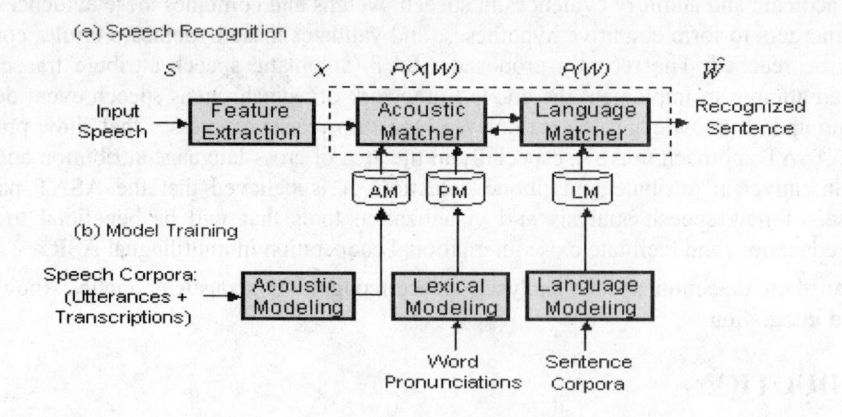

Figure 1: Data-driven approach to ASR: (a) MAP decoding; and (b) Training of models

Instead of working with the speech signal, *S*, directly, one converts *S* to a sequence of acoustic vectors, *X*, and formulates the speech decoding problem as:

$$\hat{W} = \arg\max_W P(W \mid X) = \arg\max_W P(X \mid W) P(W) \qquad (1)$$

in which the recognized sentence is obtained by searching the set of all permissible sequences of words. $P(X|W)$, often referred to as an *acoustic model* (AM), e.g. Lee [27] and Gauvain [16], is the conditional probability of the feature X, for a given W. A comprehensive review and critical look at acoustic modeling and its interactions with the MAP decision rule in Eq. (1) can be found in Lee [27]. $P(W)$ is the *a priori* probability of generating the sentence W, known as a *language model* (LM), e.g. Rosenfeld [49] and Bellagarda [4]. *Pronunciation model* (PM) can also be built from pronunciation examples to model lexical variation in spoken languages, e.g. Fosler-Lussier [13]. *Search* to efficiently solve for W in Eq. (1) can be found in Ney [42].

Moving ahead from the abovementioned state-of-the-art system design to look into the future of ASR technology development, it is instructive to examine key advances in the ASR field in the past and contemplate on potential new directions. Before the 1960's the dominating approach to ASR was based on sound classification rules developed by speech scientists. In the 1970's we saw an intensive study in applying acoustic and linguistic knowledge sources to speech recognition in the ARPA Speech Understanding Project [25]. Due to the implied rule-based scenario, expert knowledge is often required to even design a simple task. Robustness to adverse conditions in this setting was never addressed in a serious manner. Much of the knowledge accumulated in these studies was left in the background since then. Instead we saw an emergence of HMM-based continuous speech recognition in the *Dragon System* [3].

Going into 1980's and 1990's we witnessed the maturity of data-driven learning approaches to speech modeling, such as HMM [46], and ANN [5]. This *knowledge-ignorant modeling* paradigm [29] relies on collecting a large amount of task-specific speech and text examples and learning the corresponding model parameters without the need of using detailed knowledge embedded in the speech data. Using the speech knowledge hierarchy of acoustics, lexicon, syntax and semantics, it is possible to approximate some of the above knowledge sources and compile them into a single finite state network composed of acoustic HMM states, grammar nodes, and their connections [35]. ASR is then performed by matching the input feature sequences to all the possible acoustic state sequences and finding the most likely word string by traversing the above knowledge network using *dynamic programming* (DP) [42] and *heuristic search* [43]. These two collections of techniques, namely data-driven model learning and structural search over knowledge integration networks, have contributed greatly to the fast progress in the speech recognition technology.

In the meantime in the 1990's a significant portion of ASR research has gone into studying practical methods for implementation of large vocabulary systems. Much has been stimulated by the ARPA Human Language Technology Program, on three LVCSR projects, namely the Naval Resource Management (RM), the Air Travel Information System (ATIS) and the North American Business (NAB, previously known as the Wall Street Journal or WSJ) tasks. Along with large data collection efforts and algorithm development, objective technology evaluation methodology also played a key role. A recent summary of tests on all past DARPA benchmarking evaluations can be found in Pallett [44]. Furthermore, there were worldwide activities, from interactive voice services in telecommunication [7], voice dictation [23], conversational systems [63], spoken document retrieval [40], to multilingual ASR, such as Chinese spoken language processing [30] and limited-domain spoken language translation (e.g. [59]).

However when compared with *human speech recognition*, or HSR, the state-of-the-art ASR systems usually give much larger error rates even for simple tasks operating in clean environments [37]. In noisy conditions, such as in a moving vehicle, ASR systems often degrade a great deal and sometimes give an error rate more than one order of magnitude higher than HSR. Such a performance gap is unacceptable for general users and difficult for application designers. Therefore there remain great challenges the ASR research community has yet to address. In the following discussion we attempt to move away from the knowledge-ignorant approach to a knowledge-rich paradigm so that knowledge acquired from other fields, such as acoustic phonetics, can be properly integrated into speech analysis and modeling to improve performance of ASR system.

2. ASAT: A KNOWLEDGE-RICH DATA-DRIVEN PARADIGM

ASR researchers can learn a great deal from phoneticians like Prof. Wu, or speech synthesis tools, such as HTS, in order to link statistical signal processing with acoustic phonetics so that a vast collection of literature in acoustic phonetics can be utilized to enhance the performance of state-of-the-art ASR systems. Due to the difficulty of directly incorporating speech knowledge sources into HMM-based network representations of task constraints, many attempts have failed.

On another front, it has been shown that HSR performs much better than the state-of-the-art ASR systems. It is interesting to note that human beings perform speech recognition by integrating multiple knowledge sources from bottom up. It has long been postulated that a human determines the linguistic identity of a sound based on detected evidence that exists at various levels of the speech knowledge hierarchy, from acoustics to pragmatics. For example, Klatt [25] studied the so-called *acoustic landmarks* that are assumed invariant to changes in speakers and speaking environments. This is consistent with what has been documented in textbooks on acoustic phonetics, e.g. Chomsky [6], Stevens [55]. Fant [12] has consistently advocated the approach of distinctive features from an acoustic-phonetic viewpoint. Indeed, people do not continuously convert a speech signal into words as an ASR system attempts to do; instead, they detect *acoustic* and *auditory* evidences, weigh them and combine them to form *cognitive* hypotheses, and then *validate* the hypotheses until consistent decisions can be reached.

Lately there has been an interest in developing ASR systems that encode more linguistic knowledge (e.g. [22]). Two recent Johns Hopkins University Summer Workshops featured development of ASR algorithms and systems, focusing on integrating information related to articulatory or acoustic-phonetic features, e.g. in speech production [10] and landmark-based ASR [17]. Along with the discussions in Allen [1], this human-based model of speech processing suggests a candidate framework for developing next-generation speech technologies that will go beyond the current limitations. Instead of the conventional top-down, network decoding paradigm, a bottom-up event detection and evidence combination paradigm for ASR, called automatic speech attribute transcription (ASAT), is illustrated in Figure 2.

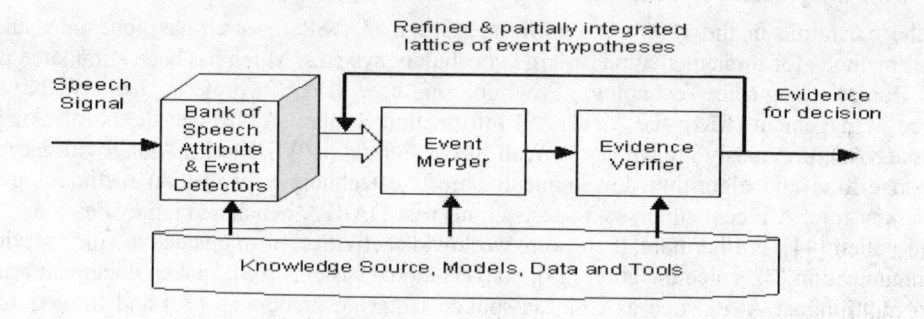

Figure 2: Bottom-up ASR based on attribute detection, event merging and evidence verification

Based on the bottom-up ASR paradigm described in the block diagram in Figure 1, ASAT [32] was recently sponsored by National Science Foundation in the US. Speech is first processed by a *bank of speech attribute detectors*, followed by a sequence of verifiers, validating evidences at every level of the linguistic knowledge hierarchy to recognize speech and other human information embedded in speech. Studies on key components in Figure 2 have been performed. A study on frame-based and segment-based speech event detectors can be found in Li [36]. An extension to word detection for any word is discussed in Ma [39]. Utterance verification based on a *generalized log likelihood ratio* (GLLR) which measures separation between models was studied as a test statistic in Sukkar [56], and used as confidence measures in Tsao [58] for speech events.

2.1 Speech Attribute Detection

An event or attribute can be the presence of a particular acoustic-phonetic cue, for example, "voicing" as a function of time. It can also characterize a speaking environment, such as an estimated confidence of how likely the noise background stays at a prescribed signal-to-noise (SNR) level, say 10dB, over time. Sometimes it can be used to represent the presence of important speech parameters, such as the gender, accent, and emotional state according to a *speaker's profile*. At the physiological response level, firing of a neuron can also be interpreted as an event. As discussed above, a properly designed score function of the detector can also be used to model the *a posteriori* probability of the event, given the observed speech signal. One key feature of the detection-based approach is that the outputs of the detectors do not have to be synchronized in time and therefore it is flexible to allow a direct integration of both short-term detectors, e.g. for detection of VOT, and long-term detectors, e.g. for detection of pitch, syllables, and particular word sequences.

An *event detector* converts an input speech signal into a time series, which describes the level of presence (or *level of activity*) of a particular property (or *attribute*) in the utterance over time. This function can be computed as the *a posteriori* probability of the particular attribute, given the signal, within a proper time window. The bank consists of a number of such attribute detectors, each being individually and best designed for the detection of a particular property. These properties are often stochastic in nature and are relevant to information needed to perform ASR.

The proposed detection paradigm, shown in Figure 2, is a "divide and conquer" strategy. It is possible for the speech science community to work together with the speech processing community in a collaborative manner to provide the best detectors for all speech attributes of interests, e.g. Lee [31]. A large body of literature exists for pitch tracking, formant estimation, voicing detection, and many other related problems. Recent efforts in classification of nasal and stop sounds demonstrated advantages of integrating speech knowledge, and signal processing techniques, e.g. Rabiner [45]. In an experiment, we show in Figure 3 that language-independent detection is feasible.

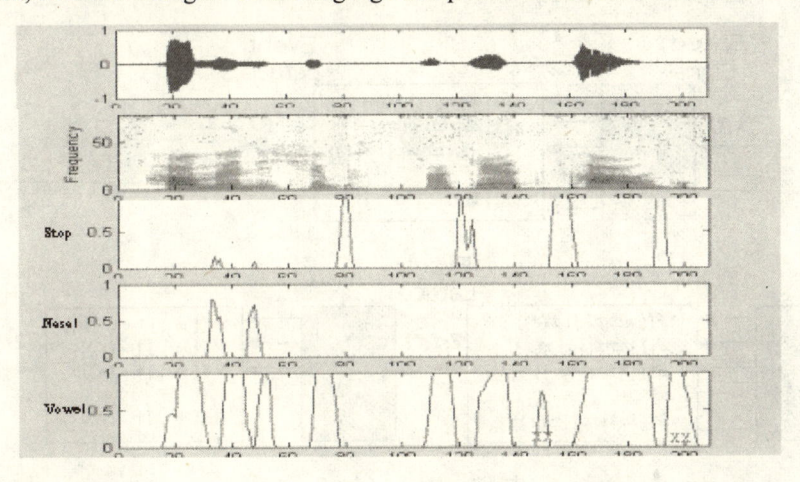

Figure 3: Detectors trained on Mandarin, tested on English spoken by a non-native speaker

In Figure 3, we show a good detection using three detectors, trained with Mandarin utterances and tested on an English utterance spoken by a non-native English speaker with a different type of microphone from the one used in recording the speech data in the training set. It is interesting to note that the four stops and the two nasals are all correctly detected. There were two false alarms in the bottom panel labeled "XX". Note both errors were caused by a mispronunciation.

In real-world event detection we have to use two competing HMMs to decode each utterance into the target and non-target segments, and compute the error rates accordingly. As shown in Li [36] the detectors optimized with discriminative training algorithms work better than the baseline HMM detectors when detectors are trained and tested using the TIMIT corpus. For silence, vowel and fricative attributes, over 96.4% accuracy was observed. On the other hand for stop and nasal manners the error rate was 5.4%. The approximant attribute with its time varying property gave the worst error rate of 6.1%. The results were quite encouraging even with only existing techniques.

2.2 Speech Event Merging

The *event merger* takes the set of detected events as input and attempts to infer the presence of higher level attributes (e.g. a phone or a word) which are then verified by the *event verifier* to produce a refined and partially integrated lattice of event hypotheses. This new lattice of hypotheses is then fed back for further knowledge integration. This iterative information fusion process always uses the original event activity functions as the raw evidence. A terminating strategy can be instituted by exhausting all the supported attributes. The procedure produces the evidence for a final decision or the recognized sentence itself, depending on the desired application.

The proposed approach, when applied to auditory processing, attempts to simulate the human auditory process by assuming that the speech signal is first converted to a collection of auditory response patterns (feature detection), each modeling the probabilistic activity level of a particular acoustic-phonetic event of interest shown in the A1 module in Figure 4. Detection of the next level of events or evidences, such as phones, is accomplished by combining relevant features from A1, as shown in the A2 module in Figure 4. Each activity function can be modeled by a corresponding neural system, or neuron. Both the activation level and firing rates have been used in neural encoding, e.g. Dayan [8]. ANNs provide a convenient mathematical tool to model neuron combinations and encoding of temporal neural information. Simulating perception of temporal events is of particular interest, e.g. Elman [11].

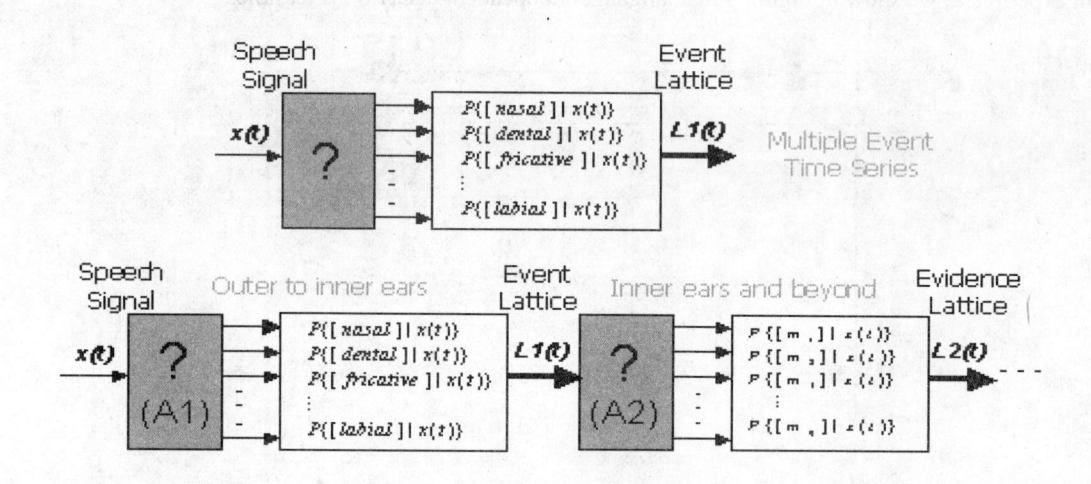

Figure 4: An auditory perception perspective of acoustic-phonetic event detection and combination

2.3 Evidence and Theory Verifiers

The plug-in MAP decoder to recognize the word sequence W in Eq. (1) is a *choose-one-of-the-above* scenario. It is not possible to cover all sentences and therefore it results in recognition errors if the sentence is not part of the set. We need to ask the question "why should we accept W as the recognized string?" and "can we assign a value to measure the confidence of our acceptance?" These two issues lead researchers to study three closely related topics, namely: (1) *keyword recognition* and *non-keyword rejection* [60]; (2) *utterance verification* (at both the string and word levels (e.g. [56, 48]); and (3) *confidence measures* (e.g. [28]).

Due to the overlapping nature of the two competing distributions, the verification performance is often evaluated as a combination of type I (*false alarm*) and II (*false acceptance*) errors. In many general speaker verification (SV) and utterance verification (UV) problems [56], the alternative assumes that X is not generated by the known source, which often means the alternative is a *composite* hypothesis as opposed to being a simple hypothesis which makes the design of optimal tests much more involved. In real-world practice, we form a test statistic $T(X)$, such that we accept the assumed target event if $T(X) \geq \omega$, where ω is a verification threshold. The *receiver operating characteristic*, or ROC, curve of a test provides a way of tuning the desired test performance, according to the choice of threshold values. Following Neyman-Pearson lemma, e.g. Lehmann [23], a *probability ratio* or *likelihood ratio* (LR) test is often performed. Likelihood functions of the distributions of the null and alternative hypotheses need to be evaluated for any input X. For verification of long *temporal* events, such as in utterance verification, consisting of a sequence of smaller events, a string-based log likelihood ratio (LLR) is usually decomposed into a sum of word- and phone-based LLR statistics computing target and anti scores [28], i.e.

$$T(X) = LLR(X \mid W) \approx \sum_i LLR(X_i \mid w_i) = \sum_i \left[\log f(X_i \mid \lambda_{w_i}) - \log f(X_i \mid \lambda_{\overline{w_i}}) \right] \quad (2)$$

$$LLR(X_i \mid w_i) \approx \sum_k LLR(X_{ik} \mid p_{ik}) = \sum_k \left[\log f(X_{ik} \mid \lambda_{w_{ik}}) - \log f(X_{ik} \mid \lambda_{\overline{w_{ik}}}) \right] \quad (3)$$

As an example, in phone detection, we can estimate the GLLR between two competing distributions given by a target phone model and a general speech filler model, e.g. Wilpon [60]. The models were built with the TIMIT training utterances. In the right curve in Figure 6, we plot the distribution for phone /d/ (using an IPA notation) and on the left we have the histogram for all the other "non-d" segments. A typical result for non-binary classification is that the curve for the target samples (on the right) is sharper than the one on the left (larger variance due to the more variety of non-target speech data). The mean of the right Gaussian density is greater than zero (the assumed verification threshold), indicating a correct detection most of the time, while the mean of the left Gaussian density is less than zero, showing a correct rejection for most "non-d" samples.

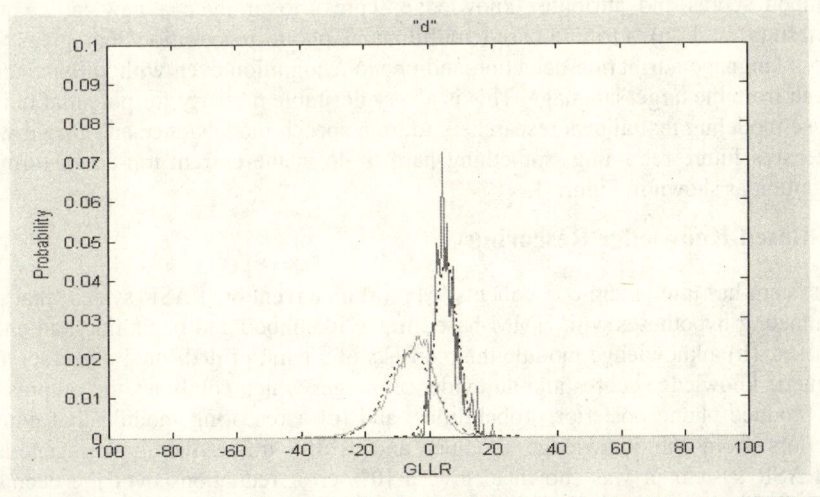

Figure 5: Verifying phone /d/ using HMM likelihood ratios trained and tested with TIMIT

In order to make use of the detected features, we must combine them in such a way that we can obtain word sequence hypotheses. In essence, this boils down to three problems: (a) combining multiple estimates of the same event to build a stronger hypothesis, (b) combining estimates of different events to form a new, higher level event with similar time boundaries, and (c) combining estimates of events sequentially to form longer-term hypotheses. While the canonical bottom-up processing sequence would be to combine multiple estimates of each feature, and then combine the features into phones, words and word sequences, we envision a paradigm that is flexible, for example, to combine a feature-based phone detector with a directly-estimated phone detector. In principle, a 20K-word system can be realized with a set of 20K individual keyword detectors [39]. An ASAT-like system has been realized with words used as detection attributes and shown to produce a system that performed partial understanding on ill-formed utterances, rejected out-of-task sentences and maintained good accuracies for in-grammar utterances [23].

Other higher-level information can also be utilized, including likelihood distributions of the phone durations as a validation criterion to help eliminate spurious hypotheses; similarly, using syllable boundary detection can cut down on the potential hypothesis space. In addition, we need to be sensitive to the phonetic variation that occurs in speech due to context. Phones that occur at the ends of syllables and/or words are more likely to be non-canonically pronounced than those in the beginning, e.g. Fosler-Lussier [13]. Similarly speech with a fast speaking rate tends to have more phonetic substitutions and deletions. Thus the sequence combination algorithm by forming words from phones in this case will need: (a) allowing some phones to be "looser" than others, and (b) being able to ask the verification question, *"does this hypothesis make sense in this environmental context?"*, similar to those asked in dynamic pronunciation modeling [13].

Decoding these sequential events will require iterative parsing of event lattices, such as the use of probabilistic chart parsers. We are usually highly confident in "islands of certainty", and then we fill in other words that are driven by top-down demands (e.g. syntax) rather than from bottom-up. Recent attempts of using conditional random fields gave good results, e.g. Morris [41].

3. SOME RECENT PROGRESS

The ASAT framework shown in the block diagram in Figure 2 is the basis for a number of recent studies. In the following we show two sets of key results: (a) a capability to improve state-of-the-art system performance by incorporating a set of acoustic phonetic detectors to provide additional information so that the hypotheses in recognition lattices can be rescored by combining frame-based HMM likelihood scores and attribute "knowledge scores" to produce a new lattice with better recognition results; and (b) attribute-based multilingual phone recognition that gives interesting results in cross-language attribution detection and phone recognition even without language-specific training speech from the target language. This is a very desirable property for potential universal and attribute phone modeling that allows researchers to train speech models once and for all without the need for extensive future retraining, something hard to do in the current top-down formulation of speech recognition as shown in Figure 1.

3.1 Lattice-Based Knowledge Rescoring

The overall system has three main components [51]: (a) a conventional ASR system that provides a lattice of competing hypotheses with HMM-based frame likelihood and beginning and end times of word hypotheses, (b) a knowledge module that consists of a bank of dedicated detectors to generate acoustic phonetic knowledge scores and an evidence merger which combines the outputs of speech detectors to produce phone posterior probabilities, and (c) a rescoring module that combines the phone posteriors from the knowledge module, and HMM frame likelihoods generated by a conventional ASR system. It was shown to give 5-10% error reductions over the decoding-based HMM systems [51] for continuous phone and word recognition. The most interesting fact was that for the WSJ evaluation, the detectors were still trained with the TIMIT data (no retraining on the

WSJ data), and for the 15 worst utterances, the knowledge rescoring system gave a 25% word error reduction, mostly on reducing substitution and insertion errors. A close look shows that conventional HMM-based systems sometimes produce recognition results that do not observe acoustic phonetic constraints as shown in the following example:

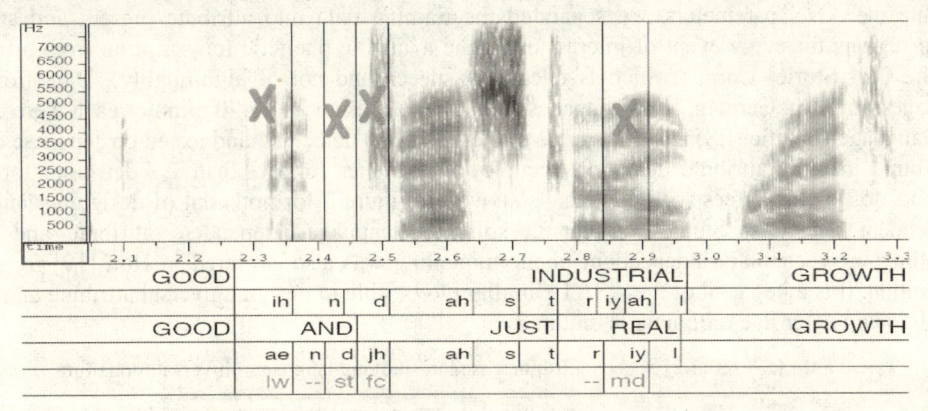

Figure 6: Diagnostic error correction by knowledge rescoring

Shown in the bottom five panels are corrected sentence, its corresponding phone sequence, wrongly-recognized sentence, its corresponding phone sequence, and the corresponding attributes that was poorly scored, respectively. The knowledge module heavily penalized the four regions marked as "x" in the top panel on the spectrogram of the speech segment displayed, because the four segments of the recognized sentence did not agree with the acoustic phonetic properties imposed by the set of attribute detectors. On the other hand, the correct sentence scored favorably for the four segments being considered, and therefore the rescoring module moved the correct sentence to the top ranked sentence and the recognition errors were all corrected.

3.2 Attribute-Based Universal Phone Modeling for Multilingual ASR

Following the ASAT paradigm discussed earlier in Figure 2 we use a phone recognition system shown in the block diagram in Figure 7, consisting of three main modules: (1) a bank of speech attribute detectors, (2) a set of phone mergers, and (3) an evidence verifier. The evidence verifier generates only the first best hypothesis as the recognized phone string for evaluating continuous phone recognition performance. Lattice rescoring has been shown to significantly improve phone and word recognition [51], and will not be addressed in the current study.

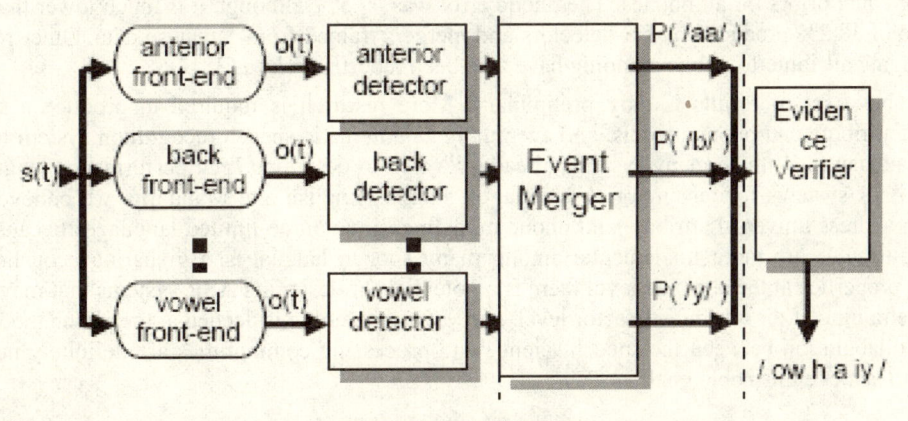

Figure 7: Overall system

Table 1 lists the set of 21 acoustic phonetic features [52] we used in our system for designing the attribute detectors. The main purpose of each attribute detector is to analyze speech and produce a confidence or posterior probability score that pertains to the acoustic phonetic attribute of interest. We built each detector with 3 feed-forward ANNs with one hidden layer of 500 hidden nodes. To estimate the ANN parameters, we separated the training data into attribute present and attribute absent regions for every event of interest using the available phonetic transcription from a training set (the OGI Stories Corpus which is telephony speech and not of high-quality). Data from five languages, English, German, Hindi, Japanese and Spanish, of about 45-70 minutes each were used to train language-specific (LS) and "language-universal" (LU) detectors, and tested on Japanese data. It was found that the attribute detection accuracy was higher for LU than LS detectors for many attributes [52]. This agrees with our results shown in Figure 3 for potential of designing language-independent detectors. Studies similar in spirit to language-independent attribute and phone modelling for vocabulary-independent phone modelling was also explored in Hon [19] for speech recognition. It is a key goal of the ASAT paradigm to be able to design universal attribute and phone models, so no extensive retraining is required.

Table 1: A set of 21 speech attributes used in studying language-universal modelling

Manner	approximant, fricative, nasal, vowel, stop
Place	anterior, back, continuant, coronal, dental, glottal, high, labial, low, mid, retroflex, round, silence, tense, velar, voiced

An attribute-to-phone merger shown in the middle part of Figure 7 produces a frame-level phone score by combining together detector outputs from attributes corresponding to the phone of interest with different weights. We call this process attribute-to-phone mapping. All phone mergers here were implemented using a single feed-forward ANN with one hidden layer of 800 hidden nodes. A softmax function was again used at the output layer. Again the merger can be trained using LS or LU data. However, training LU-based attribute-to-phone mapping is more difficult, when no target-language data are available and therefore it requires extensive knowledge shared among different languages to predict phone properties in an unseen language. A recent study was conducted on Japanese phone recognition [38] using LU-based attribute detectors trained from the five other languages from the OGI Story corpus. On the other hand the phone merger for Japanese was trained with only the Spanish data because of the shared five vowel property.

For continuous phone recognition Viterbi algorithm [46] was performed to generate a decoded sequence of phones as shown in the right part of Figure 7. The HMM state likelihoods needed were calculated from the phone posterior probabilities provided by the corresponding phone merger, assuming equal priors for all phones. The phone error was 47.5%, although it is much lower than the error rate of 38.2% produced by LS detectors and mergers trained from Japanese data. Other results on improving attribute-to-phone mapping have also been reported in Lyu [38].

The above set of results is only preliminary. More research is required to produce a set of universal attribute and phone models, and eventually an automatic speech recognition system for all spoken languages. With so many systems already devoted to designing high performance language-specific ASR systems for resource-rich languages, such as English and Mandarin, we believe it is timely to address universal attribute and phone modeling for resource-limited languages because we believe attributes are more fundamental among many spoken languages. By sharing acoustic and phonetic properties at the attribute level there is a potential for designing ASR systems that may only require retraining at the attribute detector level, and yet no retraining is needed at the phone modeling level. Collaboration between the speech science and processing communities are definitely needed in order to achieve this noble goal.

4. SUMMARY

We have briefly reviewed the present state of automatic speech recognition. Although we have learned a great deal about how to build and efficiently implement multilingual ASR systems, there remain a whole range of fundamental questions for which we have no definitive answers. We have presented an ASAT paradigm that provides a collaborative platform as a link between the two diverse communities of statistical signal processing and acoustic phonetics. This agrees in spirit with Prof. Wu Zongji's distinguished career in which speech science and processing always go hand in hand. We expect the ASAT paradigm for speech analysis and recognition be adopted by many well-established groups and new comers in both the science and processing communities to broaden speech research and education, and eventually close the performance gap between machine and human recognition of speech.

REFERENCES

[1] Allen, J. 1994. How Do Humans Process and Recognize Speech. *IEEE Trans. Speech and Audio Proc.*, Vol. 2, No. 4, 567-577.

[2] Bahl, L. R., Jelinek, F., Mercer, R. L. 1983. A Maximum Likelihood Approach to Continuous Speech Recognition. *IEEE Trans. Pattern Analysis, Machine Intelligence*, Vol. 5, No. 2, 179-190.

[3] Baker, J. K. 1975. The DRAGON System: An Overview. *IEEE Trans. Acous., Speech, Signal Proc.*, Vol. 23, No. 1, 24-29.

[4] Bellegarda, J. R. 2000. Exploiting Latent Semantic Information for Statistical Language Modeling. *Proc. IEEE*, Vol. 88, No. 8, 1279-1296.

[5] Bourlard, H., Morgan, D. 1994. *Connectionist Speech Recognition — A Hybrid Approach*. Kluwer Academic Press.

[6] Chomsky, N., Halle, M. 1968. *The Sound Pattern of English*. Harper and Row.

[7] Cox, R. V., Camm, C. A., Rabiner, L. R., Schroeter, J., Wilpon, J. G. 2000. Speech and Language Processing for Next-Millennium Communication Services. *Proc. IEEE*, Vol. 88, No. 8, 1273-1314.

[8] Dayan, P., Abbott, L. F. 2001. *Theoretical Neuroscience: Computational and Mathematical Modeling of Neural Systems*. The MIT Press.

[9] DeMori R. (ed.) 1998. *Spoken Dialogues with Computers*. Academic Press.

[10] Deng, L. 1997. Computational Models for Speech Production. In *Computational Models for Speech Pattern Processing* (NATO ASI Series), 199-214, Springer-Verlag.

[11] Elman, J. L. 1990. Finding Structures in Time. *Cognitive Science*, Vol.14, 179-221.

[12] Fant, G. 1973. *Speech Sounds and Features*. The MIT Press.

[13] Fosler-Lussier, E. 1999. *Dynamic Pronunciation Models for Automatic Speech Recognition*. PhD. Dissertation, University of California.

[14] Furui, S. 1980. A Training Procedure for Isolated Word Recognition Systems. *IEEE Trans. Acoust., Speech, Signal Processing*, Vol. 28, No. 2, 129-136.

[15] Gauvain, J.-L. Lee, C.-H. 1994. Maximum A Posteriori Estimation for Multivariate Gaussian Mixture Observations of Markov Chains. *IEEE Trans. on Speech and Audio Proc.*, Vol. 2, No. 2, 291-298.

[16] Gauvain, J.-L., Lamel, L. 2000. Large Vocabulary Continuous Speech Recognition: Advances and Applications. *Proc. IEEE*, Vol. 88, No. 8, 1181-1200.

[17] Hasegawa-Johnson, M. et al. 2004. WS04: Landmark-Based Large Vocabulary Speech Recognition, http://puccini.ifp.uiuc.edu:3455/1/Home.

[18] Haykin, S. 1994. *Neural Networks: A Comprehensive Foundation*. McMillan.

[19] Hon, H. W. 1992. *Vocabulary-Independent Speech Recognition: The VOCIND System*. PhD. Dissertation, School of Computer Science, Carnegie Mellon University.

[20] Huo, Q., Lee, C.-H. 2001. Robust Speech Recognition Based on Adaptive Classification and Decision Strategies. *Speech Communication*, Vol. 34, Nos. 1-2, 175-194.

[21] Jelinek, F. 1985. The Development of an Experimental Discrete Dictation Recognizer. *Proc. IEEE*, Vol. 73, No. 10, 1616-1624.
[22] Jelinek, F. 1997. *Statistical Method for Speech Recognition*. The MIT Press.
[23] Kawahara, T., Lee, C.-H., Juang, B.-H. 1998. Key-Phrase Detection and Verification for Flexible Speech Understanding. *IEEE Trans. Speech and Audio Proc.*, Vol. 6, No. 6, 558-568.
[24] Kirchhoff. K. 1998. Combining Articulatory and Acoustic Information for Speech Recognition in Noisy and Reverberant Environments. *Proc. ICSLP-98*, 891-894, Sydney, Australia.
[25] Klatt, D. 1977. Review of the ARPA Speech Understanding Project. *J. Acous. Soc. Am.*, Vol. 62, No. 6.
[26] Lee, C.-H., Soong, F. K., Paliwal K.K. (eds.) 1996. *Automatic Speech and Speaker Recognition: Advanced Topics*. Kluwer Academic Publishers.
[27] Lee, C.-H., Huo, Q. 2000. On Adaptive Decision Rules and Decision Parameter Adaptation for Automatic Speech Recognition. *Proc. IEEE*, Vol. 88, No. 8, 1241-1269.
[28] Lee, C.-H. 2001. Statistical Confidence Measures and Their Applications. *Proc. ICSP-01*.
[29] Lee, C.-H. 2004. From Knowledge-ignorant to Knowledge-Rich Modeling: A New Speech Research Paradigm for Next Generation Automatic Speech Recognition. *Proc. ICSLP-04*.
[30] Lee, C.-H., Li, H., Lee, L.-S., Wang, R.-H. Huo, Q. (eds.) 2006. *Advances in Chinese Spoken Language Processing*. World Scientific Publishing Co.
[31] Lee, C.-H. 2006. Back to Speech Science — Towards a Collaborative ASR Community of the 21st Century, In: P. Divenyi, S. Greenberg, G. Meyer (eds.), *Dynamics in Speech Production and Perception*, NATO Science Series. IOS Press.
[32] Lee, C.-H. 2007. An Overview on Automatic Speech Attribute Transcription (ASAT). *Proc. Interspeech-07*.
[33] Leggetter, J., Woodland, P.C. 1995. Maximum likelihood linear regression for speaker adaptation of continuous density hidden Markov models. *Computer Speech and Language*, Vol. 9, 171-185.
[34] Lehmann, L. 1959. *Testing Statistical Hypotheses*. John Wiley & Son.
[35] Levinson, S. E. 1985. Structural Methods in Automatic Speech Recognition. *Proc. IEEE*, Vol. 73, 1625-1650.
[36] Li, J., Lee, C.-H. 2005. On Designing and Evaluating Speech Event Detectors. *Proc. InterSpeech-05*.
[37] Lippmann, R. 1997. Speech Recognition by Human and Machines. *Speech Communication*, Vol. 22, 1-14.
[38] Lyu, D., Siniscalchi, S. M., Kim T.-Y., Lee, C.-H. 2008. An Experimental Study on Continuous Phone Recognition with Little or No Language-Specific Training Data. *Proc. ITRW2008*, Aalborg, Denmark.
[39] Ma, C., Lee, C.-H. 2007. A Study on Word Detector Design and Knowledge-Based Pruning and Rescoring. *Proc. Interspeech-07*.
[40] Makhoul, J., Kubala, F., Leek, T., Liu, D., Nguyen, L., Schwartz, R., Srivastava, A. 2000. Speech and Language Technologies for Audio Indexing and Retrieval. *Proc. IEEE*, Vol. 88, No. 8, 1338-1353.
[41] Morris J., Fosler-Lussier, E. 2008. Conditional Random Fields for Integrating Local Discriminative Classifiers. *IEEE Trans. Acous., Speech, and Language Proc.*, Vol. 16, No. 3, 617-628.
[42] Ney, H., Ortmanns, S. 2000. Progresses in Dynamic Programming Search for LVCSR. *Proc. IEEE*, Vol. 88, No. 8, 1224-1240.
[43] Nilsson, N. J. 1971. *Problem-Solving Methods in Artificial Intelligence*. McGraw Hill.
[44] Pallett, D. 2003. A Look at NIST's Benchmark ASR Test: Past, Present, and Future. *Proc. IEEE ASRU Workshop 2003*, 483-488.
[45] Rabiner, L. R., Schafer, R. W. 1978. *Digital Processing of Speech Signals*. Prentice-Hall.
[46] Rabiner, L. R. 1989. A Tutorial on Hidden Markov Models and Selected Applications in Speech Recognition. *Proc. IEEE*, Vol. 77, No. 2, 257-286.
[47] Rabiner, L. R., Juang, B.-H. 1993. *Fundamentals of Speech Recognition*. Prentice-Hall.
[48] Rahim, M., Lee, C.-H. 1997, String-Based Minimum Verification Error (SB-MVE) Training for Speech Recognition. *Computer, Speech and Language*, Vol. 11, No. 2, 147-160.
[49] Rosenfeld, R. 2000. Two Decades of Statistical Language Modeling: Where Do We Go from Here? *Proc. IEEE*, Vol. 88, No. 8, 1279-1296.

[50] Shinoda, K., Lee, C.-H. 2001. A Structural Bayes Approach to Speaker Adaptation. *IEEE Trans. Speech and Audio Proc.*, Vol. 9, No. 3, 276-287.

[51] Siniscalchi, S. M., Li, J., Lee, C.-H. 2006. A Study on Lattice Scoring with Knowledge Scores for Automatic Speech Recognition. *Proc. InterSpeech-06.*

[52] Siniscalchi, S., M. Svendsen, T., Lee, C.-H. 2008. Toward A Detector-Based Universal Phone Recognizer. *Proc. ICASSP-08.*

[53] Siohan, O., Chesta, C., Lee, C.-H. 2001. Joint Maximum a Posteriori Adaptation of Transformation and HMM Parameters. *IEEE Trans. on Speech and Audio Proc.*, Vol. 9, No. 4, 417-428.

[54] Siohan, O., Myrvoll, T. A., Lee, C.-H. 2002. Structural Maximum A Posteriori Linear Regression for HMM Adaptation. *Computer Speech and Language.*

[55] Stevens, K. 1998. *Acoustic Phonetics.* The MIT Press.

[56] Sukkar, R. A., Lee, C.-H. 1996. Vocabulary Independent Discriminative Utterance Verification for Non-Keyword Rejection in Subword Based Speech Recognition. *IEEE Trans. on Speech and Audio Proc.*, Vol. 4, No. 6, 420-429.

[57] Tokuda, K., Zen, H., Black, A. W. 2004. HMM-based approach to multilingual speech synthesis, In:S. Narayanan, A. Alwan (eds.), *Text to speech synthesis: New paradigms and advances.* Prentice Hall.

[58] Tsao, Y., Li, J., Lee, C.-H. 2005. A Study on Separation between Acoustic Models and Its Applications. *Proc. InterSpeech-05.*

[59] Waibel, A., Geutner, P., Tomokiro, L. M., Schultz, T., Woszczyna, M. 2000. Multilinguality in Speech and Spoken Language Systems. *Proc. IEEE*, Vol. 88, No. 8, 1297-1315.

[60] Wilpon, J. G., Rabiner, L. R., Lee, C.-H., Goldman, E. R. 1990. Automatic Recognition of Keywords in Unconstrained Speech Using Hidden Markov Models. *IEEE Trans. Acoustic, Speech and Signal Proc.*, Vol. ASSP-38, No. 11, 1870-1878.

[61] Yamagishi, J., Kobayashi, T. 2007. Average-voice-based speech synthesis using HSMM-based speaker adaptation and adaptive training. *IEICE Trans. on Inf. & Syst.*, Vol.E90-D, No.2, 533-543.

[62] Young, S., Odell, J., Ollason, J., Valtchev, V., Woodland, P. 1997. *The HTK Book.* Cambridge University.

[63] Zue, V.W., Glass, J. R. 2000. Conversational Interfaces: Advances and Challenges. *Proc. IEEE*, Vol. 88, No. 8, 1166-1180.

THE LATVIAN "BROKEN TONE"

Ilse LEHISTE

ABSTRACT

The paper reports on an acoustic-phonetic study of Latvian tones. The system is traditionally described as consisting of three tones: a falling tone, an even or level tone, and a so-called broken tone, characterized by a glottal stop in the middle of the syllable nucleus, followed by a voiceless third part. The falling and level tones turned out to correspond to previous descriptions; the broken tone showed considerable variability. Irregular phonation was almost always present, but none of the five tested speakers used an actual glottal stop.

Keywords: Latvian prosody; ternary tonal oppositions; phonetic nature of the Latvian third (broken) tone

1. INTRODUCTION

The prosodic system of Latvian includes a length opposition and a tonal opposition. Vowels can be contrastively short or long in any position of the word. The actual duration of vowels is partly dependent on tone. Standard Latvian is described as having three tones on long syllable nuclei — falling, even or drawn, and a third tone frequently referred to as "broken tone". The terms are adaptations of the German terms *fallender Ton*, *Dehnton,* and *Stosston* given by Endzelin, who was the first to describe them in his 1899 German-language publication [2]. The current paper presents the results of an acoustic-phonetic study of the prosody of Latvian, focusing on the phonetic realization of syllables bearing the broken tone.

2. PREVIOUS DESCRIPTIONS

The most recent available description of Latvian tones is given in an article by Laimute Balode and Axel Holvoet (in [1]). According to Balode and Holvoet (p. 14), the falling tone is characterized by greater intensity and higher pitch in the initial part of the vocalic segment; the drawn tone shows no decrease in either intensity or pitch, both being maintained at the same level; and the broken tone resembles the falling tone in having a more prominent first part, but this first part is followed by a glottal stop, and the second part — following the glottal stop — is voiceless (whispered).

Balode and Holvoet also describe various modifications of the prosodic system in Latvian dialects. In most of the Central dialect, the falling and broken tones have merged into a single broken tone; in High Latvian (Letgalian), the falling and drawn tones have merged, resulting in an opposition between presence and absence of glottalization, similar to Danish *stød*.

Falling and level tones are relatively common; the broken tone is rare. Its occurrence in Latvian appeared worthy of special attention, given the fact that Latvian is spoken on the shores of the Baltic Sea, and that two other languages in the same area (Danish and Livonian) have a similar prosodic feature.

3. MATERIAL AND METHOD

The study of Latvian prosody is part of a considerably more extensive project [4], of which the current paper constitutes a sample. The set of data that will be presented in this context is derived from recordings of a poem by E. Zalite, read by five speakers. The recordings were made at the University of Latvia in Riga, and analyzed at The Ohio State University in Columbus. The poem consists of six four-line stanzas, for a total of 24 lines. The odd-numbered lines of each stanza contain four disyllabic trochaic metric feet; the even-numbered lines consist of three disyllabic feet and a final monosyllabic foot. All disyllabic foot types are represented: there are 18 short-short metric feet, 17 short-long, 27 long-short, and 22 long-long metric feet, plus 12 monosyllabic feet, for a total of 96 metric feet. As there were five speakers, the total material comprises 480 metric feet.

The tones were identified by Professor Laimdots Ceplitis of the University of Latvia and three of his colleagues, both for what could be considered normative realization of the accents, and for each speaker separately.

The measurements include the following: duration of metric feet, duration of pauses between lines and between stanzas, duration of potential accent-bearing syllable nuclei (vowels and vowel+ resonant sequences), fundamental frequency at the beginning and end of the syllable nucleus, fundamental frequency at the peak of the fundamental frequency curve, and position of the peak relative to the beginning of the syllable nucleus. The results of the measurements were averaged separately for each speaker and together for the five speakers.

Intonation is liable to interact with word-level fundamental frequency at the beginning and end of the line. The fundamental frequency patterns are therefore described with reference to metric feet occurring in the second and third position within the four-foot line.

4. RESULTS

The acoustic shape of the falling and drawn tones conformed to expectations. The syllable nuclei bearing the broken tone differed from previous descriptions in numerous ways; these are summarized in Table 1.

Table 1: Acoustic characteristics of syllable nuclei expected to carry the broken tone in productions of a Latvian poem by five readers.

	Sp. 1	Sp. 2	Sp. 3	Sp. 4	Sp. 5	Total
Number expected	29	34	28	39	32	162
Negative F_0 peak	1	4	8	0	3	16
Intensity change	2	2	1	4	3	12
Falling-level F_0	0	1	4	5	2	12
Voiced/voiceless SN	0	0	0	2	6	8
Falling F_0	24	12	7	9	10	62
Even F_0	2	2	5	11	4	24
Not measurable	0	13	3	8	4	28

The features associated with the syllable nuclei that were expected to carry the broken tone included the following: a glottal stop at approximately the middle of the syllable nucleus, a "negative peak" in the F_0 curve, and a division of the syllable nucleus into two parts, which could be manifested in various ways — as an abrupt change in the intensity of the formants on a broad-band spectrogram, in a pitch curve consisting of a fall in the first half and a level pattern on the second half, and of full voicing in the first half, with devoicing, whispering or laryngealization in the second half.

Not all of the syllable nuclei marked by the Latvian linguists as bearing the broken tone had these characteristics. For each speaker, the majority of the syllable nuclei that had been marked as such actually did not differ from the other two patterns. The falling pattern appeared to be used more often than the level pattern. Also, the speakers did not necessarily agree among themselves in the realization of a word that had been marked as expected to carry the broken accent: in the speech of each some might have a falling realization, some an even realization, and one or more might have one of the characteristics described above. Incidentally, there were no clearly identifiable glottal stops in any of the productions.

Still, some generalizations can be made. Speaker 3 had the largest number of negative F_0 peaks. Speaker 4 favored an F_0 curve that falls in the first half and remains level on the second half. Speaker 5 had the largest number of instances in which the second half of the syllable nucleus was voiceless. All speakers except Speaker 4 favored the use of the falling tone as a substitute for the broken tone, but Speaker 4 preferred the even tone. As a group, the five speakers used some kind of acoustic pattern that differed from the established falling and even patterns in 48 out of 162 expected occurrences of the broken tone, or in 29.6% of the cases. In spite of the somewhat chameleon-like character of the broken tone, it seems to possess a certain amount of phonetic reality.

I should like to conclude with a reference to an earlier publication of mine [3]. In that paper I reported on an acoustic analysis of 239 Latvian utterances produced by the Latvian linguist Valdis Zeps at the Communication Sciences Laboratory of the University of Michigan in 1958 — fifty years ago. There were 117 instances of occurrences of the broken tone. I will quote now from pp. 310-311 of the earlier article:

"In most occurrences, the third tone was manifested as a change in the phonation pattern used during the production of the syllable carrying the tone. The syllable nucleus started with normal phonation; the normally phonated part lasted for approximately half of the total duration of the syllable nucleus. This first stage was followed by a second, during which the phonation pattern changed abruptly and markedly. ... The interruption was followed by a third stage, whose mode of phonation varied between regular phonation, laryngealization and voicelessness. The duration of the interruption and the third stage together was approximately as great as that of the regularly phonated first stage."

There is a generation's difference between Valdis Zeps and the speakers whose productions have just been presented. There was variability in this speech in the phonetic manifestation of the broken tone, but it was present in every instance. What can be observed in comparing the two sets of data is a gradual change of the prosodic system of Latvian. On the basis of the data summarized in Table 1, the change is in the direction of a merger of the broken tone with the falling tone.

REFERENCES

[1] Balode, L., Holvoet, A. 2001. The Latvian language and its dialects. In: Dahl, Ö., Koptjevskaja-Tamm, M. (eds.), *Circum-Baltic Languages,* Volume I: Past and Present. Amsterdam/Philadelphia: John Benjamins Publishing Company, 3-40.

[2] Endzelin, J. 1899. Über den lettischen Silbenakzent. *Beiträge zur Kunde der indogermanischen Sprachen* 25, 259-74.

[3] Lehiste, I. 1972. Some observations concerning the third tone in Latvian. In: Valdman, A. (ed.), *Papers in Linguistics and Phonetics to the Memory of Pierre Delattre.* The Hague and Paris: Mouton, 309-315.

[4] Lehiste, I. 1992. The phonetics of metrics. *Empirical Studies of the Arts* 10 (2), 95-120.

A CONTRASTIVE PHONETIC STUDY BETWEEN CANTONESE AND ENGLISH TO PREDICT SALIENT MISPRONUNCIATIONS BY CANTONESE LEARNERS OF ENGLISH

Helen MENG

ABSTRACT

This work aims to derive salient mispronunciations made by Cantonese (L1) learners of English (L2) in order to support the design pedagogical and remedial instructions. Our approach is grounded on the theory of language transfer and involves systematic phonological comparisons between the two languages at the phonetic, phonotactic and prosodic levels. Major disparities across the language pair are identified to focus on phonological contexts where transfer effects are prominent. This methodology enables us to propose salient pronunciation errors that are cross-validated with anecdotal examples observed from daily conversational interactions.

Keywords: salient mispronunciations, second language acquisition

1. INTRODUCTION

The objective of this work is to derive salient mispronunciations made by Cantonese (L1) learners of English (L2). Our long-term goal is to design effective pedagogical and remedial instructions for pronunciation improvement. The target learners are adults (university students) who are native Cantonese speakers seeking to improve their pronunciation of English. In this work, the primary language (L1) is Cantonese, a major dialect spoken by over 60 million people in Hong Kong, Macau, South China and many oversees communities. The secondary language (L2) is American English.

Pronunciation errors may be due to a diversity of factors, such as an imperfect understanding of semantics, syntax, morphology, phonology, coarticulatory effects and letter-to-sound rules. As an initial step, we focus on phonology. Our proposed approach is grounded on the theory of language transfer [2][5] and involves phonological comparisons between L1 and L2 across the phonetic, phonotactic and prosodic levels. We identify major disparities across the language pair, such as missing phones and violation of phonotactic constraints, in order to focus on phonological contexts where perceived interferences of transfer features are prominent. This procedure enables us to devise a methodology for proposing salient mispronunciations that are cross-validated with anecdotal examples observed from daily conversational interactions with university students over many years. The linguistic discrepancies may also offer an explanatory model for us to understand the cause of errors [1]. In the following, we present the results of our comparison at different phonological levels and provide illustrate examples of mispronunciations.

2. PHONETIC COMPARISON

2.1 Vowels and diphthongs

Figure 1 illustrates the Cantonese vowel charts containing the 4 short vowels, 7 long vowels and 10 diphthongs. Appendix A presents some Chinese characters whose syllable pronunciations contain these vowels and diphthongs. Meanings of the characters are parenthesized. Figure 2 illustrates the American English vowel charts containing the 13 vowels and 3 diphthongs in American English. The reduced vowel /ə/ is excluded because its quality varies considerably based on co-articulatory context [4]. Appendix B presents English words containing these vowels and diphthongs [8].

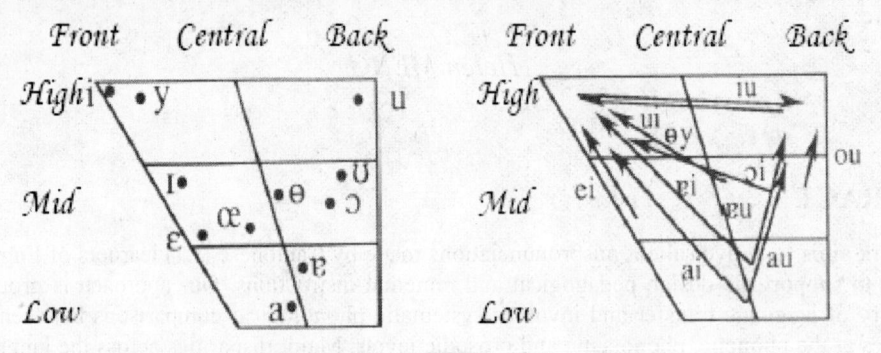

Figure 1: Cantonese vowels and diphthongs, based on [6]
Tongue positions (front, central, back, high, mid, low) are labeled.

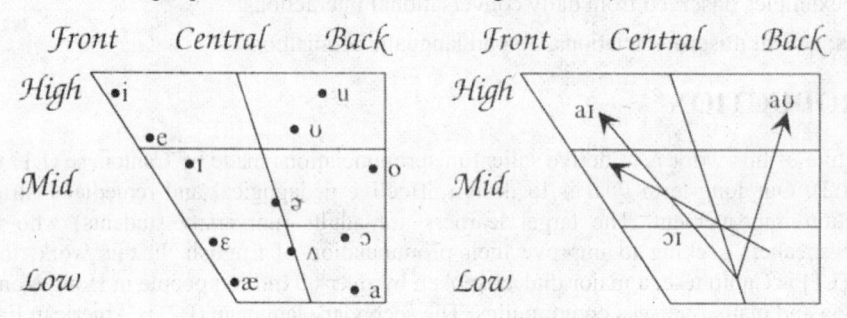

Figure 2: American English vowels & diphthongs, based on [4]

Comparison between the vowel charts in Figures 1 and 2 helps organize our observations on common mispronunciations due to English vowels that are missing in the Cantonese phonetic inventory. This missing set includes /e, æ, o, ɚ ʌ, a/. Hence when Cantonese native speakers enunciate these English vowels, they replace with Cantonese vowels that are close in terms of production and perception. Depending on the degree of resemblance, a subset of these vowels may be perceived as mispronunciations, due to prominent transfer effects from Cantonese (L1) to English (L2). Table 1 offers illustrative examples. Common substitutions for the remaining vowels in the missing set are shown in Table 2 and these are often deemed acceptable.

Table 1: Salient vowel mispronunciations of Cantonese speakers learning English

Target English Vowel	Replacement from Cantonese	Examples of mispronunciations
æ	ɛ	"had" /hæd/ is often pronounced inaccurately as "head" /hɛd/.
ɚ	œ	Retroflexion is replaced with lip-rounding, e.g., "her" /h ɚ/ is replaced by /hœ/, which sounds like 靴 (boot).
ɑ	ɐ	The English vowel /ɑ/ (e.g. in the pronunciation of "dodge") typically has lower first and second formant frequencies than the Cantonese /ɐ/ [7] (e.g. in the pronunciation of 打 "hit"). The perceived difference, however, may be subtle.
ə	variable	The chosen substitute for the English reduced vowel /ə/ varies based on the articulatory context as Cantonese does not have a reduced vowel. For example, "about" /əbaʊt/ may be mispronounced as /abaʊt/.

Table 2: Substitutions deemed acceptable between target English vowels and their Cantonese counterparts

Target English Vowel	Replacement from Cantonese	Examples of mispronunciations
e	ei	"say" /se/ versus 四 /sei/
o	ou	"sew" /so/ versus 苏 /sou/
ʌ	ɐ	"gut" /gʌt/ versus 吉 /gɐt/

Additionally, there are vowels that are present in both Cantonese and English, namely /ɪ, i, ʊ, u, ɔ/. Cantonese speakers tend to substitute the English vowels with their close L1 neighbors. Examples are shown in Table 3. The first two involve mispronunciations in terms of tense-lax confusions. We conjecture that a possible reason is due to phonotactic constraints, as will be explained in a later section.

Table 3: Substitutions among long and short vowels

Target English Vowel	Replacement from Cantonese	Examples of frequent mispronunciations
ɪ	i	"sit" /sɪt/ mispronounced as "seat" /sit/
ʊ	u	"full" /fʊl/ mispronounced as "fool" /ful/
ɔ	ɔ	"caught" /kɔt/ mispronounced and sounds like "cot" (as the Cantonese /ɔ/ has a shorter duration)

2.2 Consonants

Tables 4 and 5 shows the consonants in Cantonese and American English respectively, organized according to the manner and place of articulation. Comparison between the two tables helps structure our observations in common mispronunciations for Cantonese learners of English. We refer specifically to English consonants that are missing from the Cantonese inventory, including voiced plosives, fricatives and affricates. Cantonese learners often substitute for these missing English consonants with Cantonese consonants that have similar place and/or manner of articulation. We present details in the following subsections.

2.2.1 Missing voiced plosives

The voiced plosives /b, d, g/ are present in English but absent in Cantonese. In the *prevocalic* position, these are often substituted with the voiceless, unaspirated Cantonese plosives /p, t, k/ which serve as good approximations. However, in the postvocalic position, voiced plosives may be unaspirated and voicing may be realized as durational lengthening of the preceding syllable nucleus. This leads to the durational difference within the contrastive word pairs: "cab" versus "cap" (/kæb/ versus /kæp/), or "pad" versus "pat" (/pæd/ vs. /pæt/). These word pairs are often not clearly distinguished by Cantonese learners, e.g.

- "feed" /fid/ is pronounced as "feet" /fit/
- "bag" /bæg/ is pronounced as "back" /bæk/, etc.

2.2.2 Missing Affricates

English affricates are post-alveolar and include unvoiced and voiced tokens, namely, /tʃ, dʒ/. These are non-existent in Cantonese and are often replaced respectively with the aspirated and unaspirated alveolar affricates /tsʰ, ts/. These have close resemblance in the place of articulation, e.g.

- "charge" /tʃ a r dʒ/ is often mispronounced like 又住 / tsʰ a ts y/, which a transliteration and not a word

In this example, the voiced pre-palatal affricate /dʒ/ in English occurs in a postvocalic position and is realized as the alveolar affricate /ts/ in Cantonese. However, since Cantonese affricates must be prevocalic due to phonotactic constraints, the mispronunciation adds a syllable nucleus at the word ending. Suitable candidates may be the palatal vowels /y, i/, which have matching tongue position during articulation. The former may be preferable as it involves lip rounding, which resembles lip protrusion during articulation of /dʒ/.

2.2.3 Missing Fricatives

This subsection addresses English fricatives that are missing from the Cantonese inventory. We describe the common substitutions performed by Cantonese learners of English.

Table 4: Consonants in Cantonese, organized according to the manner and place of articulation

	Bilabial	Labio-dental	Labio-velar	Dental	Alveolar	Pre-palatal	Palatal	Velar	Glottal
Plosive	p, pʰ				t, tʰ			k, kʰ kʷ, kʷʰ	
Affricate					ts, tsʰ				
Nasal	m				n			ŋ	
Fricative		f			s				h
Approximant	w						j	(w)	
Lateral Approximant					l				

based on [Zee, 1991]

Table 5: Consonants in American English

	Bilabial	Labio-dental	Labio-velar	Dental	Alveolar	Pre-palatal	Palatal	Velar	Glottal
Plosive	p, pʰ, b				t, tʰ, d			k, kʰ g	
Affricate						tʃ, dʒ			
Nasal	m				n			ŋ	
Fricative		f, v		θ, ð	s, z	ʃ, ʒ			h
Approximant	w				r		j	w	
Lateral Approximant					l				

based on [Ladefoged, 1999]

The English /v/, a voiced, labiodental fricative, is often mispronounced either as the voiceless labiodental fricative /f/ or the sonorant bilabial approximant /w/. Examples include: "vast" /væst/ versus "fast" /fæst/

- "vest" /vɛst/ versus "west" /wɛst/.

There are two English dental fricatives. /θ/ is voiceless and is often mispronounced as the voiceless Cantonese labiodental /f/. /ð/ is voiced and is often mispronounced as the voiced alveolar plosive in Cantonese /t/. Examples include:

- "three" /θri/ versus "free" /fri/
- "there" /ðɛr/ versus "dare" /tɛr/

The English alveolar, voiced fricative /z/ is often mispronounced as the voiceless /s/, e.g.

- "seize" /siz/ versus "sees" /sis/
- "zinc" /zɪŋk/ versus "sink" /sɪŋk/

The English unvoiced post-alveolar and voiced fricatives /ʃ, ʒ/ are frequently substituted with the voiceless alveolar /s/. Examples include:

- "show" /ʃo/ versus "so" /so/
- "social" /soʃəl/ versus "soso" /soʃəl/

2.2.4 Missing Approximants

Articulation of the English approximant /r/ involves lip rounding and retroflexion. /r/ is absent from Cantonese and is often substituted with /w/ (rounded approximant) or /l/ (lateral approximant), e.g.

- "rate" /ret/ versus "wait" /wet/
- "very" /vɛri/ as /vɛli/ or /wɛli/

2.2.5 Confusion among /n/ and /l/

This subsection is different from the others as it describes a specific confusion between the alveolar nasal /n/ and the lateral approximant /l/. In colloquial Cantonese, /n/ is often substituted with /l/. This substitution is generally deemed acceptable, e.g.

- 你 (you) /nei/ pronounced as 理 (logic) /lei/

A similar substitution frequently occurs for the prevocalic nasal /n/ in English words uttered by Cantonese learners. This substitution is perceived as a prominent mispronunciation, e.g.
- "nine" /n ay n/ as "line" /l ay n/.

3. PHONOTACTIC COMPARISON

The Cantonese syllable has a simple [C]V[C] structure, where the optional syllable onset contains one consonant (except for /kw/ or /kʰw/) and the optional syllable coda also contains one consonant. Similarly, the syllable onset and coda are optional in the English syllable, but each may contain up to three consonants, such as in the word "strengths" /strɛŋθs/. Cantonese learners frequently mispronounce English consonant clusters, either with *vowel addition* in the word-final position, e.g.
- "kissed" /kɪst/ becomes /kɪstɐ/

or *consonant deletion*, e.g.
- "exact" /ɪkzækt/ becomes /ɪk-sɛk/
- "professor" /prəfɛsə/ becomes /pou-fɛ-sa/

Both processes attempt to generate syllables that are compatible the Cantonese syllable structure.

Cantonese phonotactic constraints [5] may also be a possible cause for other phonetic substitutions in mispronunciations made by Cantonese learners, e.g.
- "tone" /t o n/ pronounced as 通 (reach) /t ou ŋ/
- "bill" /bɪl/ pronounced as 标 (sign) /b iu/
- "in" /ɪn/ pronounced as 烟 (smoke) /jɪn/

The first example word "tone" contains the English vowel /o/, whose closest Cantonese counterpart may be diphthong /ou/. However, this diphthong typically occurs in an open syllable. We may substitute with the vowel /ʊ/ since it has similar quality, but if /ʊ/ should close with a nasalized coda, it must be the velar /ŋ/. These factors may cause "tone" to be mispronounced as /t ou ŋ/. In the second example, the word "bill" contains a postvocalic /l/. This consonant never closes a syllable in Cantonese but its manifestation bears similarity to lip rounding. Hence the Cantonese diphthong /iu/ may serve as a perceptually close substitute for /ɪl/ and cause "bill" to be mispronounced as /b iu/. In the third example, the word "in" contains the vowel /ɪ/. This vowel must be preceded with a syllable onset in Cantonese and insertion of /j/ offers the closest matching place of articulation. Hence "in" becomes /jɪn/.

4. PROSODIC COMPARISON

English and Cantonese have significant differences in prosodic features such as loudness, duration, and pitch. A major contributor to such differences is syllable stress. English syllables may be unstressed (reduced), or they may carry primary or secondary stress. For example, the word "aeroplane" has three syllables carrying primary stress, no stress (unstressed) and secondary stress respectively. Stressed syllables generally have higher energies, longer durations and higher pitch frequencies. The strong and weak stress patterns generate rhythm in English, to which we refer as a stress-timed language.

Cantonese syllables have approximately equal durations, i.e. it is a syllable-timed language. Stressed and unstressed syllables in English are often pronounced by Cantonese learners with largely uniform durations, but that stressed syllables often have higher tones. These tone frequencies are further influenced by the lexical (nine-)tone system that is characteristic of Cantonese. Hence, Cantonese learners tend to speak English with a different rhythm.

5. CONCLUSION

This paper describes an initial effort to derive a list of salient pronunciation errors made by Cantonese learners of English. The proposed approach is grounded on the theory of language transfer and involves phonological comparisons between Hong Kong Cantonese (L1) and American English (L2) across the phonetic, phonotactic and prosodic levels. We identify major disparities across the two languages, which are believed to heighten the perceived phonological interference of transfer features and cause mispronunciations. Systematic phonological comparisons across the various linguistic levels enable us to devise a methodology for deriving salient mispronunciations in second language acquisition, organize anecdotal examples observed from daily conversational interactions, as well as understand the cause of errors in order to design pedagogical and remedial instructions. Future work involves the design and collection of speech corpora in order to empirically verify the mispronunciations derived above. We will also generalize the proposed methodology to derive mispronunciations made by Mandarin (L1) learners of American English (L2).

6. ACKNOWLEDGEMENTS

We wish to thank Professor Eric Zee and Professor Wai-Sum Lee of the Phonetics Laboratory, Department of Chinese, Translation and Linguistics of the City University of Hong Kong, for many helpful discussions.

REFERENCES

[1] Chan, A., Li, D. 2000. English and Cantonese Phonology in Contrast: Explaining Cantonese ESL Learner's English Pronunciation Problems. *Language, Culture & Curriculum*, 13:1.
[2] Ellis, R. 1994. *The Study of Second Language Acquisition.* Oxford University Press.
[3] Ho, R. 2005. 粤音自学提纲。香港教育图书公司。
[4] Ladefoged, P. 1999. American English. *Handbook of the IPA*. Cambridge University Press.
[5] Lado, R. 1964. *Linguistics Across Cultures: Applied Linguistics for Language Teachers.* University of Michigan Press.
[6] Zee, E. 1991. Chinese (Hong Kong Cantonese), *Journal of International Phonetic Association*, 21:1.
[7] Zee, E. 2003. Frequency analysis of the vowels in Cantonese from 50 male and 50 female speakers, *Proc. ICPhS*, Barcelona.
[8] Zue, V. 1991. Notes on Speech Spectrogram Reading. *MIT Summer Course*, 1991.

Appendix A: Cantonese vowels and diphthongs in the context of syllable pronunciations of Chinese characters (Meanings of the characters are in parentheses).

Four short vowels			Seven long vowels		
ɪ	/sɪk/	色 (color)	i	/si/	丝 (silk)
ɐ	/sɐp/	湿 (wet)	y	/sy/	书 (book)
ʊ	/sʊk/	叔 (uncle)	ɛ	/sɛ/	借 (borrow)
θ	/sθt/	恤 (shirt)	œ	/hœ/	靴 (boot)
			a	/sa/	沙 (sand)
			ɔ	/sɔ/	梳 (comb)
			u	/fu/	夫 (husband)
Ten diphthongs					
ai	/gai/	佳 (good)	θy	/sθy/	税 (tax)
ɐi	/sɐi/	西 (west)	ɔi	/hɔi/	开 (open)
au	/gau/	交 (give)	ui	/fui/	灰 (gray)
ɐu	/sɐu/	收 (receive)	iu	/siu/	烧 (burn)
ei	/sei/	四 (four)	ou	/dou/	刀 (knife)

Appendix B: American English vowels and diphthongs in the context of an English word

i	beat	o	boat
ɪ	bit	ʊ	book
e	bait	u	boot
ɛ	bet	ɝ	Burt
æ	bat	aɪ	bite
a	Bob	ɔɪ	Boyd
ɔ	bought	aʊ	bout
ʌ	but	ə	about

328

AUDITORY-VISUAL PERCEPTION OF MANDARIN SYLLABLES

Hansjörg MIXDORFF

ABSTRACT

This paper presents a summary of studies by the author and his co-workers exploring the auditory-visual perception of syllables in Mandarin. Firstly, we examined the existence of visual cues for tone perception of monosyllabic tokens by reducing the tonal information in the audio-track. Secondly, we investigated the effect of masking noise on tone as well as segment perception. Results of these studies include that visual information cannot substitute information lost in the acoustic channel but facilitate tone perception in noise. Furthermore, tone information is generally more robust against noise than segmental information but recognition rates also depend on the type of the nuclear vowel.

Keywords: Mandarin, tone perception, auditory-visual speech

1. INTRODUCTION

First of all I would like to thank for this opportunity to contribute to Prof. Wu Zongji's Festschrift. I vividly remember an encounter in the year 2003 when I held a seminar at CASS and was invited to dinner by Wu Zongji and Lin Maocan. At this occasion I was presented with a cooking book from *A Dream of Red Mansions*. Although I never managed to prepare any of the complicated dishes described therein, I am still indebted to the hospitality and trust of my many friends and colleagues in China who also cooperated on a number of studies (including the ones presented here).

Syllabic tones in tone languages are connected with distinct F_0 patterns (rising, falling, etc.). Mandarin has four different lexical tones: high (1), rising (2), low (3), and falling (4), commonly used tone indices are given in brackets. A so-called neutral tone (0) lacking a clear tonal target occurs in certain function words. Research has shown that these tone contours patterns can be associated with distinct F_0 patterns which are strongly influenced by the tonal context (tonal co-articulation between subsequent syllables) [1], focus [8][3], as well as sentence intonation [6].

Although research has shown that tones can be associated with distinct F_0 patterns which might suggest that tone is a purely acoustic phenomenon, there are now auditory-visual studies that suggest that speakers also exploit visual cues when identifying tones [1][2].

This paper summarizes two earlier studies which examine visual contributions to tone and segment perception in noise. The experimental designs are similar in the sense that subjects are presented with mono-syllabic tokens and have to classify them.

2. PERCEPTION OF AUDIO-VISUAL TONES

There has been so far relatively limited research with respect to the integration of acoustic and visual information in the perception of tone. A recent production study [9] suggests certain restrictions with respect to the coordination of the laryngeal and articulatory systems which might be responsible for visual cues of tones. In the associated realm of prosody, it has been shown that there is a strong correlation between head movements and F_0 [6]. These correlations are continuous and seem to be used by multimodal perceivers during auditory-visual perception [1], but direct studies on the perception of these movements are yet to be conducted.

The corpus of monosyllabic tokens compiled for the first study [4] contains a total of 25 syllables which were uttered by a female native speaker of Mandarin with the four different tones. The 25 syllables were chosen based on the following criteria: (1) all members in each syllable set should be real words; (2) together they provide a good coverage of Mandarin vowels, as well as articulatory trajectories (for instance, tongue movements from the back to the front, from the front to the back, etc.). A list of the syllables used is shown in Table 1.

Table 1: List of syllables used in the study, Hanyu Pinyin notation

bo	ji	liu	wei	yi
cai	lang	lun	xian	ying
chuang	lei	luo	xu	yuan
Fang	liang	mao	yan	yun
Hui	lin	meng	yao	zhi

The tokens were randomized and recorded by a professional female speaker at iFlyTek Corporation Hefei with an analog video camera and digitized in MPEG2 standard (352 × 288 pixels, 25 frames per second, audio sampling rate 48kHz). Each syllable was recorded four times.

In order to segment the long video sequences into chunks of individual tokens, the audio tracks were down-sampled to 16kHz and annotated using *Praat TextGrid* [10] A tool was created for converting the *TextGrid* into a *VirtualDub* [11] script which in turn was used for automatically cutting the video as well as saving the associated soundtracks to individual wave files. The videos were cut with a window starting 400ms before the onset of the syllable and ending 400ms after the offset.

In order to determine the potential contribution of visual cues to tone perception two different audio degradation paradigms were adopted:

(1) Reduced audio, that is, stimuli which presumably do not contain acoustic tonal information

(2) Masked audio, that is, the original audio is masked by varying levels of noise

Accordingly, the original soundtracks were subjected to the following manipulations. **Devoiced stimuli** were created by LPC analysis in *Praat* (default settings: Prediction order 16, window-size 25ms, step-size 5ms) and resynthesis using pink noise as the source signal. Pink noise was chosen rather than white noise, for the resulting speech stimuli were more similar to whispered speech and more comfortable to listen to.

Amplitude-modulated noise stimuli were created by extracting the *IntensityTiers* of the **devoiced stimuli** in *Praat* and amplitude-modulating band limited noise (f_{cutoff}=2kHz). The resulting signal still contains the temporal envelope of the devoiced stimulus, but no spectral information.

Babble noise-masked stimuli were created by adding babble noise at SNRs of –3, –6, –9, and –12 dB, with SNR calculated for the speech portion only. The appropriate values of SNR were determined by preliminary trials, identifying the region between tone identification performances on clear-audio and complete masking.

A *VirtualDub* script was used for replacing the original soundtracks by clear 16kHz, babble-noise masked, devoiced and amplitude-modulated noise versions. From each syllable, two example tokens were selected, yielding 25 syllables×4 tones×2 tokens=200 stimuli of each version. For easier reference we introduce abbreviations for the types of stimuli: clean 16kHz audio, **Clean-A**, clean 16kHz audio plus video, **Clean-AV**, devoiced audio, **DeVoiced-A**, devoiced audio plus video, **DeVoiced-AV,** amplitude-modulated noise, **AmpNoise-A**, amplitude-modulated noise plus video, **AmpNoise-AV,** babble-noise masked audio, SNR=–3dB, **Noise3-A,** babble-noise masked audio plus video, SNR=−3dB, **Noise3-AV**, etc.

Experiments were conducted using the *DMDX* software [12] and employed scripts provided by Caroline Jones (MARCS, UWS) that were slightly modified. Considering the large number of stimuli and the fact that the tests were to be conducted with native Mandarin speakers, an identification task rather than a discrimination task was employed. This required participants to identify the presented stimulus by choosing one of four Chinese characters whose phonetic realizations differed only in tone.

One set of syllables was chosen for a practice session preceding the experiment proper, and the remaining 24 syllable sets were divided into four groups. During a session each subject was presented with stimuli from four different auditory, visual or auditory-visual conditions in four consecutive blocks of trials. A rolling design was employed such that the four types of stimuli presented to a particular participant in one trial set were, for instance, **Clean-A**, **Clean-AV**, **Devoiced-A**, and **Devoiced-AV**, with each block containing a different set of syllables, and the sequence of stimulus types varying between the four trial sets.

Within each block, tokens pertaining to a syllable set were presented consecutively, but in randomized order. Each combination of syllable and tone occurred four times, that is, each of two different examples of the syllable/tone combination was presented twice. Hence each trial set consisted of 24 syllables×4 tones×2 versions×2 repetitions=384 trials and took about 35 minutes to complete.

Participants listened to the stimuli over headphones connected to a PC soundcard. Each trial started with a preparation phase of one second during which the word 'ready' was displayed. Then the stimulus was presented, followed by the four Mandarin words represented as Mandarin characters. The order of the four words corresponded to the numbering conventions for Mandarin tones and was left unaltered during the experiment. Following the presentation of the four words, participants made a forced choice by hitting the appropriate number key on the keyboard.

In the practice trials (using one syllable set), feedback concerning response accuracy was given, but in the main test no feedback was given.

Participants were 20 members of staff (5 male, 15 female) at iFlyTek corporation, Hefei, China, aged 23-30. They reported having normal hearing, and four had corrected vision. Most of them were familiar with the speaker who had produced the video data. Each participant performed on two of the trial sets.

The results are discussed in two parts, first with respect to conditions employing clean and devoiced audio stimuli, and second with respect to the masked audio and amplitude-modulated noise.

2.1 Clean and devoiced audio stimuli

In the clean and devoiced audio stimulus conditions, eight participants (3 male, 5 female), all staff at CRSLP, took part. Figure 1 displays the proportion of correct responses for stimulus types **Clean-A**, **Clean-AV**, **DeVoiced-A**, and **DeVoiced-AV**.

Given that the number of possible tones is four, the statistical chance level for the current experiment is at 25%. As can be seen, the identification rate on clear audio is close to 100%. The average results suggest only slight differences between audio only and the corresponding audio plus video conditions. In the case of the devoiced stimuli the picture is rather mixed. Whereas the high tone (number 1) is recognized only slightly above chance level, the low tone (3) yields around 95% correct responses. The corresponding tonal confusion matrix for the DeVoiced-AV condition is displayed in Table 2.

As can be seen, tones 1 and 2 are highly confusable, though the confusions are not necessarily symmetrical.

Clean and Devoiced Stimulus Conditions

[Bar chart showing Proportion Correct by Tone (1-4) for Clean-A, Clean-AV, DeVoiced-A, and DeVoiced-AV conditions]

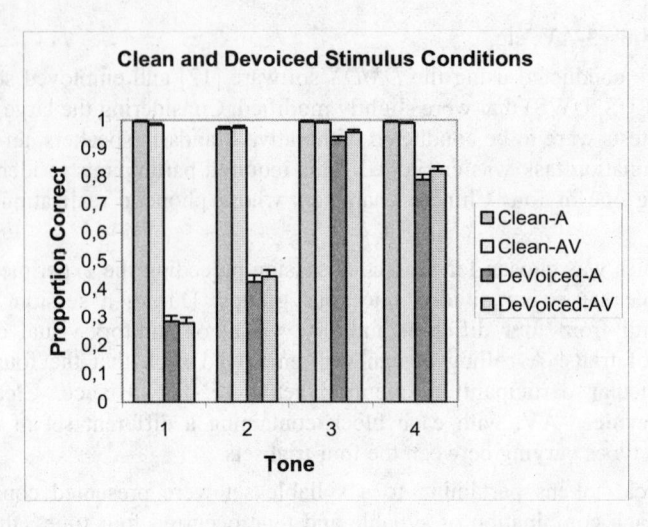

Figure 1: Results of perception experiment employing stimuli types Clean-A, Clean-AV, DeVoiced-A, and DeVoiced-AV. The table displays from left to right: The stimulus type, the underlying tone, the mean correct identification rates, the total number of judgments N and the associated standard deviations.

Table 2: Confusion matrix for stimulus type **DeVoiced-AV**. Rows indicate intended tone, columns perceived tone, and figures correspond to percent.

Intended Tone	Perceived tone in DeVoiced-AV			
	1	2	3	4
1	27.9	23.5	6.3	42.3
2	13.3	44.6	27.3	14.8
3	0.8	2.7	95.6	0.7
4	9.4	4.8	4.0	81.8

2.2 Babble noise-masked audio stimuli and amplitude-modulated noise

Figure 2 displays the proportion correct for babble noise-masked stimuli types, as well as amplitude-modulated noise. Due to space limitations results for individual tones are only displayed for **Noise12-A** and **Noise12-AV**, see Figure 3. As can be seen from Figure 2, recognition rates are still fairly high at an SNR of –3dB, and subjects do not significantly benefit from seeing the video. As the SNR decreases, however, the relative gain of the 'plus video' conditions increases, from 1.3% at –3dB to 15.3% at –12dB. The gains are highly significant (p<.01) for –9 and –12dB. The relative gain for amplitude-modulated noise is even higher at 36.4%, though this augmentation occurs for an audio only condition with recognition rates close to chance. In the break-down for individual tones in the Noise12-A and Noise 12-AV conditions, it is interesting to note that the greatest augmentation occurs for tones 3 and 4, exactly those tones that are perceived well even when de-voiced (see Figure 2). It is of interest to note that this was also the case in the amplitude-modulated noise, for in this condition, tones 3 and 4 still reach recognition rates of 73 and 75% respectively. Together this evidence suggests that these two tones may exhibit distinct extra-fundamental frequency cues, such as duration and intensity, which are even preserved in the devoiced condition.

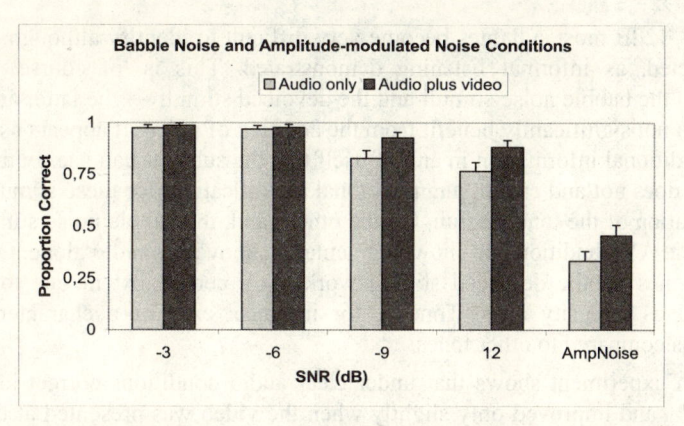

Figure 2: Pooled results of perception experiments employing stimuli types Noise3-A, Noise3-AV, Noise6-A, Noise6-AV, Noise9-A, Noise9-AV, Noise12-A, Noise12-AV, AmpNoise-A, and AmpNoise-AV.

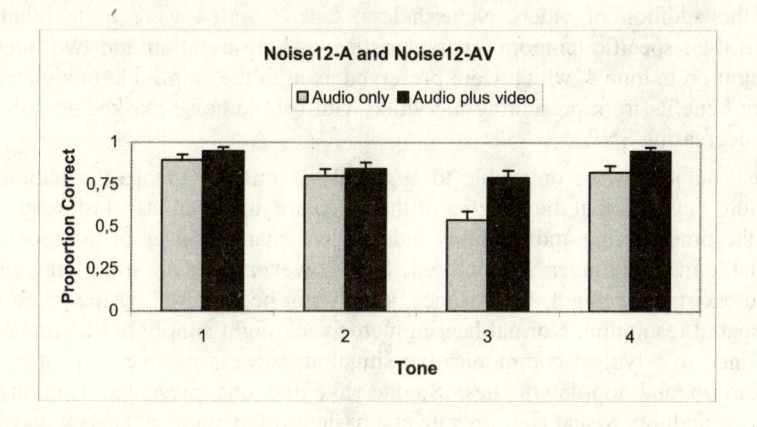

Figure 3: Results for Noise12-A and Noise12-AV as a function of tone

The recognition results for individual tones in Noise12-A and Noise12-AV shown in Figure 3 (bottom) are much more balanced than in the **DeVoiced-AV** condition, as is confirmed by the confusion matrix for the **Noise12-A** condition shown in Table 3. They suggest that tones 2 and 3, as well as tones 3 and 4 are most prone to confusion. Interestingly the latter two are much better separated in the devoiced case (Figure 1). The results of the masking experiment confirm earlier observations [2] that presenting the video along with masked audio increases the tonal identification rate. This gain appears to increase with increased masking of the speech sound.

Table 3: Confusion matrix for stimulus type **Noise12-A**. Rows indicate intended tone, columns perceived tone and figures correspond to percent.

Intended tone	Perceived tone			
	1	2	3	4
1	89.6	5.2	5.2	0.0
2	4.2	80.2	14.6	1.0
3	10.4	21.9	54.2	13.5
4	4.2	4.2	9.4	82.2

At an SNR of –12dB most syllables become very difficult to identify although the tonal contour can still be detected, as informal listening demonstrated. This is, of course, the fundamental difference between the babble noise stimuli and the devoiced stimuli — the latter are devoid of tonal information and do not significantly benefit from the addition of video. It appears as if the video does not contain any additional information in and of itself that the subjects can use. In the devoiced cases video information does not and cannot augment tonal identification, for these stimuli do not have an auditory representation of the tone gesture. On the other hand, the babble noise stimuli do have such information, and the AV conditions do show augmentation above the audio alone. On the other hand, identification of tones on the devoiced stimuli works to a certain extent due to the presence of durational as well as intensity cues. Tone 3, for instance, exhibits a characteristic two-peaked intensity contour as compared to other tones.

The perception experiment shows that under clear audio conditions correct identification rates were close to 100% and improved only slightly when the video was presented at the same time, an obvious ceiling effect.

Identification rate on devoiced audio was reduced to a mean of 60% and did not significantly improve with the addition of video. Nevertheless, tone 3 and 4 were quite reliably identified, probably due to their specific temporal characteristics — long duration and two intensity peaks in tone 3, short duration in tone 4, which were preserved even in the amplitude-modulated noise. There were significant benefits from presenting the video with babble noise-masked stimuli, and this gain increased with decreasing SNR.

The fact that subjects were only able to augment the missing tonal information in the noise-masked conditions suggests that the benefits of the video are due to an effect of early auditory-visual integration of the time varying and modality-independent characteristics of the tone even when the underlying syllable may no longer be identified. This, however, does not imply that visual-only cues for tones do not exist; they might, for instance, simply not be captured by the video due to limited temporal and spatial resolution. Normal hearing perceivers might simply not be trained to make use of tone cues, since in a typical communicative situation, success in tone perception depends on a range of bottom-up and top-down cues. Studies like the one presented here are nevertheless illustrative of how auditory-visual cues operate at a basic level to augment speech perception.

3. PERCEPTION OF TONE AND SEGMENTAL CONTENT

As shown in the preceding section we found that visual information enhances tone perception when the audio information is reduced by a masking noise. This auditory-visual gain rises as the SNR decreases. We did, however, not consider the effect of the noise on the segmental information. Therefore, strictly speaking, the so-called word identification test we performed was actually only a tone identification task as we provided the subjects with a selection of possible Chinese characters pertaining to the different choices. Subjects therefore knew the segmental content of the stimulus they had to classify. In a follow-up study [5] we therefore aimed to investigate whether tonal and segmental information is affected equally as the masking noise becomes stronger or whether the tonal information is more robust. Furthermore we wanted to examine the influence of the syllable's segmental structure on tonal identification, as well as on the auditory-visual gain.

A corpus of 220 frequent Mandarin mono-syllabic words was uttered by a male speaker of Mandarin and video-taped with a mini DV camera in portrait mode (720×576 pixels, 25 frames per second, sampling rate 48kHz) at TFH Berlin and transferred to a PC. The data were rotated by 90° and de-interlaced discarding even fields using VirtualDub [11]. The resulting video format (288×360 pixels) was compressed using the Indeo 5.1 codec at maximum quality and the audio down-sampled to 16kHz.

In order to segment the long video sequences into chunks of individual tokens, the audio tracks were annotated acoustically using Praat TextGrid [10] which were converted to *VirtualDub* scripts which in turn were used for automatically cutting the video as well as saving the associated soundtracks to individual wave files. The videos were cut with a window starting 400ms before the acoustic onset of the syllable and ending 400ms after the offset.

Babble noise was added to the speech signals at levels of 0, –3, –6 and –9dB. This range was chosen after first informal tests showed that masking on audio only stimuli started at 0dB, whereas stimuli were completely masked at –12dB.

The original audio tracks of the videos were then replaced by the noisy versions at 0, –3, –6 and –9dB SNR yielding altogether eight types of stimuli which will be referred to as follows:

Noise0/3/6/9-A, babble-noise masked audio only stimuli

Noise0/3/6/9-AV, babble-noise masked audio plus video stimuli.

As in the preceding study, experiments were conducted using the *DMDX* software [12]. The recognized phonetic content had to be specified using the romanized transcription system commonly known as Pinyin (see, for instance [13]) including the number of the tone.

A designated set of tokens other than the 220 words was chosen for a practice session preceding the experiment proper, and the 220 words were divided into four groups. During a session each subject was presented with 220 stimuli from four different auditory or auditory-visual conditions in four consecutive blocks of trials. As can be seen in Table 1, a rolling design was employed such that the four types of stimuli presented to a particular participant in one trial set were, for instance, **Noise0-AV**, **Noise3-A**, **Noise6-AV** and **Noise9-A,** with each block containing a different set of syllables, and the sequence of stimulus types varying between the four trial sets. Hence, the total number of 220×8=1760 stimuli was divided into eight different sets.

Within each block, tokens pertaining to a word set were presented consecutively, but in randomized order, and a session took less than 30 minutes to complete. Participants listened to the stimuli over headphones connected to a PC soundcard. Each trial started with a preparation phase of one and a half seconds during which the word 'ready' was displayed. Then the stimulus was presented, followed by the request to type the Pinyin sequence of the word perceived completed by hitting the <RETURN> key. Each stimulus was only presented once, and there was no time limit for the Pinyin input.

Participants were 16 members of staff (1 male, 15 female) at iFlyTek corporation, Hefei, China, aged 21-33 from the speech data department. They reported to have normal hearing, four had corrected vision. All of them had received special training for speech annotation works. None of them was familiar with the speaker who had produced the video data. Each participant performed on one of the eight of the trial sets in. After the test, participants were interviewed about their observations. Six of the subjects felt that the test had been very tiresome, only five thought that the video had facilitated the task. A rather unexpected but important comment was that the speaker on the video was not handsome enough to deserve being looked at. The data were aggregated, checked for typos or illegal inputs and subjected to statistical analysis.

Figure 4 displays the proportion of correct responses for tones and syllable segments depending on the SNR. As can be seen, the rate drops steadily as the SNR decreases. Already at 0dB the syllable recognition is only 68% compared to 95% for the tones. At –9dB tone recognition approaches chance level, whereas the segments are only correctly identified in 6% of the times.

Figure 5 displays the proportion correct for the four different tones of Mandarin. Just as shown in [9] the third tone is best identified in noise due to its relatively long syllabic duration and two-peaked intensity pattern. Tone 4 syllables in turn are relative short.

If we have a look at where in the syllable the recognition errors mostly occur, we yield the picture shown in Figure 6. As the SNR decreases, recognitions rates for all parts of the syllable, i.e. the onset, the nuclear vowel and the coda drop. In all cases but the lowest SNR of –9dB, rates are highest for the nuclear vowel, followed by the onset and then the coda. Even at –9dB about 40% of at least one part of the syllable are identified correctly. At this SNR, onset-nucleus sequences are identified correctly in 23% of cases, and nucleus-coda sequences in 26%. It should be noted that after looking at some of the typical confusion patterns we treated diphthong nuclei such as 'ai' or 'ou' for this evaluation as sequences of nucleus 'a' and coda 'i', and nucleus 'o' and coda 'u', respectively.

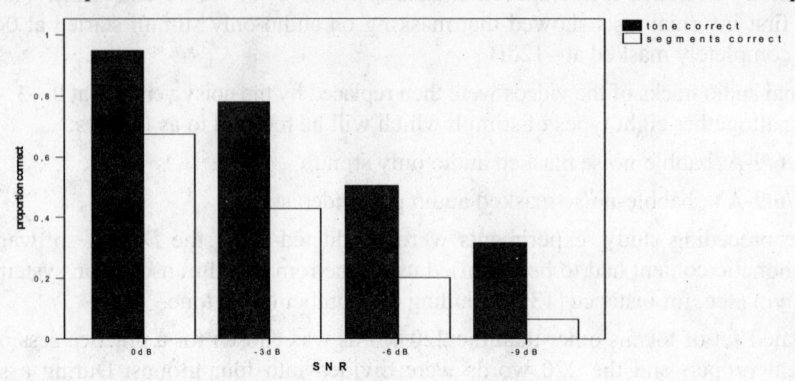

Figure 4: Pooled results from perception experiment showing the proportion correct for segmental and tonal information depending on the SNR of the stimulus.

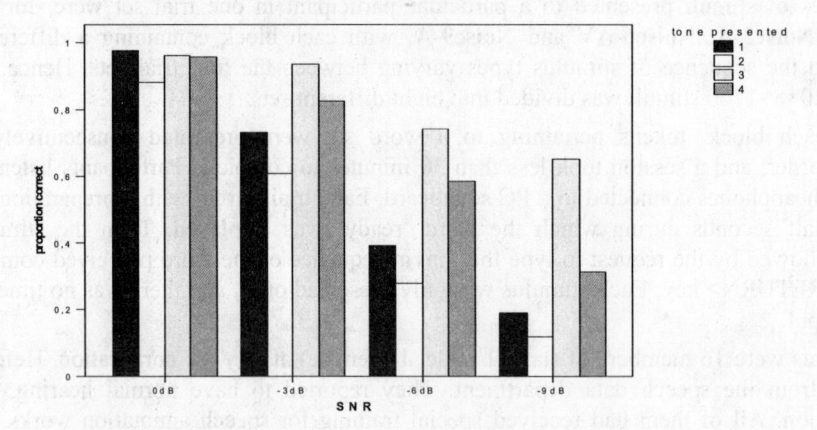

Figure 5: Proportion correct for recognition of the four syllabic tones depending on the SNR of the stimulus. As can be seen tone 3 is the most stable.

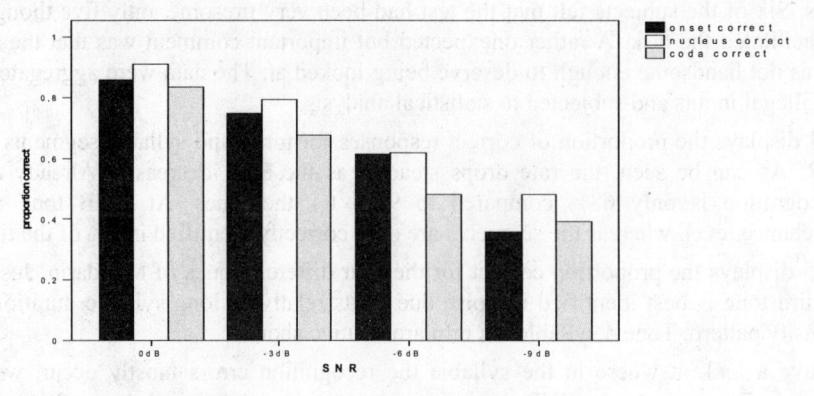

Figure 6: Proportion correct for recognition of onset, nucleus and coda depending on the SNR of the stimulus. As can be seen, the nucleus is the most stable.

We examined which syllables gained most from the visual information and looked at the proportion correct for different nuclear vowels. Results are displayed in Table 4. Since the Pinyin system is not always consistent with regards to vowel representation, we chose SAMPA-like symbols for indicating the vowel property along with Pinyin examples. As could be expected, vowels with strong lip rounding such as [o], [y] and [u] benefit most from the visual information.

Table 4: Proportion of correct nuclear vowel identification depending on the type of the nuclear vowel in audio only and audio plus video conditions.

nuclear vowel	audio only	audio plus video	Pinyin example
@	.69	.75	sh**e**ng
a	.67	.84	sh**a**n
e	.75	.84	sh**e**i
E	.49	.76	n**ia**n
i	.70	.75	n**i**
I	.82	.79	sh**i**
o	.31	.70	p**o**
u	.43	.89	sh**u**
U	.24	.69	s**o**ng
y	.50	.88	y**u**
total	.61	.79	

Figure 7 shows results concerning the potential auditory-visual gain yielded when the video image is presented along with the audio. The proportions correct for tones and segments depending on the SNR are displayed separately for audio only (video=0) and audio-visual (video=1) conditions. Different from the results found in [9] there is no tangible gain for the tonal discrimination, whereas it is obvious for the segmental information. The syllable recognition rate rises by up to 20% with the visual information.

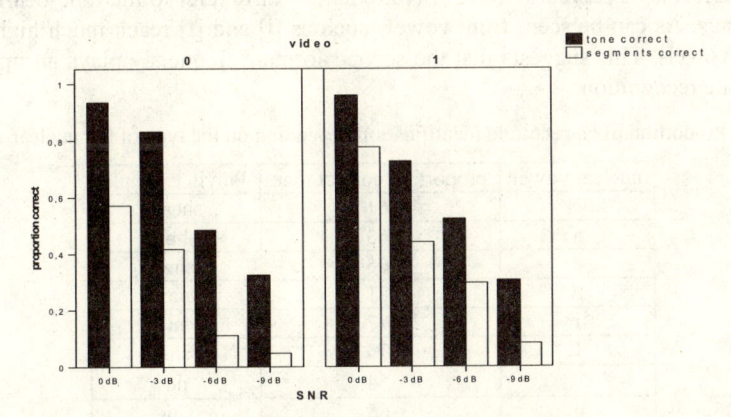

Figure 7: Proportion correct for recognition of tonal and segmental information depending on the SNR of the stimulus, split into audio only (video=0, left) and audio plus video (video=1, right) conditions. The auditory-visual gain is significant in the recognition rate for the segments, but not for the tones.

If we look at the relationship between the type of the onset consonant and the onset recognition rate, fricatives such as [s] and [S] get the highest rates, followed by plosives [p], whereas sonorants are affected most by the masking noise (see **Table 5**). In Table 6 we display a list of onsets prone to confusion and their most frequent confusion partners. The consonants are represented using a SAMPA-type notation. As can be seen most of the confusions concern candidates that either share place or manner of articulation.

Table 5: Proportion of correct onset identification depending on the type of initial consonant and SNR

vowel type	SNR			
	0dB	–3dB	–6dB	–9dB
fricatives	.90	.82	.74	.52
plosives	.87	.73	.62	.36
sonorants	.77	.64	.49	.17
total	.86	.75	.61	.36

Table 6: Most likely confusion candidates for the ten most confusable onsets, figures indicate proportion of false hits.

onset	Pinyin example	proportion correct	likely confusion candidates
w	wang	.33	f (.21), l (.08), r (.08)
l	long	.34	r (.14), y (.08), t (.07)
∅	ang	.36	r (.18), t (.11)
k'	kong	.41	h (.16), k (.10), t (.09)
m	meng	.47	p (.10), n (.10), r (.09)
n	nong	.51	r (.18), y (.13), l (.10)
k	gong	.56	h (.08), t (.07), y (.07)
h	hong	.60	k (.06)
p	bang	.63	h (.06), t (.06)
ts	cong	.63	tS (.18), tC (.09)
t	dong	.63	h (.06), r (.06)

We finally examined whether the type of the nuclear vowel influenced the tonal recognition. The result of this analysis is displayed in Table 7. Note that we only refer to the tone-bearing vowel part, even in diphthongs. As can be seen, front vowels such as [i] and [I] reach much higher recognition rates than back vowels. This suggests that the second formant frequency plays an important role in the process of tone recognition.

Table 7: Proportion of correct tone identification depending on the type of the nuclear vowel

nuclear vowel	proportion correct tone	Pinyin example
@	.61	sheng
a	.63	shan
e	.66	shei
E	.71	nian
i	.77	ni
I	.75	shi
o	.54	po
u	.66	shu
U	.52	song
y	.88	yu
total	.64	

It must be stated that the amount of data and the number of subjects are relatively small and therefore only allow tentative conclusions. Our results suggest that the tonal information is more robust against noise than segmental information. Although each tone has only three counterparts to be confused with and the potential of segments to be confused is much higher, our results show that actual confusions only occur with very few candidates that in the case of consonants share either manner or place of articulation with a segment. We found that the nuclear vowel is the part of the syllable with the highest recognition rate, followed by onset and coda.

In contrast to [4] the video image did not contribute to tone identification, but only enhanced segment recognition. This result may be explained by the different experiment design. In [4] participants were asked to identify the tone by choosing from a list of Chinese characters that all had the same segmental content. Therefore they did not experience the same cognitive load as in the current study where they had to identify both the tone AND the segments. Furthermore we examined the influence of the syllable structure on tone perception and found that front vowels facilitate recognition whereas back vowel yield lower rates.

4. DISCUSSION AND CONCLUSION

The studies presented here were focused on the way tone perception is influenced by various factors such as auditory-visual settings and background noise. We found that tonal information cannot be recovered from visual information, and visual cues are mere correlates of temporal organization. Therefore tones three and four were easily identified even in devoiced stimuli. The visual channel apparently facilitates acoustic perception, and as long as there is still tonal information available in the audio signal. Interestingly, the audio-visual gain in the tone perception task is only significant when the segmental information is already provided (Section 2). When tone as well as segment identification are required, as shown in Section 0, participants seem to yield auditory-visual gain only for the segment identification, not the tone identification. Whether speakers in a real-world conversation draw on visual information for disambiguating tones must still be investigated. In the future we plan to examine more spontaneous speaking styles that might be more prone to tonal reductions, as well as look at longer tone sequences. We are also interested in more realistic settings in which tonal confusions are likely to occur, for instance in inter-dialectal communication.

REFERENCES

[1] Burnham, D., Ciocca, V., Stokes, S. 2001. Auditory-visual perception of lexical tone. *Proceedings of Eurospeech* 2001, Aalborg, Denmark, 395-398.

[2] Burnham, D., Lau, S., Tam, H., Schoknecht, C. 2001. Visual discrimination of Cantonese tone by tonal but non-Cantonese speakers, and by non-tonal language speakers. In: Massaro, D., Light, J., Geraci, K. (eds.), *Proceedings of AVSP2001*, 155-160.

[3] Chen, G., Hu, Y., Wang, R., Mixdorff, H. 2004. Quantitative Analysis and Synthesis of Focus in Mandarin. *Proceedings of TAL 2004*, Beijing, 25-28.

[4] Mixdorff, H., Hu, Y., Burnham, D. 2005. Visual Cues in Mandarin Tone Perception. In *Proceedings of Eurospeech 2005*, Lisbon, Portugal, 405-408.

[5] Mixdorff, H., Wang, Y., Hu, Y. 2008. Robustness of Tonal and Segmental Information in Noise-Auditory and Visual Contributions. *Submitted to Speech Prosody 2008*, Campinas, Brazil.

[6] Shih, C. 2004. Tonal effects on intonation. *Proceedings of TAL 2004*, Beijing, 163-167.

[7] Xu, Y. 1998. Consistency of tone-syllable alignment across different syllable structures and speaking rates. *Phonetica* 55, 179-203.

[8] Xu, Y. 1999. Effects of tone and focus on the formation and alignment of F_0 contours. *Journal of Phonetics* 27, 55-105.

[9] Xu, Y., Sun, X. 2002. Maximum speed of pitch change and how it may relate to speech. *Journal of the Acoustical Society of America* 111, 1399-1413.

[10] http://www.praat.org.

[11] http://www.virtualdub.org.
[12] http://www.u.arizona.edu/~kforster/dmdx/dmdx.htm.
[13] http://pinyin.info.

UNDERSTANDING VARIABILITY IN SPEECH: A BRIEF SURVEY OVER 2.5 MILLENNIA

John J. OHALA

ABSTRACT

Ever since the earliest attempts to understand the nature, the form, and variability in speech, whether within one language or the variation one finds in the pronunciation of the "same" word in different but related languages, there has always been interest in explaining such variation in physical, physiological, or psychological terms. After millennia of study of this subject this goal is within reach.

1. INTRODUCTION

From distant times there has always been curiosity about the nature and the mechanism of speech and language. This is reflected in myths suggesting a divine origin of speech or positing specific deities as the patron of speech: in Hinduism, Sarasvati, in Greek mythology, Hermes, in Norse mythology, Lodur. The same motivation to understand the workings of speech led to scientific, i.e. empirically-based studies of speech. In this paper I propose to give an interpretive history of phonological science over 2.5 millennia. My purpose in attempting this audacious task is to provide some perspective on modern mainstream phonology as practiced today in the West.

First, what do I mean by "phonological science"? I believe the essence of a scientific discipline is to be found in the questions it asks. The answers to the questions (i.e. theories, hypotheses, conjectures) may change or evolve over time and the methods used to obtain these answers may also change. The perennial questions asked in phonological science, I would maintain are:

(1) How can one describe a language's pronunciation to:

a) lend it permanency in the face of apparent variation and change (there can be many motivations for this: to better interpret or understand important texts — including oral texts); simply to establish a language or dialect as standard with respect to competing languages or dialects); it is not the linguists' business or concern to pass judgment on the motivations behind linguistic description.

b) for the aid of language learners.

(2) To establish relationships — typically familial or diachronic relationships between different (mutually unintelligible) languages. Again, the motivation for this can be varied from "pure" scientific interest to chauvinistic, ethnic, or nationalistic purposes; but the motivation is less important to us than is the scientific support for the claims.

(3) To discover the psychological basis of speakers' language competence in the phonological domain.

(4) To discover optimal techniques for language instruction/learning.

(5) To discover how humans' language capacity arose, i.e. how language evolved.

(6) To understand speech pathologies such that they can be ameliorated.

(7) Understanding variation in spoken speech to the point of being able to mechanize the functions of speaking and perceiving speech, i.e. automatic speech synthesis and automatic speech recognition.

In this paper I will focus on the history of contributions to the first three questions — without denying the importance of the remaining four in which remarkable progress has been made in the past few decades.

When appeals to divine intervention don't satisfy, which domains would the interested scholar turn to? The answer, and I believe this is still true to the present day, is (1) the physical, i.e. the anatomical, physiological, and acoustic-perceptual aspect of speech, (2) the psychological elements serving speech, and (3) the social influences and functions of speech.

2. DESCRIBING SPEECH

The necessary first step — and this is true of any scientific investigation — is to reduce the huge mass of data to a manageable few entities. This is the pattern in the development of astronomy, chemistry, physics and biology. Like these domains, speech is highly variable. Pāṇini and all the phonologists after him identified what they considered the basic "building blocks" of speech. Whether these correspond to individual phonemes or CV syllables, etc., this is the start of the scientific proposal for an understanding of speech.

The earliest description of speech and its elements that we have is a quite sophisticated one, that of Sanskrit by the Hindu grammarian Pāṇini from (estimated) 3rd to 5th c BPE. In his monumental work, the Astadhyayi, the description was in quasi-phonetic terms but it was sufficient to differentiate the various phonemes and their morphophonemic variants. Pāṇini was not the first to address the sound system of Sanskrit; he refers to earlier works that did not survive.

Other notable early descriptions of the sound systems of individual languages include:

- Various Greek and Latin grammarians' descriptions of and philosophizing about their languages, including Dionysius Thrax (*Tékhnkē grammatiké*, 2nd c BPE) and Plato's Cratylus (4th c BPE; perhaps an intentionally humorous look at etymology).
- The rhyme tables of Middle Chinese (Sui Dynasty, 6th-7th c AD). Although Chinese writing is not in itself phonetically-based, the compilers of the rhyme tables demonstrated a parsing or decomposition of the monosyllabic words into initials and rhymes. These tables have proven to be invaluable in the reconstruction of earlier stages of Chinese.
- Descriptions of Arabic (e.g. by Khalīl ibn Ahmad Al Farāhīdi (أحمد بن الخليل، الرحمن عبد أبو الفراهيدي) and Sībawaihi (سيبوى) in the 8th c.
- The "Grammarian" (his name is unknown) who described Icelandic in the 12th c.

I would place in the same category as "description" the development of an orthography for a language. Instead of being an explicit description of a language's parts and how they are arranged, an orthography is in an implicit account of the same. The few orthographies that embody some sort of iconism (usually articulatory) are actually a bit more than an implicit description. Some linguistically significant orthographies representing constituent sounds are:

- Egyptian hieroglyphics — phonetically based, as first discovered and deciphered by Thomas Young (and subsequently elaborated and the decipherment finished by François Champollion).
- Devanagari (for Sanskrit and its daughter languages; ult. derived from Brāhmī script, 3rd c BCE).
- The Olmec hieroglyphs from Central America where each symbol represented a CV sequence, from 3rd c BCE [16].
- The Japanese syllabary (as a systematization in 4th ~ 5th c of parts of Chinese orthography, kanji, which in itself was not primarily phonologically based).

- Hangul, the Korean writing system, commissioned by King Sejong in the 14th c (1446). Not only sound based, but also an iconic representation of position of the vocal organs.
- The development of indigenous writing systems for Cherokee, Eskimo & Inuktitut, Amharic, and various other Native American and African languages. (In many cases, the concept of a phonologically-based writing system was previously known and the innovation consisted in developing — a nouveau — a version adapted to a new language.)

It is often claimed that such sound-based orthographies approximated what would be called in modern linguistics a phonemic description of the language's sound system. This may be a somewhat exaggerated claim: (1) syllabaries have symbols for CV (and sometimes CVC) but usually not separate C's and V's, (2) Japanese kana have a separate symbol for syllable-final /n/ but also separate indivisible symbols for /na/, /ni/, /no/, etc. (3) Egyptian hieroglyphics had symbols for long vowels but not short vowels.

3. GIVING EVIDENCE THAT DIFFERENT LANGUAGES DEVELOPED FROM SOME COMMON PARENT LANGUAGE

Here I highlight attempts which would satisfy our current sense of (some) scientific validity. (In fact there have been from ancient times wild and disreputable comparisons between one language and others, usually attributing variation to laziness and other unattractive traits of speakers of the "other" languages or dialects.) The more scientifically respectable claims made some attempt to discount borrowing as a cause of similarity and, most importantly insisted on there being many points of similarity such as lexical, morphological, etc.

The very earliest attempts made "gestalt" comparisons between lexical items and didn't take into account all morphological factors. The later accounts (by Rask, Grimm, etc.) emphasized point-by-point similarities (e.g. the word initial "p" in Greek and Latin corresponded to "f" in Germanic, etc.) I would consider that both approaches exploited a kind of intuitive notion of probability and this is the essence of the COMPARATIVE METHOD. This method is simply an intuitive application of the statistical law that the probability, p, of the collection of events, $X=x_1, x_2, \ldots x_i, \ldots x_n$, is the product of the probabilities of the separate events.

Although not used in a quantitative way by the historical linguists, it is a method capable of yielding a level of objectivity and accuracy of evidence comparable to that found in the "hard" sciences. Charles Darwin — some centuries after the linguists — used this same method of marshalling evidence in support of his theory of evolution, i.e. proof by the sheer weight and interconnection of the accumulated bits of evidence. Any discipline faced with data that is difficult to quantify and subject to distortion by a great many uncontrollable extraneous factors — and this is a characteristic of some behavioral, social and the biological sciences — must resort to this method of orchestrating the empirical support for its hypotheses. Linguistics was among the first, if not THE first, to do this.[1]

One of the earliest works linking the European languages historically was authored by Marcus Zuerius van Boxhorn (1612-1653) from the University of Leiden. Prompted by the discovery of an ancient statue which Boxhorn identified as from the "Scythian" culture, he identified Scythian as the language ancestor of the Germanic (including the Scandinavian), Romance, Greek, Celtic, Slavic and Persian languages, based on whole-word "gestalt" similarities of vocabulary. Unfortunately, he also claimed Turkish, Georgian and other languages to be part of the same family which we know in the

---

[1] As a somewhat curious footnote on the history of the application of the comparative method: it was applied in a strictly mathematical way by the great English scientist Thomas Young to support the possible relatedness of Basque and Ancient Egyptian. He claimed to find enough cognate words to judge that they were related. His error: he "cherry-picked" the cognates and used a questionable model for estimating similarity of candidate cognates. (See Poser, http://www.billposer.org/Papers/young.pdf)

light of subsequent researches is not the case. And although he pre-dated Sir William Jones in claiming a family relationship of these European languages with a member of the "Indo-"part of Indo-European[2], namely, Persian, his evidence on this latter point was erroneous.

Boxhorn himself cites Ioannes Aventinus (1477-1534) and Sigismundus Gelenius (1497-1554) as having earlier tried to demonstrate the family relationship between various European languages.

János Sajnovics (1733-1785), a Hungarian, demonstrated the relationship between Sami (a.k.a. "Lapp") and Hungarian (1770). This was taken further by Samuel Gyarmathi in 1799.

Lorenzo Hervas y Panduro (1735-1809) was a Jesuit missionary who, when the Pope rescinded the missionary "license" of the Jesuits, attempted to consolidate and archive the observations and discoveries of his fellow Jesuits about the life, lore, and the languages they encountered from around the world. Hervas is credited with discovering the Austronesian family of languages: a language family with the widest distribution geographically, stretching from Madagascar on west to Easter Island on the east and encompassing scores of languages in the Philippines and Oceania. Again the method of comparison was of the "gestalt" type.

Jonathan Edwards, Jr (1745-1801) was an American churchman who has been credited with the discovery [7] of the Algonquian family of languages in the Eastern regions of North America.

The crucial breakthrough in the history of historical linguistics and in linguistics in general comes from the fusion of phonetics and historical linguistics.

This is exemplified most notably in the work of Lambert ten Kate (1674-1731) a Dutch scholar who published an account of the relationship between Dutch (at that time) and the well-known European classical languages [29][3]. Another pioneer in this domain was Charles de Brosses (1709-1777) who, in a 1765 work, using an original iconic feature-based phonetic transcription, demonstrated sound-to-sound and feature-to-feature correspondences in the vocabulary of related European languages.

This method was applied on a significantly larger scale by Rasmus Rask [25] and Jacob Grimm [11] who also used point-by-point comparisons between the parts of words in different languages. They are generally credited with sparking the revolution in historical phonology which still flourishes.

A crucial element of the method — part of what has become known as the Comparative Method — for establishing the phonological element of a language's history was to insist that sound change tended to be regular; exceptions had to have their own regularity caused by a differing environment (this latter point furthered especially by Grassmann [9] and Verner [31]).

Some remarkable innovations and discoveries were made using the comparative method: Schleicher reconstructed a parent language no longer extant (contra to previous practice of identifying only known languages — including dead ones — as possible parent languages); Saussure reconstructed speech sounds — the so-called "laryngeals" in Proto-Indo-European — known only by their effect on adjacent sounds and the laryngeals themselves is no longer extant in any language known at the time (except that decades later Jerzy Kuryłowicz found them in Hittite texts).

Two parallel movements further strengthened the work of Historical Phonology: first, the description of more and more languages of the world, especially by those trained in phonetics and, second, the application of laboratory phonetics and other empirical studies to questions in historical phonology. In these areas there were significant contributions from Liu Fu [19], Li Fang-Kuei [18],

---

[2] In Jones' case, the "Indo" language that he put in the same family as the European ones was Sanskrit. Relevant here is that Persian and Sanskrit are both members of the Indic branch of what we now call the Indo-European language family.

[3] He had previously demonstrated the relationship between Gothic and Dutch (ten Kate 1710).

Wu Zongji [33], Y. R. Chao [2], and William S-Y. Wang [32].[4] There is now a steady tradition of the integration of laboratory phonetics and historical phonology [22][23].

Applications of the Comparative Method in Historical Phonology to other languages led eventually — by the 20th c — to the assignment of virtually all of the 6000 or so known human languages to one or another of some 20~30 families. This must surely count as one of the most significant contributions of linguistics to science, putting linguistics at the forefront of the behavioral sciences.

4. GIVING AN ACCOUNT OF THE PSYCHOLOGICAL BASIS FOR PHONOLOGICAL PATTERNS IN A GIVEN LANGUAGE, I.E. THE PSYCHOLOGICAL GRAMMAR

An interest in the psychological aspect of language was stimulated by the writings of Saussure, Baudouin de Courtenay, Sweet, among others. A notable example was the work of Meringer & Meyer on speech errors ("Versprechen und Verlesen" 1895). Originally designed as a study to find out if dissimilation could be explained as due to speech errors ("slips of the tongue"), they gathered hundreds of speech errors in unrehearsed speech. To their credit they decided that cases of dissimilation were unlike naturally-occurring speech errors.

But there was much speculation at this time (and even today) that observed sound changes were somehow implemented purposefully — that they were a product of the speaker's will — that they were teleological (e.g. to make speech easier to produce or easier to hear and understand).

My belief — the results of much of my work on sound change — is that once we understand the phonetic basis of sound change it can be understood as listener error — comparable in the auditory domain to scribal errors when copying manuscripts. That is we do not have to posit complex psychological mechanisms.

Around the end of the 19th c and the beginning of the 20th c, the theory of the phoneme was developing: the idea underneath the plethora of speech sound types that the phoneticians were discovering, there was really just a relatively small number of "phonemes" which were the psychologically distinctive elements. The rest, the "allophones" were contextually-determined variants of the phonemes.

My observation: unfortunately the principal method for discovering these alleged psychological entities was again the comparative method applied over a shallow time depth. Although the target was a psychological entity, there were no appropriate psychological methods to find them.

In the mid-20th c, generative grammar came on the scene and was suposed to be able to discover the psychological underpinnings of sound variations manifested in related words in different morphological and syntactic environments.

E.g., [ɑj] : [ɪ]
divine : divinity
sine : sinuous
revise : revision

Criteria for deciding on the architecture of these psychological mechanisms were generality and simplicity. This is what justified abstract underlying form, ordered phonological rules changing features of the underlying phonemes, markedness, and a host of other devices.

The result of mainstream phonology's abstract, imaginary conception of the elements of speech: a separation of the work of phoneticians (and other empirically-oriented studies of speech) and the

---

[4] Chao and Wang were once the author's colleagues at University of California, Berkeley.

"phonologists". And there has been a bewildering proliferation of phonological "theories" with an average a "half-life" of 7.5 years:

In short, there is no evidence that the machinery proposed to account for phonological variations like English divine ~ divinity or even "want to" ~ "wanna" has any relation to speakers' psychological mechanisms. The sole criterion of positing mechanisms with maximal generality (via maximum simplicity) has never been justified psychologically. The methods used really resemble the comparative method applied at time depth shallower than what is appropriate for, say, the Romance or Germanic languages, but deeper than what is applicable for finding the "phonemes" of a language.

This is not just my interpretation of generative phonology and its offshoots. S. R. Anderson [1] remarks:

"When we examine ... early MIT theses in phonology such as those of Foley [8], Harris [14], Kiparsky [17], McCawley [20] and Schane [27], as well as Halle's own work on Russian and Latvian (e.g. Halle & Zeps [13]), there is a common thread apart from the focus on rules in descriptions. In each case, these works draw heavily on the existing results of historical linguistics, either directly (as in Kiparsky's case) or as a source of antecedent analysis whose bearing on synchronic phonology is quite direct in a 'morphophonemic' context."

What this means is that modern mainstream phonology in the 20th c and continuing into the 21st c — insofar as it purports to discover the mental, i.e. the psychological mechanisms underlying speakers' competence, is a _scientific fraud_. Rather than uncovering what is in speakers' heads, it is conducting the same kind of descriptive studies and using the same methodology developed in the centuries before the 20th c — for the sake of establishing languages' history, not their psychological representation in the brain.

On one occasion, Chomsky has admitted the empirical weakness of the program of research that he advocated:

"... I do not think anybody actually working on language can doubt ... that sooner or later ... it is going to be necessary to discover conditions on theory constructions, coming presumably from experimental psychology or from neurology, which will resolve the alternatives that can be arrived at by the kind of speculative theory construction linguists can do on the basis of the data available to them. That is, there will come a point, no doubt, and I think in some area of linguistics it may already have been reached, where one can set up alternative systems to explain quite a wide range of phenomena. One can think that this or that system is more elegant and much deeper than some other, but is it right? ... It seems to me that in phonology that point may have been reached."

This admission was made in 1967 at conference on brain mechanisms underlying speech when there was skepticism expressed by other participants about the basis for Chomsky's claims about the psychological foundation of language competence. But more than 40 years have passed and mainstream phonology is still engaged in "speculative theory construction". Rather, an earlier view of Chomsky's [3], made à propos of syntactic research, seems to have prevailed:

"... at the present stage of the study of language, it seems rather obvious that the attempt of gain some insight into the range of data that we now have is likely to be far more fruitful than any attempt to make this data more firm, e.g. by tests for synonymy, grammaticalness, and the like. Operational criteria for these notions, were they available and correct, might soothe the scientific conscience, but how, in fact, would they advance our understanding of the nature of language or of the use and acquisition of language?"

We can be grateful that Lavoisier in the late 18th c did not adopt a similar view with respect to the weighing of the products of combustion, results from which led to an overthrow of the phlogiston theory of combustion and the ushering in modern chemistry.

5. WHAT TO DO?

As mentioned at the start of this paper, all scientific disciplines consist, roughly, of questions about the world, answers to these questions, and the methods used to evaluate the candidate answers. There is no argument that the program of inquiry about the phonological aspect of language that Chomsky (and his associates, notably Halle) initiated has been, to use a slangy term from the 1960's, "consciousness-raising". But methodologically it represents a step backwards from the impressive progress phonological studies had made previously. But what can be done to promote a truly scientific pursuit of the psychological basis of speakers' ability to produce and perceive speech? To some extent the answer has already been given: there is already a strong tradition of psycholinguistic studies that illuminate what speakers know about the sound patterns in their language and what use they make of that knowledge: Meringer & Meyer [21], Esper [7], Greenberg & Jenkins [10], Zimmer [35], Ohala & Jaeger (1986), Ohala [22], Ohala & Ohala [24], Cutler [5] to mention just a few relevant works. I do not claim that these works represent the truth: rather they show how questions of the psychological aspect of phonology can be evaluated in the empirical arena. The ascendancy of this tradition is essential for our field. It will not happen overnight: It is for the emerging generation not yet contaminated by the effete practices and delusions of the past that will usher in the new, stronger phonology.

6. ACKNOWLEDGEMENTS

I want to thank Mark Sicoli, Maria-Josep Solé, Yao Yao, and especially Natasha Warner, for giving me valuable assistance in the preparation of this paper. But the opinions expressed are mine.

REFERENCES

[1] Anderson, Stephen R. 2000. Reflections on On the Phonetic Rules of Russian. *Folia Linguistica* 34, 11-28.

[2] Chao, Y. R. 1976. My linguistic autobiography. In: Dil. A. S. (ed.), *Aspects of Chinese sociolinguistics: Essays by Yuenren Chao.* Stanford: Stanford University Press.

[3] Chomsky, N. 1964. Current issues in linguistic theory. In: Fodor. J. A. & Katz. J. J. (eds.), *The structure of language.* Englewood Cliffs: Prentice Hall, 50-116.

[4] Chomsky, N. 1967. Discussion. In: Darley, F. L. (ed.), *Brain mechanism underlying speech and language.* NY: Grune & Stratton, 100.

[5] Cutler, A. 2005. *Twenty-first century psycholinguistics: Four cornerstones.* London: Routledge.

[6] des Brosses, Charles. 1765. *Traité de la formation méchanique des langues, et de principes physiques de l'étymologie.* Paris: Chez Saillant, Vincent, Desaint.

[7] Edwards, Jonathan, Jr. 1788. *Observations on the Language of the Muhhekaneew Indians.* New Haven, Printed by Josiah Meigs. Esper, E. A. 1925. A technique for the experimental investigation of associative interference in artificial linguistic material. *Language Monographs* 1. Baltimore: Linguistic Society of America.

[8] Foley, James. 1965. *Spanish Morphology.* PhD.Dissertation, MIT.

[9] Grassmann, H. 1863. Über die Aspiraten und ihr gleichzeitiges Vorhandensein in An- und Austlaute der Wurzein. *Zeitschrift für vergleichende Sprachforschung auft fem Gebiete des Deutschen, Grieschischen und Lateinischen* 12, 81-138.

[10] Greenberg, J. H., Jenkins, J.J. 1964. Studies in the psychological correlates of the sound system of American English. *Word* 20, 157-177.

[11] Grimm, Jacob. 1822. *Deutsche Grammatik.* (2nd ed.) Göttingen: Dieterich.

[12] Gyarmathi, Sámuel. 1799. *Affinitas linguae hungaricae cum lingua fennicae originie grammatice demonstrate.* Göttingen.

[13] Halle, Morris, Valdis Zeps. 1966. A survey of Latvian morphophonemics. *Quarterly Progress Report of the Research Laboratory of Electronics,* MIT (83), 105-113.

[14] Harris, James. 1967. *Spanish Phonology*. PhD. Dissertation, MIT.
[15] Hervas, Lorenzo. 1784. *Catalogo delle lingue conoscuiute e notizia della loro affintá, e diversitá.* Cesena.
[16] Justeson, John J., Kaufman, T. 1993. A decipherment of Epi-Olmec hieroglyphic writing. *Science*, Vol. 259, No. 5102, 1703-1711.
[17] Kiparsky, Paul. 1965. *Phonological Change*. PhD. Dissertation, MIT. Published by Indiana University Linguistics Club.
[18] Li Fang Kuei. 1944. The influence of the Primitive Tai glottal stop and preglottalized consonants on the tone system of Po-ai. *Bulletin of Chinese Studies* 4, 59-68.
[19] Liu, Fu. 1925. *Étude expérimentale sur le tons du chinois.* [Collection de L'Institut de Phonétique et des Archives de la Parole, Fascicule 1] Paris: Société d'Édition.
[20] McCawley, James D. 1965. *The Phonological Component of a Grammar of Japanese*. PhD. Dissertation, MIT.
[21] Meringer, R., Meyer, K. 1895. *Versprechen und Verlesen*. Stuttgart.
[22] Ohala, J. J. 1981. Speech timing as a tool in phonology. *Phonetica* 38, 204-217.
[23] Ohala, J. J. 1993. The phonetics of sound change. In: Charles Jones (ed.), *Historical Linguistics: Problems and Perspectives*. London: Longman, 237-278.
[24] Ohala, J. J., Ohala, M. 1995. Speech perception and lexical representation: The role of vowel nasalization in Hindi and English. In: Connell, B. & Arvaniti, A. (eds.), *Phonology and Phonetic Evidence. Papers in Laboratory Phonology IV*. Cambridge: Cambridge University Press, 41-60.
[25] Rask, R. K. 1818. *Undersøgelse om det gamle Nordiske eller Islandske Sprogs Oprindelse.* Copenhagen: Gyldendalske Boghandlings Forlag.
[26] Sajnovics, Janos. 1770. *Demonstratio idioma Ungarorum et Lapponum idem esse.* Tyrnavia.
[27] Schane, Sanford. 1965. *The Phonological and Morphological Structure of French*. PhD. Dissertation, MIT.
[28] ten Kate, Lambert. 1710. *Gemeenschap tussen de Gottisch spreke en de Nederduytsch.* Amsterdam: Jan Rieuwertsz.
[29] ten Kate Hermansz, Lambert. 1723. *Aenleidning tot de Kennisse van het verhevene Deel der nederduitsche Sprake*, 2 Vols. Amsterdam: Rudolph en Gerard Wetstein.
[30] Van Boxhorn, Marcus Zuerius. 1647. *Bediedinge van de tot noch toe onbekende afgodinne Nehalennia.* Leyden: Willem Christiaens vander Boxe.
[31] Verner, Karl. 1875. Eine Ausnahme der ersten Lautverschiebung. *[Kuhn's] Zeitschrift der vergleichende Sprachforschung* 23, 97-130.
[32] Wang, William S-Y. 1969. Competing changes as a cause of residue. *Language* 45, 9-25.
[33] Wu Zongji. 2000. From Traditional Chinese Phonology to Modern Speech Processing — Realization of Tone and Intonation in Standard Chinese. *ICSLP'2000*.
[34] Young, Thomas. 1819. Remarks on the Probabilities of Errors in Physical Observations, and on the density of the earth, considered, especially, with regard to the reduction of experiments on the pendulum. *Philosophical Transactions of the Royal Society of London* 109, 70-95.
[35] Zimmer, Karl E. 1969. Psychological correlates of some Turkish morpheme structure conditions. *Language* 45, 309-321.

PHONETICS: CONSISTENCY AND VARIABILITY

Louis C.W. POLS

ABSTRACT

Spoken Language is conceptualized and produced by humans as well as perceived and understood by them in communicative situations, unless human-computer interaction is involved. This human speech is remarkably consistent and amazingly variable at the same time. Given the seemingly ease with which young children acquire their mother tongue, it is surprising that second language acquisition is so difficult for adults. The variability in natural speech is related to anatomy, speaking style and emotion, speaking rate, reduction and co-articulation, external conditions, etc. but also to word choice, grammar and syntax, education, etc. The speech consistency, with or without speaker normalization, channel normalization, rate normalization etc. together with the common language background makes it possible to understand each other nevertheless. In this short contribution in honor of the 100th birthday of the distinguished scientist Prof. Wu Zongji, I would like to report about some research projects that I jointly perform(ed) with some of my (former) PhD. students on phonetic variability and consistency.

Keywords: cowel identification, tracheoesophageal speech, diphthongs and long vowels of Dutch

1. INTRODUCTION

In large parts of the Western world it is customary and mandatory to retire at 65 years of age, which happened to me in 2006. It is then a shock to realize that in China there is this Prof. Wu who is still actively involved in phonetics research despite being almost 35 years older. I had the honor to meet Wu Zongji on several occasions; one was related to a working visit I made in 1990 to NTT Basic Research Laboratories in Musashino. This then also allowed me to participate in the first ICSLP conference in Kobe, so capably organized by Prof. Hiroya Fujisaki. Despite all his organizing obligations Fujisaki managed to be an excellent host and made it possible for Prof. Wu and me to visit a Kabuki theatre performance. In 1997 I spent a short period of time at Peking University to give some guest lectures there. On that occasion I also visited the Department of Phonetics of the Institute of Linguistics of Chinese Academy of Social Sciences. Prof. Wu actively participated in the lively discussions following my presentation and joined us for an exquisite lunch with Peking Duck, after which he took the trouble to guide me for several hours through the Forbidden City. I am still most grateful for that. The last public performance that I witnessed of Prof. Wu was a memorable keynote presentation in perfect English at the opening of the 6th ICSLP in Beijing in October 2000. This lecture, entitled 'From traditional Chinese phonology to modern speech processing — realization of tone and intonation in standard Chinese', is the perfect illustration of phonetic *variation*, this time of tone and intonation in spoken Chinese. The underling tonal patterns that have to be filtered out, comprise the *consistency* that allows for interpretation and for speech synthesis.

It is my intention in this small contribution to the Festschrift to present some recent work I jointly performed with some of my PhD students: David Weenink [18], Petra Jongmans [8] and Irene Jacobi

[4]. It is about three totally different topics, thus also illustrating the diversity and multidisciplinarity of Phonetics.

2. SPEAKER — ADAPTIVE VOWEL IDENTIFICATION

Vowels in words in sentences are generally very well understood by native listeners. Only under critical conditions, such as poor pronunciation, bad communication channel or ambiguous context, the intelligibility might become more difficult. By isolating vowel segments from their context one realizes that the remaining spectro-temporal information in such a segment is sometimes barely sufficient for identification. Koopmans-van Beinum [12] showed this for Dutch in a listening experiment where stimuli varied from vowels spoken in isolation, to vowel segments from isolated words, up to segments from unstressed vowels in free conversational speech. The percentage correct scores averaged over 100 listeners, the 12 Dutch vowels, and the 2 male and 2 female speakers were 89.6%, 84.3% and 33.0% respectively. Formant analyses of the stimuli confirmed that an additional complexity arises when stimuli from different speakers are mixed.

Weenink [18] carefully compared such 'mixed' and 'blocked' conditions with isolated Dutch vowels spoken by 5 male and 5 female speakers and 5 children. The error percentages averaged over 20 listeners, 12 vowels, and these 15 speakers are 10.9 and 4.4% for the mixed and blocked conditions respectively. Actually, he also used several other stimuli such as 50ms fixed duration, synthesized with fixed F_0, or whispered, but always the blocked condition showed better performance (lower error scores) than the mixed condition.

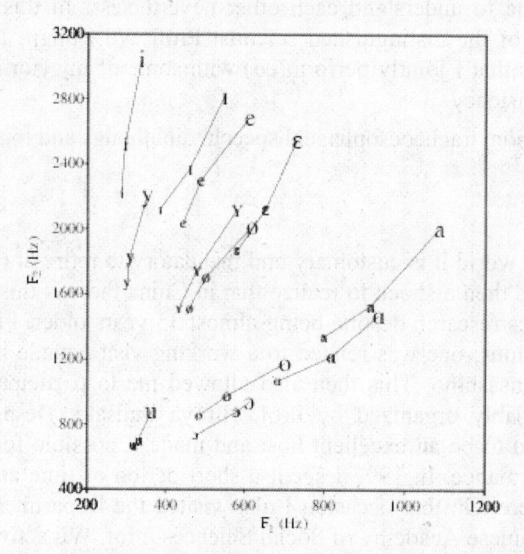

Figure 1: Average formant positions for 12 Dutch vowels spoken in isolation by 10 males (smallest size phonetic symbols), 10 females (intermediate), and 10 children (largest). From Weenink [18].

Formant analyses also illustrate the vowel variability over male, female and children speakers, see Fig. 1. Adapting to the speaker, as is possible in a blocked condition, apparently helps the listener. This is also well-known in automatic speech recognition, although the best way to do this is less well understood. Large-vocabulary speaker-adaptive systems are heavily trained for one speaker, but this does not allow for a quick switch to another speaker, whereas smaller-vocabulary multi-speaker systems generally use an average-speaker model and do not adapt. Quick adaptation would be advantageous but also has the risk over overreacting. Adapting with prior knowledge of what is said would also be helpful, but is not always realistic. Pols et al. [15] already showed that 'centering' the formant or bandfilter vowel data per speaker, clearly improves recognition performance, but this (extrinsic) normalization requires the availability of a complete set of vowel data per speaker beforehand. Weenink [18] evaluated various intrinsic (immediate, without preliminary knowledge) and extrinsic speaker normalization methods, and also looked at the benefit of using dynamic rather than static vowel information. Most of his analyses were performed with the TIMIT dataset [13], containing 630 American-English male and female speakers that each spoke 10 sentences. The 630 speakers were split into 326 male speakers in the training set and 112 in the test set, plus 136 female speakers in the train and 56 in the test set. Twenty vowel categories were considered. We used both formant and bandfilter analyses. We also used various pattern recognition procedures, such as principal components analysis (PCA), discriminant analysis (DA), procrustes normalization (PT), feedforward neural nets (FNN), and adaptive resonance theory networks (ART). Five extrinsic speaker normalization procedures were tested:

- bias adaptation in a neural net for formant data
- discriminant analysis on TIMIT bandfilter data
- neural net bias adaptation for bandfilter data
- vowel recognition with Category ART
- procrustes normalization

For details of these analyses and for many other details, I refer to Weenink [18] and Pols and Weenink [16]. Here we just present in Table 1 the discriminant classification results of the TIMIT vowels with 18-dimensional bandfilter data. On the left-hand side the training data are specified, whereas on the right-hand side the percentages correct for the various test sets are given. We distinguish 'all data', both stressed and unstressed (train set 57463 vowel segments; test set 20911), 'all summary data' implying average vowel data per speaker (train set 8498; test set 3081), and 'all stressed vowel data' (train 36328; test 13234), each time for male and female speaker separately. Furthermore we distinguish between 'static' and 'dynamic', indicating that either one central 20ms frame or three (one central and two frames 25ms before and after the midpoint) frames per vowel segment are used. The numbers between parentheses concern correct scores after speaker normalization (by simply centering the data per speaker to the group average).

Table 1: Average percentage correct scores of TIMIT vowel data using discriminant classification. For more details about the training and testing conditions, see text.

	trained with		tested with				
			Static		Dynamic		
Data	# train segments	type	Train data	Test data	Train data	Test data	# test segments
All	40468	M	47.3 (50.3)	48.4 (50.6)	56.0 (58.4)	55.7 (58.1)	13889
	16995	F	46.4 (49.3)	46.1 (48.6)	56.3 (59.0)	54.7 (57.1)	7022
All Summary	6008	M-S	65.9 (76.6)	66.8 (77.3)	84.4 (89.9)	83.6 (89.0)	2070
	2490	F-S	62.0 (73.9)	61.2 (73.6)	83.8 (88.7)	79.7 (86.6)	1011
All Stressed (+)	25706	M+	49.8 (53.0)	50.9 (53.7)	60.7 (63.1)	60.0 (62.7)	8845
	10622	F+	49.0 (51.9)	48.9 (51.3)	60.7 (63.5)	59.4 (62.3)	4389

For instance the last row in this table should thus be read in the following way: A discriminant classifier trained with the 10622 stressed vowels of 136 female speakers in the *train* part of TIMIT shows a correct score of 49.0% when tested with the same data set, and shows a correct score of 48.9% when tested with the 4389 stressed vowels of 56 female speakers in the *test* part. When three frames, rather than one frame of bandfilter data are used for training and testing, these scores are 60.7% and 59.4% respectively. Reducing individual variation, by using average data per vowel per speaker (condition 'All Summary'), leads to substantially higher correct scores. Dynamic information substantially improves the score, just as speaker normalization by centering does, under all conditions. However, one should keep in mind that for this extrinsic speaker normalization method information about the whole vowel set of each speaker was always required.

More interesting is probably our *intrinsic* normalization attempt. Such a more human-like adaptation method should have to adapt faster without preliminary knowledge about the identity of the vowel(s). One solution could be *to make local differences have global consequences*. We have implanted such a model in the following way:

- Start with a trained discriminant analyzer and suppose that an average reference vowel position is available for each vowel;
- Then an unknown vowel is presented to the classifier and the distance to each reference vowel is determined;
- The shortest distance is determined and tested against a tolerance criterion, for we want to make sure that the unknown is 'close enough' to the reference;
- If the 'close enough' criterion is satisfied, all references are moved parallel to the direction of the difference vector, otherwise no changes are made.

Applying this procedure to the male summary data we can improve the score from 66.8% (see Table 1) to 69.7% by optimizing the parameter α that defines how much the current reference positions of all 20 vowels will move. In order to achieve this improvement, all vowel data from one speaker have to be presented sequentially, thus this is similar to the blocked condition. We applied 50 different permutations of the data. If each time a new vowel item from a different speaker is presented (mixed condition), no real improvement could be achieved, although still the blocked score was always higher than the mixed score, just as in human vowel recognition.

All analyses performed in this project were done with the freely available speech signal processing package 'Praat', developed by Boersma and Weenink (http://www.praat.org/). With respect to this Festschrift, it may be interesting to refer to one specific application that was also developed within Praat, namely a system that supports beginning students of Mandarin Chinese to produce tones correctly [19].

3. THE INTELLIGIBILITY OF TRACHEOESOPHAGEAL SPEECH ANALYSIS AND REHABILITATION

In a tone language like Mandarin Chinese the proper generation of tones is mandatory for the accurate understanding of words. However, in any language, voicing and pitch variation are used to distinguish between phonemes, to produce word stress and sentence accent, to express meaning and emotion, etc. It is thus an enormous handicap if, because of laryngeal cancer, the entire larynx including the vocal folds has to be removed (total laryngectomy). This also implies that the trachea (wind pipe) is disconnected from the esophagus (digestive tract) and is bent forward and sutured in the skin at the base of the neck (tracheostoma) for breathing. Apart from the use of an electro-larynx (simple external voice source) and esophageal speech (a small amount of air is swallowed into the esophagus and then belched out again), tracheoesophageal (TE) speech is an excellent solution. This requires a prosthesis (like Provox®) to be put in a small hole made between trachea and esophagus. This prosthesis is a one-way valve allowing air (after closing the stoma) to go from the lungs via the trachea into the esophagus where the so-called neoglottis can be put into vibration, thus serving as a new voice source. This allows much longer phonation times than with esophageal speech. However, since the neoglottis is much less flexible and controllable than the natural vocal folds, the intelligibility of TE-speech is generally less good than that of natural speech. So far it is not very common to give the TE-patients speech training, since after all they can breathe and speak again. In this project of Petra Jongmans, which is a continuation of an earlier project of Corina van As [1] about the voice quality of TE-speech, the rehabilitation component (therapy program) got much attention. However, in order to know better what to train, also an acoustic analysis and a perceptual assessment of TE-speech was performed. I will present below some results of the three elements of this study. For many more details see the doctoral thesis of Jongmans [8] as well as several publications [9][10][11].

3.1 Perceptual assessment of TE-speech

Eleven male laryngectomized TE speakers using TE speech by means of a Provox® voice prosthesis [3] produced speech material consisting of syllables (CV, n=18×3; VCV, n=21×3; VC, n=11×3; some consonant clusters in initial, medial and final position; and hVt, n=15), nonsense sentences (so-called semantically unpredictable sentences, see Benoit, 1990) and 2 to 3 minutes of free monologues. Ten native Dutch naïve listeners, with no prior experience of TE-speech, performed various listening tasks for these nine sub sets.

The seven syllable sets had to be identified by using normal spelling, which fortunately is unambiguous in Dutch. Percentage correct scores as well as confusions were studied. Special attention was given to the voiced-voiceless contrast. For some results, see Table 2 below.

Also what listeners understood from the SUS-sentences was typed in normal spelling, resulting in percentage sentence correct scores. Table 3 shows the great variability in scores over the 11 TE speakers.

Table 2: Percentage correct scores for initial, medial and final *consonants*, as well as for manner of articulation. Scores are averaged over 11 TE speakers, 10 listeners and 3 vowel environments. Also percentage unvoiced *plosives* perceived as voiced and vice versa are given, as well as consonant clusters scores. One should keep in mind that the number of Dutch consonants (#) per category and per position varies. For comparison the consonant scores in CVCVC nonsense words for normal speakers are also given (Pols, 1983).

	initial	#	medial	#	final	#	overall
consonant	66	*18*	73	*20*	82	*10*	72
plosive	76	*5*	79	*6*	90	*3*	80
fricative	52	*7*	56	*7*	88	*3*	60
nasal	77	*2*	86	*3*	62	*2*	77
approximant	75	*4*	85	*4*	79	*2*	80
consonant clusters	68	*5*	82	*5*	85	*5*	78
plosives UV–>V	25		14		n.a.		
plosives V–>UV	5		7		n.a.		
CVCVC (Pols, 1983)	94	*17*	92	*17*	96	*11*	

Table 3: SUS-sentence correct score per TE speaker and overall

TE-speaker	*1*	*2*	*3*	*4*	*5*	*6*	*7*	*8*	*9*	*10*	*11*	overall
sentence score	94	78	82	74	68	55	32	26	12	46	56	57

Eleven bipolar semantic 7-point scales were used to judge the spontaneous speech segments. Seven of these were intelligibility scales, such as *easy vs. difficult to understand*, *normal vs. deviant*, and *clear vs. mumbled*. Four were voice quality scales, such as *beautiful vs. ugly*, *low vs. high* and *deep vs. shrill*, whereas the listeners also made one overall judgment (*good-moderate-poor*). A principal components analysis was performed on the correlation matrix of the mean scores for each speaker on each scale to investigate relations between the different rating scales. Only one component with an eigenvalue larger than one could be extracted, which explained almost 74% of the variance. This implies that our naïve listeners were unable to distinguish between voice quality and speech intelligibility scales. Although the principal components analysis found only one component, it seems that the scale *easy vs. hard to understand* is the most important scale for intelligibility research in TE speakers. This scale is also a good predictor for the *good-moderate-poor* judgment. Correlations were determined between the 12 semantic scales on the one hand and the various phonemes and SUS sentence scores on the other hand. Most of the phoneme tests do not correlate in any significant way with the scale judgments on spontaneous speech. However, consonants in initial and medial position, and clusters in initial and final position do correlate quite well with some of the scales. SUS-scores correlate highly with all scales except *low vs. high*.

Some of the results that may have implications for the therapy program are the following: TE-speech intelligibility is severely compromised when compared with normal laryngeal speech, see Table 2, thus strengthening the feeling that speech training may truly be beneficial. Fricatives show the lowest scores of all manner categories, so they should definitely be included in the therapy program. A large part of the therapy program should consist of training the problematic voiced-voiceless distinction, as exemplified for the plosives in Table 2. Beyond the phoneme level, attention should also be given to sentence and spontaneous-speech intelligibility.

3.2 Acoustic analysis of the voicing distinction in Dutch TE-speech

To get a better insight in the voicing distinctions as produced by TE speakers, we analyzed the temporal characteristics of all medial plosives and fricatives /p-b, t-d, f-v, s-z/. We limited this to those realizations that were perceived at least 80% correct, this number of realizations was 98. By comparison, the medial plosives and fricatives of five normal laryngeal (NL) speakers were also measured, amounting to 60 realizations. We will present only some result here for the plosives, for more details see Jongmans [8]. Eight durational correlates were measured, such as *preceding vowel duration*, *closure duration*, *burst duration*, etc. Additionally, six derived measures were taken into account, such as *phonation offset after first vowel as percentage of closure duration*, *percentage of voiced frames in the closure* and *relative burst intensity*.

A linear mixed effect model was used to calculate differences including four factors: TE vs. NL speakers, voiced vs. voiceless, vowel type, and place of articulation. All correlates differentiate significantly between voiced and voiceless. A conditional inference tree analysis showed that *relative phonation time in the closure* is the most distinguishing correlate for TE speakers. We had thought that TE-speakers would exaggerate certain segmental correlates to convey a voiced-voiceless contrast and that this would distinguish them from NL speakers. However, our results do not confirm this hypothesis. Still, consistent voicing is a problem; TE speakers show a lower percentage of voiced frames and more individual variation in voiced plosives than NL speakers. TE speakers also show a lower harmonics-to-noise ratio both for voiced and voiceless plosives. These and other results suggest that TE speakers have more difficulty to employ actual voicing than NL speakers. Some TE speakers are indeed able to use periodicity as distinguishing correlate, thus suggesting the presence of a myoelastic component, but it is not present in all speakers and it is not always used consistently.

3.3 Developing and testing an evidence-based therapy program to improve TE-speech intelligibility

Given the above results, the therapy program contains training on individual articulatory features at the phoneme and word level (6 lessons), as well as training on clear speech and optimal prosody (phrasing and use of accents) (3 lessons). Nine one-hour sessions was the maximum that was refundable by medical insurance within the Dutch system. The success of the therapy program was tested with a pre and post test (phoneme and sentence identification tests and qualitative judgments of TE-speech intelligibility by using semantic scales and study-specific questionnaires). Nine subjects completed the program. They read out loud CV and VCV nonsense syllables (for the consonants) and CVC words (for the vowels), embedded in a carrier phrase, a Dyva word list, and semantically unpredictable sentences (Benoit, 1990). They also read a story and produced a retold version. The phoneme and sentence identification experiment was performed online by 10 phonetically trained listeners. The Dyva word lists were evaluated online by six speech language pathologists. Ten naïve listeners performed the semantic scaling experiment with bipolar 7-point scales similar to those discussed above, both for the read and the retold material. Also an overall judgment (good-moderate-poor) was given. The study-specific questionnaires (four options per question) consisted of 11 questions for the TE speakers themselves and 10 questions for a close relative. All above tests were performed before as well as after the therapy program. Some results are presented in Table 4.

Table 4: Mean scores on various tests before and after the therapy program, plus an indication of the significance of the differences. For more details, see text and Jongmans [8].

	pre test	post test	sign
initial plosives	77	79	ns
initial fricatives	50	62	p<.01
initial nasals	88	87	ns
initial approximant	77	83	ns
initial mean	67	74	p<.01
medial plosives	81	86	p<.01
medial fricatives	62	69	p<.01
medial nasals	73	86	p<.01
medial approximant	90	92	ns
medial mean	73	79	p<.01
vowels	93	94	ns
SUS sentences	46	60	p<.01
Dyva word test	91	93	sign.
speakers questionnaire	2.88	3.18	p<.01
relatives questionnaire	3.21	3.35	ns
retold	4.07	3.83	p<.01
read	3.91	3.94	ns

Several of the phoneme scores as well as the sentence scores show progress. Space does not permit us to go into any detail concerning the semantic scaling. We just give the overall scores for all 18 scales together for the read and the retold material in the two last rows in Table 4 (the higher the score, the better the intelligibility). Apparently, for continuous speech there is not much progress (in the retold condition performance even degraded significantly). More time will have to be spent in the therapy program on continuous speech. Probably the retelling task was also too difficult for them: Although they were instructed to produce spontaneous speech while errors did not matter, they tried to retell the story as correctly as possible, which they felt to be a hard job to do. The speakers themselves appear to be quite satisfied with their participation in the limited therapy program.

4. VARIATION AND CHANGE IN DIPHTHONGS AND LONG VOWELS OF SPOKEN DUTCH

In the two projects discussed so far, speech variation was caused by inter- and intra-speaker differences (and the possibilities for speaker normalization) and by deviant speech quality after total laryngectomy. This third project, of Irene Jacobi, is about sociolinguistic variability. It was initiated by the earlier observation [17][2] of lowering of (the onset of) the Dutch diphthong /ɛi/ by young well-educated females and this variant was called Polder Dutch or avant-garde Dutch. This pronunciation variation was systematically studied by Jacobi [4]see also [5][6][7] for long vowel (/e:, o:/) and diphthong (/ei, ɑu, œy/ segments taken from spontaneous speech. 70 Speakers from CGN [Spoken Dutch Corpus, 14]were selected and balanced as good as possible in terms of sex (male and female), age (19-76 years), regional background (4 regions) and level of education and occupation (high and low social status). Although formant analyses were also performed, most analyses were based on principal component analyses (PCA) of bark-filtered spectra. The pc1 — pc2 plane itself was derived from a PCA on all average /a/, /i/ and /u/ bandfilter spectra of all 70 speakers. We chose to express all measured *onset lowering* and *amount of diphthongization* relative to the position of the individual corner vowels /a, i, u/. This way we applied a nice way of speaker normalization and it appeared to make our measurements also less sensitive to the noisiness of many live recordings. Actually the percentage onset lowering per realization was expressed as the pc1 (first principal component) distance to /a/ relative to the pc1 — distance between /a/ and /i/. A negative value thus represents much lowering. Similarly the percentage degree of diphthongization was expressed as the pc1 — distance between onset and offset (at 10% and 90% of the segment duration) relative to pc1 — distance between /a/ and /i/. A 100% score thus represents much dynamics, much diphthongization. It will be clear that there will be much individual variation in the data. Still there were various significant effects, but because of the large number of factors, the picture is rather complicated. Some of the main findings are: With our way of analyzing and presenting the data, there were no significant differences between male and female data. The higher-educated speakers showed more lowering and more diphthongization for all vowels than the lower-educated speakers. By grouping the continuous parameter *age* into three discrete *age groups* (young-mid-old), several more interesting effects showed up. The factor 'level of education' appeared to be the most regular main effect, followed by the factor 'age group'. When split to age groups, significant patterns of change in pronunciation between generations were found for the higher-educated generations, most salient for /o:/ and /e:/. For many more interesting details, see Jacobi [4]. There, also a same-different perception experiment is described that compares speaker realizations of vowels within words. It is shown that the most salient spectro-temporal differences in the vowel realizations are indeed perceptually relevant. Also the age of the listeners appeared to have an influence upon the judgment of the (dis)similarities of the vowel pronunciations of the speakers.

5. CONCLUSION

Although the three studies are widely different, I consider all three of them to be highly relevant for many important questions in phonetic sciences. They are all three examples of the enormous variability that occurs in the production of real speech. However, they illustrate at the same time the enormous flexibility by the listeners in coping with these differences while extracting and interpreting the relevant information for recognition and understanding.

6. ACKNOWLEDGEMENTS

Although I (co-)supervised all three projects, it will be clear that almost all the hard work has been done by the PhD. students David Weenink, Petra Jongmans and Irene Jacobi, for which I want to thank them a lot. Also the other supervisors Frans Hilgers, Corina van As-Brooks, Fred Weerman and Jan Stroop greatly contributed to these projects.

REFERENCES

[1] As, C.J. van. 2001. *Tracheoesophageal speech. A multidimensional assessment of voice quality.* PhD. Dissertation, University of Amsterdam.

[2] Benoit, C. 1990. An intelligibility test using semantically unpredictable sentences: towards the quantification of linguistics complexity. *Speech Communication* 9, 293-304.

[3] Heuven, V.J. van, Edelman, L., Bezooijen, R. van. 2002. The pronunciation of /ɛi/ by male and female speakers of avant-garde Dutch. *Linguistics in the Netherlands*, 61-72.

[4] Hilgers, F.J.M., Schouwenburg, P.F. 1990. A new low-resistance, self retaining prosthesis (Provox®) for voice rehabilitation after total laryngectomy. *Laryngoscope* 100, 1202-1207.

[5] Jacobi, I. 2009. *On variation and change in diphthongs and long vowels of spoken Dutch.* PhD. Dissertation, University of Amsterdam.

[6] Jacobi, I., Pols, L.C.W., Stroop, J. 2005. Aspects of the /ɛi/-lowering in Standard Dutch. *Proc. Interspeech 2005*, 2877-2800.

[7] Jacobi, I., Pols, L.C.W., Stroop, J. 2006. Measuring and comparing vowel qualities in a Dutch spontaneous speech corpus. *Proc. Interspeech 2006*, 701-704.

[8] Jacobi, I., Pols, L.C.W., Stroop, J. 2007. Dutch diphthong and long vowel realizations as changing socio-economic markers. *Proc. ICPhS 2007*, 1481-1484.

[9] Jongmans, P. 2008. *The intelligibility of tracheoesophageal speech. An analytic and rehabilitation study*.PhD. Dissertation, University of Amsterdam.

[10] Jongmans, P., Hilgers, F.J.M., Pols, L.C.W., As-Brooks, C.J. van. 2005. The intelligibility of tracheoesophageal speech: first results. *Proc. Interspeech 2005*, 1749-1752.

[11] Jongmans, P., Hilgers, F.J.M., Pols, L.C.W., As-Brooks, C.J. van. 2006. The intelligibility of tracheoesophageal speech, with an emphasis on the voiced-voiceless distinction. *Logopedics Phoniatrics Vocology* 31, 172-181.

[12] Jongmans, P., Wempe, A.G., Hilgers, F.J.M., Pols, L.C.W., As-Brooks, C.J. van. 2007. Acoustic correlates of the voiced-voiceless distinction in Dutch normal and tracheoesophageal speakers. *Proc. ICPhS XVI*, 1997-2000.

[13] Koopmans-van Beinum, F.J. 1980. *Vowel contrast reduction: An acoustic and perceptual study of Dutch vowels in various speech conditions*. PhD. Dissertation, University of Amsterdam.

[14] Lamel, L.F., Kassel, R.H., Seneff, S. 1986. Speech database development: Design and analysis of the acoustic-phonetic corpus. *Proc. DARPA Speech Recognition Workshop*, 100-109.

[15] Oostdijk, N., Goedertier, W., Eynde, F. van, Boves, L., Martens, J.P., Moortgat, M., Baayen, H. 2002. Experiences from the Spoken Dutch Corpus project. *Proc. 3rd LREC*, 340-347.

[16] Pols, L.C.W., Tromp, H.R.C., Plomp, R. 1973. Frequency analysis of Dutch vowels from 50 male speakers. *J. Acoust. Soc. Am.* 53, 1093-1101.

[17] Pols, L.C.W., Weenink, D. 2005. Vowel recognition and (adaptive) speaker normalization. *Proc. Specom 2005*, Patras, 17-24.

[18] Stroop, J. 1998. *Poldernederlands, waardoor het ABN verdwijnt*. Bert Bakker, Amsterdam.

[19] Weenink, D. 2006. *Speaker-adaptive vowel identification*. PhD. Dissertation, University of Amsterdam.

[20] Weenink, D., Chen, G., Chen, Z, Konink, S. de, Vierkant, D., Hagen, E. Van, Son, R. Van. 2007. Learning tone distinctions for Mandarin Chinese. *Proc. Interspeech 2007*, 2341-2344.

PROSODY MODELING OF COMMUNICATIVE INFORMATION FOR SYNTHESIS AND RECOGNITION

Yoshinori SAGISAKA, Yoko GREENBERG, Ke LI, Mingzhao ZHU,
Minoru TSUZAKI, Hiroaki KATO

ABSTRACT

This paper describes our studies on prosody modeling to treat *communicative information*, information embedded in non-reading speech, conventionally classified as paralinguistic information for its synthetic speech output and its recognition as perceptual impression. To quantitatively describe information embedded in prosody for communication, we have introduced multi-dimensional perceptual impressions and associated them with lexicons. Through dimension reduction using Multi-Dimensional Scaling, consistent correspondence was observed between perceptual impressions and prosodic characteristics of communicative speech, which gave the possibility of transcription and extraction of new communicative prosodic information used to be abandoned as paralinguistics in linguistics. Moreover, high correlations between prosody and lexicons enabled natural prosody generation from input lexicons for communicative speech synthesis. Naturalness evaluation of communicative prosody synthesized using a proposed scheme and the experiment of automatic extraction of perceptual impression suggested a new research paradigm where *communicative information* can be treated using corpus-based quantitative description and computational modeling.

Keywords: communicative prosody, paralinguistic information, speech synthesis, computing prosody, expressive speech synthesis, prosody recognition

1. INTRODUCTION

In speech communication, human use prosodic information for wide variety of speech communications that cannot be conveyed by written languages. The variety of prosody has been studied mainly in relation to linguistic structure and lexical attributes such as accents and tones, which has revealed the relation between information structure and its prosodic manifestation in speech. However, in traditional speech studies, reading style speech has been mainly employed to study linguistic correlates though there are so many different variations in real world speech such as communicative speech used in face-to-face communications. This fact reminds us of the research specification in theoretical linguistics where ungrammatical sentences frequently observed in real world have been disregarded as a problem of performance.

In speech studies, this simplification has worked well as in theoretical linguistics. It has enabled to analyze relations between linguistic components and their manifestations in speech clearly without being bothered by other factors governing speech communications in real world. However, at the same time, this specification has concealed the essential part of spoken language that cannot be fully understood by information considered for written-language based linguistics. Since there has been no efficient descriptive system to treat prosodic variations in real world, people started to study prosodic variations in communicative speech as paralinguistic or non-linguistic information independent of linguistic correlates. Though we cannot clearly formulate this dependency at this moment, we think that it is too early to put all of them out of linguistics. In so called *paralinguistic* information, there exists information highly correlated to linguistic factors. We believe that linguistics should cover some of this information in terms of communicative information to cover spoken language.

In the current speech science and technology, little research efforts have been paid for systematic description and characterization of this *communicative information* as spoken language correlates [8]. Though there have been quite many studies on prosodic variations as emotional speech or expressive speech, most of them have simply characterized the prosody of pre-specified speech category by itself but not as linguistic correlates. We consider that specification of prosody by itself and analysis with respect to linguistic correlates are two keys for effective use of prosodic information in speech communication. We need a description scheme to identify and characterize prosodic variations in communicative speech systematically.

In this article, we introduce our research efforts on the specification and the use of *communicative information* manifested in the prosody of non-reading speech [5][2][3][6][7][9]. In Section 2, we introduce a description of *communicative information* using perceptual impressions which turned out to be highly correlated to F_0 heights and dynamics of communicative speech. In Section 3, we show a communicative prosody generation scheme where additional new component is added to conventional one based on *communicative information* derived from lexicons. In Section 4, we report on the automatic extraction of multi-dimensional perceptual impression as *communicative information* from prosody of a single word utterance "n" in real world speech corpus. Finally, in Section 5, we sum up the current studies on our trials and state further possibilities speculated from current results.

2. COMMUNICATIVE PROSODY DESCRIPTION USING PERCEPTUAL IMPRESSION

2.1 Perceptual impression vector

In order to specify communicative information conveyed by prosody in non-reading style speech, we have observed prosodic variations of a single word utterance "n" which is, acoustic phonetically, a sustained utterance of either [m], [n] or [eng] and frequently used in conversations [5]. In Japanese, it can be an interjection, rejoinder, or filler depending on the context or situation. A single word "n" is used to express quite a wide variety of information coupled with different prosodic patterns though it only consists of a single phonetic category. Since single phrase utterance of "n" has neither any linguistic structure nor finer constituent, we can directly compare their prosodic features with perceptual impressions without being bothered by complex linguistic factors.

Through the analyses on prosodic variations of "n", we found that its F_0 characteristics can be classified by its height and four types of dynamics (rise, flat, fall and rise+fall). In order to specify the information conveyed by communicative prosody, we adopt descriptions of perceptual impressions. After preliminary listening tests, we decided to use twenty-six word expressions for the description of perceptual impressions. These impression words were *doubt, ambivalence, understanding, approve, deny, objection, agreement, dark, weakly, not interested, bad mood, heavy, bothering, audacious, anger, annoying, cheerful, delight, gentle, good mood, excited, happy, light, interested,* and *bright*.

Based on our observation of "n", twelve single word utterances that were controlled by three types of average F_0 height (high, mid, low) and four types of F_0 dynamics (rise, flat, fall and rise+fall) were served in a perceptual impression experiment. With respect to these word expressions for the description of perceptual impressions, we asked listeners to quantitatively evaluate speech impression in twenty-six dimensions based on the semantic differential (SD) method. Hereafter, we call this multi-dimensional expression of perceptual impressions an impression vector.

By applying multi-dimensional scaling (MDS) to the metric defined as Euclidian distance of each impression vector, we found that the perceptual impressions can be reduced to three dimensions. By carefully associating six directions determined by these three dimensions with the impression words, we decided to refer these axes as *confident-doubtful*, *allowable-unacceptable* and *positive-negative*. Though these axis names by themselves can show their own directions which may not exactly coincide to these axes in this perception space, we would like to refer them by words through its rough meaning correspondence rather than as dimension1, 2 and 3.

Interesting enough, these three dimensions were found to be systematically highly correlated to the height and dynamics of F_0 and the duration [5]. The dimension showing *positive-negative* was highly related with F_0 average heights while the ones of confident-doubtful and *unacceptable-allowable* were related with F_0 dynamic patterns. The higher/lower the F_0 average height was, the more positive/negative impression appeared to be indicated respectively. F_0 dynamic patterns were located in order of Rise, Flat, Rise+Fall and Fall, and this order was corresponded to impression of doubtful-confident. Moreover, the speech samples were located in the order of Rise+Fall, Rise, Flat and Fall from the unacceptable impressions toward allowable. This fact suggests the possibility of prosody control by multi-dimensional impressions as input information.

2.2 Generalization using real data

As stated in the previous section, the relation between prosodic characteristics and perceptual impressions was first confirmed using single word "n". Though we focused on F_0 height and dynamic patterns based on small sized preliminary data, further analyses [3] showed that these patterns were quite essential and could cover randomly selected 6271 samples among 23648 single phrase utterances of "n" from the 150 hours speech data spoken by one Japanese female in JCT/CREST ESP project [10]. From the shapes of VQ centroids of these F_0 patterns as shown in Figure 1, it was confirmed that the F_0 dynamic patterns could be classified into four categories. For F_0 heights, they were continuously distributed.

Moreover, we observed that these prosodic characteristics were not only restricted to single phrase utterance of "n", but also other phrases generally used in daily communications [2][3]. As explained in the next Section 3, in these studies, speech synthesis experiments showed the possibility of prosody generation by copying prosodic characteristics of "n" to other phrases through an

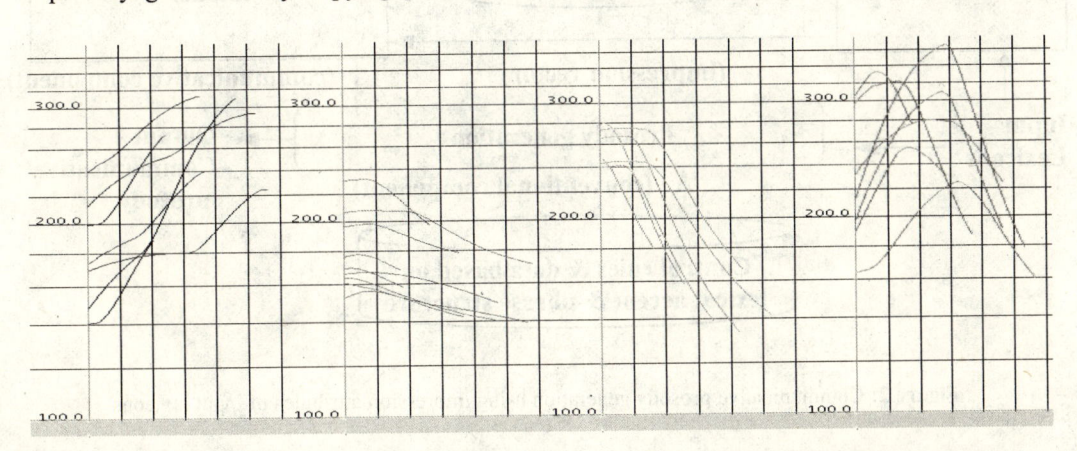

Figure 1: Typical F_0 dynamic patterns of "n" observed in daily communications

impression vector.

Since the relationship between perceptual impressions and prosodic characteristics looks quite general, we can expect that impression cues are systematically manifested in speech. This idea gives us a possibility of a reverse mapping, that is, the automatic extraction of perceptual impression from communicative prosody. If we can successfully extract perceptual impression form single phrase utterance of "n", it can be applied to other common single phrases. We introduce experimental results on the extraction of perceptual impression from "n" in Section 4.

3. COMMUNICATIVE SPEECH SYNTHESIS BASED ON INPUT LEXICON

3.1 Communicative prosody generation scheme

The relationship between prosodic characteristics and perceptual impressions was found not only in a single word "n" but also in general single phrases. In general single phrases, their lexical attributes are highly correlated to its communicative prosody [2]. For this lexical attributes, as a first step, we adopted an impression vector. Though we are treating single phrase only as a first step, we are considering a prosody generation scheme shown in Figure 2.

As shown in Figure 2, input words are not only used to compute conventional prosody control characteristics in text-to-speech modules but also their attributes can be employed to estimate communicative prosody expressed by three dimensional impression factors: confident-doubtful, allowable-unacceptable and positive-negative. For this use, we should store these impression scores for each word as lexical impression attributes. Though the current modeling is carried out for a single phrase where we use each prototypical one-dimensional attribute only, we expect that this modeling can be expanded to combinations expressed as an impression vector determined by output lexicons. The prosodic variations are newly generated in communicative prosody module using perceptual impression vectors. The communicative F_0 dynamic patterns, durations and F_0 average height are calculated from the input impression vectors.

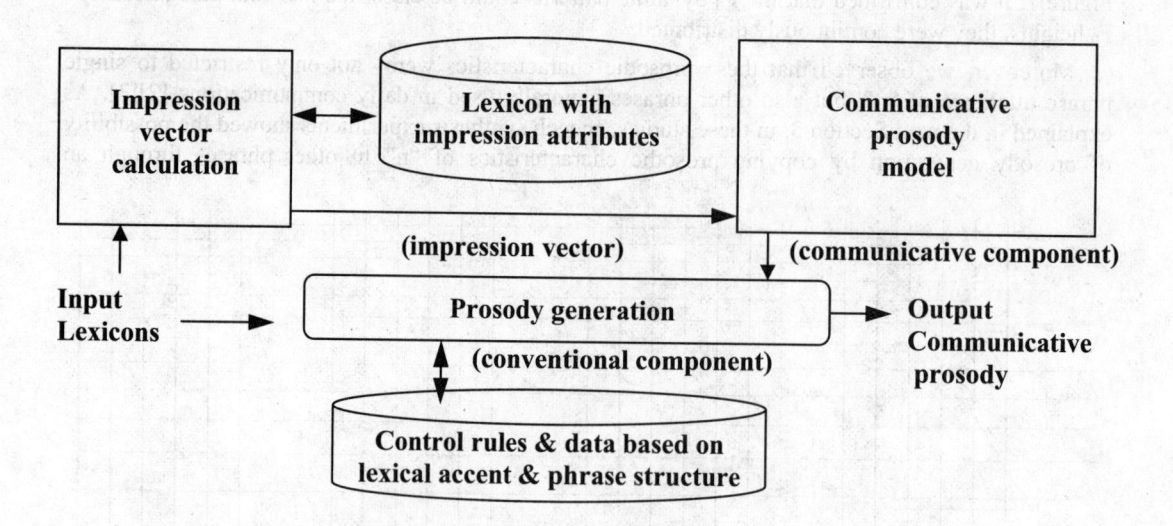

Figure 2: Communicative prosody generation using impression attributes of input lexicons

3.2 F₀ generation using a command-response model

To generate a communicative F₀ contour, we employed a command-response model proposed by Fujisaki [1]. As this model enables F₀ modification constrained by F₀ generation model in a small number of freedom, we expect natural modifications constrained by generation mechanism and clear understanding of modification. As well known, in a command-response model, an F₀ contour is expressed a sum of phrase components and accent components as shown in the following equation.

$$\ln F_0(t) = \ln F_{min} + A_p G_p(t-T_0)$$
$$+ [A_{a1}\{G_t(t-T_1) - G_t(t-T_2)\}$$
$$+ A_{a2}\{G_t(t-T_3) - G_t(t-T_4)\}]$$

where G_p, G_t, F_{min}, A_p, A_{a1}, A_{a2}, T_0, T_1, T_2, T_3 and T_4 correspond to phrase component, accent component, bias level, the magnitude of phrase command, the magnitude of accent commands, the onset time of phrase, the onset and the reset time of accent commands respectively.

In the proposed scheme of communicative prosody generation, communicative component is computed from an input word impression vector. Though we have already studied a training scheme for the mapping from an impression vector to F₀ control parameters using a neural-network for single phrase utterance of "n" [6], it still needs further studies to apply to general phrases. For the current studies of naturalness evaluation, we adopted reading style speech samples and modify their F₀ patterns using the average value of F₀ control parameters and duration obtained from single phrase utterances of "n" for the corresponding impression. We believe that this approximation by the average values would be acceptable for the current use though they are not ideal.

3.3 Naturalness evaluation of synthesized speech with communicative prosody

To confirm the validity of the proposed prosody generation scheme, we generated communicative prosody using the control characteristics of "n". As a first trial, we used twelve single phrase utterances consisting of lexicons expressing six prototypical impressions (*confident-doubtful, allowable-unacceptable and positive-negative*) [3]. These lexicons had already been confirmed to have an expected impression by a subjective evaluation test for lexicons by themselves (i.e. without speech). They were uttered in a reading style by two Japanese native speakers (one male and one female) and recorded in a quiet environment. The prosody of a read speech was used as an ideal prosody of conventional (i.e. read) component and was modified according to prosodic characteristics of "n" that has the same impression. Table 1 shows the modification of F₀ control parameters and total utterance duration. These values were obtained as differences between read-style "n" utterances and prototypical communicative "n" utterances for each impression by averaging several tens of corresponding speech samples.

Table 1: Modification of F₀ generation parameters to add communicative prosody component

	Confident	Doubtful	Allowable	Unacceptable	Positive	Negative
F_{min}	+0.3	−0.25	+0.3	−0.25	+0.3	−0.25
A_p	*1.99	*1.42	*1.99	*2.08	*1	*1
A_a	*2.26	*2.19	*2.26	*1.86	*1	*1
duration	*0.75	*1.3	*0.75	*1.3	*1	*1

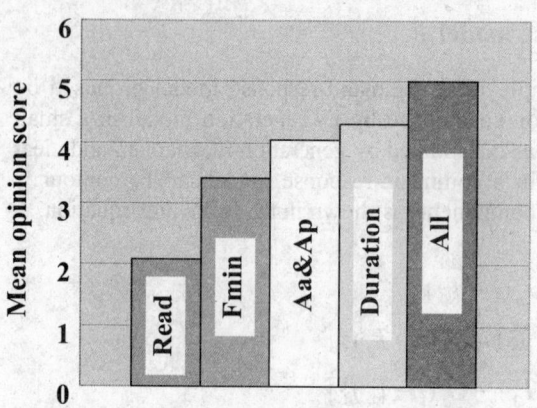

Figure 3: Effectiveness of control factors in communicative prosody component based on impression of input lexicon.

In order to see how the proposed communicative prosody generation scheme reflecting the prosody of single phrase utterance "n" would work for phrases expressing prototypical six impressions, perceptual evaluation tests were carried out. For the perceptual evaluation tests of naturalness, five different patterns of speech corresponding to two dimensional perceptual impressions: *doubtful-confident unacceptable-allowable* were prepared. Besides the neutral speech, prosody of each sample was converted to four different patterns that modified only F_{min}, A_a and A_p, and duration, and all of the four prosodic characteristics using STRAIGHT vocoder [4]. As for the speech samples expressing *positive-negative*, the F_{min} modified version was generated. Accordingly, forty eight speech samples were prepared in total.

We asked a group of subjects to put scores ranging from 0 (reading style) to 7 (conversational style) to each sample phrase. The subjects consisted of four native Japanese speakers (two male and two female). As shown in Figure 3, the results of the subjective perceptual evaluation test showed the effectiveness in increasing the naturalness of speech with communicative prosody by the proposed control scheme.

Moreover, we have conducted another perceptual experiment to evaluate the adequacy of the proposed communicative prosody generation scheme [3].Using another sixteen single phrases expressing various impressions, we synthesized sixty speech samples with various communicative prosody, not only word impression fitted one but also another randomly selected ones. Through the perceptual experiment, we found that 86% of speech samples synthesized with lexicon derived (average) prosody were judged as natural. On the other hand, 88% of the samples which prosodies do not share with the impression with the input phrase were perceived as unnatural. Among the speech samples with lexicon derived prosody, high correlation value 0.87 was obtained between word literal impression (an input impression vector) and perceived impressions. These results show the validity of proposed communicative prosody generation scheme.

3.4 Generalization towards language independent communicative prosody control

Though prosody differs from language to language not only by language intrinsic properties such as accentual properties, prosodic structures but also by other factors such as sociological differences, it is also true that we share some prosodic characteristics commonly. By observing the prosody relating to six prototypical impressions (*confident-doubtful, allowable-unacceptable and positive-negative*) for other languages, we notice that we may share these prosodic differences in other languages. The lexicon based non-literal information in communicative prosody can be easily applied to other languages. To confirm the validity of this idea, we synthesized communicative speech using inter-language prosodic style modification [7]. We synthesized communicative Mandarin speech using prosodic characteristics of communicative Japanese speech. The fundamental frequency and duration characteristics of a Japanese single phrase "n" were copied to Mandarin through an input word impression vector.

Same as communicative prosody generation shown in the previous sections, a three-dimensional vector was calculated through MDS analysis from the subjective impression of an input Chinese word. Communicative Chinese speech was synthesized as same as Japanese one. The prosody of a reading style Chinese speech was used as an ideal prosody of conventional (i.e. read) component and was added according to prosodic characteristics of the Japanese single phrase "n" that has the same impression.

Subjective evaluation showed that 85% of Chinese single phrase speech samples with the prosodies derived from the impression vector were natural. The correlation between lexical impressions of input and perceptual impressions of synthesized speech turned out to be quite high except some samples. By observing these samples, low correlations were resulting from abstractness of words expressing impressions that might allow multiple word usage. Though the inter-language prosody modification has been carried out only from Japanese to Chinese up to this moment, this experimental result suggests the possibility of generalization to language-independent communicative prosody generation through lexicons.

4. AUTOMATIC EXTRACTION OF PERCEPTUAL IMPRESSION

4.1 The inverse mapping from prosody to impression

As a series of synthesis experiments showed in the previous sections, communicative information embedded in non-reading speech can be treated through a perceptual impression vector. Since human can perceive it from communicative speech, it is likely that we can extract perceptual impression from communicative prosody. Though arbitrary phrases may be too difficult to analyze at this moment, we can start to extract it from a simple utterance. If we can successfully extract a perceptual impression vector from simple utterances, we may expect to generalize it as same as the synthesis of communicative prosody.

For this purpose, we decided to extract a perceptual impression vector from communicative speech as a first step [9]. Here again, we employed single phrase utterances of "n" used in Section 2.2. For features to extract impression, we employed prosodic parameters representing F_0 height, dynamics and duration. For F_0 height, we adopted an F_0 average and its dynamic range. To parameterize F_0 dynamics, we normalized an F_0 pattern. Whole duration was employed as duration parameter. To obtain F_0 dynamics, first, an F_0 pattern is normalized using F_0 average and range with whole duration. A normalized F_0 pattern was approximated by the values at equal interval of ten points in normalized duration.

As an output impression, we adopted three-dimensional vector expression instead of original impression word derived dimension by considering robustness of the mapping. For the prediction of perceptual impression, we adopted a three-layered feed-forward neural network. The input consists of thirteen nodes corresponding F_0 average, F_0 range, whole duration and ten parameters expressing normalized F_0 pattern. The output consists of three nodes corresponding to impression vector components corresponding *confident-doubtful, allowable-unacceptable and positive-negative impressions*. The number of hidden layer nodes was chosen to be thirteen same as input. In the network, fully connected net weights were iteratively trained using back-propagation till the reduction of prediction errors was saturated.

4.2 Experiments on perceptual impression extraction

Sixty samples of one-word utterances of "n" were selected to widely cover the samples from the VQ centroids of 1076 samples obtained as representatives of samples of "n" used in Section 2.2. To get perceptual impressions of speech samples, we asked thirteen raters to score each speech sample on the twenty-six impressions used in the previous sections. The scores had 7 levels from –3 (not at all) to 3 (very much). Using 55 samples for the training of the neural network, the other five samples were used as open test data.

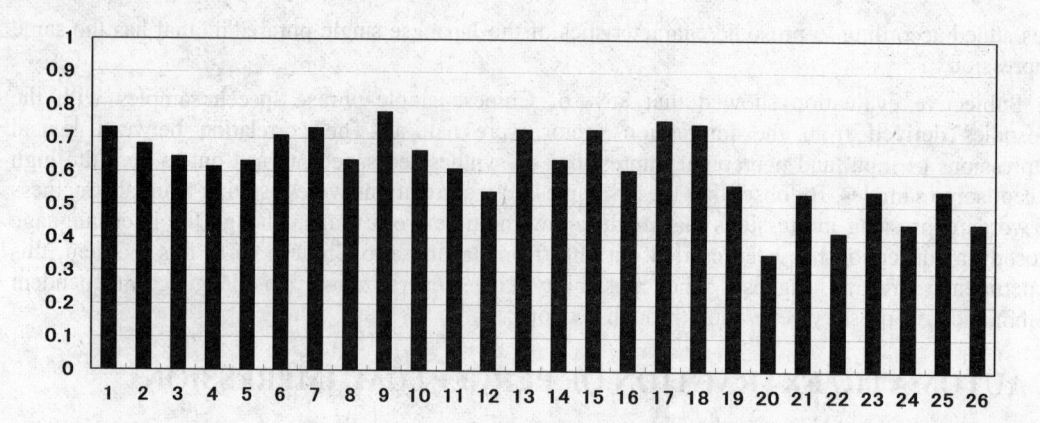

Figure 4: Correlations between the predicted values and perceived average for each component of the 26-dimensional impression expressions (prediction ability of each impression category).
(1: doubt, 2: ambivalence, 3: deny, 4: question, 5: objection, 6: approve, 7: agreement, 8: understanding, 9: bright, 10: dark, 11: cheerful, 12: weak, 13: interested, 14: not interested, 15: good mood, 16: bad mood, 17: light, 18: heavy, 19: gentle, 20: audacious, 21: exciting, 22: bothering, 23: delight, 24: anger, 25: happy, 26: annoying)

As overall prediction accuracy, we got the correlation scores of perceptual impression vectors between extracted ones and perceived ones 0.993 and 0.75 for the closed and open sets, respectively. The mean correlation between the predicted twenty-six-dimensional impressions and the observed twenty-six-dimensional perceptual impressions of the sixty samples turned out to be 0.90 and 0.69 for the closed and open set data respectively. Though the overall correlations were not so high, we found that out of the sixty test samples, more than 90% showed correlations higher than 0.75. Other samples seemed to give unclear subjective impressions. Figure 4 shows the correlations between the predicted values and perceived average for each component of the 26-dimensional impression expressions which correspond to prediction abilities of each impression category. As shown in these correlation scores, most of the impression prediction has been successfully carried out. It was also found that these correlation scores were highly influenced by the variations between raters and that low correlation impressions seemed to result from their abstractness or descriptive ambiguity.

5. CONCLUSION

Our studies on prosody modeling are introduced to synthesize and recognize *communicative information* contained in non-reading speech. To quantify *communicative* information in non-reading prosody, an impression vector has been proposed to describe multi-dimensional perceptual impressions to link prosodic characteristics to lexicons. Through dimension reduction using MDS, systematic correspondences have been observed between lexicons and communicative prosody.

The proposed communicative prosody generation scheme turned out to be effective for single phrase utterances and commonly used in other language. The success of the inverse mapping of impression recognition from input prosody confirmed the usefulness of an impression vector as an intermediate expression and revealed the possibility of bi-directional communicative information processing.

These experimental results indicate a new possibility of communicative prosody characterization in relation to lexical attributes. We prefer the treatment of these kinds of prosodic phenomena in linguistics by expanding the target field of written language to spoken language rather than treating independent to linguistics as paralinguistic information. We believe that this is one of the most important information conveyed by speech and should be studied not merely as a topic in engineering but also as an essential subject of phonetics and linguistics in future.

Furthermore, we expect that this corpus-based approach will be able to provide a new methodology in quantitative specification and analysis of speech communication through definite description of lexical attributes. In particular, we really hope that this type of information description would be of use in future to compute semantics in computational modeling of language and speech.

6. ACKNOWLEDGEMENTS

A part of this work is supported in part by Waseda Univ. RISE research project of "Analysis and modeling of human mechanism in speech and language processing" and Grant-in-Aid for Scientific Research B-2, No. 18300063 of JSPS.

REFERENCES

[1] Fujisaki, H., Hirose, K. 1984. Analysis of voice fundamental frequency contours for declarative sentences of Japanese. *J. Acoust. Soc.* Japan (E), Vol.5, No.4, 233-242.

[2] Greenberg, Y., Tsuzaki, M., Kato, K., Sagisaka, Y. 2005. Communicative speech synthesis using constituent word attributes. *Proc. INTERSPEECH2005*, 517-520.

[3] Greenberg, Y., Tsuzaki, M., Kato, K., Sagisaka, Y. 2006. A trial of communicative prosody generation based on control characteristic of one word utterance observed in real conversational speech. *Proc. Speech Prosody 2006*, 37-40.

[4] Kawahara, H., Masuda-Katsuse, I., Cheveign'e, A. 1999. Restructuring speech representations using a pitch-adaptive time-frequency smoothing and an instantaneous-frequency based F_0 extraction: Possible role of a repetitive structure in sounds. *Speech Communication* 27, 187-207.

[5] Kokenawa, Y., Tsuzaki, M., Kato, K., Sagisaka, Y. 2005. F_0 control characterization by perceptual impressions on speaking attitudes using Multiple Dimensional Scaling analysis. *Proc. ICASSP*, 273-276.

[6] Li K., Greenberg, Y., Campbell, N., Sagisaka, Y. 2007. On the analysis of F_0 control characteristics of nonverbal utterances and its application to communicative prosody generation. In *NATO Security through Science Series E: Human and Societal Dynamics*, Vol.8, The Fundamentals of Verbal and Non-verbal Communication and the Biometric Issue, 179-183, IOS Press.

[7] Li K., Greenberg, Sagisaka Y. 2007. Inter-language prosodic style modification experiment using word impression vector for communicative speech generation. *Proc. INTERSPEECH 2007*, 1294-1297.

[8] Sagisaka, Y., Yamashita, T., Kokenawa, Y. 2005. Generation and perception of F_0 markedness for communicative speech synthesis. *Speech Communication* 46, 376-384.

[9] Zhu M., Li K., Greenberg and Sagisaka, Y. 2007. Automatic extraction of paralinguistic information from communicative speech. *Proc. the 7th Symposium on Natural Language Processing* 2007, 207-212.

[10] JST/CREST Expressive Speech Processing project. http://feast.atr.jp/esp/esp-web/.

BOUNDARY AND LENGTHENING
— ON RELATIVE PHONETIC INFORMATION

TSENG Chiu-yu, SU Zhao-yu

ABSTRACT

The aim of the present study is to better understand the temporal structure of discourse prosody through relative phonetic information, in particular, phrase final lengthening and discourse boundary discrimination. Using data of fluent Mandarin narrative speech, we tested two assumptions to compare their contributions to discourse boundary discrimination, namely, independent/single vs. integrated/paired acoustic cues. Single factors included five acoustic features to see whether the identities of discourse boundaries can be discriminated, namely, (1) boundary pause (BP), (2) pre-boundary duration (PrDu), (3) pre-boundary intensity (PrIn), (4) duration contrast (DuCon) and (5) syllable intensity contrast (InCon). Relative factors were ten paired combinations from the above five features to test their respective contributions to discourse boundary discrimination as well. The results demonstrated that single discrete cues were not as discriminative as paired ones, suggesting that boundary information is related to relative combined cues. Among the paired combinations, the combined cue of pre-boundary syllable duration and the following pause, PreDu+BP, is most discriminative. We further examined pre-boundary lengthening in relation to discourse organization by three discourse prosody units: the syllable, the prosodic word (PW) and the prosodic phrase (PPh), and found pre-boundary global lengthening by the PPh is systematically related to higher-level discourse specifications. The results suggest that discourse constrained tempo modulation across speech flow is default within the same speaking rate. Therefore, we argue that temporal planning is constrained by higher-level discourse planning; higher level planning induces overall lengthening; global lengthening reflects cognitive load. In addition to phone- and syllable-contributed factors, discourse temporal organization is also constrained by discourse unit.

Keywords: discourse boundary, boundary discrimination, final lengthening, relative phonetic information

1. INTRODUCTION

In previous work on narrative prosody, we have established a hierarchical discourse framework the HPG (Hierarchy of Prosodic Phrase Group) through corpus analysis [8]. The discourse perspective allows examination of fluent speech prosody from top-down; it also makes possible clarifications of terms used for phonetic, phonological and prosody investigations. While the segments are phonetic terms [6][5], terms like syllable, prosodic word, intonation phrase (IP) are phonological terms [4][7] often used interchangeably as phonetic units or prosodic units as well [3][1]. However, in a discourse prosody framework pitch (perceived relative F_0), rhythm and tempo (temporal structure and distribution), loudness (perceived relative strength), boundary lengthening (rather than phrase final lengthening) and boundary pause are all but relative prosodic phenomena in relation to discourse organization. Therefore, by default the syllable (Syl), prosodic word (PW), prosodic phrase (PPh), breath-group (BG or compulsory change of breath during fluent speech) and prosodic phrase group (multiple-phrase speech paragraph) are all discourse prosodic units that can be analyzed and compared for relative prosodic properties. In particular, an IP is no longer an ultimate intonation unit (IU) but a discourse sub-unit; phrase intonations are no longer examined in isolation; intonations no longer examined for trajectories only but also for overall relative height and tempo. Further, the HPG framework specifies how prosodic units are constrained and governed by prosodic layers, and how theses units and layers contribute systematically and cumulatively to global output prosody, and why fluent speech prosody must include unit-dependent information in relation to discourse organization, rather than simply phone-and-syllable dependent information plus phrase/sentence intonation [8][9][10]. As a result, three major characteristics of the HPG distinguish it from other prosody studies: (1) it emphasizes the relative cross-unit prosodic association contained in fluent speech and specifies how such relative phonetic in the supra-segmental domain can be accounted for. (2) Boundary breaks across fluent speech are treated as discourse units and bear discourse identities. (3) An intonation phrase is a discourse unit subject to HPG specifications.

The HPG prosodic units from the bottom layer upward are the syllable (SYL), the prosodic word (PW), the prosodic phrase (PPh), the breath group (BG) and the multiple phrase group (PG). Two prosodic layers are higher than PPh in the hierarchy. The immediate higher node of the BG is the PG, which is the highest node in the HPG hierarchy and refers to breathing limit which corresponds to a compulsory physiological constraint. The highest node PG refers to a complete multiple-phrase speech paragraph and corresponds to the obligatory and ultimate cognitive constraint of speech. The hierarchical relationships among these nodes are SYL<PW<PPh<BG<PG. In correlation to the HPG units are respective discourse boundaries B1, B2, B3, B4 and B5 which bare the same hierarchical relationships and function as prosodic units. Hence, the relationships among the discourse boundaries are B1<B2<B3<B4<B5. The identities of these discourse boundaries are outcome of perceptual annotation by trained transcribers. The intra- and inter-transcriber consistency was over 93% [19]. Furthermore, by specifications of the HPG an intonation phrase is a discourse subunit PPh, and by default not an ultimate prosody unit. The discourse identity of a PPh is subject to three PG specifications the PG-initial, -medial or -final. As a result, output global discourse prosody must contain higher level PG information accordingly. In short, our previous work has shown that in fluent continuous speech, additional prosodic information exists in addition to tones, stress and phrase intonation in the supra-segments, and no prosodic information should be studied as discrete units; and relative associations must be accounted for.

In the following sections, we will present a study on the timing structure of Mandarin discourse prosody through boundaries and lengthening to show how higher level temporal allocation is organized by discourse units and represents discourse-relative phonetic information, and how the phrase also functions as a temporal unit in fluent speech.

2. EXPERIMENTS

2.1 Speech material

Two types of Mandarin speech corpus in different speaking rates were used. Read speech of (1) plain text of 26 discourse pieces (CNA, approximately 6700 syllables) by one male M051 and one female F051, and (2) three rhyme formats of Chinese Classics (CL approximately 1600 syllables) by one male M056 and one female F054. The speech data were recorded in sound-proof chambers. Pre-analysis annotation included automatically labeled segmental identities in the SAMPA-T notation using the HTK toolkit, and subsequent manual tagging by trained transcribers of perceived boundary breaks using the Sinica COSPRO Toolkit [11]. Annotated segments were spot-checked by professional transcribers for identities and alignments. Table1 summarizes the speech material by corpus type, speaker, and the number of the HPG prosodic units and boundaries.

Table 1: Summary of speech data by corpus type, speaker, and the HPG prosodic units and boundaries. The HPG prosodic units are the syllable (SYL), prosodic word (PW), prosodic phrase (PPh), breath group (BG) and phrase group (PG). Corresponding HPG boundaries following each of the prosodic units are B1, B2, B3, B4 and B5 respectively.

corpus	speaker	SYL/B1	PW/B2	PPh/B3	BG/B4	PG/B5
CNA	F051	6583	3468	1092	297	151
	M051	6661	3332	1207	270	129
CL	F054	1444	599	290	135	58
	M056	1551	619	318	142	47

The mean syllable durations for speakers F051 and M052 are 199ms and 189ms; the mean syllable durations for speakers F054 and M056 are 265ms and 202ms. Taken as a reference to speaking rate, we found a positive correlation by speech material than by speaker. The above materials were used for all three experiments in the present study.

2.2 Experiment 1

We have stated in Section 1 that discourse prosody is mainly about semantic cohesion through relative associative information manifested in the supra-segmental domain. The rationale implies that using relative acoustic information would result in better generalized pattern and discrimination of discourse information than discrete acoustic information. Given that boundaries are important discourse information, three discourse boundaries, PPh boundary B3, BG boundary B4 and PG boundary B5, were selected as the categories of generalization and discrimination. Three discrete acoustic variables were chosen to test the generalization and discrimination. They are (1) boundary pause (BP), (2) pre-boundary syllable duration (PrDu) and (3) pre-boundary syllable intensity (PrIn). The following two steps were employed to examine patterns of generalization and boundary discrimination.

Procedure 1. Whether a single acoustic factor is sufficient to generalize and discriminate discourse boundary identities

The procedure involved testing whether generalization and discrimination could be achieved by any single acoustic factor. The average values of specified acoustic feature for B3, B4 and B5 were derived from the speech materials by speaker and by speech type. These derived mean values across B3, B4 and B5 were plotted as reference that denotes the tendency among boundaries by speech data type and speaker. We then compared the trajectories among different speech data to look for whether the best single acoustic factor with most generalized pattern could be identified. We also tested whether discrimination of discourse boundary identities could be attributed to any one of these single discrete factors.

Procedure 2. Whether a relative acoustic factor is sufficient to generalize and discriminate discourse boundary identities

The same rationale from Procedure 1 was utilized to test boundary generalization and discrimination, but using one relative acoustic factor at a time. Between-boundary duration contrasts (BwDuCon) and between-boundary intensity contrasts (BwInCon) were calculated and used as the contributing factors. Between-boundary duration contrasts were defined by subtracted outcome of cross-boundary syllables. The same subtraction was applied to derive the between-boundary intensity contrasts as well. Both duration and intensity contrasts specify cross-unit as well as cross-boundary relative acoustic information. The same averaging and comparison methods used in Procedure 1 were employed to see if any single relative factor is sufficient to discriminate the identities of discourse boundaries.

2.3 Experiment 2

We further hypothesized that pairing of single factors would result in better generalization and discrimination than results from Experiment 1, and the discrimination varies by pair, and thus specified pairing would result in better discrimination than single factors to discriminate the three discourse boundaries B3, B4 and B4.

The five acoustic features generated from Experiment 1, namely, (1) boundary pause (BP), (2) pre-boundary duration (PrDu), (3) pre-boundary intensity (PrIn), (4) duration contrast (DuCon) and (5) syllable intensity contrast (InCon), were used as feature candidates to generate paired-combinations and as variables for ANOVA. These five features were first normalized then paired. A total of ten paired combinations were selected. These 10 paired variables were calculated by ANOVA for discriminating categories B3, B4 and B5 from each other.

2.4 Experiment 3

We have previously established that temporal templates for each prosodic unit can be derived by the HPG framework [8][9], suggesting that default temporal patterns exists in each prosodic layer in addition to phone and syllable durations. This rationale made possible a hypothesis that final lengthening is discourse unit/boundary dependent and must be addressed with boundary pause information. In other words, boundary discrimination must include both boundary pause information as well as pre-boundary duration patterns to signal discourse information. Since in fluent continuous speech, an intonation phrase is a sub-unit of discourse unit, pre-boundary lengthening is not simply constrained by phrase information alone. To test the hypothesis, we calculated pre-boundary duration patterns by the HPG prosodic units, namely, the syllable, the PW and the PPh, and compared their respective patterns to the speech data.

3. RESULTS

3.1 Experiment 1

Results from Procedure1 reveal that none of the three single factors (1) pause duration, (2) pre-boundary syllable duration and (3) pre-boundary syllable intensity is discriminative of discourse boundaries except the factor of pause duration. We noted that the factor of pause duration discriminated boundaries B3 from B4 and B5; yet at the same time it was not discriminative of boundaries B4 and B5. In other words, discrimination by pause duration is limited. Moreover, no identities of discourse boundary can be discriminated by either the pre-boundary syllable duration or the pre-boundary intensity as shown in Figure 1. The results suggest that boundary discrimination cannot be attributed to any single factor. Furthermore, pre-boundary lengthening is not a boundary feature by itself. The results thus motivated further examination of the role of final lengthening in relation to discourse information in subsequent investigations.

Results from Procedure 2 reveal that between paired single-factor contrasts, namely, the contrasts between pre- and post- PPh boundary duration and intensity by one syllable, no significant discrimination of discourse boundaries could be achieved either, as shown in Figure 2. However, we note that paired duration factor, the between-PPh-duration contrast, is discriminative of text type CAN and CL, as shown in the upper panel of Figure 2; while single duration factor, the pre-boundary duration is not, as shown in the middle panel of Figure 1. In addition, cross-speaker consistency is found by text type, thus indicating text type may be inherent to rate of reading whereas speaker difference is not, as reported in Sec. 2.1. Regarding intensity patterns, the between-boundary intensity contrasts by only one syllable also provide better discrimination than pre-boundary intensity alone. In other words, although using paired single factors to bring out minimum relative information does not produce better discrimination across the board; paired factors still perform better than single features.

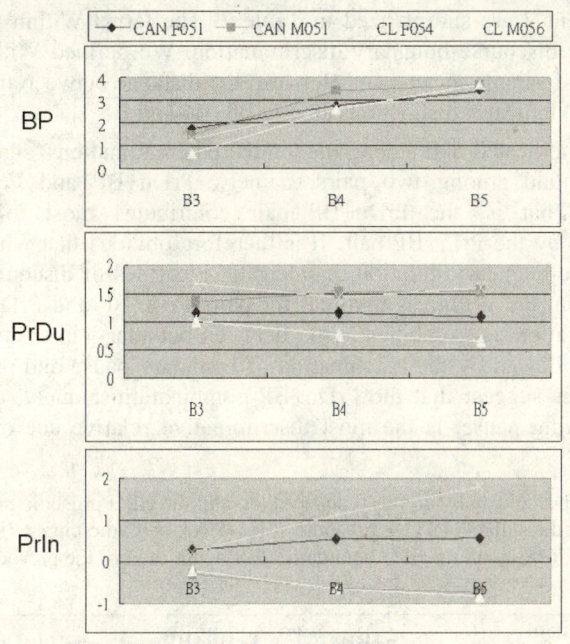

Figure 1: Cross boundary discrimination by single acoustic features. Each panel denotes one specific acoustic feature. The horizontal axis represents the prosodic boundary indexes B3, B4 and B5. The vertical axis represents the coefficient of normalized values of boundary pause (BP), pre-boundary duration (PrDu) and pre-boundary intensity (PrIn), respectively. Zero at the vertical axis is defined as the mean of syllable duration.

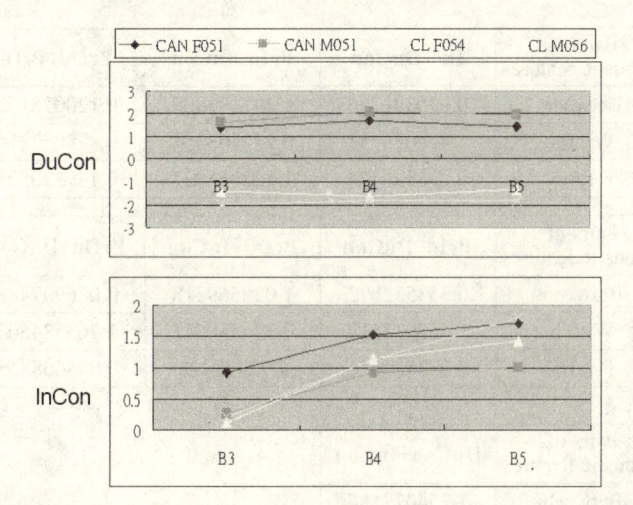

Figure 2: Cross boundary discrimination by single contrastive factors. Each panel denotes one specific contrastive feature. The horizontal axis represents the prosodic boundary indexes B3 to B5. The vertical axis represents the coefficient of normalized values between boundary duration contrasts (DuCon) and between boundary intensity contrasts (InCon). Zero at the vertical axis is defined as the mean of syllable duration and intensity.

3.2 Experiment 2

The results of Experiment 2 are summarized in Table 2. The terms Within and Between are two evaluation indicators for discourse boundary discrimination. We defined Within by the population variance of distribution of sample means; and Between the distance between the sample means. The F-ratio (Between/Within) indicates distinctions among B3, B4 and B5.

The obtained results indicated that among the ten paired combinations, significance of boundary distinction was only found among two pairs, namely, PrDu+BP and PrIn+BP, where $F(2, 40)=0.28387$, $P<0.05$. That is, the PrDu+BP pair contributes most to discourse boundary discrimination, followed by the PrIn+BP pair. It is therefore obvious that when boundary pause is combined with either pre-boundary duration or intensity, identities of discourse boundaries can be discriminated. In addition, the Within is minimal for pairs PrIn+BP and PrDu+BP, indicating that when pre-boundary duration is combined with between-boundary intensity contrast, boundary discrimination is best, followed by the combination of boundary pause and pre-boundary duration. The above results further suggest that the PrDu+BP combination, namely, the PPh-final syllable duration plus the following pause, is the most discriminative relative cue of discourse boundary identities.

Table 2: Summary of speech data by corpus type, speaker, and the HPG prosodic units and boundaries. The HPG prosodic units are the syllable (SYL), prosodic word (PW), prosodic phrase (PPh), breath group (BG) and phrase group (PG). Corresponding HPG boundaries following each of the prosodic units are B1, B2, B3, B4 and B5 respectively.

Pairs of Acoustic features	PrIn+BP	PrDu+BP	BP+InCon
Between	2.394360811	2.117735421	0.930326811
Within	0.714117065	0.479096215	1.116294559
F-ratio	3.352896784	4.420271653	0.833406204

Pairs of Acoustic features	BP+DuCon	PrIn+InCon	PrDu+PrIn
Between	0.070391796	1.297194809	0.120075103
Within	1.810655131	0.912193354	0.875052214
F-ratio	0.038876424	1.422061237	0.137220501

Pairs of Acoustic features	PrIn+DuCon	PrDu+InCon	PrDu+DuCon
Between	0.353532872	1.020569418	0.076907482
Within	1.652913517	0.374550542	1.763574503
F-ratio	0.213884676	2.72478425	0.043608865

Pairs of Acoustic features	DuCon+InCon
Between	1.254027187
Within	1.736954223
F-ratio	0.721969048

Table 3 summarizes the averaged sum of PPh-final syllable duration and boundary pause duration in seconds, where constant pattern across boundaries can be observed.

Table 3: A list of average sum of final syllable duration and pause (sec by speech data type and speaker)

corpus	speaker	B3	B4	B5
CNA	F051	0.499738	0.607713	0.684998
CNA	M051	0.519527	0.800465	0.880004
CL	F054	0.52102	0.833563	1.007355
CL	M056	0.456447	0.679508	0.774484

3.3 Experiment 3

Figure 3 shows the phrase final duration patterns by HPG prosodic units — the syllable, the PW and the PPh across speech data and speaker. We noted that by analyzing the pre-boundary duration pattern of the final syllable alone, it revealed that consistent and patterned lengthening occurs before the B3 boundary, but not before higher boundaries B4 and B5. This result does not explain why discourse boundary identities could be consistently perceived across listeners. However, if the same inconsistency was found across all boundaries, which happened to patterns found for the PW, then lengthening may not be a reliable boundary cue and is related to the lower level phrase boundary only. However, when pre-boundary duration patterns were examined by PPh, similar patterns are found across speaker and data-type, as shown in the lower panel of Figure 3. Furthermore, the lengthening patterns of pre-boundary PPh are also consistent with discourse boundary type. Such consistency can be seen as evidence of higher level overall slowing down or lengthening by phrase, thus suggesting calculation of tempo, rhythm and speaking rate merits more sophisticated considerations.

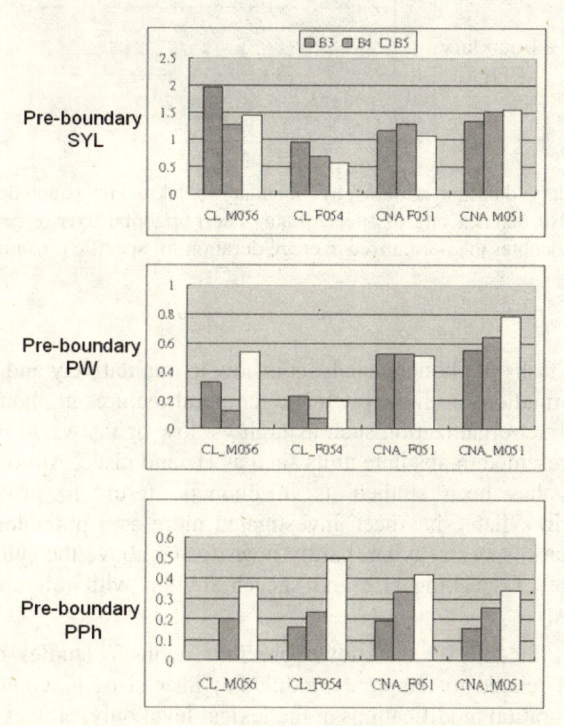

Figure 3: Cross boundary comparison of duration patterns by prosodic units—the syllable (SYL), the PW and the PPh. The horizontal axis represents indices of the speech data and speaker. The vertical axis denotes normalized average duration of prosodic units.

Figure 4 shows the results of average duration patterns by discourse boundary identities B3, B4 and B5. We found that discourse boundaries can be discriminated by pre-boundary duration patterns of higher level discourse unit (the PPh) across speaker and speech data type, as shown in the lower panel of Figure 4; but not by pre-boundary duration patterns of lower level discourse units (the SYL and PW), as shown in the top and middle panels in the same figure. In other words, the identities of discourse boundaries B3, B4 and B5 are only consistent with the pre-boundary duration patterns of the PPh.

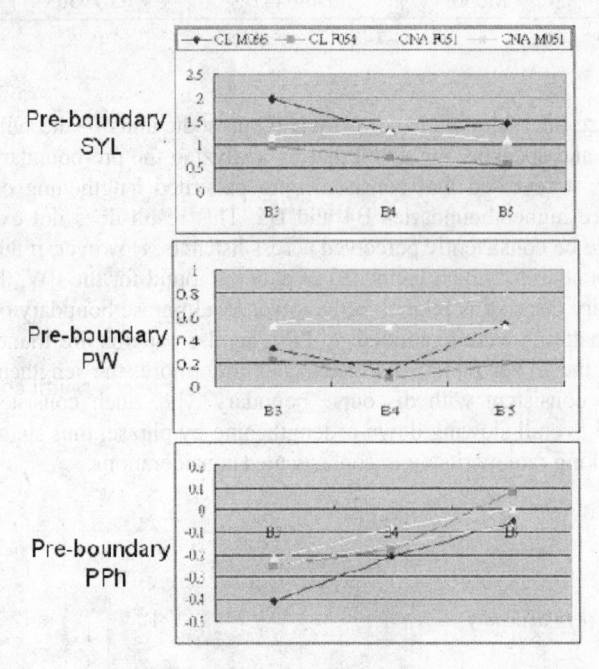

Figure 4: Cross-boundary duration patterns by boundary breaks. The panel denotes result of specific prosodic unit. Each curve denotes one of speech data. The horizontal axis represents prosodic boundary index. The vertical axis denotes the normalized average duration for specific prosodic unit.

4. DISCUSSION

One of the most difficult tasks of phonetic analysis is how to qualitatively and quantitatively account for relative phonetic information. Both the pitch and temporal features in phonological structures are presented in relative abstract organization such as high vs. low or fast vs. slow, while realization in speech signals is often presented in absolute units such as Hz and msec. Although timing structure of the Mandarin segments has been studied as in phonetic terms to provide phone-dependent information, the Mandarin syllable has been investigated more as a phonological unit instead of a rhythmic unit, and Mandarin speech rhythm hardly investigated above the syllable. In addition, little reference has been made of speaking rate and speech rhythm with reference of global duration patterns by prosodic units.

For example, one of the most well known previous acoustic studies on Mandarin duration patterns is how stress is related to temporal modulation instead of F_0 contours [16], referring to segmental and syllable-duration modifications at the lexical level only. However, much less attention has been paid to relative phonetic information at the discourse level and prosody units above segments and the syllable. Studies on boundary and lengthening were no exception. For example, a comprehensive investigation on Mandarin segment lengthening made important observations of how prosodic boundaries and pause occur between prosodic units instead of within units, and manifestation of pre-boundary lengthening bear prosodic functions to the phrase [14]. More recent studies reported on the role of lengthening with reference to prosodic boundary and its perceptual significance in continuous speech using the pre-boundary syllable [20][13], thus inadvertently suggested the syllable as the default unit of lengthening. Another study reported that lengthening is complemented by pause duration at prosodic boundaries, but the units did not go beyond the intonation phrase [17]. Perceptual studies reported that although the pause duration at sentence-final positions is significantly longer than that of phrase-final ones, the syllable duration at sentence- and prosodic-phrase-final positions was not significantly different [18]. Furthermore, although more recent studies reported how the degree of final lengthening is modulated by boundary types [2] and how segmental strengthening is relative to prosodic functions [15], little discussion with reference to discourse units and structure is discussed. In short, almost all of the previous studies have focused on modulation of segmental duration at the syllabic level. We noted also that even when the discourse factor was considered, there has been less reported account in relation to discourse organization. In particular, the relative aspect of timing structure with respect to boundary features and boundary identities in discourse prosody has been overlooked. We think that one reason of the oversight could be due to taking the phonetic or phonological unit IP (intonation phrase) as an independent prosodic unit, whereas by HPG account, an IP corresponds to a PPh which is a discourse and speech-paragraph sub-unit and therefore requires further discourse specifications by default.

Interestingly, in one of the recent studies on the PPh boundary B3, we studied the much varied B3 pause duration not by the duration of pauses, but with respect to cross-unit contrastive patterns in the acoustic signals, and discovered that within PG phrase boundaries can be accounted for by boundary immediate contrastive patterns of duration and intensity without any pause information [12]. The findings thus explained why the within-PG phrase boundary B3 was consistently perceived across listeners irrespective of pause duration, even when there was no pause at the boundary. We discussed when processing fluent speech on-line, the listener makes use of crucial relative phonetic information related to prosody organization. In short, both neighboring and cross-over prosodic references provide cues to global prosody; higher-level discourse organization is reflected in global units and boundaries in relation to each other. Therefore, discourse prosodic units should not be taken as discrete ones, nor should they be investigated when discourse context is removed and discourse organization/information absent.

The results from Experiments 1 show that single factors are not discriminative of discourse boundaries. The results of Experiment 2 show that the identities of discourse boundaries can be discriminated when pre-boundary syllabic duration or intensity is combined with the following boundary pause. In other words, pre-boundary syllabic information by itself is not sufficient for the discrimination of boundary identities, but when coupled with the following pause, the combined feature proved to be adequate. The results suggest that when prosodic context is limited, a little extra relative information goes a long way. We believe that more high-level relative information is utilized by the listener to facilitate faster and easier on-line top-down processing.

The results from Experiment 3 are most interesting because it provided evidence of how global lengthening could be represented and what its discourse function is. The results thus make direct reference to how overall timing modulation can be represented quantitatively and how lengthening occurs to the entire pre-discourse-boundary phrase. The evidences also show why in fluent speech lengthening is applied by prosody unit instead of by the syllable, and how global temporal planning is manifested. Consistent perceptual identification of discourse boundary identities echoes the finding, because listeners must make use of global relative information to facilitate on-line processing. Alternatively, the same results also imply that overall modulation of temporal allocation is regulated by discourse prosodic organization, and interact with fixed or changed speaking rate. We believe that the implications of global lengthening have shed new lights to how speakers plan and process the temporal features across fluent speech, and default discourse temporal templates could be derived and modeled.

5. CONCLUSION

We have shown that (1) overall temporal modulation within a fixed speaking rate involves the timing structure and temporal arrangement at the discourse level and result in overall lengthening of the pre-boundary phrase, (2) how lengthening is in fact an integral part of boundary information by discourse units, and when coupled with boundary pause facilitates boundary identities to emerge, (3) lengthening is relative and should be addressed as relative phonetic information, and (4) global lengthening related to overall modulation of speaking rate shows how the timing structure of discourse prosody is subject to discourse organization and discourse association. In summary, we hope to show that relative phonetic information that exists in the speech events, though usually not accounted for in phonological investigations, contributes significantly to the production and processing of fluent continuous speech, the most natural and used form of speech communication. Such relative information would not emerge, unless we adopt a discourse perspective of investigation and make use of methodological innovations.

REFERENCES

[1] Crystal, D. 1969. *Prosodic Systems and Intonation in English*. Cambridge: Cambridge University Press.

[2] Fon, J., Johnson, K. 2004. Syllable onset intervals as an indicator of discourse and syntactic boundaries in Taiwan Mandarin. *Language and Speech* 47(1), 57-82.

[3] Halliday, M. A. K. 1967. *Intonation and Grammar in British English*. The Hague: Mouton.

[4] Pierrehumbert, J. B. 1980. *The phonology and phonetics of English intonation*. PhD. Dissertation, MIT, Cambridge.

[5] Pike, K. L. 1943. *Phonetics: A Critical Analysis of Phonetic Theory and a Technic for the Practical Description of Sounds.* Ann Arbor: University of Michigan Press.

[6] Scott, N. C. 1941. Broad Transcriptions. *Le Maitre Phonetique* 76: 48-51.

[7] Selkirk, E. O. 1984. *Phonology and Syntax: The Relation between Sound and Structure*. Cambridge: The MIT Press.

[8] Tseng, C., Pin, S., Lee, Y. 2004. Speech prosody: Issues, approaches and implications. In: Fant, G., Fujisaki, H., Cao, J. and Xu, Y.(eds.), *From Traditional Phonology to Modern Speech Processing* (语音学与言语处理前沿). Foreign Language Teaching and Research Press (外语教学与研究出版社), 417-437, Beijing, China.

[9] Tseng, C., Pin, S., Lee, Y., Wang, H., Chen, Y. 2005. Fluent Speech Prosody: Framework and Modeling. *Speech Communication (Special Issue on Quantitative Prosody Modeling for Natural Speech Description and Generation)*, Vol. 46, 3-4, 284-309.

[10] Tseng, C. 2006. "Prosody Analysis" in *Advances in Chinese Spoken Language Processing.* In: Chin-Hui Lee, Haizhou Li, Lin-shan Lee, Ren-Hua Wang, Qiang Huo (eds.), *World Scientific Publishing*, 57-76, Singapore.

[11] Tseng, C., Cheng, Y., Chang, C. 2005. Sinica COSPRO and Toolkit — Corpora and Platform of Mandarin Chinese Fluent Speech. *Oriental COCOSDA 2005*, (Dec. 6-8, 2005), Jakarata, Indonesia.

[12] Tseng, C., Chang, C. 2008. Pause or No Pause? — Prosodic Phrase Boundaries Revisited. *Tsinghua Science and Technology*, 13(4), 500-509.

[13] Zu, Y., Chen, X. 1999. Segmental duration and lengthened syllables. *ICPh99*, San Francisco, 277-280.

[14] 曹剑芬（1998）汉语普通话语音节奏的初步研究。载《语音研究报告》，中国社会科学院语言研究所语音研究室。

[15] 曹剑芬（2005）音段延长的不同类型及其韵律价值。载《语音研究报告》，中国社会科学院语言研究所语音研究室。

[16] 林焘（1983）探讨北京话轻音性质的初步实验。《语言学论丛》第十辑。北京：商务印书馆。

[17] 钱瑶、初敏、潘悟云（2001）普通话韵律单元边界的声学分析。第五届全国现代语音学学术会议，北京。

[18] 王蓓、杨玉芳、吕士楠（2001）汉语韵律层级边界结构的声学相关物。第五届全国现代语音学学术会议，北京。
[19] 郑秋豫（2001）语流中韵律结构的主要征信。 第六届全国语音通讯学术会议 (NCMMSC-6)， (Nov. 19-24, 2001)，深圳。
[20] 祖漪清、陈肖霞（1999）连续语流中的音节延长及其作用。第四届全国现代语音学学术会议，北京。

IN DEFENSE OF LAB SPEECH IN PROSODY RESEARCH

XU Yi

ABSTRACT

Lab speech has often been described as unnatural, overly clear, over planned, monotonous, lack of rich prosody, and lack of emotions. Along with this view is a growing popularity for directly examining spontaneous speech for the sake of understanding spontaneous speech, especially in regard to its prosody. In this paper I argue that few of the stereotyped characteristics associated with lab speech are warranted. Instead, the quality of lab speech is a design issue rather than a matter of fundamental limitation. More importantly, since it is controlled, the potential contribution of lab speech to our understanding of the nature of human speech far outweighs that of spontaneous speech.

1. INTRODUCTION

As speech research advances, there is a growing interest in aspects of speech beyond lexical phonemes like consonants, vowels and tones. In pursuit of this interest, many turned to spontaneous speech to look for answers. A widespread view is that only by directly examining spontaneous speech can we understand the nature of everyday speech. Accompanying this view is the increasingly popular idea that the so-called "lab speech" is grossly inadequate for shedding light on the richness of spontaneous speech. In this paper, I will argue that much of this belief is based on neglect of the literature, misconceptions about scientific inquiry, lack of imagination or simply failure to think things through.

2. TERMINOLOGY

By a broad definition, lab speech refers to speech that is recorded in the laboratory, usually in the form of reading aloud scripts that are pre-composed. However, the term lab speech is often used to refer to a stereotyped speech such as:

> Say *hid* again.
> Say *heed* again.
> Say *hood* again.

where the italicized words are the ones under scrutiny. But in fact, this type of lab speech is already a big improvement over earlier recordings in which syllables are recorded in isolation [34].

The progress from isolated vowel/words to vowels in a controlled syllable frame in a carrier sentence actually highlights the possibility of improvements in designing lab speech materials. But such possibility is typically ignored when people use lab speech as a bad name. A more precise definition of lab speech should be something like *speech recorded under experimental control*, which more accurately represents the nature of lab speech.

Spontaneous speech, according to Beckman [4:7], is "speech that is not read to script". She further distinguishes between ten different types of spontaneous speech recordings, ranging from *unstructured narrative* to *instruction monologue*. The dividing line between lab speech and spontaneous speech can sometimes be blurred. For example, even when recording unscripted speech, certain levels of controls can be implemented. In what is referred to as *instruction monologue*, the speaker is asked to instruct a real or imaginary silent listener to perform a task. With this technique, some control over both content words and syntactic structure can be achieved [4]. To the extent the level of control is achieved, this type of speech could be labeled as lab speech as well. But, just as one would expect, the control is said to be achieved at the expense of naturalness [4].

3. MYTHS ABOUT LAB SPEECH

There are many myths about lab speech that pass around in the speech science community. But few of them are explicitly stated in peer-reviewed publications. They nevertheless have impacts on the way we conduct speech research. Although many researchers still use lab speech in their studies, they often do so apologetically, and are constantly thinking of ways to incorporate spontaneous speech into their research. In the following I will list a few ideas that I believe are the most popular about lab speech, and explain why they are actually just myths. Not all of these ideas are taken seriously by everyone, because some of them are so obviously false. But the more "credible" ones are in fact often closely related to the more simplistic ones, and it is thus important to point out the intimate relations between them.

3.1 Lab speech is slow and careful

This is probably one of the least sustainable myths, but many other myths are closely related to it. Speaking rate, as a matter of fact, is one aspect of speech that is among the most easily controlled in the laboratory. Numerous studies have been conducted in which speaking rate is systematically controlled, ranging from those that specifically look at the limits on the speed of articulation [23][41][56] to those that examine the effect of speaking rate on various phonetic aspects of speech [1][7][14][17][18][21][25][26][31][36][37][39][51][53][57].

Also there are different methods of manipulating speaking rate in the lab. The most straightforward is to simply ask speakers to speed up or slow down. While it is not easy to aim at a particular speaking rate as measured by, say, number of syllables per second, it is very easy to have untrained subjects speak at 2-3 different rates. My personal experience is that it is only difficult sometimes to make people speak very slowly without losing control over the aspect of speech under scrutiny. For example, in Xu and Xu [57] we had to use only two speaking rates: normal and fast, because otherwise the speakers would often insert pauses when producing focus at a very slow rate. The second strategy is to instruct subjects to speak casually or formally, or clearly or intimately, so as to elicit different speaking rates [32][33]. Yet another way of controlling the rate of specific phonetic units is to control the local rate. For example, in Mandarin, the middle syllable of a trisyllabic word is often spoken at a much faster rate than the surrounding syllables. Such local variability in rate has been explored in [40][49][53].

Also, controlling speaking style in the lab could allow us to separate variations due to speaking style and those due to other factors, such as speaking rate, as mentioned earlier. This has been done in Krause & Braida [25].

Most importantly, the laboratory manipulation of speaking rate is so effective that some of the phenomena allegedly occurring only in spontaneous speech have been elicited in the lab. They will be discussed next, for they are also relevant to the myth about clarity of lab speech.

3.2 Lab speech is clear and articulate

This is closely related to the slowness myth, but somehow a little more sensible. That is, regardless of whether speaking rate is controlled, speech recorded in the lab may tend to be clear and articulate. This is probably because, being in a laboratory, and asked to speak from a script, it is natural for speakers to speak clearly, just as they would when speaking to a foreigner or in front of a microphone for a formal occasion, or just reading aloud text in a classroom. But this kind of stylistic tendency can be controlled. Speakers can be instructed to speak either more or less formally [13][33][35] and they do not seem to have much difficulty following such instructions. In fact, for some experimental purposes, we have to instruct subjects not to slur while trying to speak naturally [55]. It is a pure myth that everyone would uncontrollably speak in a careful manner as soon as they are in front of a microphone. There might be some people like that. But I have yet to encounter one in my own research.

Speakers' flexibility in controlling their own speaking style has made it possible for researchers to manipulate their speech along the dimension of clear versus casual in quite a few studies [13][32][33][35][44]. In an ongoing study, we have successfully elicited samples of syllable contractions from nonsense words embedded in meaningful sentence frames in Taiwan Mandarin, i.e. the merger of two or more syllables into one, which is generally believed to be characteristic of only casual speech [8].

Most importantly, controlling speaking style in the lab would allow us to separate variations due to speaking style and due to other factors, such as speaking rate, as mentioned earlier [25].

3.3 Lab speech is unnatural

This may be one of the most readily conceived characteristics of lab speech, because it seems to contain an element of truth, i.e. scripted speech, by definition, is non-spontaneous. And being non-spontaneous is the opposite of being natural. But it is first of all important to point out something obvious. That is, even the most stereotypical lab speech is still human speech produced by real speakers. Regardless of what the speakers are asked to do in an experiment, their performance is based on their naturally acquired ability to speak, and is therefore a reflection of what they do every day. It is not the case, for example, that they learn from the experimenter how to produce a vowel or a consonant or a tone, or they learn from the experimenter how to make focus or ask questions. They already know how to do those things, and that's why we want them in the laboratory in the first place. An experimental set-up only provides them with a situation in which the production of certain aspects of speech is obligatory. Note that similar situations occur in natural conversations, too. The difference is that those situations are out of the control of the researchers.

Of course unnaturalness usually has a much broader connotation than not being spoken off the cuff. It is often associated with qualities such as carefulness, articulate, formalness, etc. As discussed earlier, much of these characteristics are actually controllable in the lab and are thus not obligatory aspects of lab speech. On the other hand, it has to be admitted that lab speech can be unnatural in some sense. The more important question is, then, whether the goal of the study is compromised when the recorded speech sounds "unnatural".

To answer this question, we can revisit some of the previous studies. In Peterson and Barney [34], vowels of American English are studied by embedding them in the syllable frame of h__d and asking subjects to read a randomized list of 10 such words. This is perhaps one of the most stereotypical examples of lab speech, and so one may legitimately ask, what did the study miss by using lab speech? The purpose of the study is to understand the relationship between the perceptual identification of vowels and their acoustic properties. For this purpose the type of lab speech used, unnatural as it must have sounded, seems quite adequate. In Xu [50], Mandarin tones are studied by asking native speakers to say bi-tonal combinations carried by the disyllabic sequence /mama/, which in turn are embedded in tonally balanced sentence carriers. Because the /mama/ sequences are mostly nonwords, the speech samples are by a narrow definition quite "unnatural". The goal of the study is to understand contextual tonal variations. Judging from the fact that the findings of the study have been corroborated multiple times in other studies of Mandarin [51][52][53] and other languages [15][19][28][48] using either nonsense or meaningful materials, the goal of the study was not compromised.

In general, whether anything is missing due to lack of naturalness is dependent on the match between the purpose of the study and the design of the experiment.

But the naturalness issue is still not fully resolved. If someone's speech in the lab does sound unnatural, we may further ask, what exactly has this person done to make his/her speech unnatural? Has he/she suddenly turned into a text-to-speech (TTS) system and started to generate speech like a TTS system? Of course not. Or, is the person doing something that has never been done in his/her life? Probably not either. It is more likely that the person has spontaneously assumed a speaking style that seems to be appropriate for the occasion, i.e. reading aloud text in a place where serious business is being conducted. Such a style shift is not something artificial. Rather, it is a *natural* adjustment to the situation. From a functional point of view [22][24][54], such a style shift happens along an independent functional dimension which ranges from extremely casualness to extremely formality. The nature of such a functional dimension no doubt requires research, as has been done in some recent investigations [20][32][33][35]. But the point here is that, as I have argued before, communicative functions are independent though parallel to each other [54]. The presence or absence of a particular function does not suppress the operations of other functions. Therefore, the so-called unnaturalness in lab speech is likely a manifestation of *formality*, which, though worth studying in its own right, would not invalidate the findings about other communicative functions based on lab speech, as has been shown in [6].

3.4 Lab speech is over-planned

When speakers are asked to read aloud scripted texts during a recording session, naturally there is a possibility that they can plan for the whole utterance before starting to speak. But lab speech is not always fully planned. Just as we can manipulate the amount of information given to the listener in a perception experiment, we can also manipulate the amount and timing of information given to speakers to control their planning during production [42][46]. Whalen [46], for example, controlled the amount of text subjects could see before starting to speak. By so doing he could examine the amount of anticipatory and carryover coarticulation that is plannable by the subjects. In Xu, Xu & Sun [58], although subjects were given scripts of the sentences to be read aloud, their task was to imitate the exact manner with which the sentences were spoken by the model speaker. But because various parts of the speech of the model speaker was replaced with pink noise, subjects could not do much planning ahead of time. There can also be many other ways to control the amount of planning by the speaker. Whether and how such control is exerted, again, is a matter of experimental design which is closely related to the purpose of the research.

3.5 Lab speech is monotonous with impoverished prosody

This myth is apparently based on a poor understanding of what we already know about speech prosody. First, if we adopt a broad definition of prosody so that it covers any aspect of speech that is suprasegmental, lexical tones in languages like Mandarin would be included as part of prosody. Of course nobody in their right mind would deny that tones can be produced in the laboratory. Similarly, lexical stress in languages like English, which is also suprasegmental, is also easily observable in the lab. Secondly, even if we narrow down the definition of prosody to exclude anything lexical, there are still many prosodic patterns that are readily observable in lab speech. These include patterns associated with focus [5][9][52]57], topic [27], grouping [43][44] and sentence modality [11][29][30], to cite only a few.

What is important here is that prosodic patterns are used to encode various communicative functions. When an experimental design does not include the right condition to make the encoding of a particular function obligatory, the associated prosodic pattern is not guaranteed to occur. Thus the lack of various particular prosodic patterns in many laboratory experiments is often either due to deliberate exclusion of those functions, or lack of proper methods to elicit them. But either way the issue is about how and how well an experiment is designed, not whether lab speech allows us to study prosody at all. Judging from the fruitful returns of so many studies, studying prosody with lab speech is certainly possible.

3.6 Lab speech is emotionless

This is untrue given that many studies have used speech samples with emotions enacted in the laboratory. Questions can no doubt be raised about the authenticity of the enacted emotions. But as will be argued later, to use anything that occurs naturally as an object of study, the first obstacle to overcome is the correct classification of that object. This makes emotions in spontaneous speech just as elusive as those in enacted speech. Again, however, since lab speech is controllable, the methods of eliciting emotions can be continually improved, limited perhaps only by ethnical concerns in some situations, e.g. those linked to extreme emotions. But again, similar restrictions may be applicable to spontaneous speech with extreme emotions as well.

3.7 Interim summary

The above discussion has shown that the myths about lab speech are not well-founded. In general, the characteristics attached to lab speech are related to the purpose of the study rather than to lab speech as a whole. When we want to understand vowels, consonants and tones, we have to be able to control the variation of these aspects of speech while keeping other aspects constant. What this means is that the non-manipulated aspects are left either in their neutral state, or in a state appropriate for the recording situation. But these other aspects can be also manipulated when the purpose of a study requires it. In particular, various prosodic functions can be specifically controlled, as has been done in many studies.

4. SPONTANEOUS vs. LAB SPEECH

The appeal of spontaneous speech is that it can potentially make up for what is missing from lab speech [4]. Although we have seen that some popular ideas about what is missing from lab speech are actually based on myths, is it still possible that spontaneous speech can at least offer some more? My answer to this question starts from reconsidering the fundamental motivations of examining spontaneous speech.

One of the assumptions behind the drive to look at spontaneous speech is that science progresses by accumulating observations. Thus it is hoped that by looking at more and more samples of spontaneous speech, our knowledge about speech will keep improving. But as pointed out by Popper [38], no observation can be theory free or non-selective. All observations are selective and theory-laden. What is often not pointed out is that being theory-laden does not mean that the observations are necessarily driven by a theory that is widely accepted or hotly contested. They could be based on theories that are formed "on the run". For example, suppose we have no knowledge about the intonation of a particular language and we start by directly observing the F_0 contours of the language. We may notice that there are prominent peaks and valleys in the F_0 tracks. If we report our observations by summarizing the locations and sizes of those peaks and valleys, we may think that our report is free of any grand theories. That may be true. But such descriptions of the intonation of this language are actually driven by our own petty theories formed as we made the observations. That is, we have assumed that, a) F_0 peaks and valleys are *important events* in intonation, b) they are *direct correlates* of certain important linguistic categories, and c) what is obvious to the eye, e.g. peaks and valleys, is also obvious to the ear. Note that, each of these is actually a theoretical postulation, and as such they all need further assessment as to their validity.

How, then, do we assess a theory of speech, grand or petite as it may be? Do we dive into a spontaneous speech database and look for proof ? If we do, how do we control the factors that may have contributed to the measurements we have taken? For example, we now know that the F_0 contour of a syllable is determined not only by its tone or stress, but also by factors such as tonal context, focus, sentence type, topic, etc. [54] But how do we control them in a spontaneous speech database?

Anyone who has attempted to do so would attest that the task is extremely difficult, if not impossible. In fact, to be able to find utterances that would fit the requirements of all the experimental conditions, the database would need to be almost infinitely large. In contrast, all these factors can be easily controlled under experimental conditions, as mentioned earlier.

Another motivation for looking at spontaneous speech is the belief that it is much richer than lab speech in terms of the variety of prosodic patterns. This may be true if by spontaneous speech we mean all the speech utterances produced by all speakers in a language community. By definition, a corpus of all the spontaneous utterances should indeed contain all the prosodic patterns. The problem is, no one can ever have access to such a corpus. Instead, real-life spontaneous speech corpora are all very limited in terms of the number of utterances as well as the types of prosodic patterns. More importantly, even if a particular prosodic event, say, focus, does occur in an utterance, to understand it, we need to compare it with another utterance in which focus is absent. But chances are that those utterances in the corpus which lack the equivalent focus are also different in terms of other factors, such as syllable structure, word structure, tonal context, sentence type, location in sentence, location in the paragraph and so on. In fact, finding a single minimal pair in a spontaneous corpus that satisfies all the conditions is anything but trivial. Finding multiple pairs, as typically required by a controlled experiment, is close to impossible. And, to make things worse, even if a minimal pair happens to be found based on a particular set of conditions, chances are that it is no longer a minimal pair as soon as a new condition is added. Given such limitations, it is very difficult to conduct a rigorous study using a spontaneous speech corpus.

A further difficulty with spontaneous speech is the problem of labeling. Any speech corpus needs to be carefully labeled for its internal elements before it can be subjected to research analysis. However, the labeling and analysis constitute an inherently circular process, as has been pointed out [4:12]. That is, the labeling process assumes that we already know what and how to label, but the analysis process assumes that we still don't know the nature, the identity, or even the locations of those elements. This circularity problem is exacerbated if the labeling is done on the basis of direct observations. For example, in the ToBI conventions of labeling intonation, pitch accents labels are attached to the visually prominent F_0 peaks and valleys. Thus an analysis of the corpus based on these labels is taking for granted the assumptions behind the labels, thus effectively treating a significant portion of the signal as not needing further analysis. Although this problem can be somewhat alleviated by doing what Wightman [47:28] has suggested, namely, to "label what you hear", we are still left with the assumption that the labelers *know what to listen for* in the uncontrolled speech utterances.

Of course, I would not go so far as saying that spontaneous speech corpora are useless. As collections of various natural patterns, they may be useful in motivating new hypotheses and raising questions about existing ones. But even on that ground I would also like to note that theoretical postulations do not actually need to be based on direct observations. This is because how a theory is initially conceived is irrelevant to science according to the Popperian view [38]. What is critical is that theories need to be tested through falsification. And it is the stringent requirement of the falsification process that is hard for spontaneous speech corpora to meet.

At this point it might be helpful to take an excursion out of the field of speech communication to take a look at psychology for a debate that happened about 20 years ago over whether memory research should focus on "everyday memory" as opposed to laboratory memory. The debate occurred amidst a popular drive to study everyday memory in order to increase the ecological validity of memory research. That drive is not very unlike the current popular surge in speech research to study spontaneous speech in order to increase generalizability to everyday speech. But the problems with everyday memory are also not unlike those with spontaneous speech discussed above, as pointed out by Banaji and Crowder [2:1189]:

> ...the multiplicity of uncontrolled factors in naturalistic contexts actually prohibits generalizability to other situations with different parameters. The implication that tests in the real world permit

greater generalizability is false once the immense variability from one real-world situation to another is recognized. (p. 1189)

Because of such problems, the research with everyday memory has not been fruitful:

No theories that have unprecedented explanatory power have been produced; no new principles of memory have been discovered; and no methods of data collection have been developed that add sophistication or precision. (p. 1185)

I am not in a position to jump to conclusions about the fruitfulness of research based on spontaneous speech, as I have not yet done an exhaustive survey of the spontaneous speech literature. But I am quite sympathetic to the conclusions of Garner in a report to the US Office of Naval Research, as cited by Banaji and Crowder [3:79]: "operational experimentation is more time consuming, far more expensive, and frequently cannot control experimental factors, so that as a practical matter it is very difficult to do operational experimentation which has a high degree of generality of prediction." Here operational experimentation means experimental manipulations in the operational field as opposed to in the laboratory. In the case of speech research, it may be about time for the field to do a similar assessment: Has the theoretical return been good with the vast amount of money spent on building and analyzing numerous spontaneous speech corpora?

5. CONCLUSION

Despite its increasing unpopularity, many of us are still looking at lab speech in our research on both the segmental and prosodic aspects of speech. But many of us are doing so with a guilty conscience, and frequently have to be apologetic about the speech materials that we have used. After examining the major complaints against lab speech, I hope to have shown that virtually all of them are unfounded. It is not true that lab speech is uniformly slow and articulate, unnatural, over planned, monotonous with impoverished prosody, and emotionless. Rather, these characteristics are seen in some of the lab speech samples partly due to the purpose of the study, and partly due to the crudeness of experimental design in some cases, but never due to fundamental limitations of lab speech in general. I have argued in particular that naturalness itself may be related to degrees of formality, which is likely a communicative function in its own right, and as such can be studied also in the laboratory.

I have also argued that although spontaneous speech corpora may allow us to make initial observations, true progress in our understanding of speech has to rely heavily on lab speech. This is because science progresses not by collecting more data, but by "hypothesis derivation from theory and hypothesis testing in the laboratory" [2:1192; 38]. Spontaneous speech can rarely allow us to fully control the factors that contribute to the phenomena we are interested in, which makes rigorous hypothesis testing difficult. The richness of spontaneous speech therefore may actually form impenetrable obstacles to true understanding. In contrast, experimental controls in the lab allow us to make observations by manipulating the factors under investigation while keeping other factors constant. Observed variations can then be directly attributed to the manipulated factors. This is of course by no means an easy process, and the techniques we employ need constant update in order for us to gain increasingly better insights into the full complexity of speech in general, and prosody in particular. But marginalizing lab speech is clearly the wrong way to go.

REFERENCES

[1] Adams, S. G., Weismer, G., Kent, R. D. 1993. Speaking rate and speech movement velocity profiles. *Journal of Speech and Hearing Research* 36, 41-54.

[2] Banaji, M. R., Crowder, R. G. 1989. The bankruptcy of everyday memory. *American Psychologist* 44, 1185-1193.

[3] Banaji, M. R., Crowder, R. G. 1991. Some everyday thoughts on ecologically valid methods. *American Psychologist* 46, 78-79.

[4] Beckman, M. E. 1997. A typology of spontaneous speech. In: Y. Sagisaka, N. Campbell and N. Higuchi. (eds.), *Computing Prosody: Computational Models for Processing Spontaneous Speech*. New York: Springer-Verlag, 7-26.

[5] Botinis, A., Fourakis, M., Gawronska, B. 1999. Focus identification in English, Greek and Swedish. In *Proceedings of the 14th International Congress of Phonetic Sciences*. San Francisco, 1557-1560.

[6] Bruce, G., Touati, P. 1992. On the analysis of prosody in spontaneous speech with exemplification from Swedish and French. *Speech Communication* 11, 453-458.

[7] Caspers, J., van Heuven, V. J. 1993. Effects of time pressure on the phonetic realization of the Dutch accent-lending pitch rise and fall. *Phonetica* 50, 161-171.

[8] Cheng, C., Xu, Y. 2008. Acoustic Features of Disyllabic Contraction in Mandarin. Presented at BAAP 08 Colloquium, Sheffield, UK.

[9] Cooper, W. E., Eady, S. J., Mueller, P. R. 1985. Acoustical aspects of contrastive stress in question-answer contexts. *Journal of the Acoustical Society of America* 77, 2142-2156.

[10] Crystal, T. H., House, A. S. 1990. Articulation rate and the duration of syllables and stress groups in connected speech. *Journal of the Acoustical Society of America* 88, 101-112.

[11] Eady, S. J., Cooper, W. E. 1986. Speech intonation and focus location in matched statements and questions. *Journal of the Acoustical Society of America* 80, 402-416.

[12] Ferguson, S. H., Kewley-Port, D. 2002. Vowel intelligibility in clear and conversational speech for normal-hearing and hearing-impaired listeners. *Journal of the Acoustical Society of America* 112, 259-271.

[13] Gagne, J.-P., Rochette, A.-J., Charest, M. 2002. Auditory, visual and audiovisual clear speech. *Speech Communication* 37, 213-230.

[14] Gandour, J. 1999. Effects of speaking rate on Thai tones. *Phonetica* 56, 123-134.

[15] Gandour, J., Potisuk, S., Dechongkit, S. 1994. Tonal coarticulation in Thai. *Journal of Phonetics* 22, 477-492.

[16] Garner, W. R. 1950. The validity of prediction from laboratory experiments to naval operational situations in the area of human engineering and systems research (Report No. 166-I-130). Institute for Cooperative Research, Johns Hopkins University, Baltimore.

[17] Gay, T. J. 1968. Effect of speaking rate on diphthong formant movements. *Journal of the Acoustical Society of America* 44, 1570-1573.

[18] Gay, T. J. 1978. Effect of speaking rate on vowel formant movements. *Journal of the Acoustical Society of America* 63, 223-230.

[19] Gu, W., Hirose, K., Fujisaki, H. 2007. Analysis of Tones in Cantonese Speech Based on the Command-Response Model. *Phonetica* 64, 29-62.

[20] Harnsberger, J. D., Wright, R., Pisoni, D. B. 2008. A new method for eliciting three speaking styles in the laboratory. *Speech Communication* 50, 323-336.

[21] Hirata, Y. 2004. Effects of speaking rate on the vowel length distinction in Japanese. *Journal of Phonetics* 32, 565-589.

[22] Hirst, D. J. 2005. Form and function in the representation of speech prosody. *Speech Communication* 46, 334-347.

[23] Janse, E. 2003. Word perception in fast speech: artificially time-compressed vs. naturally produced fast speech. *Speech Communication* 42, 155-173.

[24] Kohler, K. J. 2004. Prosody revisited — FUNCTION, TIME, and the LISTENER in intonational phonology. In *Proceedings of International Conference on Speech Prosody 2004*, Nara, Japan, 171-174.

[25] Krause, J. C., Braida, L. D. 2004. Acoustic properties of naturally produced clear speech at normal speaking rates. *Journal of the Acoustical Society of America* 115, 362-378.

[26] Kuo, Y.-C., Xu, Y., Yip, M. 2007. The phonetics and phonology of apparent cases of iterative tonal change in Standard Chinese. In: C. Gussenhoven and T. Riad. (eds.), *Tones and Tunes Vol 2: Experimental Studies in Word and Sentence Prosody*. Berlin: Mouton de Gruyter, 211-237.

[27] Lehiste, I. 1975. The phonetic structure of paragraphs. In: A. Cohen and S. E. G. Nooteboom (eds.), *Structure and process in speech perception*. New York, Springer-Verlag, 195-206.
[28] Li, Y. J., Lee, T. 2002. Acoustical F_0 analysis of continuous Cantonese speech. In *Proceedings of International Symposium on Chinese Spoken Language Processing*, Taipei, Taiwan, 127-130.
[29] Liu, F., Xu, Y. 2005. Parallel encoding of focus and interrogative meaning in Mandarin intonation. *Phonetica* 62, 70-87.
[30] Liu, F., Xu, Y. 2007. Interaction of word stress, focus, and sentence type in English. *Journal of the Acoustical Society of America* 121, Pt. 2, 3199.
[31] Miller, J. L., O'Rourke, T. B., Volaitis, L. E. 1997. Internal structure of phonetic categories: Effects of speaking rate. *Phonetica* 54, 121-137.
[32] Moon, S.-J., Lindblom, B. 1994. Interaction between duration, context, and speaking style in English stressed vowels. *Journal of the Acoustical Society of America* 96, 40-55.
[33] Perkell, J. S., Zandipour, M., Matthies, M. L., Lane, H. 2002. Economy of effort in different speaking conditions. I. A preliminary study of intersubject differences and modeling issues. *Journal of the Acoustical Society of America* 112, 1627-1641.
[34] Peterson, G. E., Barney, H. L. 1952. Control methods used in a study of the vowels. *Journal of the Acoustical Society of America* 24, 175-184.
[35] Picheny, M. A., Durlach, N. I., Braida, L. D. 1986. Speaking clearly for the hard of hearing II: acoustic characteristics of clear and conversational speech. *Journal of Speech and Hearing Research* 29, 434-446.
[36] Pind, J. 1995. Speaking rate, voice-onset time, and quantity: the search for higher-order invariants for two Icelandic speech cues. *Perception and psychophysics* 57, 291-304.
[37] Pitermann, M. 2000. Effect of speaking rate and contrastive stress on formant dynamics and vowel perception. *Journal of the Acoustical Society of America* 107, 3425-3437.
[38] Popper, K. 1959. *The Logic of Scientific Discovery* (translation of Logik der Forschung, 1934). London: Hutchinson.
[39] Prieto, P., Torreira, F. 2007. The segmental anchoring hypothesis revisited: Syllable structure and speech rate effects on peak timing in Spanish. *Journal of Phonetics* 35(4), 473-500.
[40] Shih, C. 1993. Relative prominence of tonal targets. In *Proceedings of the 5th North American Conference on Chinese Lingusitics*, Newark, Delaware, University of Delaware 36.
[41] Tiffany, W. R. 1980. The effects of syllable structure on diadochokinetic and reading rates. *Journal of Speech and Hearing Research* 23, 894-908.
[42] van Heuven, J. V. 2004. Planning in speech melody: production and perception of downstep in Dutch. In: H. Quené and van Heuven, J. V. (eds.), *On Speech and Language: Studies for Sieb G. Nooteboom*. The Netherlands: LOT Occasional series by Utrecht University, 83-93.
[43] Wagner, M. 2005. *Prosody and Recursion*. PhD. Dissertation, Massachusetts Institute of Techonology.
[44] Wang, M., Xu, Y. 2008. F_0 pattern and syllable grouping in Mandarin. In *Proceedings of PCC2008*, Beijing.
[45] Weismer, G., Berry, J. 2003. Effects of speaking rate on second formant trajectories of selected vocalic nuclei. *Journal of the Acoustical Society of America* 113, 3363-3378.
[46] Whalen, D. H. 1990. Coarticulation is largely planned. *Journal of Phonetics* 18, 3-35.
[47] Wightman, C. W. 2002. ToBI or not ToBI. In *Proceedings of The 1st International Conference on Speech Prosody*, Aix-en-Provence, France 25-29.
[48] Wong, Y. W. 2006. Contextual Tonal Variations and Pitch Targets in Cantonese. In *Proceedings of Speech Prosody 2006*, Dresden, Germany PS3-13-199.
[49] Xu, Y. 1994. Production and perception of coarticulated tones. *Journal of the Acoustical Society of America* 95, 2240-2253.
[50] Xu, Y. 1997. Contextual tonal variations in Mandarin. *Journal of Phonetics* 25, 61-83.
[51] Xu, Y. 1998. Consistency of tone-syllable alignment across different syllable structures and speaking rates. *Phonetica* 55, 179-203.

[52] Xu, Y. 1999. Effects of tone and focus on the formation and alignment of F_0 contours. *Journal of Phonetics* 27, 55-105.

[53] Xu, Y. 2001. Fundamental frequency peak delay in Mandarin. *Phonetica* 58, 26-52.

[54] Xu, Y. 2001. Speech melody as articulatorily implemented communicative functions. *Speech Communication* 46, 220-251.

[55] Xu, Y. 2007. How often is maximum speed of articulation approached in speech? *Journal of the Acoustical Society of America* 121, Pt. 2, 3199-3140.

[56] Xu, Y., Sun, X. 2002. Maximum speed of pitch change and how it may relate to speech. *Journal of the Acoustical Society of America* 111, 1399-1413.

[57] Xu, Y., Xu, C. X. 2005. Phonetic realization of focus in English declarative intonation. *Journal of Phonetics* 33, 159-197.

[58] Xu, Y., Xu, C. X., Sun, X. 2004. On the Temporal Domain of Focus. In *Proceedings of International Conference on Speech Prosody 2004*, Nara, Japan, 81-84.

STUDIES ON CHINESE TONE INFORMATION PROCESSING AND THEIR POSSIBLE IMPLICATION FOR AUTOMATIC PRONUNCIATION TRAINING

ZHANG Jinsong, CAO Wen

ABSTRACT

Appropriate lexical tone processing technology is desired in computer-aided pronunciation training (CAPT) technology for Chinese. As the current CAPT technology takes root in the state-of-the-art automatic speech recognition (ASR), we intend this paper to summarize our several studies on tone information processing. The studies include robust tone recognition based on multi-level tone nucleus framework, investigation on tone contribution to Pinyin-to-text conversion, design of an efficient phoneme set of tone dependent units for ASR. Based on the results of these studies, we suggest that the proposed approaches are applicable and instructive to developing tone processing technology in developing Chinese CAPT technology.

Keywords: CAPT, tone recognition, speech recognition, information evaluation

1. INTRODUCTION

The application of automatic speech recognition (ASR) technologies to computer-aided pronunciation training (CAPT) has attracted many interests in recent years, and it provides a possibility of self-learning and practicing of second language speaking skills without the need of human tutors. Chinese is a known tonal language, in which each syllable is associated with a lexical tone. There are four basic tones and a neutral tone, the same base syllables with different tones become different morphemes or words. Therefore, pitch tones play important phonemic roles in Chinese language. Appropriate technology for tone tutoring is a must for developing Chinese CAPT systems.

Experiences of teaching Chinese as a 2nd language [1] showed that it is hard for most foreigners to pronounce individual tones, and it is much harder for them to utter continuous tones. The major reason can be ascribed to the complex tonal variations, which can usually be classified into two levels [1][2][3][4]: acoustics level and tonality level. Fundamental frequency (F_0) is the main acoustic manifestation of tones. In continuous speech, it is subject to significant variations from standard tonal patterns [2][3]. Tonality variations indicate that a number of tones lose or changes their tonalities in continuous speech [4], such as tone reductions, tone sandhi phenomena and those of dialectal effects. All these tonal variations are related to the natural speaking way to convey linguistic, prosodic and other information of a speaker, so that they are necessarily to be modeled for a tone CAPT technology aiming at training of natural speaking skills.

Current CAPT literature mainly focuses on segmental pronunciations and individual tones. To alleviate this problem, we retrospect here our three different studies on tone information processing for Chinese ASR, including robust tonal acoustic modeling based on tone nucleus framework for automatic tone recognition [2][3][6]; investigation on the contributions of tone information to Pinyin-to-text conversion [5]; a flexible and informative tone dependent phoneme set design based on mutual information for ASR task [4]. These studies covered both acoustic and tonality variations for the purpose of speech recognition. We suggest that they are applicable and instructive to developing tone CAPT technology, too.

2. TONE NUCLEUS FRAMEWORK FOR TONE RECOGNITION

In continuous speech, F_0 contours are manipulated to realize not only lexical tones, but also focus, prosodic phrasing and other para-linguistic information. Furthermore, as the periodicals of the successive human vocal cords' vibrations, they are also subject to variations due to articulatory constraints of the mechanical-physiological speech production system. These make tonal F_0s in continuous speech rather different from those of isolate tones. To cope with these complex F_0 variations, an approach named as multi-level modeling based on tone nucleus model was proposed and realized to build robust tonal acoustic models for tone recognition in [2][3][4].

The approach decomposes sentential F_0 variations into different levels and uses appropriate modeling methods for F_0 variations at each individual level. The first level is sub-syllabic, the Tone Nucleus model was introduced to classify a tonal F_0 contour into the tone nucleus and possible transition loci, and then the tone nucleus was used for tone recognition. The second level is to use anchoring hypothesis based tone nucleus normalizations to cope with inter-syllable tonal coarticulation variations. The third level is above inter-syllable coarticulation, a so-called hypo- and hyper-coarticulation framework was used to model the interplay effects among tonal coarticulations and high-level articulation effects from prosodic phrase boundaries, sentential foci, etc. The three individual methods at different levels can be integrated together as one robust approach.

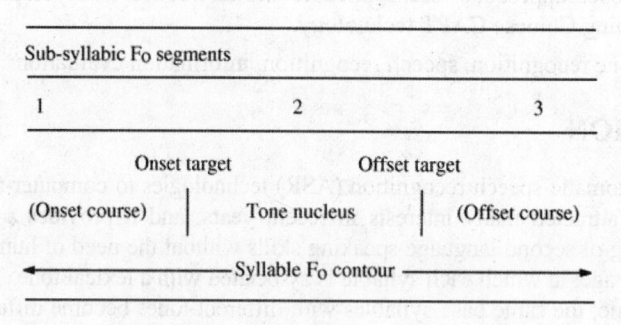

Figure 1: Illustration of Tone Nucleus model

2.1 Tone Nucleus Model

Tone nucleus model is a F_0 segmental structure model systematically accounting for F_0 variations at syllabic level. As illustrated in Figure 1, it suggests that a syllable F_0 contour may consist of three segments: onset course, tone nucleus and offset course. Among the three segments, only the tone nucleus is obligatory, whereas the other two are intrinsic F_0 transition loci, which are articulatory transition F_0s non-deliberately produced, and their appearances are optional.

- Tone Nucleus: the segment contains the most critical information for tone perception. The beginning and ending points of a tone nucleus correspond to the Tone onset and Tone offset, which may take pitch values as given in Table 1.

Table 1: Pitch targets of four basic tones. "H" and "L" stand for high and low targets respectively

Targets	Tone 1	Tone 2	Tone 3	Tone 4
Onset	H	L	L	H
offset	H	H	L	L

One merit of tone nucleus model is that it provides a systematic view of sub-syllabic F_0 variations which originate from segmental phonations. A syllable with a voicing Initial may show a significant F_0 transition locus to its onset target, whereas a syllable of the same tone may not has the locus due to its voiceless Initial part. Under the framework of Tone Nucleus model, we may only focus on the Tone Nuclei for recognizing tones, while discarding other transition loci. For example, the second syllable [yi4] in the example utterance has a significant rising locus to its high onset target, as shown in (b) of Figure 2. If we discard the transition F_0 loci and only keep tone nuclei, as shown in (c) of Figure 2, the left F_0 contours seem to conform more to the standard tonal F_0 patterns than the original ones.

2.2 Anchoring-based F_0 Normalization

In continuous speech, strong coarticulations due to a locally rapid speaking rate or weak stress may result in significant F_0 variations where both the F_0 heights and the slopes of the tone nuclei might vary significantly from the standard F_0 patterns of underlying tones. Human beings were found to be able to perceive the purported underlying tones with high consistency despite substantial F_0 variations, provided that they had the tonal context. To model the underlying perception mechanism, we proposed a hypothesis of anchoring-based tone discrimination to extract the discriminating cues in the tonal context in addition to the F_0 height and F_0 slope coefficients.

- Relative F_0 difference between the offset point of the first lexical tone and the onset of the second lexical tone may be an important discriminating cue for high or low pitch, besides the direct cue of a gliding F_0 contour.

Based on this hypothesis, a lexical tone in continuous speech can also be acoustically characterized by the patterns given in Table 2, besides the flat, rising, dipping or lowering F_0 patterns.

- Onset gap: the difference between the onset F_0 and the offset F_0 of preceding lexical tone.
- Offset gap: the difference between the offset F_0 and the onset F_0 of succeeding lexical tone.

Table 2: Anchoring-based feature patterns for the four basic lexical tones in continuous speech

Lexical tones	Onset gap	Offset gap
Tone 1	≥ 0	≥ 0
Tone 2	≤ 0	≥ 0
Tone 3	≤ 0	≤ 0
Tone 4	≥ 0	≤ 0

Furthermore, we proposed two methods to normalize a syllable F_0 contour in continuous speech. For the ith frame in one lexical tone,

- Left-to-right: $logF_0'_i = logF_{0i} - logF_0$ of the preceding tone offset.
- Right-to-left: $logF_0''_i = logF_{0i} - logF_0$ of the succeeding tone onset.

The panels (d) and (e) in Figure 2 illustrate the F_0 contours of Left-to-right and Right-to-left normalizations respectively. In (d), H onsets stay higher or nearby 0, and L onsets lower or nearby 0. We may note that the 4th and 6th syllables, both of Tone 3, originally have higher onset values than the final syllable of Tone 4 in (c). But they turned out to go to lower regions than the final Tone 4 in (d). Similarly, normalized F_0 contours in (e) also show to be consistent with the anchoring patterns in Table 2. The normalized F_0 contours $\log F_0'$ and $\log F_0''$ can be combined with the normal F_0 features to do tone recognition.

2.3 Hypo- and Hyper-articulation Intonation Model

The more complex F_0 variations are the interplay of tonality, contextual tone and high-level prosodic events such as foci and phrasing structures. An appropriate intonation model which can describe consistently (or approximately) the complex interplay variations is necessary for developing robust tonal acoustic models. Based on the tone sequence intonation theory, we proposed a so-called Hypo- and Hyper-articulation intonation model, which considers two kinds of relationships between two neighboring lexical tones: either the two tones are subject to default coarticulation variations, i.e. Hypo-articulation, or they are not, i.e. Hyper-articulation.

- Hypo-coarticulation: As can be observed in all tonal combinations of disyllabic words, there seems to be one specific coarticulation F_0 pattern for any pair of them. We assumed that they might result from the so-called articulation rule of economy of effort.

- Hyper-coarticulation: In the continuous speech, if two neighboring lexical tones do not show the defined hypo-articulation pattern, they are regarded as hyper-articulated. High-level prosodic events including phrasing boundaries, word stress and sentence focus, have been observed to break underlying hypo-coarticulations, and their inherited hierarchical structure seemed to lead to different amount of efforts for hyper-coarticulation.

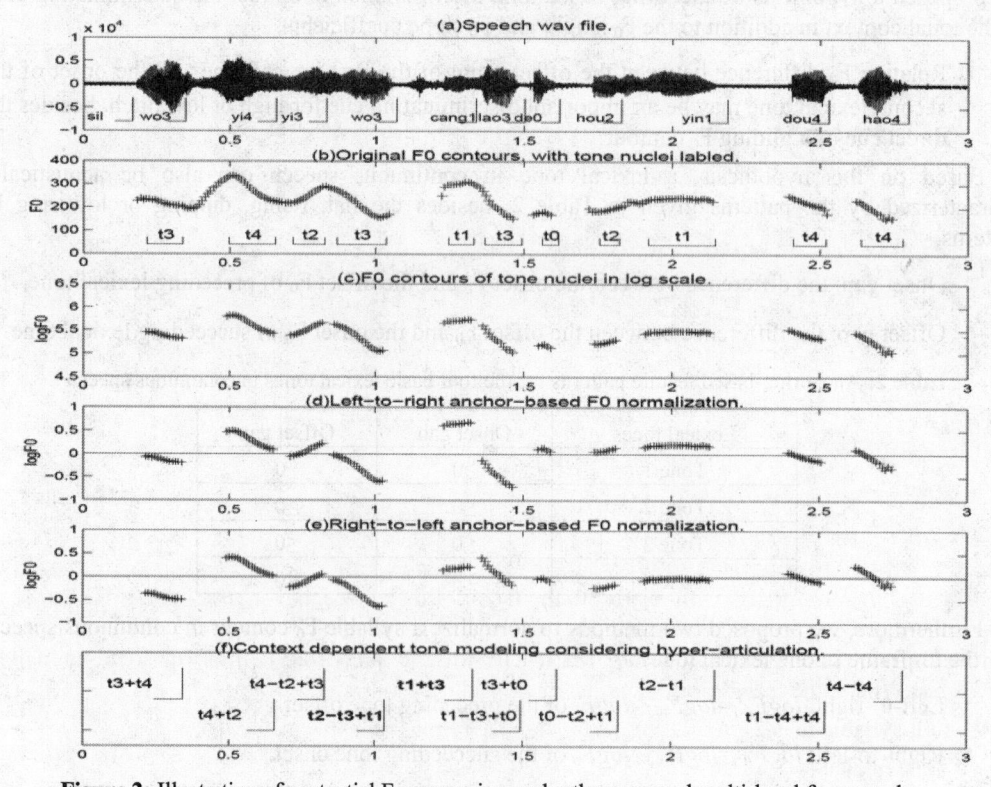

Figure 2: Illustration of sentential F_0 processing under the proposed multi-level framework

Table 3 gives the defined hypo-articulation patterns for each pair of the basic lexical tones with respect to the onset F_0 of the first lexical tone and the offset of the second tone. Assimilatory effect indicates that the preceding offset and the succeeding onset show to be assimilated. Dissimilatory effect indicates that the two points appear to depart from each other.

Table 3: Defined hypo-coarticulation patterns in our models. "A" stands for assimilatory effect, while "D" stands for dissimilatory effect.

Offset of	Onset of			
	Tone 1	Tone 2	Tone 3	Tone 4
Tone 1	A, A	D, A	D, A	A, A
Tone 2	D, D	D, A	D, A	D, D
Tone 3	D, A	D, A	D, A	D, A
Tone 4	A, A	D, D	D, D	A, A

As shown in the Figure 2, the last two syllables in (c) are two Tone 4s. The L offset of the 1st Tone 4 was raised to a higher place, while the H onset of the 2nd Tone 4 was dragged to a lower place, thus they are assimilated. If two neighboring tones do not show their hypo-articulation pattern, they are regarded to be hyper-articulated due to some higher-level effect. In the same example, the onset H target of the 5th tone was not substantially lowered by the L offset target of the 4th tone, thus hyper-articulated.

Tri-tone context dependent (CD) models are used to model the hypo-articulation F_0 variations. Mono-tone, bi-tone models are proposed to model the hyper-articulation F_0 variations. For the above mentioned hyper-articulated tone, a bi-tone t1(+t3) was used to model the 5th tone which stopped its default hypo-articulation with its preceding tone, instead of a tri-tone (t3-)t1(+t3), as shown in (f) of Figure 2.

2.4 Experimental Results

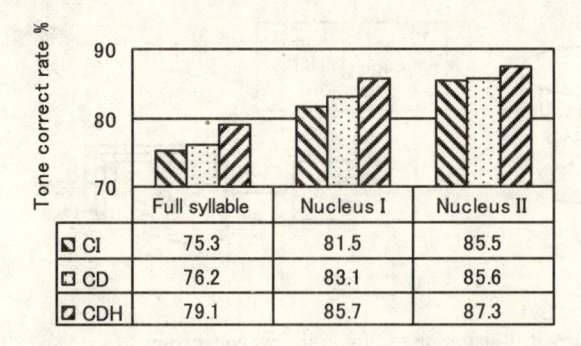

	Full syllable	Nucleus I	Nucleus II
CI	75.3	81.5	85.5
CD	76.2	83.1	85.6
CDH	79.1	85.7	87.3

Figure 3: Illustration of tone recognition performances

Tone recognition experiments were carried out using a female's data. Comparison recognition experiments have been made with respect to the factor of different acoustic features and the factor of different context dependent strategies. The results are illustrated by Figure 3. The significantly improved performances indicated the efficiencies of the proposed multi-level tonal modeling techniques. Where, the feature specification includes three kinds:

- Full syllabic features: Acoustic features of the whole syllables are used.
- Tone nucleus I: Acoustic features of the tone nuclei are used.
- Tone nucleus II: Anchoring-based normalized F_0 features: $logF_0'$ and $logF_0''$, were appended to the standard feature vector.

And the context dependent strategies include:

- CI: Context independent tonal HMMs.
- CD: Context dependent tri-tone HMMs.
- CDH: Hypo- and hyper-coarticulation based context dependent tonal HMMs.

3. TONE INFORMATION AND PINYIN-TO-TEXT CONVERSION

3.1 Tone Information and ASR

In the GB2312 standard, the commonly used Chinese characters are 6783. The base syllables without tone distinctions are about 410, and the tonal syllables are about 1300. Accordingly, the average number of homophonic characters is 16.5 per base syllable, and 5.2 per tonal syllable (exactly the numbers should be higher due to multi-pronunciations). Therefore, tone information should play an important disambiguation role for Chinese speech communication.

However, in the last decade, few Chinese speech recognition systems have made effective use of pitch tone information. Many groups reported similar discouraging results about incorporating tone processing to their ASR systems, such as about only 0.4% absolute gains. Such kinds of results let people doubt the necessity of tone processing for building Chinese ASR systems.

In order to make clear the problem why tone information was not helpful for Chinese ASR, we designed a Pinyin-to-text conversion experiment, where the relationships between tones and language models were investigated [5].

3.2 Method of Pinyin-to-text Conversion

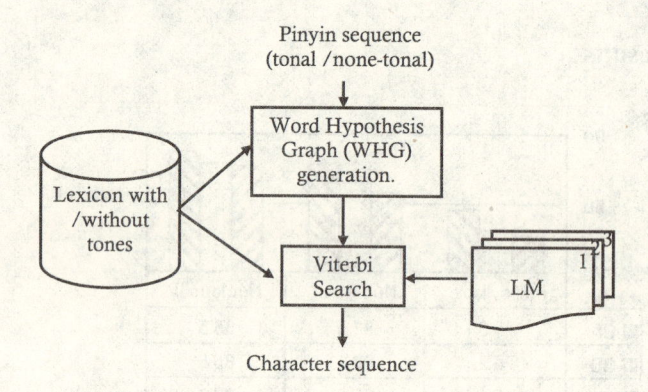

Figure 4: Illustration of Pinyin-to-text conversion

Figure 4 shows the procedure of Pinyin-to-character conversion. The input Pinyin-sequence can be regarded as the output of an acoustic matching stage in an ASR system, which has a 100% acoustic accuracy. Based on the lexicon, the Pinyin-sequence is converted into an word-hypothesis graph (WHG) containing all possible word hypotheses w for corresponding Pinyins and connections. Any path W_i from the starting point to the ending point of the WHG has an associated language model's probability as follows when the language model is in the form of n-gram.

$$P(W_i) = \prod_{j=1}^{n} p(w_{i,j}|w_{i,1},\cdots w_{i,j-1}) \tag{1}$$

The path W^* which has the highest probability is regarded as the correct output, and it can be found by a dynamic decoding algorithm like Viterbi. Therefore, this process is almost the same search stage as the one in a typical ASR system, except the previous acoustic matching stage with perfect performance. By providing the following information:

- With or without tone information: both the input Pinyin sequence and lexicon may have or haven't perfect tone information.
- Different language models (LM): a domain dependent LM, a domain mismatched LM, or a merged LM from domain dependent and mismatched LMs.

We can clarify the possible contributions to conversion rate from tone information, and the relation between them and the different LMs.

3.3 Experimental Results

We experimented on two different tasks: Phrasebook sentences for tourist information and Callhome Mandarin of family conversations through telephone. The Phrasebook includes almost orthodox sentences, while the Callhome contains spontaneous dialogues. The lexicons we used have the same 47000 word entries for both the tonal and non-tonal lexicon. Based on them, five word bi-gram language models were trained as in Table 5. The evaluation set has 1493 sentences with 15445 characters for the Phrasebook task, and 6156 sentences with 56847 characters for the Callhome task. For each evaluation, three LMs are used: the PDLM for the role of domain mismatched LM, the PhLM or the ChLM for domain dependent LM, and the PhPDLM or the ChPDLM for the merged LM.

Table 4: The developed LMs

LM	Corpus used	Number of sentences
PhLM	Phrasebook(Ph)	111200
PDLM	People Daily(PD)	307500
ChLM	CallHome(Ch)	23000
PhPDLM	Ph+PD	418700
ChPDLM	Ch+PD	330500

Figures 5 and 6 give the conversion performances for the two tasks respectively. From them, we can see that:

- In both tasks, tone information is very helpful in improving conversion accuracies.
- But the extents of contributions are dependent on the powers of the LMs used. When the LM is less powerful such as the domain mismatched PDLM, the uses of tones brought the most significant improvements in both tasks. While the LMs become more powerful such as the domain dependent PhLM and ChLM, the gains from tones reduced. The gains are intermediate in the case of interpolated LMs including PhPDLM and ChPDLM.
- In the cases of domain dependent LMs of PhLM and ChLM, tone information brought about more improvements to the task of Callhome, indicating that tone information might be more helpful in recognizing daily spontaneous speech. The reason might be due to the fact that spontaneous speech consists of more un-grammatical sentences, making its language model less predicative than that of orthodox text.

Phrasebook

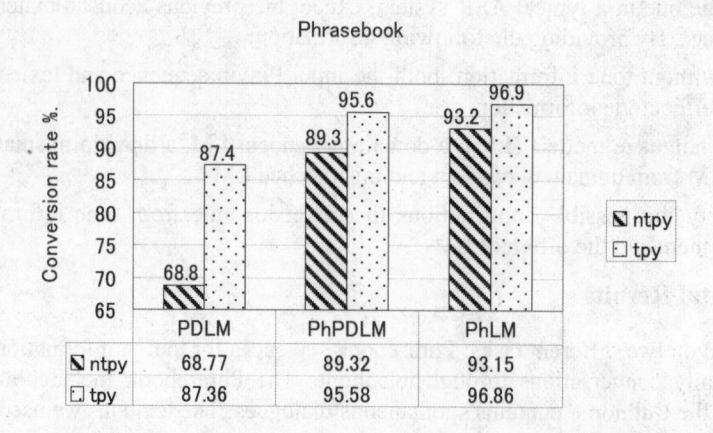

	PDLM	PhPDLM	PhLM
ntpy	68.77	89.32	93.15
tpy	87.36	95.58	96.86

Figure 5: Pinyin-to-text conversion results of the Phrasebook task

Call home conversation.

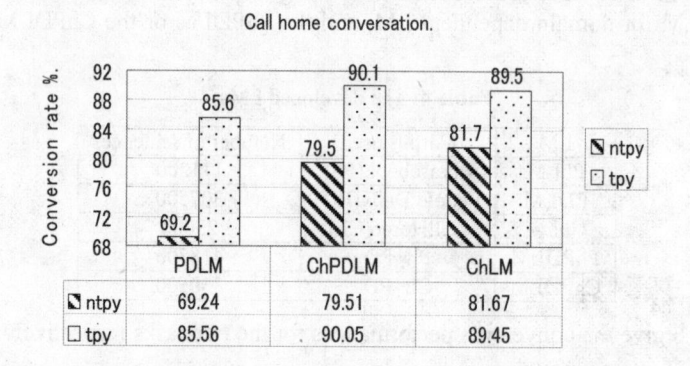

	PDLM	ChPDLM	ChLM
ntpy	69.24	79.51	81.67
tpy	85.56	90.05	89.45

Figure 6: Pinyin-to-text conversion results of the Callhome conversation task

4. INFORMATIVE TONE DEPENDENT PHONEME SET

4.1 Tone Dependent Phonemes for ASR

In the literature of Chinese ASR, the most popular approach to incorporate tone information to the ASR system is to use a phoneme set with tone dependency. This means that for a vowel "a", the system will expand it to five allophones: "a_0", "a_1" ..."a_4", for representing the vowel with the neutral tone, Tone 1 to Tone 4 respectively. The size of phoneme set usually increases by several times, and that of tri-phones increases from tens of thousands to millions. As a result, the acoustic model training and lattice decoding become rather difficult and computationally heavy.

However, we regarded that a full expansion of tone dependencies might be unnecessary. The reasons lie in that: on the one hand, speakers tend to reduce some tones from their lexical forms in daily speech when the reductions do not obstacle speech communication, and this could also partly account for why tone recognition performances of continuous speech are rather lower than isolate tones. On the other hand, the lexical and language model (e.g. n-gram) information in an LVCSR system is usually very efficient to disambiguate most of homophone words due to a lack of tone information, as showed by the results of Pinyin-to-text conversion experiments.

Therefore we proposed [4] that only those tone dependencies incorporated are necessary for disambiguating word confusions of an LVCSR system, under the condition of given lexicon and language model. In other words, a tone dependency is regarded as redundant and not included in the ASR system when the lexical and language model can disambiguate those homophone words resulting from the lack of that tone.

4.2 Method of Phoneme Set Design

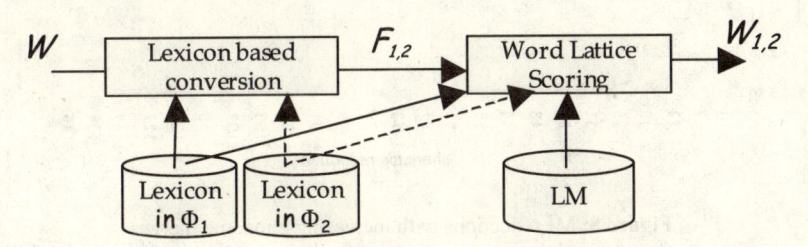

Figure 7: Illustration of phoneme optimization method

We formalize the phoneme set design problem into an information coding/decoding approach [4] as illustrated in Figure 7, where W stands for word-based text corpus, Φ_1 and Φ_2 for two different phoneme sets, $F_{1,2}$ for the different phoneme transcriptions of the W based on $\Phi_{1,2}$ lexicons respectively, $W_{1,2}$ for the decoded words from $F_{1,2}$ based on the same language model and the respective lexicons. When a coding method Φ_i is lossless, the decoded words W_i should satisfy $W=W_i$. However, when the coding is not uniquely decodable, a better coding Φ^* should be the one

$$\Phi^* = \arg\max_i I(W, F_i) \text{ where } i = 1,2 \tag{2}$$

The mutual information $I(W,F_i)$ can be calculated as

$$\begin{aligned} I(W,F_i) &= H(W) - H(W|F_i) \\ &= \log P(W|F_i) - \log P(W) \\ &= \log \frac{P(F_i|W)}{\sum_{all\ j} P(F_i|W_j) P(W_j)} \end{aligned} \tag{3}$$

$P(W)$ and $P(F_i|W)$ represent two main components in the current speech recognition system, i.e. language modeling and probabilistic pronunciation variation modeling.

4.3 Experimental Results

Based on the mutual information criterion, we designed a greedy search algorithm to merge one pair of phonemes each step [4] in order to reduce the redundancy in an initial large phoneme set. An experiment was carried on the tone dependent Initial/Final (IF) set, which initially has 206 units. The text corpus (CBTEC) we used is the Chinese version of Basic Travel Conversation Text (BTEC) of ATR. It contains about 200000 sentences with about one million words. The lexicon size is about 17000, and the language model is a 2-gram model trained from CBTEC.

Figure 8 shows the relationship between MI reductions and the increasing number of phoneme merges.

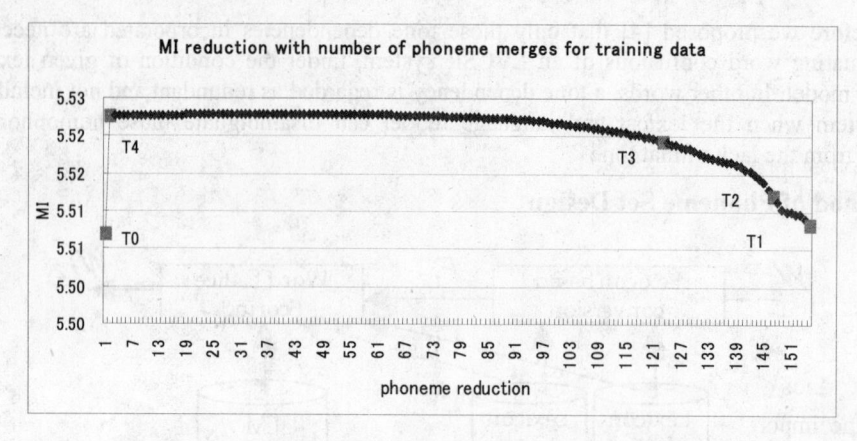

Figure 8: MI reductions with increasing phoneme merges

We selected five different unit sets to build our speech recognition systems. T0 is the conventional non-tonal IFs with 59 units; T1 has 50 units and shows a similar MI to that of T0; T2 has the same number of units as T0, but shows a better MI than T0; T3 has 80 units, and shows only slight MI loss from the initial phoneme set T4, which has the full tone-featured set of 206 units. Table 6 lists the number of Initials, Finals and logical tri-phones in the five ASR systems respectively.

Table 5: Different phoneme sets

Set	Units	Initials	Finals	Tri-phones
T0	59	21	37	107441
T1	50	18	31	70128
T2	59	18	40	114945
T3	80	20	59	292651
T4	206	21	184	3022775

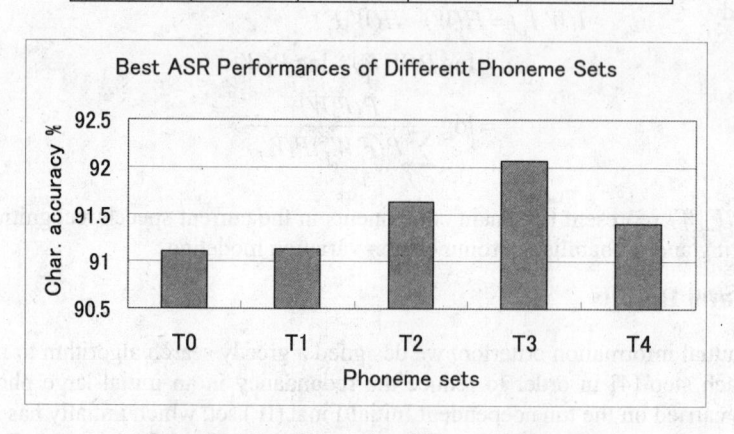

Figure 9: ASR results using different phoneme sets

Speech recognition experiments were carried out using the above five phoneme sets, and the results are shown in Figure 9. Generally speaking, the automatically derived phoneme sets show some better or similar performances compared with the non-tonal set T0, and the T3 set gets the highest performances. This indicates that derived phoneme sets are efficient for the recognition task.

5. DISCUSSION: APPLICATIONS TO CAPT

Findings and knowledge learned from the above three studies are regarded as applicable and instructive to developing tone CAPT technologies. At current stage, we consider the followings.

- Robust tonal acoustic modeling is applicable to developing tone error detection modules that play a key role in a CAPT system. Tone nucleus model, anchoring-based normalization, and Hypo- & Hyper-articulation intonation model will facilitate the task of continuous speech.
- Knowledge of the fact that contributions of tone information to Pinyin-to-text conversion are dependent on the perplexities of language models might guide us to develop keyboard input tools, which can help foreign students to acquire the pronunciations including the tones through text input exercises. Different LMs might be adopted there to meet different demands of difficulties.
- One important finding learned from the mutual information criterion based phoneme set design is that different phonemes have different communication loads in continuous speech. If we order the importance of the phonemes according to their communication loads, we can say that students should lay more emphasis on those important ones. Appropriate CAPT tools can be developed based on this principal.
- The development of any CAPT technology should suffice the requirements by the theory of second language learning.

6. CONCLUSION

This paper summarizes three studies on tone information processing for continuous speech ASR, and discusses their possible applications to Chinese CAPT study. These possibilities are the future directions we will work on.

7. ACKNOWLEDGEMENTS

The present study was supported by the MOE Project 07JJD740060 of Key Research Institute of Humanities and Social Sciences at Universities.

REFERENCES

[1] Cao Wen. 2002. *Pronunciation training of Chinese*. Beijing: Beijing Language and Culture University Press.

[2] Zhang Jinsong, Hirose, K. 2004. Tone nucleus modeling for Chinese lexical tone recognition, Elsevier Science. *Speech Communication*. 42, 447-466.

[3] Zhang Jinsong, Nakamura, S., Hirose, K. 2005. Tone Nucleus Based Multi-level Robust Acoustic Tonal Modeling of Sentential F_0 Variations for Chinese Continuous Speech Tone Recognition, Elsevier Science. *Speech Communication* 46, 440-454.

[4] Zhang Jinsong, Hu Xinhui, Nakamura, S. 2008. Using Mutual Information Criterion to Design An Efficient Phoneme Set For Chinese Speech Recognition. *IEICE Transaction on INFO. & SYST*. E91-D(3), 508-513.

[5] Zhang Jinsong, Nakamura, S., Hirose, K. 2002. Is tone recognition necessary for Chinese speech recognition—evidence from Pinyin-to-character conversion. Proc. of *ASJ-Fall*, 5-6.

[6] Wang Xiaodong, Hirose, K., Zhang Jinsong, Minematsu, N. 2008. Tone Recognition of Continuous Mandarin Speech Based on Tone Nucleus Model and Neural Network. *IEICE Transaction on INFO. & SYST*. E91-D(6), 1748-1755.

List of Publications by Professor Wu

1938a   调查西南民族语言管见，《西南边疆》第1期。
(Remarks on the survey of the minority languages in southwest China. *Southwest Frontiers*, No.1.)

1938b   拼音文字与云南边民教育，《西南边疆》第2期。
(Alphabetic writing and the education of the people living in the border areas of Yuannan province. Southwest Frontiers, No.2.)

1948   《湖北方言调查报告》（与赵元任、丁声树等合著），上海：商务印书馆。
(*A Survey Report on the Dialects in the north of Hubei Province*. Co-authored with Chao Yuen-ren, Ding Shengshu, et al. Shanghai: The Commercial Press.)

1957   华北、华东、华中十省方言普查工作现况，《中国语文》第7期。
(Status of the general dialect survey of the ten provinces in north, east and central China. *Studies of the Chinese Language*, No.7.)

1958   武鸣壮语中汉语借字的音韵系统，《语言研究》第3期。
(The phonology of the loanwords from Han dialects in the Zhuang language of Wuming, Guangxi. *Studies in Language and Linguistics*, No.3.)

1961   谈谈现代语音实验方法（用"齐鲁"笔名），《中国语文》第10-12期。
(On modern methodologies of phonetic experiments. Published with the penname Qilu. *Studies of the Chinese Language*, No. 10-12.)

1963a   《普通话发音图谱》（与周殿福合著），北京：商务印书馆。
(*Atlas of the articulation of Standard Chinese*. Co-authored with Zhou Dianfu. Beijing: The Commercial Press.)

1963b   一种分析语音的重要仪器——语图仪综述，《科学仪器》第1卷第3期。
(Introducing Sonagraph, an important instrument of phonetic analysis. *Scientific Instruments*, Vol.1, No.3.)

1964   普通话元音和辅音的频谱分析及共振峰的测算，《声学学报》第1期。
(Spectrum analysis of the vowels and consonants of Standard Chinese and the measure of formant. *Acta Acoustica*, No.1.)

1974   《湖南方言调查报告》（与赵元任、丁声树等合著），台北："中研院"史语所。
(*A survey report on the dialects of Hunan Province*. Co-authored with Chao Yuen-ren and Ding Shengshu, et al., S. F. Fang, Institute of History and Philology, Taipei.)

1979a 实验语音学知识讲话（用语音室笔名），《中国语文》第1, 2, 4, 5, 6期。
（On experimental phonetics: An introduction. Published in the name of the Phonetics Laboratory, Institute of Linguistics, CASS. *Studies of the Chinese Language*, No.1, 2, 4-6.）

1979b A preliminary study of distinctive features and their correlations in Standard Chinese. Abstract. *Proceedings of the 9th International Congress of Phonetic Sciences*, Vol. 1, Copenhagen, Danmark.

1980 试论普通话语音的"区别特征"及其相互关系，《中国语文》第5期。
（A tentative discussion of the distinctive features in the phonetics of Standard Chinese and their interrelationships. *Studies of the Chinese Language*, No.5.）

1981 实验语音学与语言学，《语文研究》第1期。
（Experimental phonetics and linguistics. *Linguistic Research*, No.1.）

1982a Rules of intonation in Standard Chinese. Reprints of Papers for the Working Group on Intonation. *Proceedings of the 13th International Congress of Linguists*, Tokyo, Japan.

1982b 普通话语句中的声调变化，《中国语文》第6期。
（Tone change in the sentences of Standard Chinese. *Studies of the Chinese Language*, No.6.）

1984 （with P. Ladefoged）Places of articulation: an investigation of Pekinese fricatives and affricates. *Journal of Phonetics*, No.12.

1985 普通话三字组变调规律，《中国语言学报》第2期。
（Rules of tri-syllabic tone sandhi in Standard Chinese. *Journal of Chinese Linguistics*, No.2.）

1986 《汉语普通话单音节语图册》（主编），北京：中国社会科学出版社。
（*A Collection of Monosyllabic Spectrographs of Standard Chinese*. As editor-in-chief. Beijing: China Social Sciences Press.）

1987 The aspirated/non-aspirated stops and affricates in Standard Chinese. *Proceedings of the 11th Interantional Congress of Phonetic Sciences*, Vol. 5, Tallinn.

1988a 普通话辅音不送气/送气区别的实验研究，《中国语言学报》第3期。
（Experiment and research on the aspirated / non-aspirated distinction in Standard Chinese consonants. *Journal of Chinese Linguistics*, No.3.）

1988b Tone-sandhi Patterns of quadro-syllabic combinations in Standard Chinese. *Report of Phonetic Research*. Institute of Linguistics, Chinese Academy of Social Sciences.

1989a 《实验语音学概要》（与林茂灿共同主编），北京：高等教育出版社。
（*Outline of Experimental Phonetics*. Co-edited with Lin Maocan. Beijing: Higher Education Press.）

1989b （with Sun Guohua） An experimental study of co-articulation of unaspirated stops in CVCV contexts in Standard Chinese. *Annual Report of Phonetic Research*. Institute of Linguistics,

Chinese Academy of Social Sciences.

1989c 补听缺斋语音杂记，《中国语文》第6期。

（Miscellaneous remarks on phonetics. *Studies of the Chinese Language*, No.6.）

1990a （with Sun Guohua）Acoustic coarticulatory patterns of voiceless fricatives in CVCV in Standard Chinese. *Report of Phonetic Research*. Institute of Linguistics, Chinese Academy of Social Sciences.

1990b Can poly-syllabic tone-sandhi patterns be the invariant units of intonation in Spoken Standard Chinese? *Proceedings of the 1st International Conference on Spoken Language Processing*, Kobe, Japan.

1990c 汉语普通话语调的基本调型，《王力先生纪念论文集》，北京：商务印书馆。

（Basic contour patterns of intonation of Standard Chinese. *Essays in Honor of Professor Wang Li*. Beijing: The Commercial Press.）

1991a 《现代汉语语音概要》（主编），北京：华语教学出版社。

（*Outline of Modern Chinese Phonetics*. As editor-in-chief, Sinolingua, Beijing.）

1991b （with Liu Mingjie）A study of pre-vocalic acoustic effects of the "zero-initial" syllables in Standard Chinese. Report of Phonetic Research, Institute of Linguistics, Chinese Academy of Social Sciences.

1991c （with Sun Guohua）A study of co-articulation of unaspirated stops in CVCV contexts in Standard Chinese, *Proceedings of the 12th Inernational Congress of Phonetic Sciences*, Vol. 3. Aix-en-Provence, France.

1992 普通话零声母起始段的声学分析（与刘铭杰合著），《第二届全国人机语音通讯会议论文集》。

（Acoustic analysis of zero-consonant initials in Standard Chinese. Co-authored with Liu Mingjie. *Proceedings of the 2nd National Conference on Man-Machine Communication*, Guilin, China.）

1993 A new method of intonation analysis for Standard Chinese Frequency transposition. processing of phrasal contours in a sentence. *Report of Phonetic Research*, Institute of Linguistics, Chinese Academy of Social Sciences. Also in: G. Fant et al.（eds.），1996. *Analysis, Perception and Processing of Spoken Language*. Elsevier Science B. V.

1994 Further experiments on spatial distribution of phrasal contours under different range. Registers in Chinese intonation. *Proceedings of the International Symposium on Prosody*, Yokohama, Japan.

1995a Tentative planning of prosodic rules for the naturalness of synthetic Spoken Chinese. *Report of Phonetic Research*. Institute of Linguistics, Chinese Academy of Social Sciences.

1995b Predictability of different attitudinal intonation in Standard Chinese. *Proceedings of the 13th*

International Congress of Phonetic Sciences, Vol. 2, Stockholm, Sweden.

1996a 为改进合成普通话口语自然度所需韵律特征规则的设计，《计算机时代的汉语和汉字研究》（罗振声、袁毓林主编），北京：清华大学出版社。

（A design of prosodic rules for improving the naturalness of synthetic Spoken Standard Chinese. In: Luo Zhensheng, Yuan Yulin（eds.）, *Studies of Chinese Language and Writing in the Computer Age*. Beijing: Tsinghua University Press.）

1996b 用于普通话语音合成的"韵律标记文本"的设计，《第三届全国语音学研讨会论文集》，北京：北京广播学院。

（The design of Prosodic Labeling Text for the phonetic synthesis of Standard Chinese, *Proceedings of the 3rd National Symposium on Phonetics*. Beijing: Beijing Broadcasting Institute.）

1996c 赵元任先生在汉语声调研究上的贡献，《清华大学学报（哲社科学版）》第13期。

（Chao Yuen-ren's contributions to the study of the tones of Chinese. *Journal of Tsinghua University Philosophy and Social Sciences*, No.13.）

1996d A new method of intonation analysis for Standard Chinese: frequency transposition processing of phrasal contours in a sentence. *Festschrift for Hiroya Fujisaki—analysis, perception and processing of spoken language*. Amsterdam, Elsevier Science.

1997a 从声调与乐律的关系提出普通话语调处理的新方法，《庆祝中国社会科学院语言研究所建所45周年学术论文集》，北京：商务印书馆。

（A new method of Standard Chinese intonation processing based on the relation between tone and melody. *Collected Essays Dedicated to the 45th Anniversary of the Institute of Linguistics, CASS*. Beijing: The Commercial Press.）

1997b （with Wang Renhua et al.）Towards a project of All-Phonetic-Labelling-text for TTS synthesis of Spoken Chinese. In: Wang Renhua and Keikichi Hirose（eds.）, *Proceedings of the first China-Japan workshop on spoken language processing*. Hefei: Press of University of Science and Technology of China.

1997c 试论"人－机对话"中的汉语语音学，《世界汉语教学》第12期。

（A tentative discussion of phonetics of Chinese in man-machine discourse. *Chinese Teaching in the World*, No.12.）

1998a 普通话语音合成中协同发音音段变量的规正处理，汉语及少数民族语言语音学研讨会论文，香港：香港城市大学。

（The formalization of segmental coarticulatory variants in Standard Chinese synthesis. *Proceedings of the Conference on Phonetics of the Languages in China*. Hong Kong: Hong Kong City University.）

1998b 普通话四字组中韵律变量的处理规则，《语音研究报告》，中国社会科学院语言研究所语音研究室。

（Rules for processing prosodic variations of quadro-syllabic groups in Standard Chinese. *Report of Phonetic Research*. Institute of Linguistics, Chinese Academy of Social Sciences. Beijing, China.）

1998c 我与语音学，张世林主编《学林春秋》，北京：中华书局。

（My life with phonetics. In: Zhang Shilin（ed.）, *Xuelin Chunqiu*. Zhonghua Book Company, Beijing.）

1998d 隋唐长安四声调值试拟，《北京市语言学会第五届年会论文提要汇编》，北京：北京语言文化大学。

（Suggestion of four-tone value for Chang'an in Sui and Tang Dynastys. *Abstract collection of the 5th annual conference of Beijing linguistics association.* Beijing: University of Beijing Language and Culture.）

2000 From traditional Chinese phonology to modern speech processing — realization of tone and intonation in Standard Chinese. *ICSLP 2000*, Beijing.

2001 普通话语音合成中有关自然度的韵律变量问题，《第五届全国现代语音学学术会议论文集》，北京：清华大学出版社。

（The problems of prosodic variations in speech synthesis in Standard Chinese. *Proceedings of the 5th National Symposium on Phonetics*. Beijign: Tsinghua University Press.）

2002a 从胡乔木的提问试论汉语的声调和节奏，《语音研究报告》，中国社会科学院语言研究所语音研究室。

（A tentative discussion on tones and rhythms in traditional Chinese. *Report of Phonetic Research*. Institute of Linguistics, Chinese Academy of Social Sciences. Beijing, China. Also, in 2002, *Collection of linguistics*, No. 28.Beijing:The Commercial Press.）

2002b 中国音韵学和语音学在汉语言语合成中的应用，《语言教学与研究》第1期。

（An application of Chinese phonology and phonetics in Chinese speech synthesis. *Language and linguistics teaching and study*, No.1.）

2002c 试论汉字草书笔法与普通话语调规则的相似性，中国声学学会2002年全国声学学术会议，桂林。

（From the Chinese cursive calligraphy to the intonation contour. *Proceedings of the National Symposium on Acoustics made by Chinese Acoustic Association*, Guilin.）

2002d 赵元任著，吴宗济、赵新那编，《赵元任语言学论文集》，北京：商务印书馆。

2003a 试从文学与艺术的韵律探索普通话的韵律规则，《第六届全国现代语音学学术会议论文集》，天津。

（Exploring prosodic rules from literature and art points. *Proceedings of the 6th National*

Symposium on Modern Phonetics. Tianjin: Tianjin Normal University.）

2003b "书话同源"——试论草书书法与语调规则的关系，《世界汉语教学》第1期。

（The same source between Chinese calligraphy and speech — the relationship between cursive script and Chinese intonation rules. *Chinese Teaching in the world*, No.1.）

2003c 《补听集——吴宗济自选集》，周奎杰、张世林主编，北京：新世界出版社。

（*Selected micellanceous of Wu Zongji*, eds. by Zhou and Zhang. Beijing: New World Press.）

2003d 试论普通话中韵律规则与其他若干学科中韵律规则的共性，《语音研究报告》，中国社会科学院语言研究所语音研究室。

（On the generality of prosodic rules in spoken Chinese and those in some other fields. *Report of Phonetic Research*. Institute of Linguistics, Chinese Academy of Social Sciences. Beijing, China.）

2004 《吴宗济语言学论文集》，北京：商务印书馆。

2006 赵元任著，吴宗济、赵新那编，*Linguistic Essays by Chao Yuen-ren*，北京：商务印书馆。

Messages of Congratulations to Professor Wu

Dear Professor Wu Zongji,

First of all, I wish to express my feeling of utmost respect and deep friendship to you on this very special occasion of your centennial birthday. As I wrote in my message for you five years ago, ninety-five years was only a milestone in your great life, and now I am so happy to see you active and productive at age 100! I can foretell again that we will surely celebrate your 105th birthday in the year 2014!

On this memorable occasion, let me review thirty years of our friendship. We met first in Copenhagen in 1979 when we were both elected to serve on the Permanent Council for the Organization of International Congresses of Phonetic Sciences. On that occasion, we discussed many problems of our common interest. I had been working on word accent and sentence intonation of common Japanese since 1969. Realizing that Chinese as an important tone language has many challenging features not found in Japanese, and that you are an eminent phonetician from China, I asked you whether you would be interested in looking into the variations of tone and intonation of Chinese. It was the start of our lasting friendship, collaboration, and mutual enlightenment.

Since then, I had the pleasure of inviting you to Japan three times. The first was in 1982 for the Working Group on Intonation in Tokyo, held in conjunction with the 20th International Congress of Linguists. Your deep insight into the entire problem was already shown in your paper for the workshop, which I organized and chaired with Eva Gårding. Then it was in 1990 for the First International Conference on Spoken Language Processing (ICSLP) in Kobe, for which I was Founder Chair. At that time, we spent almost two weeks to work together in Tokyo, Kyoto and Kobe. Thirdly, it was in 1994 for the International Symposium on Intonation in Yokohama, which I chaired in conjunction with the Third ICSLP. It was always a great pleasure for me to share my interest with you.

In addition to these occasions in Japan. I had the pleasure of meeting you many times both in China and abroad, and of discussing, not only problems of speech and language, but also of philosophy and literature of both China and Japan. In fact, you are the only scholar and friend in the world with whom I can share my deep love and admiration of Chinese culture. I treasure your poems you kindly wrote for me on numerous occasions of my life.

Dear Professor Wu, I am so glad to have taken part in the editing of this special Festschrift, and to join your many friends and admirers in dedicating it to you. I wish you many more years of active, productive, and happy life to come.

Hiroya Fujisaki
Professor Emeritus
The University of Tokyo

Tribute to Professor Wu Zongji

How wonderful it is, my friend and colleague Wu Zongji, that you have completed the one hundredth year of a very good and productive life. Although we have not spent time together very often, I relish the honor and pleasure of having known you for so many years. It is my heartfelt hope for you to have good health and the strength to keep up your interest in our cherished field of phonetics.

Arthur S. Abramson

Arthur S. Abramson
Professor Emeritus of Linguistics
The University of Connecticut
Scientist
Haskins Laboratories

I remember with pleasure the many years we served together with Professor Wu on the council for organizing the International Congresses of Phonetic Sciences. I hope that my small contribution to the Festschrift honoring Professor Wu's achievements will serve as a personal congratulation.

Ilse Lehiste

Ilse Lehiste
Professor Emeritus
The Ohio State University

Dear Professor Wu Zongji,

It is a great and very special honour and at the same time a tremendous pleasure for me to be part of the large circle of your friends, colleagues and former students who have the opportunity to contribute to this Festschrift, and to extend warm wishes, on the occasion of your 100th birthday. Phonetic Science has been extremely fortunate in reaping the fruits of your broad and innovative research, in which you have been blessed by an exceptionally long active life. Thanks to your work, our acoustic, phonetic and phonological knowledge of one of the world's major languages, Mandarin Chinese, has increased, and is still increasing through your students, by leaps and bounds, most particularly in the areas of tone and intonation. One of your especially successful students, Dr Xu Yi, is an Associate Editor of the journal *Phonetica*, and is responsible for papers dealing with prosody in tone languages and with languages of China, thus helping to disseminate research in your life-long fields of interest and activity throughout the Phonetic Science community world-wide.

Let me add a little personal note to this message of congratulation. While I am writing these lines my younger daughter happens to be on a short visit in our home. She still remembers very vividly meeting you, and sitting beside a highly esteemed Chinese scholar, at a dinner that Professor Mario Rossi, at the 12th ICPhS in Aix-en-Provence, gave for the Permanent Council for the Organization of Congresses of Phonetic Sciences, of which you were a member. She is asking me, and so is my wife, who met you on that occasion as well, to pass on their best wishes for your very special day and for the future.

With kindest regards,
Yours ever

(Message from Prof. Louis Pols received on February 16, 2009)

Distinguished Prof. Wu Zongji, dear friend,

For me as a young guy being almost 68, it is impossible to imagine becoming 100 years of age, especially with an active life as that of Prof. Wu. In our Low Countries (The Netherlands), professors are supposed to retire at 65 years of age; how then could there be in China this Professor Wu still actively involved in phonetics research despite being more than 30 years older!

I had the honor to meet Wu Zongji on several memorable occasions and I was always impressed by his joyful spirit, his great involvement in scientific matters, his critical remarks, and his scientific contributions in perfect English, most notably his memorable keynote presentation at the opening of the 6th ICSLP in Beijing in October 2000, entitled "From traditional Chinese phonology to modern speech processing — realization of tone and intonation in standard Chinese". For me this lecture was the perfect illustration of what phonetics is all about. *Variation* of tone and intonation in spoken Chinese, *consistency* in the underlying tonal patterns that allow for proper interpretation and for natural speech synthesis. I was inspired by this for the topic of my own scientific contribution to this Festschrift.

Prof. Wu can be proud of his life and of his work, exemplified in the present high quality speech research, not just in China but in the whole region. I congratulate him wholeheartedly and, as a past president of ISCA, I take the liberty to do that also on behalf of the whole international speech community.

Louis C.W. Pols

Dear Professor Wu Zongji,

The scientific community of speech researchers is celebrating your centennial birthday. Please accept this short message conveying my heartiest congratulations to you. You know how and why your successful approaches to bridging the gap between traditional phonology and modern speech processing have been so influential on my own thinking in this area, especially in my attempts to discuss the future perspectives of phonetic speech research. I am so grateful that I had the opportunity to meet you and to speak with you about your work. To express my deep gratitude let me simply say: Thank You!

I hope you are doing well and that you are continuing your important work.

Hans G. Tillmann

Dear Professor Wu Zongji,

I am delighted to learn from Professor Fujisaki that you are celebrating your 100th birthday in coming April. In fact, I sent you a congratulation message last year through a postgraduate student of mine in Seoul who attended the conference in Beijing that I knew was devoted to you.

No phonetician or linguist I know of lived for one hundred years: Daniel Jones passed away at the age of 86, Henry Sweet at 67. King Sejong the great of Korea who invented the Korean alphabet in the 15th century lived only to be 53 years of age. Dear Professor Wu ! You have in this sense surpassed all other phoneticians and linguists in the East and the West and emerged as a true victor.

I would like to congratulate you once again on your centennial birthday, and wish you many happy and healthy returns in the years to come and ever increasing research activity !

Hyun Bok Lee, CBE, PhD. (London),
Professor Emeritus of Phonetics & Linguistics,
Seoul National University,
Honorary President of the Korean Society of
Phonetics and Speech Science

It is both my honor and pleasure to congratulate Professor Wu Zongji on his 100th birthday. In his distinctive ways, Professor Wu has shown us all how a brilliant mind, a wide range of interests, a profound appreciation of art, and an unyielding zest of life could dwell harmoniously in a simple life he lives. Surrounded by a roomful of owls and books, whisking a few strokes of Chinese calligraphy, reading and re-reading a good book, savoring a hearty meal, sipping a small jug of warm rice wine, laughing out loud at a good joke, and there we see him, one of the most insightful linguists of our time. Happy birthday, Professor Wu! We will continue to draw inspirations from your passionate explorations of language, the most wonderful and unique faculty of human.

Dear Professor Wu,

Happy 100th Birthday!

As your student from 1981 to 1984, I benefited tremendously from your teaching, advice, and most importantly, your own example as a devoted scholar. I still have vivid memories of the many study sessions I had in your home, where I not only enjoyed our engaging discussion but also indulged in your gourmet cooking. Over the years I have been trying to follow your footsteps, but emulating your longevity will probably be the greatest challenge for me.

My best wishes to you for continuing to be healthy and productive and to enjoy life for many more years to come!

Xu Yi

贺吴宗济先生百岁华诞

堪称三朝元老
不愧语学权威

后学周定一敬题
二〇〇九年三月
时年九十六

贺 信

敬爱的吴老先生，

今年是您的百岁寿辰，可喜、可敬、可贺。

我在贵阳清华中学读书时的老师是您在清华大学时的同学，所以我在该校时尊称您为老师。您后在中央研究院历史语言研究所同赵元任等先生一同工作，所以我还应该尊称您为前辈。上个世纪五十年代您从事欧游访问回来，我曾听过您的演讲。语言所在端王府时我曾在您那布置很精致的小房间里拜访过您。我们在河南息县五七干校时，我亲眼目睹您在自制的小煤油炉上炒鸡蛋。回京后我曾登门品尝您亲手煮制的咖啡，欣赏您收藏的猫头鹰纪念品。您为我们所创建的语音实验室在声学语音学方面作出了卓越的贡献，这一切都深深地印入了我的脑海，也深深地印入了我国语音学研究的发展史中。当您受到国际上以及国内给予您的学术荣誉时，您却淡然处之，从不张扬。当您处于逆境受到不公正的待遇时，同样也淡然处之，从不计较。我想这也许是您高寿的因素之一。您在学术和人品方面都为我们作出了榜样。我愿意永远地向您学习，向您致敬。

祝您

平安，快乐！

晚辈 赵世开 敬贺

2009年3月1日（晚辈也已八十三岁）

恭贺吴先生百岁华诞

我是在 1959 年的夏天分配到语言所的语音组的，当时语音组已有四位先生：吴宗济先生、周殿福先生、林茂灿先生和负责设备管理的邢继禄同志。我记得到了语音组以后除了学习掌握腭位照相、X 光照相，同时还开始了元音声学分析。当时使用的是丹麦 2105 型超外差频率分析仪。这种设备只能分析稳态的元音，为了分析音节中的元音，吴宗济先生利用现有的录音机设计了一种切音机，努力从音节中分离出不同的元音，虽然这样做很困难，手续很繁复，但还是比较可行的办法。与此同时，吴宗济先生指导我学习语音学理论。他抱了一尺多高的英文版的书籍给我，我记得有：Chiba and Kajiyama 的 The vowel, its nature and structure（照片版），国际语言学家第八次年会论文集 Proc. of 8th inter. Cong. of linguists（1958），Delattre 的 The physiological interpretation of sound spectrograms（照片版），Joos 的 Acoustic Phonetics 等一批他从捷克、丹麦和瑞典购买和照相带来的资料。他首先为我选定国际语言学家第八次年会论文集中的《声学语音学的新技术对语言学的贡献》（Fischer-Jørgensen, E.,1958）What can the new techniques of acoustic phonetics contribute to linguistics。这篇文章几乎总结了当时声学语音学研究的新成果，从而成为我的语音学研究的启蒙老师。由于我的英文水平极低，又加上当时没有相应的专有术语词典，因此读这篇文章真像读天书一样。但很幸运的是得到吴先生的悉心指导，无论从英文词句翻译上，还是确定专有名词的中文定名及其概念的诠释方面，吴先生都不嫌其烦地为我解释，甚至要弄明白一个名词，吴先生要去查阅很多文章，结合当时的我们正在进行的国际音标元音和普通话元音（由周殿福先生发音）声谱分析的现象，反复思考，确定译名及含义。我现在想来最难忘的是共振峰的译名及其计算方法。大家知道，共振峰(formant)是元音和浊辅音最基本的声学特征，是元音音质（quality）及其生理舌位的声学映像。但在 1960 年，formant 这个词应译成什么成为一大难题。Fischer-Jørgensen 的文章提到"大家知道元音的特性是能量集中在一定相对狭窄的频段内，这个频段称为 formant，而且这些 formant 的位置因元音的不同而不同"。在 formant 脚注中说道，"formant" 这个词不仅表示语音声波的能量集中，而且也表示声道振动样式，两者是紧密关联的。由此吴先生确定 "formant" 译为 "共振峰"，即是声道共鸣的结果。而"峰"的含义是指功率谱上元音几个谐波峰群之最大峰值位置。这个译名非常符合汉语的语义，因而得到声学界老前辈马大猷先生的肯定，从而成为今天声学术语和语音学术语的基本词汇。

接着问题又来了，从元音功率谱上的谐波峰上怎样去确定共振峰的位置。当我们分析了国际音标的[i][ɪ]时，发现两者的 F1 最强谐波的频率位置是相同的，据此画在声学元音图上这两者处在相同的高度上。我们认为这既不符合听辨结果，也不符合国际音标元音图的位置，由此提出了怎样从谐波群中测量共振峰频率的问题。吴先生根据 Joos 的 Acoustic Phonetics 中谐波图上的一条包络线（虚线）的启示，确定共振峰应落在最强谐波和次强谐波之间的某一位置，即应处在谐波群中三条谱线组成的包络峰的重心（颠值）上。原则确定后，吴先生着手具体测量方法的制定，这就是后来首先在第一届中国声学学会上提出的报告《普通话元音和辅音的频率分析及共振峰的测算》，这篇文章后来发表在《声学学报》1 卷 1 期（1964），现收录在《吴宗济语言学论文集》中。此文详细地用图解和计算公式对国际音标元音和普通话元音，不论是男、女、童的发音（基频不同）分别给出了计算方法，都能测算得十分准确。这是一个创造，是中国语音学家对国际语音学的贡献。吴先生的这种创新精神贯彻在他 50 年的语音学研究生涯中，如自主设计研制切音机，语音声谱分析、记录中一套联动装置，还有腭位照相装置及三维分析方法（见《实验语音学概要》，118 页）。在接近 90 高龄时

（1996）还在汉语语调分析方面另辟蹊径，提出了"移调"或"转调"的方法，让我们有耳目一新、茅塞顿开之感。

今天我们纪念吴宗济先生百岁华诞之际，应该学习吴老先生一生对生活的热爱和对科学的孜孜追求，活到老学到老、创新到老的精神，推进我国语音学基本理论及其应用学科的发展。

中国社会科学院民族与人类学研究所
中国语言学会语音学分会主任

贺吴宗济教授百岁华诞！

时起上世纪 60 年代初，当我回国参与语音信号处理和声码器研究起，由于中国声学学会语言声学分会的活动，与中国社会科学院语言研究所吴宗济老师经常有联系，有机会聆听吴老师的学术报告及教导，吴先生的语言学、汉语声调和方言等研究成果奠定了汉语语言信号处理的基础，为我国语言和语音研究跻身于世界行列作出了杰出的贡献！至今已有近五十载，吴先生的乐观形象、亲和师表、学术教导仍然不时地浮现在我的心头。他是我的精神榜样。

值此百岁华诞之际，我愿以此敬祝

吴老先生永葆青春活力，寿比南山！

学生 袁保宗
于北京交通大学 2009 年 2 月 9 日(元宵节)

百岁人瑞

吴宗济先生是我尊敬的一位实验语音学家。

我认识吴先生很晚，但比较早就读过他的文章。上世纪末，我作为访问学者去美国进修，开始从事语音信号处理的研究。在此期间，为了充实自己，打好基础，我收集和阅读了一批语音学方面的文献资料，其中包括在康奈尔大学图书馆找到的几本《中国语文》期刊，上面就刊登了吴宗济先生写的有关实验语音学的几篇连载文章。这些文章对我全面了解语音信号的各种物理及非物理的属性和特征帮助很大。

回北京以后，在没有和吴先生见面以前，就听到过许多关于他的故事，例如 70 高龄的他骑着自行车往返几十里从东郊到北大讲授实验语音学的课程，甚至骑着单车长征八达岭长城等等。除了被他过人的体力和精力所"震慑"以外，更为他传播实验语音学知识、培养青年学子的精神所感动，增添了对他的钦佩之情。

我第一次见到吴宗济先生并和他简短交谈是在声学所举办的那次语音学会议上，以后又在学术会议上多次见到吴先生，每次见到他，我总喜欢和他谈上几句，大多是对会上某篇论文或某个话题的评论，虽然没有什么深入的学术上的探讨，但也从吴先生渊博的语音学知识和丰富的经验中得到教益。但特别触动我的是吴先生的不同寻常的"音路历程"，他在一篇自述性的文章中曾说过，他真正"上路"是上世纪 70 年代后期以后的事，也就是说，吴先生的主要研究成果，包括他发现的声调连读的变调规律，语调和字调的多层次的相互影响的规则，短语韵律的规律，都是在他 70 岁以后所取得的，有些成果，像提高语音合成自然度的语音变量的规正与处理的方法，还是在 80 岁以后取得的。他的学术生涯还一直延伸到了 90 高龄以后，我印象最深刻的是我参与筹办的 2000 年北京国际口语处理学术大会（ICSLP），这是国际语音处理界的一个权威性学术会议，会议邀请吴宗济先生代表中国学者作大会特邀学术报告，吴先生当时已是 92 岁，邀请这样高龄的大会报告人，在 ICSLP 的历史上还是第一次，在国际学术会议上也极少见，引起了到会者的热烈反响，传为佳话。吴先生也不负众望，生动地报告了中国实验语音学研究现状及他本人的研究成果，非常精彩，博得了长时间的掌声。

吴先生 80 年代以来，一直活跃在学术第一线，老当益壮，成果不断。他的成功的音路生涯，突显了他对于语音学事业的热爱和执着追求、奋斗不息的精神；也突显了他与现代语音学发展同步、探索求新的精神，而这些正是我们需要学习和发扬的治学精神。

中国传统尊称德高望重受人敬重的高寿长者为人瑞，吴宗济先生就是一位值得我们尊敬的在学术上有成就的百岁人瑞。

黄泰翼

恭贺吴宗济教授百岁华诞

  1958 年吴先生自欧洲游学归来，正值我们开展"语音打字机"（即语音识别）研究。当时语言所也属于中国科学院，所以就便于我就实验语音学诸多问题向先生求教。宗济先生学贯中西博古通今，加之平易近人和善可亲，久而久之遂成为忘年交。我也由此步入了语音学的殿堂。

  先生治学勤奋严谨，有两件事让我十分感佩。上世纪 60 年代初，国内还没有语图仪，只能使用一般的频率分析仪（B&K2107）作语音分析，工作起来费时费力。由于他持续大量工作，竟将仪器上调谐用电位器的线绕电阻丝磨断了。仪器生产商丹麦老板 Brüel 博士都为之惊异。还有，当语言所刚刚经历了"文革"的痛苦磨难和文改会走廊的短暂栖身之后，在北京地质学院得以从新开始工作。先生十分兴奋，立即动手筹建隔声间，以便发音录音之用。他多次跑到石景山，采购价廉的矿渣棉作吸声材料。建成后还找我来商量如何精确测量这个小房间的混响时间。这是多么可贵的敬业精神哪！真是业精于勤。

  1979 年，在科学的春天到来之际，吴先生又率林茂灿先生和我组团赴哥本哈根参加第九届国际语音科学大会，会上他当选为国际语音科学大会常设理事会成员，从此打开了我国语音学界走上国际舞台的大门。现在先生仍思维敏捷笔耕不辍，春节期间还把他搜集的有关声调的起源和发展的中外文献给我看。其间还共悟"得大自在"之快乐。

  欣逢宗济先生百岁华诞，谨祝健康长寿，并呈拙诗一首为贺：

良师益友五十年
携手同窥音韵园
且喜吉人得天相
尤望仙翁寿比山

张家騄
2009 年 2 月 15 日

音路漫漫，难忘领路人

　　值此吴先生百岁华诞之际，恭祝先生健康长寿，继续指引我们在漫漫的音路上探索、寻觅语音的真谛。

　　吴先生致力于语音学研究，但对语音工程技术十分关心。我从阅读他的著作和聆听他的讲演中受益良多。特别是每年总有几次去拜访吴先生，每次总是讨论语音学问题，以语音合成中遇到的实际问题最多。吴先生说，讨论语音学能使人长寿。希望能由此沾一点吴先生的"寿气"。

　　吴先生在论文中说：对于汉语，汉字的声调和由字组成的词或词组中的连读变调是汉语语调的基本单元，即使在语句中也不会有太大变化。给出基本单元的基本模式和变调规律，写出简明的规则，就可以达到构建语句基本语调的目标。这种独辟蹊径的语调观，和汉语合成语调控制方案确实是为解决合成语音中的自然度问题提供了基础，在初敏和我研制的语音合成系统中达到了立竿见影的效果。吴先生的语调研究是一步一个脚印，他在不同时期，给出了双音节词、三音节词、四音节词到多音节词的不同声调组合的音高、音长变化的规律。这些工作都是在实验语音学测量手段还不完备的条件下完成的。敬佩吴先生的事必躬亲，刻苦耐劳的精神。同时对吴先生的悟性，语音认知的天赋赞叹不已，因为他在上世纪六七十年代得到的结果，是现在可以用基于大规模语料库的语音参数测量和统计方法重复的。孔江平和我，以及邓丹、石锋和我在词调上的一些研究，都是在吴先生的基础上完成的。

　　前年我带几位捷通华声语音技术公司的年轻工程师和技术员去拜访吴先生，他正在给喷墨打印机灌墨水。毕竟是年近百岁的老人了，手脚不是十分灵便，年轻人要帮他，他不许，最后还是自己把打印机拾掇好了。打印机边上放了一寸多厚的语图和音高图，这是他为语言所老年基金课题准备的结题报告的一部分。忙完打印机，他对照语图和音高图，侃侃而谈他在这个基金研究中的体会，告诉我们除词调以外，语调控制中的要领。两个小时热烈的讨论在不知不觉中度过，吴先生高兴，我们满载而归。在公司经常听到员工抱怨语音分析，看得眼也花了，听得耳也聋了。这次见到了吴先生，他们再也不说什么了。后来吴先生给我寄来了他的结题报告，沉甸甸的，凝聚着老人的心血，充满着对年轻人的期望。这册结题报告是我家里最珍贵的文献资料，陈列在书柜里，是一盏音路上的指路明灯。

吕士楠

2009 年 3 月 25 日 于北京

敬爱的吴宗济先生：

恭贺百年华诞，祝您健康快乐！

如果说，是赵元任、刘复等先辈在中国土地上播下了科学语音学的种子，那么，正是吴先生您的不懈努力和卓越贡献，使中国几经劫难的科学语音学的"香火"得以继续，并引领这个学科坚持走基础理论研究跟实际应用紧密结合之路，不但迎来了中国语音学蓬勃发展的春天，而且丰富了世界语音学的宝库。正如 J. Ohala 教授曾经指出的那样，您的研究提升了国际上对汉语声调、辅音和元音以及韵律的理解，您是新兴一代追求科学地认识言语的语音学家的楷模。

30 多年前有幸拜您为师，那是我的福分！您把我领进了实验语音学的大门，给我展现了一片崭新天地，让我从此踏上了现代语音学的科学殿堂：是您，第一次手把手地教我操作语图仪，教我腭位照相，教我识读语图，教我辨识语音的 X 光照片，使我茅塞顿开，得以通过声学和生理实验的手段，认识许多扑朔迷离的语音现象；是您，在第一时间把我"扔"到了 *Speech Chain* 原著的汪洋大海之中，结果让我既收获了语音学基础理论、扩大了眼界，又习得了基本的英语技能；是您，一开始就让我跟着您在语音学理论与言语工程应用相结合的实践中摸爬滚打，一下子就把我引上了一条正确的研究与探索之路，使我得以从揭示言语产生和感知机理的高度考察音段和超音段特性，不断加深对自然言语本质的认识。还有您那诲人不倦的高尚情操，您那"老骥伏枥，志在千里"的奋斗精神，时刻激励和鼓舞着我努力拼搏。您是我们永远的学习楷模！

衷心祝愿您健康吉祥，继续引领我们前进！

曹剑芬 敬贺
中国社会科学院语言研究所语音研究室
2009 年 2 月 19 日

敬贺一代宗师吴宗济先生百龄华诞，祝先生在实验语音学学术舞台上永葆美妙青春，并在百岁寿辰后步入佛家"无量寿"之最高境界。

愚晚78岁弟子王理嘉敬上
北大刘复先生创建之语音乐律实验室
2009 年 2 月 18 日

永远创新，永远年轻
贺吴宗济先生百年寿辰

  我应该算吴先生学生辈的学生了，1979 年吴先生来北大给中文系研究生开实验语音学的课，我还只是个刚刚入校的本科生，无缘聆听。

  做学生时就听说过吴先生许多趣事，比如，因为会弹钢琴，听音能力极好，而考上清华的研究生，等等，所以一直觉得吴先生又亲切又神秘。

  吴先生 1980 年发表的《什么叫区别特征》和《试论普通话语音的"区别特征"及其相互关系》是引导我深入了解音系学区别特征理论的两篇最重要的文章，吴先生对国外理论的熟悉，给我留下很深刻的印象。

  给我最深印象的是吴先生把两字组、三字组、四字组连调跟句子语调联系起来，给出了在基本单元字组连调的基础上根据句法或语用信息"移调"而形成句调的汉语语调模型。这一模型有音系学内涵，有中国特色，吴先生的理论创造力令人叹服！后来吴先生又通过音乐中听觉音高与物理音高的关系，更好地说明了连调块高低移动所需要的物理音高上的调整，使得自己的理论模型也能够较精确地符合语音自动生成的应用需要。吴先生在音乐方面深厚的基础，跟语音学的研究相辅相成，完全融合为一体了。

  我留校并于 1991 年后开始音系学的研究后，才跟吴先生有了实际的接触，亲身体会了吴先生的幽默、乐观，对新生事物似乎是与生俱来的新鲜感，永不休止的求新精神。他以近 80 的高龄学会了计算机，并且以之为工具亲自参加了语音自动生成的工程性项目；他把汉语语音韵律的特点与中国诗文书画的特点联系起来，看出中国文化相通的特点。跟吴先生接触，总能感染到顽童式的活力，他那里没有枯燥的学问，只有无穷的趣味！

  祝吴先生永远创新，永远年轻！

北京大学中文系 王洪君

2009 年 2 月 16 日

庆贺吴宗济教授百岁华诞

  为庆贺吴宗济先生百岁华诞，中国社会科学院语言研究所出版了这本论文集。我以崇敬的心情谨表祝贺。

  30年前，当我们在清华大学建立语音识别科研组的时候，阅读了吴先生的一些学术论文，拜访过吴先生的语音研究室，得到吴先生和他的同事们的热情接待。在他们的鼓励和帮助下，开始了我们的研究工作。随后我们又陆续看到吴先生和他的同事们更多的论文和著作，也有更多机会和吴先生接触，直接得到他的指导。从别人那里又听到过很多关于吴先生的故事。耳闻目睹，我想谈谈我对吴先生和他的论文的印象和一些我觉得值得大家学习的榜样：

  1. 吴先生的论文、著作和他的所言所说都充满了与众不同的地方，就因为这样，他对现代语音学的创建、发展和推广应用作出了很大的贡献。

  2. 吴先生和他的同事很重视实验，研究工作密切联系实际，使他们的论文和著作具有很强的生命力。

  3. 这些论文和著作深入浅出，通俗易懂，特别适合我们这些做言语工程工作的人阅读和学习。

  4. 吴先生是语音学界的泰斗，却一点架子都没有，平易近人，和他讨论问题时感到特别亲切。

  5. 吴先生到老还对研究工作一直不停地耕耘，这种执着精神实在难能可贵。

  6. 吴先生在任何时候，即使身处逆境，都能乐观以待，这可能是他长寿的主要原因吧。

吴先生的学生 清华大学计算机科学与技术系 方棣棠

致語音學大師吳宗濟先生

百歲平安、春輝永綻

香港中文大學工程學院副院長
蒙美玲敬賀 3.2009.

吴宗济先生——语音界的良师益友

吴宗济先生是语音学界的泰斗，我在清华大学读书时就拜读过吴先生的大作。直到1990年神户的ICSLP学会上，我才有幸和吴先生相识，趁此去吴先生住所拜访过几次。拜访中，吴先生从做学问，做人到养身健体侃侃而谈，使我第一次领略了"听君一席话胜读十年书"的境界。从那以后，每当在国内外有相遇的机会，都忘不了向吴先生请教一番。吴先生见面打招呼总称我"老校友"，让我觉得飘飘然。

在众多的轶事中有一件小事可以说对我触动很深，影响很大。记得1997年3月中国科大王任华老师在黄山市举办了一个小型中日的语音研究会，其中一项活动是爬黄山。当时好几位60岁的先生都坐着轿子上山，89岁的吴先生自己徒步登山。爬山的中途我都感觉有点受不了，吴先生却精神充沛泰然无事。这件事让我感动不已。事后向吴先生请教养身健体之道。吴先生给我讲了他"文革"期间在"牛棚"里的健身故事。吴先生说，当时条件很差，大多数人感冒了吃点药就睡觉，他感冒了坚持"恶治"：就是跑步出一身汗再冲澡。他就是通过挑战人类自身的极限，战胜病魔，健身强体的。受到吴先生教诲和鼓舞，自那以后我也在健身强体方面积极挑战自己的极限，尽可能保持旺盛的体力去学习和工作。

吴宗济先生在做学问育人，养身健体诸方面，都为我们树立了楷模。在纪念吴老先生的百岁华诞之际，我祝愿吴先生再次挑战人类的极限，健康长寿，为我国语音界培养更多的栋梁人才。

党建武
2009年春

Messages of Congratulations to Professor Wu

恭祝吴文俊先生：

福如东海

寿比南山

郑方

二〇〇九年二月

恭贺

吴宗济先生寿登期颐

音路历程
乐在其中
百年华诞
一代宗师

学生 石锋 敬贺

二零零九年二月十六日

敬贺吴宗济先生百岁华诞

伟哉先生，百岁院士。辞旧迎新，跨越世纪。
弃武习文，六艺交融。五音擅长，遐迩振声。
既乐濯足，亦善振缨。丧乱无忧，心如怀冰。
布道四方，进退从容。行无虚饰，其道犹龙。

邈哉先生，煌煌其辉。出乎同类，拔乎其萃。
实验补听，既浊能清。吐故纳新，雕龙飞腾。
触类旁通，由博返约。声学班头，六马仰秣。
循循善诱，依依声韵。桃李芬芳，天下归心。

乐哉先生，童心未泯。夕阳愈红，桑榆晚晴。
癖好鹍鹏，出奇脱俗。吾等燕雀，岂知祸福。
杖藜名山，知足常乐。波振四海，尘飞五岳。
薪传南北，语学魁斗。幸甚至哉，海屋添筹。

吴洁敏

私淑弟子吴洁敏敬贺
2009 年 3 月 16 日

2007 年夏，我去吴先生家请他为《中国语音学报》创刊题词，吴先生欣然提笔写下"明音辨韵，北斗南针"八字。今逢吴先生百岁纪念文集出版之际，将此八字刻印两方，以表感谢和庆贺。

2004 年 5 月，刚过完 95 岁生日的吴先生访问上海，时值祝寿文集 *From Traditional Phonology to Modern Speech Processing* 正式出版，吴先生在给我的书上题了一段文字，表达了他"虽老而自认为当不朽"的好心情。其中一句写道："语音的研究，愈深入，愈觉其难，过去所认为'得意之作'，在今日必然或减重，或竟碰壁。"

的确，许多看似浅显的问题为我们制造了不少障碍；二十多载的语音研究中竟找不出像样的结果。又一个五年过去了，迎来了吴先生的百岁华诞。在语音技术日益进步的今天我愿将上面这段简单的文字拿出来与大家共享。

祖漪清
2009 年 2 月 16 日

最最敬爱的吴宗济先生：

  感谢冯隆师十年前带我登门拜访了您。

  感谢那一年您把翻译文稿与整理文集的任务交给了我。

  正是在给您译稿和整理文集时，我学到了无数的好东西——既从您的文章里，也从您的言传身教中。

  尤其是您所提出的语调基本单元的思想，那为我发现普通话调核单元起到了不可替代的指引作用。而跟您促膝谈音，通宵达旦，无拘无束，是令我回味无穷的无上享受！

  最最敬爱的吴先生，有幸成为您的忘年是我最大最大的骄傲！

  期待为您编第二本文集……然后，咱们一起，把那瓶您30多年前花7块钱买的茅台喝干如何（瞧，我还惦记着呢^_^）？

  祝您百岁竿头 更进一步！

曹文
2009年2月27日

My most respected and beloved Professor Wu Zongji,

  Thank my teacher Mr. Long Feng for taking me to visit you ten years ago. And thank you for trusting me to translate your English essays and collate your selected works then.

  It was during my work for your selections that I learned a lot – both from your articles and from your instruction.

  I must especially mention that your idea of the "basic unit of intonation" (phrasal contour) led me to find different kinds of nucleus units of Chinese intonation. And I often recall the enjoyable time when we were discussing phonetic issues freely all night long!

  My most respected and beloved Professor Wu, it has been the greatest honor for me to have your friendship despite difference in our ages!

  Looking forward to collating articles of your second selections…And after that, may we drink up the Moutai Wine, which you bought more than 30 years ago for 7 RMB yuan (Look, I am still thinking of it☺)?

  Wish you good health and success over 100th birthday!

Dr. Wen Cao

Associate Professor
Phonetics Lab
Beijing Language & Culture University

我心目中的百岁老人吴宗济先生

我认识吴先生是从他和林先生主编的《实验语音学概要》一书开始的，那是 1993 年，我刚刚开始在南大攻读硕士的时候，实验室里保存着这本书的复印件，这也是我接触的第一本语音学启蒙书籍。第一次见到吴先生，则是在 1995 年的春季，那时我来北京查阅资料，到语言所拜访了林先生，恰巧吴先生也在实验室，然而除了简单的问候，并没有机会做更深的交流，心目中只是对吴先生留下了一个和蔼的印象。

真正结识吴先生还是从我在清华念书时开始，记得在 1998 年的夏天，导师蔡老师领着我和师弟张维一起去吴先生家拜访。吴先生向我们详细地讲解了他提出的韵律移调理论、韵律协同发音模型等等，拿出许多过去发表过的文章和书籍供我们参考，给我留下了很深的印象。除此之外，我还在吴先生家里发现了一些有趣的事情，比如吴先生将他的书斋取名为"补听缺斋"，并在里面陈列着许多猫头鹰饰品。我曾经问起有什么含义，吴先生说，语音研究，除用音标记音，还必须用"实验以补听官之缺"。提起猫头鹰，他说，世人经常说夜猫子进宅，好事不来，认为猫头鹰晦气。其实，猫头鹰是益鸟，它夜里辛勤工作，干了好事还挨骂，因此他要为猫头鹰正名。现在我也养成了一种习惯，当我出国偶尔碰到这些饰品时，也会带一两个回来送给吴先生。

和吴先生认识一晃已经过了十年，和他在一起的时候，总是让人心情愉悦。吴先生有时会和我们说起他传奇的人生，比如他的求学和研究经历，以及人生中的一些坎坷。这些故事从吴先生口中叙述起来，却往往会变成一件件有趣的事情，让人在欢笑中，从心里钦佩着吴先生的这份豁达。

有一次我在吴先生家一起吃午饭时，问起吴先生有没有长寿的秘诀，他说其实什么都没有，只需要有一副好心情。吴先生形容他是"赤橙黄紫又青蓝，但将绿色看人间"，也许这就是这位百岁老人最真实的写照，真心希望这种豁达和快乐的人生永远陪伴着吴先生。

陶建华
2009 年 4 月于北京

祝福故事老人——吴宗济先生百年华诞

衷心地祝愿吴先生生活之树常绿，生命之水长流。

认识吴先生，是由于步入语音研究的缘故。对吴先生印象最深的，却是他满腹的故事。初次见吴先生，还是我在声学所攻读博士学位的时候。导师吕士楠先生带着我们几个学生去参观社科院语言所。当时的吴先生，已 80 多岁，精神矍铄、步履如飞。老先生热情地给我们讲解各式各样的声学设备，从音叉到浪纹仪、到声调推断尺，从设备的声学功能，到其背后的人物故事。吴先生侃侃而谈，我们这些听众也是如痴如醉。这是我终生难忘的一课。

第二次听吴先生讲故事，是 1998 年在香港，参加一个学术会议。利用会议间隙，吕老师和我一起陪着吴先生游尖沙嘴。出门时天气还好，玩了一半却下起雨来。只好躲进一家文化广场喝杯咖啡。趁这工夫，就又请吴先生讲故事。从清华求学讲到抗战逃难，从摄影、拍电影讲到语音研究。听了这些故事，我真是感慨万分。以前只知吴先生在语音学界成就非凡，这才发现，我所知之实乃冰山一角。故事听得越多，就越觉着吴先生高深不可测也。

2009 年春节前夕，约着吕老师一起给吴先生拜个早年。吴先生依然那么精神和健谈。闲谈之中，我又听到了很多"新"故事。同去的王老师问吴先生，您这一辈子经历了那么多磨难，灰心过吗？老先生说：我这一辈子有好几次站在生死的边缘上，各 50%的机会，能走过来就是幸运的，还有什么可抱怨的？这就是吴先生的长寿、健康的秘诀。一个人若能豁达如吴先生，怎能不康健长寿，若能对事业孜孜以求如吴先生，又怎能不硕果累累。

初敏

2009年2月14日

贺吴宗济先生百岁寿辰

  2009 年 4 月吴宗济先生就 100 岁了。他历经了丰富而精彩的整整一个世纪的生命之旅。

  我自 1990 年开始研究普通话声调和语调的关系，那个时候我是法国 Aix-en-Provence 大学的研究生。我不断地看吴宗济先生的文章，其中他发表的两字组、三字组、四字组连调跟句子语调的文章给我很深的印象。

  1991 年我们和吴宗济先生认识了。我爱人梅山乐在北京和吴宗济先生见面了，那个时候他还自己骑自行车，从北京回来以后我爱人跟我说了，吴宗济比我还健康……

  那年八月 在 Aix-en-Provence 举行了第 XII ICPhS。吴宗济先生和林茂灿先生在我们家住了一个星期。我们一起去了 Marseille，至今都记忆犹新。从那个时候开始我们家和吴宗济先生的友谊不断加深。

  我们每次来北京，不论是访问还是工作都一定去看他。孩子们叫他北京老爷爷。我们每次去旅游的时候都帮他买他的收藏柜里还没有的猫头鹰。

  我们最喜欢的是跟他一起游览颐和园，他什么故事都知道，我们也喜欢他讲他自己的故事。吴宗济先生学富五车，尽管是一个高级研究员，他待人非常热心，重视培养年轻人的能力，把所有的知识传授给他们。

  祝吴宗济先生百岁为上寿，一言乃千金！
JOYEUX ANNIVERSAIRE !!!

葛妮和全家

上海，2009 年 3 月 5 日

贺吴先生百岁

自 1982 年师从吴宗济先生和林茂灿先生起，弹指整整 27 年过去了。如今，恰值吴老先生百岁寿诞。借此良机，特写此短篇恭贺吴先生老人家生日快乐，身体健康，寿比南山！

古语说得好，有德者寿！寿星吴先生是一位德高望重、治学严谨、平易近人的学者。他与我在瑞典皇家工学院的博士论文导师方特先生一样，都是语音学界的世界级泰斗，都是对语音研究不断奉献的长者。

仔细比较一下，还可以发现我的两位良师，吴先生和方特先生，还有更多相似的地方。譬如说，他们原先都是学理工科的，后长期从事实验或声学语音学的研究，再专功韵律学（Prosody）。他们都长期担任国际语音学会常设理事。他们俩都非常重视语音知识的积累，重视培养新人。

同时，他们都很健康、长寿，虽然一个主要以骑自行车来代步、健身，而另一个是常驰骋在网球场上、或整理前庭后院。

另外，两位尊师都十分好客。记得我曾在方特先生的家宴中，遇见丹麦的著名语音教授 Eli Fischer-Jørgensen。当她得知吴先生是我的国内导师时，就给我谈起当年吴先生作访哥本哈根大学的逸事。有一天，吴先生热情地邀请她和别的同事去中国驻哥本哈根的大使馆做客并欣赏中国电影。当影片中出现祖国群山峦叠时，吴先生即兴地说，这跟我们早上看到的二维语谱图好像！还有一次也是在方特先生的家宴中，我见到了日本东京大学的 Hiroya Fujisaki 教授。那时吴先生正好在 Fujisaki 教授的实验室作访问学者。Fujisaki 教授提起吴先生时，非常兴奋，连连说吴先生是现代汉语韵律学的先驱，造诣颇深，和吴先生合作十分愉快并富有成果。Fujisaki 教授还对我说："你真幸运，能当吴先生的学生。"

一日为师终身为师，我在吴先生身上学到了很多宝贵的东西。如今吴先生寿登期颐，我衷心地祝良师 Happy Birthday！

Qiguang Lin

敬贺吴宗济先生百岁寿辰

今年 4 月 4 日是吴宗济先生的百岁寿诞，作为他的学生，我感到万分欣喜。吴先生这样的老师是可遇不可求的，虽然我已有十余年未在吴先生身边受教，但他的为学和为人我终生难以忘怀。

我从 1995 年到 1998 年在语言所语音室跟随林茂灿先生读研究生，吴先生为我讲授一年的《语音学》课程。因为只有我一个学生，又是面对吴先生这样的大学者，起初我还真有些紧张。但是一次课上下来，我的紧张便荡然无存，因为他总是那么亲切，让你丝毫感觉不到任何距离感。听吴先生讲课是一种享受，他渊博的学识和传奇的人生经历都深深地吸引着我，每次课都在不知不觉中就过去了。我至今还保留着吴先生发给我的课程提纲，授课内容主要包括汉语音韵学、现代语音学和普通话语音学三大方面，提纲上面列举的授课题目密密麻麻地写了三页，可见吴先生所花费的心血。1998 年我到 MIT 攻读语言学博士学位，先后修了一些语音学课程，都不觉得太吃力。这都是吴先生和林先生为我打下的好基础。

吴先生的学问可以说是横贯中西、纵贯古今，从传统音韵学、方言调查到现代语音学、自然语音处理，他在普通话语音研究方面的工作都是具有开创性的，是公认的世界知名的语音学家。但是吴先生的思想是开放的。1996 年 Ken Stevens 的学生陈芸菲刚从 MIT 毕业，得到 MIT 的资助，在语音室作两年研究工作，她就来旁听吴先生的课。吴先生每次都称芸菲为陈小姐，得知芸菲是电子工程背景出身后，他马上说希望芸菲可以在这方面教教他。还有一次我跟吴先生对上声在句中位置的某种特殊音变有不同的看法，吴先生鼓励我做一个小实验来验证一下。

我在国内上大学和上研究生时，常有胃痛的毛病。吴先生和林先生对此都很关心。有一次吴先生告诉我，他年轻时也有同样的毛病，于是他就吃很多辣椒，后来胃病就好了。

2007 年中央电视台对吴先生作了一个专访，我岳父在国内看到后马上告诉了我。承蒙李爱军的帮忙，我在央视网站上也看到了。吴先生跟十年前几乎没有任何变化，思维还是那么敏捷，谈吐还是那么妙趣横生。我很自豪地跟我爱人说：吴先生在采访中讲到的故事，90% 我都听他讲过！我还注意到里边有一个片段：吴先生说今天有一个人给他带来了一些泰语的材料，他要去看一下。不了解吴先生的人一定会觉得这很不可思议，但这正是我所熟悉的吴先生，他的探索不止的研究精神是我最钦佩的。而吴先生对世事坦然平和的心态，更是我可望而不可及的。

值此吴先生百岁文集出版之际，谨祝吴先生身体康健！

美国旧金山大学 李智强
2009 年 2 月 28 日
于美国加州旧金山

恭賀

吴宗济
百岁辉煌
福寿双全

藤崎博也
曹剑芬
林茂灿
沈家煊
李爱军
许长江
李瑞华
祖子晰